VALLANDIGHAM.

SPEECHES,

ARGUMENTS, ADDRESSES,

AND

LETTERS

OF

CLEMENT L. VALLANDIGHAM.

"Do right; and trust to God, and truth, and the people. Perish office, perish honors, perish life itself, but do the thing that is right, and do it like a man."—*Speech of January* 14, 1863.

NEW YORK:
PUBLISHED BY J. WALTER & CO.,
19 CITY HALL SQUARE.
1864.

PUBLISHERS' NOTICE.

The very large sale, last year, of an imperfect compilation of the speeches of the Hon. Clement Laird Vallandigham, justifies the publication of the present full and authentic edition. And just now is the fitting moment to offer to the public the patriotic words of warning and wisdom which, for now nearly four years, have been not only rejected, but denounced as "treason." Defeated armies, an enormous public debt, and intolerable taxation, a decaying commerce, ruined currency, and bankrupt country—these are indeed severe but most instructive schoolmasters.

The "Biographical Memoir" prefixed was prepared by Mr. Vallandigham's brother, and is accurate. Every statement in it, personal or otherwise, can be strictly verified.

J. W. & Co.

New York, *July*, 1864.

CONTENTS.

PAGE

BIOGRAPHICAL MEMOIR, ... 11

SPEECHES, ETC.

Power of the Legislature to alter Legislative Districts 68
Constitutional Reform 77
History of Abolition Movement 97
Argument in Fugitive Slave Rescue Case 134
Argument in Contested Election Case—Vallandigham and Campbell 157
Speech on Contested Election 169
Remarks on Impeachments 189
" " the Tariff 192
Letter on the Invasion of Harper's Ferry 201
There is a West; for the Union forever; outside of the Union, for Herself 205
Newspapers—the Mails.—Letter to Postmaster-General 225
Remarks on Death of the Hon. W. O. Goode 227
Remarks on Bill for Arming Militia of the States 230
Remarks on the "Hour Rule" 236
Report on the Franking Privilege 245
Justice to the North-West.—Remarks on Motion to excuse Hawkins, of Florida, from "Committee of Thirty-three" 258
Response, upon being called out at Serenade given to Mr. Pugh 263
Revolution of 1861 265
Letter to Hendrickson and Others 302
Executive Usurpation 306
Remarks on his Proposition to appoint Commissioners to accompany the Army 324
The Tariff—Tea, Coffee, and Sugar 326
Charges of Disloyalty Repelled 327
Speech on the "United States Note" Bill 340
Address of Democratic Members to the Democracy 362
On Public Debt, Liability, and Expenditures 369
Speech before the Democratic Convention, Columbus, O. 384
State of the Country.—Speech at Dayton 397
Address accepting Nomination for Congress 415
Address accepting Cane presented by Ladies of Dayton 417
The Great Civil War in America 418
The Conscription Bill—Arbitrary Arrests 454
Peace—Liberty—The Constitution 479
The Right of the People to Keep and Bear Arms 502
Protest before the Military Commission 505
Address to People of Ohio, upon going into Exile 506
Address to People of Ohio upon arriving in Canada 507
Letter to the Democratic Meeting at Toledo 510
" " " " at Dayton 514
" " " " at Carthage 518
Address after Election of 1863 520
Address to the Students of Michigan University 521
Speech after his Return 527

SUPPLEMENT.

PAGE

Benevolent Institutions of the State....535
Patience, Firmness, and Truth....536
Retrenchment—Salaries....537
Legislation—Its Mysteries....539
Sepulture—Cemeteries....539
The Public Debt of Ohio—Repudiation....541
The Character of the true Statesman....542
The Mexican War....543
Slavery—the Wilmot Proviso—the Union....546
Political Position and Principles....547
The Clergy and Politics....549
Right of Revolution—"Dorrism"....549
Conservatism and Progress—the True and the False....550
Compromise Measures of 1850....551
Moneyed and Municipal Corporations....552
Campaign of 1860....554
Position on the War, April, 1861....554
Private Conference on the War and Usurpation, proposed....555
Letters to Sabin Hough....555
Mason and Slidell—the "Trent" affair....556
"Loyalty"—Patriotism....558
Finances and Taxation....559
Proscription—Redress....560
Peace Resolutions....562
Invasion—Arrest—The Times....564
True Position and Duty of Democratic Party.—Letter to Sanderson....566
The Military Commission—the "Charge and Specification"....567
Reception at Windsor, C. W....568

MISCELLANEOUS.

The Union. From Dayton *Empire*....568
Not "for Peace before the Union." Card to Cincinnati *Enquirer*....569
The Union—against Bill for abolishing Slavery in District of Columbia....569
Soldiers—Pay—Pensions.—Note to Dr. McElwee....569
Laws—Rights—Duties—Reception at Dayton....570
The Sanitary Commission.—Letter to McLaughlin....570
Self-defence—Protection—Reprisals.—Letter to Hubbard & Brother....570
Late, grudging, and imperfect Justice. From New York *Tribune*....571

PERSONAL NOTICES.

As a Member of Ohio Legislature. From Ohio *Statesman* and Cincinnati *Signal*....572
Speech of January 14th, 1863—Opinions of the Press....573
After his Arrest—Time on Vallandigham. From Springfield *Republican*....576
On his Nomination for Governor. From Albany *Atlas and Argus*, and Boston *Post*....576
His Personal Appearance. From Seneca Falls *Reveille*....576
At Niagara Falls. From New York *News*....577
At Windsor, C. W. From *Plaindealer*, *Sentinel*, and *Press*....577
Visit of Students of Michigan University. From Hillsdale *Democrat*....578
Vallandigham's Birthplace. From Wellsville *Patriot*....579
"The Name of Glory." By Thomas Hubbard....580

BIOGRAPHICAL MEMOIR.

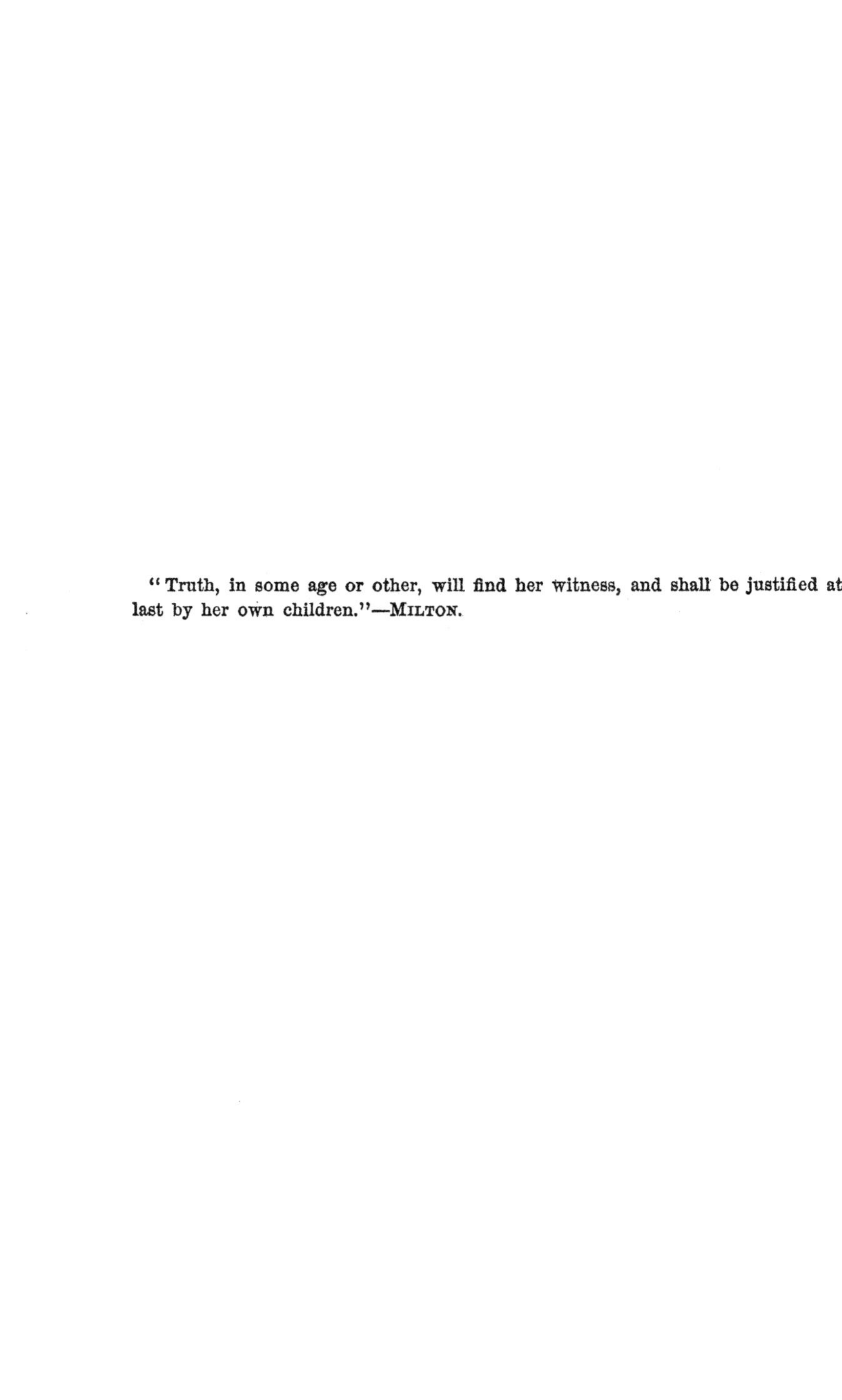

"Truth, in some age or other, will find her witness, and shall be justified at last by her own children."—MILTON.

BIOGRAPHICAL MEMOIR.

THE maternal family of Mr. VALLANDIGHAM (pronounced Val*lan*'dig-ham) is Scotch-Irish, his grandfather, James Laird, having been born in the county Down, north Ireland. His mother, Rebecca Laird, was born on the Susquehanna, in York county, Pennsylvania, and still survives at the age of seventy-five, residing in New Lisbon, Ohio. She had two brothers, Episcopal clergymen, and one a member of the bar, John Laird, who died in 1824, while an Ohio State Senator from Columbiana county. She is a woman of superior intellect, strong will, and much force of character, and of singular piety.

Mr. VALLANDIGHAM'S paternal ancestors were Flemings, the name being originally VAN LANDEGHEM. One of that name was one of the four most distinguished Flemish knights at the battle of "the Golden Spurs," fought by the "Lion of Flanders," near Courtrai, in 1302. There is still a village, Landeghem by name, near Ghent, in East Flanders. In the reign of Louis XIV. they were French Protestants, or "Huguenots." Michael Van Landeghem emigrated to Virginia previous to the year 1690, an exile for religious opinion's sake, and settled in what was then Northumberland county. He became a considerable land-owner in that and the adjoining counties. His son Michael was born in the same county, in 1705, but died in Fairfax county, not many miles from the now classic stream of "Bull Run," where his son George Vallandigham (the spelling of the name being now changed) was born about 1736. He studied law in Prince George county, Maryland, where he married a daughter of Colonel Joseph Noble, whose mother's name was Dent (of English descent, and one of the oldest families in the State); and about 1773 removed to what was then Youghiogheny county, Virginia, near Pittsburg; where his second son, Clement, was born in 1778. About the time of his migration West, the "Logan War" with the Ohio Indians, broke out; and from that time till Wayne's victory, in 1794, Colonel Vallandigham was obliged, with a brief interval now and then, to lay aside his Blackstone for the rifle or the sword. He marched as an officer under Lord Dunmore, the last colonial Governor of Virginia, in his expedition, in 1774, against the Chillicothe Towns. In 1789, having meantime been surveyed by Mason and Dixon, a few miles into Pennsylvania, he was admitted to the bar at Pittsburg. He zealously supported the Federal authorities in the "Whiskey Insurrection," and a year or two afterwards was beaten for Representative in Congress, in consequence of it. During the canvass he was threatened with violence if he should dare attempt to speak at a certain place. But he went and spoke unmolested. He was a man of fine personal appearance, particular in his apparel, scrupulous of his honor, pious, and of most gentlemanly address.

His son Clement was educated at Jefferson College, Pennsylvania, graduating in 1804. He was licensed to preach as a Presbyterian clergyman and in 1807, emigrated to New Lisbon, Columbiana county, Ohio, where, after a most faithful and laborous ministry of more than thirty years, he died in October, 1839. He was a man of talents and learning, of great firmness of purpose, singularly conscientious, and of spotless purity of character.

Clement Laird Vallandigham was born in New Lisbon, July 29, 1820. At the age of less than two years he had learned the alphabet, and when but eight, commenced the study of Latin and Greek, at home; completing the usual course in both languages before he had reached the age of twelve. The next five years he spent in reading and study, and in fishing, hunting, and other youthful sports, passing little time at school. Indeed, nearly his entire education was acquired under his father's roof. At the age of seventeen he entered the junior class at Jefferson College, Pennsylvania, and soon acquired, as a speaker and debater, a high reputation in the Franklin Literary Society, of which he became a member. At the end of one year he left college, and in October, 1838, took charge, as principal, of the "Union Academy," Snow Hill, on the Eastern shore of Maryland; many of his scholars being older than himself. Here he remained for two years, spending his time, in addition to the discharge of his regular duties, in close study and reading (largely oratorical and political), but enjoying also with zest the refined society and elegant hospitality of the Eastern shores of Maryland and Virginia. In August, 1840, he returned to New Lisbon, and at the age of twenty was soon drawn fully into the fierce contests of the memorable Presidential campaign of that year. His first effort at extempore speaking was in a politicial debate at Calcutta, in his native county; where he spoke for an hour with such success, that his Democratic friends bore him off in triumph upon their shoulders. He was thenceforth a champion of the cause.

In November, 1840, he returned to Jefferson College to graduate; but soon after, being grossly insulted by the President, in the progress of a controversy which originated in the expression by him of certain political opinions, in the course of the usual recitation on Constitutional law, he demanded and received an honorable dismission, and returned home in the latter part of January, 1841. Some five years later, when a member of the Ohio Legislature, he was twice offered a diploma as a graduate, but refused it. Previous to leaving college he had been chosen by his society as their "debater" for the annual "contest" of 1841, and in March returned to discharge his duty. The form of the question was, in substance, whether our Federal system of Government was in more danger of perishing from Disintegration than Consolidation; but it opened up the whole question of STATE RIGHTS. Mr. VALLANDIGHAM maintained the strictest doctrine of the "Resolutions of '98," in the boldest and most decided manner, and "lost the honor," to his society. But nothing daunted, he changed neither his opinions nor his purpose to succeed in life. His argument remained for several years on the records of the society, and was much admired. He, we are sure, is certainly not ashamed of its doctrines now.

Returning home, he began the study of the law with his eldest brother, then practising in New Lisbon. He was a diligent and painstaking student, though still devoting much time to literature, politics, and oratory, and participating in the election contests of each year, not neglecting manly exercise and sports.

In the winter of 1842, borrowing money for the purpose, as he had borrowed also to defray his expenses at college, he went to Columbus, Ohio, making the journey in a hack; and there on the fifth of December, was admitted to practice in the supreme and other courts of the State. Returning in a few days, he went into partnership with his brother, who at the end of a year retired from the bar to enter the ministry. Mr. VALLANDIGHAM applied himself diligently to his profession, with such success that, within four years from his admission, his practice was equal to that of any member of the New Lisbon bar. But he still devoted much of his time to literature, politics, and public speaking. He took an active part especially in the Presidential campaign of 1844, yet never descending to either rant or vulgar denunciation.

In the summer of 1845, he was unanimously nominated by the Democratic party of his native county, as one of their candidates for Representative in the State Legislature; and in October of the same year, having just attained the constitutional age, was elected without opposition. The Legislature met on the first day of December, 1845, and Mr. VALLANDIGHAM took his seat the youngest member of the body. Previous to leaving home he laid down the following "Rules" for his conduct as a legislator: "1. To avoid interfering in merely local matters, unless they involve a grave *general* principle. 2. To avoid, with persevering resolution, all connection or mingling with the petty factions or personal jealousies and quarrels of politicial friends; and of foes also: if *necessary* to act in any way in them, to do it as an "armed neutral," manifesting at the same time, that I act as a patriot from a sense of duty, and not from feeling as a partisan. 3. To speak but rarely, and *never* without having made myself complete and thorough master of the subject—so that when I rise, every one may expect to hear something worth listening to. No error is more fatal to influence in a deliberative assembly, than the violation of this plain rule: 'Verily, ye are not heard for your much speaking.' 4. Always to bear in mind the dignity and responsibility of my station, remembering that by the favor of my fellow-citizens, I am a part of the government, and that human government is the vicegerency of Heaven, and the highest exertion of human power."

Mr. VALLANDIGHAM'S first effort was made on the 8th of December, upon a motion to print the reports of the Benevolent Institutions of the State. The subject was selected by him purposely, because it did not involve party feeling, and the speech was extremely well received by members of both parties. On the first day of the session, he had been appointed a member of the Committee on Privileges and Elections, and on the 9th submitted a carefully prepared report upon the question of the eligibility of officers of the State Bank to a seat in the Legislature, maintaining, in opposition to a majority of his party, that they were not constitutionally disqualified. Soon after, on the 18th, from the minority of the committee, he made a very elaborate report upon the question of "Legislative Districts," in the Morgan county contested election. The report attracted great attention in the House and throughout the State. Hon. Samson Mason, a distinguished Whig, who, as chairman of the committee, had submitted the report of the majority, said in debate, that "the report of the minority was an able one, and highly creditable to the talents of the gentleman who had made it." And Mr. C. C. Hazewell, then editor of the *Ohio Statesman*, now of the Boston *Traveller*, speaking of it, said, "Columbiana county may well be proud of her young member, who has already achieved for himself an enviable name as a debater, for skill and fairness, and as a writer at once powerful and dignified. He is one, also, who does not think it necessary to disgrace great talents by buffoonery and immorality in order to achieve a sudden notoriety."

On the 30th, Mr. VALLANDIGHAM spoke briefly in favor of the bill to repeal the Ohio State Bank Act—referring, in calm and determined language, to his confidence in the power of Truth, and his readiness to wait patiently and even long, till she should be vindicated. He continued to take an active part in all important debates, carefully observing the rules which he had laid down for himself; and on the 11th of February, in a speech which was most flatteringly received, defended the sanctity of cemeteries and other places of human sepulture; and again, on the 24th, in an elaborate speech against the Tax Bill, drew the character of "the True Statesman," as he conceived it.

Mr. VALLANDIGHAM's first vote, given a few hours after he was sworn in, was in support of a resolution to open the sittings of the House with prayer, a majority of his party voting against it. Soon after, in reply to a member of his own side, who complained that he (Mr. V.) was quite too courteous to the Whigs, he said, paraphrasing Burke, "that *he* hoped always so to be a Democrat as not to forget that he was a gentleman." About the same time a Whig correspondent of a newspaper, writing in reference to a violent speech by a Democratic member, said, "He was suitably replied to by C. L. Vallandigham, a young gentleman who is always as near right as party trammels will permit him to go, and sometimes a little more so." Thus his high moral character and urbane manners, together with diligent and laborious attention to his duties, secured to him the respect and good-will of all; and, entering the House utterly unknown and the youngest member of it, his reputation was in three months established throughout the State.

Returning home in March, 1846, he resumed the practice of the law with redoubled diligence; but in June, was required to canvass the county throughout, in order to secure a renomination to the Legislature. At the preceding session, Columbiana had been entitled to two members; this year to but one. Mr. V.'s former colleague appeared against him, and a vehement contest followed, the nomination being equivalent to an election, and made by ballot. The cause of the opposition to him was this: Some two years previously the Legislature had passed a so-called "Retrenchment Act," reducing all salaries to a contemptibly low standard; Common Pleas Judges being paid seven hundred and fifty dollars a year, and members of the Legislature two dollars (or eight shillings) a day. Mr. VALLANDIGHAM had taken some money with him to the State capital, had lived "righteously and soberly," abstaining totally from liquors and other similar indulgences, and yet had been obliged to borrow money to enable him to return home. He voted and spoke earnestly for the repeal of the "Retrenchment Act." Fully aware that his course would be unpopular with many of his constituents, he said: "Entertaining these opinions, and believing that I am about to do right, I enter fearlessly upon the discharge of my duty, satisfied to abide the judgment of a constituency I am proud to represent. If that judgment be against me, I shall be content; having still within my bosom the consoling consciousness that I dared to do what appeared to me just." After an animated contest of several weeks, Mr. V. was renominated by a vote of two to one; and at the following October election, in spite of a very vigorous opposition by the Whig party, was re-elected by a large majority.

The Legislature met on the 7th of December, 1846, and Mr. VALLANDIGHAM was complimented by the unanimous vote of his party for Speaker. The session was marked by the discussion of three most important subjects, Mr. V. taking a leading part as to all.

To the prosecution of the war with Mexico, then vehemently opposed by the Whig party, he gave an earnest support. But in the resolutions which he offered on the 15th of December, he took care to establish the grounds of his support, declaring it "a war brought about and commenced by the aggressions and acts of Mexico;" "*a constitutional war;*" "*a war carried on in pursuance of the Constitution and laws;*" and a war the object of which was not conquest and subjugation, but "*a speedy, honorable peace.*" These resolutions he supported in a strong speech; and being assailed personally in reply by a Whig member, he retorted sharply in a second speech of considerable length, in the course of which he answered the objection that the Legislature was intermeddling in that which did not concern it; saying that "as a friend to our peculiar system in its true spirit, and as a State-Rights man, he would be sorry to see the day when the individual States should cease to feel the deepest solicitude in the acts of the Government of the Union."

At the same session, the "Missouri Question" was revived in the form of the "Wilmot Proviso," or proposed exclusion of Slavery from the Territories. In fourteen years the agitation terminated in CIVIL WAR. On the 16th of January, resolutions in favor of the "Proviso" were introduced by a Whig member from the "Western Reserve." Mr. VALLANDIGHAM promptly moved to lay them upon the table, which was done. A few days later, being called up for discussion, he opposed them in an impassioned speech (briefly and imperfectly reported), declaring that the agitation could result only in civil war and disunion, and that he had spoken with great earnestness and feeling, "because he felt called upon, as a patriot and citizen, to resist and expose every measure which might work incalculable mischief, not only to ourselves, but to generations yet unborn." He further declared that whenever any question might arise, involving the Union in the alternative, he would go with his might on that side—on the side of the Union, now and forever, one and inseparable. During the session two several petitions were presented by Whig members, praying the Legislature, because of the annexation of Texas, to "declare the Union dissolved, and withdraw the Ohio Senators and Representatives from Congress." Mr. V. voted for the motion, in each case, to reject the petition.

But his ablest speech at this session was made in support of his bill to provide for calling a Convention to amend the State Constitution. The bill received a majority, but not a two-thirds vote as required, and therefore failed; but the speech attracted much attention throughout the State, and ultimately led to the passage of the bill at a subsequent session.

Taking an active part upon all important questions, Mr. VALLANDIGHAM again found it necessary to separate, now and then, from his party friends. Upon one of these occasions—on a bill to promote the cause of popular education, in which he took a deep interest—he said "he was sorry to part company with them on any question; but was not afraid to vote according to the dictates of his conscience. He had stood upon the floor before, and was ever proud to stand, even in a minority, when he could feel, as he now did, that he stood on the vantage-ground of truth."

Upon the question of the so-called "Black Laws," relating to the disabilities of negroes and mulattoes, Mr. V. voted against their repeal, but supported a bill to submit the question to a vote of the people; expressly declaring that he so voted because the measure "would result in the most effectual putting down of this vexed question for perhaps twenty years to come. It would probably fall out as the question of negro suffrage in New York, where the people had voted against it by a majority of fifty thousand."

Throughout this his second session, Mr. VALLANDIGHAM maintained and added to the reputation which he had acquired at the first. A gentleman (then as now an eminent lawyer and politician), writing to a Cincinnati neutral paper, said of him, in March, 1847: "Although the youngest member of the Legislature, he came to be regarded, long before the close of his first session, as the leader of his party on the floor, which position he maintained during the late short and active session. . . . . . . Courtesy and urbanity in public as well as in private life, have secured for him the esteem of all who know him, without regard to party; while his abilities have commanded their respect. In all his intercourse with men, there is evinced a frankness and an obliging, generous feeling which, above all other traits of character, create and retain warm personal friends."

Upon his return home in February, Mr. VALLANDIGHAM resumed the practice of the law diligently, declining to be a candidate for re-election; but during the summer, determined to remove to Dayton, Ohio, where he arrived on the 28th of August, and immediately assumed the editorial charge of the "Western Empire," a weekly Democratic newspaper. In a carefully prepared "Salutatory," he defined his principles, and the manner in which he proposed to conduct it; accurately distinguishing between true constitutional Democracy and mere popular licentiousness; declaring his fixed purpose to stand fast to the Constitution strictly construed; to maintain the doctrine of State Rights as taught in the Resolutions of '98; and to defend the Union; and further declaring that he would "pander to the sectional prejudices, or the fanaticism, or wounded pride, or disappointed ambition, of no man or set of men, whereby that Union should be put in jeopardy." "In our editorial intercourse with the public," he added, "we shall seek no personal controversy, nor shall any one draw us into any controversy unbecoming a gentleman. Towards all adversaries between whom and us there shall arise any matter of difference, we will exhibit proper respect—sometimes for their sakes, always for our own." And speaking of despotism, he said: "We will war against it in all its forms, and to us the despotism of the many is no more tolerable than the despotism of the few." *

Among his leading articles while editor of the *Empire*, was one denouncing political preaching and partisan clergymen; another affirming the right of revolution, but opposing what was then called "Dorrism," or the asserted right of a mere numerical majority, at any time, to set aside existing rules and forms as prescribed by constitutions, and by spontaneous movement, without form or color of law, to set up a new constitution and government; and another against the repeal, then agitated by the Abolitionists, of the Fugitive Slave Law of 1793.

In June, 1849, Mr. VALLANDIGHAM sold out his interest in the "Empire;" and after spending the summer and autumn in travel and the winter in general reading and study, resumed the regular and diligent practice of the law, in April, 1850, with reputation and success. During the winter preceding, he had been proposed and voted for, by his party in the Legislature, for Judge of the Common Pleas Court of the Montgomery circuit; but defeated by "the balance of power party," because of his views upon the question of Slavery.

In the fall of 1850, he defended the Compromise or Adjustment measures of that year, at a very excited public meeting, called to denounce the Fugitive Slave Act then recently passed; and a week later, at another most important and respectable meeting, offered a series of resolutions in support of the Union, the Constitution, and the Laws, which were unanimously adopted. His speech at the first meeting called forth the highest commendation from both parties.

In the summer of 1851, after the adoption of the new Constitution, he was a candidate before the Democratic State Convention, for the

* The newspaper organ of the Whig party of Dayton, thus noticed Mr. V.'s connection with the "Empire:" "Mr. VALLANDIGHAM presents himself to our people as a political editor, in the temperate and gentlemanly manner, which from previous representations of his character, we had been led to expect."

office of Lieutenant-Governor, but after an animated contest and a most flattering vote, was defeated. In August, 1852, notwithstanding a very bitter opposition, he was nominated by a large majority, as the Democratic candidate for Representative in Congress, from the third or Dayton district; but after a most exciting canvass, was beaten by a majority of one hundred and forty-seven, in a poll of some twenty thousand. His competitor secured the "third party" or Abolition vote, and also the aid of several treacherous Democrats who "bolted" the nomination. Two weeks after the election, the Central Committee of the third or "Liberty party" issued a circular referring to Mr. V. in these terms: "In opposition to Mr. Campbell, the Democratic party had nominated C. L. Vallandigham, a lawyer of high standing, an eloquent and ready debater, of gentlemanly deportment and unblemished private character, and untiring industry and energy. But he was known, to all, to be an ultra pro-slavery man (anti-Abolitionist); he undertook, with a relish, to carry the load of the Compromise measures, the Fugitive Slave Law included, and he broke down under the burden."

Two years afterwards he was unanimously renominated by his party for the same post; but it was the well-remembered Kansas-Nebraska and "Know-Nothing" campaign, and he was beaten by nearly twenty-six hundred votes. Incapable of discouragement, he again accepted a unanimous nomination by the Democratic party of the district, in 1856. It was the year of the first struggle for the Presidency, by the Republican or Abolition party, now consolidated by the total dissolution of the Whig party. The Presidential canvass was extremely violent; but in the third district, it was wholly forgotten in the terrible bitterness of the Congressional contest. Nothing equal to it had ever occurred in the United States. The Abolition party had renominated Mr. CAMPBELL, who had twice before been Mr. VALLANDIGHAM's successful competitor. For three months, day and night, every energy of the candidates and their respective parties, was exhausted; and at the end of the canvass, Mr. CAMPBELL appeared by the official count to be elected by nineteen majority. Gross and palpable frauds had been committed by the successful party; and upon this ground, and because a number of negro votes had been cast for his competitor, the friends of Mr. V. demanded that he should contest the election. He consented, and on the first of December, 1857, giving up his law-practice which had every year, notwithstanding his devotion to politics, become larger and more lucrative, he appeared in Washington to prosecute the contest. But the "Lecompton Question" was absorbing all attention, and had divided the Democratic party. He was in great danger of having the justice of his case sacrificed to the interests of faction; but after a tedious and most harassing contest of six months, trying both patience and temper, and requiring the utmost tact and ability, he was declared entitled to the seat, by a majority of seven votes; and accordingly, on the 25th of May, 1858, was sworn in as a member. But the session was nearly at an end, and he soon after returned home; and being accepted by his party as a candidate without the formality of a convention, was, in October following, re-elected over Mr. CAMPBELL, by a majority of one hundred and eighty-eight votes. This was his first political success since the renewal of the Anti-slavery agitation in 1846. Because of his determined hostility to abolition fanaticism, and his unbending purpose never to yield principle to mere policy or expediency, he had failed repeatedly in every political aspiration. He himself in his speech of January 14, 1863, thus records his position and his experience: "Sir, I am one of that number who have opposed abolitionism, or the political development of the Anti-slavery sentiment of the North and West, from the beginning. In school, at college, at the bar, in public assemblies, in the Legislature, in Congress, boy and man, as a private citizen and in public life, in time of peace and in time of war, at all times and at every sacrifice, I have fought against it. *It cost me ten years' exclusion from office and honor, at that period of life when honors are sweetest.* No matter; I learned early to do right and to wait." He did wait, and was finally successful, and so continued, till the whirlwind of civil war changed every thing, and again compelled him to appeal to truth, justice, and time. But this long interval was not unprofitably spent. These repeated contests and defeats disciplined and strengthened and hardened him for the yet severer struggle to come; and meantime, besides the assiduous and successful practice of his profession, he devoted himself to political science and philosophy, and especially to the reading of history, always his favorite study. During this period he completed a full course of history from the earliest records in the Bible, down to the present time. A part also of his leisure was occupied in modern literature and the ancient classics. And he always found time for all; yet spent the hot months of each summer in travel and recreation.

Subsequent to the October election in 1855, Mr. VALLANDIGHAM delivered, before a Democratic meeting in Dayton, one of the ablest speeches of his life. It is a searching and exhaustive review and exposition of the rise, progress, and full development of the Abolition movement in the United States. After several years of halting and trimming before that party, then holding the balance of power, during which the Democracy of Ohio had obtained a precarious control of the State government, they were, at last, badly beaten at two elections; and the purpose of the speech was to bring the party up to meet the

Slavery issue fairly and boldly, and thus to restore it to sound doctrine and discipline, and therefore to power and usefulness. He concluded with these warning words: "If thus, sir, we are true to the country, true to the Union and the Constitution, true to our principles, true to our cause and to the grand mission which lies before us, we shall turn back yet the fiery torrent which is bearing us headlong down to the abyss of disunion and infamy, deeper than plummet ever sounded; but if in this, the day of our trial, we are found false to all these, false to our ancestors, false to ourselves, false to those who shall come after us, traitors to our country and to the hopes of free government throughout the globe, Bancroft will yet write the last sad chapter in the history of the American Republic."

At the following State Convention, the halting policy on that question was abandoned. Mr. V. was chosen a delegate from the State at large to the Cincinnati Convention, and took an active part in its proceedings, especially as a member of the committee on the "Platform."

In June, 1857, occurred the "Ohio Rebellion" of that year. The deputies of the United States Marshal for the southern district of that State, were resisted in the execution of regular judicial writs issued under the Fugitive Slave Act. They were pursued by a body of armed men, more than fifty in number, from Champaign County, through Clark into Green, and there overpowered, and the prisoners rescued. They were also themselves arrested on State process. To discharge them from imprisonment, a habeas corpus was issued from the United States District Court at Cincinnati. The Attorney-General of Ohio was sent down by Mr. Chase (then the Governor), to argue the case for the State. Mr. Pugh, Mr. Vallandigham, and another, appeared for the United States. Mr. V.'s argument called forth the highest commendation. Maintaining the vital doctrine of State Rights to the fullest extent, he yet asserted and upheld the absolute supremacy of the Federal Government within its constitutional limits.

During the wearisome contest at the first session of the Thirty-Fifth Congress, Mr. Vallandigham had been assiduous in attendance upon the sittings of the House, diligently observing and studying the usages and rules of parliamentary bodies, as he had also done while a representative in the State Legislature. At the second session, 1858–'9, he took little part in the current debates, but continued the study of parliamentary law; addressing the House, however, upon the subjects of Impeachments and the Tariff, and successfully defending himself against a charge made at the preceding session, in regard to his vote upon the repeal of the "Black Laws," while a member of the Ohio House of Representatives.

In October, 1859, returning from a visit to Washington and Baltimore, it was his ill fortune to hear the first gun and witness the first conflict of the great Civil War which soon after convulsed the whole country in revolution. He arrived at Harper's Ferry upon the train which passed just after the capture of "John Brown," by Colonel Robert E. Lee. Delaying a few hours, he, by accident, saw this first martyr of Abolitionism, and held some conversation with him, which being made public by the reporters, he was bitterly assailed by the abolition press, as though guilty of some great sacrilege. To these assaults he replied in a letter, stating the occasion and nature of his interview, and giving a brief description of Brown, and a narrative of his raid. It is a valuable part of the history of that memorable affair.

The Thirty-Sixth Congress met in its first session, amid great excitement, on the 5th of December. In the House, neither the Democratic nor "Republican" or Abolition party, had a majority, the balance of power being held by the so-called "American" or "Know-Nothing" party. By the Abolitionists, John Sherman, of Ohio, a man of much pretension and small ability, was put in nomination for Speaker. He was an indorser of "Helper's Impending Crisis," that manual of assassination and robbery, which aided much to foment the "John Brown Raid," and, along with other causes, to kindle the flames of civil war between the North and South. A violent, and, at times, almost bloody struggle for two months, ensued over the speakership. The debates, after the first two weeks, became most turbulent in their character. The hostile parties glowered upon each other. More than half the members came to the House heavily armed. Knives projected from men's bosoms; pistols were dropped upon the floor, and personal collision several times was most imminent. Mr. VALLANDIGHAM rose to address the House late on the evening of December 14. He asked the usual courtesy of an adjournment. But because of the extreme bitterness towards him on part of the Abolition members, in consequence of his interrogation of "old John Brown," it was refused. He began his speech amid great confusion upon their side of the Chamber, but soon yielded to a motion to adjourn. It was again refused; whereupon he declined to continue the speech which he had intended to make, and, there being no "hour rule," contented himself with speaking against time upon the "Helper Book," yielding every little while to motions to adjourn. Amid the utmost confusion, but with arms calmly folded, standing at the head of the middle aisle, he continued this line of remark until the opposition were glad to yield to an adjournment.

The next morning he resumed and finished his speech without interruption, and amid the most respectful silence. Referring to the scenes of the night previous, he said:

"Though a young man still, I have seen some legislative service.

One of the earliest lessons which I taught myself as a legislator, and which I have sought to exemplify in every department of life, was so to be a politician as not to forget that I was a gentleman. There is a member of this House, now present, with whom, some years ago, I served in the Legislature of my State, and to him I might with perfect confidence appeal to verify the assertion that no man ever was more exact in the observance of every rule of courtesy and decorum, not only in debate, but in private intercourse with his fellows. I might appeal, also, to the members here present of the last Congress, and to every member of this House of Representatives, and demand of them whether I have offended in any thing, in public or private, in word or by deed. That courtesy which I thus readily extend to others, I am resolved to exact for myself, at all times and at every hazard."

The great struggle terminated finally in the compulsory withdrawal of Sherman, and the election of a Republican not an indorser of Helper's Crisis.

In the midst of this contest, Mr. VALLANDIGHAM had occasion to defend successfully, in a letter to the Post-office Department, the freedom of the mails, in favor of a constituent, the publisher of a political-religious newspaper hostile to him in sentiment and party. In February he delivered a brief eulogy upon the occasion of the death of Mr. GOODE, of Virginia, and, in March, spoke at length against the "hour rule," denouncing it as a chief source of evil in legislation and parliamentary proceeding. The speech was listened to with great attention from all parties. About the same time he spoke in support of his bill to provide for the better arming of the militia of the States. It was a subject to which he had always devoted much attention—having, while a student of law, held the position of division-inspector in his native county, with the rank of lieutenant-colonel. In 1857, upon the reorganization of the volunteer militia of Ohio, he had been chosen a brigadier-general, and had spent no small amount of money and time to bring his command into good condition and discipline. He now labored earnestly, at this and the succeeding session, to procure arms from the Federal Government, though without success. An appropriation of three hundred thousand dollars was more difficult to be obtained then than three hundred millions now.

In April, 1860, as Secretary of the National Democratic Committee, he attended the Presidential Convention at Charleston, South Carolina. Though never an indorser of Mr. Douglas's peculiar views in reference to "Squatter Sovereignty," or the power of the inhabitants of a Territory over the institution of Slavery, yet for personal reasons and because he believed him to be the fittest man to meet the impending crisis, he sincerely supported that gentleman for the nomination. At the same time he saw, with anxiety and alarm, that the unwise counsels and ill-advised measures of some of Mr. D.'s friends, were about to be used by his extreme Southern opponents to break up the Convention, and did not hesitate to speak his mind freely. Foreseeing in this, as in so much else, the approaching storm of civil war, he earnestly labored to avert the mischief. Men over-zealous in support of their favorite, took occasion to question his sincerity. This coming to the notice of Mr. Douglas, he replied in a letter to a friend, declaring that he never had a moment's doubt of Mr. V.'s honor and fidelity; adding, "Whenever I know a man to be a gentleman, I always regard his word as conclusive."

Mr. Douglas having been nominated by the main body of the adjourned Convention at Baltimore, Mr. VALLANDIGHAM supported him earnestly throughout the canvass. He was himself, for the fifth time, the Democratic candidate in his district for Representative in Congress, and again without the formality of a convention. Though not quite the most bitter, it was the most difficult and delicate of all his canvasses; inasmuch as the opponents of the Republican party were divided into three sections, supporting respectively Bell, Breckinridge and Douglas. Yet he was returned by a majority nearly the same as in 1858. Shortly afterwards he went to New York and New Jersey to speak in behalf of the "Union Ticket" in those States. And it was at the great meeting of November 2d, at the "Cooper Institute," that he made the declaration that "he never would, as a Representative in the Congress of the United States, vote one dollar of money whereby one drop of American blood should be shed in a civil war;" which declaration he says, in a card published soon after, "was received with vehement and long-continued applause, the entire vast assemblage rising as one man, and cheering for some minutes." Six months later, when he had made the declaration good, that same "vast assemblage" would have torn him in pieces had he ventured to set foot in the city of New York. Yet "after some time be past," sobered by the chastening ordeal of blood and of financial and commercial ruin, they will again rise up to do him honor, because he kept his faith and word. Late in the afternoon of the day of election, he reached home and gave his vote, remarking to a friend that "he feared it was the last which any one would give for a President of the *United* States."

In a speech at Dayton, on the 19th of May (while at home on a brief visit), he had denounced Lincoln's doctrine of "the irrepressible conflict" in a vehement and impassioned manner, as "revolutionary, disorganizing, subversive of the Government, *and ending necessarily in disunion.*" "Our fathers," he said, "had founded a government expressly upon the compatibility and harmony of a union of States 'part slave and part free;' and whoever affirmed the contrary, laid the axe at the very root of the Union." And in a later speech at the same place, he said: "Kill the Northern and Western anti-slavery organization (the Republican party), and the extreme Southern pro-slavery, 'fire-eating' organization of the Cotton States (its offspring), will expire in three months. Continue the Republican party—above all, *put it in power, and the antagonism will grow till the whole South will become a unit.*"

On the first of August, he had addressed a very large Democratic meeting at Detroit, in Michigan. In the course of the speech, he said: "Northern sectionalism and fanaticism has been approaching nearer and nearer to Mason and Dixon's line, while Southern fanaticism, starting in the Cotton States, has been creeping northwardly, until the two factions have nearly met. What will be the inevitable result of the conflict which must ensue? They must meet, if the floods of fanaticism be not checked. When they meet on the southern borders of Illinois, Indiana, and Ohio, how long can the country endure? *Human nature has been misread from the time of Cain to this day, if blood, blood, human blood, be not the result.* But, thank God, between the two sections there is a band of national men, patriots, who love their country more than sectionalism, ready to stay this conflict. Our mission is to drive this sectionalism of the North back towards the Lakes; and that of the South back to the Gulf of Mexico." It was upon this occasion that he first crossed the river to Windsor, little imagining that in three years it was to be his place of sojourn while in exile for the exercise of his constitutional rights as a citizen. He foresaw the Civil War, but not the immediate overthrow of personal and political liberty.

Soon after the Presidential election, referring, in a card, to his declaration in the speech at the Cooper Institute, he said: "I now deliberately repeat and reaffirm it, resolved, though I stand alone, though all others yield and fall away, to make it good to the last moment of my public life. No menace, no public clamor, no taunts, nor sneers, nor foul detraction, from any quarter, shall drive me from my firm purpose. Ours is a government of opinion, not of force—a Union of free will, not of arms; and coercion is civil war—a war of sections, a war of States, waged by a race compounded and made up of all other races, full of intellect, of courage, of will unconquerable, and, when set on fire by passion, the most belligerent and most ferocious on the globe—a civil war, full of horrors, which no imagination can conceive and no pen portray. If Abraham Lincoln is wise, looking truth and danger full in the face, he will take counsel of the 'old men,' the moderates of his party, and advise peace, negotiation, concession; but if, like the foolish son of the wise king, he reject these wholesome counsels, and hearken only to the madmen who threaten chastisement with scorpions, let him see to it, lest it be recorded at last that none remained to serve him 'save the house of Judah only.' At least, if he will forget the secession of the Ten Tribes, will he not remember and learn a lesson of wisdom from the secession of the Thirteen Colonies?"

Congress met, in second session, on the 3d of December. The next day a member from Virginia moved that a committee of thirty-three, one from each State, be appointed to consider and report upon the "perilous condition of the country." Mr. VALLANDIGHAM voted for the motion; because, as he remarked, it was an expedient; and though totally inadequate, he was willing to support any and every expedient, trusting that something might be yet done to avert the impending dangers. Mr. Hawkins, of Florida, being named one of the committee, moved to be excused. A debate followed, and Mr. V. spoke briefly but earnestly in protest against the composition of the committee; criticising it also as too numerous, and therefore discordant and slow; and asking what kind of conciliation and compromise that was, which began by forcing a member to serve upon a committee raised for the very purpose of peace? He spoke also earnestly in defence of the Northwest, declaring that the people of that section, to secure a maritime boundary, would, if necessary, "cleave their way to the sea-coast with the sword." They might be a nation of warriors, but a tribe of shepherds never. He closed with a solemn warning that the time was short and the danger imminent, and that standing in the forum of history, acting in the eye of posterity, all duties should be discharged instantly and aright, if we would be

"Medicined to that sweet sleep
Which yesterday we owed."

The House refused to excuse Mr. Hawkins; but he did not serve. It was in this debate that Mr. Sickles repeated, substantially, Mr. V.'s declaration against supporting a civil war, pledging that no man should ever pass through the city of New York to coerce a seceded State, and threatening that that city would assert her own independence. He recanted, and is a major-general: Mr. VALLANDIGHAM made his declaration good, and is now an exile. But in proud conscientiousness he could exclaim in Congress, after two years of desolating and disastrous war, "To-day I bless God that not the smell of so much as one drop of its blood is upon my garments."

A stormy session ensued. All compromise was first delayed and then finally rejected by the Abolition party, and the secession of seven States and the establishment of the Confederate Government followed. Mr. Pugh spoke against coercion in a powerful and most eloquent speech on the 20th of December; and at a serenade given in his honor a few days later, Mr. V. earnestly advocated conciliation, not force; peace, not civil war; saying that although they who so counselled "might be prostrated for a time by the heavy tide of public opinion which would run against them, yet upon the gravestone of every such patriot would be written '*Resurgam;*' and it would be a glorious resurrection."

On the 20th of February, 1861, he spoke at length in a very elaborate speech, in behalf of compromise and especially in support of his own proposed amendments to the Constitution. No propositions were ever so grossly misrepresented. Mr. VALLANDIGHAM had prepared, in advance, an abstract of them for the telegraphic agent of the "Associated Press" at the capital, who transmitted it correctly to the Eastern papers; but at Philadelphia the knavish agent of the Association telegraphed it to the Western press as a proposition to divide the United States into four separate republics. Mr. V. demanded a correction; but the perversion was only repeated in a form still more false. This was but the beginning of that persistent and aggravated misrepresentation in every form, by telegraph as well as otherwise, to which, for more than three years now, he has been subjected. The propositions are published in full in this volume along with the speech. They were amendments only to the existing Constitution. They proposed "sections" within the Union; not distinct nationalities or republics outside of it. The preamble itself recites, as the purpose of the propositions, that "it concerned the peace and stability of the Federal Union and Government, that a division of the States into mere slaveholding and non-slaveholding sections, causing hitherto—and from the nature and necessity of the case—inflammatory and disastrous controversies upon the subject of Slavery, ending already in present disruption of the Union—should be forever hereafter ignored." And he himself, in a card published a few days after their introduction, declared: "My propositions look solely to the restoration and maintenance of the Union forever by *suggesting a mode of voting in the United States Senate and the electoral colleges*, by which the causes which have led to our present troubles may, in the future, be guarded against, *without secession and disunion;* and, also, the agitation of the Slavery question, as an element in our national politics, be forever hereafter arrested. My object—the sole motive by which I have been guided from the beginning of this most fatal revolution—is to maintain the Union, and not to destroy it." So far as any suggestion has ever been made respecting a possible future division of the American Republic "into four distinct nationalities," it came from the pen of Lieutenant-General Scott, who even went so far as to name the probable capitals of three of the "nationalities."

At the time this speech was delivered, the voice of nearly the whole country was decidedly for peace. At the opening of the session, Mr.

V. had found himself almost alone against "coercion;" but in February, the sentiment had greatly changed both in Congress and out of it. Immediate danger of civil war seemed to have passed by. Yet satisfied that all hope of present adjustment was at an end, and separation or disunion an existing, though, as he hoped, a temporary fact, he spoke chiefly in review of the more remote and hidden but real cause which had led to the crisis; and from these sought to deduce the true nature of the searching and decisive remedies which he believed essential. But in the whirlwind of the hour, neither the House nor the country was in a temper to hear philosophy, and the speech attracted then no part of the attention which it has since received. It was appropriately entitled, in the pamphlet edition published at the time, "The Great American Revolution of 1861"—a revolution which he pronounced "the grandest and the saddest of modern times." It is almost useless to add that he voted for the Crittenden Compromise propositions, and for all others which, in his own language, "so much as promised even to heal our troubles and to restore the Union of the States." But he voted also steadily, in common with nearly the whole body of the Democratic and Conservative members, against the Force Bill and all other measures of coercion; believing that threats would avail nothing to intimidate the seceded States; while justice and fair compromise would satisfy the vast majority of their people. During the course of the session, Mr. Corwin having without provocation, attempted to raise a laugh at the expense of his "unhappy colleague," Mr. V. retorted sharply: "Sir, this is the most important question ever debated in the American Congress, and too serious every way for jest. It ought to make every man 'unhappy;' and I am very sorry that my facetious colleague is not unhappy over it, too. It is a pity, sir, that he cannot lay aside his levity long enough to consider it with a little of the seriousness which it demands. This is no time for smartness, but for sadness and solemnity rather."

Mr. Vallandigham returned home in March, trusting that peace at least might be, for the present, maintained. On the 15th of that month, Mr. Douglas, who during the early part of the second session had inclined strongly towards coercion, made his memorable speech, the most statesmanlike of his life, declaring, "War is disunion; war is final, eternal separation." But the necessities, if not the purposes, of the Administration and of the Republican party, required civil war, and they found means to precipitate it. A fleet threatened Charleston; Sumter fell, and the proclamation of the 15th of April followed. Mr. V. did not hesitate for one moment to maintain his position. It is scarcely possible to realize the howl of denunciation which forthwith was raised against him, or the ridiculous and preposterous reports—among others that his house had been destroyed and that he himself had fled—which were circulated. He noticed them in a card on the 17th of April, declaring that his position had long since been taken, was well known, and would be maintained to the end. Some days later he wrote two strictly private letters to a gentleman in Cincinnati, who, having been arrested for "treason" upon a judicial warrant a few months afterwards, was tried before a United States Commissioner; the sole proof against him being the production of these letters. Yet the Federal District-Attorney, Flamen Ball by name, was not ashamed to urge on the case upon this evidence. His argument was after this fashion, doubtless: Mr. VALLANDIGHAM is, of course, a "traitor:" the accused corresponds with him; "argal" the accused is a traitor. The letters themselves, very brief, contain not any thing of note except that they suggest a *fear* or *apprehension* (common to almost all men before that time) that war being disunion, nothing remained but separation. But they do not express *desire* or *wish*, or any thing similar, for disunion. On the contrary, Mr. V. distinctly says that "he would watch the first favorable chance to move publicly for peace and restoration."

During the latter part of April and the months of May and June, as also for many months afterwards at Washington, in his journeyings and at home, Mr. VALLANDIGHAM was exposed day and night to imminent danger of personal harm or death. Even his assassination was publicly invited by men holding responsible official positions under the Administration. In his own language, "he carried his life in the hollow of his hand." But no evil befell him or came nigh his dwelling.

On the 3d of May, the proclamation of the President, calling out volunteers and increasing the regular army and the navy, without act of Congress, was issued. It was a bold and most dangerous usurpation, which, if submitted to without remonstrance, could end only in the final subversion of the Constitution in every part. Mr. V. immediately issued a private circular, addressed to some twenty or more of the most prominent Democratic politicians of the State, proposing a conference at Chillicothe on the 15th of the month, to concert measures to arouse the people to a sense of the danger which was so imminent from the bold conspiracy to usurp all power into the hands of the Executive, and thus to "rescue the Republic from an impending military despotism." But four answers were received—three favorable, and one adverse to the conference. It was not held.

Certain of his constituents having addressed him a letter, requesting his views more at length, he replied on the 13th of May, quoting from and adopting Mr. Douglas's speech before referred to, and declaring: "As for the conquest and subjugation of the South, I will not impeach the intelligence of any man among you, by assuming that you dream of it as at any time or in any way possible. Remember the warning of Lord CHATHAM to the British Parliament: 'My Lords, you cannot conquer America.' A public debt of hundreds of millions, weighing us and our posterity down for generations, we cannot escape. Fortunate shall we be if we escape with our liberties. Indeed, it is no longer so much a question of war with the South, as whether we ourselves are to have constitutions and a republican form of government hereafter in the North and West. In brief: I am for the CONSTITUTION first, and at all hazards; for whatever can now be saved of the UNION next; and for PEACE always as essential to the preservation of either."

Such were his sentiments, his conception of the impending dangers, and his convictions as to the final issue of the war during the first month after the proclamation, and when, amid the storm which swept over the whole land, scarcely ten men in the country dared confess that they were of the same opinion.

On the 4th of July, the Thirty-Seventh Congress met in first or extraordinary session. The Speaker elect delivered a ferocious and bloodthirsty address, declaring that territorial unity must be maintained though the "waters of the Mississippi should be *crimsoned with human gore*, and every foot of American soil *baptized in fire and blood*." This atrocious sentiment was received, according to the official report, with "vociferous applause upon the floor and in the galleries, which lasted for many minutes." Indeed, the entire scene reminded one of some of the maddened spectacles exhibited by the French National and Constituent Assemblies, rather than the sitting of a Congress of sober and rational statesmen. It was the purpose of the Administration leaders to prevent all debate, and there seemed to be a general disposition among the members on both sides to acquiesce. But Mr. VALLANDIGHAM was resolved to be heard, and he obtained the floor on the 10th of July. No speech was ever delivered in the midst of greater personal danger—not even Cicero's oration for Milo, or Curran's defence of Bond. The galleries and lobbies were filled with an excited soldiery and infuriated partisans, threatening assassination. A leading Administration paper in New York had, two days before, declared, that if an attempt was made to speak for peace, the "aisles of the hall would run with blood." Arbitrary arrests for opinion and speech had already been commenced. Almost without sympathy upon his own side of the House, and with a fierce, insolent, and overwhelming majority upon the other, Mr. VALLANDIGHAM, calm and unawed, met every peril, and spoke as firmly, solemnly, and earnestly, as under ordinary circumstances. "My duty," said he, "shall be discharged—calmly, firmly, quietly, and regardless of consequences. The approving voice of a conscience void of offence, and the approving judgment which shall follow, 'after some time be past,' these, God help me, are my trust and my support." The "motto" from Lord Bacon's will, prefixed to the pamphlet edition of the speech, is significant; interpreted, as it has now been, by the light of three years' experience. A very large number of copies was circulated in various forms, North and South, and it was published also in England and on the continent. The peroration has been especially admired; but it fell upon hostile or unwilling ears. His fit audience was to be gathered in the presence-chamber of Time. But comparative freedom of speech, which otherwise might have perished, was made secure, at least within the halls of Congress.

On the 12th, in debate on the Volunteer Army Bill, he moved for the appointment of seven commissioners to accompany the army, to receive and consider propositions from the Confederate States or any one of them, looking to a suspension of hostilities, and the return of those States or any of them to the Union. He supported the motion in a few remarks, saying, that while he would not in the beginning have given a dollar or a man to commence the war, he would now vote as many men and as much money as might be necessary to defend and to protect the Federal Government; but he would not support a war of aggression or invasion. His proviso received but twenty-one votes upon a count. The only terms of peace then, as proclaimed on the floor by a "war Democrat," amid frantic applause in the galleries, were that the people of the South should lay down their arms, sue for peace, and surrender their leaders for execution. Similar terms had once before been demanded by George the Third and Lord North. Mr. VALLANDIGHAM voted for the second part of the celebrated "Crittenden Resolution" of July 22d, the day after the rout at Bull Run; but for reasons which he assigned in his speech at Dayton, of August 2, 1862, refused to support the first. It was a solemn day; the Gascon insolence, and vociferous levity of July 4th, had been succeeded by craven fear. Every moment members sat in anxious suspense, lest the sound of Beauregard's cannon should awaken the echoes of the Capitol. Mr. Crittenden's resolution had been scouted out of the House three days previously; it passed now with but two dissenting voices.

Upon a question relating to army chaplains, Mr. V. testified his devotion to religious toleration, by moving to strike out the clause which required them to belong to some "Christian denomination," and insert "religious society," so as to include men of the Hebrew faith; remarking that "while we were in one sense a Christian people—and yet in another not the most Christian people in the world—ours was still not a Christian *Government*, nor a Government which has any connection with any one form of religion in preference to any other form." The amendment was rejected.

The Military Academy bill being under consideration, Mr. VALLANDIGHAM denounced the new-fangled oath of allegiance which it proposed to require of the cadets. "I am especially opposed," he said, "to the unheard-of and execrable oath required by one of its sections. There is no inconsistency, not the slightest, between the allegiance which every man owes to the State in which he lives, and that which he bears to the United States. They are perfectly reconcilable. Yet it requires the renunciation of the allegiance which every cadet owes, by birth or adoption, to his State. It is an oath which ought not to be required of any young man of honor, or of any citizen of a free country. I denounce it, too, as unconstitutional. All that that instrument provides for, is an oath to support it." Here his remarks were arrested and declared out of order, whereupon he resumed his seat, saying, "Then, sir, I propose to discuss it in that GREAT HEREAFTER to which I have so often had occasion of late to appeal." Before the adjournment he introduced a joint resolution providing for the calling of a Convention of the States, to adjust all controversies in the mode prescribed by the Constitution; but never, during the entire Congress, was able to secure any action upon it. He had taken a most active and vigilant part in the proceedings throughout the session, and although with the sympathy and support of but some eight or ten members, was always upon the alert, and on the day of the adjournment, was aptly described by a Republican member, as "the young man standing in the aisle, where he has stood nearly all the session—on the frontier." The House adjourned on the 6th of August, in the midst of the most fatuous and childish levity.

On the 7th of July, Mr. VALLANDIGHAM'S courage and presence of mind had been severely tested. He had that day visited the Ohio camps on the west side of the Potomac, where several hundred of his constituents were stationed. Soon after arriving upon the ground, some members of a Cleveland company approached and notified him to leave. He refused indignantly: a tumult ensued. Several of the officers and a large majority of the men soon rallied to his support, and the rioters retired to their own limits. He remained an hour or two, and then returned to Washington. A substantially correct statement of the affair, referring to "the nerve and courage" shown by him, was telegraphed from Alexandria to Baltimore and Philadelphia; but at the latter place suppressed, and a false and distorted version substituted by the agent of the "Associated Press," and thence duly transferred to that shameless compilation of falsehood and trash, Putnam and Moore's "Rebellion Record."

The adjournment was followed by one of those periodic and spasmodic reigns of terror, with which the Administration has so often afflicted the country during the war. But Mr. V. was not molested. In contempt of all threats of violence, he addressed several public meetings in his own district, during and after the canvass, which resulted in overwhelming defeat to the Democratic party in every State.

Upon the meeting of Congress in second session, in December, the House, in hot haste, indorsed the act of Captain Wilkes in seizing Mason and Slidell on board the British mail-steamer Trent. Two weeks later, news arrived of the preparation of England for war, and Mr. V. for the purpose of exposing the shallow but blustering and cowardly statesmanship of the Abolition party in the House, offered a preamble reciting the action of the Navy Department and the resolutions of the House, and proposed to pledge Congress to support the Executive in maintaining the position thus assumed; but his resolution was summarily referred to a committee, and thus suppressed.* "Before three months," said he, "these men will be surrendered in face of a threat." It was done in ten days. In a subsequent debate, he deprecated the surrender thus made, but in strong language condemned the original seizure as against international law, maintaining that they should have been given up at first. During this debate, January 7, 1862, his "loyalty," as usual, was called in question, and he replied: "Consistency, firmness, and sanity in the midst of general madness—these make up my offence. But 'Time, the Avenger,' sets all things even; and I abide his leisure. . . . . I appealed then, as I appeal now, alike to the near and to the distant future; and by the judgment of that impartial tribunal, even in the present generation, I will abide; or if my name and memory shall fade away out of the record of these times, then will these calumnies perish with them."

On the 3d of February, he addressed the House on the subject of finances and the United States Note or "Legal Tender" bill, in a searching and exhaustive argument against a forced Government paper currency; predicting the inevitable result—depreciation and final explosion. Just at this time, such and so great had been the flood of denunciation and falsehood poured out upon him, that it is safe to say that in Congress and out of it, he was the most unpopular, best abused, most execrated man in America. He was himself fully conscious of the fact; and one of the opening paragraphs of the speech freely confesses it. "Nor am I to be deterred," he said, "from a faithful discharge of my duty, by the consciousness that my voice may not be hearkened to here, or in the country, because of the continued, persistent, but most causeless and malignant assaults and misrepresentations to which, for months past, I have been subjected. Sir, I am not here to reply to them

* A false and corrupted copy will be found in the "Rebellion Record."

to-day. Neither am I to be driven from the line of duty by them. 'Strike, but hear.'" He was barely listened to in the House; yet the speech was received very favorably among the better class of bankers and financiers in New York and Boston.

On the 19th of the same month, John Hickman, of Pennsylvania, moved a resolution of inquiry into Mr. VALLANDIGHAM'S "loyalty," founded upon a local item in a Baltimore newspaper of the lowest class. An intensely interesting and exciting scene followed. The resolution, although wholly without notice, gave him the fit occasion, long waited for, to defend himself from the suspicions and calumnies to which he had so long been exposed, and he instantly improved it to the utmost; and with undisturbed self-possession and dignity, but in tones the most earnest and indignant, retorted with so much vigor and spirit upon his accuser, that he was glad to escape by withdrawing the resolution. The rencontre was of very great advantage to Mr. V., and was the first break in the cloud which hitherto had rested over him. His allusion to the flag which hung above the Speaker's seat, forced admiration from even a hostile House and galleries. As he sat down he overheard a friend say, "He has not made a mistake nor spoken an ill-advised word from the beginning."

In April, Mr. Wade, of Ohio, in a speech in the Senate, assailed Mr. VALLANDIGHAM as "a man who never had any sympathy with the Republic, but whose every breath was devoted to its destruction, just as far as his heart dare permit him to go." Patiently waiting a few days for a fitting opportunity, Mr. V. read the sentence and said: "Now, sir, here in my place in the House, and as a representative, I denounce—and I speak advisedly—the author of that speech as a liar, a scoundrel, and a coward. His name is Benjamin F. Wade." An effort was made to censure him, but he had the resolution ruled out upon a point of order. This was the only occasion upon which he ever departed from the strictest decorum and propriety of language in the House; but the provocation was extreme, and Wade was the first responsible indorser whom he had found, of the accumulated falsehoods and detraction of a whole year. Petitions, finally, for his expulsion as "a traitor and a disgrace to the State of Ohio," were presented from Cincinnati and Springfield, and referred to the Committee on the Judiciary, but reported back and laid upon the table, as unfounded. Seven times, during the session, these attacks were renewed, and as often failed. Indeed, he has himself said that for months he never heard an Administration member address the Chair, without looking up to see if a resolution for his censure or expulsion was about to be offered. But he escaped the trying ordeal unscathed. It was said afterwards that "he could not be detected because he was too sharp to leave his tracks uncovered."

"Never make any tracks," said he, in reply, "and none will ever be found out." During this session also, his vigilance was never for a moment relaxed. Powerless in numbers and influence, he had but one weapon—knowledge of the rules of the House, and skill in parliamentary law; and he used it with the utmost efficiency. "I am always uneasy," said a member, not originally friendly to him, "when Vallandigham is out of his seat, lest some mischief should be slipped in contrary to rule."

A concerted effort, for election purposes, having been made by the Secretary of the Treasury (Mr. Chase), and several Administration members of the House, to underestimate the public debt and expenditures, Mr. V., on the 30th of June, in a statistical and carefully premeditated speech, exposed the cheat, and exhibited the real extent of the liabilities incurred up to that date.

The violent public commotion which followed the proclamation of the 15th of April, 1861, the apparent unanimity in support of the war, the desertion of many of the old Democratic leaders and the fatal timidity of others, together with the specious cry of "No party," had greatly paralyzed the Democratic organization. Its disastrous defeat that year in every State where the elections were contested, almost dissolved it. Repeated efforts had been made by Mr. VALLANDIGHAM and the little band with which he acted, to restore the party; but all had failed, and two several "caucuses" of the Democratic members of Congress had broken up in disorder. The case was still more hopeless in December. But he closely watched and calmly waited for the opportune moment; and in March, 1862, taking advantage of the rapid and bold development of the real purposes of the party in power in their various schemes for Confiscation and Emancipation, he drew up a call for a conference of the Democratic Senators and Representatives, and obtained signatures to the number of thirty-five. The meeting was held on the 25th of March, and after a full discussion and some altercation, it was resolved that the organization of the party should be perfected, and on motion of Mr. V. ordered that a committee be appointed to prepare an Address to the People of the United States. But previous to this, a secret and concerted effort was being made by certain Eastern politicians of the Democratic party, in combination with others of the old Whig and "American" parties, to disband the former, and to consolidate a new "conservative" organization with a new name. They who were in this movement managed, upon the pretext that Mr. VALLANDIGHAM was too unpopular to be on the committee, or, indeed, to be recognized as a member of the party, to postpone, and finally to defeat the appointment of the committee ordered by the conference. But he, and those who acted with him, were not to be thus beaten. He prepared an Address, which, after much delay and difficulty, was signed by twelve Democratic Representatives from the West (six of them from Ohio), and by two from Pennsylvania, and one from New Jersey: all the other Eastern members except one, and four of the Western, refusing peremptorily to sign it. It was issued on the 8th of May; and three days later, the new "Conservative" movement culminated in a caucus in the hall of the House of Representatives, John J. Crittenden presiding. But the "Address" was already before the public, and to the Democratic masses it was as the call of the trumpet to battle. Few political documents have ever produced a greater effect. The effort to supersede the Democratic organization utterly failed. In every State Democratic tickets were put in nomination, and the extraordinary and almost universal successes of the year followed. About the time of the publication of the "Address," Mr. V. visited Philadelphia and New York for the first time since the commencement of the war, and was in both cities and along the route, received with honor by his friends. In the latter, he was tendered a serenade at the Metropolitan Hotel; but apprehending that the war-fury had not yet sufficiently subsided, he declined it.

On the 2d of July he left Washington for Columbus, Ohio, to attend the Democratic State Convention on the Fourth. It was one of the largest, most enthusiastic, and harmonious, ever convened in the State. From the east side of the State House, at the close of the business proceedings, he addressed it in a speech wholly extemporaneous, but most impassioned, and delivered with voice and gesture terribly in earnest. Its effect upon the audience was very great. One delegate described his shoulders as bruised and blue for several days, from the spasmodic working of the fingers of a stalwart countryman behind him during the delivery. At the beginning, throughout, and at the close, the applause was unbounded. In fact, his entire reception at Columbus was one of the proudest and most gratifying. He arrived in that city on the evening of the 3d, and after midnight responded to a serenade; the next day addressed the convention, and again at night spoke from the hotel to an immense assemblage—three speeches within twenty hours.

McClellan had just been defeated and hurled back upon the James river, though after a gallant and stubborn resistance, and a most masterly retreat. Pope's short but disastrous and disgraceful campaign began. More troops were demanded, and the reign of terror was renewed with greater violence than ever before. Two clergymen from the "Union" Slave States, who had been upon a visit to Mr. Vallandigham, were arrested on their way home. It had been the intention to arrest them at his house, and to seize him with them. Arrangements were made subsequently to effect his arrest separately, and officers came up for that purpose from Cincinnati. Mr. V.'s friends rallied to his support, and his house, and all approaches to it, were securely guarded. For several weeks he sat up or lay whole nights in his day-clothes. Regular reports of the arrival of all trains were brought to him, and ward and watch kept continually till break of day. Not a footfall upon the pavement escaped his ear. He himself, in his speech at Newark, New Jersey, in February, 1863, has described "that most terrible of all apprehensions, haunting you, walking with you, abiding with you—the fear of arrest." "I felt it," he adds, "when night after night, in my own house—which one of the noblest of Englishmen told me, which my father told me, which the Constitution of my country told me, was my castle—when night after night from the setting of the sun, from the hour when the gray starlight had gathered around that which should have been a peaceful and undisturbed home, until day dawned, I watched in suspense for every footfall upon the pavement, and the sound of every carriage which rumbled along the street, lest some execrable minion should dare attempt to cross the threshold of that castle. 'Not while memory holds a seat in this distracted globe,' shall the vigils of those terrible nights be forgotten."

The intention to arrest him was abandoned. Meantime, however, he resolved to address the people of Dayton, to whom he had not spoken since the war began. It was a bold movement, exhibiting the highest moral as well as physical courage; since repeated threats had been made, during the preceding eighteen months, that he would not be allowed to speak; and, independent of this, the deed of assassination might easily be done under cover of darkness. Uncertain as to the number who would attend, the meeting was announced for a public hall in the city; but as evening approached, an immense concourse of people, numbering some eight thousand, assembled. The hall was speedily filled to overflowing, but not an eighth part of the audience could gain entrance. The meeting was adjourned to the south side of the beautiful stone court-house of the city; and thence Mr. VALLANDIGHAM addressed the vast and excited multitude for nearly three hours, in a speech which was received with exalted enthusiasm, and which, when published, called forth the highest encomiums. "Elevated in tone, statesmanlike in conception, full of pathos, and pure in diction," said the editor of the *Crisis*, "it thrills the reader as though fresh from a Roman Senate in the hour of Rome's most terrible trials for freedom and existence." At the close, the people accompanied him in triumph to his home. The victory was won, and he was secure. One passage only need be quoted here:

"I, too, have sworn to support the Constitution; and more than that, *I have done it.* I demand that all men, from the humblest citizen up to the President, shall be made to obey it likewise. In no other way can we have liberty, order, security. I was born a freeman. I shall die a freeman. It it appointed to all men once to die; and death never comes too soon to one in the discharge of his duty. I have chosen my course—have pursued it—have adhered to it to this hour, and will to the end, regardless of consequences. My opinions are immovable; fire cannot melt them out of me. I scorn the mob. I defy arbitrary power. I may be imprisoned for opinion's sake—never for crime, never because false to the country of my birth, or disloyal to the Constitution which I worship. Other patriots, in other ages, have suffered before me. I may die for the cause: be it so; but "the immortal fire shall outlast the humble organ which conveys it, and the breath of liberty, like the word of the holy man, will not die with the prophet, but survive him." And, meantime, men of Dayton, the opinions which I entertain, the deep convictions that control me in that course which, before Almighty God, I believe can alone maintain the Constitution and restore the Union as our fathers made it, I never, never will yield up. Neither height nor depth, neither death nor life, nor principalities, nor powers, nor things present, nor things to come—no, nor the knife of the assassin, shall move me from my firm purpose."

In September he was nominated the sixth time, and by acclamation, as the Democratic candidate for Congress. He accepted in a brief address, and referring to the dangers of the canvass and the threats that he would not be permitted to speak in certain localities, said: "Let it be understood, once for all, that wherever in any part of any county in the district, it is deemed convenient and proper to announce a Democratic meeting, *it will be held; and, God willing, I will address it.*" He made his declaration good, canvassing every county, and addressing large and enthusiastic meetings of the people. But since the election in 1860, a hostile Legislature had changed the district, adding thereto a county giving always an overwhelming Abolition majority. The sole struggle, therefore, was to carry his original district, and in this he succeeded by a largely increased majority.

The fall elections in all the States resulted in Democratic triumphs. The reign of terror was broken down and free speech once more secured. Mr. VALLANDIGHAM addressed many immense meetings in Ohio and Indiana, continuing his labors up to the day of his departure for Washington. He was everywhere received with extraordinary honors and enthusiasm. But at one of these meetings in Indiana, arrangements were made by the Governor and United States Marshal to arrest him on his way home at night. His friends urged that under cover of darkness, he should be taken in a carriage past the point where the arrest was to be made; but he answered, "I came by the cars, and in that way I mean to return, arrested or not—so help me God." He took the train, and although the marshal and a company of soldiers were at the depot, no arrest was attempted. He subsequently addressed a meeting near the same place and upon the same road, but was not even threatened. Soon after this an elegant gold-headed cane was presented to him, with appropriate ceremonies, by the ladies of Dayton. Replying to the address, he referred in fitting but delicate terms to his mother, saying: "If, indeed, sir, I have exhibited any of the high qualities of courage, fortitude, and immovable devotion to THE GOOD AND THE RIGHT, which, on behalf of these ladies, you have so kindly attributed to me, it is to one of their own sex, more than to any other human agency, that I am indebted for them—MY MOTHER. In childhood, in boyhood, and in youth, in the midst of many trials, from her teachings, and by her example, I have learned those lessons and formed the character and habits—if it be so—which fitted me, with courage and endurance, and unfaltering faith, to struggle with the terrible times in the midst of which we live."

The Thirty-Seventh Congress met in third session, in December. From May down to that period, scarcely any thing but disaster had befallen the Federal arms. The elections had nearly all terminated adversely to the Administration. All was alarm, almost terror. Arbitrary arrests were suspended; Forts Warren and Lafayette and other Bastiles gave up their prisoners; and Mr. Seward graciously announced in an official dispatch, the return of the country to its "normal condition," when all citizens might freely oppose and criticise the measures and conduct of the men in power. But one more effort was yet to be essayed against Richmond. The fortunes of battle were committed to the "weak but presumptuous Burnside," who, on the 13th of December, for five hours, with frantic recklessness, drove on his columns against the Confederate intrenchments, and at nightfall, after the loss of fourteen thousand of his best troops, had earned the well-deserved cognomen of "The Butcher of Fredericksburg." The day before the battle, Mr. VALLANDIGHAM had arrived in New York. Affairs were now changed; and accepting a proffered serenade at the New York Hotel, he addressed a very large assembly, and there, amid great applause, first uttered the word "PEACE" in public meeting in that city.

Returning to Washington, he found the Administration and their friends in Congress casting about for some mode of escape from the struggle, with safety to themselves. Negotiation, armistice, mediation, peace, were no longer treasonable words. At this time he introduced a series of resolutions in favor of peace and reconstruction, and in condemnation of the doctrine of "State suicide or extinguishment," and also of all attempts, direct or indirect, to supersede the existing constitutional government, by a dictatorship. One of these resolutions was an almost literal transcript of a motion concerning the American war, made in the British House of Commons, by the Marquis of Granby, in November, 1777,and rejected by a vote of 243 to 86, in the third year of that war.

The Christmas recess of 1862 soon after occurred, and members separated. Reassembling in January, the drawn battle at Murfreesboro and the costly but total failure before Vicksburg had been added to the long list of disasters. About this time Mr. V. was approached by letter and personal interview, on the part of one of the most eminent and influential supporters of the Administration, to ascertain whether some means could not be devised to bring about a cessation of hostilities through foreign mediation, leaving the terms of adjustment to foreign arbitration. Whatever the design of this proposition, the effect and issue were palpable—*final peaceable separation.* Mr. V. was ready and anxious for any thing which would stop the war, and believing that mediation would at that time be "the speediest, easiest, most graceful mode" of effecting his object, he agreed to support it, but rejected "arbitration" as both impracticable and dangerous, insisting that "the people of the several States here, at home, must be the final arbitrators of the great quarrel in America; and the people and States of the Northwest, the mediators who should stand, like the prophet, betwixt the living and the dead, that the plague of disunion might be stayed." Pending this correspondence and conference, he addressed the House on the 14th of January, reviewing the great Civil War from the beginning to that date, and maintaining the practicability and necessity of reconstruction through peace and compromise. The speech was listened to by the House and crowded galleries with the profoundest attention; and when published, found millions of readers and admirers. A political enemy describing the delivery of it, wrote: "He waxes more earnest as he approaches the key note of his harangue, and with an energy and force that makes every hearer—as his moral nature revolts from the bribe—acknowledge all the more, the splendid force with which the tempter urges his cause, with flashing eye and livid features and extended hand, trembling with the passion of his utterance, he hurls the climax of his threatening argument again upon the Republican side of the House: 'Believe me, and accept it as you did not the solemn warnings of years past, *the day which divides the North from the South, that self-same day decrees eternal divorce between the West and the East.*'" But that part of the speech which he himself, no doubt, preferred to any other, was the following:

"I had rather my right arm were plucked from its socket and cast into eternal burnings than, with my convictions, to have thus defiled my soul with the guilt of moral perjury. Sir, I was not taught in that school which proclaims that 'all is fair in politics.' I loathe, abhor, and detest the execrable maxim. I stamp upon it. No State can endure a single generation whose public men practise it. Whoever teaches it is a corrupter of youth. What we most want in these times, and at all times, is honest and independent public men. That man who is dishonest in politics, is not honest at heart in any thing; and sometimes moral cowardice is dishonesty. Do right; and trust to God, and truth, and the people. Perish office, perish honors, perish life itself—but do the thing that is right, and do it like a man. I did it. Certainly, sir, I could not doubt what he must suffer who dare defy the opinions and passions, not to say the madness, of twenty millions of people. Had I not read history? Did I not know human nature? But I appealed to TIME; and right nobly hath the Avenger answered me."

He rejected utterly at that time, both in private letters and interviews, and in his speech, the idea of final separation as the object of a cessation of hostilities; and in this he uttered but the almost universal sentiment of the Democratic party. He believed that the Administration was then willing to make peace upon the basis of such separation, and only desired to have their opponents commit themselves to the same policy, thereby sharing the odium and relieving them, in part, from the responsibility of the act. Failing in this, they rallied late in January, and resolving upon a more "vigorous prosecution of the war" than ever before, resorted, at last, to a formal suspension of the habeas corpus, an indemnity to the President and all under him, and the Conscription. At the same time a formidable effort was made to revive the scheme of a new "conservative" party to supersede the Democratic organization and oppose radicalism, but support the war. This time the movement was to comprehend a portion of the Abolition or "Republican" party; and chief among its leaders were to be Thurlow Weed and William H. Seward. Mr. V. could, at that time, obtain no opportunity to address a public meeting in New York; but being invited to speak in Newark, New Jersey, very near to the former city, he gladly availed himself of the occasion to denounce, in the severest terms, the proposed arrangement. Whatever may have been the effect of the speech, it is certain that the movement utterly failed.

Meantime, in Congress, all the various war measures were pushed to the utmost. The Conscription bill called forth a vehement debate. By accident it had passed the Senate without opposition, while in the House it was announced that no debate would be allowed, and the "previous question" was moved, to force an immediate vote upon it. But the minority were resolved to be heard, and by parliamentary manœuvre called, in cant phrase, "fillibustering," compelled the majority to yield the point of discussion and amendment. One of the ablest debates ever heard in the House of Representatives followed. Crittenden, Pendleton, Voorhees, Biddle, and others, put forth their whole strength Mr. VALLANDIGHAM addressed the House at night on the 23d of February, in a speech, unprepared and without a single note except the paging of the extracts which he read, but which, in the language of Mr. Voorhees, "held the House spell-bound;" many upon both sides regarding it as his ablest Congressional effort, surpassing in argumentative force and concise vehemence, his speech of the 14th of January. His rebuke of an Administration member, for an offensive interruption soon after he took the floor, called forth applause, for the first time for him in that Congress, from the galleries. The bill, unconstitutional and odious as it still is as an act of Congress, was stripped of some of its worst features. Thus much, at least, was gained by the debate; though at last "the dumb eloquence of numbers" prevailed against the vehement oratory of Truth.

During the session he had occasion to defend his speech of the 20th of February, 1861, and the constitutional amendments in support of which it was delivered, from the gross perversions of a colleague; and just at the close of the session, to reply to a personal assault and refute a petty falsehood repeated in the House by another colleague.

The day after the adjournment of Congress he arrived at Philadelphia, and was there first entertained at dinner at the Girard House; then in the evening he briefly addressed an immense concourse of people in front of the hotel, and finally, later at night, partook of the elegant hospitalities of the "Philadelphia Club." Visiting New York city next, he addressed a large and enthusiastic assemblage at the rooms of the Young Men's Democratic Union Association, in a speech devoted to a review of the legislation of the session which had just closed (especially of the Conscription act), and a fuller development of his theory or plan of reconstruction through peace and negotiation. The next day he visited Albany on invitation for political conference, and a day or two later spoke at a Democratic meeting in Stamford, Connecticut, in support of Thomas H. Seymour, then a candidate for Governor of that State. Returning home on the 13th of March, he was met at the depot by thousands of his constituents, and borne amid great cheering to the court-house, where he was honored with an enthusiastic reception, which he duly acknowledged in a brief address, in the course of which he said: "I would resist no law by force, but would endure almost every other wrong, as long as free discussion, free assemblages of the people, and a free ballot remain; but the moment they are attacked, I would resist." Soon after, at a very large meeting in Hamilton, he vindicated the right of the people to keep and bear arms, and denounced, in just and indignant terms, a recent military order, "Number 15," forbidding citizens to purchase arms or ammunition. He declared it to be in direct conflict with "General Order Number One, the Constitution of the United States, George Washington commanding," and concluded thus: "Sir, I repeat now what I believe to be the true programme for these times: try every question of law in your courts, and every question of politics before the people, and through the ballot-box; maintain your constitutional civil rights, at all hazards, against military usurpation. Let there be no resistance to law, but meet and repel all mobs and mob violence by force and arms on the spot."

During the month of April he addressed large public meetings in various parts of the State; and in a bold and candid letter to a gentleman of Lancaster, Pennsylvania, urged that *antagonism* was the great element of party enthusiasm and strength; and that as the Administration were now contending solely for *unity and a strong government through war, and failing in that, then disunion*, both policy and duty required that the Democratic party should put itself in direct antagonism by declaring at once for *Union and constitutional liberty through an honorable peace.*

Meantime the renewed conspiracy of the Administration to suppress freedom of speech and of the press, and to break down all party opposition, and thereby to perpetuate their power by force, became, every day, more and more palpable. For obvious reasons, it was resolved that the Democratic party in the Northwest should be first crushed, and the Northwestern States reduced to the subjugated condition of the Border Slave States. A fit instrument for this execrable work was speedily found. Ambrose E. Burnside, "a name infamous forever in the ears of all lovers of constitutional liberty," was sent out from Washington, reeking with the blood of his own men massacred at Fredericksburg, as commander or military satrap of the Department of the Ohio, comprising the States of Kentucky, Ohio, Indiana, and Illinois. A native of Indiana, but of New England parentage, and "raised" in Rhode Island; weak in intellect and with an hereditary taint of hypochondriac insanity; a renegado from the Democratic party; ignorant of the first principles of civil liberty, and servile in his sycophancy to power, he entered upon his task with the violence of a military fanatic, and at the same time, the superserviceable zeal of a minion eager to anticipate the secret desires of his master, and earn the approving

> "Hubert, I love thee;
> Well, I'll not say what I intend for thee."

Incapable of public speaking, his first appearance, nevertheless, was as an orator at an Abolition meeting at Hamilton; his next, as author of "Order Thirty-Eight," with which his name will forever remain associated. It was a comprehensive and sweeping edict, under which every act of atrocity and outrage, including murder itself, could be and was perpetrated. For the first time a permanent "military commission" for the trial of citizens, men and women, was established in a State not in insurrection, and where the process of the courts never for a moment had been interrupted. One of the earliest victims was a delicate and elegant lady from Kentucky, and soon the military prisons were crowded. Full of the insolence of his satrapy, Burnside resolved to arrest Mr. VALLANDIGHAM. The State Convention had been fixed for the 11th of June. Aware of the purpose and plan to subjugate the Northwest, that gentleman had, along with others, labored earnestly to anticipate the movement, by bringing the convention forward to April, and making nominations before the conspiracy was ready for development. He expected to be nominated for Governor, and was satisfied, that if the Democratic party should place its candidates before the people, and open the political campaign first, neither himself nor any one else would be molested. Unfortunately, the proposition failed by a tie-vote in the committee. In the last week in April, a third "General Order" was announced at Indianapolis, expressly forbidding, in so many words, any criticism of the policy or conduct of the Administration. Mr. VALLANDIGHAM was at the time in Columbus, and immediately held a consultation with a number of his friends, declaring to them that the crisis had now arrived, and that some one must take the responsibility of meeting it at once, and endure the consequences. It was material to ascertain whether the spirit of the people was utterly broken, and ready for unlimited aud slavish submission. Accordingly, it was agreed that a meeting for Thursday evening, the 30th of April, should be held in front of the State House; and here, in a calm and well-considered speech, he announced his firm purpose to criticise and condemn any and all acts and policies of the party and men in power, whenever, in his judgment, they deserved censure, and in precisely the same manner and with the same freedom as in times past. "If it be really the design of the Administration," said he, "to force this issue, then come arrest, come imprisonment, come exile, come death itself, I am ready here to-night to meet it." But it was not for this speech that he was to be molested. Burnside had made other arrangements, better suited to his narrow intellect and crooked propensities. Mr. V. had at first declined to speak at the Mount Vernon meeting to be held on the 1st of May; but finally, the day before, had yielded to the urgency of a special messenger sent down to him at Columbus. His presence, therefore, was almost accidental; but his name had been announced, and Burnside had ordered two of his subaltern officers to strip themselves of their uniforms, and attend the meeting in the disguise of citizen's clothes as spies, and report his speech.* He spoke briefly and without special effort. Returning home the next day, he first heard rumors of his intended arrest. On Sunday, the 3d of May, they became more rife, and his friends proposed to organize to resist as in the year preceding, but he declined, saying, that if this were done now, he should be again obliged to remain in Dayton all summer, and thus be unable to canvass the State; since, if it was the purpose of the Administration to arrest him, it would be effected the first time he should leave home, and when he would be incapable of resistance. On the 4th, an Administration journal announced that officers had been sent up in disguise to Mount Vernon to watch and report him, and that he would have trouble. At half-past two o'clock the next morning, May 5, 1863, he was aroused from his slumbers by a loud knocking at his front door. Rising and inquiring from the window what was wanted, the officer in command of the detachment of soldiers,† answered that he had been sent by General Burnside to arrest him. Mr. V. denied the right of military arrest, and refused to come down. After repeated threats to shoot, intermingled with entreaties, the officer ordered the front door to be forced, but it was found too strong, and a door in the rear was finally broken down with an axe, and next the door of an upper bedchamber, and finally a third door opening into the room where, after dressing, he had retired. The house was now full of soldiers, though the officer in command had not ventured himself to enter. Half a score of muskets were pointed instantly at him, whereupon he said, "You have now broken open my house and overpowered me by superior force, and I am obliged to surrender." He then passed out through the shattered panels of his doors into the street; the bugle sounded the recall, and, surrounded by soldiery, he was marched to the depot, and thence carried by the cars to Cincinnati, where, soon after daylight, he was taken to the military prison, Kemper Barracks. Here he remained till evening, when, by order of Burnside, who had become greatly alarmed lest there should be a popular outbreak and rescue, he was hurried across the river to Newport Barracks, and there locked up for the night Next morning he was obliged to witness from his window the "roll-call" at reveille, with the "Stars and Stripes" waving over him and the band playing "Hail Columbia, Happy Land!" Soon after he was taken again across into Cincinnati, and thrust before the military commission, upon a "Charge and Specification," setting forth that, in vio-

* The names of these two miscreants were H. R. Hill and John A. Means, both captains in the 115th Regiment of Ohio Volunteers.

† Captain Charles G. Hutton, of Burnside's staff.

lation of Order Thirty-Eight, at Mount Vernon, on the 1st of May, in a public speech to the people, he had declared the war to be cruel and unnecessary; not waged for the preservation of the Union, but for the purpose of crushing out liberty and erecting a despotism—a war for the freedom of the blacks, and the enslavement of the whites; that he had denounced Order Thirty-Eight as a usurpation of power, and declared that the sooner the people should inform the minions of usurped power, that they would not submit to such restrictions upon their liberties, the better; and had asserted that he was at all times and upon all occasions resolved to do what he could to defeat the attempts which were being made to build up a monarchy upon the ruins of free government. Such was the "crime," and none other, and no more, upon which he was to be mocked with a "trial." Denying the authority and jurisdiction of the military commission,* he refused to plead; but the case was ordered to proceed. One only of the members was a citizen of Ohio; one was an unnaturalized foreign adventurer; another had been convicted of being the keeper of a disreputable house, while the Judge Advocate subsequently plead guilty to certain "nimble caperings" at the transom-light of a lady's bed-chamber in the Burnett House. They had been fitly selected for their work, and they did it accordingly. Two days were spent nominally in the "trial," at the end of which Mr. V. presented a brief and pointed "protest," repeating his denial of the jurisdiction of the Court, demanding a judicial trial by jury, and vindicating his right to make the speech for which ostensibly he had been arrested. Beyond this he declined to submit any thing. The finding and sentence of the military commission were not made public till the 18th. Meantime he had been removed to the Burnett House (Burnside's head-quarters), where in room "246," in the attic, he was kept under a strong guard, who were ordered, in case of any attempt at rescue or escape, to put him to death. Similar orders had been issued to his captors previous to his arrest.

During the few hours he was in Kemper Barracks prison, Mr. VALLANDIGHAM wrote a brief address to the Democrats of Ohio, and found means to pass it out for publication. He knew that the object of his arrest was to strike terror into others, and he was anxious to make it known that he himself was calm and unmoved, and to enjoin upon his friends to "stand firm and falter not an instant." The day of his arrest was one of intense excitement in Dayton. Thousands thronged the

* The members of this military commission (which sat at the St. Charles Restaurant on Third Street), were Brig.-Gen. Robert B. Potter, Col. John F. De Courcy, Lieut.-Col. E. R. Goodrich, Maj. John Mason Brown, of Kentucky, Maj. J. L. Van-Buren, Maj. A. H. Fitch, Capt. P. M. Lydig, and Judge-Advocate Capt. James Madison Cutts.

streets, and, at nightfall, the agitated mass broke out into violence. But meantime, Burnside, in great alarm, had sent up several companies of soldiers to suppress the disturbance, and the next day declared martial law throughout the county. More than thirty citizens were arrested and dragged down to the military prisons at Cincinnati; and for six weeks, every Democrat of Montgomery was at the mercy of an inebriate military commandant. Burnside's own brutal conduct towards the prisoners was consistent with his real character. He visited them more than once, and with oaths and curses, and, in one instance, with blows, vented his rage upon them. During the whole time that Mr. VALLANDIGHAM was in his custody, he was in constant fear of assassination, or, at least, of a popular outbreak and rescue; and while his prisoner enjoyed calm and unbroken slumbers aloft, the jailor trembled below, "afraid for the terror by night." A guard of soldiers, with fixed bayonets, and loaded muskets, marched with Mr. V. to and from the "Commission," and a squad of ten regulars kept watch day and night, over his room, while sentinels paced the pavements below. The author of the arrest had greatly misread the feelings of the people. Nearly everywhere, and by all parties, the act was at first condemned. But one newspaper in New York city, the Daily *Times*, justified it. Immense and violent public meetings were held all over the country in denunciation. Every day the popular indignation grew stronger and more intense. It had been Burnside's intention to arrest all the chief Democratic leaders of the Northwest; and in some cases, the orders had been made out. In alarm, he was now obliged to pause. His attempt soon after to suppress the Chicago *Times*, called forth so powerful an insurrectionary feeling, that the President was forced to revoke the order. Thus, through premature and too violent development, the whole conspiracy to break down party opposition to the men in power, and subjugate the Northwest, utterly failed. "Order Thirty-Eight" died. The counter-revolution, at last, fairly set in, and continued with increasing violence, till the Confederate invasion of Pennsylvania and the consequent fall of Vicksburg reversed the whole current, and revived the failing fortunes of the war-party and the Administration.

Two days after the "trial" before the military commission, the Hon. George E. Pugh, on behalf of Mr. VALLANDIGHAM, moved for a writ of habeas corpus, before Humphrey H. Leavitt, Judge of the United States Court for the Southern District of Ohio. No suspension of the privilege of the writ had, at that time, been declared under the act of Congress, and the pretence of a Presidential right to suspend it had been exploded. Judge Leavitt required that notice of the application should be first given to Burnside, who submitted an extraordinary paper, justifying the act, and claiming a constitutional and legal right to commit it, as military commandant of the Department of the Ohio, which he chose to regard as a vast camp, every citizen within its limits being subject to military law. The case was opened on the 11th, by Mr. Pugh, in an argument of great ability and consummate eloquence. He was replied to, on behalf of Burnside, by two members of the Cincinnati bar, in elaborate speeches, appropriated and modernized from the crown lawyers of the reign of Charles the First and James the Second.* Mr. Pugh rejoined in an argument of even greater ability than his first; and Judge Leavitt, after two or three days' consideration, and upon consultation with Burnside, refused the writ upon the grounds—first, that the arrest was legal; and, second, that though it had been illegal, it was "morally certain that the writ would not be obeyed," and therefore ought not to be issued. Not since the days of Empson, Dudley, or Jeffreys, had such judicial servility to executive power been exhibited. Never, except upon the trial of John Hampden, in the ship-money case, was a like "opinion" pronounced from the bench. Let a single sentence suffice: "The sole question," says this most righteous judge, "is whether the arrest was legal; and, as before remarked, *its legality depends on the necessity which existed for making it*, and of that necessity, for the reason stated, this court cannot judicially determine." And yet this monstrous doctrine is among the most moderate utterances of the opinion. The twelve judges of the First Charles were not more complaisant. "There is a rule of law," said one of them, "and a rule of government; and many things which may not be done by the rule of law, may be done by the rule of government;" and they all agreed that "when the good and safety of the kingdom in general is concerned, and the whole kingdom in danger, the king is the sole judge both of the danger, and when and how the same is to be prevented and avoided." The English judges held their offices during the pleasure of their master, the king. The American judge held his for life, and under a written constitution, which expressly declared that no citizen should be arrested, "except upon due process of law."†

Two days after the refusal of the habeas corpus, the "sentence" of the military commission and the approval of it by Burnside, was made public, condemning Mr. VALLANDIGHAM to "close confinement" in Fort Warren, Boston harbor, during the war. Imprisonment on the Dry

* Their names were Flamen Ball and Aaron F. Perry.

† Judge Leavitt, while a member of Congress, had received his appointment nearly thirty years previously from President Jackson; but soon after, upon the currency question, deserted him, and never afterwards claimed to be, or was recognized as a member of the Democratic party.

Tortugas Islands had, at first, been contemplated; and many believed that sentence of death had been Burnside's original purpose, from which he was deterred alone by the violence of the popular indignation which the arrest had excited. Whether this be true or not, he certainly insisted to a distinguished gentleman of Cincinnati, that he might justly put Mr. V. to death for a speech delivered by him at Batavia, in April.

On the 19th of May, Mr. VALLANDIGHAM was transferred from the Burnett House to the gunboat "Exchange," then lying in the Ohio, opposite Cincinnati, near Newport Barracks. The same evening Abraham Lincoln changed the "sentence," and ordered Burnside to send him under secure guard, to General Rosecrans, to be by him put beyond the Federal military lines; ordering further that in case of his return within the lines, he should be arrested and kept in close custody for the term originally specified. This order was executed a day or two after, and he arrived by rail from Louisville, on Sunday night, May 24, at Rosecrans's head-quarters, Murfreesboro, Tennessee. By that officer, after a few moments plain but respectful talk upon both sides, he was properly received and hospitably entertained for several hours; and at two o'clock on the morning of the 25th, under a numerous guard of cavalry, left for the Confederate lines, by way of the Shelbyville pike, halting at the house of a Mr. Butler till daybreak, and then resuming the march to the "neutral ground," where, at the house of a Mrs. Alexander, he breakfasted, while the Federal officers, under a flag of truce, made known their purpose. After some delay they returned, and he was taken to within a short distance of the extreme picket-line, and there set down at the house of Jeremiah Odell, first in presence of the Federal officers, having addressed these words to the Confederate soldier who had been sent out to meet him: "I am a citizen of Ohio and of the United States. I am here within your lines by force and against my will. I, therefore, surrender myself to you as a prisoner of war." He knew well the shallow object of Abraham Lincoln in banishing him within the Confederate lines, and the moment it was announced to him on board the gunboat at Cincinnati, had resolved to defeat it at the outset.

For several hours, while the answer of General Bragg, who was sixteen miles distant, was being obtained to the question whether he should be received, he remained in the "neutral ground." They were hours of solitude, but calmly spent—the bright sun shining in the clear sky above him, and faith in God and the future burning in his heart. At noon, a favorable answer having been returned, he was received within the Confederate lines, and passing, under cavalry escort, through numerous camps, reached General Bragg's head-quarters, at Shelbyville, soon after dusk. Here he was kindly received, and directed to the house of Mrs. Eakin, where a spacious and pleasant room had been provided for him. "I retired at once," he wrote to a friend, "having slept but half an hour since Saturday night, and was awakened early next morning by the rays of a bright Southern sun piercing the eastern window of my room. There were no sentinels at my door, and I walked out unchallenged." In Shelbyville he remained a week in almost entire seclusion, passing his time in reading. On the 1st of June he was directed to report on parole, to General Whiting, at Wilmington, North Carolina; and the next day left by the cars, passing through Tullahoma, Chattanooga, Knoxville, and Bristol, to Lynchburg, where he was met by Colonel Robert Ould, the Confederate commissioner of prisoners, and by him accompanied through Petersburg to Wilmington, where he reported to General Whiting. At every depot from Shelbyville to the end of his journey of more than a thousand miles, large numbers of the people were assembled to meet him; but no public demonstration was attempted, and he passed quietly to his destination. Before leaving Cincinnati, he had resolved to reach Canada at the earliest moment; and in case he found blockade-running from the Eastern ports impracticable or too hazardous, then to cross the Mississippi and make his way through Texas to Matamoras, and thence by steamer to Havana and Halifax. But at that time vessels were running to and from Wilmington almost with the regularity of packets; and after a sojourn there of a few days, he took passage on the steamer "Cornubia," Captain Gayle, and on the evening of the 17th of June, ran out in safety through the blockading squadron, and arrived in Bermuda on the 20th. In these quiet and very pleasant islands he remained ten days, and thence by steamer went to Halifax, landing on the 5th of July. From Halifax by way of Truro, he travelled to Pictou, and thence by steamer up the Gulf and River Saint Lawrence, to Quebec, where, as in Bermuda and at Halifax, he was cordially and honorably received. At the Club-House he was tendered and accepted a very handsome entertainment, at which he met a number of the most distinguished gentlemen of Canada. The same evening he left by special train generously provided for him, for the Clifton House, Niagara Falls, where he arrived on the 15th of July, after a journey of more than four thousand miles by land and sea, and twelve days earlier than the day which he had designated to his friends previous to leaving Cincinnati. Of the incidents and adventures of this long journey the time has not yet come to write.

The day he left for the South upon the gunboat, he published a brief address to his party in Ohio, in which he declared that in vain the malice of enemies should contrive to give color to the calumnies and misrepresentations of the past two years; that no order of banishment executed by superior force, could release him from his obligations or deprive him of his rights as a citizen of Ohio and of the United States;

that he should maintain his allegiance as such citizen, wherever he might be, till his return; and that meantime he did not doubt that the people of Ohio, not cowering for a moment before either the threat or the exercise of arbitrary power, would in every trial prove themselves worthy to be called freemen.

The Democratic State Convention of Ohio assembled at Columbus, on the 11th of June. In many respects it was the most remarkable political meeting ever held in the United States. Although but a delegate convention, the people came up from every county, to the number of more than twenty thousand. Even from parts of the State traversed by railroads, many travelled in wagons, and bringing provisions with them, camped out. At daylight on the morning of the 11th, three several orators, from as many different stands in the State Houseyard, were haranguing the people. Mr. VALLANDIGHAM was nominated for Governor, by a vote of four hundred and eleven to thirteen, and the nomination ratified by the assembled multitudes, by acclamation. Unfortunately, the committee on resolutions refused to make the direct issue of PEACE, and chose to put the campaign solely upon the question of personal liberty—one of the noblest, certainly, and most momentous ever submitted to any people. Throughout the entire canvass it was pressed to the utmost, but the subject of peace almost totally ignored.

In every State, by the Democratic and Conservative parties and press, the nomination was hailed with extraordinary enthusiasm, and few, at that time, doubted his triumphant election. But when he had arrived at Niagara Falls, a month later, all was changed. The invasion of Pennsylvania, and the victories of Gettysburg, Vicksburg and Port Hudson, had reversed the counter-revolution; the "rebellion" was, in the belief of nineteen-twentieths of the people, at last really crushed out, and the whole country once more was made to cry aloud for war. No man was more conscious of the immense change in public affairs and the popular sentiment which three weeks had brought forth, than Mr. VALLANDIGHAM. Yet his fixed convictions were not shaken for a moment, and in the "Address" published by him at that time, he alluded to the subject in these words, which were then to the Republicans foolishness, and to his friends a stumbling-block. But he knew them to be well founded, and events since have more than justifed him:

"If this civil war," he wrote, "is to terminate only by the subjugation or submission of the South to force and arms, the infant of to-day will not live to see the end of it. No, in another way only can it be brought to a close. Travelling a thousand miles and more, through nearly one-half of the Confederate States, and sojourning for a while at widely different points, I met not one man, woman, or child, who was not resolved to perish rather than yield to the pressure of arms even in the most desperate extremity. And whatever may and must be the varying fortune of the war, in all which I recognize the hand of Providence pointing visibly to the ultimate issue of this great trial of the States and people of America, *they are better prepared now every way to make good their inexorable purpose, than at any period since the beginning of the struggle.* These may indeed be unwelcome truths; but they are addressed only to candid and honest men."

At the same time, nominated while still in the Confederate States, and thus honored by the most distinguished testimony of public confidence which could be bestowed, he felt constrained to accept the issue just as it had been tendered in the "platform" of the Convention; and for the moment to ignore, though never to retract, his well-known and long-settled opinions and convictions upon the question of the war and peace. And this position he consistently maintained throughout the canvass; alluding again, and only casually, to that question, in the letter of July 31st, to the Toledo meeting, in this language: "Continual war and strife are the forbidden fruit of our political Eden, and bear still the primal curse, uttered in tones louder than the voice of the mighty cataract in whose presence I now write—*In the day that thou eatest thereof thou shall surely die.*"

Soon after Mr. VALLANDIGHAM's arrest, a large and potential indignation meeting had been held at Albany, New York, to which Governor Horatio Seymour had addressed a remarkable letter, very decided and even revolutionary in its tone and language. Strong resolutions were adopted, and a committee appointed to transmit them to Mr. Lincoln, calling upon him, at the same time, to discharge Mr. V. from imprisonment. The Ohio State Convention also selected a committee of nineteen, one from each Congressional district, composed of some of the very first men of the State, to present to him the resolution requesting, not as a favor but a right, the revocation of the order of banishment. These gentlemen repaired to Washington, and in person discharged their duty. To both committees, Mr. Lincoln returned separate replies in writing, justifying the outrage, and insisting gravely and without a "joke," upon his constitutional right to commit and repeat it. In these extraordinary letters he maintained the whole doctrine of "military necessity," insisting that the Constitution in time of war, varied "in its application," from the Constitution in time of peace, so that its limitations upon power, and the rights secured by it to the States and the people ceased, in cases of rebellion and invasion involving the public safety, to be applicable, and that "the man whom, for the time, the people had, under the Constitution, made the commander-in-chief of the army and navy, was the man" who was to decide when the public safety was involved, and what in that case ought to be done. He went further, and forgetting his high position as President, resorted to deliberate falsehood, subterfuge, and prevarication, in order to justify the particular act of which the committees complained. Wholly ignoring the "charge and specification" upon which alone Mr. VALLANDIGHAM had been arrested and subjected to trial by the military commission, and conceding in so many words, that if the arrest were made for language addressed to a public meeting in criticism of the Administration, or in condemnation of the military order of the General, "it was wrong," he did not scruple to assert that Mr. V. was arrested "because he was laboring with some effect, to prevent the raising of troops, *to encourage desertions from the army*, and to leave the rebellion without an adequate military force to suppress it." No such charge had been preferred against him, and it was without the slightest foundation in truth. He repeated, also, the false statement that the Judge who refused the habeas corpus, was a member of the Democratic party; and in his reply to the Ohio committee, with mingled falsehood and hypocrisy, and in the form of solemn adjuration, charged the man who, under his own edict, executed by force, was absent where his voice in self-defence could not be heard, with complicity with armed combinations to resist the conscription and the arrest of deserters, and with numerous acts of assassination which he declared had been committed. These were his words: "And now, under a sense of responsibility more weighty and enduring than any which is merely official, I solemnly declare my belief that this hindrance of the military, including maiming and murder, is due to the course in which Mr. VALLANDIGHAM has been engaged, in a greater degree than to any other cause; and is due to him personally in a greater degree than to any other one man. These things have been notorious, known to all." And yet, while they constituted distinct and overt acts of crime, easy of proof if true, they formed no part of the "charge and specification" before Burnside's military commission, to prove which he had stripped two of his officers of their uniform, and sent them as spies to Mt. Vernon. Did ever official insolence and mendacity go further? Nor was this all: with a full knowledge that Mr. VALLANDIGHAM's speeches, including the very one for which ostensibly he was arrested, were full of injunctions to obey all laws and to respect all rightful authority, Mr. Lincoln did not hesitate to add that with all these acts of violence and resistance "staring him in the face, he (Mr. V.) had never uttered a word of rebuke or counsel against them." Yet after all these assertions, he declared in his reply to the Albany committee, and repeated it in his letter to the committee from Ohio, that Mr. VALLANDIGHAM's arrest "had been for *prevention*, and not for *punishment*; not so much for what had been done, *as for what probably would be done*." He concluded his letter to the Ohio committee, with an offer to revoke the order of banishment, upon the condition that the several members of the committee should bind themselves to certain propositions in writing submitted by him, which implied nothing less than support of the war, and indorsement of the Administration; but he added, with despotic insolence, that "in regard to Mr. VALLANDIGHAM and all others, he would thereafter as theretofore, do so much as the public safety might seem to require." To the propositions thus made, the committee replied that they "were not authorized to enter into any bargains, terms, contracts, or conditions, with the President of the United States to procure the release of Mr. VALLANDIGHAM." The entire correspondence was conducted, on the part of both committees, with great dignity and consummate ability; and but for the stirring military events at that time transpiring in Pennsylvania and the Mississippi Valley, would have produced a powerful effect upon the public mind. But delusive and unsubstantial successes in the field had revived, to a large extent, the popular delirium of war; and again, amid arms, as well reason as laws were silent.

In August, Mr. VALLANDIGHAM, after a brief tour down the lakes and the River St. Lawrence to Montreal and Quebec, selected Windsor, in Canada West, opposite Detroit, Michigan, as his place of sojourn. It was easy of access and convenient for communication with Ohio and the Northwest; while the beautiful Detroit River and Lakes Erie and St. Clair, full of fish and fowl, and the thick forests around abounding in game, could afford healthful exercise for the body, and pleasure to the mind. He arrived on the 24th, and the next day was visited by a large delegation of his fellow-citizens from Detroit, who gave him a cordial welcome. "How priceless is this exile," said the gentleman selected to speak on behalf of the delegation, "since it has caused the usurpers of power to pause in their mad career, and has nerved the arm and aroused the vigilance of freemen to defend the great corner-stone of free institutions—free speech and a free press!" Mr. V. replied in appropriate terms, but, with rare delicacy and forbearance, declined to speak in personal denunciation, in a foreign country, of those by whom he had been so deeply wronged. "Claiming the fullest right at home," he said, "to criticise and condemn the men and acts of the Administration, and meaning there and at the proper time to again exercise it to the utmost, I yet, on foreign soil, have no word of bitterness to speak. I only remember now that they represent my country, and forbear."

At this time the political canvass in Ohio had become intensely excited. Nothing equal to it had previously been witnessed—not even in 1840. The meetings of Mr. VALLANDIGHAM'S friends numbered from ten thousand to thirty thousand, and in some instances even fifty thousand, in attendance. For weeks, all except political agitation and discussion, was laid aside and forgotten. A body of public speakers second to none in any State, and including several of the highest national reputation, addressed the people day and night. Gallantly and with matchless eloquence, Mr. Pugh, as candidate for Lieutenant-Governor, bore the Democratic standard in the fight. It had been Mr. V.'s earnest desire and purpose to return home early in September to aid in the canvass; but the judgment of his friends was decidedly against it, because of political considerations, and he felt obliged reluctantly to acquiesce. But from Windsor during the canvass, he addressed two earnest letters to his party in the State—one in reply to the threat that civil war in Ohio should follow his election, and the other in warning and denunciation of the formal suspension, on the 15th of September, of the privilege of the writ of *habeas corpus* in every State. At this time many of his friends believed that his triumph was certain. The Administration were greatly alarmed. "Don't ask me to do any thing," said Lincoln to Wendell Phillips, "till after the Ohio election." It was his design, at one time, to attempt to control the election by force, as in Kentucky; and the suspension of the writ of *habeas corpus* was the first step in that direction. But the firm front shown by the Democratic party, and their fixed purpose to resist by arms, if necessary, compelled him to change the scheme from force to fraud, and through the joint aid of secret "Union Leagues" and the War Department, his success was complete. For although Mr. VALLANDIGHAM received a larger vote by many thousands, than was ever before given to a Democratic candidate for Governor of Ohio, yet the vote of the State was recorded against him, by a majority of sixty-one thousand, exclusive of thirty-nine thousand returned from the army. The friends of the Administration had repeatedly declared that they could better sustain the loss of a battle, or even of a whole campaign, in the field, than to lose the political control of Ohio, by his election. But success attended them everywhere; and in every State, except New Jersey, the Democratic party, no matter upon what platform or with what candidates, whether for peace or the war, suffered a decisive defeat. Even in the army, the Democratic vote of Ohio was no less than that received by the candidate of that party in Iowa, though he held a brigadier's command at the time, in actual military service in the Southwest.

Mr. VALLANDIGHAM had well known that his election was impossible, and therefore could have been surprised only by the majority against him. But he calmly heard the announcement of his defeat, and the same day published an Address to the Democrats of Ohio, saying: "You are beaten; but a nobler battle for constitutional liberty and free popular government, never was fought by any people. And your unconquerable firmness and courage, even in the midst of armed military force, secured you those first of freemen's rights—free speech and a free ballot. The conspiracy of the fifth of May, fell before you. Be not discouraged; despair not of the Republic. Maintain your rights: stand firm to your position; never yield up your principles or your organization."

In November, a large delegation of the students of the University of Michigan, at Ann Arbor, called upon him at Windsor. To the sincere and glowing speech of the young gentleman who presented the delegation, Mr. VALLANDIGHAM replied in an address which by men of all parties, was regarded as a rare example of wise and moral counsel and scholarly eloquence. He appreciated the tribute thus paid to one who had no rewards to bestow, saying: "The applause of the young is the highest praise. They speak the language of the coming generation, and anticipate the judgment of posterity." But he preferred to change the visit of ceremony into one of profit; and besides sound advice in regard to study and the pursuits of after-life, enjoined the highest morality. "Remember," said he, "that ability, however eminent, and intellectual discipline, however exact, are not enough. Without pure morals, correct habits, and fixed integrity, you cannot endure the trial. Be virtuous. Be pious. I use the word in no narrow, sectarian, or theological sense; but in that which Virgil means when he calls Æneas, '*pius*'—a piety which belongs to no one sect, nor clime, nor time, nor country, but which everywhere and at all times, renders to God, and self, and man, whatever is due, and does in the very spirit of the Sermon on the Mount." But that which most nearly disclosed one of the chief traits of his own character, was the injunction: "Have faith—absolute, unquestioning, immovable—that faith which, speaking to itself in the silence and calm of the heart's own beating, says, 'If not to-day, or this time, then to-morrow, or next, or some other day, at some other time, in some other way, all will be well.' Without this, no one ever achieved greatness." Such were the sentiments, amid persecution, in exile, and after defeat, of the man whom his competitor for gubernatorial honors graciously consigned, after the election, to oblivion.

At Niagara Falls Mr. VALLANDIGHAM was daily overwhelmed with visitors from every State, and the throng was but little diminished at Windsor. Spies, too, beset him at every step; but to no purpose. The Administration seemed to fear him somewhat as Châteaubriand said the gray coat and cocked hat of the First Napoleon was feared by the Legitimists of Europe. The United States gun-boat Michigan, with loaded cannon and steam up, lay opposite his bed-room window for four weeks, lest he should, perchance, land in Detroit, and, possibly, capture and destroy the city; while a score of detectives, provided with his photograph, kept watch in every public place. At all this he could smile in calm contempt.

Since the election, Mr. VALLANDIGHAM has lived in great quietude and seclusion in Windsor. Like the Master of Ravenswood, he has chosen for his motto, "I bide my time." In a letter to a friend, written in November, he thus describes his daily way of life: "I am here as calm, as determined, as steadfast, and as hopeful as ever, and as busy too. I am reviewing history and political philosophy; dipping a little into the ancient classics again; making notes and memoranda of the times; writing letters; and closely, day by day, watching the course of events at home and abroad; ready for any fortune, and, I hope, equal to it. I see many visitors also, and spend not an idle moment—for my recreations, riding, walking, fishing, hunting, &c., I do not count idleness."

In February, 1864, Mr. Pugh applied in the Supreme Court of the United States at Washington, for a writ of *certiorari* to review and annul the proceedings and sentence of the military commission before which Mr. V. had been tried. But that tribunal, having under the Constitution no appellate jurisdiction of any kind, except in cases first ascertained by law, and Congress not having given such jurisdiction in any proceeding before courts-martial or military commissions, was obliged, and upon this ground expressly and alone, to deny the writ. No American legislator had ever before imagined that any mere citizen would, under any circumstances, be subjected to trial by military law, in a State where judicial process and courts had never been interrupted; and, therefore, no mode of redress had ever been provided.

In 1846, Mr. VALLANDIGHAM was married to Miss Louisa A. McMahon, a sister of the Hon. John V. L. McMahon, of Baltimore, Maryland. and daughter of William McMahon, one of the purest and best of men, who lived and died a pious and honored citizen of Cumberland in the same State. He has but one child living, a bright, noble boy of ten years of age. He has only two brothers—one the Rev. James L. Vallandigham, of Newark, Delaware; and the other, Dr. George S. Vallandigham, residing in New Lisbon, Ohio. A younger brother died many years ago. His own personal appearance is thus described by an Englishman writing from Niagara Falls: "A more thorough gentleman in manner, appearance, and language, it would not be easy to find; certainly it would be difficult to get many such among those who assail him so bitterly. He is a man of medium height and build, fresh in complexion—that freshness which betokens health—and exceedingly intelligent-looking, without that massiveness of brain which frequently, though not always, accompanies great intellectual power. Exceedingly amiable in disposition, he is respected by all who know him. Refined in manner and language, he impresses you on the instant as few American politicians impress you. Were I to describe him in a word, not knowing his native country, I would say he was an English gentleman of good education and training, of great probity, and much more than an average share of ability and political acquirements. A schemer, even in politics, I could not conceive him to be." But, perhaps, the most concise and accurate personal description of him, is the following, from a Southern paper, written in May, 1863: "Whilst in Shelbyville, I seized the opportunity of seeing Mr. VALLANDIGHAM. Without impertinently intruding upon that distinguished man, I heard him converse for an hour or so, upon one topic and another. His manner has nothing studied or affected; he speaks without effort or hesitation, and his face bears a permanent expression of good humor and friendship. His eyes are blue, full, and look right into yours; and whilst they beam with vivacity and intelligence, there is an earnest honesty in them which has won your regard and admiration before you know it. His complexion is florid, his nose rather hooked (Roman), chin and lips well chiselled and firm, teeth strong and white, hair and whiskers dark chestnut and close trimmed, height about five feet ten. His frame is robust, compact, and graceful. Altogether he is certainly a man of extraordinary mental and physical vigor; of great natural abilities improved by cultivation, combining impulse with deliberation, and enthusiasm with remorseless determination of purpose."

As a speaker, Mr. VALLANDIGHAM is thus described by a correspondent of the Boston *Herald*, an Administration paper: "His method of speaking is very attractive. Added to fine appearance of person, he has a good voice and gesture, and always speaks without notes. I might add, also, that his great coolness amid the most heated discussions, is one of his peculiarities, and gives him decided advantages over more impassioned antagonists." Another hostile correspondent, referring to the delivery of a particular passage in one of his speeches, says: "With flashing eye and livid features, and extended hand trembling with the passion of his utterance, he hurls the climax of his threatening argument upon the Republican side of the House."

Since the foregoing was written, Mr. VALLANDIGHAM has returned to his home in Dayton, Ohio. He came of his own act and pleasure, appearing, unknown to all, before the Democratic District Convention at Hamilton, Ohio, on the 15th of June. He was received with the most extraordinary demonstrations of enthusiasm and joy, and having first been appointed a delegate to the Democratic Presidential Convention, at Chicago, addressed the people; soon after which he took the train for Dayton, where he arrived late in the afternoon, and drove immediately to his own home, which he had not seen for thirteen months. In the evening hundreds called, and day and night ever since, his house has been thronged with cordial and determined friends. The evening after his return he was serenaded, and addressed from his own portico an assemblage of some two thousand persons, called together upon a few hours' notice. So far no attempt has been made to rearrest or in any way to interfere with him.

July, 1864.

From Mr. VALLANDIGHAM's private note-book we are permittted to copy the following, dated in August, 1843. How closely he has adhered to these resolutions of his early youth, his subsequent public and private life abundantly attest. He pursued them faithfully till, just twenty years later, they led him into exile, and yet he clings to them still:

"FIXED RULES

Of political conduct to guide me as a statesman; *in no instance and under no circumstances whatever* to be relaxed or violated; and this by the blessing of Almighty God:

"1. Always to pursue what is honest, right, and just, though adverse to the apparent and *present* interests of the country; well assured that what is not *right*, cannot, in the long run, be expedient.

"2. Always to prefer MY COUNTRY, and the whole country, before any and all considerations of mere party.

"3. In all things coolly to ascertain, and, with stern independence, to pursue the dictates of my judgment and my conscience, regardless of the consequences to party or self.

"4. As far as consistent with the national honor and safety, and with justice to the country, to seek PEACE with all nations and to pursue it; persuaded that a pacific policy is the true wisdom of a State, and war its folly; yet as resolved to demand nothing but what is right, so to submit to nothing that is wrong.

"5. Sedulously, at all times and in every place, to calm and to harmonize the conflicting interests and sectional jealousies of the different divisions of the Republic, and especially of the North and South; and with steady perseverance, under all circumstances, to uphold and cement the Union of the States as "the palladium of our political safety and prosperity"—except at the sacrifice of the just constitutional liberties and inalienable rights of oppressed minorities.

"6. Without infringing the rights of conscience, always to countenance and support religion, morality, and education, as essential to the well-being of a free Government; and in all things to acknowledge the superintending Providence of an All-Wise, Most Just, and Beneficent God, in the affairs of the Republic."

SPEECHES.

"I appealed to Time; and right nobly hath the Avenger answered me."

Speech of Jauuary 14, 1863.

SPEECHES, ETC.

THE CONSTITUTIONAL POWER OF THE LEGISLATURE TO ALTER LEGISLATIVE DISTRICTS.*

The minority of the Committee on Privileges and Elections, to which was referred the memorial of Daniel Chandler, contesting the right of Jordan Betts, the sitting member from the county of Morgan, to the seat which he at present holds in this House, respectfully report: That they have bestowed upon the case, submitted to them, all that attention which its importance demanded. They regret the necessity which compels them to differ wholly with the majority of the committee. But since a difference—a wide, though an honest difference—separates them, in their conclusions, from that majority, it remains only for them to present, for the consideration of the House, the reasonings by which they have been governed, in their judgment upon the papers referred to the committee.

It has been a matter, also, of surprise and regret, that, in a case partaking so much of the nature of a judicial proceeding, efforts should have been made, out of doors, to prejudge the rights of the parties to this contested election: still more, that such efforts should have been countenanced within the House. This, in the opinion of the undersigned, is not a matter in which the deference or the allegiance which every man ought, and can honorably owe to party habitudes, or to the wishes and opinions of his fellows of a kindred political faith, ought to be allowed the smallest influence. Upon the facts, the law, and the Constitution, it behooves every member to decide in his own individual judgment, since the Constitution of the State, by the eighth section of the first article, has made him a "judge" of the qualifications and the election of his fellow-members.

* Report submitted by Mr. Vallandigham, from the minority of the Election Committee, in the Ohio House of Representatives, December 18, 1845, in the Morgan county contested election, *Daniel Chandler* against *Jordan Betts.*

The papers and other documents referred to, or in possession of the committee, present the following state of facts:

An act of the General Assembly, passed December 29, 1817, erected certain portions of the counties of Washington, Guernsey, and Muskingum, into a new county, called by the name of Morgan, comprising within its territory, as prescribed in the act, the townships of Bloom, Bristol, Brookfield, Centre, Deerfield, Jackson, Malta, Manchester, Morgan, Meigsville, Noble, Olive, Penn, Union, York, and Windsor, together with two other townships, subsequently attached to an adjoining county.

In the year 1843, in pursuance of section 2, article 1, of the Constitution of Ohio, an enumeration was made of all the white male inhabitants above twenty-one years of age, residing within the State.

On the 12th day of March, 1844, the Legislature passed "an act to fix and apportion the representation of the General Assembly of the State of Ohio," the first clause of which act is in the words following: "Be it enacted, &c., that the General Assembly of this State shall be composed of thirty-six Senators, and seventy-two Representatives, to be apportioned as follows": The 19th clause, section 1st, of that act, fixes and apportions "to the counties of Perry, Morgan, and Washington, one Senator, to be elected in the years 1845 and 1847; to each of said counties one Representative, and an additional Representative to the county of Morgan, in the year 1847." Morgan county, which, by this act, was thus organized into an electoral district, and declared entitled to one Representative in the years 1844, '45, and '46, and to an additional one in the year 1847, was composed, at the time said act was passed, of the territory including the townships before named. No other territory, and no white male inhabitants above twenty-one years of age, other than such as were living at that time, constituted the territory, and the white male inhabitants, above twenty-one years of age, of the county called Morgan, at the date of the act before recited.

By a local law, passed March 11th, 1845, the townships of Homer and Marion, being parts of the territory within the county of Athens, together with seven sections of the township of Roxbury, in Washington county, were attached to the county of Morgan. Four and a half of these sections were subsequently incorporated, by the commissioners of Morgan county, with Windsor township, in that county, and the remaining two sections and a half, with the township of Marion. The act made no provision requiring the votes of the electors within the townships and sections annexed by it, to be polled or counted for Representative in Morgan county. It is silent, altogether, upon that subject.

On the 14th of October, 1845, in pursuance of the Constitution, and of the laws of the State, an election was held in Morgan, as in other counties, for certain officers, and among these, for Representative in the General Assembly. Two candidates for the office were presented to the people—Jordan Betts and Daniel Chandler. Of the votes cast in the townships of Morgan county, before enumerated, together with the townships and sections attached by the act of 11th March, 1845, Mr. Chandler received two thousand one hundred and eighty-seven, Mr. Betts two thousand one hundred and fourteen, exhibiting a majority of seventy-three votes for Mr. Chandler. But of the votes polled in the townships, comprising that county, at the period of the fixing and apportionment of the representation, by the act of March 12th, 1844, two thousand and fourteen were cast for Betts, and one thousand eight hundred and fifty-eight for Chandler, showing a majority for Mr. Betts, of one hundred and fifty-six votes.

Assuming that the votes polled in the townships of Homer and Marion could not, in conformity with the Constitution, and with law, be deemed votes legally cast for Representative, in the county of Morgan as an electoral district, the clerk of the Common Pleas, and the justices whom, in pursuance of the statute, he had called to his assistance, refused to count the votes so polled; and accordingly, Mr. Betts, having a majority of all other votes, received from the clerk a certificate of election to the seat which he now holds in the House. Mr. Chandler contests the right of Mr. Betts to that seat, and presents his memorial, which has been read by the clerk.

Upon this statement of facts, two questions are presented for the judgment of the House—

1. Was it *the intent* of the act of 11th March, 1845, or did it *so operate*, as to make the townships and sections enumerated in it, *so far a part of the county of Morgan*, as to entitle the white male inhabitants above the age of twenty-one, residing in those townships and sections, to vote *for Representative in that county*.

2. If such were the intent or the operation of the act, is it, so far, an act which the Legislature has constitutional power to pass?

Preliminary to the consideration of these questions, and for the purpose of disembarrassing the subject of all matters either not controverted, or not necessarily connected with the issue joined upon the case, and of ascertaining the precise points of controversy, the undersigned here state what is or might be safely, and with truth, admitted.

It is admitted, that if the votes polled for Representative in the townships of Homer and Marion, be counted as votes legally cast in the county of Morgan, Mr. Chandler is entitled to the seat which he claims in his memorial; otherwise, Mr. Betts is entitled to that seat.

It is admitted that the Legislature may constitutionally establish new counties, or alter the boundaries of old ones, incorporating parts of the territory of one county into the territory of another. With all this, we have nothing do.

It might be admitted that the votes polled in the townships and sections annexed by the act of '45, for *county* officers, ought to have been, and were, rightfully received and counted as votes given in Morgan county:—it might equally be admitted that they were illegally and improperly so received and counted; and yet, Mr. Betts be entitled to his seat.

It might be admitted that the votes of the sections above referred to, were improperly counted among the votes polled in Morgan county *for Representative.* Four and a half of these sections were incorporated, as before stated, with Windsor township, in that county. It was, and is, impossible to distinguish between the votes legally and those illegally so polled in that township. But the dilemma is readily solved. In Windsor township, Mr. Betts received 116 votes; Mr. Chandler, 125. Now let *all* the votes cast in that township for Mr. Betts be *rejected*, and all the votes received in it by Mr. Chandler be *counted;* still, Mr. Betts has a clear majority of forty votes; and therefore, so far, is entitled to his seat.

It might be admitted that the act of March, '45, was passed at the instance of the people, *without distinction of party*, residing in the territory annexed by it to Morgan county—that it was passed for their convenience—that said territory and its inhabitants were received and treated as part of that county, for county purposes—that the property within that territory was placed for taxation upon the duplicate of the county of Morgan—all this may be admitted, and still, Mr. Betts be entitled to his seat.

It might be admitted that the former distribution of Representatives was unjust and unequal, so far as to the counties named in the act of 1845;—that the act only so altered that distribution, as to remove the inequality; and still, Mr. Betts be entitled to his seat.

It might be admitted that the electors of township number four, which, by an act passed January 29, 1827, was incorporated with the county of Lorain, voted with that county for its Representative in the General Assembly, though of that fact there was no evidence presented to the Committee. But since no question was raised in the case, it cannot be regarded as a precedent of any great value. So that, still. Mr. Betts may be entitled to his seat.

And finally, as a matter to which the undersigned entreat the very earnest and candid consideration of the House—it might even be conceded that the clerk of the Common Pleas of Morgan county had violated the most solemn responsibilities of his office—trifled with the obligation of his oath—trampled upon the Constitution, and set at defiance the laws, the whole statute-book, violating flagrantly every page of it, from the first syllable to the last—nay, he might even have done what he did do, for a *pecuniary recompense—for money*, thus superadding the crime of bribery to the accumulated guilt of a violation of all other moral, constitutional, and legal responsibilities;—and yet, under the laws and the Constitution, Mr. Betts be entitled to his seat. With the action of the justices and the clerk, the House has just nothing to do. For had Mr. Chandler received the certificate of election, beyond a doubt, Mr. Betts might have appeared at the bar of the House as contestor. And in such event, it is plain as the sun at broad noon, that the question would have been precisely what it now is. The question is *not*, who ought to have had the certificate from the clerk, but, who is *now* entitled by the law and the Constitution, to a seat as the Representative from the county of Morgan? In respect to the action of the justices and the clerk, the minority have this only now to say:—that if the townships of Homer and Marion constituted *no part*, under the Constitution or the law, of the county of Morgan, for the purposes of the election of a Representative for [illegible] county, the clerk and the justices whom he called to his assistance, had no more right, and were under no greater obligation to receive the poll-books from those townships, than from any other township in any other county in the State; and were bound to refuse them so far as to the votes cast for Representative.

The undersigned ask now the attention of the House to the first point before submitted. Nothing can be clearer, than that there is no *express intent* declared in the act of March 11, 1845, to the effect that the electors of the territory annexed to the county of Morgan, should vote for Representative, with that county. Neither is there in any part of it, any provision whatsoever, from which such intent can rationally and fairly be inferred. All the known and settled rules for ascertaining the intent of statutes, fail wholly, when applied to that act, to establish an intent such as above supposed. The words do not declare it; it cannot be presumed from the context, nor from the subject matter, nor the reason or spirit, nor yet even from the title of the act.

But, though such be not the intent of the law, does it *so operate* as to entitle the electors of the several townships and sections attached by it to the county of Morgan, to vote for a Representative from that county? The apportionment act of March 12, 1844, 19th clause, section 1st, organized the counties of Athens and Meigs into an electoral district, and assigned to them one Representative in the General Assembly. At the date of that act, the townships of Homer and Marion were parts of that electoral district, and the inhabitants of those townships were, by that law, and the general election laws of the State, entitled to vote, in common with the other white male inhabitants of the district, for one Representative *for the counties of Athens and Meigs.* Now, it will hardly be pretended that the law of March 11, 1845, undertakes *expressly*, to repeal, in whole or part, the act of March 12, 1844. Such pretence would be in broad contradiction of the evidence of every man's senses. Does it, then, so operate as to repeal the latter, by *way of implication?* This it might effect in two ways—either by requiring, expressly, something contradictory to the provisions of the former law, or by being, in its nature, repugnant to, and irreconcilable with, that law. But, as already has been shown, the act of '45 contains no clause in any part of it, pointing out in what county or electoral district the electors of the territory annexed shall vote. Total silence, in every respect, on a subject so important as the right of suffrage, cannot, by any torture of interpretation, be construed into a contradiction, either express or implied, of the requirements of former laws upon that subject; laws, also, which were known to be in force at the time. And further: the journals of the last session show that, while the law of March 11th was pending before the Legislature, amendments were proposed, pointing out the effect which the law should have upon the electoral rights of the inhabitants of the townships and sections annexed to Morgan county; but these amendments were rejected by decisive majorities. So that not even was this silence accidental. It may also not be amiss, here to observe, that the language of the act of last session differs, very widely, from the language of the act of 1827, before referred to in this report.

But neither is there any thing in the nature of the act of 1845 repugnant to the apportionment law of 1844. The former act does not affect to deal at all with the electoral rights of the inhabitants in the territory annexed by it; it is a local act, passed for local purposes, by local influences, perhaps, and for the convenience of those inhabitants, in ordinary county and township affairs. The latter deals wholly with the inhabitants of the State as electors, and it deals with them in no other capacity. It treats of the distribution of political power, and it does not pretend to treat of any thing else. And further, the electors of the townships and sections attached to Morgan county, had hitherto voted for Representative with the electors of the county of Athens. Nothing in the act of 1845, prohibited them from continuing so to vote, or required them to vote elsewhere. They might, in all other respects, have become citizens of the county of Morgan. They might have voted even for county officers with that county, and for Representative, have voted with Athens. Nothing could have been easier. The 22d section of the general election law of 1831, points out the mode of so voting in the case of new counties, organized between the regular periods of apportionment. The like has been done repeatedly. And the law made no change in their township officers, or in the time, manner, or place of holding elections. Here was no burden; no hardship; no disfranchisement.

To sum up all in a few words: the act of the last session declares no express intent to alter, in any manner, the apportionment or election laws in force at that time, or to change, lessen, or extend the boundaries of electoral districts, as fixed by those laws. Neither is there any thing in its requirements contradictory to those laws. And, finally, nothing in the nature or character of that act, can be pointed out, repugnant to the rights conferred, or the obligations imposed, by the laws first named.

So conclusive does this view of the case seem to the minority, that they might well here rest, and confidently demand the judgment of the House in favor of the right of Mr. Betts. But considerations, graver far, and, if possible, still more satisfactory, remain yet to be presented.

By the second section, article 1st, of the Constitution of Ohio, it is ordained that "within one year after the first meeting of the General Assembly, and within every subsequent term of four years, an enumeration of all the white male inhabitants, above twenty-one years of age, shall be made in such manner as shall be directed by law. The number of Representatives shall, at the several periods of making such enumeration, be fixed by the Legislature, and apportioned among the several counties, according to the number of white male inhabitants above twenty-one years of age in each, and shall never be less than twenty-four, nor greater than thirty-six, until the number of white male inhabitants above twenty-one years of age, shall be twenty-two thousand; and after that event, at such ratio, that the whole number of Representatives shall never be less than thirty-six, nor exceed seventy two." Upon this part of the Constitution, the minority, with all be coming deference to the honest opinions of others, claim with very great confidence, and in perfect assurance of being sustained in the construction they set up, that it is not within the constitutional power of a subsequent Legislature to alter or repeal a law fixing and apportioning representation in the General Assembly, passed, in good faith, in pursuance of the section above quoted, except at the several periods of making the enumeration in the section provided for. An examination of the section, applying to it the known and common-sense rules of interpretation, will enable every man to decide, in his own judgment, upon its true meaning. And, first, it provides for "an enumeration of all the white male inhabitants (of the State) above twenty-one years of age," within one year after the first meeting of the General Assembly. That enumeration was made in 1803, the Assembly having first met in the spring of that year. The same section further provides, that such enumeration shall be made "within every subsequent term of four years." It is then further provided, that "the number of Representatives shall be fixed and apportioned among the several counties" of the State. But when so fixed and apportioned? "At the several periods of making such enumeration;" that is, once in every term of four years. And how fixed and apportioned among the several counties? "According to the number of white male inhabitants above twenty-one years of age in each." How is that number to be ascertained? By an enumeration. When is that enumeration to be made? Once in every term of four years. Is it the number of inhabitants throughout the whole State which is to determine the apportionment? No; but the number in each county. Thus it will be perceived that the Legislature has the power expressly given, to take once in four years, at regular periods, the census of certain inhabitants of the State; and according to that census, to fix and apportion the Representatives among the several counties, according to the number of such inhabitants in each. But it may be argued that the Legislature is not prohibited from taking an enumeration and apportioning Representatives at periods other than those fixed; and that, if so, it may alter or amend, at any time, the periodical apportionment acts. True, it is not prohibited by express words—but is such the intent of the Constitution? Is it the theory of that instrument? Far from it. The bill of rights, section 28, in words pointed and emphatic, ordains, that "to guard against the transgression of the high powers which we have delegated, we declare that ALL powers not hereby delegated, remain with the people." Such powers only, therefore, as are, by the Constitution, delegated to the Legislature, can be exercised by it. No part of that instrument, except the 2d section of article 1st, provides for the enumerating of the white male inhabitants of the State, above the age of twenty-one; or for fixing and apportioning the representation of such inhabitants in the General Assembly. By this section, therefore, the extent of that power must be judged. Unless from the fair interpretation of its terms, the power claimed for the Legislature can be inferred, such power does not exist. Keeping steadily in view the express and solemn reservation in the Bill of Rights, together with that rational strictness of construction, without which Constitutions are of little value, we may safely lay down as principles which commend themselves to the common sense of every man, that—

1. Where a power is conferred by our Constitution, and the manner of its exercise is, at the same time, expressly pointed out and limited, such power cannot be exerted in any other manner.

2. Where a power conferred, is expressly defined in point of the

time when it shall be exercised, such power cannot be exerted at any time other than that so defined.

3. Where a power is delegated to be exercised at certain periods pointed out, the exercise of the power so delegated, at the time specified, exhausts such power, and leaves it, until the period prescribed shall again come round, without any present existence in the Constitution.

Tested by these principles, nothing can be clearer than that the power claimed for the Legislature, to alter the limits fixed for electoral districts by the periodical apportionment law, at other times than those expressly prescribed, has no shadow of existence in the Constitution. The power to apportion, conferred by the second section, article 1, of that instrument, is in so many words, circumscribed as to the manner of its exercise. The apportionment must be made according to the number of the white male inhabitants, above the age of twenty-one in each county. The time when it may be exercised, is with equal exactitude pointed out. The apportionment is to be fixed once in every term of four years. And, by a natural corollary, the power, when so exerted as prescribed, is exhausted and gone, until the case contemplated by the Constitution shall again arise. All this may, in like manner, be affirmed of the power to enumerate, as conferred in the section before quoted; for, although the minority do not mean to deny, for other purposes, an enumeration of the inhabitants of the State may be made at any time, yet, it seems to them free from all doubt, that for the purpose of apportioning representation in the General Assembly, the Legislature can neither take nor recognize any enumeration of the electors of the State, or of any county within it, except at the several periods ordained by the Constitution. And the undersigned state here, as a proposition not to be disputed, that if it is not competent for the Legislature to alter the boundaries of electoral districts, by direct legislation, such power cannot, in any way, be exerted by legislation indirect.

Let the facts of the case, before stated, be now applied to the Constitution. In 1843, being at the regular period prescribed by that instrument, an enumeration was had of all the white male inhabitants of the State above twenty-one years of age. In the year following, and so soon as the census was returned to the General Assembly, a law was passed, fixing and apportioning the representation of the State. That law assigned to the county of Morgan, one Representative in the years '44, '45, and '46, with an additional Representative in 1847—thereby erecting that county into an electoral district. And the law thus, by its very terms, professed to fix the representation of the county till the year 1848. It also assigned to the counties of Athens and Meigs one Representative for the same period, and to Washington county one also. It has before been shown what the limits were at that time, of the territory embraced within the county of Morgan. Now, by the number of white male inhabitants above the age of twenty-one, within those limits as they then were defined, the Legislature was governed in apportioning the representation of that county. Any alteration, therefore, of those limits, by taking from or adding to the number of such inhabitants, would derange wholly and set aside the rule of apportionment by which the express words of the Constitution declare that the Legislature shall proceed in such apportionment. But it might be urged that the law of March 12, 1844, gave to the county of Morgan one Representative in the year 1845, and that on the day of election, the townships of Homer and Marion were parts of that county. He who would urge such an argument, mistakes wholly the law and the Constitution. He forgets the distinction between a county so called, and an electoral district. He forgets, too, that "county" is a name, not a thing—a name affixed, for sake of convenience, to describe certain territory, and that it is the territory—the thing, not the name, which the Constitution and law mean. The rule or basis of representation places this beyond controversy, for assuredly, the electors of the territory annexed to the county of Morgan, formed no part, at the period of enumeration in 1843, of the electors of that county, to whom, and to whom alone, a Representative was apportioned. The same is true, also, of the county of Athens, from which the townships of Homer and Marion were taken. Those townships were, at the enacting of the apportionment law of 1844, parts of the county last named. The inhabitants residing within them at that time, were a portion of the inhabitants of Athens; and under the law were, together with its other inhabitants, entitled to a Representative from that county, and from no other, and had a right to vote for such Representative, and for no other. If it be the mere name "county," and not the territory, which the law and Constitution mean, then it would follow that the Legislature might, at any time, constitutionally consolidate a half dozen of counties into one called Morgan, for example, and then, by an appeal to the letter of the Constitution, and of the apportionment law, decide that such county was entitled to but one Representative. And why not? Washington, Athens, Perry, Meigs, Monroe, and Belmont, have all been incorporated with or annexed, or, if the word be better liked, attached to Morgan; and the white male inhabitants above the age of twenty-one, formerly residing in those counties, have now become, by operation of law, inhabitants of Morgan county, entitled to vote in that county, and that only for its Representative. For if the Legislature may attach townships to electoral districts, for electoral purposes, it may in like manner, and for a like purpose, attach whole counties. But this reasoning may legitimately, and without violence, be run a step further. Suppose the General Assembly change the name of a county, or consolidate a number together, and give them a new name, Middlesex, for example; now, there being no such county or name found in the apportionment law, no representation whatever could be allowed to the electors who might reside within its limits. Is not this absurd?

The undersigned here farther observe, that a very wide distinction is to be drawn between the power to alter county lines, or change territory or townships from one county to another, and a power to effect such changes in representative districts, and for purposes of representation. The existence of the one by no means involves the existence of the other. Certainly, the Legislature, instead of employing the term "county" alone, in the apportionment law, might describe the territory embraced within such county, in the words of the statute defining the limits of the county, and erect that territory, so described, into an electoral district. But, for the sake of convenience and brevity, the simple term county, with its name annexed, as implying that territory, is employed; and thus, the same territory is both a county so called, and an electoral district, according to the capacity in which it is considered. And from the different capacities or functions assigned to them, arises the plain difference in the power which the Legislature may exert over them. The one may be altered at any time—the other, only at the periods ordained by the Constitution.

If any doubt yet remained as to the unalterable nature, for four years, of the limits of electoral districts when once established, such doubt ought, in the opinion of the undersigned, at once to be yielded up, in view of the unambiguous and emphatic words of the Constitution. "The number of representatives shall, at the several periods of making such enumeration, be FIXED by the Legislature, and apportioned among the several counties" of the State. Now, if there be any significancy in language—if words mean one thing, and not another,—nay, if they mean any thing at all, to fix cannot, by any refinement of construction, signify to loosen, to set afloat,—and to fix for four years, cannot mean to leave open for change, at the caprice of legislators, at any time within the period so prescribed. But it may be argued that it is only the number of representatives which is to be fixed, and that the term does not apply, in grammatical construction, to the apportioning of representation among the several counties. Be it so. Yet both the number of the representatives and their apportionment, are provided for in the same section—the same clause,—the same member of the same sentence; and if the apportionment may be altered at a time other than the regular period of enumeration, then, by a like process of reasoning, and by the fair rules of constitutional construction, the number, also, of representatives, may be altered, though that number, by a word, than which there is none more significant within the whole compass of the Anglo-Saxon tongue, be declared FIXED for the term of four years.

There remains, yet, one point further to be considered. By the latter clause of the 3d section, article 7th, of the Constitution, it is ordained, that "every new county, as to the right of suffrage and representation shall be considered as a part of the county or counties from which it was taken, until entitled by numbers, to the right of representation." The attention of the House is here directed to this part of the Constitution, with the design of affording, if possible, by way of analogy, some light upon the question which the House is called upon to decide. The undersigned had presumed that there could be but one opinion as to its meaning. In this they erred, and are now compelled to differ totally with the majority in the construction which they put upon it. The clause itself, in no dubious language, expressly points out where the electors of a new county shall vote for representative, until entitled to representation themselves. True, the words are, "until entitled by numbers." But how are their numbers to be constitutionally ascertained? By enumeration. And when is such enumeration to be made? At the several periods provided for by section 2d, article 1st, of the Constitution—namely, once in every term of four years, and at no other period. Such, also, the minority here add, appears to have been the uniform construction hitherto put upon the clause above set forth. The 22d section of the general election law of 1831, sanctioned by the Legislature of that year, and by subsequent concurrence, and by practice, provides, "that at all elections for State and county officers in any county laid off or organized between the periods at which the ratio of representation is fixed by law, and before the next subsequent period for apportionment shall arrive, two set of poll books shall be provided, etc., and one of the poll books of such set shall be sealed up by one of the judges of election, and be carried to the old county from which such part of the new county was taken, etc." Such language needs no commentary. The undersigned have, with great labor and research, examined sixty-two acts of Assembly, laying off or organizing sixty new counties, beginning with the first General Assembly of the State, in March, 1803, and ending in December, 1832, a period of thirty years, and find not one case in all this mass of legislation, in which the Legislature has undertaken to grant representation in the General Assembly, to any one of the sixty new counties above referred to, as distinct counties, except at the constitutional periods, and by the general periodical apportionment acts. Such a uniformity of precedent, upon a construction really doubtful, could not, perhaps, be found in the legislation of any State.

As to precedents or practice, in regard to the constitutional provision, more directly touched by the question which the House is to decide; the minority have examined twenty-nine acts, beginning with the year 1804, and ending in 1828, altering the boundaries of counties, or attaching portions of one county to another, in like manner as done by the law of last session; and have found no one instance in which any of those acts assume to change the general apportionment law, or to interfere, in any way, with the electoral districts defined by it, or make any enactment as to the county or district in which the electors of the territory annexed shall vote for representatives in the General Assembly. These acts differ little, in substance, from the law of March, 1845.

The minority further report that they have found no case where, by contested election or otherwise, the question now presented to the House, has, at any time, before arisen. So far as they are advised, it is a question entirely novel, and which must be adjudged upon its own merits, as they appear in the facts, the law, and the Constitution.

The undersigned have all along argued as though the Constitution were the supreme law of the State, and beyond the power of the Legislature to supersede. This is a doctrine which will not, either here or elsewhere, be openly denied. An attempt to elevate the occasional will of the legislator exercising a vicarious and delegated function, above the permanent and exactly defined will of the people in their primordial and sovereign capacity, will, in this generation, find no foothold in America; still less will efforts be now made to overthrow constitutions by tumultuary violence. But it is not by the sword, nor by any open and physical force, that constitutions, in a comparatively virtuous and healthy age, are most likely to be subverted. A more slow, but equally dangerous and certain, engine of attack has been devised—the insidious sap and mine of construction. If constitutions are to be rasped, and frittered, and pared down into nothingness, by the constructive process, they had far better be abolished at once. If, through such process, they cease to be a barrier to the occasional and rampant impulses of majorities, let not our public records be, henceforth, encumbered with such instruments. The undersigned can present in no stronger light the necessity of preserving, unimpaired, the exact boundaries of the Constitution, than by setting before the House the dangers of the interpretation claimed by the majority of the committee. Grant to the Legislature but the power to alter, at any time, the electoral districts, and, still more, to establish new counties, and provide them at once with a separate representation in the Assembly, and where shall be the end? The whole political power of the State is at the command of a temporary, and it may be, a reckless and unprincipled, majority. From all this, nothing can deliver us but a resort to the *ultima ratio populi*, the inalienable though formidable right of Revolution. The minority will pursue these consequences no farther.

Confident, therefore, that the right of the sitting member, from the county of Morgan, to the seat which he now holds, is clear and unquestionable, the undersigned report accordingly.

The following notice of the foregoing Report, was from the pen of C. C. HAZEWELL, now of the Boston *Traveler*, and was published in the Ohio *Statesman*, of December 25, 1845, of which paper he was then editor:

This Report is from the pen of Mr. VALLANDIGHAM, the young but most able member from Columbiana. It is one of the most clear, logical, and convincing arguments that it has ever fallen to our lot to read, and should be circulated in all parts of the State. It cannot fail to carry conviction to every impartial mind, and to raise the reputation of its author to a very high point indeed. Columbiana may well be proud of her young member, who has already achieved for himself an enviable name as a debater, for skill and fairness, and as a writer at once powerful and dignified. He is of that class of men whom the Ohio Democracy need, to place them in the position which they occupied a few years ago, and which has been lost, not through any dislike of the people to Democratic principles, but because the party has been unhappily identified with the names and character of two or three detestable individuals, whose utter worthlessness was enough to sink any party. In Mr. VALLANDIGHAM we have such a man as the Democracy of Ohio can rely upon, one who does not think it necessary to disgrace great talents by buffoonery and immorality, in order to achieve a sudden notoriety. A gentleman and a scholar, and thoroughly attached to the principles of Democracy, we can always rely upon him for good services, especially when grave and important matters come up, requiring the action of the highest order of mind, to have them properly discussed and settled.

SPEECH ON CONSTITUTIONAL REFORM,

In the Ohio House of Representatives, January 16, 1847.*

THIS bill, Mr. Speaker, proposes the initiatory step towards a change in the Constitution of the State. It provides a way for resolving again into its original elements the machinery of our State government, for the purpose of its reorganization by those from whose hands it came, and whose creature it is. With that object in view, and in pursuance of the mode pointed out in the existing constitution, it proposes to submit to THE PEOPLE whether they desire any amendment or change in that instrument.

It is now forty-four years, Mr. Speaker, since our present constitution was established. At that period of our history, the State of Ohio, stretching from Pennsylvania to the Indiana line, and from the Ohio River to the northern lakes, with an area of thirty-nine thousand square miles, was an almost unbroken wilderness, with a population of but forty-eight thousand inhabitants, settled at intervals, in the openings, where "the arm of the frontier-man had levelled the forest and let in the sun." Few in numbers, these inhabitants were simple also in their habits, and fewer still in their wants. The hardy pioneers, who, penetrating this wilderness, had expelled its native savage occupants, and built a few log cabins in its solitudes, till then undisturbed by the reforming axe of the European race, made few contracts, committed not many crimes, and needed but the simplest forms of government. Courts of justice were held, at that early period, at not above nine or ten different points within the whole territory of Ohio; and the lawyers of the Cincinnati bar of that day practised regularly in the courts of Detroit (then within our limits), traversing for that purpose the whole distance on horseback, and sleeping often in mid-winter upon the bare snow of the forest, because in many places, for forty miles together,

* This speech was made in support of Mr. VALLANDIGHAM'S bill for calling a Convention to amend the Constitution of Ohio. The bill received a majority, but not two-thirds, and therefore failed. At a subsequent session, a similar bill was passed. To the people of Ohio this will be a document of permanent value and interest, as having indicated certain important and necessary changes in the organic law of the State, which, having been made, have done much toward securing the more prompt and efficient administration of justice. To the general reader this speech will show that Mr. Vallandigham early discovered and appreciated the important truth that all genuine progress is the outgrowth of a wise and judicious conservatism which gathers up, appropriates, and improves upon the lessons of wisdom and experience.

neither cabin nor other dwelling of white man or savage, cheered with its friendly smoke the inhospitable quietude of that unbroken wilderness.*

It was for such a people, living in such a territory, and with habits such as I have described, that the convention, assembled at Chillicothe on the first day of November, 1802, ordained a constitution. The men who sat in that convention were men of great singleness of purpose, great native intelligence, and earnest, for the most part, in their attachment to the true principles of republican government. But, assembling at a period when written constitutions were comparatively an untried experiment; destitute of that political science, the amazing progress of which is one of the characteristics of the age, and of that experience which enlightens and directs the more fortunate generation of this day, it is not to be expected that a perfect system of government should have been ordained by them. And, more than this, circumstanced as they were, and without that foresight and amplitude of mind which a profound and comprehensive survey of the wants and necessities, as well prospective as present, of mankind in organized society can alone give to the statesman, it is still less to be expected that, framing a constitution adapted to the government of fifty thousand pioneers in the midst of a wilderness, they should have looked forward half a century, and so moulded it as to be fitted to the condition of two millions of people of every diversity of habit and education, and following every occupation and pursuit known in a highly civilized State. The most sagacious among them could not have foreseen—it was not within the limits of human foresight, for history had then furnished no example—that within little more than the ordinary lifetime of a generation, a change so prodigious should mark the social and political condition of the commonwealth which they were about to establish. Not foreseeing it, they could not provide for its occurrence; and, not having provided, the evil is upon us. They were ordaining a written constitution, and written constitutions, unlike those which are the slow growth of centuries of usage, cannot adapt themselves to the ever-varying wants and circumstances of a young and growing people. But they did know that their work was not perfect, and foresaw the necessity for a change which might at some future day exist; and accordingly provided that way for securing such change or amendment, in pursuance of which this bill has been introduced.

I have meant no disparagement, Mr. Speaker, to the wisdom and ability of those who sat in the convention of 1802. They framed a constitution full of much that is valuable, and well suited to the necessities of the people in their day. But we have outgrown it. The

* Burnet's letters, 1837.

swaddling-bands of the infant have become badly fitting to the stalwart limbs of the grown-up giant. The convention adjourned on the twenty-ninth of November, 1802. Forty-four years of continued and rapid progress in all that belongs to man as an individual or a citizen, have obliterated almost every vestige of that condition of things to which the result of their labors was adapted. The forty-eight thousand inhabitants have grown to two millions, spread over the entire extent of the territory now comprised within the limits of Ohio. In agriculture, in commerce, in manufactures, in the arts and sciences of all kinds, in literature, merchandise, litigation, in all the wants and all the luxuries of civilized life—from nothing in that day, we have risen to place ourselves in the front rank among the States of this Confederacy. Having thus outgrown long since the institutions prepared for us in the infancy of our State, efforts repeated and persevering have been made for years past to secure a change in those institutions, conformable to the great and multiplied changes in our necessities and condition as a people. I claim no originality for this measure. Scarce a session has passed in many years, at which it has not been proposed. Repeatedly and earnestly the executives of our State have urged upon the legislature the propriety, and necessity even, of providing for a change in the constitution; but without success. Once only—in 1819—the proposition was submitted to the people. Even then the necessity for amendment was felt to be great. The subject was pressed upon the attention of the legislature by Ethan A. Brown, then Governor of the State, and passed with but little opposition. This, however, was but seventeen years from the formation of the constitution; that event was then too recent, and accordingly the people rejected the proposition. But I need only remind gentlemen that twenty-eight years have passed since that rejection. A new generation has grown up. Our population has doubled within that period. Changes in all that go to make up the varied condition of a populous and civilized State, greater far than within the seventeen years preceding, have since marked the progress of the State. Every year has added to the necessity for a radical change in many parts of the constitution. That necessity is at last everywhere admitted. Conviction has forced itself upon the minds of the people. And now, sir, as yet another effort in behalf of peaceable reform, and deeply impressed with the responsibility which I have taken upon myself, perhaps too lightly, I have brought forward this measure, with a hope and anxiety for its success in this house, which I cannot find language to express. I would, if I could but embody and unbosom the deep feelings of my heart, speak to this house in words which, like the Egyptian darkness, might be felt as with the hand, and implore the passage of this bill.

I have said that this measure is but the initiatory step towards the great reform to which I have referred. That step is discretionary with the Legislature; and although such discretion, operating as a control upon the people, ought to be employed with a liberal hand, approaching to facility, yet there ought to exist also, both some propriety or necessity for its exercise, and a fitness in the time proposed, before the people are called upon to decide a question of such great importance. And if I do not succeed in establishing both these requisites to the entire satisfaction of the House, I will consent to abandon this bill, earnest as my desire is that it may become a law.

The defects of the present constitution—defects most of which might readily be inferred, and which arose chiefly from the time and circumstances of its formation—are so freely and generally admitted, that I need spend little time in argument, and may content myself for the most part with but briefly pointing them out.

I begin with THE JUDICIARY. And first, as to the SUPREME COURT, the highest judicial tribunal of the State.

This court consists of but four judges, any two of whom constitute a quorum, and are empowered to hold courts. By consequence of this strange anomaly, no decision, in case of their disagreeing, can be had upon the circuit. But, besides this, it is manifest that four judges, though more than enough in the early times of the State, when there was not a thousandth part of the litigation which presses now, in enormous mass, upon our courts—indeed, prior to 1808, three only were appointed—are quite too few to dispose, even with the most summary haste, of a tithe of the business brought before them.

Nor is this all. These self-same judges, by a provision growing out of local jealousies in the convention of 1802, are required to hold the Supreme Court once a year in every county in the State. Now the number of these counties—and they are rapidly increasing—is eighty-two: so that these four judges are required to hold no less than eighty-two several courts, in each and every year; flying for that purpose over the whole of the vast territory of Ohio. The Supreme Court usually begins it sittings about the first of March, and closes about the first of December, so that nine months only are allowed within which to determine upon the innumerable judgments and decrees which are, or rather ought to be, given in the immense mass of business depending before this court. Within those nine months also, these judges are compelled to traverse the entire eighty-two counties of the State, passing over some two thousand or more miles of territory, holding eighty-two courts, hearing, or pretending to hear, and deciding upon—still oftener continuing—the thousands of cases upon the docket, every one of which touches the property, the liberty, or the life even, of the citizen. To accomplish all this, requires powers of action and endurance not vouchsafed to mortal man. This is positively the very worst part of the system. Only think, sir, of your Supreme Court, the last depositary of the tremendous powers and responsibilities of the judiciary, turned into a flying express, and running a tilt against the wind on a trial of speed; to-day at Cleveland, on the lake, hanging a man by the neck till dead; to-morrow at Cincinnati, consigning some hapless wretch to the ignominy and horrors of the penitentiary, or ejecting an unlucky suitor in that great city from a homestead worth millions perhaps, on which he has spent the most valuable part of a lifetime! Nothing is equal to it —except it may be the military exploits of the great Frederick, of whom it has been said: "Yesterday he was in the south, giving battle to the Austrian; to-day, in Saxony or Silesia—instantly he was found to have traversed the electorate, and was facing the Russian and the Swede, on his northern frontier. If you looked for his place on the map, before you had found it he had quitted it. He was always marching, flying, falling back, wheeling, attacking, defending, surprising, fighting everywhere, and fighting all the time."

But I have not done yet with the defects. To avoid the consequences of a division among the judges upon the circuit, and to secure something like uniformity and weight to their decisions, the Legislature some years ago devised an annual session of all the judges, to wit, *four*, at Columbus, to compose what is called a COURT IN BANK. Nothing could illustrate and enforce one-half so well the utter inefficiency of the system, as so paltry an expedient. The very evils to be remedied are but made more apparent and worse. Four judges composing the court, the same equality of division may arise, with this superadded evil, that two upon a side instead of one stand arrayed against each other, while the unfortunate litigants, meantime, after years of litigation, at the cost, perhaps, of half their fortunes, are compelled at last either to arbitrate their disputes, or to wait till the expiration of the term of service of one of the judges, or perchance his death, or, what is still less probable, his resignation—for "few die and none resign"—may afford a chance for a rehearing of the cause, and another division of opinion, to be terminated, or protracted it may be, after the same fashion.

Again: this court convenes in the month of December. So that these same judges, after nine long months of session as a Supreme Court, and of fatigue and travel and mental harassment, "in journeyings often, in weariness and painfulness and in watchings often," are hurried away in a whirlwind of judicial activity, to find themselves transformed suddenly into a Court in Bank, with one hundred and half as many cases more, to sit just four weeks, for the purpose of revising *their own decisions*, made in the hurry of their blood-stirring gallop through eighty-two counties in the course of nine months. Thus, sir, after this long period of judicial reconnoitring by this corps of flying artillery, the grand attack is ordered, and the whole citadel, outworks and all, of accumulated litigation, is to be carried by assault, in the space of four weeks. But seriously, Mr. Speaker, fatigued and exhausted by their labors beyond endurance, the judges of the Supreme Court are convened at the very close of these labors, and without a moment's respite, to begin the investigation of a hundred and fifty cases, enveloped amid a mass of written or printed arguments whose number and bulk would almost put the blush of inferiority upon the ponderous tomes of Thomas Aquinas, or any of the schoolmen. Now, I beg to know, sir, if it be within the limits of possibility to obtain, in such a condition of things, such decisions as alone become the oracles in the last resort of the law? Who that has spent a moment in reflecting upon the nature and effect of judicial adjudications but must know that they ought to be the work of leisure and deliberation, and pronounced upon a full knowledge only of the law and the facts; since, if by an unjust decision my property, my liberty, or my life is taken away, the consequences are none the less calamitous to me than if they had been brought about by the arm of despotism or the power of the sword. But upon the circuit there is neither time nor opportunity for the acquisition of this knowledge, and in Bank the case is perhaps worse.

But the evil is two-fold. The "law's delay" has long since passed into a byword and a reproach upon courts of justice in other times and countries. Here it is a matter of necessity, ordained in effect by the very constitution of the State. Hitherto, sir, I have spoken as though the dispatch of business by the Supreme Court, even without a becoming consideration, were physically possible. But what is the fact? Between March and December—sometimes between April and December, as in the present year—this court sits in eighty-two different counties extending throughout the entire State. The number of cases on the docket in these counties is estimated at about three thousand. Now, the number of weeks the court is usually in session upon the circuit is thirty-six; so that an average of just about two and a half days, Sundays included, is allowed to each county. Hamilton alone requires four weeks—thirty-two only remain to be distributed among the other eighty-one counties, and from these is to be deducted the time necessarily spent in travelling over so many hundred miles of territory. Now, sir, I ask in all earnestness, if it be in the nature of things that the one-twentieth part of the business before the court should be disposed of, even with the most headlong haste, in so short a space of time? That man never lived—the Almighty never put powers of action and endurance into breathing human clay—equal to the task.

And now, sir, what is the result of all this, and how does it accord with the rights of the citizen and the intent of the constitution itself? That instrument never meant to interpose such a barrier between the citizen and his rights. Its preamble declares it to be ordained, "*in order to* ESTABLISH JUSTICE." Again says the Bill of Rights, "That the general, great, and *essential* principles of liberty and free government may be recognized, and forever *unalterably established*, we declare:

"Sec. 7. That *all courts shall be open*, and *every person*, for an injury done him in his lands, goods, person, or reputation, *shall have remedy* by due course of law, and right and justice administered WITHOUT DENIAL OR DELAY."

Such was the design of the constitution, and such the earnest and emphatic language in which that design was expressed. But how is it now carried out? "All courts shall be open." True, there is no literal infringement of this injunction. Your courts are open. The docket is there, and the clerk to issue, and the sheriff to serve your process. But the mockery is only the more galling. Open! ay, too open. But beware, unfortunate suitor, beware; there is no regress from this worse than Cretan labyrinth. The footprints around this den of the lion all point towards its entrance.

"And *every person*, for an injury done him, SHALL HAVE REMEDY." Could words more significant be marshalled together in any language? But what is the effect of a practically contradictory provision of the same instrument? Every person shall have remedy. Now, does not every lawyer know that none but the more wealthy and influential can afford the "expensive luxury" of protracted litigation? Take but a single example of daily occurrence. You commence suit in the Common Pleas at its April term. Your cause is just, but your adversary's lawyer thinks he detects a flaw in the declaration. A demurrer is put in. The June term comes; business presses; law arguments can be heard only at the end of the term, and then in the hurry and confusion you either deem it unsafe to hazard your case, or the court are unable to hear it. You suffer a continuance. November term arrives, and the demurrer is argued and overruled. Surely you will now have justice and remedy without further denial or delay. But stop; that remedy is to be by "due course of law," and the courts will not dispose of two several issues in the same cause at the same term. Again continued, is the mandate of the judge. It is now April term, and the issue is made up, when, lo, a material witness is suddenly found absent by the defendant, beyond the process of the court. What then? an affidavit, and yet another continuance. Or worse; after waiting, perhaps, a whole fortnight with your witnesses, expecting the trial every hour, the court is compelled to adjourn without reaching your case. A whole year is now already gone since you began suit, confident behind the constitutional shield against delay. But skilful legal tacticians have turned the flank of the constitution. Disheartened and vexed almost beyond endurance, you yet make another effort, and the June term brings the consummation of your hopes. Trial is had, and you have obtained a verdict. But a new trial is moved for; the court hear the argument, and coolly pocket the motion, telling you in vulgar law Latin, *Curia vult advisare.* In November the motion is overruled. But lo, a bill of exceptions has been provided by your adversary and you are transported to the Supreme Court, that lazar-house of litigation, where "hope never comes that comes to all." Well, sir, some time between the next March and December, the "angel visit" of that august flying squadron is announced, and you repair to the court-room just in time to find the court adjourned and on horseback for the next county. Another year revolves—the third since you applied for that remedy which you thought to obtain without "denial or delay"—and your case is heard. But behold, the judges disagree, and the case is reserved to Bank. The scales now fall from your eyes, and you find yourself involved in what you deem interminable litigation. It is too late, however, to retreat, and after one or two years more, or three it may be, you again obtain a tardy decision in your favor, and enter upon the enjoyment of your rights. But the end is not yet. Yours may have been a *chancery* suit, and just at the moment you begin to sit down in repose from the fatigues of litigation, a *bill of review* is filed by your indomitable adversary. And after passing again through the same courts, and the same tedious process of procrastination, after five or six years more, an *adverse* decision is obtained against you; and stripped at last of every thing, worried, exhausted, indignant, you give up in despair. Now I appeal to every lawyer to say whether the process I have described may not be passed through in almost every case, and whether it is not passed through in every fiercely litigated case brought into court.

Such, Mr. Speaker, is the "due course of law" by which "every person" shall obtain remedy for an injury done to person, property, or reputation. Sir, I will not stop to gauge the dimensions of a purse long enough and wide enough to support the enormous expense of such litigation—to say nothing of the mental fatigue and harassment worse than any pecuniary consideration.

But, again: "Right and justice are to be administered WITHOUT DENIAL OR DELAY." Sir, I have said enough already to satisfy every man that the practice of our courts is but a solemn mockery of the constitution, though the fault is in that instrument itself. Without denial or delay! Not so; a mockery, mere mockery, every word of it What, no delay, when one, two, five, eight, twelve years even are exhausted in insupportably protracted litigation, the miserable litigant stretched, meantime, upon the rack of a mental torture, enough to divide soul and body? Call you that administering right and justice without delay?

But is there not a practical denial also? If the delay, and expense, and mental harassment of a heavy and protracted lawsuit, are such as to drive suitors from our courts, and compel them to forego the submission of their controversies to the constitutional tribunals of the land, acquiescing rather in every species of injustice and oppression, how much better is their condition than if you were to wall up the doors of your court-rooms, or to forbid entrance except to the favored few who are rich? The denial, the practical denial, is just the same, and the ruinous results upon public faith and to private right just as aggravated. Why, sir, it is of no moment to the suitor, so far as it affects his life, or person, or property, or reputation, whether the injury be done him by open despotism, or, though forbidden by the letter of the constitution, yet compelled by the force of circumstances. The end alike of both is death, death to his rights. Rather, then, let us abolish the mere form of government, and go back to the first law of might, since, escaping thus the pretended benefits of political organization, we shall escape its burdens also.

Having now pointed out briefly the two great opposite evils of our system, namely, haste and delay, as exhibited in the Supreme Court, I pass to the Common Pleas. And here it need hardly be remarked, that not a few of the evils spoken of flow necessarily from the organization of these courts also. But I shall not weary the House with repetition, adding only that to them, in the first resort, is committed almost the entire mass of judicial business in the State, both at law and in chancery; requiring, therefore, in the judges of these courts, an extent of ability and learning, and of aptitude for the office of judge, which it is given chiefly to the Mansfields, the Eldons, and the Marshalls of the profession, to possess. The great fault, then, of the Common Pleas consists in the constitutional necessity for having not less than two associate judges for each court. Usually there are three, and these are almost always men of no legal knowledge or education whatever—frequently of no knowledge or education at all, and who are rarely consulted upon law points, or if consulted (and then only for form's sake) acquiesce readily in the opinion of the presiding judge. I speak in general terms, for I have seen associates now and then, whose natural dignity and good sense made them, in all but the forms and niceties of the law, an overmatch for the lawyer who had been elevated, unhappily, to a seat upon the bench. But these are exceptions, and even if they were found in every court, they could not make the system much the less defective. For of what use are these men, not learned in the law? except, indeed, in the mere formal business of probate and administration, or in the granting of licenses to keep tavern. At best they are but an unnecessary encumbrance, and if erected into an Orphan's Court, with the powers now exercised chiefly by them in the Common Pleas, apart from the president-judge, might very easily and to much advantage be dispensed with.

I come now to the mode of election and tenure of office. That election is by the Legislature on joint ballot, and for the term of seven years. To all this I am opposed. If you do not come back to the ancient method of Executive nominations to be confirmed by the Senate, with a tenure for life, or during good behavior, a mode and tenure altogether adverse to the genius of our institutions, and tolerated in the federal constitution only because it is better to tolerate some evils there, than to run the hazard of evils far worse, by too frequent and great changes in an instrument founded upon so tender and delicate a compact, and embracing so many and such varied conflicting interests—if, I say, you cannot come back to this, I see nothing to be gained by withholding the election of Judges from the people. The present system has no one advantage over the mode I speak of—a mode adopted long ago, without pollution to justice, or prejudice to the sacred and elevated character of the judiciary, in Mississippi, and more recently, by the new constitutions of Louisiana, Texas, Iowa, and New York. I admit that once I entertained and expressed apprehension for the purity and safety of the judiciary, in the event of popular elections. But my little experience and my observation of judicial appointments within a few years past (I may add very recently), have satisfied me that as good and better selections will be made by the people, than by this or by any Legislature. Political connection with the party in the majority, is now and always has been made a prerequisite in the candidate: for when, I beg to know, did a whig Legislature elect democrats to judgeships, or a democrat Legislature elect whigs? In elections by the people it could be no worse. *And Ambos's saloon would find fewer patrons then.* The general principle surely is that all elections ought to be by the people direct; and the case should be a strong one to justify a departure from the rule. I admit that the judiciary is by far the strongest; and that there are reasons peculiar to it, and not applicable to the other departments, in favor of the exception. But I repeat and insist that unless you can secure the full benefit to be derived from a different method of appointment, it is both wrong and vain to abandon a general principle so vital, and so consonant with the spirit of our institutions. Give but a sufficient term of years to the tenure, and above all, fixing a *minimum* compensation liberal enough to secure the best virtues and talent of the bar, thus place the salary of the Judge beyond the tampering of vulgar demagogues, and you have nothing to fear from a popular election. In these opinions and in the conviction which forced them upon me, I am both honest and sincere. I do not know, indeed, that the mode of electing Judges just pointed out, would at this time meet the approbation of the people of this State, or even of a majority of this House. I think the people are with us. I know they will be, and that right speedily. But I entreat most earnestly that no man here vote against this bill because there might arise a diversity of opinion as to the particular provisions of the constitution to be framed, and because he is afraid *his* views of political organization might not prevail in the convention. Such diversity must of necessity exist; but the majority should govern; and if the people to whom the constitution would be submitted, approved, whose voice should be lifted up in complaint?

I turn now from the judiciary, to point out defects in other parts of the constitution. And first, THE WANT OF A CHECK UPON THE LEGISLATIVE POWER TO INCUR PUBLIC DEBTS. Made wise by a wholesome but severe experience, in nearly every constitution adopted within the last ten years, the people have provided some such restriction: and surely we in Ohio have had good cause to lament the want of it in ours. The principle of the check is plain. The property of the whole people is *confiscated* in the shape of taxes, to provide for the liquidation of the debt. Foremost indeed, it is mortgaged, "pledged," and then the alternative is either payment or repudiation: the first is onerous; the last iniquitous and disgraceful. Now assuredly it is but fair that they who must pay, should first give express consent to the debt; and the especial reason why express consent should, in this case, first be obtained, by direct vote of the people, is to be sought for in the fact, that *every citizen* is compelled to bear his proportion of a burden from which, except in hopeless poverty, there is no escape. I desire to be understood; the penalty of the law against murder may readily be avoided by refraining from the perpetration of the murder. Not so with tax laws. Now to unlimited power in the Legislature over this subject, I object. Combinations and local influences and interests, have too powerful a control in legislative assemblies, to make them the safe depositaries of so tremendous a power. Providently, therefore, and wisely did the constitution recently submitted to the people of Missouri (though rejected) provide that,

"The General Assembly shall have no power to pass any law whereby any debt shall be created, that shall cause the entire indebtedness of the State, contracted under this Constitution, to exceed at any one time twenty-five thousand dollars, except in cases of war, insurrection, or invasion.

"But the General Assembly may propose by a vote of a majority of all the members elected to both branches thereof, the creation of a debt for any specified purpose, which shall be submitted to the direct vote of the people at the next general election thereafter, and if approved by a majority of the qualified voters voting on such question, shall be of full force and effect; provided that each proposition shall be for one object alone, and shall propose the ways and means by taxation for the payment of the debt and interest, as they become due; and provided further, that no more than one proposition shall be submitted by any one session of the General Assembly, and that the debt proposed shall not have a longer time to run than twenty years."

Somewhat similar also is the restriction in the recent constitution of New York. Now, whether such provision were adopted in so many words or not, some restriction certainly ought to be imposed upon the legislative exercise of a power so delicate and momentous.

The requirement of AN ANNUAL SESSION OF THE LEGISLATURE is the defect in the present constitution to which I next advert; and the remedy proposed will, I know, meet the almost unanimous concurrence of the House. I mean BIENNIAL SESSIONS, with a provision for extraordinary sessions in great emergencies. This also is a modern and highly popular improvement in constitutional science. Into most of the constitutions recently organized it has been freely admitted, and at the late general election in Maryland it was ordered by a large majority to be incorporated into the constitution of that State by special amendment. Though by no means persuaded that it is the all-healing remedy for the many ills of legislation, I need not argue long to satisfy this House that those worst and most costly of all the evils of a representative system of government, *hasty, excessive, and unstable legislation*, must, of necessity, be greatly diminished were the Legislature to assemble but once in two or three years. Most also of this legislation is special and private. Here, sir, is the volume of local laws for the session of 1844–'45, numbering in all, together with the resolutions, four hundred and seventy, while the number of laws of a general character passed at the same session, reached to but eighty-nine. The former embrace almost every variety of subject from the incorporation of a bank down to the changing of a man's name, or the laying out of a back alley in a paltry village. The assembling annually of the Legislature would seem to remind the citizens of this State that they may now find a ready instrument wherewith to have that done which nobody and nothing else will do. A thousand schemes of crude, or absurd, or useless, perhaps iniquitous legislation, are thus projected, which otherwise would never have been devised. Self-reliance is forgotten. The individual man, living, breathing, God-created, exulting in the might and majesty of an immortal and almost omnipotent nature—the man God made in his own image, and into whose nostrils He breathed the breath of life—man, conquering the elements, making the lightnings his messengers, and thrusting the storms under his feet, is lost sight of, and the graven images, the base gods of legislative creation, which, "having eyes see not, and ears hear not," are bowed down to and worshipped, till none other are deemed able to save. To the government all eyes are directed; by it all the ills of life are to be dispelled, and from it all blessings to flow. Not a bridge can be erected, not a highway laid out, nor a turnpike graded, without the intervention of the Legislature. Hercules is always invoked, and a god brought upon the stage even when there is no "nodus" worthy of such agency. The "let alone policy," that first and most ennobling of all political maxims, which teaches man to rely mainly upon the powers and attributes of his own nature, and to distrust the omnipotence of government to dispel evils and create blessings, is cast aside, and soul-debasing prostration before political and corporate organization, substituted in its stead. I say nothing of the cost to the people. The evil strikes deeper: the corruption reaches that which is more delicate than the purse; and there is no medicine nor surgery equal to the cure.

But besides the excess of legislation, much of it is necessarily hasty, and, worst of all, unstable. The law of yesterday is annulled to-day; and one Legislature meets only to set aside the acts of its predecessor. The sound of the hammers, tinkering perpetually at the laws, is heard at all hours in the halls of the Legislature. Acts amendatory, supplementary, constructive, declaratory, repealing, explanatory, are piled upon acts, till not unfrequently the parts in force have to be traced back through ten successive volumes, and meantime every thing like uniformity and certainty is lost, and courts, lawyers, and litigants, floundering in a sea of conflicting and contradictory legislation, are alike driven to despair. No man, not even the legal profession, can keep up with the striding progress of law-making. Cases are begun under one statute, heard upon a second, and decided upon a third. Is not all this an evil and an oppression not to be endured? But it is fastened upon you by the constitution: it is ordained and established as part of the fundamental law of the State; and the remedy is through that measure only, which with as earnest entreaty as ever came from human lips, I now urge upon the house to adopt. There is no other remedy for evils which are corrupting the people, and poisoning the fountain of legislation. Here, in this remedy alone, is there enough, amply enough to compensate for all the cost and hazard of a reorganization of our political system. And I implore gentlemen as they love liberty, as they reverence, and would hand down our free institutions to their children unimpaired, not to defeat this bill.

[Mr. V. then said that there were many other evils and defects in substance in the constitution, which would need a remedy, but he would pass to the consideration of those which, though in matter of form, arrangement, and style, were yet not to be disregarded. He then took up the constitution, reading and commenting at some length upon sections two, four, seven, nine, nineteen, and twenty-six, of the first article; and upon article four, article seven section five; and sections six and twenty-seven of article eight—more minutely and earnestly upon the seventh section of the first article, showing that so carelessly was this as well as other sections drawn up, that it literally *excluded* every person from the Senate "who is a citizen of the United States," or who "shall have resided two years in the county or district immediately preceding the election;" or who "shall have paid a state or county tax," unless such person "shall have been absent on the public business of the United States or of this State," in which event he might, if *not a citizen of the United States,* be eligible to the Senate, *though he had resided* the two years preceding his election in the county or district.* Mr. V. then proceeded:]

The necessity and propriety of a change in the constitution of this State are so readily and universally admitted, that I have spent too much time, perhaps, in speaking to this point of my argument. But I desired to present them the more vividly before the members of this House, because no mere cold conviction or assent of judgment, I feared, could command their support to this measure, without an accompanying impulse from the will. Scarce a man who has spent one moment's reflection upon this great question but will tell you, "I admit the necessity of amendment, but the time is not favorable." Sir, when will the time be favorable, if not now? Within forty-four years—since the formation of the present constitution—not less than five-and-twenty, perhaps thirty, constitutions have been either reorganized or adopted anew. Scarce one State of the "old thirteen" but has changed its fundamental law, and some among them twice or three times. Massachusetts, old, sober, conservative Massachusetts, where change and progress in politics are feared as the breath of the pestilence, has amended hers. Virginia and Pennsylvania, also, have done likewise, and Virginia is convulsed now again, by the efforts of her reformers, toward yet another change. Rhode Island, slumbering as she did, for nearly two centuries, under the charter of a British King, has waked up at length, and framed anew her organic law. New Jersey, Louisiana, Texas, and, more recently still, New York, have each reorganized their constitutions. And shall Ohio, YOUNG OHIO, fall behind? Sir, the progress of constitutional science (the great bulwark of liberty), within half a century, has amazed the civilized world. Nothing in any other department of politics has equalled it. The capacity, once doubted, even in this country, of the people for self-government, in its most expanded limits, has been demonstrated;

* The section is in these words:

"SEC. 7.—*No* person shall be a Senator who has not arrived at the age of thirty and *is* a citizen of the United States—shall have resided two years in the county or district, immediately preceding the election, unless he shall have been absent on the public business of the United States, or of this State; or shall moreover have paid a state or county tax."

while, meantime, the tyrants and legitimists of the old world have looked on with blanched cheek and cowering eye at the progress of the democratic principle, which, scorning to tread the beaten track of ordinary politics, has stricken out a new path, crushing to the ground before its giant strides, all the sluggard opposition of that false conservatism which sits like the unhappy Triton on its fast-bound rock, and weeps in envy and malevolence at the Genius of Improvement going forth as the strong man rejoicing in his strength. This spirit of progress, let me admonish gentlemen, it is vain to resist. You may retard, but you cannot arrest it. I know it will be opposed, and that all the might and skill of that conservatism will conspire for its fall. Men are slow to give up what they delight to call "the wisdom of their ancestors." Sir, there is a wisdom which sometimes becomes madness. But we do not teach forgetfulness of the lessons of the past. We would go back to that fountain, but we would desire, also, to grow wise from experience, and to correct the errors which that experience points out. Experiment is the great laboratory of politics; but its results must be carried into practice by reforms, or they are of no value. True, sir, in the midst of all this soul-gladdening march of improvement, we should rejoice to look back also to the instructions of those who have gone before us. I belong, indeed, to what is sometimes sneeringly called the "progressive" school of politics. I am proud to belong to it. It teaches faith in man as God made him. Progression, too, is a law of our race. But not that progression which forgets all the teachings of the past, and spurns all the dangers of the future. The true law of progress, if I understand it, demands not so much the originating of new principles in politics, as the varied application of the old and established principles to the ever and rapidly changing circumstances which distinguish every year in our history from the years which have preceded it, altering our policy and conduct of affairs, and *even our institutions*, accordingly as these changes demand it, directed throughout, however, by the same great leading principles which reason and prescription alike combine to make authoritative and venerable. On just such principles would I desire that the great reform here proposed, should be conducted. And now, too, we have all that wisdom can devise, or the experience of our own or other States can teach, to guide us. The times are propitious. Why then delay? Do your fear the introduction of party into this great question of reform? Never will there be a time less exposed to its influences. This proposition will be submitted to the people at the fall election of '47, at a season when there will be neither president, governor, nor members of Congress to elect, and when no disturbing causes, therefore, will combine to trouble the pool of politics, National or State. Nothing of so generally an agitating character, as to arouse even the ordinary political excitement throughout the State, will or can be brought before the people. I know of nothing to break the calm of that election. And if the people should decide for a convention, the election of its members, and the commencement of its sessions, must both take place before the presidential canvass of '48. When will a time so auspicious come again? Do you mean to wait till parties shall no more exist? Sir, such vain imaginings are the very worst sort of political "Millerism." That day will never come. You must first alter man's nature, or, striking down the spirit of liberty, must compel the uniformity of inexorable despotism. Parties will always exist in a free country, and it is the business of wise men not to attempt to eradicate, but to regulate and control them. But why shall party enter at all into this question? It is a question for the whole people of the State, and concerns them, not as whigs, or as democrats, but as citizens. Other States have met as one people in this great matter of constitutional reform. In Louisiana, where parties are nearly balanced, but three thousand votes were cast against the new constitution of '44. In Iowa and Missouri the new constitutions proposed were rejected—in the former twice rejected—though the party whose friends had submitted them, was largely in the majority. Even in New York, where, if in any State, partisan influence was most to have been expected—in New York, where the despotism and corruption of party are carried as far surely as in Ohio, the call for a convention was sustained by a vote of two hundred and thirteen thousand to thirty-three thousand, or a majority of not less than one hundred and eighty thousand votes, while the constitution which that convention submitted received a majority of fifty thousand at an election where a whig Governor and a democratic Lieutenant-Governor were each elected by about ten thousand majority. Why, sir, even in the convention of Pennsylvania too—old democratic Pennsylvania—I mean the Pennsylvania of '38, not '46—John Sergeant was chosen President. And is it in Ohio alone that the thraldom of party is so monstrous that a convention is not to be called, and not even the people consulted whether they desire it, for fear that the influence of partisan politics will corrupt its deliberations? Sir, I was born in Ohio, and I will never consent to brand upon her brow the infamy of such an imputation. Your best and purest men will find seats in this convention, and they will vote and speak as honest men and as patriots.

But if the fear of party is to defeat this measure, when will it pass? Now I submit it to gentlemen as to members earnest in their desire to vote for the best interests of the people;—if this bill is never to pass—if the constitution needs no amending, and is never to be amended—this objection is at least consistent. But if you look forward to a time when the constitution of this State *is* to undergo the process of revision, then let us hear no more of party, for its corrupting influence will be far greater and more perilous half a century hence, than in this comparatively healthy age of the commonwealth—certainly as great in five years or ten as at this day. Sir, I protest earnestly against the defeat of this measure by the votes of those who, admitting the necessity of a change in our constitution, desire and expect to see it carried out at some future day. What! object to this bill now, and vote against it because you are afraid that party corruption will steal into the convention and fasten upon the State a constitution worse than the present, and yet think to call just such convention, for just the same purpose, at some other time—as if party spirit and party distinctions were at their last gasp and never more to be heard of! Sir, I repeat it: that day will never dawn. I have no faith, not the slightest, in the coming of a political millenium when the lion and the lamb shall lie down together. Such visions are just "the stuff that dreams are made of." The "moonshine's watery beams" have ten times the substance of such shadows. But why fear a worse constitution? The people are first to resolve whether they will have a convention. They are then to elect the members of that convention, and finally the constitution itself is to be submitted to them for their approval or rejection. The people are to decide that question also. And how and whence comes this fear of a worse constitution, but from secret distrust in their virtue and intelligence?

Again: I have heard it said, "New York has just adopted a new constitution; let us wait till we see how it works." What kind of an argument is this? This bill does not propose to adopt the New York constitution, or any other already formed. What has it or what have they to do with the question of a convention in Ohio, that we shall wait till they have been tried? Their principles are not new; and if they were, how know you that they would be introduced into ours; or if they were introduced with the sanction of the people, who should say aught against it? Wait? And how long? One, two, five years? How long shall the test be? Why, sir, by that time Virginia shall have reorganized her constitution, and then we shall be told, "wait till she has tried how it works." Every year some new constitution is framed, and thus this objection may be forever applied.

When the proposition similar to this, Mr. Speaker, was under debate, at the last session, the argument most urged against it, and that which I feel and know will go farther toward the defeat of this bill than all others put together, was the fear of untried and dangerous innovations. The dire spirit of radicalism, they told us, and some now will tell us, is abroad in its rage, and threatens, like the Apostles of old, to turn the world upside down. Sir, this fear of innovation, or rather of progress, is a morbid affection to be dealt with as other hypochondriac diseases.

And I would lament beyond the power of words to express, that its influence should be allowed to defeat this measure. But how comes such an objection to be urged by those among the majority of this House? Have not the whig party sworn upon the horns of the altar, eternal hostility to all such innovations as are thus feared and abhorred, and does not that party boast of a permanent majority in this State reckoned by thousands? Have we not heard it proclaimed times out of number, that Ohio is unalterably a whig State? Now, sir, this question must first be submitted to the people; and upon the new constitution also they must decide. And think you, sir, the people, a large majority of whom are claimed to be whigs—conservative whigs, and opposed to all innovations and radicalism, to hard money and legislative supremacy over "vested rights," so called—will first demand such convention, thus exposed to such dangers, then elect a majority of members to serve in it, who will propose a radical, impracticable constitution: and finally, support that constitution by their free suffrages? No, sir, let gentlemen be consistent. If in truth you have confidence in your majority, vote for this bill. It is we, we who should fear, if any. But we are not afraid to trust this question to the people of Ohio. Ours is a living faith in their virtue and intelligence. We believe, and mean this day to prove the sincerity of that belief by our votes, that they will choose just such a convention and such a constitution as will best promote the true principles of free government, and the real interests of the State. Afraid! and of whom and what? Sir, this bill proposes no more—and I desire to write it upon the hearts of the members of this House, as with a pen of iron—no more than simply to submit to the people, whether they desire a convention to amend or change the constitution. It calls no such convention. We have no authority to call it. And if the people of this State do not desire it, they will vote this proposition down, and that, too, with little trouble and at no expense. If they mean to demand a convention, they will signify that demand through the ballot-box—that "weapon surer set, and better than the bayonet." And who shall interpose between them and their will? Shall the agent become greater than his principal, or the creature dictate control to the creator? I repeat it, this bill does not propose to call a convention. Look at its title—"*A bill to provide for ascertaining the will of the people of this State, upon the question of calling a convention to amend or change the Constitution of the same.*" That, sir, is its object—its sole object. And who shall dare rise up and say, "We care not to know the will of the people upon this question? *We* are opposed to a convention: that is enough. *We* are afraid of it, and *their* voice shall not be heard." Yet such, in effect, will be the language of him who shall this day record his vote against the measure.

But there are those who, admitting in all their force the defects of the present constitution, the necessity of amendment, the fitness of the time, the nature of this proposition, the right of the people to decide upon it, the propriety of submitting it to their decision, and all the other great considerations, in view of which I have plead with this House for the passage of this bill, yet folding their hands to sleep, tell us in sluggard accent, "better wait a little longer." Wait! Why, and for what? Sir, I abhor the word. "Howlings attend it." It is a bad word, and sounds dismally of the ruin of great enterprises. It smacks of death, all over of death. It has the hollow moan of the sepulchre of all good, about it. There is ruin in its accent. "Wait a little," said the First Charles when the Commons of England knocked loud at the palace, and demanded reform of abuses and redress of grievances—and the storm of civil uproar bore him headlong to the scaffold. "Wait a little," said the Second James, to the enraged Protestants of his kingdom, crying out for security to their religious rights and form of worship—and the throne rotted away from under him, and he died miserably an exiled King. "Wait a little," said Louis of France, as the cloud of popular discontent arose no bigger than a man's hand;—and it began to blacken the horizon. "Give us our rights and protect us against the monstrous wrongs perpetrated upon us," said the people, as they thundered at the gates of the Bastile. "Wait a little," murmured the King;—and the storms came, and hail-stones, and coals of fiery indignation from the people, swept over France; and throne, and king, and government, and nobles, all went down in blood, before the whirlwind of revolution. "Wait a little!" There is danger in the words. Sir, the people of this State demand this reform, and will ere long come thundering about this capitol, also, if denied. The present constitution was never submitted to them for their approval, and exists only by connivance. True, it points out a mode of amendment, and provides for submitting that question to the people, as we now demand at the hands of this House, and in their name, that it may be done. But I warn gentlemen not to carry refusal and delay too far. Look to Rhode Island. Though her cause fell into unsafe hands who betrayed it, yet, reckon not, I beg you, too largely upon its failure. The people of Ohio will not be hurried rashly into a mode of reform other than that prescribed by even the present constitution, to which they have yielded no more than a tacit assent. Nor yet, be assured, will they slumber forever upon those rights which constitutions can neither give nor take away. But this constitution has declared in so many words, the rights of the people to be above the authority of their representatives, and recognized their inalienable and full power at all times over their forms of government. And though we should forget, yet they will remember it. Let me remind gentlemen of this provision of our bill of rights—there is fearful significancy in it. I read from the constitution:

> "That the general, great, and essential principle of liberty and free government may be recognized and forever unalterably established, we declare,
>
> "SEC. 1. That all men are born equally free and independent, and have certain natural, inherent, and inalienable rights, amongst which are the enjoying and defending life and liberty, acquiring, possessing, and protecting property, and pursuing and obtaining happiness and safety; and every free republican government, being founded on their (THE PEOPLE'S) *sole authority*, and organized for the great purpose of protecting *their* rights and liberties, and securing *their* independence; to effect *these ends* THEY HAVE AT ALL TIMES A COMPLETE POWER TO ALTER, REFORM, AND ABOLISH THEIR GOVERNMENT WHENEVER THEY MAY DEEM IT NECESSARY."

Now, sir, I do not undertake to say that this provision, comprehensive and emphatic as its purport and language are, authorizes a change of the constitution, by the people of this State in their *unorganized* capacity, and in a mode other than that pointed out by the instrument itself. But with this provision in it, and with the fact palpable, that the constitution never received the direct approval of the people, and is not their constitution except by acquiescence, I will not answer for doctrines which may be taught, and movements which may be made, if this Assembly shall persist in obstinate refusal to carry out the intent of that constitution, and the will of the people. It is the part of wisdom not to press measures like this to extremes. Sir, this bill must and will some time or other become a law. You may vote it down now. You may look the people in the face and say to them, "We care not to know your will upon this question, for we are adverse to it." But be assured, be assured, that sooner or later, and in a day perhaps when you think not of, this bill will pass. If passed now, your constitution will be framed in the midst of calm, by the sober second thought of a convention of cool-headed men and patriots, and passed upon by a people undisturbed by agitation. But if this Legislature shall wait, and wait, and wait, till with safety they can wait no longer—till forced by the thunderings and knockings of the people, which will not be denied; know well, your constitution will be "born in bitterness and nurtured in convulsion." For let me admonish this House, in the crooked but significant Anglo-Saxon tongue of Carlyle, that here, too, as in France, if rulers and representatives refuse the timely correction of the abuses, errors, and defects of Government, "SOMETHING WILL SOME DAY DO ITSELF IN A WAY TO PLEASE NOBODY." If, then, in truth, you are afraid of the spirit of an impracticable radicalism—if really you fear a constitution worse than the present, wait not, I beseech you, till the whirlwind and the storm of popular commotion shall sweep over the State; but pass this bill now—to-day, and claim to yourselves the honor and gratitude of other times, and make this session memorable, and this day long to be venerated in the State of Ohio. Let no man ask us to wait longer. Pass this bill; be not afraid of the people. Trust to them the decision of this question, and proclaim by your votes this day, the sincerity of your faith in their virtue and intelligence to frame a constitution worthy of this great commonwealth.

HISTORY OF THE ABOLITION MOVEMENT.

Speech delivered at a Democratic Meeting held in Dayton, Ohio, October 29, 1855.

Fuit hæc sapientia quondam,
Publica privatis secernere, sacra profanis. HORACE.

Æternas opes esse Romanas nisi inter semet ipsi seditionibus sæviant. Id unum venenum, eam labem civitatibus opulentis repertam, ut magna imperia mortalia essent.
LIVY.

Then only both Commonwealth and Religion will at length, if ever, flourish in Christendom, when either they who govern, discern between civil and religious (religion and politics); or they only who so discern, shall be admitted to govern. Till then nothing but troubles, persecutions, commotions, can be expected, the inward decay of true religion among ourselves, and the utter overthrow, at last, by a common enemy. MILTON.*

AFTER some preliminary remarks, explanatory of the object of the meeting, and the reasons why it was proper and expedient thus early to discuss before the people the great question which must make up the chief issue in the campaign of 1856, and to organize preparatory thereto, Mr. VALLANDIGHAM said that he proposed as the text or "rubric" of what he had to say to-night, the following inquiries:

WHY HAS THE DEMOCRATIC PARTY SUFFERED DEFEAT IN OHIO? WHY IS IT SO GREATLY DISORGANIZED? WHAT WILL RESTORE IT TO SOUND DOCTRINE AND DISCIPLINE, AND, THEREFORE, TO POWER AND USEFULNESS?

These, Mr. President, are grave questions. I propose to answer them plainly—boldly—not as a partisan, but as a patriot; and for the opinions which I shall this night avow, I alone am responsible. I speak not to please, but to instruct, to warn, to arouse, and, if it be not presumption, to save, while to be saved is yet possible. The time for plain Anglo-Saxon out-speaking is come. Let us hear no more the lullaby of peace,

* These mottoes were prefixed to the pamphlet edition of the Speech, when first published in 1855.

when there is no peace; but rather the sharp clang of the trumpet stirring to battle; at least, the alarm-bell in the night, when the house is on fire over our heads. Or, better still, give us warning while the incendiary is yet stealing, "with whispering and most guilty diligence," and flaming torch, toward our dwelling, that we may be ready and armed against his approach.

First, then: The Democratic party of Ohio suffered defeat because it became disorganized; and it was disorganized because it held not, in all things, to sound doctrine, vigorous discipline, and to true and good men. It began to tamper with heresy and with unsound men—to look after *policy*, falsely so called, and forget sometimes the TRUE and HONEST; not mindful, with Jackson, that the right is always expedient—at least, that the wrong never is; and that an invigorating defeat is ever better than a triumph which leaves the victor weaker than the conquered. This is a law of nature, gentlemen, and we may claim no immunity from punishment for its infraction. I speak of the Democratic party of Ohio, because we are our own masters, and have a work of our own to perform. But the evil, in part, lies outside the State. It infects the whole party of the Union, as such. It ascends into high places, and sits down hard by the throne. But I affect the wise caution of Sallust, remembering that *concerning Carthage it is better to be silent, than speak too little.* Yet we, as members, must partake of the weakness and enervation of other parts of the system; and atrophy is quite as fatal, though it may not be so speedy, as corruption and gangrene.

The inquiries, gentlemen, which I have proposed, assume the truth of the facts which they imply. Are they not true? That we have been defeated, is now become history. But defeat did not disorganize us. Had not discipline first been lost, we could not have been overpowered. I know, indeed, that some have affirmed that we, too, are an effete party, ready to be dissolved and pass away. It is not so. Dissolution and disorganization are wholly different things. The Democratic party is not a thing of shreds and patches, organized for a transient purpose, and thrown hap-hazard together, in undistinguishable mass, without form, consistency, or proportion, by some sudden and temporary pressure, and passing away with the occasion which gave it being; or catching, for a renewed, but yet more ephemeral existence, at each flitting exigency, as it arises in the State; moulding itself to the form of every popular humor, and seeking to fill its sails with every new wind of doctrine, as it passes, either in zephyr or tempest, over the waves of public caprice—born and dying with the breath which made it. No; the Democratic party is founded upon PRINCIPLES which never die: hence it is itself immortal. It may alter its forms; it must change its measures—for, as in principle it is essentially *conservative*, so in policy it is the party of *true progress*—its individual members and its leading spirits, its representative men, cannot remain the same. But wherever there is a people wholly or partially free, there will be a Democratic party more or less developed and organized. But no party, gentlemen, is at all times equally pure and true to principle and its mission. And whenever the Democratic party forgets these, it loses its cementing and power-bestowing element; it waxes weak, is disorganized, is defeated—till, purging itself of its impurities, and falling back and rallying within its impregnable intrenchments of original and eternal principles, it returns, like "eagle lately bathed," with irresistible might and majesty, to the conflict, full of hope, and confident in victory. Sir, it is this recuperative power—this *vis medicatrix*—which distinguishes the Democratic party from every other; and it owes this wholly to its *conservative element*, FIXED POLITICAL PRINCIPLES. I say *political* principles—principles peculiarly belonging to government—because it is a POLITICAL party, and must be judged according to its nature and constitution. Recognizing, in their fullest extent, the imperative obligations of personal religion and morality upon its members, and also that, in its aggregate being, it dare not violate the principles of either, it is yet neither a Church nor a lyceum. It is no part of its mission to set itself up as an expounder of ethical or divine truth. Still less is it a mere philanthropic or eleemosynary institution. All these are great and noble, each within its peculiar province, but they form no part of the immediate business and end of the Democratic party. And it is because that party sometimes will forget that it is the first and highest duty of its mission to be the depositary of immutable political principles, and steps aside after the dreams and visions of a false and fanatical progress—sometimes political, commonly philanthropic or moral—that it ceases to be powerful and victorious; for God has ordained that truth shall ever, in the end, be vindicated, and error chastised.

Forgetting the true province of a political party, the Democracy of France and Germany has always failed, and ever must fail. It aims at too much. It invokes *government* to regenerate man, and set him free from the taint and the evils of sin and suffering; it seeks to control the domestic, social, individual, moral, and spiritual relations of man; it ignores or usurps the place of the fireside, the Church, and the lyceum; and, emulating the folly of Icarus, and spreading its wings for a too lofty flight into upper air, it has melted like wax before the sun. *Indirectly* indeed, government will always, sir, affect more or less, all these relations for good or evil. But departing from its appointed orbit, confusion, not less surely or disastrously, must follow, than from a like departure by the heavenly bodies from their fixed laws of motion. And, indeed, the greater, and by far the gravest part of the errors of Democracy everywhere, are to be traced directly to neglect or infraction of the fundamental principle of its constitution—that man is to be considered and dealt with by government strictly in reference to his relations as *a political being.*

These reflections, Mr. President, naturally lead me to the first inquiry:

Personal dissension; a turning aside after mere temporary and miscalled expediency; a faith in and following after weak, or uncertain, or selfish, or heretical men; neglect of party tone and discipline as essential to the *morale*, and hence the success of a party, as of an army, and just as legitimate; these, and the like minor causes of disorganization and defeat, I pass over. They are incident to all parties, and, although never to be too lightly estimated, yet rarely occasion lasting or very serious detriment. Commonly, indeed, sir, they are but the *diagnostic*, or visible development of an evil which lies deeper—just as boils and blotches upon the surface of the body show that the system is tainted and distempered within. Neither do I pause, gentlemen, to consider how far the final inauguration of the grand scheme of domestic policy, which the Democratic party so many years struggled for, and the consequent prostration and dissolution of the Whig party, have contributed to the loss of vigilance and discipline; since an organization healthy in all other things must soon recover its wonted tone and soundness. Sir, the Democratic party has principle to fall back upon; and it has, too, a trust to execute, not less sacred, and almost as difficult as its first work. It is its business to preserve and keep pure and incorrupt that which it has established. And this, along with the new political questions which, in the world's progress, from day to day spring up, will give us labor enough, and sweat enough, without a wild foray into the province of the benevolent association, the lyceum, or the Church; to return thence laden, not with the precious things, the incense, and the vessels of silver and gold from off the altar, but the rubbish and the offal—the bigotries, the intolerance, the hypocrisies, the persecuting spirit, and whatever else of unmixed evil has crept, through corruption, into the outer or the inner courts of the sanctuary.

I know, indeed, gentlemen, that every political party is more or less directly affected, as by a sort of magnetism, by all great public movements upon any subject; and it is one of the peculiar evils of a democracy, that every question of absorbing, though never so transient interest—moral, social, religious, scientific, no matter what—assumes, sooner or later, a political shape and hue, and enters into the election contests and legislation of the country. For many years, nevertheless, sir, questions not strictly political exerted but small influence upon parties in the United States. The memorable controversies which preceded the American Revolution, and which developed and disciplined the great abilities of the giants of those days—founded, indeed, as all must be, upon abstract principles drawn from the nature of man considered in his relation to *government*—were yet strictly legal and political. The men of that day were not cold metaphysicians, nor wicked or mischievous enthusiasts—else we had been subjects of Great Britain to this day. Practical men, they dealt with the subject as a practical question; and deducing the right of *revolution*, the right to institute, alter, or abolish *government*, from the "inalienable rights of man," the American Congress summed up a long catalogue of injuries and usurpations wholly *political*, as impelling to the separation, and struck out of the original draught of the Declaration of Independence the eloquent, but then mistimed, declamation of Jefferson against the African slave-trade. Sir, it did not occur to even the Hancocks and the Adamses of the New England of that day that the national *sins and immoralities* of Great Britain could form the appropriate theme of a great state paper, and supply to a legislative assembly the most potent arguments wherewith to justify and defend before the world a momentous political revolution. Discoveries such as these are, belong to the patriots and wise men—the Sewards, the Sumners, the Hales, and the Chases—of a later and more enlightened age.

Our ancestors went to war, indeed, about a preamble and a principle: but these were political—the right of the British Parliament to tax America. And they did not stop to inquire whether war was humane and consistent with man's notion of the Gospel of Peace. Their political rights were invaded, and they took up arms to repel the aggression. Nor did they, sir, in the temper and spirit of the pharisaic rabbins and sophisters of '55, ask of each other whether, morally or piously, the citizens of the several Colonies were worthy of fellowship. They were resolved to form a POLITICAL UNION, so as to establish justice and to secure domestic tranquillity, the common defence, the general welfare, and the blessings of liberty to themselves and posterity. And the Catholic of Maryland and Huguenot of Carolina, the Puritan Roundhead of New England and the Cavalier of Virginia—the slavery-hating, though sometimes slave-trading, saint of Boston and the slave-holding sinner of Savannah—Washington and Adams, Rutledge and Sherman, Madison and Franklin, Pinckney and Ellsworth, all joined hands in holy brotherhood to ordain a Constitution which, silent about *temperance*, forbade *religious tests and establishments, and provided for the extradition of fugitive slaves.**

The questions which engaged the great minds of Washington and the men who composed his cabinets were, also, purely political.

* Both these provisions were carried unanimously, without debate and without vote.—3 *Mad. Pap.*, 1366, 1447, 1456, 1468.

"*Whiskey*," indeed, sir, played once an important part in the drama, threatening even civil war; but it was as the creature of the tax-gatherer, not the theme of the philanthropist or the ecclesiastic. Even the *Alien and Sedition Laws* of the succeeding administration—renascent now by a sort of Pythagorean *metempsychosis*, in the form of a secret, oath-bound conspiracy—were defended then solely on political grounds. "The principles of '98," which, at that time, convulsed the country in the struggle for their predominance, were, indeed, *abstractions*, though of infinite *practical* value—but they were constitutional and political abstractions. Equally is it true that all the capital measures, in every administration, from '98 to 1828, were of a kindred character, except only the *Missouri Question*, that "fire-bell in the night" which filled Jefferson with alarm and despair. But this was transient in itself; though it left its slumbering and treacherous ashes to kindle a flame, not many years later, which threatens to consume this Union with fire unquenchable.

But within no period of our history, gentlemen, were so many and such grave political questions the subject of vehement, and sometimes exasperated discussion, as during the administrations of Jackson and his successor, continuing down, many of them, to 1847. Among these I name Internal Improvements, the Protective System, the Public Lands, Nullification, the Removal of the Indians, the United States Bank, the Removal of the Deposits, Removals from Office, the French Indemnity, the Expunging Resolutions, the Specie Circular, Executive Patronage, the Independent Treasury, Distribution, the Veto Power, and their cognate subjects. Never were greater questions presented. Never was greater intellect or more abundant learning and ingenuity brought into the discussion of any subjects. And never, be it remembered, was the Democratic party so powerful. It was the power and majesty of principle and truth, working out their development through machinery obedient to its constitution and nature. True, Andrew Jackson was then at the head of the party, and his name and his will, moving all things with a nod, were a tower of strength. But an hundred Jacksons could not have upheld a party one day which had been false to its mission.

Within this period, indeed, Anti-masonry rose, flourished, and died; the first, in the United States, of a long line of *third* parties—the *tertium quid* of political sophisters—based upon but one tenet, and devoted to a single purpose. But even in this, the professed principle was solely political.

Following the great questions of the Jackson era, came the Annexation of Texas, the Oregon question, and the Mexican War; during or succeeding which, that pestilent and execrable sectional controversy,

Respublicæ portentum ac pæne funus, was developed and nurtured to its present perilous magnitude.

Here, gentlemen, a new epoch begins in our political history. A new order of issues, and new party mechanism are introduced. At this point, therefore, let us turn back and trace briefly the origin and history of those grievous departures from the ancient landmarks, which, filling the whole country with confusion and perplexity, have impaired, more or less seriously, the strength and discipline of the Democratic party.

In the State of Massachusetts—not barren of inventions—in the year 1811, at a meeting of an ecclesiastical council, a committee was appointed, whereof a reverend doctor, of *Salem*, was chairman, to draught a constitution for the first "Temperance Society" in the United States. The committee reported in 1813, and the society was established. It languished till 1826; and, "languishing did live." Nathan Dane was among its first presidents. In that year of grace, sir, at *Boston*, died this association, and from its ashes sprang the "American Society for the promotion of Temperance"—the parent of a numerous offspring. This association was, in its turn, supplanted by the Washingtonian Societies of 1841, and they, again, by the Sons of Temperance. The eldest of these organizations taught only *temperance* in the use of ardent spirits; their successors forbade, wholly, all spirituous, but allowed vinous and fermented liquors. The Washingtonians enjoined *total abstinence* from every beverage which, by possibility, might intoxicate, and so, also, did the Sons of Temperance. But all these organizations, gentlemen—in the outset, at least—professed reliance solely upon "moral suasion," and denied all political purpose or design in their action. They were voluntary associations, formed to *persuade* men to be temperate. This was right, was reasonable; was great, and noble; and immense results for good rewarded their labors. The public was interested, everywhere. The cause became popular—became powerful. Designing men, not honest, were not slow to discover that it might be turned into a potent political engine for the advancement of personal or party interests. Weak men, very honest, were dazzled and deluded by the bright dream of intemperance expelled, and man restored to his original purity, by the power of human legislation. And lo, in 1855, in this, the freest country upon the globe, fourteen States, by statute—bristling all over with fines, the jail, and the penitentiary—have prescribed that neither strong drink nor the fruit of the vine shall be the subject of contract, traffic, or use within their limits. Temperance, which Paul preached, and the Bible teaches as a religious duty, and leaves to the Church, or the voluntary association, is now become a controlling element at the polls and in legislation. Political parties are perverted into great temperance societies; and the fitness of the citizen for office gauged now by his capacity to remain dry. His palm may itch; his whole head may be weak, and his whole heart corrupt; but if his tongue be but parched, he is competent.

And now, sir, along with good, came evil; and when the good turned to evil, the plague abounded exceedingly. I pass by that numerous host of lesser *isms* of the day, full—all of them—of folly, or fanaticism, and fit only to "uproar the universal peace, confound all unity on earth," which, nevertheless, have excited much public interest, numbered many followers, and, flowing speedily into the stream of party politics, aided largely to pollute its already turbid and frothy waters. I come to that most recent fungus development of those departures from original and wholesome political principle, Know-Nothingism—as barbarous in name, as, in my judgment, it is dangerous in essence.

The extraordinary success, gentlemen, which had attended political temperance and abolition, revealed a mine of wealth, richer than California *placer*, to the office-hunting demagogue. Ordinary political topics were become stale—certainly unprofitable. But he, it now appeared, who could call in the aid of moral or religious truths, touched an answering chord in the heart of this very pious and upright people—a people so keenly sensitive, too, each one, to the moral or religious *status* of his neighbor.

Not ignorant, sir, of the corroding bitterness of religious strife, and mindful of the desolating persecutions, for conscience' sake, of which governments, in times past, had been the willing instruments, the founders of our Federal Constitution forbade, in clear and positive language, all religious tests and establishments: and every State, in terms more or less emphatic, has ordained a similar prohibition. The Constitution of Ohio, declaring that all men have a *natural and indefeasible right* to worship Almighty God according to the dictates of their own conscience, provides that "no preference shall be given, by law, to any religious society, nor shall *any interference* with the rights of conscience be permitted; and no *religious test* shall be required as *a qualification for office.*"

By prohibitions, positive and stringent as these are, gentlemen, our fathers, in their weakness, thought to stay the flood of religious intolerance. Vain hope! The high road to honor and emolument lay through the "higher law" reforms of the day. Moral and religious issues alone were found available. The roll of the "drum ecclesiastic" could stir a fever in the public blood, when the thunders of the rostrum fell dull and droning upon the ears of the people. It needed but small sagacity, therefore, to foresee that the *prejudices* of race and sect must prove a still more powerful and wieldy engine. The Pope of Pilgrim's Progress grinned still at the mouth of the cave full of dead men's bones; and Fox's Book of Martyrs lay shuddering yet, with its hideous engravings, under every Protestant roof. How easy, then, to revive, or, rather, to fan into a flame, this secret but worse than goblin dread of Papacy and the Inquisition. Add to this, that a majority of Catholics are foreigners—obnoxious, therefore, to the bigotry of race and birth also; add, further, that silence, secrecy, and circumspection are weapons potent in any hands: add, still, that to be over-curious is a controlling element in the American character. Compound, now, all these with a travesty upon the signs, grips, and machinery of already existing organizations, and you have the elements and mechanism of a great and powerful, but assuredly not enduring party.

In the month of January, 1854, the telegraph, on lightning wing, speeds through its magic meshes the astounding intelligence that, at the municipal election of the town of *Salem* (not unknown in history), in the Commonwealth of Massachusetts, men not known to be candidates were, by an invisible and unknown agency, said to be a secret, oath-bound society, without even so much as a name, elected by heavy majorities over candidates openly proclaimed. In March, and in April, similar announcements appear from other quarters. The mystery is perplexing—the country is on fire—and lo, in October, nine months after this Salem epiphany, from Maine to California, the mythic "SAM" has established his secret conclaves in every city, village, county, and State in the Union.

And here, again, sir, the Protestant clergy, forgetting, many of them, their divine warrant and holy mission—I speak it with profoundest sorrow and humiliation—have run headlong into this dangerous and demoralizing organization. They have even sought, in many places, to control it, and through it, the political affairs of the country: and, sad spectacle! are found but too often foremost and loudest and most clamorous among political brawlers and hunters of place. I rejoice, sir, that there are many noble and holy exceptions—ministers mindful of their true province, and preaching only the pure precepts and doctrines of that Sacred Volume, without which there is no religion, and no stability or virtue worth the name, in either Church or State. Nevertheless, covertly or openly, the Protestant clergy and Church have but too much lent countenance and encouragement to the order. And the truth must and shall be spoken both of Church and of Party.

In seizing upon the Temperance and other moral and religious movements, party invaded the territory of the Church. The Church has now avenged the aggression, and gone into party—not with the might and majesty of holiness—not to purify and elevate—but with distorted feature, breath polluted, and wing dripping and droiling in mire and stench and rottenness, to destroy and pollute, in the foul embrace, whatever of purity remained yet to either Church or the hustings. The Church has disorganized and perverted party; and, in its turn, party has become to the Church as "dead flies in the ointment of the apothecary." Church and State, each abandoning its peculiar province, and meeting upon the common ground of fanaticism and proscription, have joined hands in polluting and incestuous wedlock. The Constitution remains, indeed, unchanged in letter; but this unholy union has rendered nugatory one among its wisest and most salutary enactments.

But, gentlemen, all these are, in their nature and from circumstances, essentially ephemeral. No powerful and controlling interests exist to cement and harden them into strength and durability. They are among the epidemic diseases which for a season infect every body politic—leaving it, if sound in constitution and not distempered otherwise, purified and strengthened. In all these, too, the Democracy, as a party, has stood firm and uncontaminate; although, indeed, individual members have, in every State and county, been beguiled and led astray, and thereby the aggregate power and influence of the party greatly impaired.

Especially, sir, is the present order of "Know-Nothings" evanescent. Even now it totters to the earth. In the beginning, indeed, it was, perhaps, the purpose of its founders to hold it aloof from the great sectional controversy between the North and the South, and to mould it into a permanent national party. But circumstances are stronger than men—and already throughout the North it has become thoroughly abolitionized. Hence, it must speedily dissolve and pass away, or remain but a yet more hateful adjunct of that one stronger and more durable organization, in which every element of opposition to the Democratic party must, sooner or later, inevitably terminate—THE ABOLITION HORDE OF THE NORTH; for, however tortuous may be its channel, or remote its fountain, into this turbid and devouring flood will every brook and rivulet find its way at last.

The consideration of this great question, Mr. President, I have naturally and appropriately reserved to the last. It is the gravest and most momentous, full of embarrassment and of danger to the country; and, in cowering before, or tampering with it, the Democratic party of Ohio has given itself a disabling, though I trust not yet mortal wound.

I propose, then, sir, to trace fully the origin, development, and progress of this movement, and to explore, and lay open at length, its relations, present and prospective, to the Democratic party and to the Union.

SLAVERY, gentlemen—older in other countries also than the records of human society—existed in America at the date of its discovery. The first slaves of the European were natives of the soil; and a Puritan governor of Massachusetts—founder of the family of Winthrop—bequeathed his soul to God, and his Indian slaves to the lawful heirs of his body. Negro slavery was introduced into Hispaniola in 1501, more than a century before the colonization of America by the English. Massachusetts, by express enactment, in 1641, punishing "man-stealing" with death—and it is so punished to this day under the laws of the United States—legalized yet the enslaving of captives taken in war, and of such "strangers," *foreigners*, as should be acquired by purchase; while confederate New England, two years later, providing for the equitable division of lands, goods, and "*persons*," as equally a part of the "spoils" of war, enacted also the first fugitive slave law in America.* White slaves—convicts and paupers some of them; others, at a later day, prisoners taken at the battles of Dunbar, and Worcester, and of Sedgemoor—were, at the first, employed in Virginia and the British West Indies. Bought in England by English dealers, among whom was the queen of James II., with many of his nobles and courtiers—some of them, perhaps, of the house of Sutherland—they were imported and sold at auction to the highest bidder. In 1620, a Dutch man-of-war first landed a cargo of slaves upon the banks of James River. But the earliest slave-ship belonging to the English colonists was fitted out, in 1645, by a member of the Puritan Church, of Boston. Fostered still by English princes and nobles, confirmed and cherished by British legislation and judicial decisions, even against the wishes, and in spite of the remonstrances, of the Colonies, the traffic increased;

* SLAVERY IN MASSACHUSETTS.—"There shall never be any bond slavery, villeinage, or captivity among us, *unless* it be lawful captives taken in just wars, and such *strangers* as willingly sell themselves, or *are sold to us*."—*Massachusetts Body of Liberties*, 1641, § 91.

"It is, also, by these confederates agreed, that, etc..... and that according to the different charge of each jurisdiction and plantation, the whole advantage of the war (if it please God so to bless their endeavors) whether it be in lands, goods, or *persons*, shall be proportionably divided among said confederates."—*Articles of Confederation, etc., May* 19, 1643; § 4; *and Bancroft's United States*, vol. 1, p. 168.

THE NEW ENGLAND FUGITIVE SLAVE LAW.—"It is also agreed that if *any servant run away from his master* into any of these confederate jurisdictions, that, in such case, *upon certificate* of one magistrate in the jurisdiction out of which the said servant fled, or upon due proof, the said servant *shall be delivered up* either to his master or *any other that pursues* and brings such certificate or proof."—*Ibid.*, § 8.

slaves multiplied, and, on the Fourth of July, 1776, every Colony was now become a slave State; and the sun went down that day upon four hundred and fifty thousand of those who, in the cant of eighty years later, are styled "human chattels," but who were not, by the act of that day, emancipated.

Eleven years afterward, delegates, assembling at Philadelphia, from every State except Rhode Island, ignoring the question of the sinfulness and immorality of slavery, as a subject with which they, as the representatives of separate and independent States, had no concern, founded a Union and framed a Constitution, which, leaving with each State the exclusive control and regulation of its own domestic institutions, and providing for the taxation and representation of slaves, gave no right to Congress to debate or to legislate concerning slavery in the States or Territories, except for the interdiction of the slave-trade and the extradition of fugitive slaves. The Plan of Union proposed by Franklin, in 1754, had contained no allusion, even, to slavery; and the Articles of Confederation of 1778, but a simple recognition of its existence—so wholly was it regarded then a domestic and local concern. In 1787 every State, except, perhaps, Massachusetts, tolerated slavery either absolutely or conditionally. But the number of slaves north of Maryland, never great, was even yet comparatively small—not exceeding forty thousand in a total slave population of six hundred thousand. In the North, chief carrier of slaves to others, even as late as 1807, slavery never took firm root.* Nature warred against it in that latitude; otherwise every State in the Union would have been a slaveholding State to this day. It was not profitable there, and it died out—lingering, indeed, in New York, till July, 1827. It died out; but not so much by the manumission of slaves as by their transportation and sale in the South. And thus New England, sir, turned an honest penny with her left hand, and with her right modestly wrote herself down in history as both generous and just.

In the South, gentlemen, all this was precisely reversed. The earliest and most resolute enemies to slavery were Southern men. But climate had fastened the institution upon them; and they found no way to strike it down. From the beginning, indeed, the Southern colonies especially had resisted the introduction of African slaves; and, at the very outset of the revolution, Virginia and North Carolina interdicted the slave-trade. The Continental Congress soon after, on the 6th of April, 1776,

* The North and the Slave Trade.—The number of African slaves imported into the port of Charleston, S. C., alone, in the years 1804, 1805, 1806, and 1807—the last year of the slave-trade—was 39,075. These were consigned to *ninety-one* British subjects, *eighty-eight* citizens of New England, *ten* French subjects, and only *thirteen* citizens of Charleston.—*Compend. of U. S. Census*, p. 83.

three months earlier than the Declaration of Independence, resolved that no more slaves ought to be imported into the Thirteen Colonies. Jefferson, in his draught of the Declaration, had denounced the king of England alike for encouraging the slave-trade, and for fomenting servile insurrection in the provinces. Ten years later, he boldly attacked slavery, in his "Notes on Virginia;" and in the Congress of the Confederation, *prior to the adoption of the Constitution, with its solemn compacts and compromises upon the subject of slavery*, proposed to exclude it from the territory northwest of the river Ohio. Colonel Mason, of Virginia, vehemently condemned it, in the Convention of 1787. Nevertheless, it had already become manifest that slavery must soon die away in the North, but in the South continue and harden into, perhaps, a permanent, uneradicable system. Hostile interests and jealousies sprang up, therefore, in bitterness, even in the Convention. But the blood of the patriot brothers of Carolina and Massachusetts smoked yet upon the battle-fields of the Revolution. The recollection of their kindred language and common dangers and sufferings, burned still fresh in their hearts. Patriotism proved more powerful than jealousy, and good sense stronger than fanaticism. There were no Sewards, no Hales, no Sumners, no Greeleys, no Parkers, no Chases, in that Convention. There was a *Wilson*, but he rejoiced not in the name of *Henry;* and he was a Scotchman. There was a clergyman—no, not in the Convention of '87, but in the Congress of '76; but it was the devout, the learned, the pious, the patriotic Witherspoon; of foreign birth, also—a native of Scotland, too. The men of that day and generation, sir, were content to leave the question of slavery just where it belonged. It did not occur to them, that each one among them was accountable for "the sin of slaveholding" in his fellow; and that to ease his tender conscience of the burden, all the fruits of revolutionary privation, and blood, and treasure—all the recollections of the past, all the hopes of the future—nay, the Union, and with it, domestic tranquillity and national independence—ought to be offered up as a sacrifice. They were content to deal with political questions, and to leave cases of conscience to the Church and the schools, or to the individual man. And, accordingly, to this Union and Constitution, based upon these compromises—execrated now as "covenants with death and leagues with hell"—every State acceded; and upon these foundations, thus broad and deep and stable, a political superstructure has, as if by magic, arisen, which, in symmetry and proportion, and, if we would but be true to our trust, in strength and durability, finds no parallel in the world's history.

Patriotic sentiments, sir, such as marked the era of '89, continued to guide the statesmen and people of the country, for more than thirty years, full of prosperity; till, in a dead political calm, consequent upon temporary extinguishment of the ancient party lines and issues, the MISSOURI QUESTION, resounding through the land with the hollow moan of the earthquake, shook the pillars of the Republic even to their deep foundations.

Within these thirty years, gentlemen, slavery, as a system, had been abolished by law or disuse, quietly and without agitation, in every State north of Mason and Dixon's line—in many of them lingering, indeed, in individual cases, so late as the census of 1840. But, except in half a score of instances, the question had not been obtruded upon Congress. The Fugitive Slave Act of 1793 had been passed without opposition, and without a division in the Senate; and by a vote of forty-eight to seven in the House. The slave-trade had been declared piracy, punishable with death. Respectful petitions from the Quakers of Pennsylvania, and others, upon the slavery question, were referred to a committee, and a report made thereon, which laid the matter at rest. Other petitions, afterward, were quietly rejected, and, in one instance, returned to the petitioner. Louisiana and Florida, both slaveholding countries, had, without agitation, been added to our territory. Kentucky, Tennessee, Louisiana, Mississippi, and Alabama, slave States each one of them, had been admitted into the Union, without a murmur. No Missouri Restriction, no Wilmot Proviso, had as yet reared its discordant front to terrify and confound. NON-INTERVENTION was then both the practice and the doctrine of the statesmen and people of that period; though, as yet, no hollow platform enunciated it as an article of faith, from which, nevertheless, obedience might be withheld, and the platform "spit upon," provided the tender conscience of the recusant did not forbid him to support the candidate, and help to secure the "spoils."

Once only, sir, was there a deliberate purpose shown, by a formal assault upon the compromises of the Constitution, to array the prejudices of geographical sections upon the question of slavery. But, originating within the secret counsels of the Hartford Convention, it partook of the odium which touched every thing connected with that treasonable assembly,* till, set on fire by a live coal from the altar of jealousy and fanaticism, it burst into a conflagration, six years later. And now, sir,

* THE HARTFORD CONVENTION.—"*Resolved*, That it is expedient to recommend to the several State legislatures certain amendments to the Constitution, viz.:

"That the power to declare or make war, by the Congress of the United States, be restricted. That it is expedient to attempt to make provision for *restraining* Congress in the exercise of an unlimited power *to make New States, and admit them into the Union. That an amendment be proposed respecting* SLAVE REPRESENTATION AND SLAVE TAXATION."—*The third resolution of the Hartford Convention, reported Dec.* 24, 1814, *and subsequently adopted.*

It was also resolved "that the *capacity of naturalized citizens to hold offices of trust*, honor, or profit, ought to be restricted."

for the first time in our history under the Constitution, a strenuous and most embittered struggle ensued, on the part of the North—the *Federalists* of the North—to prevent the admission of a State into the Union; really, because the North—the Federalists of the North—strove for the mastery, and to secure the balance of power in her own hands; but ostensibly because slaveholding, which the Missouri Constitution sanctioned, was affirmed to be immoral and irreligious. In this first fearful strife, this earliest departure from the Constitution and the ancient sound policy of the country, *the North*—for the truth of history shall be vindicated—THE NORTH was the aggressor; and that, too, without the slightest provocation. Vermont, in New England, Ohio, Indiana, and Illinois, out of territory once the property of slaveholding Virginia, had been admitted into the Union; and Michigan organized into a territorial government, without one hostile vote from the South given upon the ground that slavery was interdicted within their limits. Even Maine had been permitted, by vote of Congress, to separate from Massachusetts, and become a distinct State. But now Missouri knocked for admission, with a constitution not introducing, but continuing slavery, which had existed in her midst from the beginning; and four several times, at the first, she was rejected by the North. The South resisted, and the storm raged. Jefferson, professing to hate slavery, but living and dying himself a slaveholder, or, in the delicate slang of to-day, a "slave-breeder," loving yet his country with all the fervid patriotism of his early manhood five and forty years before, heard in it "the knell of the Union," and mourned that he must "die now in the belief that the useless sacrifice of themselves by the generation of 1776, to acquire self-government and happiness to their country, was to be thrown away by the unwise and unworthy passions of their sons;" consoling himself—the only solace of the patriot of fourscore years—that *he* should not live to weep over the blessings thrown thus recklessly away for "an abstract principle;" and the folly and madness of this "act of suicide and of treason against the hopes of the world."*

* THE MISSOURI QUESTION A FEDERAL MOVEMENT—THE NORTH THE AGGRESSOR.—"The slavery agitation took its rise during this time (1819–'20), in the form of attempted restriction on the State of Missouri—a prohibition to hold slaves to be placed upon her as a condition of her admission into the Union, and to be binding upon her afterward. *This agitation came from the North, and under a Federal lead,* and soon swept both parties into its vortex. . . . . *The real struggle was political, and for the balance of power,* as frankly declared by Mr. Rufus King, who disdained dissimulation. . . . . The resistance made to the admission of the State, on account of the clause in relation to free people of color, was *only a mask* to the real cause of opposition. . . . . *For a while this formidable Missouri question threatened the total overthrow of all political parties upon principle, and the substitution of geographical parties, distinguished by the slave line,* and, of course, destroying the just and proper

But the incantations of hate and fanaticism had evoked the hideous spectre, and it ought to have been quelled, never to reappear. The appalling question was now stirred; and it should have been met and resettled forever, by the men of that day, on the original basis of the Constitution—not left, as a legacy of discord, a Pandora's box full of all evil, of mischief and pestilence, to the next generation. They were not true to themselves; they were not true to us. They cowered before the goblin, and laid before it peace-offerings and a wave-offering, and sent us, their children, to pass through the fire in the valley of Hinnom. Setting aside the compromises of the Constitution, and usurping power not granted to Congress, they undertook to compromise about that which had already been definitely and permanently settled by that instrument. This was the beginning, sir, of that line of paltry and halting compromises; of fat-brained, mole-eyed, unmanlike expedients, which put the evil day off only to return laden with aggravated mischief. They hushed the terrible question for a moment; and the election machinery moved on, and the spoils of the Presidency were divided as before. But it was "a *reprieve* only, not a *final sentence.*" The "geographical line" thus once conceived for the first time, and held up to the angry passions of men, was, as Jefferson had foretold, never obliterated, but rather, by every irritation, marked deeper and deeper. And, after fifteen years' truce, it reappeared in a new and far more dangerous form; and, enduring already for more than half the average lifetime of man, has attained a position and magnitude which neither demands, nor will hearken to any further compromise. Nevertheless, sir, but for the insolent intermeddling of the British government and British emissaries—continued to this day, with the superaddition now of Napoleon the Third—it might have slumbered for many years longer.

In England, gentlemen, the form of personal bondage disappeared even to its last traces from her own soil, about the beginning of the seventeenth century; its legal existence continued till 1661; its worst

action of the Federal Government, *and leading* eventually *to a separation of the States.* It was a *Federal movement*, accruing to the benefit of that party, and, at first, was overwhelming, sweeping all the Northern Democracy into its current, and giving the supremacy to their adversaries. When this effect was perceived, the Northern Democracy became alarmed, and *only wanted a turn or abatement in popular feeling at home, to take the first opportunity to get rid of the question, by admitting the State, and re-establishing party lines upon the basis of political principles.* . . . . It was a political movement for the balance of power, balked by the Northern Democracy, who saw their own overthrow, and the eventual separation of the States, in the establishment of geographical parties divided by a slavery and anti-slavery line. . . . . In the Missouri controversy, the North was the undisputed aggressor."—*Benton's Thirty Years*, pp. 5, 10, *and* 136, *of volume first.*

realities remain to this day; for although, in that very humane and most enlightened Island, there be no involüntary servitude except as a punishment for crime, yet in England poverty is a crime, punishable with the worst form of slavery, or by starvation and death. Three hundred years ago, she began to traffic in negro slaves. Queen Elizabeth was a sharer in its gains. A hundred and fifty years later, at the peace of Utrecht, England undertook, by compact with Spain, to import into the West Indies, within the space of thirty years, one hundred and forty-four thousand negroes, demanding, and with exactest care securing, a monopoly of the traffic. Queen Anne reserved one-quarter of the stock of the slave-trading company to herself, and one-half to her subjects; to the king of Spain the other quarter being conceded. Even so late as 1750, Parliament busied itself in devising plans to make the slave-trade still more effectual, while in 1775, the very year of the revolution, a noble earl wrote to a colonial agent these memorable words: "We cannot allow the Colonies to check or discourage, in any degree, a traffic so beneficial to the nation." Between that date, and the period of first importation, England had stolen from the coast of Africa, and imported into the new world, or buried in the sea on the passage thither, not less than three and a quarter millions of negroes—more, by half a million, than the entire population of the Colonies. In April, 1776, the American Congress resolved against the importation of any more slaves. But England continued the traffic, with all its accumulated horrors, till 1808; for so deeply had it struck its roots into the commercial interests of that country, that not all the efforts of an organized and powerful society, not the influence of her ministers, not the eloquence of all her most renowed orators, availed to strike it down for more than forty years after this, its earliest interdiction in any country, by a rebel congress. Nevertheless, sir, slavery in the English West Indies continued twenty-seven years longer. But the loss of her American Colonies, and the prohibition of the slave-trade, had left small interest to Great Britain in negro slavery. Her philanthropy found room now to develop and expand in all its wonderful proportions. And accordingly, in 1834, England—England, drunk with the blood of the martyrs, stoning the prophets, and rejecting the apostles of political liberty, in her own midst—robbed, by act of Parliament, one hundred millions of dollars from the wronged and beggared peasantry of Ireland, from the enslaved and oppressed millions of India, from the starving, overwrought, mendicant carcasses of the white slaves of her own soil, to pay to her impoverished colonists, plundered without voice and without vote in her legislature, the stipulated price of human rights; and with these, the wages of iniquity, in the outraged name of God and humanity, mocked the handful of her black bondsmen in the West

Indies with the false and deluding shadow of liberty. Exeter Hall resounded with acclamation; bonfires and illuminations proclaimed the exultant joy of an aristocracy fat with the pride and lust of domination. But in that self-same hour—in that self-same hour, from the furnaces of Sheffield and the manufactories of Birmingham; from the wretched hovels of Ireland, full of famishing and pestilence; from ten thousand work-houses crowded with leprous and perishing paupers, the abodes of abominable cruelties, which not even the pen of a Dickens has availed to portray in the full measure of their enormity, and from the mouths of a thousand pits and mines, deep under earth, horrid in darkness, and reeking with noisome vapor, the stupendous charnel-houses of the living dead men of England, there went up, and ascends yet up to heaven, the piercing wail of desolation and despair.

But England became now the great apostle of African liberty. Ignoring, sir, or putting under, at the point of the bayonet, the political rights of millions of her own white subjects, she yet prepared to convict the world of the sinfulness of negro slavery. Exeter Hall sent out its emissaries, full of zeal, and greedy for martyrdom. The British government took up the crusade—not from motives of religion or philanthropy. Let no man be deceived. No, sir. Since the days of Peter the Hermit and Richard the Lion-hearted, England, forgetting the Holy Sepulchre, had learned many lessons; and none know better now their true province and mission, than English statesmen. But the American experiment of free government had not failed. America had grown great—had grown populous and powerful. Her proud example, towering up every day higher, and illuminating every land, was penetrating the hearts of the people, and threatening to shake the thrones of every monarchy in Europe. Force against such a nation would be the wildest of follies. But to be odious is to be weak, and internal dissension had wasted Greece, and opened even Thermopylæ to the Barbarian of Macedon. The Missouri Question had revealed the weak point of the American Confederacy. Achilles was found vulnerable in the heel. *In spem ventum erat,* INTESTINA DISCORDIA *dissolvi rem Romanam posse.*

The machinery which had effected emancipation in the British West India Islands, of use no longer in England, was transferred to America. Aided by British gold, encouraged by British sympathy, the agitation began here, in 1835; and so complete was it in all its appointments, so thorough the organization and discipline, so perfect the electric current, that, within six months, the whole Union was convulsed. Affiliated societies were established in every Northern State, and in almost every county; lecturers were paid, and sent forth into every city and village; a powerful and well-supported press, fed from the treasuries, and working up the cast-off rags of the British societies, poured forth a multitude of incendiary prints and publications, which were distributed by mail throughout the Union, but chiefly in the Southern States, and among the slaves. Fierce excitement in the South followed. And so great became the public feeling and interest, that President Jackson, so early as the annual message of 1835, pressed earnestly upon Congress the duty of prohibiting the use of the mail for transmitting incendiary publications to the South. But, prior to the sitting of Congress, the Abolition societies, treading again in the footsteps of the emancipationists in England, had prepared, and now poured in a flood of petitions, praying Congress to take action upon the subject of slavery. The purpose was to obtain a foothold, a fulcrum, in the capital; for without this, the South could not be effectually embroiled, and little could be accomplished, even in the North. But no appliances were left untried. Agitators, their breath was agitation; quiescence would have been a sentence of obscurity and dissolution. And accordingly, in May, 1835, the American Anti-Slavery Society was established in New York, its object being the immediate and unconditional abolition of negro slavery in the United States. It was a permanent organization, to be dissolved only upon the consummation of its purpose. The object of attack was the South, the seat of war the North. Public sentiment was to be stirred up here against slavery, because it was a moral evil, and a sin in the sight of the Most High, for the continuance of which, one day, the men of the North were accountable before heaven. Slaveholders were to be made odious in the eyes of Northern men and foreign nations, as cruel tyrants and task-masters, as kidnappers, murderers, and pirates, whose existence was a reproach to the North, and whom it were just to hunt down and exterminate, as so many beasts of prey, to whom even the laws of the chase extended no indulgence. To hold fellowship and union with slaveholders, was to partake of all their sins and enormities; it was to be "in league with death and covenant with hell." The Constitution and Union were themselves sinful, and, as such, they ought forthwith to be abrogated and dissolved. And thus, sir, the earlier Abolitionists, who were zealots, began just where their successors of to-day, who are traitors, have ended.

A separate political organization was not, at the first, proposed, and each man was left to his ancient party allegiance. The revolution was to be a moral and religious revolution, and its principles, propagated by petitions, lectures, societies, and the press, in the North, were, through these instrumentalities, to penetrate Congress and the legislatures of the South, and if not hearkened to there, then to effect a dismemberment of the Union by secession of the North, or secession forced upon the South.

Slavery, gentlemen, had, before this, been the subject of earnest and sometimes angry controversy in Congress, and elsewhere. But a powerful and permanent organization, founded for such a purpose, and working by such appliances, had never yet existed. Coming thus in such a questionable shape, even the North started back aghast, as at "a goblin damned;" and it was denounced as treason and madness from the first. Its presses were destroyed, its assemblies broken up, its publications burned, and its lecturers mobbed everywhere, and more than one among them murdered in the midst of popular tumult and indignation. The churches, the school-houses, the court-houses, and the public halls were alike closed against them. Misguided men, fanatics, emissaries of England, traitors—these were among the mildest of epithets which, in every place, and almost from every tongue, saluted their ears. The very name of "Abolitionist" became a byword and a hissing. Not an advocate, and scarce even an apologist, for the men, or their course, was found in either hall of Congress. Members presented their petitions with great reluctance; and, as late as the twenty-eighth of December, 1837, Mr. Calhoun rejoiced that "every senator, without exception," had confessed himself opposed to the agitation. A bill to punish, by severe penalties, any postmaster who should knowingly put into the mail any incendiary publication directed to the South, had, by the casting vote of Vice-President Van Buren, been ordered to a third reading. The Senate declined to refer, or in any way act upon, the numerous petitions presented, while the House, refusing to read, print, or refer, laid them forthwith upon the table. In January, 1838, the Senate, by a majority of four to one, adopted a series of resolutions denouncing the Abolition movement "on whatever ground or pretext urged forward, political, moral, or religious," as insulting to the South, and dangerous to her domestic peace and tranquillity; and further, condemning all efforts toward the abolition of slavery in the District of Columbia and the Territories as a breach of good faith, a just cause of serious alarm to the States in which slavery exists, and of most mischievous tendency. At the following session, the House of Representatives, by a majority of more than one hundred and fifty, passed resolutions, stronger, if possible, than these, and, some time later, censured, and almost expelled, John Quincy Adams, for presenting an abolition petition looking to a dissolution of the Union.

Outside of Congress, also, sir, Abolition received, up to this period, just as little countenance or support. By both of the great political parties it was utterly and indignantly repudiated; while from none of the political, and scarce any of even the religious journals and periodicals of the day, did it find either aid or comfort. Especially, sir, was the Democratic party then sound on this question. General Jackson had already denounced, in strong language, officially, the "wicked and unconstitutional attempts of the misguided men, and especially the emissaries from foreign parts," who had originated the Abolition movement. President Van Buren, in his inaugural address, had volunteered a pledge to veto any bill looking to the abolition of slavery in the District of Columbia. Benton, Buchanan, Wright, Allen, all concurred; and voted, also, for the resolutions which passed the Senate. In Ohio, the Democratic State Convention of January 8, 1840, planted itself firmly upon the rock of the Constitution, and taking high and patriotic ground, condemned the efforts then being made for the abolition of slavery in the District of Columbia, "by organizing societies in the free States, as *hostile to the spirit of the Constitution, and destructive to the harmony of the Union*:" and resolving that, "We, as citizens of a free State, had *no right* to interfere" with slavery *elsewhere*, denounced the Abolition movement and Abolition societies, declaring, that while they "ought to be discountenanced by every lover of peace and concord, *no sound Democrat* would have any part or lot with them." It was, also, further resolved, as if in the very spirit of prophecy, that "political Abolitionism was but *ancient Federalism*, under a new guise, and only a new device for the overthrow of Democracy."

These resolutions, sir, were adopted with but *three* dissenting voices, in a more numerous assemblage of delegates than had ever before met in the State.

[Here GEORGE W. ELLS, Esq., one of the old Liberty (Abolition) Guard, interrupting, said, that historical statements ought to be correct; that he had been a member, from Licking County, of the convention referred to, and that he knew that the resolutions quoted had never passed, but were smuggled into the proceedings, in order to be circulated through the South, to aid Mr. Van Buren.]

Mr. VALLANDIGHAM :—Sir, I have before me the *official record* of the proceedings of that convention, signed by the late lamented Thomas L. Hamer, president of the convention, a man too candid, too brave, and too true to lend himself to so base and detestable a fraud for any such purpose. You libel the gallant dead; and it is quite too late in the day, after the lapse of *fifteen years*, for you, sir, by your own parol testimony, to seek to impeach the absolute verity of the record. And I repeat now again, and desire you to hear and understand it, that these resolutions *did* pass that convention, and pass, too, with but three dissenting voices, in that, the largest State convention ever before assembled in Ohio. And if you, sir, happened to be one of the *three* who voted against these resolutions, I can only say that you had the misfortune to find yourself in a very small and most inglorious minority. I assert further, that three weeks after that convention, Benjamin Tappan, then a senator in Congress from Ohio, quoting these same resolutions, and affirming the statement which I have just made concluded a speech of remarkable precision and clearness, by declining even to present a petition from citizens of the State, praying for the abolition of slavery in the District of Columbia.*

A few months later—mark you, Mr. President, Ohio then took the lead in denouncing the treason and fanaticisms of Abolition—the Democracy of the Union, assembled in general convention at Baltimore, passed, without a dissenting vote, that memorable resolution, penned by that pure and incorruptible patriot, Silas Wright; and which penetrated then the heart also, and not the ear only, of every Democrat, to the full and utmost significancy of every word and letter, repudiating "incipient steps," even by Congress, in relation to "questions of slavery," of every sort, as calculated to lead to the most alarming and dangerous consequences, and such as ought not to be countenanced by any friend of our political institutions.

Such, Mr. President, was Abolition in the North, fifteen years ago —*such it is not now.* To the philosophic historian, who, in a future age, shall sit amid the ruins of my country, to write her decline and fall, I leave the sad but instructive office of tracing its progress, and exploring the causes which, step by step, have led to its present portentous development. I propose but a brief and hasty summary.

Slowly emerging from obscurity and odium, abolition began to fix attention, not as hitherto, by its sound and fury, but, losing none of these, rather now by its increasing numbers and influence. Designing men soon foresaw that, of all the movements of the day, none promised so abundant and perhaps durable a harvest to him who should organize and discipline its wild crusading forces into a regular political party. Fanaticism, and a false religious zeal, conjoined with that pestilent, but ever-potent spirit, which is so sorely offended at the mote that is in our

* THE OHIO RESOLUTIONS.—"*Resolved*, That in the opinion of this convention, Congress ought not, without the consent of the people of the District, and of the States of Virginia and Maryland, to abolish slavery in the District of Columbia; and that the efforts now making, for that purpose, by organized societies in the free States, are hostile to the spirit of the Constitution, and destructive to the harmony of the Union.

"*Resolved*, That slavery being a domestic institution, recognized by the Constitution of the United States, we, as citizens of a free State, have no right to interfere with it; and that the organizing of societies and associations in free States, in opposition to the institutions of sister States, while productive of no good, may be the cause of much mischief; and while such associations, for political purposes, ought to be discountenanced by every lover of peace and concord, no sound Democrat will have part or lot with them.

"*Resolved*, That political Abolitionism is but ancient Federalism, under a new guise, and that the political action of anti-slavery societies is only a device for the overthrow of Democracy."

brother's eye, and which makes each man jealous over his neighbor's conscience, could easily be arrayed under the banner of sectional hate and bigotry, and thus a distinct political faction be compounded out of these elements. Such a party, sir, united by these, the strongest, though not most durable ties, was soon shuffled together, and not long after, supplanted the system of affiliated societies. It formed separate tickets, and, in 1844, supported a candidate for the Presidency. But, prior to 1848, it attained as a party comparatively small weight in elections. The vehement contests and grave political questions which convulsed the two great parties of the country, overshadowed all interest in the feeble, but still earnest and active abolition band; but that band, meantime, was steadily increasing, by accessions, now and then from the Democrats, but chiefly from the Whigs; some honest men, and the discontented and rejected spirits of each, naturally dropping off, and falling into its ranks. Abolitionists—many of them styling themselves, at this period in their history, the "Liberty Party," gained now, in some counties, the balance of power; and hence became there an object of courtship to the other parties; in New England yet earlier, but all over the North, in 1844, the Whig party began to trim and falter upon the question. The defeat of Clay, and the annexation of Texas, gave a new impetus to abolition, and many more, upon these pretexts, fell into its ranks. Meantime, the steady, persistent, never-wearying labors of its orators and press, full of grossly false and exaggerated portraitures of slavery, and libels upon Southern society, working by day and by night, in the Church, the schools, and the lecture-room, at the public meeting, the fireside, and the sick-bed, fomenting thus hate and jealousy of the South everywhere, and that, too, for the most part, without counteracting influence from any quarter, had poured the leprous distilment deep into every vein and artery of the Northern body politic.

Just at this point, sir, in the history of the Abolition movement, came the Oregon controversy, and after that the Mexican war, embroiled by the now terrible question of the acquisition of a very large tract of Mexican territory. Pride or vanity, wounded by the settlement of the Oregon boundary at forty-nine, ambition, disappointed of office, the nomination of Generals Cass and Taylor in 1848, and the manifestly approaching dissolution of the Whig party, all contributed to throw a large portion of that party in the North, and not a few from the Democratic host, into the ranks of the Abolitionists; who, swelled now by such great accessions, threw off wholly the odious name of Abolition, and, organizing into one body, under a new title, at Buffalo, announced Martin Van Buren as their candidate for the Presidency. In the midst of all this chaos in the political elements, arose that pernicious bubble, the "Wilmot Proviso," which, convulsing the country for more than four years, in its various forms, had well-nigh precipitated us headlong into the bottomless gulf of disunion.

Assuming now the specious name of "Free Soil," and disguising its odious principles and its true purposes, under the false pretence of No Extension of Slavery, the Abolition party addressed itself to minds full now of hate toward the South and her institutions, and ready alike to forget the true mission of a political party, and the limitations of the Constitution. But the united patriotism, talent, and worth of the North and South rallied to the rescue of this the last grand experiment of free government, from the thick darkness of failure and of ruin by the parricidal hands of its own children. The Compromise of 1850 followed: intended and believed to be a final adjustment of this appalling controversy. It was designed to be a covenant of peace forever—sealed and attested by the self-sacrifice of Webster, Clay, and Calhoun, the most illustrious triumvirate of great men and patriots, in any age or any country. But to no purpose: the yawning gulf did not close over them. The origin of the evil lay deeper, and it was not reached. No great question of a like nature and magnitude was ever adjusted by a legislative compromise, in a popular government. The evil lay in that great and most pernicious error which pervaded and penetrated so large a portion of the Northern mind, that the men of the North, if not under the Constitution, yet, by some "higher law" of conscience, had a right, and, as they would escape that fire which is not quenched, were bound to intermeddle, and, in some way, to legislate for the abolition of the "accursed system." No act of Congress, no number of acts, could heal a malady like this, rooted in presumptuous self-righteousness, and aggravated by the corroding poison of sectional jealousy and hate. For such, sir, there is no sweet oblivious antidote in legislation. Set on fire by these passions, applied now to that case which, coming nighest home, appealed most plausibly and most strongly to their impulses and their prejudices, a large part of the North resolved to render nugatory the chief slavery compromise of the Constitution, by trampling under foot and resisting or obstructing the execution of the Fugitive Slave Act of 1850. And three years later, re-enforced now by many recruits from the Democratic ranks, and by almost the entire Whig force of the North, disbanded finally by the overthrow of 1852, but reorganized in part under the banner of Know-Nothingism, the Abolition handful of 1835, swelled now to a mighty host, rallied in defence of the Missouri Restriction, and shook the whole land with a rocking tempest of popular commotion, more dangerous than even the storm of 1850.

Here, then, gentlemen, let me pause to survey the true nature and full extent of the perils which thus encompass us, and to inquire: What remains to be done, that they may be averted?

In January, 1838, Mr. Calhoun spoke, with alarm—then derided as visionary—of the danger which, to him, seemed already as certain as it would be disastrous, from the continued, persevering, uncounteracted efforts of the Abolitionists, imbuing the rising generation at the North with the belief that the institutions of the South were sinful and immoral, and that it would be doing God service to abolish them, even should it involve the destruction of half her inhabitants, as murderers and pirates at best. Sir, what was then prophecy, is now history. More than half the present generation in the North have ceased to look upon Southern men as brethren. Taught to hate, first, the institutions of the South, they have, very many of them, by easy gradations, transferred that hatred to her citizens. Learning to abhor what they are told is murder, they have found no principle, either in nature or in morals, which impels them to love the murderer with fraternal affection. Organized bands exist in every Northern State, with branches in Canada, which make slave-stealing a business and a boast: and that outrage which, if any foreign State, or any State of this Union even, in any thing else, were to encourage or permit in any of her citizens, would, by the whole country, with one voice, be regarded as a just cause of instant war or reprisals, is every day consummated without rebuke, or by connivance, or the direct sanction of many of the members of this Confederacy; by school-books, and in school-houses; in the academies, colleges, and universities; in the schools of divinity, medicine, and law—these same sad lessons of hate and jealousy are every day inculcated. Even the name and the fame of a slaveholding Washington have ceased to cause a throb in many a Northern heart. The entire press of the North, in journals, newspapers, periodicals, prints, and books, with not many manly and patriotic exceptions, has either been silent or lent countenance and support, knowingly or carelessly, to the systematic and treasonable efforts of those who are resolved to pull down the fabric of this Union. Literature and the arts are put under conscription, for the same wicked purpose. Not a Northern poet, from Longfellow and Bryant, down to Lowell, but has sought inspiration from the black Helicon of Abolition: and the poison from a hundred thousand copies of false and canting libels, in the form of works of fiction, is licked up from every hearthstone, while the "Tribune" of Greeley—one among ten thousand "sold to do evil," at once the tool and the compeer of Seward in his traitorous purpose to make himself a name in history—the antithesis of Washington—by the subversion of this Republic—gathering up, with persevering and most devilish diligence, every murder, every crime, every outrage, every act of cruelty, rapine, or lust, upon white or upon black, real or forged, throughout the South, sends it forth winged with venom and malice, as a faithful witness of the true and general state of Southern society, and the legitimate fruit of slaveholding. In the public lecture and anniversary address; at the concert hall, and upon the boards of the theatre; nay, even at the festivals of our ancient charitable orders, this same dark spirit of mischief is ever present, dropping pestilence from his wings. Even history is corrupted, and figures marshalled into a huge lie, to compass the same treacherous end.

Here, again, too, the clergy, and the Church, gentlemen, mindful less than ever of their true province and vocation, have, one by one, joined in the crusade, till nineteen-twentieths of Northern pulpits resound every Sabbath, in sermon or prayer, with imprecation upon slaveholders. Already has disunion and consequent strife ensued in all the chief religious sects, three only excepted. Outside of these—and sometimes within them, too—the religion of the Bible is but too often superseded by the gospel of Abolition, and the way of salvation taught to lie through sympathy with that distant portion of the African race which is held in bondage south of Mason and Dixon's line. Thus the spirit of persecution is superadded to the jealousies of sectional position, and the furnace of hate heated seven times hotter than is wont.

They who would not turn a deaf ear to the express requirements of the Constitution, are beguiled and drawn astray by the hollow pretence of Opposition to the Extension of Slavery—a pretence alike false and unmanly, and opposed to the spirit of the Constitutional compact, and the principle which forbids to intermeddle with slavery in the States.

Others, sir, who may care nothing for the sinfulness or immorality of slaveholding, are wrought to jealousy by the false and impudent outcry against the "aggressions of the slave-power," "the grasping spirit of the South," "Southern bluster and bravado;" and many an arrant coward hires himself to be written down a hero, for his wondrous courage in lending the eye a terrible aspect on his own hustings, at the mention of a "fire-eater" from the Carolinas, or repelling, indignantly, six weeks after the offence, on the floor of Congress, the insolence of some "slave-dealing" member from Virginia, who is, perhaps, at the moment, a hundred miles from the capitol. Thus the claim of the South to participation in the common territory purchased by the common blood and treasure of the Union—nay, even her demand that the solemn compact of the Constitution be fulfilled and her fugitives restored to her, are denounced alike as arrogant "slave-driving" assaults and aggressions upon the rights of the North.

Others, again, are persuaded that the South is weak, is unwilling, and dare not resist—is afraid of insurrection, and dependent for safety and bread and existence upon the proverbial fertility and magnanimity of New England. As if no Henry, no Lee, no Jefferson, no Pinckney, no Sumpter, no Hayne, no Laurens, no Carroll, no George Washington had ever lived—as if the spirit of Marion's men lingered not yet upon the banks of Santee, and the fierce courage of the Butler who rose pale and corpse-like from the bed of death, to lead the Palmetto regiment to battle at Churubusco, foremost in the ranks and "nearest the flashing of the guns," was already become extinct.

The political parties, also, at the North, gentlemen, have faltered, and some of them fallen, before Abolition. The Whig party, bargaining with, courting, and seeking to absorb it into its own ranks, has, itself at last, been swallowed up and lost. Political Temperance and Know-Nothingism are rapidly drifting into the same voxtex. The spirit of Anti-Masonry transmigrated, some years ago, into the opaque body of Abolitionism. Fourierism, Anti-Rentism, the party devoted to Women's Rights, and all the other *isms* of the day, born of the same generating principle, are already fully assimilated to their common parent: for all these isms, sir, like the nerves of sense, run in pairs. Even the Democratic party, never losing its identity, never ceasing to be national, and even now the sole hope of the country, if it will but return to its ancient mission and discipline—the only organized body round which all true conservatives and friends of the Constitution and Union may rally—has, nevertheless, in whole or in part, at some period or another, in every State, cowered before or tampered with this dark spectre.

Just such, too, as public feeling in the North is, so is its legislation. Vermont has passed a law repealing, in effect, within her limits, the Fugitive Slave Act of 1850, and abrogating so much of the Constitution as requires the rendition of fugitives from service. Connecticut, enacting a similar statute, has gone a step farther, and outraged every dictate of justice, in the effort to make it effectual. Massachusetts, the "model Commonwealth" of the times, improving yet upon the work of her sister States, provides, also, that whatsoever member of her bar shall dare appear in behalf of the claimant of a fugitive slave, shall ignominiously be stricken from her court rolls, and forbidden to practise within her limits. Legislation of a kindred character exists, sir, in other States also; and New England will, doubtless, yet find humble imitators even in the West. Already, indeed, the Supreme Court of Wisconsin has deliberately released from her penitentiary, upon *habeas corpus*, a prisoner convicted, on indictment before a United States court, of resisting the laws and officers of the United States in a slave case. Judges, elsewhere, have held that no citizen of the United States living South may dare set his foot, with a slave, upon the northwest shore of the Ohio, at low-water mark even, without by that act, though but for a moment, and from necessity, working instant emancipation of the slave. Not many months ago, a mingled mob of negroes, white and black, at Salem, in Ohio, entered a railroad train, and by violence tore from the family of a slaveholder, passing through the State from necessity, and at forty miles an hour, the nurse of his infant child. A Massachusetts legislature has demanded of her Executive the removal of an able, meritorious, and upright judge, for the conscientious discharge, within her limits, of the duties of an office which he held under authority of the United States; and a Massachusetts ecclesiastical conclave, three hundred in number, rose as one man on the announcement of the outrage, and shouted till the house rang again with their plaudits. And a Massachusetts university rejected, also, the same judge, for the same cause, when proposed for a professorship in the institution.

Thus, sir, within little more than two years from the death of her noblest son—whose whole life, and whose dying labors were exhausted in defending the Union and holding the Commonwealth of his adoption up to the full measure of her Revolutionary patriotism and greatness—has the star of Massachusetts been seen to fall from heaven and begin to plunge into the utter blackness of disunion. In vain now, sir, from the grave of the Statesman of Marshfield there comes up the warning cry, "let her shrink back; let her hold others back, if she can; at any rate, let her keep herself back from this gulf, full at once of fire and blackness—full, as far as human foresight can scan, or human imagination fathom, of the fire and the blood of civil war, and of the thick darkness of general political disgrace, ignominy, and ruin." No; she is fallen. Sumner has supplanted Winthrop; and a Wilson crawled up into the seat which Webster once adorned.

And add, now, to all this, gentlemen, that, already, that portentous and most perilous evil, against which the Father of his Country so solemnly and earnestly warned his countrymen, a party bounded by geographical lines—a Northern party, standing upon a Northern Platform, doing battle for Northern issues, and relying solely for success upon appeals to Northern prejudices and Northern jealousies, is now, for the first time in our history, fully organized and consolidated in our midst. Add farther, that, to the Thirty-Fourth Congress, fourteen Senators and a majority of Representatives have been chosen, who in name or in fact, are Abolitionists; Ohio contributing to this dark host her entire delegation in House and Senate, one only excepted; and thus, for the first time, also, since the organization of our Government, has the House of Representatives been converted into a vast Abolition conventicle, full of men picked out for their hatred of the South, and who cannot be true to the Constitution and the Union without treachery to the expectations and the purposes of those who elected them. And then reflect yet further, that this vast and terrible magazine of explosive elements is gathered together just upon the eve of a Presidential election, with all its multiplied and convulsing interests; and that soon

Kansas will knock for admission into the Union, thus surely precipitating the crisis; and who, tell me, I pray you, may foresee what shall be the history of this Republic at the end of two years from to-day?

All this, gentlemen, the spirit of Abolition has accomplished in twenty years of continued and exhausting labors of every sort. But, in all that time, not one convert has it made in the South; not one slave emancipated, except by larceny, and in fraud of the solemn compacts of the Constitution. Meantime, public opinion has wholly, radically changed in the South. The South has ceased to denounce, ceased to condemn slavery—ceased even to palliate—and begun now, almost as one man, to defend it as a great moral, social, and political blessing. The bitter and proscriptive warfare of twenty years has brought forth its natural and legitimate fruit in the South. Exasperation, hate, and revenge, are every day ripening into fullest maturity and strength; and, throughout her entire extent, she awaits now but the action of the North to unite in solemn league and covenant to resist aggression even unto blood.

But the South, sir, has forborne a little. I say, she has forborne a little. She has not yet associated and formed political parties to put down Masonry and Odd Fellowship in the free States and in the Territories, upon the pretext that these institutions are sinful and immoral. She has not yet organized societies, and fostered and protected them by her legislation, to steal that which our law recognizes as property, and refused restitution on the pretext that by the "higher law" of conscience, no right of property exists in the thing stolen. Neither sir, has any Southern State, no, not even "fire-eating" South Carolina, sought as yet to compensate herself for the fugitives which we have abducted, by enacting laws to encourage the slave-trade, by punishing with fine and imprisonment in her penitentiary for years any one of her citizens who should aid in enforcing the laws of the United States against the traffic, striking from her court rolls any attorney within her limits, who should appear in behalf of the prosecution, and excluding all who hold the office of United States Commissioner or Judge, from any office or appointment under her authority. How long before all this shall have been done, is known to Him only whose omniscient eye penetrates and illumines the clouds and thick darkness of the future.

Thus, then, Mr. President, by little and little at first, but now, as with a flood, fraternal affection is wasted away; hate and jealousy and discord, nourished and educated into maturest development; and, one by one, the real and strong cords which bind us together as a Confederacy snapped asunder, or stretched to their utmost tension. It needs no spirit of prophecy, not even a human sagacity above the ordinary level, to foretell just how long the habits, forms, and paper parchments of a union can last when its life-giving principle and nourishing and sustaining virtue are wasted and gone. Sir, he is yet but in the swaddling bands of infancy, who does not already see that there is wanting but some strong convulsion, or even but some sudden jar in the system, to hurl us headlong down into the abyss of disunion.

I know, gentlemen, that to many all this is as "a twice-told tale, vexing the dull ear of a drowsy man." They hearkened not to the voice of Webster, Clay, and Calhoun, while yet among the living; neither would they believe, though these three men rose from the dead. Being dead, they yet speak. The dead of all ages speak. All history lifts up its warning voice. Livy and Tacitus are full of saddest and most instructive teachings. But let us not deceive ourselves. It is not in their pages that we are to read the lessons of that danger which threatens us with destruction. There has been to us no slow and gradual progression of five hundred years to the full growth and stature of a great nation; neither is it in reserve for us to pass through the mellowing and softening gradations of luxury, vice, corruption, and enervation for five hundred years more, to our final fall as an empire. No. The history of Greece is the true study for the American statesman. There he will find the chiefest lessons of political wisdom, adapted to our peculiar exigencies. He will learn there how internal dissension and discord may prostrate a state in the full vigor of its manhood; and, indeed, that it is only in the manhood of a confederacy that there is strength enough, and energy enough, in the members, to rend each other in pieces, and that in the decadence of a state, in decay and atony, it is a Cæsar within, or a Macedonian phalanx, or Roman legions from without, which overwhelm the state. In Thucydides, he may learn how a thirty years' civil war exhausted Greece, and prepared her first for the haughty domination of the conquering member of the confederacy; and finally, for that yoke of foreign despots which galls and burns into her neck to this day.

Let us improve these lessons. It is not yet too late to be saved. The current may still be turned back, and the Union restored to its former sound and healthy condition, though many a gaping scar shall attest the wounds she has received from the hands of her own children.

WHAT THEN REMAINS TO BE DONE?—I answer this momentous question, Mr. President, by declaring first, what will not heal the sick man of America.

First, then, closing our eyes and our ears to the truth, and laughing all danger to scorn, will not do it. The scoffs and derision of the diluvian world did not stay the fountains of the great deep, nor seal up the windows of heaven.

Professions and resolutions of love for the Union and Constitution, whether hypocritical or sincere, will not do it, while, at the same moment, we strike the blow which destroys both. Nor will legislative compromises and finalities, nor yet national conventions and presidential elections. None of these.

Least of all, sir, will platforms, of themselves, avail any thing. Time was when they had a meaning, and when the partisan who repudiated or doubted even an abstract principle, was stricken down by a surer and heavier blow of popular wrath than he who "bolted" a nomination. But that day is past. The best of platforms is now too often but a spider's snare; the weak and unsuspecting house-fly is caught and devoured, the stout, blue-bottle, carrion insect breaks through its meshes. A sound system of faith is, indeed, still proclaimed, but mental reservation is now tolerated. The Thirty-nine Articles are subscribed, but a wide margin and much space between the lines allowed for liberal interpretation. Obedience is no longer expected or required to the platform, if the professor will but support the candidate. And thus, sir, the aged worshipper who lingers yet around the altar, and the simple-minded convert of yesterday, whose burning faith receives the creed as an enunciation of eternal principles, the sacred canon of political scripture, are alike amazed to learn from the organ of the œcumenical council, interpreting by authority, that it is only the gospel according to Judas, whereby a general amnesty is proclaimed to all rebels and deserters;—a cumbrous but convenient piece of machinery, whereby apostates may be restored, if not to favor, at least to position and office in the party. Witness the bold and impudent fraud of the platform promulgated by the Grand Council of the Know-Nothings of Philadelphia, which yet a subordinate State Council of the same Order, assembled at Cleveland, and bound by the most stringent oaths to obedience, had assumed, in advance, to repudiate. And need I but allude to that State Democratic Convention of Ohio, which, resolving to adhere to and support the Baltimore platform, rugged all over as it is, with denunciations of all and every attempt, of whatsoever shape, or color, or pretence, in Congress or out of it, to keep up the slavery agitation, did yet, with amiable and most refreshing consistency, resolve that the people of Ohio would use all power, under the Constitution, "to prevent the increase, to mitigate, and *finally to eradicate*—tear up by the roots—the evil of slavery."

Either away, then, with platforms, at least as a sanative process, and until a sounder public virtue be restored, or require a strict and ready and honest obedience to the principles which they proclaim.

What then remains to be done?—I answer, first, that whatever it may be, it is to be done by and through the DEMOCRATIC PARTY, and the national Whigs and others who may act with it in this crisis; for, "when bad men combine, good men must associate." There is no hope, none, in any other organization. To that party, therefore, and through it to all true patriots and conservatives, I address myself, and answer further: We must return to the principles, follow the practice, imitate the good faith and fraternal affection, and restore the distinctions with which our ancestors set out at the commencement of this government. We must learn a wise and wholesome conservatism; learn that all progress is not reform, and that the wildest and most pernicious and most dangerous of all follies is to attempt to square our political institutions and our legislation by mere abstract, theoretical, and mathematically exact, but impracticable truths. We must remember, also, our true mission as a political party, and retrace our steps from outside the territories of the lyceum and the Church, and drive back the clergy and the Church to their own domain. We must build up again the partitions which separate sacred things from profane, and begin once more to "*Render unto Cæsar the things that are Cæsar's, and unto God the things that are God's.*" We must set out again to pronounce upon political questions, without essaying to try them by the touchstone of our own peculiar notions of moral or divine truth, and thus relegate temperance to the voluntary association, religion to the Church, and slavery to the judgment and conscience of those in whose midst it exists, or is sought to be established, casting aside that false and dangerous and most presumptuous self-delusion, that we are to give account, each one as citizens, for the sins or immoralities of our fellow-men. Slavery, indeed, sir, where it exists, or to the people among whom it is proposed to introduce it, may be, and it is to them, a political subject in part. To us of the North, it is and can be none other than an ethical or religious question. For, disguise and falsify it as you will; marshal and array your figures and your facts to lie never so grossly, it is the sinfulness and immorality of slaveholding as viewed by the Northern mind, and this alone, which has stirred the people of the North to such a height of folly and madness. And yet, if immoral, it concerns only the people of the States and Territories where it exists; if sinful, they only are the offenders, and even if a political evil, it is they alone who feel the curse. It is, therefore, and can be of no possible concern to us, except, indeed, upon the principle of that self-sufficient, self-righteous, and most pernicious egoism which it is time now to purge out of the system.

But a high and imperative constitutional obligation, also, Mr. President, devolves here upon the Democratic party.

The accidents and the necessities of its settlement determined the political character of this continent, and divided it into separate colonies, as perfectly independent, one of the other, as any foreign states. A common subjection to the crown of Great Britain gave the first notion of a common Federal Government; and the aggressions of that crown, and of Parliament, compelling civil war, forced our fathers into a union and articles of confederation. The Constitution of 1789 extended the powers and the efficiency, but did not alter the nature of the General Government. That instrument, sir, was framed by delegates appointed not by the old Congress, but by the States, as sovereign and independent communities. State conventions ratified it; and it was binding only as between those States which acceded to it. They consented to yield up to a common government, certain delegated powers, for the good of the whole; reserving all others, each to itself. We are a Confederacy, sir, of sovereign, distinct, independent States; in all things not brought into the common fund of power, just as thoroughly foreign to each other (except only in a common language and fraternal affection), and as subject to the obligations and comities of the law of nations, as France and England. With the domestic police and institutions of Kentucky, or any other State, the people of Ohio have no more right to intermeddle, than with the laws or form of government in Russia. Slavery in the South is to them as polygamy in the Turkish Empire; and for the political evils, or the sinfulness and immorality of the one, they are in nowise more responsible than for the other. Or—to select the same subject-matter—they have no more right to interfere with, nor are they in any degree more accountable for, the continuance of slavery in Virginia, than for its existence in Persia. Neither, sir, have the people, of the Northern States any greater right, under the Constitution, to deny admission into the Union to a State, because its laws sanction involuntary servitude, or to prescribe that slavery shall not be tolerated in a territory, than to abolish it in a State already in the Union. The converse of this proposition is sheer, rank, unmixed, unanointed *Federalism*—just the Federalism of Alexander Hamilton, who, in the convention of 1787, would have made the States wholly subordinate to the General Government—mere adjuncts—"corporations for local purposes." The reasons, sir, are obvious, and they are conclusive. It is a fundamental principle of the Democratic theory, and of our institutions, that to the people of each particular State, county, township, city, and village, shall be committed, as far as possible, the exclusive regulation of their more immediate and local affairs. In other words, that power, whenever it is practicable, shall be diffused to the utmost, and never centralized beyond urgent necessity. Again, the only limitation prescribed in the Constitution, for the fitness of a State for fellowship with us, is that such State shall establish a "republican" or representative form of government. Now, it is too late to allege, at this day, and quite too absurd, that the existence of the domestic institution of slavery in a State makes its form of government anti-republican, and, therefore, unconstitutional. Such an argument is not worth a serious refutation. Again: The territories are the common property of the States in their Federal capacity, purchased by the common blood and treasure of all, and as much the property of South Carolina as of Massachusetts. They are tenants in common of this property; and for one State to demand the exclusion of another from participation in their use in common, in every respect, is arrogant and unfounded assumption of superiority; and fifty-fold more offensive, when the pharisaic pretence is set up that they are more holy than that other State, whose inhabitants are sinners before God exceedingly, and who would pollute the territory, by the introduction of their wickedness upon its soil; assuming thus to be keeper of the conscience and custodian of the morals of the people of the territory, putting on the robes, and ascending into the judgment-seat of the Almighty. Sir, if the inhabitants of Cape Cod are not satisfied with the coparcenary, let them seek, by partition, to hold in severalty; and, obtaining thus the very small and almost infinitesimal portion which is their share, exert over it such acts of ownership as to them may seem meet; but not attempt insolently to take possession and control of the whole.

Manifestly, then, sir, the agitation of the slavery question finds no warrant or countenance, but direct and emphatic condemnation, in the Constitution. That part of the instrument which apportions the representation and taxation of slaves, for the most part executes itself, and admits only of direct attack by amendment or nullification. The clause which empowers Congress to prohibit the slave-trade, has long since been quietly carried into effect; and the South has never sought to disturb it. The sole remaining instance in which Congress may legislate in reference to slavery, is for the extradition of fugitives. From its very nature, sir, this presents a capital point for assault by Abolitionists. Long before the act of 1850, they had, by state legislation, or public odium, rendered nugatory the act of 1793, and were laboring for its direct repeal by Congress. They openly repudiated that part of the Constitution upon which it was founded; and, as early as 1843, a general convention of Abolitionists, assembled at Buffalo, and composed of the ablest and most distinguished members of the party, resolved that whenever called upon to swear to support the Constitution, they would, by mental reservation, regard that clause in it as utterly null and void, and forming no part of the instrument.* Nevertheless, sir, in the ad-

* THE BUFFALO RESOLUTION, 1843, *offered by a committee of which* SALMON P. CHASE, *of Ohio, was a member.*—"*Resolved,* That we hereby give it to be distinctly under-

justment of 1850, provision was made to enforce this solemn compact. And hence, the popular tumults, the mobs, the forcible rescues, and the nullifying acts of the New England States, and other parts of the North, which yet find countenance and applause even from a thousand presses and tens of thousands of citizens, upon the pretext that the rendition of fugitives is distasteful and revolting to the North. Yes, Abolitionist, it is the *Constitution* which you attack, not the act of 1850. It is the extradition of "panting fugitives," under any circumstances, or by virtue of any law, at which you rebel. Be manly, then, and outspoken, and honest. Act the part of cowards and slave-stealers no longer. Assail the Constitution itself, and do it openly—it is the Constitution which demands the restoration—and cover not up your assaults any longer, under the false and beggarly pretence that it is the act of Congress which you condemn and abhor.

I know, sir, that it is easy, very easy, to denounce all this as a defence of slavery itself. Be it so; be it so. But I have not discussed the institution in any respect—moral, religious, or political. Hear me; I express no opinion in regard to it; and, as a citizen of the North, I have ever refused, and will steadily refuse, to discuss the system in any of these particulars. It is precisely this continued and persistent discussion and denunciation in the North, which has brought upon us this present most perilous crisis; since to teach men to hate, is to prepare them to destroy, at every hazard, the object of their hatred. Sir, I am resolved only to look upon slavery outside of Ohio, just as the founders of the Constitution and Union regarded it. It is no concern of mine—none, none—nor of yours, Abolitionist. Neither of us will attain heaven by denunciations of slavery; nor shall we, I trow, be cast into hell for the sin of others who may hold slaves. I have not so learned the moral government of the universe; nor do I presumptuously and impiously aspire to the attributes of Godhead, and seek to bear upon my poor body the iniquities of the world.

I know well, indeed, Mr. President, that in the evil day which has befallen us, all this, and he who utters it, shall be denounced as "pro-slavery;" and already, from ribald throats, there comes up the slaveling,

stood, by this nation and the world, that, as *Abolitionists*, considering that the strength of our cause lies in its righteousness, and our hopes for it in our conformity to the laws of God, and our support for the rights of man, we owe to the sovereign Ruler of the Universe, as a proof of our allegiance to him, in all our civil relations and offices, whether as friends, citizens, or as public functionaries, sworn to support the Constitution of the United States, to regard and treat the third clause of that instrument, whenever applied in the case of a fugitive slave, AS UTTERLY NULL AND VOID, and, consequently, as forming no part of the Constitution of the United States, WHENEVER WE ARE CALLED UPON AS SWORN TO SUPPORT IT."

drivelling, idiot epithet of "doughface." Again; be it so. These, Abolitionist, are your only weapons of warfare; and I hurl them back defiantly into your teeth. I speak thus boldly, because I speak in and to and for the North. It is time that the truth should be known and heard, in this the age of trimming and subterfuge. I speak this day, not as a Northern man, nor a Southern man; but, God be thanked, still as a United States man, with United States principles; and though the worst happen which can happen—though all be lost, if that shall be our fate, and I walk through the valley of the shadow of political death, I will live by them, and die by them. If to love my country; to cherish the Union; to revere the Constitution; if to abhor the madness and hate the treason which would lift up a sacrilegious hand against either; if to read that in the past, to behold it in the present, to foresee it in the future of this land, which is of more value to us and the world for ages to come than all the multiplied millions who have inhabited Africa from the creation to this day—if this it is to be *pro-slavery*, then, in every nerve, fibre, vein, bone, tendon, joint, and ligament, from the topmost hair of the head to the last extremity of the foot, I am all over and altogether a PRO-SLAVERY MAN.

To that part now, Mr. President, of the Germans who have been betrayed upon this question, I address a word of caution. Little more than a year ago, availing themselves of the Nebraska question as the pretext, mischievous and designing demagogues, just at the moment they prepared to deny you the full enjoyment of your own political rights here in Ohio, persuaded some of you to trail in the dust at the heels of the Abolition rout. They told you, and you believed it, some of you, that, failing to establish civil liberty against the crowned oppressors of your fatherland, and seeking for it as exiles in America, you had the right, nevertheless, to intermeddle with personal liberty among the inhabitants of other States and Territories, to form political associations exclusively German, to adopt platforms of your own as such, to instruct us in the science of government, the nature of free institutions, and the value of freedom, to require of us to give away our public lands to all alike, naturalized or alien, white or *black*, to denounce the people of the South, because of the "curse of slavery," to repeal the Fugitive Slave Law, to abolish slaveholding *throughout the States, in conformity with*, as you alleged, and perhaps by virtue of power *derived from*, the Declaration of Independence, and finally to propose to convert your good old German May festival into an Abolition mass meeting, in our very midst. These things, they persuaded some of you to believe and to do. But at this very moment, and by the self-same demagogues, was the knife put to your own throats, and you were quietly guillotined, and your heads thrust into the basket, upon just the principles they had persuaded you that you had the right to intermeddle with the domestic, moral, and religious concerns of other States and Territories. Opening now your eyes to the fraud thus practised upon you, learning the true character of the men who beguiled you, and remembering that the first State which breasted and turned back the torrent which was sweeping you, and your hopes, and your rights before it, was the *slaveholding* State of Virginia, through the Democratic party of Virginia, followed up by every Southern State, Kentucky alone excepted, retrace your steps now into the ranks of that party, stand fast to your true interests and true position, concern yourselves no longer with the business of others, but quietly enjoy, and calmly defend your own rights, remembering always those who have ever sustained you in whatsoever truth and liberty and justice demand for you.

Addressing myself now, finally, Mr. President, to the Democratic party of Ohio, I say: You are a political party; hence, all your principles must as well take shape and color, as reflect them, from the fundamental institutions of the country; and those principles which belong to Democracy, universal and theoretical, are to be modified and adjudged by the Constitution. It has always been your boast, that you are peculiarly the party of the Constitution and of that Union which results from, and exists only, by the Constitution. And just in proportion as you value these, will you mould and modify your doctrine, and your practice, to sustain and preserve them in every essential element. Sure I am, at least, that you will not, for the sake of an abstract principle, purely, or mainly moral, or religious, and to us not political, and urged now in the very spirit of treason and madness, and far removed from every personal concern of yours, sacrifice or even imperil these priceless legacies of a generation at least as good and as wise as we. Trust not to past success. Times have changed. For four years you filched inglorious triumphs by fomenting dissensions among your enemies, and by exhausting all the little arts of partisan diplomacy, to keep the Whig and Abolition parties asunder. You wasted your time striving to pluck out of the crucible of politics the fluxes which they threw in, seeking thus vainly to prevent or impede a fusion which was inevitable, and which, when it came, overwhelmed you as with a flood of lava, in disastrous, if not ignominious defeat. Was this conduct befitting a great and enduring party—conduct worthy the prestige of your name? Learn wisdom from Virginia, your mother State; she is ever invincible, because she is always candid and manly and true to principle. Look no longer now to availability; above all, be not deceived by the false and senseless outcry against that most just, most Constitutional, and most necessary measure—the *Kansas-Nebraska Act.** The true and only question

* See *post*, page 282.

now before you is: Whether you will have a Union, with all its numberless blessings in the past, present, and future, or Disunion and civil war, with all the multiplied crimes, miseries, and atrocities which human imagination never conceived, and human pen never can portray?

I speak it boldly—I avow it publicly—it is time to speak thus, for political cowardice is the bane of this, as of all other republics. To be true to your great mission, and to succeed in it, you must take open, manly, one-sided ground upon the Abolition question. In no other way can you now conquer. Let us have, then, no hollow compromise, no idle and mistimed homilies upon the sin and evil of slavery in a crisis like this; no double-tongued, Janus-faced, Delphic responses at your State conventions. No; fling your banner to the breeze, and boldly meet the issue. PATRIOTISM ABOVE MOCK PHILANTHROPY; THE CONSTITUTION BEFORE ANY MISCALLED HIGHER LAW OF MORALS OR RELIGION; AND THE UNION OF MORE VALUE THAN MANY NEGROES.

If thus, sir, we are true to the country, true to the Union and the Constitution, true to our principles, true to our cause and to the grand mission which lies before us, we shall turn back yet the fiery torrent which is bearing us headlong down to the abyss of disunion and infamy, deeper than plummet ever sounded; but if in this, the day of our trial, we are found false to all these, false to our ancestors, false to ourselves, false to those who shall come after us, traitors to our country and to the hopes of free government throughout the globe, Bancroft will yet write the last sad chapter in the history of the American Republic.

ABSTRACT OF ARGUMENT IN THE OHIO "FUGITIVE SLAVE RESCUE CASE,"

*In the Circuit Court of the United States for Southern Ohio, at Cincinnati, June 25, 1857; on Habeas Corpus.**

AFTER a few introductory remarks, and a reply, at some length, to some technical objections made by the Attorney-General in the morning, to the writ and proceedings in the case, and also a brief discussion

* This case was argued for the United States, by Hons. GEORGE E. PUGH, and C. L. VALLANDIGHAM, and Judge STANLEY MATTHEWS; and for the State by Attorney-General C. P. WOLCOTT, sent down for that purpose by SALMON P. CHASE, then Governor of Ohio.

of several minor points claimed for the United States, Mr. VALLANDIGHAM, proceeded as follows:

The question of excess and abuse of authority, by the marshals, is the only one of real importance lying in advance of the great question of power and jurisdiction, in this controversy between the State and the United States. If the marshals used no more force or violence than was necessary, to prevent the execution by the sheriff of the *habeas corpus*, and a rescue of their prisoners, they are clearly entitled to protection in this proceeding under the seventh section of the act of March 2, 1833; otherwise not. Up to that piont, they were acting plainly "in pursuance of a law of the United States, and the process of a judge thereof." I will not discuss the testimony in the case; it is before the court; but will affirm that the weight of the evidence distinctly establishes that no more was done by the deputies than was necessary, or certainly at the moment and under the circumstances, appeared necessary, to prevent the rescue of the prisoners, and to defend themselves against violence, if not loss of life. It is proper, however, to advert to the point made, and, with some earnestness, pressed by the Attorney-General, that the return by the sheriff to the writ is *conclusive* as to the facts in the case, and that the courts cannot look to any testimony outside of it. True, in the absence of any statute of Congress regulating the writ and proceedings on habeas corpus, or any rule of court adopting the statutes of the State, the court here is bound by the principles of the common law as they are recognized in such cases. But it is not merely these principles as received and interpreted in Westminster Hall, but as modified and accepted in the United States. The books are full of cases where the courts of the States and of the Union, exercising a common law jurisdiction, have gone behind the return where the party was held in custody under judicial process, and inquired, by affidavit or otherwise, into the true facts of the capture and detention of the party in custody. Judge McLean allowed it in *Nelson* vs. *Cutter*, 3 McLean, 326 (1845), so also in *ex parte Robinson* (the Rosetta case) 6 McLean R., 355. Judges Grier and Kane permitted it in *ex parte Jenkins*, 2 Wall. Jr. R., 525; and so also Judge Leavitt, in *ex parte Robinson*, 4 Law Reg., 617 (the Gaines case). These are but a few of the numerous precedents which, if need were, I might produce. Upon principle also, and the reason and necessity of the case, it is assuredly proper; and in addition to many other examples, I will put the case of a member of the Federal Senate or House, who, except for treason, felony or breach of the peace, is by the constitution protected from arrest during the sitting of Congress and in going and returning. Suppose that nevertheless, while on his way to the capital of the Union, he is arrested for debt, how, without proof outside of the return, is he to secure his discharge? If the law be, indeed, as claimed by the Attorney-General, it would subject the whole proceeding to the control of the officer, with no redress for the prisoner except the poor privilege of an action for false return.

Having thus disposed of these preliminary points made in the case, I now proceed to the GREAT QUESTION to be discussed, first assuming that the Fugitive-slave Act of 1850 is constitutional, and the process in the hands of the marshals regular, and issued by proper authority. These facts I believe are not controverted.

I. *If this were an ordinary habeas corpus, which issued from the Probate Court of Champaign County to the Sheriff—if it were the true, constitutional, old-fashioned writ of habeas corpus, would the Deputies have been bound to obey it?*

I will not put the question in the usual form—Had the State Judge or Court, power to issue it? The two are, no doubt, in fact, equivalent; but I prefer the form in which I state it, as presenting the true issue more fairly. If it nowhere appears to the State Judge that the party claiming custody of the prisoner, detains him by virtue of law or process of the United States, of course he has a right, and is bound to grant the writ; it is so said by Judge McLean in *Norris* vs. *Newton*, 5 McLean R., 99. No one doubts it. But whenever the sheriff holding the writ ascertains—and it is his duty to ascertain it—that the prisoners are held by United States marshals, under process of the Federal Courts, he should desist at once from all attempt to execute it, if issued under the act of 1847, and return the facts. Such a return would be good and valid. No writ can issue to the sheriff, except under the act of 1856, without fraud, perjury, or concealment of the facts, because the copy of the warrant or commitment required to be furnished to the judge will disclose on its face that it is United States process under which the petitioner is held in custody.

It has been said that the right of the State Courts to issue writs of this sort is well settled by usage on part of the State Courts, and acquiescence on part of the United States. I deny it. As to *authority*, there is no case, I believe, till the present, where a prisoner has been charged with a *crime* under the penal laws of the United States, and jurisdiction assumed by a State Court or Judge to interfere, except the notorious "Booth Case," in Wisconsin, which no respectable lawyer will condescend to cite as authority, and the case of *The Commonwealth* vs. *Holloway*, 5 Binney's R., 512. This last was a charge of misprision of treason in 1813, and a commitment thereon by a *Justice of the Peace of Pennsylvania*, under the thirty-third section of the Judiciary Act of 1789; and the court in taking jurisdiction of the case, which they did with much hesitation, put it expressly upon the ground that the officer committing, was an officer of the State. So, too, *Clark's* case (9 Wend. R., 212), arose upon a requisition addressed to the Governor of New York. But the usual case is that of minors enlisting in the army or navy of the United States. These cases are numerous, but there are only two or three where the question of jurisdiction has been discussed or considered at all. In the first three cases reported (*Husted's* case, 1 John. Cases, 126; *Roberts*, 2 Hall's L. Journal, 192, and *Ferguson's*, 9 J. R., 229,) the application was denied or the proceeding dismissed. It has indeed been said or supposed that the latter case was overruled in 10 J. R., 328, *Stacy's* case. This is a mistake. The Court did not refer to 9 Johnson at all; nor was the principle of the case in any respect similar. It expressly appeared in the application and upon the return, that Stacy was not held under any law or process of the United States, but against all law. There never was a case more strongly demanding the interference of a Court. In the matter of *Carlton*, 7 Cowen, 471, the only question was, whether the State process could run into West Point. So in the *United States* vs. *Wyngals*, 5 Hill, 16, the sole matter raised and decided was a point in the law of evidence. Many cases have occurred in Massachusetts; but in one only has the question of jurisdiction been raised in argument, and in none has it been considered by the court. (11 Mass. R., 63, 67, 83; 24 Pick. R., 227.) Several cases also have arisen in Pennsylvania, but in one only has the question been suggested and briefly considered. (*Commonwealth* vs. *Fox*, 7 Pa. St. R., 336.) And here the Court adopt the distinction made by the Virginia Court of Appeals; that they have jurisdiction where the custody is not claimed under *process* of the *Courts* of the United States; impliedly, therefore, denying jurisdiction where it is under process of a Federal Judge or Court. It is difficult indeed to distinguish between these two classes of cases. The same legislative authority which requires the marshal or officer of a Court to keep safely his prisoner on civil or criminal process, commands the officers of the Army and Navy to hold under their authority and control, the soldiers, seamen and marines of the United States. If the Courts of the State have no power to discharge from imprisonment under process of the United States Courts, and the marshal, as repeatedly has been adjudged, may disobey the order of discharge, equally may a military or naval officer disobey and be protected.

Once, also, in a case of extradition under a United States treaty, a Judge of the Supreme Court of New York, assumed jurisdiction on *habeas corpus*. (In the Matter of *Metzger*, 1 Barb., S. C. Rep., 248.) But, this case is very much in the same spirit and style as the Booth case in Wisconsin. A United States Judge had, under the treaty with France, examined into the charge and committed the prisoner. The President issued his mandate under the treaty; a *habeas corpus* was applied for in the Supreme Court of the United States and refused. Metzger then took out a writ of *habeas corpus*, returnable before Judge Edmonds, who reversed Judge Betts, overruled the Supreme Court, rebuked the President and discharged the prisoner. This is the third time Judge Edmonds, before he became lost in the occult mysteries of *Spiritualism*, has overruled the Supreme Court; but he stands alone, except in Wisconsin, and before his Honor, Burgoyne, of the Probate Court of this city.

State Courts, in other cases, have uniformly denied even the application, when it appeared that the custody was under color of process from the United States Courts. It was so in the matter of *Sims*, before all the Judges of the Supreme Court of Massachusetts; 7 Cush. R., 285: so, also, in Pennsylvania, in *ex parte Williamson*, before Lewis, Ch. J., 3 Law Reg., 741; and, again, in *ex parte Williamson*, 26 Pa. State Rep., 1, by all the Judges of the Supreme Court, one only (Knox) dissenting. So in Georgia, in *The State* vs. *Plime*, the direct question was decided against the jurisdiction. (T. U. P. Charlton's Rep., 142.) The N. Y. Revised Statutes also forbid it.—(Vol. 2, p. 563, sec. 22.) No case is reported in Ohio; but Judge Swan, now of the Supreme Bench, questioned the right soon after the act of 1847. (2 Swan's Pl. and Prac., 1245.) So, then, even upon the authority of the State Courts, the question remains still open and doubtful, at least, in any case; though the weight of authority and the respectability of Courts is decidedly against the jurisdiction where it appears that the party was held under claim or color of process or authority from the United States.

How, then, stands the case in the Federal Courts? There is no decision by the Supreme Court directly upon the question: but the case of *Duncan* vs. *Darst*, 1 How. R., 301, in effect decides it. It was there held that a person in custody under a *capias ad satisfaciendum*, issued under the authority of the Circuit Court of the United States, could not be legally discharged from imprisonment by a State officer, acting under a State insolvent law.

Mr. Justice Nelson seems, indeed, in 1 Blatchford, 642, to concede the right to the State Judges or Courts; but this was not in a case arisen, and after argument and upon consideration, but *obiter* in a charge to the grand jury. Pope, J., in *ex parte Joe Smith* (the Mormon Prophet), 3 McLean, 121 (1843), doubts the power, even in the case of a requisition upon the Executive of a State. McLean, J., considers the question in *Norris* vs. *Newton*, 5 McLean, 92, 98; but as he qualifies and explains it, the point is not decided at all. He admits the right where the State Judge or Court, *does not know* that the confinement is under color of process or authority of the United States. This is not denied. But he says: "These facts being stated, as the cause of detention, would have *terminated* the jurisdiction of the judge under the writ."

Surely, then, if these facts appear in the *first instance*, the jurisdiction never attaches; otherwise the whole proceeding is a farce. To the same point may again be cited the Sims and Williamson cases, in 7 Cushing and 26 Pennsylvania State Reports. So the Ohio statute of 1811 expressly excepts from the benefit of the writ persons convicted, &c. In such case the Court or Judge has no jurisdiction to issue the writ. But suppose it is not disclosed to the Judge that the party applying is a convict, but only generally that he is "illegally imprisoned" (and such is the showing in this case), he is bound to issue; but the Warden of the Penitentiary is not bound to obey. Again, Judson, J., of the Southern District of New York, in the matter of *Veretemaitre*, 13 Law Rep., 608 (1850), expressly denies the jurisdiction of the State Courts, even in cases of enlistment (p. 616–618). The decisions of Judges McLean, and Leavitt, in the Rosetta and Gaines cases (6 McLean, 355; 4 Law, Reg., 617) surely, are *conclusive* of this question, in its real form. In both these cases the marshal was justified in disobeying the order of a State Court or Judge made in the proceeding on *habeas corpus*, upon the ground of his *paramount duty* to obey the laws and process of the United States. Now, if a State Judge or Court cannot enforce obedience to any order made in such a proceeding, why allow that there is any jurisdiction in the case at all? What is the writ of habeas corpus worth, if, after the prisoner is brought before him, and he is satisfied that the party is illegally confined, he has yet no right to deliver him. Is it not a mockery? Is not the majesty of the State insulted and trifled with far more by allowing the party to be brought into Court and then to defy its power? Far better that the jurisdiction be denied altogether. If, then, the real question be, is the marshal bound to obey the writ, it is surely settled and settled in the negative—a denial, therefore, of the right to issue, since that right and the right to enforce obedience ought always to be coextensive.

The doctrine here contended for is the only doctrine consistent with our complex system of government. I agree heartily and throughout, with the States-Rights doctrines, which the Attorney-General with so much ability has advocated. I yield to no man in devotion to those doctrines. Perhaps I even carry them farther than many others. But this is not a question of State rights. We live under two governments, which are only parts of one great whole. Neither government possesses all the attributes of sovereignty. Every citizen of Ohio—and especially because of a peculiarity of our State Constitution—is a citizen of the United States. As citizens of Ohio we do not exercise the right to declare war and make peace, to maintain an army and navy, or other similar acts of sovereignty. In the quality of citizens of the United States we do exercise these powers, though as such citizens we are wanting in others which belong to us in our character as citizens of the State. Sovereignty is, therefore, divided among the governments of the States and the Union. The boundaries are defined and marked out in the Constitution of the United States. Each is supreme within its own limits. Neither can be interfered with by the other while each keeps within its own proper orbit. The Constitution of the United States, and all laws in pursuance of it, are, indeed, the supreme law of the land, and where constitutional, bind the Judges of the State Courts, in case of conflict. All State officers are sworn to support it. Thus the Constitution of the Union is a part of the Constitution of Ohio; the laws in pursuance of it are a part of the legislation of the State, and the decisions of its courts within their sphere, a part of the jurisprudence of the State; and all are to be construed together. So long as each government keeps within its constitutional and legitimate sphere, such is the admirable beauty and the perfection of the system, that there never can be a collision. Wherever, then, the courts or authorities of the United States have constitutional power to act, their process and action ought to be wholly free from all control, temporary or permanent, in any way or to any extent, by State action or State process. It is of no moment what the purpose is, or how long the intermeddling, whether for an hour, a day, or six months. And, in this point of view, a writ of habeas corpus is no more sacred, and has no more power or authority to control, or delay, or affect in any way, or for any purpose, or any time, the process of the United States, than a capias, an execution, or an attachment.

I now proceed to apply these principles to the argument of the Attorney-General this morning. *Assuming the very point in controversy*, Mr. Attorney has selected his ground and built up a most able and ingenious, and, I will say, unanswerable argument. I give him the whole benefit of it in its utmost strength. *He* finds the collision which confessedly exists in this case between the State and the United States, in an attempt by this proceeding on habeas corpus, under the act of Congress, in 1833, to obstruct and render useless and powerless the penal laws and jurisprudence of the State, and to protect hereby the marshals of the United States from punishment for an infraction of those laws—the laws against assault and battery and the attempt to murder. He has argued, and most conclusively—and it is his whole argument—that the Government of the United States cannot interfere with the penal laws or process of a State, and rescue offenders from the penalty for offences against those laws. But does not Mr. Attorney see, I ask, that the *very question* to be argued is, whether the acts done by the marshals were, under the circumstances, an offence against the laws of the State! If they were, then this Court has no power, by habeas corpus or otherwise, to shield them from punishment. But let that question be tested. *Prima facie* every homicide is murder. (Wright's Rep., 75.) The statute against murder is general; it contains no excepted cases. How, then, does the sheriff, who hangs a man by the neck till dead, escape? Because the same statute book commands that he shall do it, and the different statutes and sections being construed together, it appears to be lawful. Again, the statute against homicide is general. How, therefore, is the Warden of the Penitentiary justified, who takes the life of a prisoner while attempting to escape? Because the law sanctions it. Or how comes the State Officer to stand acquit, who in executing process, is obliged from necessity to kill the party resisting? Because the law allows it. It is, therefore, not every beating that is an assault and battery, nor every killing that is murder, nor every shooting with intent to kill, that is an offence against the penal laws of the State. Now, the Constitution of the United States is a part of the Constitution of Ohio; the law of 1850, under which the process was issued to the marshals in this case, is a part of the laws of Ohio, and must be taken and construed together with the statutes against assault and shooting with intent to kill. The Constitution authorized the law, and the law the process, and the process justified the officer in using all the force necessary to execute it. If he used this force and no more, then what he did, though there were beating and shooting, was no offence against the penal laws of Ohio. And all that the court proposes to do here, is to inquire into the truth of these matters.

But Mr. Attorney has argued that this Court or Judge has no constitutional power, *on habeas corpus*, to inquire into these facts, and that this inquiry can be made only by the Supreme Court of the United States, under the twenty-fifth section of the Judiciary Act of 1789, after the case has passed through the highest State Court. Not having denied the constitutionality of that section, I have only to remind him that the Constitution has not conferred the power specially upon the Supreme Court, but left it to the discretion of Congress; and that the same legislative authority which, in 1789, prescribed the mode by writ of error to the Supreme Court, did, in 1833, confer a like power in particular cases, by *habeas corpus*, upon the Judges of the Supreme and District Courts of the United States. It is, indeed, befitting the dignity of a State that, after a case has gone through its highest tribunal, the judgment should be reviewed only by the Supreme Court, and upon error. But I see no disparagement of State pride in allowing an inquiry, on habeas corpus by a Circuit or District Court, or Judge of the United States, into the cause of imprisonment of a United States marshal—an officer of those courts—by order of a State justice of the peace. The sovereignty of the State is not very deeply wounded.

But the Attorney-General has contended, farther, that even if constitutional, the act of 1833 does not confer jurisdiction upon the court or judge in a case like this. He has argued—and in arguing has drawn his proof from the peculiar exigencies which called for the act—that it is only where it appears upon the face of the warrant or mittimus that the offence charged was the attempt to execute a law or writ of the United States, that jurisdiction attaches upon *habeas corpus.* But does not Mr. Attorney see here also, that so narrow a construction of the statute would render it nugatory? The language of the law is broad enough to include *every case* where the act done or omitted, by the reason of the doing or omitting to do which the party is imprisoned, was so done or omitted in the discharge of any duty under authority of the United States; but according to the argument urged this morning, only let the real offence be described by some other name, or concealed under some other charge, and there is no remedy by this summary proceeding. To so construe the act, is to hold out a premium for fraud and subterfuge. I will venture to affirm that not once in a hundred instances, will the warrant or commitment disclose the true nature of the charge, or the circumstances attending it. In neither the Jenkins, the Rosetta nor the Gaines cases did the facts, or the official character of the parties, appear in the papers returned by the State officer; and yet in all of them, the judges, under the act of 1833, and after objection urged, received testimony disclosing the true nature and circumstances of the accusation preferred; and upon that testimony discharged the prisoners. So, too, in the Williamson case (4 Law Reg., 5), the court upon habeas corpus received even *oral* testimony at the hearing, to explain or contradict the return. The purpose of the Act of 1833 is to enable the judges and courts of the United States to protect themselves from encroachment by other authorities, and must be reasonably construed with reference to that purpose. And upon this point I will refer the court again to Williamson's case in 26 Penn. State Reports, 27, where Lowrie, J., speaking of this Act, said: "This is not a strange way of protecting one court against the encroachments of another, 1 Rolle, 315; 2 Chit. Gen. Pr., 317—1 Madd. Ch. Pr., 135. And it is certainly *most effectual, for it would protect the marshal in disobeying an order by us to discharge the prisoner;* and thus it very plainly forbids us to discharge him."

But further: The Courts of the United States have very generally respected the doctrines which I have maintained. They have, in many instances, been even tender and delicate of the authority and process of the State Courts. The act of 1789 expressly excepts writs of habeas corpus when the party was imprisoned under color of State process or authority. In *ex parte Cabrera* (1 Wash. C. C. R., 232), the Court refused to interfere in favor of a Foreign Secretary of Legation, who was charged with forgery, under the penal laws of Pennsylvania. So in *ex parte Dorr*, the Supreme Court refused a habeas corpus to bring Dorr into court to obtain the benefit of a writ of error under the twenty-fifth section of the Act of 1789. (3 How. R., 624.) So in Massachusetts, where a man, indicted in the Circuit Court for a capital offence, was at the time imprisoned for debt under the authority of the State, Judge Story refused to interfere, and Judge McLean approves the refusal. (5 McLean, 100; 6 McLean, 363.) So where defendants, indicted in the Circuit Court of Ohio, for counterfeiting, were at the same time held in custody for an offence under the laws of the State, Judge McLean held that the United States Court had "no power to take them from such custody, nor a State Court power to remove, by habeas corpus, a defendant from the custody of a court of the United States." (5 McLean, 174.) So, also, Grier J. held in *ex parte Jenkins*, 2 Wall, Jr. R., 525.

The seeming exceptions in the twelfth and twenty-fifth sections of the Judiciary Act of 1789, and the seventh section of the Act of March 2, 1833, are intended chiefly to protect the United States from aggression upon its powers. As to the "McLeod Act" of 1842, I think that rests upon a very different principle from the other acts.

Upon authority and reason and analogy, then, I deny the right of a State Court or Judge, either by habeas corpus, or in any way, to interfere with the process or judicial proceedings of a Court or Judge, or other officer of the United States, when in the discharge of his legitimate and constitutional duty. They have no jurisdiction, in any form, in such case, and neither is the officer of the State bound to execute, nor of the United States to obey, any such process. (10 Coke's R., 76, b; 5 Watts' R., 144; 1 How. R., 308.)

Nor is there any danger of denial or delay of justice in such cases. The government of the Union is no alien within the territory of Ohio. It is no foreign tyrant or usurper, although in the region round about the head-waters of Mad River, it seems to be so regarded. Every citizen or inhabitant of the State is also an inhabitant or citizen of the United States and under their protection. Their courts, too, are open at all times; and their judges and juries surely quite as learned, as just and as upright and impartial as the juries and judges of the State courts. If false and groundless or otherwise illegal detention or imprisonment shall in any case occur, relief by *habeas corpus* or upon the trial, may with certainty be obtained there, and without danger of collision and strife.

II. So far I have argued the case as if the writ issued by the State Judge in this case, *was* a writ of habeas corpus. But it was not; and the principles I have already laid down, apply with fifty-fold force to this nondescript process issuing to the sheriff, commanding him to take the prisoners from the custody of the marshals. It was not a habeas corpus; not the high prerogative writ of old England; not the great writ secured by the Constitution, having none of its sanctity, and entitled to no part of its charities. It was not within the constitutional protection against suspension, and no court will so decide. It was not directed to the party who detained the prisoners in custody. This is of the very essence of a habeas corpus, it is descriptive of it, and enters into the definition of the writ. (1 Bouvier's Law Dict. "Hab. Corp.;" 3 Blackst., 131; Ohio Act of 1811, Sec. 1, transcribing the 31st, Charles II., C. 2, 1679.) The writ of habeas corpus was borrowed from—at least all authorities agree that it is the same in substance as the "Interdict" of the Roman law. That, too, was addressed to the person having the custody of the prisoner. It ran thus: "Ait prætor, *quem liberum dolo malo retinens exhibeas*"—that *you* produce whom *you* detain. (Dig. 43, 29, 1.) So the very name of our writ imports: "habeas," that you have. But when a writ issues to the Sheriff, not having already the custody of prisoners, it is "capias," that you take; and this is the very word of the writ in this case. The mode, too, of serving a habeas corpus, is conclusive. The original is delivered to the party having the custody and to whom it is directed, and it is he who makes the return. It is in the nature of a rule to show cause. Not so with other writs. Not so with the writ here. What, then, is it? In 1847 an act was passed by the Ohio Legislature purporting to be an amendment to the Habeas Corpus Act of 1811, requiring that the writ should, in the case of detention by private persons, be addressed to the sheriff, and require him to take the party detained into his custody, and summon the party detaining him. It is called a habeas corpus, but it is not. It is a personal replevin; the old common law writ, *de homine replegiando*, revived and a little altered. But it requires no security, as at common law; and although it makes the return a *plea* in the case, it does not provide, as at common law, for trial by jury, but leaves the matter to the Judge. This act also grew out of fugitive-slave cases (2 West. L. Jour., 279); but it had in ten years *unhappily* produced no collision. It was, therefore, out of date. The heat of the times demanded something of a higher mettle; and the act of 1856 is produced from the same loins, and engendered in the same spirit, but an offspring of far lustier and more vigorous birth. This act requires the writ in certain cases to be addressed to the Sheriff or Coroner, even where the party is in custody of an officer by virtue of judicial process. It is therefore a hybrid—a monstrosity in legislation and jurisprudence—a sort of "cross" between *habeas corpus* and *de homine replegiando*—a veritable *mulatto* among writs. It is not a *habeas corpus*, because it is not addressed to the party who detains the prisoner; and it is not a personal replevin, because that issues only in the case of imprisonment or detention by a private person (3 Blackst., 129), and specially excepts the case of imprisonment under judicial process. (3 Reeves, Hist. of Com. Law, 83.—*Replegiari facias*, &c.,—not *habeas corpus—nisi captus sit per speciale præceptum nostrum, vel capitalis justitiarii nostri*, &c.) But it is called a writ of HABEAS CORPUS, because that is a holy name and embalmed in the hearts of the people. It has a wicked and treasonable purpose to subserve, and it must assume a sacred name and garb. Its author well understood the philosophy of Mirabeau, and, after him, Byron. He knew that—

> "Words are things, and a small drop of ink,
> Falling like dew upon a thought, produces
> That which makes thousands, perhaps millions think."

But the motives and the results expected from it cannot be thus concealed; and, in a court of law, it must be stripped of its disguises, and set forth in its true character—a statute of sedition and discord. Very different was the spirit of the Act of 1839. That act provided for carrying out the compacts of the Constitution. Its preamble sounds strangely enough in this age of Higher-law fanaticism:

"*Whereas*, the second section of the fourth article of the Constitution of the United States, declares, that no person held to service or labor in one State, under the laws thereof, escaping into another, shall in consequence of any law or regulation therein, be discharged from such service or labor, but shall be delivered up on claim of the party to whom such service or labor may be due," and, "whereas, the laws now in force within the State of Ohio are wholly inadequate to the PROTECTION PLEDGED by this provision of the Constitution to the Southern States of this Union; and, whereas, it is the duty of those who reap the largest measure of benefits conferred by the Constitution, to recognize, to their full extent, the obligations which that instrument imposes, and, whereas, it is the deliberate conviction of this General Assembly, that the Constitution can only be sustained, as it was framed, by a spirit of just compromise; therefore be it enacted," &c.

Now, I most respectfully commend this preamble to the people of Clark, Greene, and Champaign, and to the learned counsel upon the other side. But before I pass from the subject of writs I will call the attention of our legislators, who extend their researches back into the musty and murky realms of the dark ages for precedents, to the writ *de odio et atia*—a writ older than either personal replevin or habeas corpus—a writ to which, possibly, the Government of the United States may yet be obliged to resort, if her officers are in like manner again imprisoned within the "infected" counties.

To resume: The law of 1856, so far as it was intended to affect or so executed as to affect the process of the Courts of the United States, I maintain is unconstitutional and void. Its effect must be to subordinate the General to the State Government, to render the officers of the former amenable to the process and authority of the latter—exactly to reverse the position of the two governments, where the former was by the Constitution supreme, and ultimately to subvert it altogether. It is opposed to the whole theory and practice of our system of government, and without repeating, I beg to remind the Court of the true nature of our system, as before described.

But especially is it opposed to the rule admitted and recognized in civil suits, without a case to the contrary, by the courts of both the States and the Union, even in cases of concurrent jurisdiction. In disputes also between courts of law and equity, under the same sovereign, it has always been conceded that, in cases of concurrent jurisdiction, the court which first takes the matter in hand is to control it exclusively and to the end. (9 Wheat. R., 532.) In cases between the Federal and State Governments, this rule is well settled and universal. In *Hagan* vs. *Lucas*, 10 Pet. R., 400, the court said: "A most injurious conflict of jurisdiction would be likely often to arise between the Federal and State courts, if the final process of the one could be levied on property which had been taken by the other." And to the same point I cite, 9 Peters' R., 330; 12 Peters' R., 102, 13 Peters' R., 136—151; 1 How. R., 308; 4 How. R., 4; 8 How. R., 107; 10 How. R., 56, 14 How. R., 52, also 368; and Pulliam vs. Osborne, 17 How. R., 471 (1854), where the cases are collected and reviewed. Also 1 Gall. R., 168; 3 Ohio State Rep., 119; 17 J. R., 4, and 1 Kent's Com., 401. I will add also the case cited by the Attorney-General from 11 Peters' R., 102, as directly in point.

So too in criminal cases, the same rule obtains, and by the Federal Courts at least has been rigidly adhered to. 5 McLean, 100, 174; 2 Wall. Jr., 525.

But the case is much stronger where the power is exclusive. Such is the case here, the warrant held by the marshals having been issued under the Fugitive slave Act of 1850. (*Prigg* vs. *Pennsylvania*, 16 Pet. R., 530; affirmed 14 How. R., 13.) The Court in *Slocum* vs. *Mayberry*, 2 Wheat. R., 1, speaking of the act giving exclusive jurisdiction to the Federal Courts over seizures, say:—"Any intervention of a State authority which by taking the thing seized out of the possession of the officer of the United States, might obstruct the exercise of the jurisdiction, would, unquestionably, be a violation of the act; and the Federal Court having cognizance of the seizure, might enforce a redelivery of the thing by attachment or other summary process, against the parties who should divest such a possession." *Gelston* vs. *Hoyt* is to the same point, affirming the foregoing case "after a very deliberate consideration." (3 Wheat. R., 216.) And to the same effect also is the very able opinion of Ranney, J., in *Keating* vs. *Spink*, 3 O. St. Rep., 119.

This rule results necessarily not only from the nature of our system, but the express provision of the Constitution, Art. VI., par. 2, declaring that instrument, and "all laws made in pursuance of it, the supreme law of the land," and binding upon all judges in every State, "any thing in the Constitution or laws of any State to the contrary notwithstanding." That provision was moved in the convention of '87, by Luther Martin, as able a lawyer and sound a State Rights man as the country ever produced. (2 Mad. Pap., 1119.) Nobody ever doubted or cavilled about it. (1 Calh. Works, 252.)

If, then, the law be constitutional, and the authority conferred by it exclusive; if it be, indeed, the supreme law of the land, then, when the process issued to enforce it is regular and valid and from a court of competent jurisdiction, it follows as an irresistible logical necessity, that that process is supreme over all process of the State, and the officer executing it, beyond all control of State authorities, Judges or Courts, or State officers or State writs of any kind.

But there is an especial reason why, in the very cases to obstruct which the act of 1856 was enacted, any interference by State process or authorities is peculiarly against both the spirit and letter of the Constitution. That class of cases is specially provided for in the compact, and in language of peculiar significance. It is not in the ordinary form. "No person held to labor or service in one State escaping to another, shall, in consequence of any law or regulation therein, be discharged from such service or labor, but shall be delivered up on claim of the party to whom such service or labor may be due." The letter—certainly the spirit—of this section is violated by any State law, or any State process which delays, hinders, or obstructs the right of the master to reclaim his slave. It was so said by the Supreme Court in *Prigg* vs. *Pennsylvania* (16 Peters' Rep.) "Its true design," said Mr. Justice Story—and did he not love liberty quite as ardently as the Duchesses of Sutherland, the Mrs. Jellabys and the whole tribe of humanitarian idolaters of the present day—"its true design was to guard against the doctrines and principles prevalent in the non-slaveholding States, by preventing them from intermeddling with or obstructing or abolishing the right of the owners of slaves. The clause manifestly contemplates the existence of a positive, unqualified right on the part of the owner of the slave, which no State law or regulation can in any way qualify, regulate, control or restrain. . . . . .

Any State law or State regulation which interrupts, limits, delays, or postpones the right of the owner to the immediate possession of the slave and the immediate command of his service and labor, operates *pro tanto* a discharge of the slave therefrom. The question can never be how much the slave is discharged from, but whether he is discharged from any, by the natural or necessary operation of State laws or State regulations. The clause contains a positive and unqualified recognition of the right of the owner in the slave, unaffected by any State law or regulation whatsoever." TANEY, Ch. J., said: "Every State law which proposes, either directly or indirectly, to authorize resistance or obstruction, is null and void, and affords no justification to the individual or the officer of the State who acts under it. Every State law which authorizes a State officer to interfere with him (the master) when he is peaceably removing his slave from the State, is unconstitutional and void," (626–7). To the same effect, also is the opinion of Judge Wayne (pp. 646, 647, 648) and of Judge McLEAN, (pp. 661, 662); and I would ask the marked attention of the Court to what they have said; especially to the declaration of Judge McLean, that "if the effect of it (the clause before read) depended in any degree upon the construction of a State by legislation or otherwise, its spirit, if not its letter, would be disregarded." And yet this was in 1842—fifteen years ago.

I next refer the Court to two cases in which the writ *De Homine Replegiando* has been resorted to in the case of fugitive slaves—one in Pennsylvania, in 1819, *Wright* vs. *Deacon*, 6 Serg. and R., 62; and the other in New York, in 1834, *Jack* vs. *Martin*, 12 Wend. R., 311–324. In the former the writ was quashed, as having been issued "in violation of the Constitution of the United States," (per Tilghman, Ch. J.) In the other, judgment was rendered for the defendant upon the same grounds. Nelson, J., delivering the opinion of the Court, said: "Here is a direct conflict between the powers. The very question in the case is, which shall give way? Shall the certificate of the magistrate, under the law of 1793, which declares it shall be a sufficient warrant for removing the fugitive from labor to the territory from which he fled, be permitted to perform its office, or shall the writ under the State law prevent it? They are antagonistic and irreconcilable powers," (324.) Both these cases met the strong approval, in 1851, of Shaw, Ch. J., and the whole Supreme Bench of Massachusetts in the Sims case, 7 Cush. R., 285; and I rely confidently on the principle upon which they were decided. I believe, also, that the principles settled in the cases before cited in 7 Cush., 26 Pa. State, 5 McLean, 6 McLean, and 4 Law Reg., are conclusive upon this point too. The opinion of Judge Nelson, in 1 Blatchf., 643, is direct and most emphatic: "When the prisoner is in fact held under process issued from a Federal tribunal, under the Constitution, or a law of the United States, or a treaty, it is the duty of the officer not to give him up in any stage of the proceedings. He should stand upon his process and authority, and, if resisted, maintain them with all the powers conferred upon him for that purpose."

[After briefly summing up the points made in the case, Mr. VALLANDIGHAM then concluded as follows:]

I have now, may it please your Honor, finished what I have to say upon the law and the facts of the case. Its magnitude, the deep public interest which it everywhere excites, and the momentous results which, with the certainty of the grave, must follow from a failure by the Judiciary or the Executive of the Union, to assert and maintain the principles and the rights which are involved in it, are my apology for having so long detained the Court in this argument. I concur with the Attorney-general in all that he has said of the vast importance of the case now and hereafter, and the more especially if the menaces which he, the law officer of the State and her representative in this forum, has seen fit to more than insinuate in case of an adverse decision, are, in the hour of madness, to be carried out by her authorities as they are now constituted. Never before has any part of the Judiciary of the United States been called upon, in the same way and to the same extent, to affirm and to vindicate these rights and principles, so essential to the peace and harmony and the existence of that beautiful complex system of government under which for so many years we have flourished and grown great and happy as a people.

In another forum and in other forms they have, indeed, been repeatedly and vehemently agitated and discussed. Similar cases have, also, now and then, arisen recently in your courts, wherein these same doctrines have been brought incidentally into debate; but never before have they been presented in the case of direct and absolute antagonism between the laws, process and authority of a State, and of the United States. The insurgents in Western Pennsylvania, in the last century, did not assume to act under any law of that Commonwealth, and found no countenance or support from any of her legally constituted authorities. No State in the Union gave aid or comfort to the conspiracy of Aaron Burr, nor was the murder of Gorsuch, and the rescue of his slaves, pretended to have been done under any statute or process of the State of Pennsylvania. Neither did that ancient and loyal Commonwealth, in the yet later cases from the county of Luzerne, require or permit her Attorney-general, or any of his deputies, to appear in her behalf. The rescue of Crafts, and the attempted rescue of Sims and of Burns, all occurred before the age of personal liberty bills and statutes of treason, miscalled acts of habeas corpus; and the Rosetta and Gaines cases both were decided before the Capitol and Legislative Halls of Ohio were prostituted to the wicked and incendiary purposes of domestic treason and discord.

State Judges and Courts have, indeed, before this, now and then called upon officers of the United States to appear at their bar, bringing with them the prisoners held in custody; and, in one instance, the Supreme Court of a State, and in another a tribunal of this city, certainly not the highest in rank and dignity, and a Judge bearing a name not the most honored in military annals, assumed to overrule the Congress, the Executive, the inferior Courts of the Union, the highest judicial tribunals of most of the States, and the most respectable of the States, and the Supreme Court of the United States, and pronounce the Fugitive Slave Act of 1850 unconstitutional, null and void. But, these things were done as in the green tree; these were the pioneers, the advance guard of the army of sedition and civil discord. Other States also, have, indeed, enacted what, in that hour of madness and folly which confounds all distinctions and misapplies all names, they have chosen to call "Personal Liberty Bills," organizing resistance to the authority and process of the Courts of the Union, instead of the bold and manly nullification of South Carolina, where resistance to what she deemed and declared unconstitutional legislation, put on the form and assumed the virtues and the heroic courage of patriotism. New England set the example, and we have followed it, of instituting the petit treason of a small and contemptible warfare of process; of writs and of counter-writs; a war, not of soldiers and artillery, with the pomp and circumstance of ordinary warfare, but of sheriffs, and constables, and bum-bailiffs, and justices of the peace, and probate judges; of marshals and deputy-marshals; a war of dirk-knives and single-barrel pistols, and revolving six-shooting pistols, with or without powder, caps and ball: a warfare in which, just the reverse of what happened at the battle of Pavia, nothing is lost except honor. It is easy, indeed, to see, and melancholy to reflect, that this small and contemptible warfare of process, must soon bring us to the sterner conflicts of regular and organized military array, when the armies of the State and the United States shall meet in deadly, and most bloody, and most disastrous battle. We see here and now but the beginning of the end. In other States, far removed from the mysterious line or parallel which separates the slave and the free States, where this insane and belligerent legislation has prevailed, no case, happily, of collision has as yet occurred. But to us here in Ohio, most unfortunately, it has been reserved—as was and is inevitable from our position geographically, bordering nearly five hundred miles upon the slave-holding States of Virginia and Kentucky—to exhibit the first example of that conflict of law and authority which the miscalled *habeas corpus* act of 1856 has rendered inevitable. Here, just before and in the midst of us, behold the first fruits of this pernicious and baleful legislation. It was said, the other day, that for more than forty years, and until the nullification ordinance and acts of South Carolina, no power to issue writs of *habeas corpus*, in cases such as this is, was conferred upon the Judges of the Federal Courts; and that for some years afterwards, it lay dormant and unexercised. Very true, very true; but legislation is always the offspring of the general or the special and temporary circumstances and necessities which surround us.

For sixty-eight years, also, the people of Ohio lived happily, freely, prosperously and in neighborly intercourse with her sister States and Territories. Without Slavery in her own limits, she yet had no quarrel and waged no war with those who had. Slaves repeatedly escaped into her territory, and were always peaceably and quietly, and ofttimes without officer or warrant, recaptured and remanded. Ohio herself, not many years ago, volunteered to enact a "fugitive slave law," not less stringent, and certainly far more odious than the now "accursed" act of 1850. But times have changed, and we are changed with them. Men, wise above what is written—wiser than the fathers; men of large capacity and a wisdom and sagacity more than ordinary—more than human, or, of intellects narrowed and beclouded by ignorance and fanaticism, or seduced by a corrupt and most wicked ambition, have discovered that the Constitution is all wrong, and its compacts all wrong; or, rather, that there is a higher law than the Constitution, and that discord is piety and sedition patriotism. They have resolved to annul and set at naught an important and most essential part of the Constitution and of its compacts; and to compel the Government of the United States to succumb to their resolves, or to bring the authorities of the State and of the Union into deadly and most destructive conflict. This was the spirit which dictated the Statute—the Personal Liberty Bill—the so-called habeas corpus act of 1856. There was no pretence of necessity for its enactment, by reason of any thing occurring in the ordinary administration of justice by the Courts of the State. No ministerial officer of the Territory or State of Ohio had ever in any one single instance during a period of sixty-eight years, refused to obey a writ of habeas corpus. But very recently a marshal of the United States had refused obedience to the order of a State Court in such a proceeding; and that most eminent and upright judge, who, for so many years, has adorned the Supreme Bench of the Union, and of whom I may say, as Mr. Webster said of John Jay, when the spotless ermine of the judicial robe fell upon him, it touched nothing not as spotless as itself—had justified him in the refusal and discharged him from confinement by order of the State Judge. And, moreover, a second time in a like case, the same marshal had declined submission to an order by another Court of this City—a Court of Probate, appointed to administer upon the goods and chattels of dead men—requiring him to release his prisoners, because the Fugitive Slave Act, under which he held them in custody, was unconstitutional and void; and again had been sustained in this very forum and by your Honor, now upon the bench. Thus the firmness and integrity of the judiciary of the United States had, so far, triumphed in the conflict, and saved the laws, process and authority of the Union from violation and disgrace. The bulwark of the Constitution remained impregnable. Possession was found full nine points in the law. Certainly, therefore, if possession could but be had, in the first instance, of the bodies of the fugitives or others in custody, the great end of obstructing and defeating the constitutional provision for the reclamation of escaping slaves, and the act in pursuance of it, would be attained, and, accordingly, as I have already established, for the first time in the history of this State, or, indeed, of any State, the writ of personal replevin in the case of prisoners held under judicial process, was introduced into our legislation, and one officer commanded to take, by force, from another officer, the prisoners held in his custody. Collision between State officers was not expected, and, indeed, cannot well arise. But in the case of independent sovereignties exercising authorities and executing independent process within the same territory, it was expected and intended—I stand justified by the facts in affirming it—that a direct and absolute conflict would and should occur. To this State of Ohio, therefore, I am sorry to say—in this district of the State—and to the county officers of Clark, Greene and Champaign, it has, in an evil hour, been allotted to exhibit the first example of the collision, which was inevitable between the two Governments to which, in equal right, though unequal degree, the rights and powers of the people of this State have been committed. The case has arisen—the direct issue has been presented—and it must be met. It is a question of power between these two depositaries. I repeat it—a question of *Power*, not of right. When South Carolina undertook to nullify a statute of Congress, and to set herself in array against the government of the Union, she made it a question of Constitutional right. Recognizing her duty to obey the Constitution and all laws in pursuance of it—no matter how odious or unjust—she denied the power of Congress to enact the Statute. But the learned doctors and professors of modern nullification—the whole *Collegia ambubiarii et pharmacopolæ*—forced to admit the constitutionality of the Fugitive Slave Act; or, at least, the right of the people and the States of the South, under the Constitution, to demand of us the reclamation of their fugitives—appeal to a "higher law" than the Constitution, and denounce the rendition of fugitives from slavery under any law or any Constitution, as against this higher law of conscience, and therefore null and void. Why have they who control just now the legislation of the State, sought to bring about this conflict between the Courts and ministerial officers of the two Governments, and by State Statutes and State process—through the machinery of writs of habeas corpus and replevin—by sheriffs, and constables, and probate judges, and justices of the peace, to harass, impede, and obstruct or prevent the execution of this law?

What argument have we heard here in this Court? Not that the Act is unconstitutional. If it were, the process held by these deputies was void process, and they were engaged in the commission of an illegal act. That would have been a conclusive answer to this whole proceeding. But it has not been alleged. That question is settled,—absolutely put at rest. Mr. Webster said six years ago, that no "respectable lawyer" would maintain the unconstitutionality of the Fugitive Slave Act of 1850. I am confident your Honor would not have heard an argument upon the question. No; we have been told that the law is harsh; that it is cruel and unjust; that it is odious and distasteful to the people. This is the apology for personal liberty bills, and acts of habeas corpus, so called, and all the other hindrances and obstructions, which have been interposed to its execution. For this cause, and this cause only, it has been declared—not here, certainly, but elsewhere—that it cannot and shall not be put in force—at least within the "sovereign states" of Clark, Greene and Champaign: that wheresoever else it may be obeyed, there it is, and shall remain, a dead letter forever. Upon pretexts and by appeals and seditious declarations such as these are, the people, or a part of the people, I trust a very small part, but enough, nevertheleless, to do, or to threaten, great mischief—have been stirred up to the madness and folly of setting themselves in array against the Government of the United States, and under the color and forms of State statutes and State process, of resisting the execution of its laws and the process of its courts, and thus of precipitating upon us the crisis which wicked and designing men have so long labored to bring about.

I have no instruction, may it please your Honor, here, before this tribunal, to discuss the question whether the Act of 1850 be justly obnoxious to these reproaches or not. With that question, this Court has no concern. Your Honor, I am sure, is no authorized expounder of the "higher law" as it is taught in this day, and still less sits here to enforce it. But I may be permitted to suggest, that in its present form substantially, it has been the law of the land for more than sixty years; that by nearly one-half of the States of this Union it is regarded as both reasonable and just; by a large portion of the people of all the States as alike necessary and proper, and by all the States except one, and by all "respectable lawyers"—I quote the words of Mr. Webster, *non meus hic sermo est*, he is responsible for it, not I,—as in strict conformity with the Constitution. If it be, indeed, harsh, cruel and unjust, it is not because it provides means improper or more than adequate to attain its end—they have, indeed, proved 'scarce sufficient as they are—but because it remands the "panting fugitive" to slavery,—"the head and front of its offending hath this extent; no more." If so, then it is the Constitution which is harsh, cruel and unjust. It is the Constitution which is odious and distasteful to that portion of the people of this State, who entertain these sentiments, and who make them the reason or the pretext for their resistance to the process and authority of the United States. It is the Constitution which must be abrogated or nullified, and they who execute or would maintain and defend it, made odious and set at defiance.

But these are doctrines and notions that find no countenance or support within these walls. Here, at least, they may not, and will not, be hearkened to with patience. I have a right then, to repeat again that this is solely a question of power between the two Governments, and it is fortunate, perhaps, for us, that this issue is thus clearly and directly presented here and in this case. It is here, and here in all its breadth and fulness and extent,—a direct and inevitable conflict of law and process between the State and the United States. It is here, the first, the natural, the necessary fruits of the insane and aggressive legislation which, for some years, has prevailed in several of the States of this Union, itself both the effect and the cause, the offspring and the parent of the violent and highly-excited public sentiment which has already resulted, first, in this resistance to the process of your courts, and finally in the melancholy and murderous tragedy of the other day. The exigence of the writ to the marshals commanded them to take and bring the bodies of their prisoners to Cincinnati, before a commissioner of the United States. The exigence of the writ to the sheriff commanded him to take those same prisoners from the custody of the marshals, and carry them to Urbana, before a State Judge. Both could not be obeyed. Resistance and collision were inevitable; and they followed, aggravated and embittered exceedingly by the violent and fanatical hostile sentiments of those who pursued and denounced the marshals as ruffians, while they encouraged and applauded the prisoners as the martyrs of liberty.

The case is here, and to the marshals concerned, it is of the last and most vital importance. Their liberties are at stake. If the Government of the United States is powerless, or is unwilling to protect them in the discharge of the duties which it has imposed upon them, it is easy to see what the result of a trial must be in the midst of the deep excitement which prevails in the counties where these acts were done—

stimulated, as that excitement has been, day by day, through the press, in public assemblies, and upon the public highways, by the most wilful and reckless misrepresentation of facts, and the most savage and wanton denunciation of those deputies as pirates and outlaws. In ordinary times, and upon other subjects, the people of the counties concerned, are no doubt as honest, as intelligent, as upright, as the people of any other counties. But in this case and upon the question involved in it, they have been wrought up to madness and folly. In resisting the execution of the Fugitive Slave Act, they think they do God's service. With them, or rather the honest but misguided portion of them, it is a sort of superstition—a species of religious fanaticism; a motive and an element in popular commotions, as all history attests, the most powerful and controlling. There are, doubtless, hundreds among them, as among others elsewhere, who, in the crusade against this law of the United States, are ready to adopt and repeat the rallying battle-cry of the Saracens: "Paradise is before us and hell-fire at our backs!" In such a state of public sentiment, I have no confidence in any class of men. It is this self-same spirit which, in every age, has lighted up the fires of persecution, and put thousands to death with every aggravation of torture and cruelty. It is this spirit—the true spirit of the "Higher Law"—which sets at defiance every claim of justice, every call of humanity, every law of God, of nature, and of man. In the ninth century, in the earlier ages of the Mohammedan faith, other religions being also tolerated, the fire worshippers of Persia possessed a temple in the city of Herat; which, in the midst of a religious tumult, was attacked and razed to the ground, and a mosque erected upon the site where it had stood. The Magi appealed for justice and restitution to the Caliph; but four thousand Mohammedan citizens of Herat, of a grave character and mature age, deliberately and unanimously swore that the idolatrous temple had never existed. Human nature is the same in every age. The people of the times and country we live in, are no better, by nature, than the people of any other country, or any other period of the world's history. The people of the counties of Clark, Greene, and Champaign, though no worse, are no better, either, than the people of other counties and States of this Union; and, pardon me, gentlemen, they have already prejudged this case and pronounced upon the guilt of these deputies.

But great, may it please your Honor, as the interest of the deputies' stake in this question may be personally, it is not they who are chiefly concerned. The whole people of the district, of the State, of the United States, of other nations, and of the ages which shall succeed the age we live in, are alike and most profoundly interested in the result.

It is a question of the peace and prosperity of our Government, and, with it, of free government all over the globe, and in all coming time. If any one State of this Union may disregard or annul any one part of the Constitution of the United States, or any one law in pursuance of it, because in its judgment it is harsh, cruel and unjust, any other State may, in like manner and upon like pretexts, disobey and set at naught any other part of this same Constitution, or any law under it. If the people, or part of the people, of Ohio may prohibit or practically prevent the execution of the Fugitive Slave Law within her limits, the people, or a part of them, of South Carolina, may also annul and disobey the acts to abolish the slave trade; and by State statutes and State process, by habeas corpus and replevin, through her ministerial officers and her courts, vex and harass, and finally beat down and render powerless the Judiciary of the Union. How long, then, can the governments of either the States or the United States endure; and what, above all, are they worth while they do endure? The end of these things is death.

But I am confident that this Court is prepared, that the whole Government of the United States is prepared to meet this issue just as it is presented. And I tell Mr. Attorney-General, and through him the Executive of the State, whose vain defiance he has this day borne here to this presence, that it is not to be awed by threats, nor to be put down by denunciation, nor to be turned aside from its firm purpose to enforce its laws and the process of its courts, in any event, at all hazards, and without respect to persons or to States, whether those States be Rhode Island or Ohio. And whenever this Court or any other court of the Union shall have judicially ascertained and declared the rights and powers of the Government to execute its process in any pending case, I know that the Executive of the Union stands prepared faithfully, fearlessly, and sternly, if need be, and by the whole power of the Government, to preserve, protect and defend the Constitution from all the assaults of its enemies.

ARGUMENT

In reply to the counsel for the Returned Member, in the Contested Election Case of Vallandigham and Campbell, before the Committee of Elections, February 27, 1858.

I.—As to the sufficiency of the notice of contest.

The specific objection urged is, that the *names* of the *illegal voters* are not set forth.

I answer, that even prior to the act of 1851, in a majority of cases, this had not been required; that the act is silent upon the subject, substituting a provision that ten days' notice of the names of the *witnesses* proposed for examination shall be given; that the language of the act is "specify particularly the *grounds* upon which he relies in the contest;" that *grounds* are one thing, and *names* of voters quite another; that every "ground" of illegality, known to the Ohio constitution and statutes relating to elections, is set forth, and cases under nearly all of them established by the testimony, and that there are many obvious reasons against requiring the names of illegal voters to be set forth in the notice of contest, or the answer; and among them this: That as the notice and answer cannot be renewed or amended, the parties would be precluded from proof of any illegal votes discovered after the thirty days limited in either case.

I answer, further, that the returned member himself has not, in his answer, set forth the name of so much even as one illegal voter.

As to precedents: fifteen cases, including those of the present session, have arisen under the law; nine of which, excluding the one now in hearing, were contested upon the ground of illegal voting, and yet in *not one* have the names of the illegal voters been set forth. Twice the objection has been directly made and overruled. In the very first case under the act, *Wright* vs. *Fuller*, 1851–'52, it was so held, (House Report, No. 136;) and yet again in *Otero* vs. *Gallegos*, 1855–'56. Objection in this case had been taken, in the answer of the returned delegate, to the omission of the names of the illegal voters. Yet the committee said: "The notice was quite sufficient to authorize the taking of the testimony. No such objection was made by the sitting member or his counsel at the time of taking the depositions; on the contrary, he appeared and cross-examined the witnesses without any objection whatever; and if he had no notice at all, but had appeared and cross-examined, he would have been estopped from setting up the want of notice."—(House Reports, 1855–'56, vol. 1, No. 90, p. 2.) Three times, also, it has been urged in contested elections in Philadelphia; Lelar's case, 1846; Kneas's case, 1851; Cassidy's case, 1857; and each time overruled by the court.

If there be any, the remotest resemblance between the notice in this contest and the one in *Archer* vs. *Allen*, in the last Congress, it might be an ingenious though perplexing intellectual exercise to point it out; yet even that notice the majority of the committee held sufficient.

II.—As to the validity of the election in the second ward, Dayton.

I leave this upon the argument heretofore submitted, adding the case of *Otero* vs. *Gallegos*, just cited, wherein the prior congressional precedents are referred to and approved.

I remark also as to the case so strongly relied on by the counsel for the returned member, *The People* vs. *Cook*, 14 Barb., 245:

1. That that was not an ordinary contested election, but a proceeding in *quo warranto* known to the common law, the parties upon the record being the *State* and the incumbent; and it is expressly said by one of the judges (p. 326) that "the result of an election, when controverted *in court*, is like a judgment sued upon. *We* have *no power* to reverse it for errors in conducting it, and thus give those concerned in it a re-trial." If this be the doctrine in contested elections before Congress, it is time, after the lapse of seventy years, that it should begin to be known and acted on. It is contradicted by every precedent from 1789 to this day.

2. There is a broad distinction, wholly overlooked by the court, between the want of authority on the part of an inspector of elections to act as such, and a mere irregularity by him in conducting it. Yet the omission to take the oath of office has always, in Congress, been held a fatal defect. The objection made in the case from Barbour was to the *form* only of the oath. It was an *apex juris* not fit to be urged; for if a Jew be sworn on the Gospels, and testify falsely, he may be convicted of perjury.—(1 Greenleaf Ev., § 371.)

But the case is chiefly remarkable for a most extraordinary misapplication or perversion of the rule that the acts of an officer *de facto* are good and valid as regards the public and third persons. It may, indeed, be sound and pertinent in proceedings on *quo warranto*, but never, never in an ordinary contested election before a legislative tribunal; otherwise, every intruder into the responsible office of inspector of elections would become invested at once with authority which could not be questioned elsewhere. By violence alone, and that at once and at the polls, could the remedy be applied and the intruder ousted. If this is to be the doctrine in cases like this, then, in a little while, at every hustings, the only struggle will be to secure at the outset, and by force or fraud, the judges of election; and in such a conflict, not the will of the people, but the strength or cunning of the party first upon the ground, must prevail.

III.—As to the non-production of the poll-books, or certified copies of them, to prove that the alleged illegal voter did vote.

I answer, first: That the poll-books may be the best evidence to prove that a name corresponding with that of the person challenged is upon the list of voters; but they do *not* prove that that identical person voted. Suppose the name of John Smith to be found upon them, and it is proved that a John Smith living within the same precinct or township was not entitled to vote; *non sequitur*, that the John Smiths are the same. There must be in every case some parol proof, therefore, that the person challenged did vote. The production of the list is, at best, but *corroborative* or cumulative evidence. The testimony of John Smith that he did vote, is better evidence of the fact than the production of a list containing the name of one John Smith.

It is said that the law requires the list to be kept, and that, therefore, the fact can be proved only by the production of the record. *Non sequitur*, again. The fact is still "did *the* John Smith, who is challenged, vote at the election?" and not "is the name of one John Smith upon the list of voters?" And, accordingly, it has been repeatedly held that where registers of marriage, birth, death, and the like, are required by the law to be kept, it is not necessary, nor yet sufficient, to produce them even in a criminal prosecution.—(1 Greenleaf Ev., § 86; 9 Mass., 493; 11 Mass., 92; 3 Har. & McH., 393; Rus. & Ry., 109.) So, also, that a man was elected to and holds a certain office may be proved by parol; and I concede that the fact that no name corresponding to that of the person alleged to have voted appears upon the poll-list, is presumptive evidence that no such person did vote.

2d. As to the congressional precedents, the point has never been made or decided, so far as I have been able to find, and the usage has not been uniform. Proof upon this point, such as is produced here, was repeatedly received in the Broad Seal case, as in the instance of the vote of Ezekiel Patterson, a colored person. "Jacob W. Davis, a witness sworn on the part of John B. Aycrigg and others, saith: I am clerk for the township of Mansfield, and was in 1838; I have the poll-list here; the names of Isaac N. Zerwilliger, Charles T. Poole, James Wamsly, William V. Schureman, and Christopher Patterson, usually called Eke, (on the assessor's duplicate it is Ezekiel,) *are on the poll-list*." —(3 House Rep., 1839, 1840, No. 541, p. 95; and see the Report *passim.*) And as to *declarations* of a person that he had voted, the poll-list not being produced, and no proof of its contents given, and *no other* evidence of the fact of voting, except his own declarations proved by third persons.—(See p. 73 of Report, and 23 of the Journal of the Committee.)

As to the only precedent cited by the counsel, *Otero* vs. *Gallegos*, poll-books were produced from only three counties. From six counties there were none introduced, and yet a part of the testimony related to illegal votes cast in those counties.

IV.—THAT THE ABSTRACT OF VOTES IN THE DISTRICT AT THE ELECTION, OR COPY OF THE RETURNS, WAS NOT "OBTAINED OR TAKEN" WITHIN THE SIXTY DAYS LIMITED.

I answer, 1st, that it is at least doubtful whether it be my place to produce it at all. It is no part of my case. I claim nothing under it. Upon its face it shows nineteen majority against me, and by so much would diminish my vote as it appears upon the testimony. In the first case under the law, *Wright* vs. *Fuller*, 1851, it appears from the report of the committee that it was the *sitting member* who produced the returns before them.—(House Report No. 136, page 1; and see *Munroe* vs. *Jackson*, House report, volume 2, page 403.)

But what is the true construction of the act of 1851? I maintain that the restriction in the ninth section applies solely to *oral testimony.*

I argue this, 1st, *from the language* of the restriction: "No *testimony* shall be taken after sixty days," &c. Testimony means the declaration or affirmation under oath, of a living witness.—(Webster's Dict.; 2 Bouvier's Law Dict.; 2 Burrill's Law Dict.; 1 Greenleaf Ev., §§ 1, 307, 308; 2 Daniel Chy. Prac., 1003, 1030.) The distinction is not between testimony and evidence, but between testimony and documentary evidence. 2d. *From the context.* The entire act, except the first and second sections, refers exclusively to the examination of witnesses. The eighth section provides for the production of documentary evidence *in connection* with the testimony of witnesses. Examples of this may be found on pages 53 and 59 of the printed testimony. So, too, under the act of January 23, 1798, of which the statute of 1851 is but almost a literal transcript, the House, by resolution on the 5th of the June following, provided for the introduction of documentary evidence during that Congress, as a matter not included within the law.—(Journal, page 323; and Cont. Elec., 16.) 3. *From the object of the act.* Judge Strong, the author, or at least reporter of the bill, said, during the debate upon it: "*The testimony is wholly that of witnesses.*"—(Cong. Globe, 1850–'51, page 109.) 4. *By analogy to the chancery practice.* There, although no testimony can be taken after "publication," yet documentary evidence, even when a witness is to be examined along with it, may be introduced at the hearing.

Upon the precedents in Congress, since the law and prior to the present session, the question is plain. In only two cases has the "abstract" been procured or taken within the sixty days. In one case it was before the service of the answer. In five, including *Archer* vs. *Allen*, it was months subsequent to the expiration of the time limited for "taking testimony." In one of these five, *Clarke* vs. *Hall*, no notice of contest was served, other than the memorial of the contestant, nearly eighteen months after the election; yet the committee of the last Congress received and considered the documentary evidence procured in the cases. So, too, in another, *Milliken* vs. *Fuller*, the notice was not served till near thirteen months after the election; yet the same kind of evidence was received and acted upon by the same committee. And in the contested election for sheriff in one of the counties of this same third district, in 1856–'57, the book of returns was brought into court and received on the third day of the hearing, although the time for "taking testimony" had expired more than two months previously. And, in addition to all this, the returned member himself evidently so construed the law as to admit of the production of documentary evidence at any time; for, although in his answer he claims under the governor's *certificate*, he did not put it in evidence during the time limited, and in the answer expressly proposes to confine his proof during that period to matters provable by witnesses.

If this "abstract" could be established only by witnesses, then there might be more plausibility in the objection. But coming authenticated by the great seal of the State of Ohio, it proves itself upon production.—(1 Greenl. Ev., §§ 4, 479, 489; 4 Dal. Rep., 416.)

The Secretary of State is the proper person, and is authorized to make the copy here produced.—(Swan's Statutes of Ohio, 345, §§ 36, 37, 38, 39; 867, § 1; and 361, § 1.)

V.—As to the admissibility of evidence called "hearsay."

The importance of the question in all cases, but especially where the election is by ballot, rather than its bearing upon this particular contest, demands for it a full consideration.

I remark, however, 1. That much of what is included by the returned member's counsel within the term, is not hearsay, but original evidence. 2. That a part of this hearsay—for example, that relating to residence—is such as is continually received by courts in ordinary litigation.—(5 Harris & J., 97; 2 Bing., 104.) Declarations made at the polls, whether under oath or not, are also clearly within this proposition as part of the *res gestæ*. 3. That both parties offer the same kind of testi-

11

mony in this regard. 4. That it is not the *adequacy*, but the *admissibility*, of the evidence which is in question.

But to the main point.

This is not the first time this question has been presented in legislative bodies; and had it been tested by the principles and precedents which have prevailed there, I should have added nothing to the argument heretofore submitted. It has not been so argued, but upon rules and precedents known only to forensic courts, where a like case never did and never can arise in the exercise of its ordinary jurisdiction. I propose to meet the argument, *first*, upon this very ground, and to discuss it just as I would had the case arisen now for the first time in the usual course of litigation in a court of common law.

All evidence to be admissible must be *relevant*—that is, tend to prove or disprove the issue. All relevant evidence is *prima facie* admissible; its rejection is always the exception. Thus, whenever a court is equally divided, the objection to evidence fails.

Among the exceptions is a class denominated "hearsay," which is always heard in the ordinary affairs of life, but which, in judicial proceedings, is rejected.

Upon this rule excluding hearsay evidence, the returned member's counsel relies. I rest upon the exceptions, of which there is a vast number; none, indeed, of course, presenting the exact question here; but this is solely because it never arose or could arise in ordinary litigation.

What would have been the decision had it so arisen, may readily be inferred from a summary of the numerous cases constituting exceptions, adjudicated in a long series of years, as each several exigency arose.

These exceptions are founded primarily upon the doctrine that "all rules of evidence are adopted for practical purposes in the administration of justice, and must be so applied as to promote the ends for which they were designed."—(1 Greenleaf Ev., § 83.)

Hearsay consists *strictly* of the declarations of persons not parties to the controversy. Admissions by the parties are *substitutionary* evidence. —(*Ibid.*, § 169.)

Now, assuming, what is not true in any legal sense, that the parties to this controverted election are the returned member and myself, no others having an interest in it, I proceed to consider the exceptions, begging again that it be remembered that I apply and argue from them solely by analogy.

Some of them are regarded by Greenleaf rather as original evidence, though usually treated as hearsay. It is not necessary here to distinguish between them.

In actions for malicious prosecution, and in cases of agency and trusts, the information upon which the party acted, though from third persons, is admissible. So, also, are letters and conversations of strangers to the record, where sanity is the question. And evidence of general reputation, reputed ownership, public rumor, general notoriety, is considered within the exceptions.—(*Ibid.*, § 101.) Expressions of bodily or mental feeling are admitted, and it is left to the court or jury to determine whether they were real or feigned. Thus, in trial for criminal intercourse, the correspondence and conversations of the husband and wife with third persons are received. So, also, are representations by a sick person, of the nature, symptoms and effects of his malady.—(*Ibid.*, § 102.) And not only is general repute in a family receivable in all questions of pedigree, including, also, birth, marriage and death, but the declarations of a single member of the family are admitted; and more than this, even *hearsay upon hearsay*. Thus the declarations of a deceased lady, as to the declarations made to her by her husband, were received in *Doe* vs. *Randall*, 2 M. & P., 20; and see also 2 Russ. & My., 165; Bull. N. P., 295; 1 Pet. Rep., 328, 337.

Inscriptions upon rings, family portraits, tomb-stones, and other funereal monuments, and charts of pedigree, are also admitted, and some of them provable even by *copies*; courts acting here upon the common sense principle, that when a fact *cannot* be proved in one way, it *may* be proved in another.—(*Ibid.*, § 105.)

Again: entries, in many cases, made by third persons are evidence of the facts set down in the entry; and this, whether made in the course of official or professional employment, or as mere private memoranda. And Greenleaf lays it down broadly that, "generally contemporaneous entries made by third persons in their own books, in the ordinary course of business, the matter being within the peculiar knowledge of the party making the entry, and there being no apparent or particular motive to pervert the fact, are received as *original* evidence," and this though the party be living and present as a witness, and not himself remembering the fact.—(*Ibid.*, § 116.)

Again: in matters of public interest, though confined to a particular district, parish, or neighborhood, the declarations of persons not parties to the suit are receivable in evidence, upon the principle that they "are the natural effusions of a party who must know the truth, and who speaks upon an occasion when his mind stands in an even position, without any temptation to exceed or fall short of the truth."—Lord Eldon, 13 Vesey, 514.)

In questions of boundary, therefore, hearsay is admitted. The language of Chief Justice HENDERSON, of North Carolina, in *Sasser* vs. *Herring*, (3 Dever. Law Rep., 340,) is strong and pertinent here: "We have, in questions of boundary, given to the single declaration of a deceased individual, as to a line or corner, the weight of common reputation, and permitted such declarations to be proven, under the rule that, in questions of boundary, hearsay is evidence. * * * * * * * From necessity, we have in this instance sacrificed the principles upon which the rules of evidence are founded." The same doctrine is held in New Hampshire, Connecticut, Pennsylvania, South Carolina, Kentucky, and Tennessee.—(1 Greenl. Ev., § 145, note 1.)

A very large class of exceptions is included under the head of *declarations against interest*, made by strangers to the litigation. They are admitted when it is shown that the declarant is dead, and therefore cannot speak; that he possessed a competent knowledge of the facts, and that the declarations were at variance with his interest. "When these circumstances concur," says Greenleaf (§ 147), "the evidence is received, leaving its weight and value to be determined by other considerations." This exception extends to declarations of any kind, whether oral or in writing (Ibid., §150); it includes within it other statements, made at the same time, though not against interest, (§ 152;) it is not necessary that the declarant, if living, should have been competent (or compellable) to testify to the facts, since it is regarded as a *confession*, § 153; it extends in favor of the successor, or party in the same interest, of a deceased rector or vicar, or corporation aggregate, (§ 155;) and it is not necessary that the fact should have been stated on the personal knowledge of the declarant, nor is it material whether it is provable by other testimony, (§ 153.)

Dying declarations also are receivable; the solemnity of the occasion being deemed to stand in the place of an oath and cross-examination.

Again: where other proof is made that a voter cast his ballot for a particular candidate, there is another technical but well settled rule under which his declarations are receivable as against that candidate. The office, in the point of view in which I am now treating it, being one of profit as well as trust in a legal sense, is an individual right; it is, in some sense, individual property, but a right or property derived from those who voted at the election. The returned member claims under each and every one who voted for him; and the contestant, in like manner, under those who voted for him. Hence the declarations of every voter are admissible against the party for whom he voted, since the right of the party to the office depends upon the right of the voter to confer it.—(3 John. R., 449; 1 Greenl. Ev., § 180.)

There is yet another class of declarations—those made by bankrupts—which are admitted *in favor* of the assignees against creditors. A strong case is *Ridley et al.* vs. *Gyde*, (9 Bing. Rep., 349,) where declarations made by White, the bankrupt, not a party to the record or in interest, a month after the act of bankruptcy, and without any intervening circumstances to connect them with it, were yet received by the English common pleas in 1832, Chief Justice Tindal, Park, and Bosanquet concurring. The chief justice said: "To shut out this conversation, would be to shut out the best evidence in the cause;" and Park, J. adhered to his decision in *Rawson* vs. *Haigh*, (2 Bing., 104,) where he had said: "I am satisfied that declarations made during departure and absence are admissible in evidence to show the motive of the departure. It is impossible to tie down to time the rule as to declarations; we must judge from all the circumstances of the case."—(And see 1 Bing., 585 1 Index to Eng. C. L. Reports, "Evidence.")

So, also, in settlement cases, declarations by parishioners as to matters of residence are held admissible in evidence, and that, too, without calling the party, though within the reach of process.—(1 M. and S., 637; and see especially the *King* vs. *Inhabitants of Hardwick*, 11 East Rep., 588.)

Other examples, many in number, might be added; but enough have been summed up to show how often and in what a variety of cases courts, even of common law, have set aside the rule excluding hearsay.

It was to establish this proposition, and not because they are direct precedents or cases in point, for of such there are none in "the books," that I have cited these examples, reasoning from them by analogy.

But the *conditions* of the exception, admitting declarations by third persons against their interest, do, in the reasoning upon which they are founded, clearly include the testimony objected to in this case.

1. The declarant must have competent knowledge of the facts, otherwise he has no right to speak. This condition is fulfilled here. 2. He must be dead. Why? Because, if alive, he ought to speak. But in this case he has a constitutional right to be silent, and cannot be compelled to speak, either, first, as to his vote, since it is by ballot; or second, as to his qualifications, since he might subject himself to a criminal prosecution. 3. The declarations must have been at variance with his interest. Now, it is true that in courts, by analogy to the now generally exploded rule disqualifying a witness because of interest in the suit, the interest in cases within this exception must usually be pecuniary, although Greenleaf seems to recognize also that danger of punishment may be a fitting element in it.—(§ 150, *note;* and see 24 E. C. L. Rep., 467.) But upon what principle of human nature is this condition of the rule founded? *That all men are eager to increase and slow to diminish their estate.* And yet how much more eager are they to retain their political rights and personal liberty. Now, in the testimony, here are two classes of declarations: first, as to the qualifications; second, as to the person for whom the declarant voted. The latter are not within the rule unless made at the same time as the former. The former are

within it; and this for two reasons: 1. Whether made before or after the election, they equally are admissible against him in a criminal prosecution for illegal voting, which in Ohio, is a penitentiary offence. 2. If *before* the election, they also subject the declarant to danger of loss of his vote, since, by statute in Ohio, witnesses may be examined at the polls, and thus the declaration of the party be there given in evidence against his right to vote.

Here, then, is the highest interest of the voter against the declaration —loss of liberty, infamous punishment, loss of suffrage. Shall one pennyworth of pecuniary interest suffice to render the declaration admissible; and yet these momentous considerations, involving the most valuable rights of the citizen, be reckoned but as the small dust of the balance?

But whether within the special conditions of the exception or not, these declarations, both as to qualifications and vote, but particularly the former, are emphatically within the *broad principle* upon which the exception itself is founded. What is it? "*The extreme improbabiity of their falsehood.*"—(1 Greenleaf Ev., § 148.) And this improbability, says the author, is strengthened by the circumstance that "it is always competent for the party against whom such declarations are adduced *to point out any sinister motive* for making them." "It is true," he adds, "that the ordinary and highest tests of the fidelity, accuracy and completeness of judicial evidence are here wanting; but their place is in some measure supplied by the circumstances of the declarant; and the *inconveniencies resulting from the exclusion* of the evidence having such guaranties for its accuracy in fact, and for its freedem from fraud, are deemed *much greater*, in general, than any which would probably be experienced from its admission." For similar reasons, doubtless, it was that in *Powell* vs. *Harter*, (24 E. C. L. Rep., 467,) an action for libel upon a charge of receiving stolen goods, knowing them to have been stolen, upon justification pleaded, the court allowed the declarations of the alleged thief to be given in evidence by the defendant to prove that he (the thief) had stolen the goods received by the plaintiff. And see also *Doe & Davy* vs. *Haddon*, (3 Doug. Rep., 310.)

There is yet another principle recognized by the common law, upon which the declarations here objected to are admissible—*necessity*. On this principle, in part, some of the hearsay which I have already considered, is admitted to prevent a failure of justice. In like manner the testimony of the wife in proceedings to keep the peace, or for assault and battery upon herself, instituted by her against the husband, is received, and thus one of the earliest, firmest, and most sacred rules of evidence—a rule not even yet swept away by the relentless hand of modern reform—is so far relaxed. So, also, the contents of a trunk lost by a common carrier may be proved by the owner.—(1 Greenleaf Rep., 27.) And in Ohio and Pennsylvania the *wife* of the owner is received as a competent witness for that purpose.—(20 Ohio Rep., 318; 8 Serg. & Watts, 369; 3 Barr, 351.) In many other cases, also, upon this principle of necessity, persons excluded by the general rules of evidence are yet admitted to testify.

Apply the principle here, and, first, as to declarations concerning disqualifications.

Upon this point it is enough to say that, besides the difficulty, sufficiently great just after an election, and increasing continually the longer the delay in taking the testimony, of securing the attendance of voters challenged as illegal, none of them of any class can be compelled to testify, even if present and on oath, as to their disqualification, because they might thereby criminate themselves. This protection extends to every question the answer to which might *tend* to convict them of having voted illegally.

To exclude the declarations of voters in any case would, therefore, tend greatly to embarrass the rights of both parties and of all concerned.

2. This necessity applies with especial force to the declarations of the voter as to the person for whom he voted; because that is a fact which he cannot be compelled to disclose where the election is by ballot. This has been repeatedly decided. I refer especially to *Easton* vs. *Scott*, 1816, Cont. Elects., 272, 276; the *Broad Seal* case, 1840; *Farlee* vs. *Runk*, 1845–46; *Monroe* vs. *Jackson*, 1847–48; and the case of *H. R. Kneas*, district attorney, whose election was contested in 1851, on behalf of *William B. Reed*, in one of the judicial courts of Philadelphia.

This, then, is a constitutional right of the voter; but there is also another high constitutional right, pertaining not to one man only, but to thousands—the right to see that the purity and integrity of the elective franchise shall be preserved by a *contest* before the appropriate tribunal. It is a private right; it is much more a public right. And of what value is the vote by ballot, if the purity of the ballot-box be not made sure?

How, then, shall these two conflicting rights both be maintained? Only by permitting the voter to withhold his own testimony, and allowing the fact in dispute to be established by other proof.

It has, indeed, been doubted whether the constitutional right of secret ballot be not infringed by admitting *any testimony* to prove the fact. So it would seem to have been held by the Committee of Elections, in *Easton* vs. *Scott;* but the House, on motion of Mr. Webster, and after a long debate, in which the contrary doctrine appears to have been maintained by Randolph, Webster and Calhoun, recommitted the report, with instructions to consider the testimony presented by the parties upon that point. And see *Otero* vs. *Gallegos, ut supra.*

The same objection was urged also in the Philadelphia contested election of 1851, just cited; and, in deciding it, Judge KING said: "What is the object here? It is important to prove how a given individual voted. How is it to be proved? First, undoubtedly, if he chooses to waive the protection given by the constitution he may state it himself. But supposing it became of vital importance to prove how he voted, cannot that be established by clear and satisfactory testimony? He may have an interest in protecting his ballot; another may have an interest in showing what that ballot was. We are to preserve his rights by protecting him in the secrecy the law contemplates; but we are equally bound to serve the general community, or the individual, by enabling him to prove it. Where we resort to other testimony than the party himself, we go upon the principle of obtaining the best testimony the nature of the case will admit. * * * * * In adopting this course, I don't understand myself as infringing upon the right of the citizen or the security of the secret ballot."—(*Report*, p. 17.)

It has always been conceded, however, that the voter may waive his right and give evidence; but surely, if his own voluntary testimony can be received because it is a waiver of his right, the next best and least objectionable testimony, and upon the same principle, is his declarations. And I here remark, also, that if, as is claimed, all evidence except his own, which cannot be compelled, is *secondary*, then, as there are no degrees in secondary evidence, why, I ask, may not his declarations be received?

And at this point I quote also from the opinion of the court in the case of LEWIS C. CASSIDY, district attorney, whose election was contested in Philadelphia, in 1857. Objection was made to certain evidence upon the ground that it "amounted to *nothing more than hearsay*," and that "to admit the evidence of the witness would tend to allow him to *prove admissions* of parties who might have been legal voters, yet subsequent to the election might have declared, from motives better known to themselves, that they did not vote at all, or were not qualified voters.' JUDGE THOMPSON, overruling the objection, said, "that the question was very simple—that to comply with the notions of counsel would be to require of the contestants an absolute impossibility. It is alleged by the contestants that fraudulent votes were polled; and it is contended that the fact can be shown in no other way than by proving it by the persons themselves who perpetrated the fraud. Now, to compel them to prove this by them would effectually put a stop to the investigation. But the law does no such thing."—(*Report*, p. 33.)

If it be said that the voter ought himself to be first summoned, so that it may be seen whether he will not waive his privilege to be silent, I answer, that wherever a witness cannot be compelled to testify, the party is under no obligation to call him. It was expressly so decided by the Supreme Court of the United States in *Reyburn's* case; 6 Peters Rep., 352, 367. JUDGE THOMPSON, delivering the unanimous opinion of the court, said: "A subpœna to compel attendance as a witness would have availed nothing, and the law does not require the performance of an act perfectly nugatory. But suppose Chase (the witness) had been within reach of a subpœna, and had actually attended the court, he could not have been compelled to produce the commission, and thereby furnish evidence against himself."

The same doctrine prevails in settlement cases also, where it is held "not necessary first to call the inhabitant (of the parish) and show that he refused to be examined, in order to admit his declarations;" 1 M. & S., 637; 10 East., 395; Greenl. Ev., § 153, 175.

So far I have argued this case as I would have argued had it arisen for the first time in the course of ordinary litigation in a court of common law, the only parties to it being the returned member and myself. Even there, with great confidence, I affirm that the evidence would be received as a new application merely of very ancient doctrines.

But I now submit that this question is not to be decided upon the strict common law rules of evidence applied in private litigation; that the real parties in this contest are the people, or certainly the electors of the district; and that the parliamentary, congressional, and legislative precedents for a great number of years, are clear and uniform in favor of the admissibility of this evidence. All this, however, I leave upon the oral and written arguments heretofore submitted upon this subject to the committee.

SPEECH ON THE OHIO CONTESTED ELECTION,

In the House of Representatives, May 22, 1858.

Mr. SPEAKER: Unused to this presence, and limited by your rules to one hour, I beg, as a special indulgence from members of this House, the liberty to proceed without those interruptions which custom seems to approve in ordinary debate. When the time allotted me shall have expired, I will readily and with pleasure reply to such interrogatories as, in that same spirit of courtesy and candor which has generally been extended to me here throughout this investigation, may consistently with your rules be propounded by any member of the House.

I appear in this forum to-day, Mr. Speaker, as the Representative of nearly ten thousand of the qualified electors of the third congressional district of Ohio; and not in my own right. I propose to speak in their name and in their behalf alone; and trust that, without suspicion of affectation, but solely for convenience and to avoid continual personal allusion, I may be permitted to refer to myself in the third person and as the contestant in this controversy, and to speak as one having no individual interest in it.

Within the time limited it is not possible to discuss, in a manner satisfactory to any one, either the facts or the question involved in this controverted election. The facts, indeed, I do not propose to consider at all. They have been found fully in the report of the gentleman from Mississippi, (Mr. LAMAR.) If any member of the House be not satisfied with that finding, it is his right, as it is also his duty, to investigate them for himself; but, till called in question, I shall assume them precisely as found in that report.

Resolved, Mr. Speaker, to confine myself wholly to those matters which appear in the papers, testimony, and reports in the case, and which are essential to its just decision, and to avoid all allusion to whatever lies outside of these limits, and is not pertinent to the issue in the cause, I propose, briefly, and imperfectly of course, within the time allowed, to speak to *two points* mainly, which are presented for the judgment of the House. And I select these because, upon the face of the adverse reports, if *either of them* be resolved in favor of the contestant, he is entitled to the seat here in controversy.

The first of these points relates to the *admissibility of testimony* affecting a number of votes, sufficient, even upon the showing of those reports, not only to turn the scale against the returned member, but to elect the contestant. I refer to the DECLARATIONS or admissions by voters as to their qualifications, and as to the candidate for whom they voted. Many of the votes here controverted, some upon both sides, depend in whole or in part upon testimony of this character. In a large majority of cases indeed where it is offered, there is other and corroborating proof. But twelve votes on part of the contestant depend solely upon this sort of testimony; and of these nine only are allowed in the report of the gentleman from Mississippi (Mr. LAMAR):—which report finds also a majority in favor of the contestant, *without these nine, and upon what is regarded as clear and satisfactory proof.* The adverse reports reject all these twelve votes, as also many others—in all to the number of more than thirty—where these declarations are offered along with direct or circumstantial proof. But upon the face of these reports, if this evidence be admissible, the contestant is entitled to the seat.

It is the misfortune, Mr. Speaker, of all American legislative assemblies, that, composed almost wholly of lawyers, every question, even the gravest problems of Government and public policy, are argued as upon special demurrer, and tried by the narrow rules of a common law jurisdiction. Certainly, sir, the skill and discipline of the bar are available in every department of life, and nowhere more valuable than in legislation; but they ought to be here used as the discipline and skill of the athlete when transferred to military warfare; his strength, and courage, and powers of endurance are all just as valuable as in the *campus*; but the weapons, the strategy, and the tactics are totally changed. A controverted election resembles, indeed, a trial at law, far more than ordinary legislation; nevertheless, there is a wide difference, as I shall attempt by and by to establish; and a more liberal rule is to be adopted in its investigation. But the first and natural impulse of every lawyer here, fresh from the dust and toil of forensic courts, is to test every question, especially of evidence, by the mere technical rules of the common-law jurisdiction with which he has, every day, been accustomed to deal. And thus, too, a civilian would in like manner try every question by the principles of the Code and the Pandects; and the practitioner at Doctors Commons by the Gregorian Institutes and the Clementine constitutions, and finding no "case in point," each would pronounce judgment accordingly. Sir, this is one of the "idols of the cave," against which the greatest of philosophers has warned us. No case like this ever has arisen, or ever can arise, in a forensic court, in the exercise of its ordinary or common-law jurisdiction. Yet I venture to affirm that it would not be difficult, in just such a case, and before just such a tribunal, to establish the admissibility of this evidence. Very true, sir, hearsay evidence—if, indeed, these declarations could be regarded as hearsay at all—is said not to be admitted. Certainly this is the general rule; but the exceptions are as numerous as the variety and the exigencies of litigation; and every day for centuries has brought forth some modification of the rule, or some new application of the multiplied exceptions; and it is a significant fact, that one hundred and seventy-eight pages of the first volume of Greenleaf upon Evidence are devoted to these exceptions alone. It is no new thing, therefore, that hearsay or declarations should be received. It is the every-day practice of your courts to receive and act upon just such evidence in the most important trials, not of property or liberty only, but of life also. In actions for malicious prosecutions; in cases of agency and trusts; in criminal conversation; in questions of sanity, sickness, pedigree, birth, marriage, death, boundary; in matters of public interest, though pertaining only to a district, parish, or neighborhood, it is regularly received. Inscriptions on family portraits and funeral monuments; entries by third persons; dying declarations; declarations by bankrupts; declarations in settlement cases, in questions of residence, or as a part of the *res gestæ*; declarations by privies in law, in blood, in estate; declarations against interest; and, of course, admissions and confessions, are all equally admissible; and whole volumes of reports and treatises are filled with them.

So, also, upon the principle of *necessity*, evidence otherwise inadmissible is received. Thus, besides much of the hearsay to which I have referred the testimony of the wife is, in certain cases, admitted against the husband; and the owner of a trunk, and in some States the wife of the owner, is received as a witness to prove the contents in an action against a common carrier. So, too, in many other cases, parties to the record, parties in interest, and others, excluded by the general rules of evidence, are yet admitted to testify.

Apply the principle here, and the declarations of a voter, both as to his qualifications and his vote, are clearly admissible. I say as to both; because the largest class of voters challenged in contests from States where, as in Ohio, there is neither registry nor property qualification of any kind—a class which, in this very case, embraces one half the whole number controverted—consists of *non-residents of the State or county*, sojourners for a day, or "pipe-layers" if you please, colonized for the purposes of the election, and who, as soon as their mission is performed, leave the country for parts unknown, or beyond the jurisdiction of the officer appointed to take the testimony. But, more than all this, neither these sojourners, nor any other voters, whose rights are called in question, even if forced to attend, can be compelled to testify, either as to their votes, since they are by ballot, or their qualifications, because they might thereby subject themselves to a criminal prosecution. Both these exemptions are high constitutional rights in Ohio, which no tribunal is permitted to disregard. The former, if not as ancient, is yet just as sacred and binding as the latter; since the very object of the secret ballot, that ungentlemanly mode of election, not founded certainly in the highest notions of human virtue and independence, and tending still less to foster and develop them, is to enable the elector to conceal what he ought never to be ashamed or afraid to avow. Nevertheless, that such is his right has been repeatedly adjudged. Add now to this the protection against self-crimination, by any compulsory admission or confession, and it is palpable that, without just such evidence as is here offered, there must, for the most part, be an utter failure of justice, and the right to purge the ballot-box by a scrutiny be rendered a delusion and a snare. And I beg to repeat here to the House, what I stated to the committee, that so far as the testimony of the voters themselves was procured—and no small part of the evidence in the case consists of it—it was upon a tacit or express pledge or understanding, not binding, certainly, but volunteered, nevertheless, that no prosecutions should be instituted.

Examples such as I have referred to, might be multiplied without number, and the proposition clearly established, that in every instance where, in a given class of cases, a failure of justice would otherwise probably occur, courts even of common law, both in England and America, have uniformly departed from the rule—itself, indeed but an exception—which excludes hearsay; and thus the oath and cross-examination been obliged to yield to other tests of veracity, where justice and the public interest demand it. It is not enough to say that the common law excludes hearsay evidence. It once excluded all who had an interest in the suit: it shut out the parties to the record; and in other respects it was hemmed in and circumscribed. But one by one, all these limitations have been abrogated, and the whole tendency of courts and legislatures now is to admit all evidence, and to allow the court or jury to judge of its credibility and its sufficiency, in view of all the surrounding circumstances of each particular case. But in an argument submitted to the committee and printed with the reports, I have discussed this part of the question at full length, and sustained the proposition by numerous citations from the highest authorities; and to that argument I respectfully refer the House.

Such, Mr. Speaker, are the rules, decisions, and course of reasoning from them, upon which, even in a court of common law, the admissibility of the declarations here objected to might be maintained. But I propose to ascend now to higher principles; to a more liberal tribunal and more enlarged jurisdiction; to a forum where public rights are investigated, and where the parties are the people. The House, in respect to contested elections, is, as one of the earliest writers upon the subject has observed, "as well a council of State, and court of equity and discretion, as a court of law and justice;" and applies, therefore, the legal rules of evidence rather by analogy and according to their spirit, than with the technical strictness of the ordinary judicial tribunals. Very early in the history of the Government—in 1793—Mr. Smith, of South Carolina, an able lawyer and sound statesman, said, in a contested election, that—

"The House had been told that *hearsay testimony* was unworthy of attention, but he wished to remind them that they were not, like a court of law, restricted to proceed upon regular proof, and not go beyond the letter of it; *they were entitled to hear and weigh every thing advanced*, and to form their opinion from the *general conviction arising upon the whole circumstances*."—*Cont. Elections*, 80.

And in a controverted election tried in Philadelphia in 1851, under a special statute of Pennsylvania, the learned judge who heard the case said: "*This is a great public inquiry* in which the community are most deeply interested, bearing upon and affecting rights and the exercise of them that lie at the basis of our whole Government." * * * "*It is not a suit, but a public investigation;*" and upon that ground, his colleague concurring, he set aside the common-law rule upon the subject, and admitted the parties to the record to testify. And this same distinction between these two jurisdictions, was recognized by the court of Queen's Bench as far back as the reign of Queen Anne.

Such a tribunal, then, is not to be circumscribed by the narrow technicalities of the common law. It has its own *cursus curiæ*, its practice and its precedents; and where these are silent, it ascends up to the principles of human nature and the springs of human conduct; to that law which is "the collected wisdom of ages, combining the principles of original justice with the boundless variety of human affairs."

And who, Mr. Speaker, are the parties before this august tribunal? Not the returned member and myself. No; we are but the John Doe and Richard Roe of the Record. We claim only on demise by the people. Every elector and every citizen, nay, each inhabitant of the district, certainly every voter at the election of 1856, is a party. They are the constituency who are here demanding representation in this Hall. It is not the paltry salary, the "provoking gold," nor yet the honor, high though it may be, of a seat upon this floor, to one or the other of us, that gives value and moment to this controversy. It is because the rights of a hundred thousand people are concerned. We are but their agents and attorneys; neither of us is the only or real party in interest; but every voter and all the voters at the election here controverted are the true parties before your tribunal. And applying now even the ordinary principles of the common law to this testimony, *every voluntary admission or confession*, whether as to qualification or as to vote, by any one having voted at that election, is receivable in evidence. The proposition is too clear for argument.

Upon what principle, then, is this testimony to be rejected? Because it is said to be *hearsay*, and to come without the sanction of the *oath and cross-examination*. Sir, however valuable or necessary these tests may be in mere private judicial investigations, if they were to be required in the ordinary affairs of life, neither the political, social, nor business relations of the world, nor even individual existence, could be maintained for a single day. From the first breath we draw in infancy to the last moment of our lives, we are dependent for all, except what lies within the narrow circle of our own vision or experience, upon this selfsame hearsay testimony. The whole history of the world, from the creation down to the events of yesterday, is founded upon it. Most of our knowledge of the arts, sciences, geography, astronomy, is derived from it. From the highest and most momentous transactions of government down through successive gradations to the most trivial concerns of individual life and conduct, we are accustomed to act upon it. Do you tell me that great empires and States—Persia, Greece, Rome—rose, flourished and fell hundreds of years ago? that historians, philosophers, statesmen, artists, potent monarchs, and famous poets, lived and died centuries since? How do you know it? Do you believe in the Copernican system of astronomy, and teach your child that the earth turns upon its axis, and revolves round the sun? How do you know that? Do you tell me that many thousand miles off beyond the ocean there lies a vast empire called China, with more than a hundred millions of people? Have you seen it? Did you hear it sworn to? How do you know that Washington lived, or that the Declaration of Independence was adopted by the Continental Congress, or that the siege of Yorktown occurred? Has some old man of a hundred years told you? and did you stop to administer the oath and subject him to a cross-examination? Are you sure to-day that Napoleon is Emperor of France? or Victoria Queen of England? Do you believe that rebellion exists in India? or that the Palmerston Ministry fell the other day from power? Sir, in all these things, as in that which pertains to the world to come, *we walk by faith and not by sight*; and to discard and cast aside whatsoever does not come to us under the ordinary sanctions of judicial investigation, is to banish all books, to dry up all the fountains of knowledge, to arrest all progress, to subvert all civilization, and to degrade mankind, and each particular man, to the lowest depths of ignorance and skepticism.

Why, sir, the very existence of that rule of the common law which excludes hearsay is proved or known only by that same kind of evidence itself. It is found in books not written or published under the usual sanctions of forensic courts. It is traditionary—*lex non scripta*—and, like a custom, it is of the very essence of its validity that, in theory at least, it should have existed *from a time whereof the memory of man runneth not to the contrary*. But I pursue this inquiry no further. My purpose has been solely to meet and repel the notion that this testimony is to be treated only with contempt.

I proceed now, Mr. Speaker, to what will, no doubt, be regarded by the lawyers of the House as of much more importance—I mean the parliamentary and congressional precedents upon this subject. Sir, this is no longer an open question in England. It was settled one hundred and fifty years ago, just as I claim it. It was the ancient practice—it is the modern practice. On a single shelf in your library are twenty-six volumes of reports and treatises on election cases decided in the Parliament of Great Britain during that long period, from 1699 to 1853, presenting an almost unbroken array of authorities in favor of the admissibility of this evidence. By resolution of the House of Commons in the great Grimsby case, in the former year, it was admitted; and again in the Bedfordshire case in 1715, by a vote of ninety-eight to sixty-six; and yet again in the Yorkshire case in 1735, by a vote of one hundred and eighty-one to one hundred and fifty-two, the petitioner was allowed to give evidence of what a voter confessed of his having no freehold, who, at the election, had sworn that he had. Subsequent to these decisions a new mode of conducting contested elections was instituted by the Grenville act of 1770—a mode continued substantially till to-day. By that act, election committees are made a sort of judicial tribunal, acting under special oath, and deciding the case in secret and by ballot; but before whom counsel, and oftentimes the ablest lawyers of the realm, are heard. Forty-nine members are selected by lot; and from this list, thus chosen, each party strikes a name alternately till thirteen remain. These constitute the committee, and a separate committee is selected in each case. Regular reports, as in courts of common law, have been preserved of the decisions of these committees. I select cases from the earliest, the middle, and the latest of these reports. From the *Worcester* case, decided in 1776, I read the following:

"The counsel for the sitting members objected, in the beginning of the cause, to the admission of evidence to prove the *declarations of voters* that they had been bribed," [and, therefore, under the bribery act, forfeited the right of suffrage.]

"The committee, however, admitted such evidence as against the voters themselves, *so as to annul their votes*, but not as against the sitting members so as to disqualify them."—3 *Dougl. Elec. Cases*, 276.

Again, from the *Leominster* case, in 1796, I read the following:

"Francis Weaver was objected to by the sitting member as having received parish relief within the year (and thus, as being a *pauper*, not qualified to vote); and John Gethin was called to prove a *confession* of Weaver made *after* the election, that his wife had been relieved by the parish. This was objected to, as being *subsequent to the election*, [it being thus impliedly conceded that if made *before*, it would be admissible.] But the committee resolved, 'that the *declaration of a voter which tends to destroy his vote*, is admissible, whether made *before* or *after* the election, unless that declaration goes to affect the voter with penal consequences.'"—2 *Peckw. Elec. Cases*, 296.

But as will presently appear, the distinction here taken by the committee has since been overruled.

Again: from the *Ipswich* borough case, in 1835, I read the following:

"In this case (Brown's case) the voter was objected to by the petitioners, on the ground of bribery, and in the course of the investigation, a question was put to the witness who came to prove the *declarations* of the voter as to his being bribed, what was the purport of the certain conversations he had with the voter relative to a bill. The question having been objected to, and counsel heard on both sides, the committee resolved, 'that evidence of declarations of voters in the admission of bribery, *whether before, during, or after the election*, is admissible.' The vote was ultimately struck off the poll."—*Knapp & Ombl. Election Cases*, 387, 388.

And the same decision was made upon another vote in the same case. And yet again: from the county of *Carlow* contested election, in 1837, I read the following:

"Mr. Maule objected that *declarations* of John Nowlan were not evidence against the sitting member." * * * * * * * *

Mr. Thesiger, [recently elevated to the Lord High Chancellorship of England, in reply, said:]

'In the Southampton case, it was held that evidence may be given of the declaration of a person even *after* voting, though it may tend to affect him with penal consequences; the dividing point was there made at the time of striking the ballot. In the Ripon case, the voter had stated to two persons in the months of June and July, 1832, that he had no vote, and that his aunt was tenant of the house; the election took place in the beginning of 1833, and the declarations were held admissible. A voter who has voted for the sitting member, is always considered as a party, and it is on that ground that his declarations are admissible. *The question is always considered to be between the voter and the party questioning his vote, and not merely between the sitting member and the petitioner.*' The committee resolved that the evidence be received."—*Falc. & Fitzh. Election Cases*, p. 72.

And the same ruling was adopted in 1842 in two cases; in 1843; in 1848 in two cases; and finally in the St. Alban's case in 1851. And between the first of these decisions in 1699, and the last, seven years ago, I find and refer to the following additional cases also:

[Mr. Vallandigham here read a list of the cases.]

Here then, sir, are thirty-six cases in all, running through a period of one hundred and fifty years, and presenting thus an array of authorities scarce ever found on any subject in any court. And besides all these, in the treatises upon this subject by Simeon, Chambers, Male, Rogers, Montague and Neale, Clerk, and Samuel Warren—the last as late as 1853—this evidence is recognized by *all* as admissible in every case of *scrutiny of the poll*, or election contested because of illegal votes; and one of the latest of these writers expressly says, that in such cases "the *statements* of voters are not open to objection as hearsay, as they are looked upon then as *parties to the suit*."

And so they all say. I find also the same doctrine—though founded upon a very small part of the authorities to which I have referred, and they the earlier—laid down in a note by the learned reporter, in 3 McCord's South Carolina Reports, 230, 233:

"The following heads may be made when declarations (or hearsay) may be given in evidence, namely: * * * * * * * *

"22. The *declarations* of a voter may be given in evidence to set aside the election; *as to diminish the poll by taking an incompetent vote off*, or to prove bribery, &c.; but they are not admissible on a charge against the candidate for bribery, &c. They are admitted to annul votes, but not to set aside the election by disqualifying the member on account of his bribery," &c.

Finally, sir, it is recognized and adopted as sound law—though founded again upon but a small part of the authorities I have cited, and they again the earlier, and confined here to but a single class among those cases where it is admitted—in that standard practical treatise upon evidence by Phillips, with Cowen & Hill's notes, more weighty and valuable even than the text. From the third volume, page 322, I read the following:

"7. Another exception to the rule that hearsay is not evidence, has been adopted in summary inquiries into the validity of elections to the Legislature, on complaint that votes were obtained by bribery. *The declarations of voters may be received as evidence of the bribery.* This is, however, only to *annul votes*, but not to sustain a charge of bribery against the candidate, with a view to disqualify or affect him, otherwise than by vacating his election."

I trust now, Mr. Speaker, that this long series of adjudications by the Parliament of Great Britain, the high character of the committees, the great men—some of them of historic renown—who have composed these committees, the yet greater lawyers who have practised before them, and the high authorities by which their rulings have been recognized, are enough, in the judgment of the House, not only to rescue this evidence from the contempt with which it has sometimes been treated, but to establish, beyond all doubt, that it is the right and the duty of the House to receive and act upon it.

I pass now, sir, to the American precedents; and here a new or additional application, in part, of the rule is, in some cases, presented. In England, as in several of the States of this Union, elections are now, as they always have been, *viva voce.* Proof of the declarations of voters as to how they voted, can, in such cases, rarely become necessary, and hence the decisions and authorities there, of course, do not often present this application of the rule. But, in every instance where the question has arisen, as in the Windsor case, in 1807, where, by mistake, the poll-lists failed to show for whom the voter challenged had voted, the evidence has been received just as in any other case. And, besides, the *nature* of the evidence is precisely the same. It is equally hearsay, *if at all.* But the voters being parties to the proceeding, any declarations or admissions by them, pertinent to the issue, are equally admissible; and accordingly the distinction does not appear ever to have been set up.

I have already quoted from the speech of Smith, of South Carolina, in 1793, upon this question. I refer also, in brief, to the cases of Kelly and Harris, in 1813; Easton and Scott, in 1816; Reed and Cosden, in 1821; Letcher and Moore, in 1834; in all of which this question was considered, and the evidence, with or without qualification, received; and I find no case where, as to either qualification or vote, it has been wholly rejected, except Newland and Graham, in 1836. But subsequent to this came up the great New Jersey "Broad Seal case" of 1840, where the direct question, especially as to the *vote*, was considered, and solemnly decided unanimously by the committee. I read from the report of the majority, as follows:

"Although in numerous instances the voter being examined as a witness, voluntarily disclosed the character of his vote, yet in many cases he either did not appear, or appearing, chose to avail himself of *his legal right* to refuse an answer on that point. In such cases the proof of *general representation as to the political character of the voter*, and as to the *party to which he belonged* at the time of the election, has been considered *sufficiently demonstrative of the complexion of his vote.* Where no such proof was adduced on either side, proof of the DECLARATIONS of the voter has been received, the date and all the circumstances of such declarations being considered as connecting themselves with the questions of credibility and sufficiency. In every instance where the proofs under all the circumstances were not sufficient to produce conviction, the vote has been left unappropriated."—*House Reports*, 1839–'40, *No.* 541, p. 699.

From the report of the minority, page 749, I read the following:

"If an unlawful vote be cast, how are we to ascertain who had the benefit of such vote? It is obvious that in many cases it will be impracticable to obtain positive proof. In some cases the voter may be willing to appear and disclose the fact under oath; in other cases it may be in the power of the party to produce a witness who can swear to the character of the vote given; but in many more no evidence of that description can be obtained to ascertain the fact in controversy. *It seems to the undersigned to be indispensable to receive secondary evidence*—['substitutionary' they should have said, for it is not secondary in a technical sense, being the confession or admission of a party]—to this point, such as the DECLARATION of the voter, either at the election or *soon after*, and also proof of his *political character*, which, when well defined, will be a sufficient guide to the truth. But we ought to be very careful not to receive and act upon evidence of an equivocal character, which may have been created or manufactured for the occasion."

Such, Mr. Speaker, was the solemn and deliberate decision, unanimously, of the ablest and perhaps the most partisan election committee ever appointed—a committee which agreed in scarce any thing else—and certainly in the most bitterly contested partisan election case ever brought into the Halls of Congress—a committee numbering among its members John Campbell of South Carolina, Truman Smith of Connecticut, Gov. Medill of Ohio, John M. Botts of Virginia, Governor Thomas of Maryland, Aaron V. Brown of Tennessee, and Millard Fillmore of New York. And the precedent thus established by them—I say *established*, for if ever a congressional precedent can be regarded as authority, this is the highest—has been generally approved and acquiesced in ever since. It has never been overruled by either a committee or the House: and never but once—in the last Congress—has a contrary doctrine been suggested, and that in a minority report, and in a case where but one vote was involved; where the question was not discussed; where no authorities, not one, appear to have been examined; and where also, as to that single vote, there was hearsay upon hearsay offered as proof. But, upon the other hand, this New Jersey precedent was distinctly approved by the minority in Farlee and Runk in 1846, and Munroe and Jackson in 1848; and in neither case questioned by the majority.

I come now, Mr. Speaker, to the second point which I proposed to discuss. Sixteen "mulattoes and persons of color" are proved to have voted at the election here controverted. The report of the gentleman from Mississippi (Mr. LAMAR) finds that *fifteen* of these persons (one being left unappropriated) voted for the returned member, and deducts them from his poll. The separate report of the gentleman from Illinois, (Mr. HARRIS,) upon the ground of alleged want of evidence as to the others, deducts only one; while the other adverse report, by the member from North Carolina (Mr. GILMER), silently refuses to deduct any of the sixteen. It ignores the whole question of colored voters, assigning no reason for the refusal to deduct them from the poll of the returned member. But the argument submitted in his behalf before the committee, and printed with and expressly made a part of that report, places it partly upon the ground that these persons of color were qualified electors of Ohio, and partly because of the alleged insufficiency and incompetency of the evidence. The proof as to one of these mulattoes is direct: as to four others it consists of their declarations or admissions; as to all it is circumstantial, also. The evidence is summed up in the report to which I have first referred, and is there shown to be just such as is recognized by all the precedents and authorities, and has been heretofore received and acted on by committees and the House. I shall not discuss it. If, after having duly considered all the several facts and circumstances thus summed up in that report, any member of the House can conscientiously say in his heart that he is not satisfied that these mulattoes and persons of color voted for the returned member, let him act accordingly. One circumstance only I will allude to—a fact disclosed in the testimony. In the third ward of Dayton there was carried to the polls, and placed upon the table where the ballots were being received, an old man of ninety—an imbecile, slavering in idiocy, the wreck of a once intelligent and most respectable citizen. With eyes wandering in vacancy, without power of mind, without power of limb—almost without power of speech—with more than the weakness every way of earliest infancy, he is not able to recognize even the friends whom he has known for twenty years—he sees nothing, hears nothing, knows nothing. But he was one of the old "Liberty-Guard," an original "Free-Soiler." And he is at last asked: Don't you want to vote against *slavery?* Don't you want to vote an *anti-slavery* ticket? A dim and shadowy recollection of the past stirs his brain; a glimmer of light breaks in upon the silent and deserted chambers of his mind. He answers "Yes;" and a *Republican ticket*, with the name of the returned member upon it, is placed in his palsied hand, and the arm moved towards the judge of election, who receives and puts the ballot in the box, exclaiming just afterwards: "I ought not to have taken that vote." Such, sir, was the spirit of the canvass of 1856. And what was the slavery against which he was thus asked to vote? *The enslavement of the African race*, which we of the North, who pro fess the Democratic faith, are continually charged with seeking to extend. And yet, am I now to be told, and by those, too, in defence of whose just constitutional rights, the political highways of the North are this day strewed every furlong with the victims of fanaticism, that those of the African race who voted at that same election are not *sufficiently* proved to have voted for the candidate of the *Republican party*, whose professed mission is perpetual warfare against those "twin relics of barbarism, polygamy and slavery?"

Were these mulattoes and persons of color, qualified electors of Ohio? That, sir, depends upon the constitution and laws of the State. I do not purpose now to discuss the question whether a State can confer the right of suffrage as to elections to this House, upon any but citizens of the United States. Fourteen years ago, a committee of elections unanimously decided, and were by a unanimous vote of this House sustained in it, that the naturalization laws of Virginia could not, or did not, confer that right. But it is enough to know that Ohio has chosen to make *citizenship of the United States* a qualification for her electors. The language of the constitution of 1851, is: "Every *white* male citizen of the United States." Two qualifications are here prescribed—color and citizenship of the United States. Were these mulattoes and persons of color "*white*," within the meaning of the constitution? That, sir, is a term of ancient and established signification in constitutional language. It needs no gloss; it has no synonym; it admits of no definition. It means *white—pure white*; and not any shade or any variety of shades between white and black. Such it is in philology and in the arts. White and black are the two extremes between which there is a large variety of colors. No artist ever confounds these terms; no man in ordinary conversation confounds them. He may speak of a dark blue, or a light brown, or a bright yellow; but never of a dark white, or a light black.

But the term "white," in constitutions, is a designation of race rather than color; and it is used in this country to distinguish primarily between the African race and all others—between a servile race and races which are free. Strictly, indeed, it may refer to the several varieties of the Caucasian race. But in constitutions, and in popular language in the United States, it is a word of exclusion against the whole negro race in every degree. Whoever has a distinct and visible admixture of the blood of that race, is not white; and it is an utter confusion of language to call him white. Sir, it is a question of vision, of autopsy: it is to be resolved upon actual view and by personal inspection rather than by pedigree. And the Almighty has marked the distinguishing character istics of the race so strong, he has furrowed them so deep, that they are not eradicated in several generations. The constitution of North Carolina has fixed the degree at the sixteenth: and this corresponds in fact, with the rule adopted generally by courts, North and South, that a distinct and visible admixture of negro blood, without reference to the exact proportions, degrades to the class of persons of color. I am aware, sir, that in Ohio a different rule was once declared: and a mere predominance of white blood held to make a man white. Sir, it would be easy to prove, as indeed in the unanswerable argument by the counsel for the contestant, it was proved before the committee, that this decision was never regarded as binding authority, even in Ohio: that it was absurd in terms and contrary to the whole course of legislation and adjudication in the United States and the several States; and above all, that no court of Ohio, or any other State, can bind this House by an interpretation of the term "white," a word of ancient and continual use in the constitutions, laws, and judicial decisions of nearly every State, and in the legislation and executive acts of the Federal Government, for a long series of years, down even to the last month. But it is enough, and more than enough for my purpose, that *since that decision a new constitution* has been adopted in Ohio, prescribing *citizenship of the United States* as a new and additional qualification for her electors, and that the Supreme Court of the United States has decided that men of the African race are not citizens of the United States.

Sir, as a State-rights man, I do not affirm that that decision is absolutely conclusive upon this House, or upon the Executive outside of the ordinary judicial proceedings, or upon the country. I was taught to deny that the Supreme Court is the final and absolute interpreter of the Constitution. Nevertheless, that tribunal, and the judges who compose it, are entitled to the highest respect; and their decisions upon any subject are very persuasive evidence of what the Constitution means, and what the law of the land is, in any court, and before every department of the Government. And in this particular case, so far, at least, as the question now before the House is involved, they have but affirmed the almost universal understanding of every one—lawyer, judge, statesman, and layman—from the beginning of the Government. In the constitutions and legislation of the States; in the judicial decisions and executive acts of the States; and in the legislation and executive acts of the Federal Government, the African has, from the first, been treated and dealt with, every way, as an inferior, degraded, and outcast race. No man dreamed that he had part or lot in the Government; and that, too, even where there were no words of direct exclusion. Sir, fifty years after this Government was organized, the Supreme Court of Pennsylvania resolved that persons of color were not qualified electors of that Commonwealth, although her constitution did not, in express terms, confine the right of suffrage to those who were white. And about the same time, Connecticut, through her highest tribunal, anticipated the Dred Scott decision by a quarter of a century.

But I will not re-argue the case. It stands to-day the law of the land; and, so far at least as the question now before the House is concerned, it enunciates the sentiment of a vast majority of the people of this country.

But it has been said that the judgment of the Supreme Court denying citizenship to Africans and their descendants is not applicable here, because those of that race who voted at the election were *nearer white than black*, and therefore not within the Dred Scott decision.

To this I might well answer that there is no proof, except as to one, of the shade of color or proportion of blood; that they are all described by every witness as "mulattoes and persons of color"—men "of mixed negro blood," with a "distinct and visible admixture of negro blood," and so admitted to be by the judges of election; and that, if there be any such distinction or exception, the testimony must show affirmatively that they are within it. But I take broader ground. I deny that any such absurd distinction is recognized, or even intimated, in the letter or the spirit of the decision. In the judgment of the court, and in the several opinions of the judges, McLean and Curtis included, the whole race is spoken of interchangeably throughout, and described as "negroes," "mulattoes," "persons of color," "Africans and their descendants"—men "of African descent," without once, anywhere, in any one single line or syllable, so much as an allusion to any such distinction. The entire race is continually put in contrast with the white race named in the Articles of Confederation, in the naturalization laws, in the constitution and laws of nearly all the States of the Union. The court followed but the legislation, the jurisprudence, and the common understanding of the whole country. Sir, when Massachusetts—I mean antediluvian Massachusetts—Massachusetts in the egg—in 1705 enacted a law "for the better preventing of a spurious and mixed issue," providing, among other things, that if any "negro or mulatto should presume to smite or strike any person of the English or other *Christian* nations," such presuming African should be "severely whipped" at the discretion of the justice before whom convicted, did it ever occur to any of the Dogberrys of that age that the spurious and mixed quadroon and mustee, Ethiopian visibly all over, was yet not included in the act because nearer white than black? No, sir; that refinement in constitutional jurisprudence was reserved to their descendants a hundred years later in northern Ohio.

Again, the naturalization laws of the United States provide only for the admission of *white* aliens to citizenship. May your courts, I ask now, under those laws naturalize the quadroons, and mustees, the bright mulattoes of Hayti? Sir, some of you "Americans" think it quite enough to naturalize the Irish and German emigrants who land upon our shores; and are you prepared now to extend the rights of American citizenship, by a liberal interpretation of the word "white," to the "spurious and mixed" subjects of Faustin Solouque, and to send them to fill up your Territories under new and improved emigrant aid societies in New England?

Again, the several acts of Congress abolishing the slave-trade, forbid the traffic in "negroes, mulattoes, and persons of color." Are the Representatives of New England willing that the mixed and spurious colored population, slave or free, of Brazil, shall be made the subject of the "traffic in human flesh," under the pretext that they are nearer white than black? Would a Northern judge, or a Southern judge, or any judge, discharge a prisoner indicted under those acts, upon this miserable subterfuge? Again, is this same spurious and mongrel population to gain admission under this pretense, from any quarter, into those States of the Northwest, whose constitutions forbid residence to persons of color within their limits? Or do your Masonic lodges, in refusing membership to men of the African race in that ancient and accepted brotherhood, recognize a distinction or exception in favor of those of that race who are "more than half white?" Then why, I ask, shall it be set up or tolerated only at the BALLOT-BOX, that peculiar institution of the FREE WHITE MEN of this country? Sir, even Ohio has begun to retrace her policy; she has changed her constitution, and two years ago passed a law defining the term "persons of color" to mean those who, "in whole *or in part*," are of the African blood.

Finally, sir, if these sixteen mulattoes and persons of color *are* white male citizens of the United States, because they are nearer white than black, then they are eligible to membership of this House, and to sit upon this floor as your peers. Sir, the time may yet come when they shall meet you here at the threshold, clad in "the shadowed livery of the burnished sun," but without so much as the modesty of "mislike me not for my complexion:" without even the proffer of the Prince of Morocco to "make incision *for these seats*, to prove whose blood is reddest;" but with rude boldness dash in, demanding their rights in this Hall. Are you prepared for that? Sir, you have already been threatened with Fred. Douglas, whiter than the lightest of these sixteen; and in his person, in a little while longer, you may have to meet this question again.

But it has been said that the decision of the Supreme Court app es only to those persons of color whose ancestors were imported into this country and sold as slaves; and that it is not made to appear affirmatively in the testimony that these mulattoes and persons of color who voted, were descended from such ancestry. Very true, sir, the plea in abatement upon which the issue was made up averred that Dred Scott was descended of African ancestors thus imported and sold; and the letter of the decision, of course, conforms to it. But, in the absence of proof to the contrary, the court might well have assumed the fact as a part of the public history of the country and of the world, which needed not to be proved. But be that as it may, this House, in a matter pertaining to its own peculiar jurisdiction, and in the exercise of its high powers as a part of this Government, has a right, and is bound to take notice of the great public facts in its history. Now, does not every man know, as a part of that history, that no African of the negro race ever came to America by voluntary emigration? So said the Supreme Court. I quote from the opinion by the Chief Justice, page 411:

> "No one of that race had ever migrated to the United States voluntarily; all of hem had been brought here as articles of merchandise."

And even since the abolition of the slave-trade, none have ever come of their own accord or as freemen. England and France, indeed, have both pretended to open up facilities for a free emigration from Africa. And with what result? At the bar of public opinion in each country—before the great forum of the world, they stand condemned as restorers of the slave-trade in disguise. The miserable juggle has been exposed. On the 11th of December last, Lord Clarendon said, in debate on this subject, that "there *could be no such thing* as a free emigration from Africa, and that the plan had utterly and entirely failed." And the Earl of Derby, now Prime Minister, in the same debate, denounced the scheme as identical in substance, if not in form, with the slave-trade itself; and in this sentiment Earl Grey concurred. And later still, on the 16th of March last, Lord Brougham and the Earl of Malmsbury, both declared in debate that it was impossible to regard the scheme of a free emigration of negroes in any other light than as an indirect revival of the slave-trade.

But, apart from all this, the reason of the rule applies equally to all of the African race, no matter how they may have come to our shores. No negro emigrant could be naturalized. It is not alone his descent from slaves in this country, that degrades him in the scale of social and political being. It is his color and his blood. It is because he is the descendant of a servile and degraded race almost from the beginning of time. The curse of Ham pursues him in every age, and all over the globe. Bayard Taylor—no apologist for slavery—speaks but the testimony of history when he writes from Nubia, in Upper Egypt, that—

> "The only *negro features* represented in Egyptian sculpture are those of slaves and captives taken in Ethiopian wars of the Pharaohs; and the temples and pyramids throughout Nubia, as far as Daref and Abyssinia, all bear the hieroglyphy of monarchs; and there is no evidence in all the valley of the Nile, that the *negro race* ever attained a higher degree of civilization than is at present exhibited in Congo and Ashantee."

Sir, no wise people will ever in any manner encourage the attempt to elevate such a race to social or political equality. And if the question of law were here doubtful, I might well demand upon these high motives of public policy, that the doubt should be resolved against the race. Above all I would urge these great considerations now and in future, against this same spurious and mongrel issue, in whose behalf a relaxation of the policy is demanded. Look to Spanish America. Look at Mexico. The blood of the conquerors was lost in the veins of inferior and outcast races, and Mexico has no "people" to-day. With no tyrant strong enough to bind her down, and no yeomanry fit for self-government, she is the sport of faction, and the prey of anarchy and bloodshed; and to-day the spirit of the murdered Guatemozin, wandering three centuries through the halls of the Montezumas, gluts itself with revenge.

Sir, it is this same spurious and mongrel race who constitute your "free negroes," North and South. They will not be slaves, and they are not fit for freemen. And when this Government shall be broken up, and the fanaticism of the age shall have culminated in the North in Red Republicanism and negro equality, and the South shall have driven out her free negroes upon you, and you shall have stolen away her slaves, then your troubles with this race, which already has plagued America for a century, will but have begun. They are your petty thieves now; they rob your larders and your sheep-cotes; they do fill up your penitentiaries, and they would fill up your hospitals and your alms-houses, *if you would let them*. *Then* they will be your highwaymen; your banditti; they will make up your mobs. With just enough of intelligence, derived from a white ancestry, to know, and enough of brutishness, inherited from the old African stock, to avenge, in any form, the ignominy and degradation of four thousand years; with fetish ideas of religion and fanatic notions of politics, they are the *sans culotte*, who, led on by the worst of white men, will make your revolutions and overturn your governments. Sir, such things have already occurred in history. They are not the baseless fabrics of a vision. No wonder the States of the Northwest have begun to erect constitutional barriers stronger than ever against a negro population. In all this there is eminent wisdom and a statesmanlike foresight.

But I have no time to pursue this subject farther. I thank the House now for the courtesy and attention with which they have heard me throughout, and regret only that I have been obliged to appear, for the first time in this Hall, in the character of a contestant.

REMARKS ON IMPEACHMENTS,

In the House of Representatives, December 14, 1858.*

MR. SPEAKER:—I do not rise to speak upon the facts of this case, nor, indeed, to discuss any thing; but rather to state briefly the conclusions at which I have arrived, and the reasons which control my vote.

I begin just where the gentleman from New York (Mr. C. B. COCHRANE) began. Before inquiry into the facts in any case, it is essential first to comprehend clearly the law or the principles to which they are to be applied. By what law, then, are we governed? Upon what principle ought this House to proceed in ordering an impeachment? In what scale shall we weigh, by what rule shall we measure, the facts in this case? What, sir, is an impeachment under the Constitution of the United States, and by the House of Representatives? Sir, this case has been heard and argued all along as though it were a *trial*, and a trial by criminal law, under a penal statute, and it has just been so argued by the gentleman from New York. Certainly the mistake is most natural; and the course pursued by the committee—I speak it most deferentially—a course sustained by but one precedent, and that not in the United States—has, in my judgment, caused all this embarrassment. They have heard the whole case; have examined witnesses in full and at length on behalf of the accused, and have reported not only the whole testimony before them, but elaborate arguments in defence of the conclusions at which they have severally arrived. But all this does not change the nature of an impeachment; nor the duty of the House.

And here, sir, at the very threshold, it becomes us to lay aside old habits and associations. Whoever hears of an impeachment, thinks involuntarily of great orators and great criminals; of Cicero and Verres, of Burke and Hastings; splendid visions rise up before him. Every lawyer, too, turns at once to Hale's Pleas of the Crown, or Chitty's Criminal Law, for the rule and practice governing impeachments. Now, sir, against all this, I maintain that impeachment with us is not a criminal

* These remarks were made on the resolution to impeach Judge WATROUS, of Texas.

proceeding at all. We are not a grand inquest; we are not a grand jury; and all analogies drawn from them, tend only to mislead and confuse. Impeachments in England and the United States are two essentially different things. They differ in the persons who may be impeached; they differ in the object of the impeachment; they differ in the nature and jurisdiction of the tribunal, and in the punishment that follows upon conviction. In England, the high court of Parliament is strictly a criminal court, and a court of public and general jurisdiction. It is so treated in all the books; and it is as much, and as closely bound by the rules of law and evidence, as is the Court of King's Bench. All persons—Lords and Commons, officers and private persons—may alike be tried by it; they may be tried for any offence, and may be put under arrest pending the trial.

The punishment is the same as upon conviction, in any other court, extending even to the death penalty; and the nature and the purpose of the tribunal is the punishment or suppression of crime.

Not so under our Constitution. The Senate of the United States is not a criminal court established for any such purpose. It has no criminal jurisdiction. It exercises no judicial power other than impeachment; and even here its power is not strictly judicial. None but civil officers are subject to impeachment, and the judgment—not the punishment, for that word is not used—extends no further than removal from office and political disability. The accused is not liable to arrest, and the case may proceed, though he should refuse to appear. There can be no conviction unless two-thirds of the Senate concur; and neither life, liberty, nor estate is affected by it. Though the offender were the President of the United States, a great State criminal, convicted of treason, hatched and consummated here within the very capital; yet could not a hair of his head be touched. You could not even put him under arrest pending the trial, and more than this, neither conviction nor acquittal by the Senate can be plead in bar of an indictment for the same offence, pending in a court of ordinary criminal jurisdiction; nor can the judgment of the Senate be given in evidence on such trial.

These incidents, sir, all indicate unmistakably that impeachment with us is not a criminal proceeding, and that we are not to look for the rules and practice which govern it to the common law of England, nor yet even to the usages of Parliament, but only to the Constitution of the United States and our own practice under it. By that instrument it is limited and defined; and we are as much bound to respect the definitions and limitations as any other part of the Constitution.

What, then, palpably, are the objects of impeachment under our Government? I answer, first, restraint upon public officers; and secondly, the removal of such as shall in any manner misdemean. Except, indeed, so far as it may be regarded as a restraint upon those who hold office for a fixed term, it is of value only or chiefly to offices held for life. These are the judges of our Federal Courts, and they are answerable before no other tribunal; they are subject to no other check; our Constitution has exacted no other security for their good behavior, and even this is not imperative to its full extent upon the Senate. Political disability does not necessarily follow upon conviction, since the Senate may do no more than remove from office. Impeachment, sir, is no engine of oppression here. There is no danger of its abuse. Indeed, the difficulties which attend upon its successful prosecution render it of little value even as a restraint. Tyranny is always simple in its appliances, and will never resort to such cumbrous machinery as impeachment.

What, I inquire next, are the *offences* for which impeachment lies under our Constitution? Gentlemen have argued as though some great crime must be charged, in order to justify it. Not so; treason, bribery, and high crimes, are indeed enumerated; but that is not all. Misdemeanors, also, are included. Whoso shall *misdemean* himself in any civil office, shall be liable to impeachment, and this is especially so in the case of the judges of our Federal Courts. They hold office "during good behavior." Misdemeanor is misbehavior. It is so in lexicography, and it is so in law. I read from Blackstone:

> "In common usage, the word 'crime' is made to denote such offences as are of a deeper and more atrocious dye; while smaller *faults* and *omissions* of less consequence, are comprised under the gentler name of misdemeanors only."

What, then, is judicial misbehavior or misdemeanor? That, sir, depends wholly upon the standard which you shall fix for judicial character and conduct. Mine, I confess, is the highest. I would have both as pure as the "fann'd snow, that's bolted by the northern blasts twice o'er," and as spotless as the ermine which was once the emblem of judicial purity. The integrity of the judge ought to be above suspicion in his great office. I would have him the *sanctissimus judex* of the Romans; for to the litigant in his court he stands in the place of God. Save impeachment, he is subject to no responsibility except an enlightened conscience, and a religious sense of duty. Theoretically, indeed, the judiciary is in every country, to a great extent, of necessity an arbitrary power. Even when hedged in by law, there yet remains the vast field of "judicial discretion;" and beyond all that lies the boundless ocean of the "interpretation of Laws"—the great business of the judge. Sir, there are ten thousand ways in which a corrupt, a weak, or a prejudiced judge—a judge hostile or friendly to the litigant, or what is more common, the lawyer, may pervert justice, pollute its pure fountains, and do foul wrong in the cause; and yet none but he who has suffered know it. These are the false weights which it is so easy, unperceived, to throw into the scales of justice. Add now, to all this, that the judicial power, like the invisible and impalpable air which surrounds, penetrates everywhere and affects every relation of life; that it extends even to life itself, to liberty, to property in all its infinite complications; to marriage, divorce, parentage, master and servant, and finally pursues us even after death in the distribution of estates; nay, that the very monuments of the dead, the dull, cold marble in which they sleep, are the subjects of its destroying or protecting hand.

There is no department of the Government, therefore, which is so liable to abuse as the judiciary; but, to the honor of America and human nature be it said, there is none where so little abuse prevails. In seventy years this is the first example of the impeachment of a judge demanded because of alleged corruption in office for private gain. Arbitrary and dissolute judges have indeed been impeached, though but in two or three instances during that long period; yet none for corruption. But if infrequent, it is nevertheless the most atrocious, and in its consequences to the judiciary and to the public the most dangerous crime which a judge can commit: for "there is no happiness, there is no liberty, there is no enjoyment of life, unless a man can say, when he rises in the morning, I shall be subject to the decision of no unjust judge to-day."

What, I inquire next, is the province of the House of Representatives here? The Constitution defines it. You have the sole power of impeachment. What is it to impeach? Certainly not to try; that is the sole right of the Senate. To impeach is simply to accuse. We do not try, we have no right to try, the question of the guilt or the innocence of the accused. I have not in this case made up my mind definitely upon that point, because I am not willing to usurp the province nor anticipate the judgment of the Senate.

We are not judges; we are not grand jurors; we do not act under special oath; we are not here exercising judicial power; we are not acting in our representative capacity. Our province is to accuse—to prosecute; and when your Committee shall appear at the bar of the Senate, they will impeach or accuse in the name of the House of Representatives. In that high court of impeachment, also, we sit during the trial as accusers. We are bound, therefore, by no mere technical rules of law and evidence. We are under no obligation other than that highest of obligations—a sense of duty alike to the people and the accused. Into our hands the Constitution has committed the guardianship—and in the case of offices held for life, the sole guardianship—of the rights of the many who do not hold office against the few who do. Certainly, sir, no man ought to be lightly accused of even official misconduct or abuse of public trust. But where there is no other restraint or redress; where the office is judicial and for life; where the trust is so delicate and momentous in its nature, and so open to abuse; where public opinion usually is silent, and even the Press cares not to speak out; this House ought, in my judgment, to be, if not swift, certainly not slow to listen to the complaints of those who invoke its process to summon the accused into court. All other courts stand open, night and day, and it is the high constitutional right of every citizen to demand their process as of course. But between this high court of impeachment, which alone under our Constitution holds the power of redress of official wrong and oppression, stands the House of Representatives. Am I not right, then, in saying that we ought not too hastily to deny the only process by which such oppression and wrong may be redressed? If, indeed, the case be palpably frivolous, or the prosecution plainly malicious, it is our duty promptly, if not indignantly, to refuse. Can any one, will any one, say that this is such a case?

But it has been said that there is too much doubt and perplexity in this case, and that, therefore, there ought to be no impeachment. Not so. We have no power to try and acquit; and these very perplexities and doubts, if, indeed, any such there are, especially after the accused has been heard fully in his defence, are, of themselves, enough to justify this House in sending the case to the Senate for adjudication. What! shall we deny to Judge Watrous's accusers the only process by which he can be brought into court and put upon trial.

Let it be remembered that the charge is corruption, and the accused a judge. Sir, I, too, am for the independence of the judiciary; but I am for its purity first. Howsoever I might vote upon the question of the life tenure and mode of appointment of the judiciary, in a convention assembled to frame a new Constitution for the United States, I am opposed to any change of that instrument in these respects now. But I will be the more exact, fifty-fold, in enforcing the only other restraint and remedy which the Constitution has devised. Corruption, moneyed corruption—and we have heard it from high authority—is steadily, though with noiseless but most guilty tread, stealing into other departments of our Government. Legislation here, it is said, has been controlled by it; and this House has not been slow to appoint committees of investigation founded upon but rumor alone. Sir, some years hence—I dare not say centuries—seats in this House may perhaps be openly bought and sold. They have long been merchandise in the House of Commons. But in England the judiciary is pure and incorrupt, and England still survives. For one, Mr. Speaker, wheresoever else in this Government corruption may come, or how far soever elsewhere it may be carried, I demand that there shall be preserved one citadel at least, within which public virtue may retire and stand intrenched.

These, then, in my judgment, are the principles, and these the considerations, upon which the House ought to proceed and be governed in ordering impeachment; and applying them now to the testimony reported by the Committee, I am obliged to vote for this impeachment.*

REMARKS ON THE TARIFF.

In the House of Representatives, February 24, 1859.

Mr. Chairman: I would very much prefer to speak upon the tariff, when a bill relating to that subject shall be under consideration; but it is evident that at this late day either no such measure will be brought in, or if brought in, then under such circumstances as will of necessity preclude debate. I feel obliged, therefore, to speak to-night, and in Committee of the Whole.

Five parties, Mr. Chairman, are interested in all that pertains to a tariff: the Government, the consumer, the shipper, including of course the importer, the producer of raw material, and the manufacturer. The immediate interest of these several classes, except shipper and consumer, is diverse. It is the immediate interest of the Government—and I begin with it because it is for its sake alone that the power to create tariffs is conferred—that the duties laid shall yield the largest amount of revenue; of the consumer and shipper, that there should be no tariff at all; of the producer of raw material, that the highest rate of duty should be laid upon it; of the manufacturer, that the raw material should be free, and the highest rate of duty laid upon the article manufactured, which goes forth to the consumer. A similar division, having reference to the different sections of the Union, might no doubt also be made; but I do not

* "There is much force in the remark, that an impeachment is a proceeding *purely of a political nature.* It is not so much designed to punish an offender, as to secure the State against *gross official* misdemeanors."—1 *Story on the Constitution*, § 803.

"It [impeachment] is designed as a method of *national inquest into the conduct of public men.* If such is the design, who can so properly be the inquisitors for the nation as the representatives of the people themselves? They must be presumed to be watchful of the interests, *alive to the sympathies, and ready to redress the grievances of the people.* If it is made their duty to bring official delinquents to justice, they can scarcely fail of performing it without public denunciation and political desertion on the part of their constituents."—*Ibid.*, § 689.

propose to consider the subject directly, in that particular view, at this time.

In every tariff, the conflicting interests of these several classes, to which I have just referred, ought to be adjusted in accordance with the proportional importance of each. The wants of Government are, indeed, to be restricted to the lowest standard of rational economy; and no more revenue collected than is sufficient for these wants at that standard; for it is not the business or right of this peculiar Federal Government of ours to protect for the sake of protecting, or to encourage for the sake of encouraging, any of the great interests, as they are called, of the country. To do that belongs to the reserved rights and powers of the States. Commerce, even, is not an exception. Congress may "regulate" commerce; but to regulate, is not to foster it at the expense of other interests not enumerated in the Constitution. Congress may "promote the progress of science and useful arts, by securing for limited times to authors and inventors the exclusive right to their respective writings and discoveries." But even here, though a class—not, indeed, of the great industrial interests, as in political economy they are called—is named, yet the right to promote science and useful arts is expressly limited to patents and copyrights. Congress may also "dispose" of the public lands; but it must dispose of them in a constitutional way, and for a constitutional purpose.

Nevertheless, it is the sacred duty of this Government, in the exercise of the high powers committed to it, to have the strictest care that none of these great interests suffer detriment by its action; and, accordingly, in laying a tariff, Congress is under the highest obligation, first, to limit the aggregate of revenue to the lowest amount consistent with the necessities of economical government; because it is the interest of shippers, and, above all, of the consumers, who constitute the vast mass of the community, that there should be no tariff at all. Second. To select as well the raw material, when produced in this country, as the manufactured article, for taxation; because it is the interest of the producer, also, to have the highest price for the thing produced. Third. To select the manufactured article; because otherwise the consumer of manufactures would escape his just proportion of the burdens of government; and in selecting the several articles, and fixing the rate, it is the duty of Congress to regard that fundamental principle of republican government, the greatest good to the greatest number; or, better yet, the least evil to the greatest number; and that other capital rule of just taxation everywhere and in every form: *the least burden upon those least able to bear it.* And if, sir, we would but divest ourselves, in laying duties, of the notion that they are any thing else but *taxes*, that the object is taxation, and all tariffs but tax-laws—if we would call things by their right names, we should have less controversy, and less evil, too, to the country, because of false notions and false action upon this vexed question.

Theoretically, indeed, it may be maintained that Congress ought, under the Constitution, to regard the revenue only in the selection and the rate imposed. But this is not now, never has been, and never will, in practice, be strictly observed. Why are not coffee and tea taxed? Neither is produced in the United States. The consumption is great, and the demand and importation, of course, great also. They would yield a handsome revenue. But they are not taxed because they are reckoned now among the necessaries of life, and the burden, therefore, would fall upon millions little able to bear it. Then, sir, there is a departure, there must be a departure, the people will have a departure in practice, from the strict theory of revenue alone. And such, too, is the usage among the several States in enacting tax laws. There is no "protection" there in taxation, and by no vote of mine shall there be "protection" here, falsely so called, in the form of a tariff. But every wise legislator and economist consults the temper, the interests, and the necessities of the people whom he would tax.

But it has been the natural, perhaps, certainly the common mistake of all, and the universal mistake of the friends of what is called "protection," that tariffs are to be laid peculiarly with reference to the interests, and for the benefit, of the manufacturer; and, from the beginning of the Government to this day, the debates in Congress, and books, pamphlets, and newspapers, throughout the country, have been filled with statistics and arguments founded upon this assumption. I am aware, sir, that it is argued, also, as it has just been argued by the gentleman from Pennsylvania [Mr. KUNKEL], that whatever benefits the manufacturer benefits the whole country; and that a "home market" is fraught with numberless blessings to the consumer. Well, sir, all this sounds very fine in theory; but, until it shall be established that fostering manufactures tends necessarily to the multiplication of the human species, or an increase in the capacity of the human stomach, pardon me, sir, if I do not believe it. Will he who manufactures iron or wool eat more than the man who grows flax or raises sheep? Can the operative of Lynn or Lowell digest better than the operative of Leeds or Manchester? Will there be a greater demand for flour, beef, and pork, in New England and Pennsylvania alone, than in all the rest of the world and Pennsylvania and New England together?

But I return to the direct question. I am no friend to the act of 1857. It is peculiarly a manufacturer's tariff, and a highly protective tariff, too; in my judgment for them the most "protective" tariff ever enacted. It "protects" in two modes; for there are two modes of "protection." It admits the raw material free, and it lays also a duty upon the manufactured article. Never was there sharper practice than in the passage of that act. It is entitled "an act *reducing* the duty on imports:" and it does reduce duties, and the reduction is apparently great. Revenue it certainly has reduced. But mark you, sir; how does that reduction work? Select the single article of wool. Under the act of 1846, all wool paid thirty per cent., and manufactures of wool twenty-four per cent. But now wool under twenty cents a pound, is free; and manufactures of wool reduced from twenty-four to nineteen per cent. Thus, the manufacturer yields six and gains thirty per cent. by the dexterous manœuvre of the 3d of March, 1857. And thus, too, are the interests of the producer, and especially of the agriculturist of the West, sacrificed for the benefit of the manufacturing interests of New England; and to-day, New England would have no change in the tariff.

I concede very readily, that in the aggregate of taxation, viewing it solely as a tax, the act of 1857 is less onerous than any former tariff, and in two years, perhaps, and with a heavy importation, it might yield a revenue sufficient for an economical Government. But as a tax, simply, it is not equal and just; and in modifying it, whensoever it shall be modified, I insist that it shall be made to conform throughout, to the just principles of taxation which I have laid down. Sir, it is my good fortune to represent, in part, an agricultural State, and especially an agricultural district. We have two millions and more of consumers, and a vast multitude of producers; and if there must be, and I think that there ought to be, at an early, but fit time, a revision of the tariff upon just principles of taxation, and for the purposes of revenue, after a reduction of expenditures to the lowest rational point, I demand that, in adjusting it, you shall regard the interests of Ohio and the West.

Sir, I have said that Ohio is peculiarly an agricultural State. With two millions and a half of people, she has twenty-five millions of acres; twenty millions occupied by or attached to farms; eleven millions actually cultivated; four hundred thousand land owners; a greater number of farms, and more tillable surface, proportionally, than any State in the Union. The cost value of her land is $600,000,000; her agricultural products worth $132,000,000, equal to the whole cotton crop of the South; and her entire taxable property is $900,000,000. She is the first wheat, the first wool, and the first corn growing State; the first wine-producing, also; and, as my Cincinnati colleagues will attest, the foremost in the production of swine. Her animal products, alone, equal $40,000,000, and the value of her butter, poultry, and eggs, would of itself support half the State governments of New England.

And yet, Ohio is a part, and a small part only, of the great Mississippi valley, that most wonderful of all the portions of the globe, the very Garden of Eden in the new creation in the political apocalypse of the Bishop of Cloyne, "time's noblest empire:" the seat, too, doubtless, of empires older than Thebes, prouder than Tyre, nobler than Nineveh, but whose memorials have perished even beyond ruins or tradition; yet destined once again to become the seat of an empire to which you, ye proud men and wise men of the East, will yet come, bearing your frankincense and your tribute.

But I rose, not, sir, to descant upon the opening glories of the West. I was speaking of my own State and of her agricultural greatness. Nor will I abate one jot or tittle from her manufacturing interests, for she is rich in all that constitutes a State. And I beg Pennsylvania to remember that the area of her coal-fields but little exceeds the area of the coal-fields of Ohio; that Illinois and Virginia are both before her; and that, in the production and manufacture of iron, Ohio, if not the second, is certainly the third State in the Union. Yet right here let me add, that her hay crop alone equals the whole value of her manufactures of iron in all its forms. But, Mr. Chairman, the coal dealers, and the ironmongers of Ohio are not here besieging Congress for tariffs and bounties to protect them from ruin. They are content—I am sure they ought to be content—with the four-and-twenty per cent. already levied upon the consumer. They scorn, as I think they ought to scorn, your favors, and will earn still, as they always have earned, their bread by the sweat of their brows. Nor do I believe that Pennsylvania has fallen from her high estate, her revolutionary greatness, when one of the most eminent of her sons repelled the bribes of George III., saying, with the true spirit and in the very language of a patriot, "Sir, I am not worth purchasing; but such as I am, the King of England is not rich enough to buy me." I commend Pennsylvania to her early virtue and her ancient independence. Let her go home and look to the sturdy and the manly industry of her sons, and not to the favors and largesses of Government for protection and for riches.

Iron is more in common use, and more a necessary of life, than coffee and tea; and is it not quite enough that the consumers, who are the many, should pay twenty-four per cent. or one-fourth its value? Sir, whoever pays his blacksmith a bill of forty dollars, pays nearly ten dollars, or one-fourth, in duty, for the benefit of the manufacturer. And right here, let me say to the people of Pennsylvania, to whose "sober second thought," borne down now by depression of trade everywhere, I look with just confidence, and to her politicians, too, who are pressing this question to the utmost, but whom that self-same sober second thought will send back into obscurity, bringing again to public life the men who shall be found true to principle and to the Constitution, but who may perish now before the storm, that the import of coal into the United States very little exceeds the export; that it already pays a duty of twenty-four per cent., or nearly one-fourth of its value; and that every year the quantity drawn from her mines has steadily increased; but especially that the depression in her iron interest, at this moment, is not attributable to the reduction of duty (only six per cent.) upon that article by the act of 1857, since the importation last year of iron and its manufactures of every kind, was $9,000,000 less than in the year preceding, and $12,000,000 less than in 1854. It is because the consumption of iron is diminished, and therefore the demand less, amid the general depression of trade and business for the last eighteen months, by reason, too, of which, all other interests, also, have suffered, that her furnaces languish. But returning trade and reviving business will put them all again into blast, without the aid of tariffs and contributions levied upon her sister States.

But, Mr. Chairman, I have pursued this line of remark further than I intended. I rose not to discuss the tariff generally, but to select and speak upon two particular products in which my own State is especially interested, but which are utterly sacrificed in the tariff of 1857, for the benefit of the manufacturer and the dealer, and to give notice that should a bill be brought before the House, I will, at the proper time, propose the necessary amendments—I refer to LINSEED and WOOL.

I do not know, sir, by whose fault it happened, but so it is, that a distinction is made in the act of 1857 between linseed and flaxseed. The language of the schedule is "linseed, but not embracing flaxseed, free." Now, sir, there is not a practical agriculturist who does not know; there is not a professor of theoretical, scientific agriculture, who ought not to know; there is not, I venture to affirm, a member even of that assemblage of agricultural savans who convened in this city the other day, under the auspices of the Commissioner of Patents, who is ignorant that linseed and flaxseed are precisely one and the same thing. It is so in every lexicon and in every cyclopedia. It is so in your "Commerce and Navigation," and in your finance reports; and it was so regarded in the earlier tariffs. Linseed is *linen semen*—the seed of flax; and the result has been that every bushel of flaxseed is admitted duty free.

Mr. DAWES. Will the gentleman from Ohio allow me to explain the difference?

Mr. VALLANDIGHAM. I understand the gentleman from Massachusetts; but he will pardon me. I have been too long accustomed to observe, if not to practice, agriculture, not to know that whatever nice distinctions may be drawn by dealers for their own benefit, there is no difference. And let me say to him, that the same happy blunder occurred in the act of 1846, linseed being rated at ten per cent., and flaxseed at twenty; but no "linseed" was ever imported at ten; the Government taking good care to collect the twenty per cent. upon it, by whatever name called vulgar or classic. The Secretary of the Treasury held to Shakspeare's notions, about names and roses, and struck for the highest revenue. But, under the tariff of 1857, "linseed, not embracing flaxseed," being made duty free, the draughtsman of the act, marvellous to relate, quite forgot to provide a separate schedule for flaxseed which he had so carefully distinguished from "linseed." There was no reciprocity here, sir; no "flaxseed, but not embracing linseed." And the result has been that *neither* has paid a dollar of duty to the government since.

Mr. COMINS. Who was the draughtsman of the act? Where did it come from?

Mr. VALLANDIGHAM. I cannot say of a certainty. I always suspected it to be of New England paternity—possibly from the firm of "Stone, Lawrence & Co."

But to resume. Here, then, is a heavy loss of revenue, and an unjust discrimination also against an article in which the people of Ohio and of the Miami valley are, above all others, interested. The sum total of flaxseed, or linseed, raised in the United States in 1850, was 562,307 bushels. Of this, Ohio alone produced 188,000, or more than one-third of the whole amount. After her, in the table, Kentucky stands next; and after her, New York and Virginia; but Ohio equals all three. The quantity has no doubt increased since, Ohio still retaining her pre-eminence. And Indiana now is also largely interested in the article. But the demand is much greater than the home supply, which is not great; because flax is an exhausting crop, and never will be extensively cultivated unless it commands a liberal price. Accordingly, the importation of flaxseed during the fiscal year ending in 1858, amounted to $3,243,174, a slight increase—$40,000—upon the imports of 1857. Under the tariff of 1846, flaxseed was rated at twenty per cent., and the duty in 1857 amounted to $600,764.80; and, had it remained at the same rate, it would have yielded a revenue last year of $648,000.

Unmanufactured flax is in the same category. Under the tariff of 1842, it paid $20 a ton; in 1846, fifteen per cent.; but, under the act of 1857, it is free. Here, again, besides the unjust discrimination against the producer in favor of the manufacturer, is a loss of revenue to the Government, amounting last year to more than $30,000.

But I pass on to the other and far more important article of wool. I have said that Ohio is the heaviest wool-growing State. The whole number of sheep in the United States in 1850 was 21,723,220. Of this number, Ohio had 3,942,929. In 1854, the number had increased to 4,845,189. It has decreased since; but still is 3,308,803. Now, it so happens that I represent the smallest wool interest of all the nineteen rural districts of the State; for out of the 3,300,000 sheep, Montgomery, Butler, and Preble number but 26,201. The immediate interest of my constituents in wool, therefore, is comparatively small; but the interest of the State is great. The wool clip of last year a little exceeded 10,000,000 pounds, valued at $3,000,000. The whole clip in the United States in 1850, was estimated at 65,169,660 pounds, worth $20,000,000. It hardly equals that amount, or sum, now; almost certainly, it does not exceed it; so that Ohio probably yields more than one-sixth of the entire quantity grown in the country.

Now, sir, from 1816 to 1857, wool costing ten cents a pound and over, had always paid a duty; and, during the greater part of that time, all wool paid some duty, more or less, according to the scale of the tariff. Under the Act of 1846 it was rated at thirty per cent., without reference to quality or cost. But, by the tariff of 1857, wool worth twenty cents a pound and under, at the port of exportation, is admitted duty free. Now, sir, in 1857, wool was imported to the value of $2,125,744, and being all subject to a duty of thirty per cent., paid in revenue the sum of $637,723.20. In 1858, the first year of the present tariff, the importation of wool of the value of twenty cents and under rose to $3,843,320, upon which a duty would have been levied under the Act of 1846, of $1,152,996. In the same year, wool worth more than twenty cents, was imported to the value of only $179,315; paying a duty of twenty-four per cent., of only $43,035.60. Thus the excess of free over dutiable wool in the first year of the Act was $3,664,005. Practically, therefore, all wool is free. And thus it is that the revenues of the Government are largely diminished; and, at the same time, the interests of the producing classes, and especially in Ohio, utterly disregarded in the Act of 1857. Sir, upon these two articles alone, the loss of revenue last year was $1,800,000.

Mr. PURVIANCE. Will the gentleman allow me to say this? The bill to which he refers, as framed in this House, did give the gentleman the protection which he demands. When it went to the Senate it was there taken in charge by Mr. HUNTER, and it was through the gentleman's own friends in the Senate that the protection which he claims was denied.

Mr. VALLANDIGHAM. I am not claiming "protection" at all. I demand only just and equal taxation. But the bill which first passed this House did admit wool worth fifteen cents duty free; and, more than that, if the value exceeded fifty cents, it was also free. It was this bill, and not that which finally became a law, which my colleague [Mr. STANTON] so vehemently assailed on the 20th, and again upon the 23d of February, two years ago yesterday in a debate to which I listened as a spectator in the galleries of the old Hall.

Mr. PHELPS, of Missouri. I would suggest, however, to the gentleman from Pennsylvania, [Mr. PURVIANCE] that the predecessor [Mr.

CAMPBELL] of the gentleman from Ohio was upon the committee of conference which agreed to that tariff bill in its present shape.

Mr. VALLANDIGHAM. Certainly my predecessor was on that committee of conference consenting to the report, and, as chairman of the committee of Ways and Means, conducted it through the House, to which it was reported on the 2d of March, and passed, as so much other mischievous legislation is passed, in the last hours of the session, under the Previous Question, having been read only at the desk of the Clerk.

Mr. COMINS. I wish to ask the gentleman if there is a pound of wool grown in his State, which is not protected at the rate of twenty-four per cent.?

Mr. VALLANDIGHAM. Perhaps not; and, according to the theory of the gentleman and his friends, the influx of foreign wool will forever forbid the production of cheap wools in the State; and thus the small farmer, without capital enough to deal in sheep of the finer breeds, be driven from the market. But upon the higher-priced wools the effect of admitting the article, when worth twenty cents and under, duty free, is indirect rather than direct. It is a premium for the manufacture of coarse woolens, and therefore—

Mr. COVODE. Will the gentleman allow me to correct him right here?

Mr. VALLANDIGHAM. No, sir, I cannot. I will yield to no one, friend or foe, in the midst of a sentence. I interrupt no one thus, and I will consent to no such interruption for any purpose. The dignity and decorum of this body, as an assembly of statesmen, are utterly degraded by these continual and persistent interruptions, corrupting all legitimate debate, and converting every speech into a maze or convolution of disjointed dialogues, and this Hall into a stage where each man plays many parts, but with none of the genius or the delicacy and refinement of the classic drama. Our debates, sir, are becoming now but empty or angry wrangles, in which assurance, petulance, bluff repartee, and mediocre smartness, assert supremacy over modesty, logic, learning, eloquence, and all the other qualities which become a statesman. I mean no disrespect to the gentleman from Pennsylvania, but he must pardon me for declining to yield.

To resume: I was about to say that the effect upon the costlier wools of admitting cheap wool duty free, was incidental rather than immediate, inasmuch as it directs capital to the manufacture of the coarser woolens, upon which there is a greater profit, to the neglect of the finer cloths, thus diminishing the demand for the higher priced wool, and of course decreasing the price.

But this is not all; for while the interests of the producer are thus disregarded in the admission of flax, flaxseed, and wool, free, good care is had that the several manufactures of these articles shall pay a sufficient duty; and accordingly flaxseed, oil and oil-cake, are rated at fifteen, and manufactures of wool at nineteen per cent.; and thus the producer is permitted to purchase back his linens, oil, oil-cake, and woolens, with the addition of fifteen and nineteen per cent. to the price at which he might have purchased them had they been placed in the free list, alongside of his free linseed, free flax, and free wool.

I have now said what I intended to say on this subject at the present time; and conclude with the notice that, should any tariff bill be reported at this session, I shall move, as a substitute, that the tariff of 1846 be revived for two years from the 1st day of July next, so that, meantime, a revision of the Act of 1857 may be had, adhering to the principle of *advalorems*, and also to all the other rules of equal and just taxation.

LETTER ON THE INVASION OF HARPER'S FERRY, 1859.*

DAYTON, OHIO, *Saturday, October* 22, 1859.

To the Editor of the Cincinnati Enquirer:

THE *Cincinnati Gazette* of yesterday contains what purports to be a conversation between John Brown, the Harper's Ferry Insurgent and myself. The editorial criticism in that paper, while unjust, is, nevertheless, moderate and decent in temper and language. Not so the vulgar but inoffensive comments of the *Commercial* and the *Ohio State Journal* of to-day. Self-respect forbids to a gentleman any notice of such assaults. But the report and editorial of the *Gazette* convey an erroneous impression, which I desire briefly to correct.

Passing of necessity through Harper's Ferry, on Wednesday last, on my way home from Washington City, I laid over at that place between morning and evening trains for the West. Through the politeness of Colonel Lee, the commanding officer, I was allowed to enter the armory inclosure. Inspecting the several objects of interest there, and among them the office building, I came to the room where Brown and Stevens lay, and went in; not aware till I entered, that Senator Mason or any

* Returning from a visit to Washington in October, 1859, Mr. VALLANDIGHAM was detained on the way, by the "John Brown" Raid, and was thus compelled to hear the first gun and witness the first shedding of blood in the great civil war in America. He held a short conversation with Brown, which being reported in the papers, he was violently assailed, and in reply wrote the letter here published.

reporter was present, and without any purpose of asking a single question of the prisoners; and, had there been no prisoners there, I should have visited and inspected the place just as I did, in all these particulars.

No "interview" was asked for by me or any one else of John Brown, and none granted, whether "voluntarily and out of pure good will" or otherwise. Brown had no voice in the matter, the room being equally open to all who were permitted to enter the Armory inclosure. All went and came alike, without consulting Brown; nor did he know either myself or the other gentlemen with whom he conversed. Entering the room I found Senator Mason, of Virginia, there, casually, together with eight or ten others, and Brown conversing freely with all who chose to address him. Indeed he seemed eager to talk to every one; and new visitors were coming and going every moment. There was no arrangement to have any reporters; nor did I observe, for some minutes after I entered, that any were present. Some one from New York was taking sketches of Brown and Stevens during the conversation, and the reporter of the *Herald* made himself known to me a short time afterwards; but I saw nothing of the *Gazette* reporter till several hours later, and then at the hotel in the village.

Finding Brown anxious to talk and ready to answer any one who chose to ask a question, and having heard that the insurrection had been planned at the Ohio State Fair held at Zanesville, in September, I very naturally made the inquiry of him, among other things, as to the truth of the statement. Learning from his answers that he had lived in Ohio for fifty years, and had visited the State in May or June last, I prosecuted my inquiries, to ascertain what connection his conspiracy might have had with the "Oberlin Rescue" trials then pending, and the insurrectionary movement at that time made in the Western Reserve, to organize forcible resistance to the execution of the Fugitive Slave Law; and I have now only to regret that I did not pursue the matter further, asking more questions, and making them more specific. It is possible that some others who are so tenderly sensitive in regard to what was developed, might have been equally implicated. Indeed, it is incredible that a mere casual conversation, such as the one held by me and John Brown, should excite such paroxysms of rage and call forth so much vulgar but impotent vituperation, unless there be much more yet undisclosed. Certain it is that three of the negroes, and they from Oberlin, and at least six of the white men, nine in all out of the nineteen, including John Brown, the leader of the insurrection, were, or had been from Ohio, where they had received sympathy and counsel, if not material aid in their conspiracy.

But the visit and interrogation were both casual, and did not continue over twenty minutes at the longest. Brown, so far from being exhausted, volunteered several speeches to the reporter, and more than once insisted that the conversation did not disturb or annoy him in the least. The report in the *New York Herald*, of October 21st, is generally very accurate, though several of the questions attributed to me, and particularly the first four, ought to have been put in the mouth of "Bystander," who, by the way, represents at least half a score of different persons.

As to the charge preferred of "breach of good taste and propriety," and all that, I propose to judge of it for myself, having been present on the occasion. There was neither "interview," "catechising," "inquisition," "pumping," nor any effort of the kind, but a short and casual conversation with the leader of a bold and murderous insurrection, a man of singular intelligence, in full possession of all his faculties, and anxious to explain his plans and motives, so far as was possible without implicating his confederates otherwise than by declining to answer. The developments are important: let the galled jades wince.

And now, allow me to add, that it is vain to underrate either the man or his conspiracy. Captain John Brown is as brave and resolute a man as ever headed an insurrection; and, in a good cause and with a sufficient force, would have been a consummate partisan commander. He has coolness, daring, persistency, the stoic faith and patience, and a firmness of will and purpose unconquerable. He is tall, wiry, muscular, but with little flesh, with a cold gray eye, gray hair, beard and mustache, compressed lips, and sharp aquiline nose; of cast iron face and frame, and with powers of endurance equal to any thing needed to be done or suffered in any cause. Though engaged in a wicked, mad, and fanatical enterprise, he is the farthest possible remove from the ordinary ruffian, fanatic or madman; but his powers are rather executory than inventive, and he never had the depth or breadth of mind to originate and contrive himself the plan of insurrection which he undertook to carry out. The conspiracy was unquestionably far more extended than yet appears, numbering among the conspirators many more than the handful of followers who assailed Harper's Ferry; and having in the North and West, if not also in the South, as its counsellors and abettors, men of intelligence, position, and wealth. Certainly it was one among the best planned and executed conspiracies that ever failed.

For two years he had been plotting and preparing it with aiders and comforters a thousand miles apart, in the slave States and the free; for six months he lived without so much as suspicion in a slave State, and near the scene of the insurrection, winning even the esteem and confidence of his neighbors, yet collecting day by day large quantities of arms, and making ready for the outbreak. He had as complete an equipment, even to intrenching tools, as any commander in a regular campaign, and intended, like Napoleon, to make war support war. He had Sharpe's rifles and Maynard's revolvers for marksmen, and pikes for the slaves. In the dead hour of night, crossing the Potomac, he seized the Armory, with many thousand stand of arms and other munitions of war; and, making prisoners of more than thirty of the workmen, officers, and citizens, overawed the town of Harper's Ferry with its thousand inhabitants. With less than half a score of men surviving, he held the Armory for many hours, refusing, though cut off from all succor and surrounded upon all sides, to surrender, and was taken with sword in hand, overpowered by superior numbers, yet fighting to the last. During this short insurrection eighteen men were killed and ten or more severely wounded—twice the number killed and wounded on the part of the American forces at the battle of New Orleans.

John Brown failed to excite a general, and most wicked, bloody, and desolating servile and civil war, only because the slaves and non-slaveholding white men of the vicinity, the former twenty thousand in number, would not rise. He had prepared arms and ammunition for fifteen hundred men, and captured at the first blow enough to arm more than fifty thousand; and yet he had less than thirty men—more, nevertheless, than have begun half the revolutions and conspiracies which history records. But he had not tampered with slaves, nor solicited the non-slaveholding whites around him, because he really believed that the moment the blow was struck they would gather to his standard, and expected furthermore the promised re-enforcements instantly from the North and West. This was the basis upon which the whole conspiracy was planned; and had his belief been well founded, he would unquestionably have succeeded in stirring up a most formidable insurrection, possibly involving the peace of the whole country, and requiring certainly great armies and vast treasure to suppress it.

Here was his folly and madness. He believed and acted upon the faith which for twenty years has been so persistently taught in every form throughout the free States, and which is but another mode of statement of the doctrine of the "irrepressible conflict," that slavery and the three hundred and seventy thousand slaveholders of the South are only tolerated, and that the millions of slaves and non-slaveholding white men are ready and eager to rise against the "oligarchy," needing only a leader and deliverer. The conspiracy was the natural and necessary consequence of the doctrines proclaimed every day, year in and year out, by the apostles of Abolition. But Brown was sincere, earnest, persistent; he proposed to add works to his faith, reckless of murder, treason, and every other crime. This was his madness and folly. He perishes, justly and miserably, an insurgent and a felon. But guiltier than he, and with his blood upon their heads, are the false and cowardly prophets and teachers of Abolition.

THERE IS A WEST; FOR THE UNION FOREVER; OUTSIDE OF THE UNION, FOR HERSELF.

SPEECH IN THE HOUSE OF REPRESENTATIVES, DECEMBER 15, 1859, UPON THE QUESTION OF ELECTING A SPEAKER.

Mr. Clerk: Desiring to speak at some length, and with some regard to method, upon the more important subjects which have been introduced into this debate, I cannot consent to yield the floor except upon a point of order, or for a strictly personal explanation. I claim no right myself to interrupt others for the purpose of interrogatory or catechising, and in return acknowledge no right in them to subject me to cross-examination as a witness upon this floor. I trust, along with other reforms, to see the ancient decorum and propriety of legitimate debate restored within these walls. In nothing, therefore, which I propose to say, do I mean to offend, by personal reflection upon any member of this House.

And now, in the first place, Mr. Clerk, allow me to say that I do not regret this discussion. I lament, indeed, that it has not, at all times, been conducted in a better temper. Had it been possible to avoid it altogether, certainly it would have been preferable that it had never been commenced; but no one familiar with the temper of the whole country, reflected back in the Representatives of the country, and concentrated here into one intense focus, could have expected a week to pass after organization without an explosion more formidable, perhaps, and in a more questionable shape. This, in my judgment, is a better time and mode in which to meet it than any other. But, gentlemen of the House of Representatives, let us conduct it at all times with the temper and courtesy which become a legislative assembly. And yet the admonition is almost needless here. Although within these walls are assembled the two hundred and forty-two Representatives and Delegates from the thirty-eight States and Territories of the Union, bringing with them every variety of personal and sectional temper and peculiarity; assembled, too, in the midst of a popular feeling more pervading and more deeply stirred up than at any former period, in one-half at least of these States, and upon the eve of startling, and, it may be, disastrous events, yet without organization, without rules, without a Speaker to command, or a Sergeant-at-Arms to execute—without gavel or mace—the instinct of self-government peculiar to the Anglo-Saxon race, and the habit of self-command and of obedience to but the shadow even of law and authority, have, for now these ten days past, secured us not only from collision and violence, but, for the most part, from breach even of the strictest decorum observed by our predecessors in this Hall at any period of our history. How sublime the spectacle! how grand this illustration of the spirit of free government! There is but one other country upon the globe where a similar spectacle could be exhibited.

I do not, then, regret this debate; it is fit and proper in itself. It is strictly parliamentary. You have a right by English precedent; you have a right by American precedent; by the usages of this House, to discuss the qualifications of your candidates for Speaker. If any member of this House has indorsed and recommended a book full of sentiments insurrectionary and hostile to the domestic peace and tranquillity of the country—a book intended or tending to stir up discord or strife between the different sections of this Union, or servile or other insurrection in any one or more States of this Union, and refuses still to disavow sympathy with the sentiments and purposes of such book, he is not fit to be Speaker or member of this House. Whether any one who has recommended such a book for wholesale circulation, not knowing, or caring to inquire into its character and contents—who has indorsed insurrection and violence in blank, and given a cordial letter of credit to whatsoever the Abolition authors of the "Helper book" might choose to say and to circulate throughout the South, is competent for Speaker, or fit to be trusted in the Speakership, this House must determine; and the country, gentlemen, must sit in judgment upon the decision.

But, Mr. Clerk, this whole subject and controversy has assumed a character and magnitude which impel me to break the silence which I thus far have observed. Sentiments have been avowed and statements made upon this floor which demand notice and reply.

[At this point Mr. VALLANDIGHAM gave way to a motion to adjourn, which was negatived. He then said that he should decline to pursue any farther that night the line of remark which he had proposed to himself; and, the House having again refused to adjourn, he proceeded to read and refer to matters which, forming no part of what he designed to say in the first place, are omitted here. (See Congressional Globe, page 159.) The House, after several other motions, having finally adjourned, the next morning he resumed as follows:]

Though a young man still, I have seen some legislative service. One of the earliest lessons which I taught myself as a legislator, and which I have sought to exemplify in every department of life, was so to be a politician as not to forget that I was a gentleman. There is a member of this House, now present, with whom, some years ago, I served in the legislature of my State, and to him I might with perfect confidence appeal to verify the assertion that no man ever was more exact in the observance of every rule of courtesy and decorum, not only in debate, but in private intercourse with his fellows. I might appeal, also, to the members here present of the last Congress, and to every member of this House of Representatives, and demand of them whether I have offended in any thing, in public or private, in word or by deed.

Now, Mr. Clerk, that courtesy which I thus readily extend to others I am resolved to exact for myself, at all times and at every hazard. I had a right, yesterday, especially after yielding for a ballot, at a time when the Republican party with confidence anticipated the election of their candidate for Speaker, to expect the usual courtesy, scarce ever refused, of an adjournment. If any gentleman, this morning, after a night's calm reflection, sees, in any thing that I have ever said or done, here or elsewhere, any justification for the extraordinary yet very discreditable scenes of yesterday, enacted by grown-up men and Representatives, I do not envy him the mental or moral obliquity of his vision.

Mr. Clerk, I heard it said many years ago, and my reading and observations of the proceedings of this House and of the Senate have taught me the truth of the declaration, that there was a marked difference between the deportment of the anti-slavery men in Congress toward slaveholders and their own Democratic colleagues from the free States. Sir, I want no better evidence of that fact than the occurrences of yesterday.

I said then, that if any member of this House had indorsed a book full of sentiments which were insurrectionary and hostile to the domestic peace and tranquillity of this country—a book intended or tending to incite servile insurrection in one or more of the States of this Union, and refused still, either by himself or through another, to disavow all sympathy with such sentiments, he was not fit to be Speaker or member of this House. That judgment I, this morning, deliberately reaffirm in all its length and breadth and significance. The other day the gentleman from Virginia (Mr. Millston), a slaveholder, distinctly declared upon this floor, with all the emphasis he could command, that any one who would incite a servile insurrection, or knowingly distribute books or papers with that design, was not only not fit to be Speaker, but not fit to live. There was then upon that side of this Chamber no sign, not even a whisper, of indignation or resentment. No, gentlemen, you sat in your seats, under that just but scathing denunciation, mute as fishes, and gentle as lambs. Even your candidate for Speaker started to his feet, and, with manifest trepidation, disavowed every purpose and sentiment of the kind. Now, gentlemen of the Republican party, once for all and most respectfully, not in the language of menace, but as sober truth, receive this message from me, greeting: I am your peer; I represent a constituency as brave, as intelligent, as noble, and as free as the best among you upon this floor—and in their name and in my own name, I tell you that just whatsoever rights, privileges, courtesies, liberties, or any thing else, you—whether from apprehension of personal danger or from any other cause—you, brave men at home vaunting arrantly there your rebukes here of Southern insolence and bravado—you, who return to your constituents at the end of every session bearing with you the scalps of half a score of fire-eaters from Alabama, Mississippi, or the Carolinas—you are accustomed to extend to slaveholders and Southern men upon this floor, I, as your peer, demand and will have at your hands. If you think otherwise, you have much yet to learn of the character of the man with whom you have to deal. I am as good a Western fire-eater as the hottest salamander in this House. (Laughter and applause.)

I have been served with a notice this morning that the Republican party here do not intend to listen to any further discussion. Very respectfully, I care not whether they listen or not. Let me tell them that the country holds its breath in suspense at the lightest word uttered in this Hall. The people of the United States are listening at this moment to catch every syllable which falls from the lips of the humblest member here.

I propose now, sir, to address myself to those subjects only which I designed, from the beginning, to discuss.

I have said, and repeat, that the sentiments which have been avowed and the statements made upon this floor demanding notice and reply impel me to break the silence which I have thus far observed. The North and the South stand here arrayed against each other. Upon the one side I behold numerical power; upon the other, the violent, even fierce spirit of resistance. Disunion has been threatened. Sir, in all this controversy, *so far as it is sectional*, I occupy the position of ARMED NEUTRALITY. I am not a Northern man. I have little sympathy with the North, no very good feeling for, and I am bound to her by no tie whatsoever, other than what once were and ought always to be among the strongest of all ties—a common language and common country.* Least of all am I that most unseemly and abject object of all political spectacles—"A Northern man with Southern principles;" but, God be thanked, still a United States man with United States principles. When I emigrate to the South, take up my abode there, identify myself with her interests, holding slaves or holding none; then, and not till then, will I have a right, and will it be my duty, and no doubt my pleasure to maintain and support Southern principles and Southern institutions.

* See *post*, page 442.

Then, sir, I am not a Southern man, either—although, in this unholy and most unconstitutional crusade against the South, in the midst of the invasion, arson, insurrection, and murder to which she has been subject, and with which she is still threatened—with the torch of the incendiary and the dagger of the assassin suspended over her—my most cordial sympathies are wholly with her.

Mr. Clerk, I have heard a good deal said here and elsewhere, about "Southern Rights." Sir, I have no respect—none—none—for Southern rights merely because they are Southern rights. They are yours, gentlemen—not mine. Maintain them here, within the Union, firmly, fearlessly, boldly, quietly—do it like men. Defend them here and everywhere, and with all the means in your power, as I know you will and as I know you can. Yorktown and New Orleans—the end of the Revolution and the end of the war of 1812—are both yours, and there is no power on earth that can subdue or conquer you.

But while I have no respect for Southern rights simply because they are Southern rights, I have a very tender and most profound and penetrating regard for my own obligations. Your rights impose upon me corresponding obligations, which shall be fulfilled in their spirit and to the very letter—three-fifths rule, fugitive slave law, equal rights in the Territories, and whatsoever else the Constitution gives you. (Applause). Our fathers made that compact, and I will yield a cordial, ready, and not grudging obedience to every part of it.

I have heard it sometimes said—it was said here two years ago, not on this floor certainly, but elsewhere—that there is no man from the free States, North or West, who is "true to the South." Well, gentlemen, that depends upon what you mean by being true to the South. If you mean that we, the Representatives of the free States of this Union, North and West, shall sit here within this Chamber, uttering Southern sentiments, consulting Southern interests, sustaining Southern institutions, and giving Southern votes, reckless of our own identity and our own self-respect, then I never was, am not now, and never will, while the Representative of a free State, be "true to the South;" and I thank God for it. If that be what is meant by "rottenness," in the other end of the capitol, commend me to rottenness all the days of my life.

But if you mean—and I know that a large majority of you do mean—true to the Constitution, without which there cannot be, and ought not to be any Union—true to our own obligations—ready and sedulous to fulfil every article of the compact which our fathers made, to the extremest inch of possibility, and yielding, gracefully and willingly, as in the earlier and better days of the Republic, every thing which comity and good-fellowship, not only as between foreign States, but among brethren demands at our hands, then I tell you, and I tell the gentleman from Tennessee, [Mr. Nelson,] that the great mass of the Democratic party in the free States, and especially in the West, and thousands and tens of thousands of others, not members of that party, are now, and I trust ever will be, true to the South.

Allow me to illustrate my proposition. There are in this Hall, as elsewhere, three classes of men. The Republican or anti-slavery man—and you, gentlemen, have, or have had, not a few of that number in the South—asks, whenever a measure is proposed here, will it tend to injure and hem in the institution of slavery? or rather, will it weaken or offend the South, because it is the South? and he subordinates every other consideration to the great object of suppressing slavery, and of warring on the South. Upon the other hand, the merely Southern man, and especially the Southern extremist, asks, how will this measure advance the interests of slavery, or, rather, how will it aggrandize the South as South? and his vote is determined or insensibly influenced by this consideration. There is yet another, a third class, who ask none of these questions, and are moved by none of these considerations; political Gallios, perhaps, the gentleman from Ohio (Mr. Corwin) would call them, who care for none of these things. To that class, Mr. Clerk, I am glad to belong. Outside of my own State, and of her constitution, I am neither pro-slavery nor anti-slavery; but maintain, as was said upon a memorable occasion, "a serene indifference" on this subject between these two sections. And here I stand upon the ancient, safe, constitutional, peaceable ground of our fathers. For many years after the foundations of this Republic were laid by wiser and better men—pardon me, gentlemen—than I see around me, no man ever thought of testing any measure here by its effects upon the institution of slavery. Never till the fell "Missouri question" reared its horrid front, begotten in New England, and brought forth in New York, was slavery made the subject of partisan and sectional controversy within this capitol. And we had peace in the land in those days, and patriotism and humanity and religion and benevolence; faith and good works. We neither had, nor demanded then, an anti-slavery Constitution, an anti-slavery Bible, nor an anti-slavery God; but the Constitution of the land, the Bible of our fathers, and that great and tremendous Being, who, from eternity, has ruled in the armies of heaven, and among the children of men.

Then, sir, I am not a Northern man, nor yet a Southern man; but I am a Western Man, by birth, in habit, by education; and although still a United States man with United States principles, yet within, and subordinate to the Constitution, am wholly devoted to Western interests. Sir, this is no new enunciation of mine here. I proclaimed it upon this floor one year ago, and now congratulate myself and the West in having found so able and eloquent a coadjutor in the person of the distinguished gentleman from the seventh district of Ohio (Mr. Corwin). Sir, I am o and from the West; the great valley of the Mississippi; of the free States of that valley, seated in queenly majesty at the head of the basin of that mighty river; yet one in interest, and one by the bonds of nature, stronger than hooks of steel, with every other State in that valley, full as it is, of population and riches, and exultant now in the hour of her approaching dominion. Seat yourself, denizen of the sterile and narrow, but beautiful hills and valleys of New England, and you, too, of the great cities of the North, whose geography and travel are circumscribed by the limits of a street railroad; seat yourselves upon the summit of the Alleghanies, and behold spread out before you a country stretching from the Alleghany to the Rocky Mountains—from the Gulf of Mexico to the Canada frontier—with limitless plains, boundless forests, fifteen States, a hundred rivers, ten thousand cities, towns, and villages, and twelve millions of people. Such a vision no man ever saw; no, not even Adam, when, in the newness and grandeur of God-made manhood, he stood upon the topmost hill of Paradise, and looked down upon a whole hemisphere of the yet unpeopled world. That, sir, is my country; if I may speak it without profanity, God's own country; yet, in this war of sections, I am of the free States of that valley.

Mr. Clerk, when I came to this city two years ago, I brought with me an intense nationality; but I had been here only a little while till I learned that a man without a section to cling to, was reckoned but as a mere cipher in the account; and from that hour, subordinate always to the Constitution, I became and am a WESTERN SECTIONALIST, and so shall continue to the day of my death. I, too, propose with the Leather Stocking of the "Prairie," to fight fire with fire. I learned here, Mr. Clerk, that while there was a North and a South, there was no West. I found her individuality sunk in the North. I saw that you of New York and New England entertained a profound respect for the citizen of South Carolina or Georgia, slaveholder though he might be, because he was east of the Alleghanies; and that you of Georgia and South Carolina reciprocated the good opinion, abolition aside, because the New Yorker and the Yankee lived very near to the rising of the sun; while the Western man was held to be a sort of outside barbarian, very useful to count in a trial of numerical strength, but of no value for any other purpose. We of the great valley of the Mississippi are perpetually ignored. Sir, if all this were done of studied purpose, it would at least be tolerable; but not so, there is no design in it. It is a cool, silent, persistent, unobtrusive, but most offensive disparagement. Gentlemen, you do not know us. It is but a few months ago that a great paper in the city of New York spoke of Judge Douglas as attempting—and it was in the very capital of the State—"to impose his absurd theories upon the honest *foresters* of Ohio." And about the same time another great paper in the North referred to Governor Chase as a public man of merely "provincial reputation."

Let not the gentleman from the Mansfield district (Mr. Sherman) flatter himself that he is to be an exception. No, Sir; he sees the parting rays of the setting sun too late in the day. A distinguished predecessor of his attained once the same point of greatness, but only to be let down gently in favor of Cape Cod. Do not deceive yourself. You were only put forward to be killed off; you were merely detailed as a follorn hope, to be shot down in front of that Malakoff which you never will capture. Oh no! though two thousand miles east of the Rocky Mountains, you are quite too far West. Your distinguished colleague from the seventh district (Mr. Corwin) is gazing now wistfully through a spy-glass in the direction whither your eyes are turned; but he, alas, any more than you, will never wake up from that delicious revery in which he now sits buried, to realize that—

> 'Tis distance lends enchantment to the view,
> And robes the Speaker's tribune to its radiant hue.

We did, indeed, gentlemen, once elect a Western President: but him you killed in a month—and a Southwestern President, too, and he survived you but fifteen months.

But, gentlemen of the West, the dayspring of our deliverance begins to dawn. Let us rejoice. The long period of our minority is about to terminate. Within the Union, after the next census, we of the Mississippi Valley will hold in our own hands the political power and the destinies of this country, and we will administer them for the benefit of the whole country. The day of our political independence is right now, while I speak. If you of the North and Southeast will conspire, as for the last seventy years, to control the power and patronage of this Government for your own benefit, we of the Mississippi Valley will combine to rescue them from your hands. If you of the whole North will continue your sectional warfare upon the whole South, know ye that we of the Northwest hold the political balance of power between you, and that we will use it to crush out and annihilate forever the fanaticism and treason which are threatening now to overspread the whole North, and very speedily to destroy this Republic. We will be ignored no longer. And here let me warn the Republican representatives from the West, that they have loaned themselves too long already to this proud and domineering North. You permit yourselves to be identified with the North, and to make common cause with her against slavery. *Cui bono?* Not yours; ah, no! You help to win the fight; you make good soldiers—excellent food for powder—but your Northern officers and Northern masters will divide the spoils. When William H. Seward threatens the South with the power and domination of the North, he means you; but when he would distribute office and patronage, he will know no West. Some of you dream that your Governor Chase will be the candidate of the Republican party for the next Presidency. Miserable infatuation! Cease, then, I beseech you, this unmanly vassalage to the North. If you will not hearken to the voice of patriotism, listen, at least, to the demands of independence and self-respect. If you will be sectionalists, lay aside this pestilent fanaticism on the subject of slavery, which you borrow servilely from the clergy, lecturers, and other demagogues of the North, and which they use for the purpose of their own aggrandizement—lay it aside, and be Western sectionalists. Talk not to me about humanity and benevolence. I have as profound and delicate an appreciation of them as you can have, but I will not be insulted with the miserable pretence. Are there no objects of charity in your own midst—no poor, no sick, no lame, no halt, no blind, no widows and orphans—to whose necessities you may administer, and thus find vent for that abounding river of humanity which wells up and flows out from the fountain of your hearts? Pardon me, but I despise and contemn your vassalage to the North as much as you can contemn and despise any man's servility to the South.

And now, one word to the gentleman from Pennsylvania (Mr. Hickman), who took refuge, the other day, in the "engine-room" of the left side of this Chamber, whence, through new and rudely-constructed port-holes, to send his missiles whistling into the camp which he so lately deserted. I admire his discretion—the better part of valor. Sir he spoke about precipitating eighteen millions of people upon eight millions. Whence does he propose to get his eighteen millions? Did he mean to include us of the Northwest? Does he imagine that we are militia-men to be drafted, or conscripts to be enrolled, and march forth at the sound of his drum, or to the notes of his bugle? I tell him that, if he means to raise the black standard of internecine war upon the South, he must find his recruits nearer home.

Mr. Florence (in his seat). He will not find them there. (Applause in the galleries.)

Mr. Vallandigham. I rejoice to hear it. But I tell the gentleman further, that, if the Territories of this Union are to become the subject of controversy after dissolution, we of the Mississippi Valley propose to keep them ourselves, and then to make fair and honest partition with each other.

I approach now, Mr. Clerk, a painful and most difficult subject—*periculosæ plenum opus aleæ.* A word which, for very many years after the organization of this Government, no man ever dared to breathe within this capitol, has now become as familiar as the most ordinary words of salutation. Not a day nor an hour passes, but the hoarse croaking of this raven is heard, piercing the fearful hollow of our ears, with mourning and dirge-like wail, the "NEVER MORE" of the Union of these States. Sir, in this war of sections, standing here between the living and the dead, we, the Democratic representatives of the West, and I, as one of that number, have a duty to perform, which, in all humbleness, but in all faithfulness, shall be fulfilled But too many of you of the North are striving with might and main to force the South out of this Union; and too many of you of the South are most anxious to be forced out. Do not deny it, either of you. I know it. Sir, if any member should rise here and tell me that there are no disunionists in the South, could I believe it? And when the gentleman from New York (Mr. Clark), or any one else, would persuade the South that there are no Abolitionists, or disunionists, in the North or the West, he only insults the intelligence of the men upon whom he would impose. Sir, if any colleague of mine, or any other gentleman from the free States upon this floor, will so far forget the solemn responsibilities of his office, in the midst of the great and most alarming dangers wherewith we are at this moment encompassed, and unintentionally, of course, misrepresent the true state of public sentiment and public action in the North and the Northern portions of the West, I, at least, will not consent to be a party to the deception. I tell gentlemen of the South that the doctrines of Hale, Banks, Seward, Giddings, Chase, Lincoln, and, above all, of the New York *Tribune*, are the doctrines of a large majority of the people of the North, and of a powerful and, for all efficient purposes of political action, a controlling minority, just now in the West. One column of editorial in the recognized organs of the Republican party of Ohio, circulating every day among the masses of the people, penetrating into the homes and hearts of every family, acting and reacted upon by the public opinion which they help to create, and by which the public men of this country are set up, or pulled down, at the ballot-box, is better evidence of the true Republican sentiment of Ohio than a thousand speeches from the distinguished member for the seventh District of that State (Mr. Corwin). Sir, I listened the other day, as I alway listen, with very great pleasure, to the genial and gushing eloquence from the lips of that gentleman, touched, as they are, as with a live coal from the altar of oratory. In the sentiments which he uttered here, there is much, very much, which meets my hearty concurrence; but I regret that truth and candor compel me to say that he does not represent the opinions and sentiments of the party to which he belongs. He claims, indeed, the leadership of that party. Pardon me—he is not only not a eader, but not even a respectful follower of the Republican party in that State. (Applause in the galleries.) Kentuckian as he is by birth, nobleman by nature—patriot as he is, and Whig as he once was, I know that he never will consent to "guard the baggage" of that vandal host. Yet am I sorry to say that, to him, more than to any other man in the State, the Republican party to-day are indebted for their political supremacy in Ohio. He it was, who, without power in his own party, yet controlled, at the late election, the fifty thousand conservative voters of that State who are not of the Democratic party, and misled them into the support of an organization and of principles with which he has no real sympathy at all. He went into the Republican party to control it for good—but he was only as a straw before the whirlwind. He finds now a barren sceptre in his gripe; and let me, with great respect, remind him that it is not conservative speeches which are needed here to save us, but conservative votes at home. Certainly, the vast majority of the people of Ohio, of all parties, are at heart opposed to insurrection and disunion; but I tell the gentleman that, if he would conquer abolition and sectionalism, he must fight them at the ballot-box.

Mr. Clerk, I do not propose to follow the gentleman into a discussion of the local politics of Ohio. I resolved, a good many years ago, to make no speech within a legislative assembly fit only to be spoken upon the "stump;" and to that resolution I propose steadily to adhere. But, inasmuch as the mere partisan politics of my State have already been drawn into a debate here, a passing remark may not be inappropriate from me as a Representative, in part, from that State—though, in truth, I can add little to what has been fitly, strongly, eloquently spoken by the gentleman from the twelfth District (Mr. Cox).

Something has been said—more, I understand, is to follow—in regard to the soundness of the Democratic party in Ohio, and in other States of the Union. Sir, I will spare gentlemen all trouble upon that point. The Democratic party in Ohio, some years ago, was not sound, as men count soundness now. You need not go back to the records, and reproduce them here. Open confession is good for the soul, and I make it. I speak the more freely, because I think—and there are hostile witnesses here present to attest it—that my own record, from the very beginning of this whole controversy concerning slavery as a political question, is as unimpeachable as the record of any man in the North or the West, and, I may add, the South, too; for let me admonish gentlemen from that section that many of the people of the free States were for a good while misled by the precepts, if not the practice, of some of the earlier, and the later fathers, too, of the Southern political church. A little charity, I pray you, upon this subject. The Democratic party of Ohio, very much after the fashion described by the gentleman from the seventh District (Mr. Corwin), adopted, in 1848, a certain resolution, in which they denounced slavery in the abstract, and, with valorous earnestness, declared that the *people* of Ohio would use all power clearly given in the constitutional compact to "eradicate," tear up slavery by the roots; *but*—there is much virtue in "but," as well as "if"—they further resolved, with refreshing consistency, protesting the highest regard for the Union, the Constitution, and the rights of all the States, that the *Democracy* of Ohio were of opinion that no power was conferred by the constitutional compact to institute any process of eradication at all. Sir, I am not here to commend the superior honesty of such a platform. The gentleman (Mr. Corwin), who is well posted and of mature years, has explained luminously how these things are done, even in Republican conventions; but I will not disingenuously pretend—of course, I have no allusion to my colleague—that these resolutions did not at that time express the sentiments of the Democracy of my State. I think that, so far as they were supposed to be anti-slavery in their character, they did express both the opinions and the feelings of a very large majority of the people of the State. Sir, I was a member of that convention, and of the committee on resolutions, and voted many times in committee, during a protracted session of two days, against any and every expression of opinion upon the question of slavery in any form. Like my colleague, I was overpowered; like him, I endeavored to make the best of it, seeking consolation in the second and sound part of the resolution, and whiling away my idle hours in the delicate task of reconciling the two branches with each other. My success in this somewhat difficult work was just about equal to the success of the gentleman (Mr. Corwin) who undertook a similar contract here, the other day. But, Mr. Clerk, at every subsequent convention I exerted myself to the utmost to procure a rescission of these resolutions; and, finally, in January, 1856, they were rescinded, and a sound platform adopted in their stead. From that hour the Democratic party has steadily gained strength. I pass by the election of Mr. Chase to the Senate, in 1848, the refusal by a State Convention to indorse the Baltimore platform, in 1853, and other unsound things, in faith or in practice, whereof the Democracy of my State were guilty in times past. "Let the dead past bury its dead." *Ernst ist das Leben.* Our business is to grapple manfully with the living realities of the present moment. Sir, in my judgment, the wisest man that ever lived was the author of the statute of limitations; all things adjust themselves equitably in periods of just about six years. Politicians, indeed, in later times, require, and, perhaps, are entitled to a shorter limitation. No man's record ought to be revived or called in question after the lapse of six months.

Allusion has been made to the present state of parties and of public sentiment in the North and West. Sir, I do not propose to speak at any length upon this subject. The events are recent, and no public man anywhere can have failed to observe them. It is folly to deny that, all through the North, and in many portions of the West, distinct and very earnest sympathy has been exhibited for John Brown in his recent insurrectionary and murderous invasion of Virginia; and that, too, not by the vulgar and low, but by men very high in political, social, and religious positions. Funeral processions, halls draped in mourning, tolling of bells, sermons, eulogies, orations, public meetings, adjournment of courts of justice, attempted adjournment of Senates and Houses of Representatives, and all the other usual insignia of public sorrow, bestowed only hitherto upon the great and the good, the patriots, the heroes, and martyrs of the world—all these tributes, and more, have been paid to the memory of a murderer and felon. Even in my own native State, and in a part of my own district, I lament to say that these sad evidences of a corrupted public sentiment have been exhibited. In Cleveland, fertile in revolutionary conventions, in Akron, in Cincinnati, and elsewhere, in public assemblages, and by other means equally public and significant, the sympathy of thousands has been expressed. Sir, it is vain to attempt to conceal what all this means. There is a public sentiment behind it all, or it never would be tolerated. Thirty years ago, John Brown, hung like a felon, would have been buried like a dog.

Allusion has been made also to the Union meetings held, or to be held, in the great cities of the North. Sir, I would not abate one jot or tittle from the true value, least of all, from the patriotism of these assemblages. When public meetings run along with public sentiment, they are powerful to mould and to give it efficiency; but when they do not beat responsive to the popular heart, they are of no value. No; one single page of election returns is worth more, as an index of real public sentiment, than all the Union resolves which shall be passed between this and the 4th of March, 1861. Let no man be deceived. If the distinguished gentleman from Tennessee (Mr. Nelson) be sincere—and I know that he is—in believing that the great mass of the people of the free States are opposed to the agitation of the slavery question in any form, and are ready to strike hands with any party which will put it down forever; if he really thinks that but a very small part of the people of the North sympathize with John Brown, or yield assent—a cordial and working assent—to the doctrines of William H. Seward, the "irrepressible conflict" included, full as it is of insurrection, treason, and murder; if he believes that, without the strong arm of the Federal Government, powerfully and in good faith stretched forth, fugitive slaves could be recaptured in one-half the free States of this Union, under any law of Congress, I can only say, that he has the mild virtue of an honest heart—most marvellous credulity. Sir, I entertain for that gentleman the very highest respect, but he must allow me to say that, aside from that portion of his remarks, the other day, which breathed so much of earnest, sincere, and eloquent eulogy upon the Union—one such speech, blinding the eyes of the people of the free States to the real public sentiment at the South, does more thus to keep alive the flames of civil discord between the South and the North and West, than a hundred speeches, vehement and impassioned though they may be, of the gentleman from South Carolina (Mr. Keitt). Sir, when a member of this House, of fine personal appearance, of sonorous voice, of classic education, and approved rhetorical excellence, tells us, with a magnificence of rhythm which regurgitates through these aisles, peals along these galleries, pierces the ceiling, and loses itself amid the columns and scaffolding of the unfinished dome of the capitol, that he will shatter this Republic "from turret to foundation stone," we are apt to understand that he is executing a grand rhetorical fugue, and that he is not half so much in earnest as he would have us imagine. But when a gentleman, mature in years, with a cold logic, a calm demeanor, but a sincere heart and earnest purpose, tells us, in the midst of invasion and murder—the legitimate and inevitable fruits of the "irrepressible conflict," which has been proclaimed against his own section—that he is not alarmed, and believes that no mischief is intended, we only understand that he invites aggression.

Sir, I am this moment reminded, by the appearance of the gentleman before me (Mr. Briggs), that I need no better illustration of the melancholy change in public sentiment, at the North, within the past few years. Here he sits, upon the only national side of this chamber, sole exemplar of the "lost politics" of the Whig party, faithful among the faithless, only he; sole representative of the flag of our country, solitary and alone, *e pluribus unum.* (Laughter.) Sir, does not all this mean something?

But I will pursue this subject no further. I find no pleasure in it. I have said, and I think the dullest among us cannot fail to discern it now, that there is danger, great and most imminent danger, of a speedy disruption of the Union of these States. Too many of you of the South desire it, and but too many of you of the North are either striving for, or reckless whether it comes or not.

Sir, I will not consent that an honest and conscientious opposition to slavery forms any part of the motives of the leaders of the Republican party. In the earlier stages of the Abolition agitation, it may have been otherwise, but not so to-day. This whole controversy has now become but one of mere sectionalism—a war for political domination, in which slavery performs but the part of the letter *x* in an algebraic equation, and is used now, in the political algebra of the day, only to work out the problem of disunion. It was admitted, in 1820, in the beginning, by Rufus King, who hurled the first thunderbolt in the Missouri controversy, to be but a question of sectional power and control. To-day it exists, and is fostered and maintained, because the North has, or believes that she has, the power and numbers and strength and wealth, and every other element which constitutes a State, superior to you of the South. Power has always been arrogant, domineering, wrathful, inexorable, fierce, denying that constitutions and laws were made for it. Power now, and here, is just what power has been everywhere, and in every age. But, gentlemen of the North, you who ignorantly or wittingly are hurrying this Republic to its destruction, you who tell the South to go out of the Union if she dare, and you will bring her back by force, or leave her to languish and to perish under your overshadowing greatness, did it never occur to you that when this most momentous but most disastrous of all the events which history shall ever to the end of time record, shall have been brought about, the West, the great West, which you now coolly reckon yours as a province, yours as a fief of your vast empire, may choose, of her own sovereign good-will and pleasure, in the exercise of a popular sovereignty, which will demand, and will have non-intervention, to set up for herself? Did you never dream of a WESTERN CONFEDERACY? Did that horrid phantom never flit across you in visions of the night, when deep sleep falls upon men? Sir, we have fed you, we have clothed you, we have paid tribute to, and enriched you, for now these sixty years; we it is who have built up your marts of commerce; we it is who have caused your manufacturing establishments to flourish. Who made Boston? What built up New York, till now, like Tyre of old, she sits queen of the seas, and her merchant-princes and traffickers are among the honorable of the earth? THE COTTON OF THE SOUTH, AND THE PRODUCE OF THE WEST. Maintain this Union, and you will have them still. Dissolve this Union, if you dare; send California and Oregon to the Pacific, compel the South into a southern confederacy, force us of the West into a western confederacy, and then tell me what position would you assume among the powers of the earth? Where then would be your pride and arrogance, your trade and business, your commerce and your dominion? Look at the map spread out before you. Behold yourselves, as Mr. Webster said of Austria, "a mere patch upon the earth's surface." And, gentlemen of New England, let me ask you, What if New Jersey, Pennsylvania, and New York should refuse to go with you? They may refuse. You are a peculiar people. (Laughter.) I cannot say God's peculiar people; for you have dethroned Jehovah, and set up a new and anti-slavery god of your own; and before one year, you will inaugurate the statue of John Brown in the place where the bronzed image of Webster now stands. (Applause and hisses.) But, suppose these three States refuse your fellowship. Then would be fulfilled the prophecy, uttered many years ago, of the re-annexation of New England to the British crown.

I know well, Mr. Clerk, that within the Union, we of the West are now, and, so far as business and trade are concerned, must ever remain, tributaries to the North. You have made us so by that magnificent network of railroads which stretches now from the Atlantic to and beyond the Mississippi. But be not deceived. That "vast inland sea" is *mare nostrum*—it is our Atlantic ocean. Once cut off from the powerful and controlling ties of a United Government, aliens and foreigners to each other, with police and espionage and armed force at every dépôt upon the frontiers, nature, stronger than man, would reassume her rights and her supremacy. You made the railroad and the telegraph, but God Almighty made the Mississippi and her hundred tributaries.

Is it not, I appeal to you, better then for you of the North, better for you of the South, better for us of the West, better for all of us, that this Union shall endure forever? Sir, I am for the Union as it is, and the Constitution as it is. I am against disunion now, and forever; against disunion, whether for its own sake or for the sake of any thing else, equal, independent, constitutional liberty alone excepted. Do you ask me when the hour for disunion will come? I tell you never, never, while it is possible to avert it; never, while we can have, within the Union, the just constitutional rights which the Union was first made to secure; never certainly, till the hour shall come wherein to vindicate the glorious right of revolution. I speak not of the abstract right of secession. Do you ask me when that hour will come? I cannot tell you. Of that every State and every people must judge for themselves, before God and the great tribunal of history. Our fathers, in their day and generation, judged of it for themselves in our great Revolution. There, gentlemen, is one precedent, at least, hallowed by success, and canonized in the world's history. American citizens dare not call it in question. I commend it to you. Study it; ponder over it; profit by it. I know, indeed, that it has been sometimes said that our fathers went to war about a preamble, and fought seven long years to vindicate a principle. But, gentlemen, I am not sure that there is not, in all this, somewhat of the flourish of rhetoric; a little of the "glittering generalities" of the Declaration of Independence. I fear it may not be safe for you to follow that precedent too closely.

Do you ask me whether the election of an anti-slavery, sectional, Republican president, upon a sectional platform, pledged to administer the Government for sectional purposes, would, *per se*, be a justifiable cause of disunion? I cannot tell you. But I do tell you, as a Western man, and I tell the gentleman from Tennessee (Mr. Nelson), that, when you of the South shall have attained the numerical power and strength in this Union, and shall then organize a Southern party, on a Southern basis, and, under the forms of the Constitution, shall elect a Southern President, for the purpose of controlling all the vast power and patronage and influence of the Government, by action or non-action, for the advancement of Southern interests, and, above all, for the purpose of extending slavery into States now free, with the design of making them all slave States, I will meet you as the Irish patriot would have met the invaders of Ireland—with the sword in one hand, and a torch in the other; dispute every inch of ground, burn every blade of grass, till the last intrenchment of independence shall be my grave. (Applause.) I will not wait for any overt act. What! Do I not know that fire will burn, that frost will congeal, that steel and poison will do their work of destruction to the human system, that I shall await the slow process of experiment to ascertain their natural and inevitable effects? Never—never! *Experimentum in vili corpore.*

These, Mr. Clerk, are no new doctrines in the country whence I come. Stronger sentiments, if possible, were uttered here upon this floor, ten years ago, by a distinguished predecessor of mine, the Hon. Robert C. Schenck, of Dayton, my fellow-citizen still, and the familiar friend of the eloquent gentleman before me (Mr. Corwin), an old-line Whig now, with a slight, very slight varnish of Republicanism.

Allow me, sir, to read what he said in a similar, though not so alarming, crisis in public affairs, on the 27th of December, 1849:

"If we of the Northern States"—

We had no West then, sir; her existence and geography have been ascertained, and settled since—

"If we of the Northern States would not vote for a Southern man, merely because he is a Southern man, and men of the South will not vote for a Northern man, merely because he is a Northern man; and if that principle is to be carried out from here into all our national politics and elections, what must be the result? Disunion. THAT ITSELF IS DISUNION. You may disguise and cover up as you please, but that it will be. It may, perhaps, be regarded as but the first step in disunion; but its consequence follows as inevitable as fate. One section—the North or the South—must always have the majority. Disfranchise all upon the other side, and the Union could not hold together a day; *it ought not to hold together upon such conditions a day.* On this floor we now have from the free States one hundred and forty Representatives, and ninety from the slave States. Suppose the relative numbers were reversed; would we submit to be denied all participation in privileges here? NOT FOR AN HOUR. And should we ask for such submission from others? NEVER. The Whig party say—never. The true people of the North say—never."

That, sir, was good Whig doctrine ten years ago. It was good American doctrine in 1856; and I aver here, upon my responsibility as a Representative, that it is good sound Democratic doctrine everywhere, and all the time.

Then, sir, I am against disunion. I find no more pleasure in a Southern disunionist than in a Northern or Western disunionist. Do not tell me that you of the South have an apology in the events and developments of the last few months. I know you have. War—irrepressible war, has been proclaimed against your institution of slavery; it has been carried into your own States; arson and murder have been committed upon your own soil; peaceful citizens have been ruthlessly shot down at the threshold of their own doors. You avenged the wrong; you executed the murderer and the felon; but he has risen from the dead a hero and a martyr; and now the apostles of this new Messiah of Abolition, with scrip and purse, armed with the sword, insolent from augmenting numbers, apostles rather of Mahomet, disciples of Peter the Hermit, are but gathering strength, and awaiting the hour for a new invasion. Certainly—certainly, in all this you have ample justification for whatsoever of excitement and alarm and indignation pervade now the whole South, from Mason and Dixon's line down to the Gulf of Mexico. But will you secede now? Will you break up the Union of these States? Will you bring down forever, in one promiscuous ruin, the columns and pillars of this magnificent temple of liberty, which our fathers reared at so great cost of blood and of treasure? Wait a little! Wait a little! Let us try again the peaceful, the ordinary, the constitutional means for the redress of grievances. Let us resort once more to the ballot-box. Let us try once again *that weapon, surer set, and better than the bayonet.*

Mr. Clerk, I am not, perhaps, so hopeful of the final result as some other men; but I was taught in my boyhood that noblest of all Roman maxims—never to despair of the Republic. I was taught, too, by pious lips, a yet higher and holier doctrine still—a firm belief in a superintending Providence, which governs in the affairs of men. I do believe that God, in his infinite goodness, has foreordained for this land a higher, mightier, grander destiny than for any other country since the world began; *Time's noblest empire is the last.* From the Arctic Ocean to the Isthmus of Darien; from the Atlantic to the Alleghanies; stretching far and wide over the vast basin of the Mississippi, scaling the Rocky Mountains, and lost at last in the blue waters of the Pacific, I behold, in holy and patriotic vision, ONE UNION, ONE CONSTITUTION, ONE DESTINY. (Applause.) But this grand and magnificent destiny cannot be fulfilled by us, except as a united people. Clouds and darkness, indeed, rest now over us; we are in the midst of perils; rocks and quicksands are before us; strife and discord are all around us. How then, sir—mighty and momentous question, pregnant with the fate of an empire—shall we bring peace to this divided and distracted country? Sir, in my deliberate and most solemn judgment, there is but one way of escape; and that the immediate, absolute, unconditional disbandment of this sectional, anti-slavery, Republican party of yours. (Applause in the galleries.) If not, then upon your heads, and upon the heads of your children, be the blood of this Republic. You have organized a political party, based upon geographical discriminations, and for the purpose of administering this Government for the benefit of a part. You have neither strength, nor organization, nor existence even, in one-half, nearly, of the States of this Union. Look around you. Behold upon this side of the house every section represented. Here are THE UNITED STATES. What do we see upon the left side of this chamber? Not one solitary Representative of your faith or party from fifteen States of this Union. What does all this mean? It never was so before in the history of this Republic. What does it all tend to? Sir, there died, not many years ago, in New England, a man whom you all once idolized as approaching a little nearer in intellect to our notions of divinity than most men in any age. Died, did I say? No, he "still lives;" lives in history, lives in the public records, lives in his published works, lives in his public services, lives upon canvas, and in marble, and in bronze. Seven years ago, he wrote to a citizen of his native State:

"*There are, in New Hampshire, many persons who call themselves Whigs, who are no Whigs at all; and no better than disunionists. Any man who* HESITATES *in granting and securing to every part of the country its just and Constitutional rights, is* AN ENEMY TO THE WHOLE COUNTRY."

I know, gentlemen of the Republican party, that you profess, many of you, that you would not deny any Constitutional right to the States of the South. Admit it. But let me ask you by what rule of interpretation do you propose to ascertain these rights? I appeal to your platforms, to your speeches, to your acts. Like the learned doctor of Padua, you confess the bond; the Venetian law cannot impugn it; but you would give the exact pound of flesh, shedding no blood, cutting nor more nor less, under penalty of death and confiscation, than the just pound, not to be made light or heavy in the balance, or the division of the twentieth part of one poor scruple, nor in the estimation of a hair. You well know that rights thus yielded are rights withheld; and withheld, too, with every aggravation of insult and wrong. Is that the spirit of the Constitutional compact? Is that the spirit which animated the great man and patriot whose ashes repose upon the banks of the Potomac, or of that other hero and patriot who finds a resting-place, in his long sleep, amid the shades of the Hermitage? How long, think you, can such a Union last? and what, above all, is it worth while it does last?

I have now finished what I desired to say upon the momentous subjects which have been introduced into this discussion. I have spoken freely of DISUNION. The time, most unhappily, has gone by when that melancholy theme can any longer be ignored or evaded. It must be met—met promptly, and met not with affected contempt, nor with real indifference. I have not spoken of it with any unmanly terror, but only with that sad and solemn alarm and apprehension which every patriot ought to feel in contemplating the overthrow of a Union so grand, a Constitution so admirable, a Government so vast, and institutions so noble, as these under and in the midst of which we are still permitted to live.

Sir, a Southern paper, not many miles from this capitol, has been pleased to say that there is no Southern State contemplating secession, in any possible contingency. No; they are only "coolly calculating the effect of disunion threats upon the nerves of the Northern and Western States." I do not believe it. Whoever utters it, libels the South and the North and the West. Idle threats and menaces will no longer frighten any one. Mutual interests and mutual fears do, indeed, bind us together still; but fraternal affection and good-will are the only bands which can keep us a united people. They are the silver cord and the golden bowl which are now so well-nigh broken at the fountain. If they be, indeed, snapped asunder, then nor threats, nor fears, nor interests, nor any thing else can keep us together. My nerves, at least, are of the hardest and the toughest. I am no more to be moved from my propriety by clamor and menace from the South, than by denunciation and fanaticism from the North or the West. Standing here—I repeat it—an armed neutral in the midst of this conflict of sections, I propose, in all humility, but in all justice, to hold even and impartial the scales between them. I have spoken freely and plainly, but have spoken justly and truly. I have not sought to conceal the evil which afflicts us—still less to exaggerate it, but only to exhibit it just as it is; for be assured—be assured there is no medicine nor surgery which can heal it without the utmost disclosure and knowledge of the true cause and character and extent of the disease. I have spoken briefly of the present evil state of public sentiment in the North and the West; in Ohio, my own native State. Yet, mother as she is, I have sought rather to imitate, not the rude and obscene behavior of Ham, but the filial piety and modesty of the elder sons of the Patriarch when mellowed with wine, and quietly, with averted eye, to cover her nakedness with the mantle of silence. Yet, as a Representative here in this Chamber, I have a duty to perform for the whole country, for the sake of the Constitution, for the perpetuity of the Union, and as its last hope.

I know well, indeed, that much that I have said to-day, will here, as elsewhere, be denounced as *pro-slavery*. Be it so. I have heard that too often, already, to feel the slightest apprehension or alarm; but I tell you, gentlemen, as a thousand times I have told those who sent me here that: If to love my country, to revere the Constitution, to cherish the Union; if to abhor the madness and hate the treason which would lift up a sacrilegious hand against either; if to read that in the past, to behold it in the present, to foresee it in the future of this land, which is of more value to us and to the world, for ages to come, than all the multiplied millions who have inhabited Africa from the creation to this day—if this it is to be pro-slavery, then in every nerve, fibre, vein, bone, tendon, joint, and ligament, from the topmost hair of the head to the last extremity of the foot, I am all over and altogether a PRO-SLAVERY MAN. (Applause from the Democratic benches and the galleries.)

NEWSPAPERS.—THE MAILS.*

HOUSE OF REPRESENTATIVES,
WASHINGTON, D. C., *Jan. 5th*, 1860.

Hon. J. HOLT, *Postmaster-General:*

SIR:—The Rev. John Lawrence, editor of the *Religious Telescope*, published in Dayton, Ohio, and within the district which I represent and the city where I reside, has advised me that the paper above named, a religious paper advocating the faith and practice of the United Brethren in Christ, is no longer delivered to its subscribers by the postmaster at Luney's Creek, Hardy County, Virginia, but is committed to the flames. He asks me to solicit the interposition of the Department to redress what he complains of as a grievance. The *Telescope*, though *anti-slavery* in sentiment when the subject is alluded to, is not an anti-slavery paper, and is not, as I am informed and believe, "incendiary" in its character in any respect, nor directly or indirectly insurrectionary in its teachings.

Certainly, every State has the right to protect itself, by all constitutional and just means, from insurrection and domestic violence. It has a right, by police laws and regulations, to secure the health and property, guard the morals, and insure the peace of its citizens. Congress and the courts of the United States have repeatedly recognized this right.

* In December, 1859, a postmaster in Hardy County, Virginia, having suppressed the *Religious Telescope*, of Dayton, O., at his office, as an Abolition paper, Mr. VALLANDIGHAM, at the request of the editor, addressed the following letter to the Post-Office Department, remonstrating against the act. The Virginia postmaster was immediately commanded to obey the law, and the *Telescope* had no further trouble.

Each State may also, in the exercise of this right, determine by law what are "incendiary" publications, tending to incite servile or other insurrections, and adopt such measures, not inconsistent with the Constitution, laws and treaties of the United States, as it may think proper to prevent their introduction or circulation. This was assumed, or conceded, by Calhoun, Clay, Webster, and by every other Senator in the debate upon this question in 1836. But, admitting all this, I suggest that an abuse, *in his official capacity, by an officer of the Federal Government*, of authority derived from a State law acting upon him as a citizen of the State, though the law be strictly constitutional and necessary, is clearly remediable by the power whence he derives his appointment. If "under the responsibilities resting upon him as an officer and a citizen," he is to "determine whether the books, pamphlets, newspapers, &c., received by him for distribution are of the incendiary character described in the Statute," does it not follow, that an appeal lies from the subordinate to his superior, to review the decision and, subject to final adjudication by the State and Federal courts, to interpret the State law under which he acts? If not, then the most flagrant abuses and usurpations of authority may, with impunity, be committed by inferior, and it may be, irresponsible officers, in the discharge of official duties under the General Government, and these usurpations and abuses not be confined to the mail service alone. Under cover of executing State police regulations and State laws, guarding against insurrection and mischief of any sort, would it not be in the power of any other Federal officers to disregard the laws of the United States in other respects? If the Federal Executive cannot intervene to supervise or control the action of its own subordinate officials, may they not be used by the States as instruments whereby to nullify the laws and expel the authority of the Federal Government itself? If subject exclusively to State control in the delivery, by postmasters, of mail matter, why not also in the transportation of the mail by mail-carriers? and if in both these particulars, or in either, why not also in the rendition of fugitive slaves, by controlling, under pretext of preventing kidnapping, the United States marshals in the several States? Is not this a doctrine fraught with danger to the peace and harmony of the Confederacy?

But surely the Government of the United States has a right and is bound to see that its officers, in the exercise of official powers conferred upon them by the Federal Constitution and laws, shall not in the least be permitted to abuse even the just and constitutional duties required of them as citizens of States, by State laws and regulations. By act of Congress in 1796, collectors and other revenue officers of the United States, masters and crews of revenue cutters, and military officers commanding upon the sea-coast, are authorized and required to aid in executing the quarantine and health laws of the several States; but "*as they shall be directed from time to time by the Secretary of the Treasury.*" Congress has passed no similar statute in the case of publications prohibited by any of the States; but if postmasters act without such law, and under State regulations alone, still their action must, in my judgment, be subject equally to the supervision and control of the Post-Office Department or of the President. The State authorities and officials are subject of course to no control by the Federal Government in this particular, except by due course of law through the State Courts and Courts of the United States.

I ask, therefore, on behalf of the gentleman above referred to, who represents a large class of the most orderly, peace-loving, and law-abiding of my constituents, that such instructions may be issued to the Postmaster at Luney's Creek, as in the discharge of his duties under the laws of Virginia, will nevertheless prevent "unreasonable searches and seizures," and compel a wise and just discretion and discrimination on his part, as a Federal officer, in executing the laws and regulations which that State has found it necessary to enact, for protection against murderous and incendiary efforts and combinations in other States to stir up civil dissensions or excite servile insurrections in her midst. They, at least, whom I have the honor to represent, have always obeyed and respected, and ever will respect and obey, every requirement and obligation of the Constitutional compact. The vast majority of them, certainly, regard none of its obligations and requirements as either odious or onerous, and they ask only that their rights also under that compact, shall be in like manner and fully protected and enjoyed.

REMARKS ON THE DEATH OF THE HON. WILLIAM O. GOODE, OF VIRGINIA.

In the House of Representatives, February 20, 1860.

THE act which we perform to-day, in memory of the deceased Representative from Virginia, is an ancient and befitting observance. It does honor to the dead; it reminds us of our own mortality. No more impressive scene is ever witnessed in this Chamber. Envy holds her breath; partisan bitterness is hushed for a moment, and even SILENCE, that rare visitant here, extends her tranquillizing wings for a little while over us. In this spirit let us approach this last solemn office of fellowship, and with the sobered earnestness which becomes these sad ceremonies, and the chastened moderation due to historic truth, let us discharge it. Exaggerated eulogy, however pardonable in mere partial friendship, has long since been exhausted upon these occasions, and we but too often repeat the folly of the barbarians, who, worshipping a fly, offered up an ox in sacrifice. Honoring the dead, let us who yet live, learn at the same time to be wiser and to do better for the rest of our lives, from the study of his character and example.

My acquaintance with the deceased member from Virginia was but limited. I knew him personally as a Representative in the Thirty-fifth Congress; but I had from boyhood known him by name as one among the most eminent of the public men of the Ancient Dominion. His life and public services I do not propose to rehearse. The gentleman from South Carolina (Mr. MILES) has anticipated me in saying that they have already been exhibited in fitting terms by the eloquent gentleman (Mr. PRYOR) who succeeds to his seat.

Although I may not say that Mr. GOODE was one of those great historic characters who mark the eras in a nation's annals, yet he unquestionably possessed more than one of those high and rare qualities without which no man and no statesman can be truly great. Born in Virginia, and soon after the Revolution, reared in "the honestest and most virgin times" of the Republic, and among the great and good men of an age and a State full of great men and patriots, certainly without these qualities he could not have commanded the confidence of the people for nearly forty years, in so many and such distinguished public stations.

WILLIAM O. GOODE was an honest man in public and in private life. Sincere in his convictions, earnest in his purposes, he meant always to be and to do right. He was neither a demagogue nor a mere partisan. While he had wisdom enough and consistency enough to respect party habitudes, he obeyed not blindly the behests of party. He scorned that vulgar and polluting partisan school of ethics which would lay down one rule of conduct for private, and another for public life, and which proclaims in execrable cant that "all is fair in politics." Far higher and nobler were the political philosophy and morals which he had learned and which he practised. He recognized in theory and in action, that great modern fact, so slowly acknowledged and so continually ignored, that there is a code of ethics in political life, as well defined, as firmly settled, as pure and elevated, and as obligatory upon the citizen and upon the public man alike, as the sublime doctrines of Socrates and of Cicero, or the holier and sublimer precepts still of the Sermon upon the Mount.

But Mr. GOODE was something more than honest: he was JUST. Many an honest man is yet unjust; and justice in public life and in the private political relation is rarer than honesty. Honesty springs from the heart, and is, in some degree, an impulse: justice belongs to the head, and is a fixed principle of conduct. It renders to every man his due. Honest himself, he was just enough to concede honesty of purpose and rectitude in action to other men and parties in antagonism to him. He acted continually, too, under a sense of duty, and he acted, therefore, always well. A German writer has said, delicately, that there are two things supremely beautiful in this world—the starry sky above our heads and the sense of duty in our hearts. This sense of duty seemed ever present in his heart to whom we pay now these honors. And he had, also, that firmness of purpose without which every virtue loses more than half its worth. Thus he united in himself the *justus et tenax* which filled the measure of poetic eulogy, even in the declining age of the Roman commonwealth. And to all this I may add that though not of brilliant genius, he was yet a wise, prudent, and sagacious public man.

Mr. GOODE was also a pure man—pure in private morals and in public morals; pure in spirit and pure in speech. He was a quiet man, too, and did the business of this House quietly. He was a pious man, in the ancient and nobler sense of the word—pious in his relations to the Supreme Being, to his family, to his friends, his country, and the world at large. Moreover he was a man of honor, and a gentleman in his manners and in his instincts. Without all these, duly blended and combined into one, no man, however eminent his abilities, can be a truly great statesman. The ancient rhetoricians had a maxim that no one could be an orator except he were a good man. Far more strictly ought this rule to be applied to him who would mould the manners, habits, opinions, and the laws, and control the destinies of a whole people.

Combining thus within himself these several excellencies, in a degree which I have not exaggerated, of WILLIAM O. GOODE it may be justly said: In him was *virtus Scipiadæ et mitis sapientia Læli*—the virtue of the Scipios and the mild wisdom of Lælius.

REMARKS ON HIS BILL FOR ARMING THE MILITIA OF THE STATES.

In the House of Representatives, March 13, 1860.

I DO not know, Mr. Speaker, whether it is strictly in order here to discuss any thing but the issues of Democracy and Republicanism, or the vexed question of slavery; but at the hazard of being deemed singular, if not disorderly, I propose to depart now, for a little while, from the beaten pathway of debate. This motion, sir, to reconsider opens up the general merits of the proposed measure, and I ask the attention of the House for about fifteen minutes, while I explain it; I will not detain you longer, and, that I may not, I desire to speak without interruption.

Mr. Speaker, if there was any one sentiment more deeply fixed in the minds of those who founded this Republic than any other, it was jealousy of standing armies. It passed into a maxim among them that large military establishments in time of peace, were dangerous to liberty. That maxim remains to this day in the bill of rights in many of our State constitutions. It has left its impress also upon the policy and legislation of this Government to the present time, when, with twelve thousand miles of land and water frontier, encircling three millions of square miles, we have a standing army numbering less than twelve thousand effective men. And yet no statesmen were more sensitive to national honor, or more awake to the necessity of national defence. Hostile to standing armies, but zealous to provide for the public safety, they looked to the MILITIA of the several States for protection against foreign and domestic enemies; and it stands a part, though a forgotten part of the Constitution of the United States, that "*a well-regulated militia is necessary to the security of a free State.*" Though that maxim, sir, was not a part originally of that instrument, yet it is impliedly acknowledged, in all its force, in the several clauses relating to that subject. Congress has power to provide for calling forth the militia to execute the laws of the Union, to suppress insurrection, and repel invasion. Congress is also specially empowered "to provide for organizing, arming, and disciplining the militia, and for governing such part of them as may be employed in the service of the United States, reserving to the States respectively the appointment of the officers, and the authority of training the militia according to the system prescribed by Congress."

No subject, sir, engrossed the attention of the earlier Presidents of the Republic more than this very power, thus amply, but cautiously, conferred. General Washington, in every formal communication to Congress during his term of office, earnestly invoked their attention to it; and, in his seventh annual message, or address, he refers to it as an object of so much moment, in his estimation, as to excite a constant solicitude that the consideration of it might be renewed until the greatest attainable perfection should be accomplished. President John Adams also, in his special message, in 1797, again pressed the subject upon the attention of Congress; and Mr. Jefferson was importunate, even, in urging upon that body additional and more effective legislation in regard to the militia. In his first annual message, in 1801, he uses this strong language:

"These considerations render it important that we should at *every session* continue to amend the defects which from time to time show themselses in the laws for regulating the militia, until they are sufficiently perfect. Nor should we *now, or at any time*, separate until we can say that *we have done every thing for the militia which we could do were an enemy at our door*."

And this recommendation he earnestly renewed in every annual message during his term of office. After him, Madison, speaking of the militia as "the great bulwark of public safety," and Monroe, and the younger Adams, and Jackson, and Van Buren, and later Presidents still, down to within the last eight or ten years, did, with pertinacious importunity, again and again press this subject upon the consideration of Congress. And, indeed, it is safe to say, that no question of public policy whatever has at any time called forth such united and persistent recommendation from the Executive Department for fifty years together; and it is equally true, that no Secretary of War has failed during that period to bestow earnest attention upon it. Yet, strange to say, no subject has been more utterly neglected by Congress. The Constitution gives us the power—exclusive, if we choose to exercise it—of organizing, arming, and disciplining the militia. In 1792, an act was passed to organize and arm the whole body of white male citizens of the respective States between the ages of eighteen and forty-five. It was very imperfect in its details, and made no adequate provision for the discipline according to which they were to be trained by the several States. Though still nominally in force, it is now everywhere, for the most part, disregarded. Indeed, if it were to be strictly executed, every white male citizen of the United States, over the age of eighteen and under forty-five, would be required, within six months after enrolment and notification, to provide himself with a good musket or fire-lock, bayonet and belt, "two spare flints," and a knapsack; or with a good rifle, knapsack, shot-pouch, powder-horn, "twenty balls, and a quarter pound of powder." Every commissioned officer would, in like manner, be required to arm himself with a sword, or hanger, and "espontoon;" or, if a dragoon officer, to provide himself with a horse fourteen and a half hands high, sword and pistols, and "holsters covered with bearskin caps;" and every private among dragoons would be required to find a serviceable horse, of the same height, with bridle, saddle, mailpillion, valise, holsters, breastplates, crupper, boots, spurs, pistols, sabre, and cartouch-box. That, sir, is literally what the law of 1792 exacts of every white man in the United States between the ages of eighteen and forty-five, except members of Congress, ferrymen, stage-drivers, clergymen, and a few others specially exempted from its operation; and all this, let it be remembered, at the individual cost of each citizen enrolled under the law. And the Congress which passed it refused, by a vote of fifty to six, upon a motion specially made for that purpose, to strike out the provision. Some progress was, indeed, made a few years later, when, by the act of 1798, thirty thousand stand of arms were ordered to be purchased by the United States, and *sold* to the States, for the purpose of arming the militia. But it was not until 1808 that Congress recognized the duty, clearly imposed upon it by the Constitution, of providing arms at the expense of the United States for the militia of the several States. It was in that year that the act, which I propose now to amend and make more effective, was passed, appropriating the sum of $200,000 for that purpose. It has never been changed in this respect; nor has there ever been any enactment to faithfully and sufficiently execute the other provisions of the Constitution empowering, and indeed requiring, Congress to organize and discipline the militia. We have, in these respects, virtually abdicated our power over the subject. Sir, I do not ask or expect Congress to take action in either of these particulars. The States themselves have been compelled, by your negligence, to provide for them by their own legislation; and it is better, perhaps, that the subject should remain where it now is, in their hands, Congress having so totally abandoned all attention to it, that the very title "militia" has disappeared for years from the index to your Statutes at Large. Indeed, if any one will venture now to introduce the subject here, or speak the name, constitutional as it is, he is in great danger of being made the object of ridicule by valiant gentlemen, inside of this house and out of it, who, but for "vile guns and villanous saltpetre," would themselves have been soldiers.

Judge Story, Sir, eminent chiefly as a civilian, but deeply imbued with the spirit of the revolutionary period of our history, and full of an enlarged patriotism, has warned us solemnly of the danger to be apprehended from the growing indifference to this great bulwark of our public liberties. "Is there any escape," he asks, "from a large standing army, but in a well-regulated militia?"

But, Mr. Speaker, while the citizen soldiery of the country, looked to in the beginning of this Republic as the very right arm of its national defence, has been thus persistently neglected, and sometimes despised, not so the standing Army of the United States. It, sir, has been the foster child of Congress. While you have passed but half a score of acts for the encouragement of the militia, since the beginning of this Government, you have enacted more than one hundred for the support, the increase, or the efficiency of the Army. While, in fifty-two years, from the 23d of April, 1808, you have appropriated just $10,400,000 for the militia, you have, within that same period, expended $500,000,000 upon the Army. Sir, I am no enemy to your Army; I am its friend. I am for its continuance; for its increase; for its efficiency every way. I am for the Military Academy, too, and for more of them, and for military academies established and fostered by the several States. I glory, sir, in the skill and discipline and valor and the achievements in times past of that gallant little Army, dotted, as it is now, all over the vast area of these States. But I remember that there are brave men and good soldiers outside of that Army, and in the various walks of civil life. I know, too, that for the purpose of national defence, or even for protection from domestic violence and insurrection, your Army is as nothing; and that your main reliance is now, as it ever has been, and must ever continue to be, upon the militia and volunteers to swell the ranks of the Army and make it effective for victory.

I will not detain the House to discuss this point at length now. But allow me, for a moment, to contrast the action of Congress in regard to these two great arms of the public defence, for the past fifty years. I take the date of the act of April, 1808, for a starting point; because it was then that, through the most strenuous exertions of Mr. Jefferson, the first appropriation for arming the militia was made by Congress. I close with the year 1858; thus including, within this brief review, a period of just half a century.

In 1808 there were seventeen States in this Confederacy; now we have thirty-three, with others just at our doors. In 1808 the population of the United States numbered about seven millions; now it exceeds thirty millions. Your Army, in 1808, mustered, all told, 3,204; on the 1st of July, 1858, it numbered 17,498. In 1808 the militia was returned at 636,386; in 1858 at 2,755,726, or seventeen times as great; and the actual number, no doubt, exceeds this return by nearly a million. In 1806 the militia of Ohio was returned at 15,351; in 1845, the date of the last return from that State, at 176,455, or eleven times greater. In 1808, under the act of that year, the appropriation equalled the sum of thirty-one cents to each militia-man in the United States; in 1858 it had fallen to less than seven cents. But the contrast is far more striking in the item of expenditures. Remember that the appropriation for arming the militia has remained stationary during all the wonderful mutations in numbers, wealth, territory, States, improvements, and whatever else has made us a great people, at just $200,000, for half a century. Not so the standing Army. For the year ending September 30, 1808, the expenditures of the War Department, including Indian affairs, fortifications, and armories, and the expenses of the new army rendered necessary then by the impending hostilities between Great Britain and the United States—and it was the year after the attack upon the Chesapeake—were just $3,023,759 55. For the year ending June 30, 1858, the expenditures of the War Department sum up thus: Army proper, $17,455,976 85; fortifications, $2,667,448 11; armories and arsenals, $1,443,235 74; in all, $21,566,660 70, or more than the entire expenditure of this whole Government thirty years ago; and that not including the expenses of the Indian department.

Thus, sir, while the militia have increased in fifty years from six hundred thousand to certainly three million, or more now, the appropriation for arming them has remained stationary at $200,000; while your Army, increasing within the same period from three thousand two hundred to seventeen thousand four hundred, has increased its expenditures from $3,000,000 to $21,500,000.

Sir, these facts and figures need no commentary. Is it not time, then, I appeal to you, that some attention, at least, should be bestowed upon the militia of the country? I repeat, that I do not ask or expect Congress to provide at all for the discharge of its high constitutional duty of organizing and disciplining the citizen soldiery of the States; although General Washington said, some seventy years ago, that the "devising and establishing of a well-regulated militia would be a genuine source of legislative honor, and a perfect title to public gratitude." But I am too well aware of the many and most serious difficulties in the way of perfecting such a system, to hope to see it accomplished. No; better leave it still with the States, and the more especially, inasmuch as to discipline or even to organize efficiently the whole body of the militia of the United States, numbering now nearly four millions, is utterly impracticable. But some of the States have introduced the system, which they are slowly perfecting—and, within the past eight years, Great Britain has followed their example—of VOLUNTEERS, enlisted of their own accord, for a term of years. These, sir, will, in time, become the NATIONAL GUARD of America. They are deserving of the utmost encouragement. But it is not right that Congress should abdicate its entire power, or rather its entire duty, in regard to this subject. It is not just that the States which already have been compelled by your negligence to take upon themselves the burden of organizing and disciplining the militia, and the heavy cost attending it, should be required also to provide arms out of their own treasuries. It is still more grossly unjust to demand that the individual volunteers, who are always young men, and usually workingmen of limited means, and who incur large expense in procuring uniforms, as also loss of wages and of time while upon duty, should furnish arms, and equipments for themselves. You abdicate your high constitutional duty to organize and discipline the militia. Is it not, then, just as little as you can do to provide arms for these volunteers who are in a sort of actual service? Sir, it was for this very purpose that your armories were, in part, originally established, and afterwards greatly enlarged. Upon this point, Mr. Jefferson, in his annual message of November, 1808, said:

"Under the acts of March 10 and April 23, respecting arms, the difficulty of procuring them from abroad during the present situation and disposition of Europe, induced us to direct our whole efforts to the means of internal supply. The public factories have, therefore, been enlarged, additional machinery erected, and in proportion as artificers can be found or formed, their effect, *already more than doubled*, may be increased *so as to keep pace with the yearly increase of the militia.*"

And yet, sir, so far from carrying out the purpose for which your public factories, if not established, were at least enlarged, and even then more than doubled, Congress has permitted them to be used almost wholly to supply the demands of the regular Army; and the annual appropriation, instead of being made to keep pace with the yearly increase of the militia, remains now in this, the fifty-second year from the date of the act, still at the $200,000 at which it was first established.

Sir, Congress has been utterly derelict in its duty, and in every particular, in regard to the militia; and, by your neglect, you have forced the States to organize and discipline, and now, at last, to appropriate money out of their own treasuries for the purchase of arms. Virginia has done it; and Maryland, the other day, appropriated $70,000 for that purpose. I repeat, that this is unjust, burdensome, and oppressive. But if you will abdicate your power and your duty in this particular, at least give your consent—and the Constitution provides for it—that each State may "keep troops and ships-of-war in time of peace," and thus may participate, to some extent, at least, in this the highest exercise of sovereignty known to independent States.

REMARKS ON THE "HOUR RULE."

In the House of Representatives, March 15, 1860.

I WILL detain the committee but a few minutes. I do not propose to discuss the subject at length. I am not ambitious of the character of a reformer. But I am sure that wise and wholesome reforms are needed in the rules of this House. I object to the report of the committee, that it is not sufficiently radical; it does not go far enough. In my deliberate judgment, he would be one of the greatest benefactors of the legislation of this Government, who would introduce and carry through a proposition to abolish the whole system of rules and of practice under them, and allow a return to the equitable and common-sense law and usages of Parliament. Our system, sir, is not half so democratic—not half so republican, if you please—as that which obtains in the House of Commons. There, every member who can catch the eye of the Speaker is at liberty to propose a measure, and address the House in support of it as long as the patience of the House will tolerate his speech, or his own good sense allow him to proceed. He may move for leave to introduce a bill, and if the House look so far favorably upon the proposition as to grant that leave, he is then, by parliamentary usage, the chairman of the select committee appointed to bring it in, and is, by virtue of that chairmanship, invested with the same privileges which are extended to chairmen of standing committees here. Thus, sir, is equality there accorded to every member, and an equal chance to participate in the business of legislation.

But how is it here? Your Speaker, whatever his natural disposition may be, is, by the necessities of his office, a despot. Your rules make him a despot. And the chairmen of your twenty-eight committees are but twenty-eight sub-despots, acting under him. They are entitled by the custom of the House to be recognized by the Speaker in preference to any other member, whenever the measures which they have severally reported are pending. No proposition can be introduced here, unless by unanimous consent or a suspension of the rules, except from a committee. The result is, that to the hands alone of the privileged few who are chairmen of the committees, is consigned the whole trade and mystery of legislation here. Our business, sir, is to register the decrees of committees. And twenty-eight men, or rather, looking to the more important committees, eight or ten out of the twenty-eight, are the organs or mouth-pieces of this House. They are the engineers and conductors who run this train, and generally it is a "lightning express train," and we, the other members, are but passengers, with checks in our hats. I repeat, then, that it would be a wise and most wholesome reform to abolish all these rules, worse now than the early Roman forms of action or English special pleading, and return to the ancient and well-tried parliamentary law and usage, allowing every member to introduce whatever proposition he may please to introduce—as Mr. Burke did his celebrated measure for economical reform—and, at least, lay before the House and the country his exposition of the principles upon which the measure is based, whether the House give its consent that he may bring in a bill or not.

But I rose, Mr. Chairman, mainly to urge the adoption of the amendment which I have proposed. I would prefer—if written speeches could be prohibited altogether—that the hour rule should be entirely abrogated. But apprehensive that the committee may not consent to go that far directly, I propose now only to mitigate the evil. No one, I think, who has observed and reflected upon the business of legislation here for some years past, will deny that very many of the evils of which the country has so much and so justly complained, and which have contributed so much to bring this House into disrepute, have arisen from the operation of this very hour rule. I might, did time permit, go back to the history of the past, and demonstrate the uniform and inevitable mischief resulting from that rule wherever it has obtained. At Athens, in her legislative assembly, there was no limit to public debate, and hence those splendid remains of Grecian eloquence which challenge the admiration of the world to this day. But in the judicial courts of Athens the rule did prevail; the "clepsydra" cut down the orator in the midst of his address, and, by consequence, forensic eloquence attained but small importance in Greece, and but little which is known or read remains of it to this day. The "hour rule" precluded advocates, and the want of advocates dwarfed the forum and the jurisprudence of Athens into comparative insignificance. Demosthenes, who "fulmined" in the public assemblies of that renowned city, shrank at the bar into a mere writer of speeches for litigants to read. Limitation upon debate was not known in the Roman Senate or at the Roman bar in the earlier days of the Republic; but as she began to fall into decay, and wicked emperors succeeded to the seats of virtuous consuls, the "hour rule" was applied in judicial trials, and it is the testimony of Tacitus and Pliny, that from that moment forensic eloquence perished. Despotism thirsted for treasure or for blood, and free speech was no longer tolerated at her bar. Dispatch is the great weapon of tyranny.

But I come down to our own times, and ask of the older members of the House, whether the effect of this rule here has not been unmixed evil? I am well aware that the usual argument urged in support of the limitation is, that it diminishes the *quantum* of debate. Is that a consideration, I ask, fit to be urged in a deliberative assembly? Why protect members from question for words spoken in debate, if no debate is to be allowed, or even if it be an object to suppress or to limit it? But I deny the fact. I affirm, on the contrary, that the aggregate amount of speaking has been vastly increased by it. I shall say nothing myself of the quality of the speaking; but I have the authority of a predecessor of mine (Mr. Schenck), who served some eight years in this House, and who has been eight years now a citizen in private life, observing the course of debate and legislation here, for the statement, as the result of his sixteen years' observation, that the speaking in this House has very much increased in quantity, and very greatly deteriorated in quality, since the adoption of the hour rule. Sir, the rule was assailed vehemently by Mr. Benton, in his Thirty Years' View, and I refer gentlemen to his observations upon it. Mr. Calhoun also denounced it as "destroying the liberties of the people by *gagging* their Representatives;" and Mr. William R. King declared that he would resist it in the Senate "even unto the death." In the House it was opposed persistently by many of the oldest and ablest members, and among them, by John Quincy Adams.

I propose, Mr. Chairman, that the hour rule shall be limited in its application only to speeches which are read. According to the law of this House, as laid down in the Manual, no member has a right now to read a speech if it be objected to; but courtesy will not tolerate an objection. So long has the custom prevailed, and to such an extent has it been carried, that it would be regarded, doubtless, as highly discourteous to demand an enforcement of the rule. Now, I believe that this proposed amendment will prove a wise provision; and that, by removing the restriction, or confining it rather to essays read in this House, a premium will be held out to legitimate debate, which I long to see restored in this Chamber, to take the place of those carefully-prepared, elaborately-constructed, and, for the most part, elegantly-written lectures which so often weary the patience of the House, admirable as they may be—for, sir, I am not one of those who join in the false and senseless outcry that the speeches which are read, or spoken upon this floor, are mere "trash." This, sir, is an accusation unjust and unfounded. But these essays or lectures are not fit for this presence; they are not delivered in the proper place. They belong to the lyceum, and not to legislation.

Allow me, sir, to refer, by way of illustration of the evil of which I complain, to what occurred when the gentleman from Alabama (Mr. CURRY) had concluded his very earnest and elaborate speech yesterday. The House was on fire, and eager for the debate to proceed. You, yourself, Mr. Chairman (Mr. STANTON), rose to reply upon the spur of the moment; and had the floor been given you, we should have had, I doubt not, one of those interesting and exciting *debates*, so highly dramatic in their character, which are now heard only in the Senate of the United States, or in the Parliament of Great Britain; but which, sir, in an evil hour for the legislation of the country, have almost wholly disappeared from this Chamber, and linger only in the memory or the records of the past. Yet, under the custom, more honored in the breach than the observance, which has grown up under the hour rule, and which is one of its most odious excrescences, the Chairman had his roll of members prepared long time in advance. You, sir, were not upon that roll; or, if upon it, not next in order. You rose first and were recognized. But the Chairman's promise was out, and the gentleman set down in the programme, claimed "specific performance." You yielded, and he proceeded amid great disorder, and very soon to empty benches, to read a speech, which, if spoken, would have commanded, as it deserved, the closest attention. They who had listened with interest so intense to the oral speech of the gentleman from Alabama (Mr. Curry), crowding these seats in silence even beyond the allotted hour—for you relaxed the rule by unanimous consent in his favor—immediately, at the very sight of the manuscript, fled from the Hall, and retired to their boarding-houses. And when the committee rose last night there were but five members present in all this vast Chamber.

I appeal for a moment here, Mr. Chairman, upon the point of the alleged abuse of unlimited debate, to the experience of this House, not only previous to the adoption of the hour rule, but during the interregnum of eight weeks which occurred at the commencement of this session. Was the patience of the House ever abused more than once, at most? Sir, we had but two speeches of really inordinate length—very able ones, indeed—within that period; and one of them, at least, I am sure, commanded the attention of the whole House, as fully and intensely throughout as any speech which has been delivered within this Capitol for more than twenty years. The average length of the speeches during those eight weeks of unrestricted debate—and I have made an estimate fairly—did not exceed from half an hour to forty minutes. Very many of them did not equal half that limit. And yet we had no hour rule then; but had it been in force, every member who obtained the floor would have felt himself under an imperious necessity of speaking full an hour, lest he should be deemed to have "broken down." And that, sir, is precisely the evil which afflicts us now under its operation.

Yet another grievance growing out of this rule, is the persistent and offensive interruptions to which every member upon the floor is subjected. No one can arise and address the House for a moment, but some gentleman interposes, not upon a point of order, not for personal explanation, but that the member who interrupts may propound an interrogatory to the member interrupted, and thus thrust him into the witness-box to extract from him, by a process of cross-examination, something not at all relevant to the subject; or perhaps to interpolate a speech of his own. Sir, this happens here, and it happens every day; because the rules of politeness, which prevail in conversation and in social intercourse, are forgotten in this House. Nothing was once, and perhaps is still, deemed more rude than to interrupt a gentleman in conversation, at least in the midst of a sentence; yet it is continually done here. And it is done because members are anxious to speak, whether prepared to speak or not; and the best opportunity to "catch the Chairman's eye," is when there is but one member upon the floor, and no one struggling for it. Then it can be secured. Thus it is that speeches by one member are thrust into the speeches of another member, to go out with them. It is done sometimes, perhaps, to divert the attention of a gentleman from the subject he is discussing, or to extract from him some troublesome answer relating to a personal matter or opinion, it may be, wholly foreign to the business of legislation. This is an evil grievous to be borne, and I think it is the result very much of the hour rule—certainly it is a part of the system of evils which have grown up since the adoption of that rule.

It may be that the solution proposed by the gentleman from Mississippi (Mr. McRae) is correct; that there are so many gentlemen upon the floor who think themselves so much better "posted" than the particular member speaking, that they are anxious to communicate some portion of the valuable surplus of their information to that member, or rather, perhaps, through him to the country.

Certainly, Mr. Chairman, I do not intend to apply these remarks personally to the gentleman from Virginia (Mr. Bocock), who sought two or three times to interrupt me some time ago. No, sir; they are the result of close observation and reflection upon what I have seen and heard from the time I first had the honor of a seat upon this floor.

[Mr. Bocock, of Virginia, here made some remarks in reply, after which Mr. Vallandigham resumed as follows:]

The speech of the gentleman from Virginia would no doubt have been very captivating in the region of Appomatox and upon "the stump" anywhere [laughter]; but surely it was quite inappropriate here; indeed, I ask no better practical illustration to enforce what I said a few moments ago than this entire interruption from a gentleman who has served in the House now these ten years, and, I fear, has fallen into all its bad habits.

In reply to his last observation, I will tell him how it comes that our speeches are of a character totally different from legitimate debate, and why members prepare speeches in writing because of the hour rule. It is important, of course, for every member to compress as much as is possible within that limit. Every man knows in his own experience that he can condense an amount of matter within an hour when he writes, which it would require an hour and a half to deliver orally. Yet, for one, I must say, in passing, I would rather listen to the dullest speech from any member here for two hours, orally delivered, than to sit for one hour under the infliction of the finest and best composed essay ever read in the House.

The gentleman from Virginia has read me a lecture on democracy, monarchy, republicanism, and the other forms of government. Sir, he himself stands here to-day the advocate of despotism. He is upon this floor defending a rule, the whole purpose and tendency of which is to prevent the free and legitimate deliberation and debate, so essential a part of legislation. But, in speaking of the previous question, he himself forgot the very wide difference between that question as it obtains here and in Great Britain. In Parliament it is used for the purpose of removing a subject from before the House, so that there shall be neither vote nor debate upon it. Here it is employed solely for the purpose of bringing the House to vote directly upon the proposition, and without debate at all. Now, if we should return to parliamentary usage, of course we would go back also to the ancient and legitimate use of the previous question, and abandon the dangerous and tyrannic perversion and abuse of it which have grown up under our own system. And yet, limited and comparatively innocuous as it is there, the previous question has not been resorted to in the House of Commons for many years; and a motion, in 1849, to limit speeches in Parliament to one hour, was rejected. And just here allow me to add, that no legislative body, anywhere, or at any time, in a free country, except the House of Representatives assembled in this Capitol, has ever submitted to this most mischievous restriction upon the freedom of debate.

The gentleman finds an apology, sir, for all these most vexatious restrictions and intricacies in the rules which preclude a member from bringing forward business, or discussing it when it is brought forward, in the number of Representatives of which this House consists. Sir, does he forget that the British House of Commons is composed of six hundred and fifty-eight members, and yet that more business is transacted there in two or three days than by this House in six weeks; and that, too, usually there in a full House. It is very true that forty members constitute a quorum for the transaction of business; and that private business, that in which the whole empire is not interested, is usually passed upon in a thin House; but whenever any great question is pending before Parliament, the House is full, and the members are nearly all present. Even the very important commercial treaty recently concluded between France and Great Britain was discussed and disposed of by the first orators and statesmen of Parliament, in two nights, only some few weeks since. How long would it have occupied this House? How much time do we usually consume in discussing great public questions? The debate on the Kansas-Nebraska bill, including the reading of essays, was continued for six or eight weeks. The discussion upon the Lecompton constitution, in which from one hundred and seventy to two hundred speeches were delivered or read, occupied the time, if not the attention, of the House from the 16th of December until the 30th of April. And why is this? Because we have no legitimate debate. The speech of one member does not follow that of another. One set of ideas or arguments are not provoked by another set urged by the speaker who preceded. We hear none, and have none, of that kind of debate. Disconnected lectures, written weeks before, and concealed in the desks of members, are continually produced here, and read to empty benches, and yet go forth to the country as speeches which thrill the hearts of members and of those who throng our galleries.

Sir, I remember, as an illustration this moment occurring to me, that a member from Illinois (Mr. Lovejoy) read an essay upon this floor, in the month of February one year ago, late at night, to three members and five pages [laughter]; yet the next day it was telegraphed to a leading paper in the city of New York, as one of the most thrilling speeches ever delivered in the House; remarkable, especially, for its fearlessness, and the boldness of its denunciation [renewed laughter], and perfectly electrifying every one present. Now, is it not time that this evil was remedied? I repeat again, that the *quantum* of speaking will not be increased by the abrogation of the hour rule; the number of pages which make up your Congressional Globe will not be multiplied; and what difference is it to us or to the country, whether one man shall speak for two hours, or two men shall speak for one hour each? It may be of some moment to our particular constituencies; but it is of none to the whole country. Let gentlemen who would discuss mere partisan or local topics, go back to the ancient usage which prevailed some forty years ago, of publishing addresses upon such questions to their constituents. Let us agree henceforth that what is said upon the floor here shall relate to the great measures of public policy and legislation which may come before us and not to mere fleeting and temporary subjects of controversy between parties. No reform which we can devise will tend so far to bring the House back to its ancient dignity and decorum, and to that high repute which belonged to it in the earlier days of the Republic.

I desire to call the attention of the committee to the fact that for thirty years after the organization of this Government, the Senate was not the centre of attraction. It was the House upon which the eyes of the country were turned. It was here, sir, that in those days there were gathered an Ames, a Madison, an Ellsworth, a Randolph, a Sherman, and others of a like fame, who have made the history of our country illustrious. But, for thirty years now, and especially within the twenty years past, since the adoption of the hour rule, along with other evils, the importance and even the equality of the House has been lost; and it is the Senate whose galleries the people throng now; it is the Senate which has drawn upon itself the chief attention of the country; it is the debates in the Senate for which the public look; it is the speeches delivered in the Senate which circulate throughout the land; and, finally, it is the Senate, as the gentleman from Virginia [Mr. GARNETT] suggested, which is not only absorbing all the legislation of the country, but is moulding that public opinion which controls the Government. Is it not apparent then, I ask, that there should be found, and right speedily, a remedy for the disrepute into which this House has fallen? What that remedy may be, I leave to your wisdom, gentlemen, to devise; but, I repeat, that the abrogation of the hour rule is, in my opinion, the first and a most important step in that direction.

Mr. COX. I wish to ask my colleague a single question. He seems to have taken the British House of Commons as his model of a parliamentary body.

Mr. VALLANDIGHAM. Not altogether, although this House was certainly modelled after it,

Mr. COX. My colleague has, no doubt, read in Ten Thousand a Year, of one Tittlebat Titmouse, who broke down a ministry by crowing at an inopportune time. [Laughter.] I suppose that, to carry our the system in this House, it should be the duty of the Speaker to appoint persons who are to perform that duty. But, as my colleague refers to classic authorities, I ask him whether it was not true that the hour rule always prevailed in the Roman Senate?

Mr. VALLANDIGHAM. Certainly not.

Mr. COX. I ask if it was not extraordinary that those great declamations of Demosthenes and Æschines always came out in exactly sixty minutes?

Mr. VALLANDIGHAM. My colleague is, as Titmouse would say, a most "respectable gent;" and no doubt the incident to which he has referred in that gentleman's parliamentary career, illustrating his powers of crowing, was called to mind by the similarity between my colleague's name, and the barn-yard fowl called

"Chanticleer, who wakes the morn."

He is the very bird for the new office he proposes. [Laughter.] But I regret that he has exhibited such lamentable forgetfulness at least, in regard to the Roman and Grecian eloquence, to which I had made allusion by way of illustration. If he had recently read the speeches of Demosthenes and Æschines, to which he refers, hewould not have asked whether they were not spoken in sixty minutes. Certainly they cannot now be read in two hours, and that without including the documents quoted by the orators.

Mr. Cox. That depends upon whether they are read in the original. [Laughter.]

Mr. VALLANDIGHAM. I do not profess to be as familiar with Greece as my colleague. He has seen the "isles of Greece," visited the classic shores of Attica, walked the streets of Athens, and stood upon the Acropolis. I have not. He visited Rome, too; though I may not speak of what he saw or heard in the Eternal City. He has written it in a book. [Laughter.] But I will not occupy the time of the committee longer. By reason of the very evil of interruptions of which I complained, I have been forced to speak at far greater length than I intended. I beg pardon, gentlemen.*

* NOTE BY MR. VALLANDIGHAM.—Not aware that the report on the rules of the House was made a special order for this day, and obliged to speak, therefore, without recent examination of the subject, I append now certain extracts to which I would otherwise have referred in my remarks:

1. Many of the extant orations written by Demosthenes for prosecutors or the accused, were in State trials or impeachments; and some of them in support of the repeal of certain laws, as for example, the Leptinean oration, were read before "committees," as we would say at this day. A longer time (if indeed there were any limit), it would seem, was allowed in such cases.

2. The first example of limitation of time for argument at the bar in Rome, was by Pompey, upon the trial of Milo, and for the purpose of securing his conviction; but the limit then was fixed at three hours. Under the Emperors it became a settled usage, and sometimes two hours, sometimes one hour, or even half an hour, were allowed, at the discretion of the judge. Pliny assigns as the reason, that "the advocates grew tired before the business was explained, and the judges were ready to decide before they understood the question." And he asks, and the inquiry is just as pertinent now, "Are we wiser than our ancestors? are the laws more just at present? Our ancestors allowed many hours, many days, many adjournments in every cause? and, for my part, as often as I sit in judgment, I allow as much time as the advocate requires; for would it not be rashness to guess what space of time is necessary in a cause which has not been opened? But some unnecessary things may be said, and is it not better that what is unnecessary should be spoken, than that what is necessary should be omitted? And who can tell what is necessary

FRANKING PRIVILEGE.

December 6, 1860.

Mr. Vallandigham, from the Select Committee of Five on the franking privilege (Mr. Charles F. Adams and Mr. William Kellogg concurring), made the following

REPORT.

The Select Committee of the House of Representatives, to whom was referred Senate bill No. 35, *entitled "An Act to abolish the Franking Privilege," have had the same under consideration, and report:*

This bill is at least equal and exact, inasmuch as it proposes to prohibit the transportation of any free matter through the mail, except to the widow of James K. Polk, late a President of the United States, cutting off congressional franks, and providing no means for the payment by government of postage on official communications of any kind. It requires every officer, civil, military, and naval, now entitled to frank, from the President of the United States to deputy postmasters, to prepay, out of his own money, postage on all matter transmitted upon official business. It forbids the free exchange of newspapers, which has been admitted by law or regulation since 1753, and proposes thus, by one annihilating act of six lines, full of manifest haste and want of consideration, to reverse the settled policy of the government from its beginning. A graver question is seldom submitted to Congress, and duly impressed with its importance, your committee has given anxious and patient attention to it.

Though the post-office system, as it exists at this day, is essentially a modern institution, yet posts are of very ancient date, and in every instance have been either established or regulated by the State. In Arabia and Persia they existed long before the Christian era, and their

till he has heard? Patience in a judge ought to be considered as one of the chief branches of his duty, as it certainly is of justice." (Book 6, Epistle 2.) These considerations apply still more strongly to debate in a deliberative assembly.

3. Cicero says in his "Brutus," that he never heard of a Lacedæmonian orator, and adds, "brevity, upon some occasions, is a real excellence; but it is very far from being compatible with the general character of eloquence."

4. Referring to the adoption of the hour rule by the House, July 7, 1841, Mr. Benton says:

"This session is remarkable for the institution of the hour rule in the House of Representatives—*the largest limitation upon the freedom of debate which any deliberative assembly ever imposed upon itself*, and presents an eminent instance of *permanent injury done to free institutions* in order to get rid of a temporary annoyance."—2 *Benton's View*, 247.

speed, in Oriental figure of speech, was outstripped only by the flight of time. Under the Roman emperors the postal system was, as to expedition at least, brought to great perfection, and Tiberius was accustomed to indignantly reject all dispatches which had been longer on the way than twenty days from the extremest provinces of Asia. In the middle ages, also, posts were established in various countries of Europe, and in Peru, at its discovery in 1527, the orders of the Inca were regularly dispatched by couriers posted at convenient distances along the principal highways. In India also, and earlier still in Tartary, a postal system existed which, in the latter country, was very extensive and complete. And at this day the post-office is an established institution of every State in Europe and America, and in all it is under the control of government. More than this, it has in almost every instance been first established by the State for its own exclusive service in the transmission of public dispatches and other official intelligence. The use of it by private persons has, for the most part, been an incident growing up under it, first from the necessities or conveniences of trade and commerce or of social correspondence, and ultimately for the sake of income to the State; and Blackstone treats of it in his Commentaries as a fixed and important part of the King's revenue. In no country is postage paid on public dispatches or communications by government officers out of their own private means. Even in Great Britain the abolition of franks in 1839 extended only to parliamentary and not to executive franking.

Within a few years after the first British settlements in America, posts were established by the legislatures of several of the colonies. In 1639, by authority of the general court of Massachusetts, a postmaster was appointed in Boston; and in 1657, Virginia provided for the transmission by each planter, under the penalty of a hogshead of tobacco (the currency of that day), of government dispatches from one plantation to another, till they should reach the place of their destination. One of the earliest acts of William Penn was the establishment, in 1683, of a post-office in Pennsylvania; and a monthly post was appointed, in obedience to the King's command, between New York and Boston, in 1672. As early as 1692 a postmaster-general for all the colonies was appointed by letters patent, with power to erect post-offices, but no efficient system was established till 1710, when, by act of Parliament, the postmaster-general was authorized to set up a general letter office in New York and other chief offices in each of the colonies. Dr. Franklin served in the post-office department for nearly forty years, and from 1753 to 1774 was postmaster-general for all British America, during which period he reduced the service to a system, and for the first time made it to yield a revenue to the government.

Throughout the war of the revolution, by order of the Continental Congress, and under the direction of postmaster-generals appointed by them, postal arrangements, more or less imperfect, were continued, and the Articles of Confederation, ratified finally in 1781, gave to Congress "the sole and exclusive right and power of establishing and regulating post-offices from one State to another throughout the United States, and exacting such postage on the papers passing through the same as might be requisite to defray the expenses of the office."

The convention of 1787 found the post-office an existing institution, and in five words empowered Congress "to establish post-offices and post-roads." Under this express grant, and the power to make "all laws necessary and proper" for carrying it into execution, has grown up that vast and stupendous system of postal arrangements by which intelligence of every kind, political, commercial, social, and intellectual, is transmitted with certainty, safety, and speed throughout the United States, over routes estimated at 260,000 miles in length, with an annual mail transportation of 82,000,000 of miles, and at a cost of nearly ten millions of dollars.

Why was it, we may well inquire, that the Constitution conferred a power so peculiar and so immense? How comes it that any government, above all that a republican government, founded upon the fundamental principle of committing nothing to government which the individual man can as well accomplish, is the sole carrier of mail matter, and yet carries nothing else? Unquestionably the primary reason is that every State has the right to provide the necessary and proper means of communicating to public officers, and in a popular government, to the people, its own dispatches and other public intelligence. The State has just the same right to establish and control the machinery used for this purpose as to construct and own the arms and munitions of its army, or the ships and equipments of its navy, or the buildings necessary for executive and legislative purposes. But for public objects the power ought never to have been given; and when the post-office is no longer used by government, except in the same way and upon the same terms as by the individual citizen, the whole of this costly and stupendous machinery, with all its vast political power and patronage, ought forthwith to be abolished. As well might the government be required to pay the market price for the arms and munitions of war fabricated at its public factories, and yet these factories be kept up for the purpose of meeting the wants of private citizens, and made "self-sustaining" by the means thus supplied. As well might government be required to pay passage money and board for its naval officers and seamen, in order that the navy may be made "self-sustaining" by the transportation of passengers, for fare, from one port to another. As well might government pay rent for its own court-houses and custom-houses in order that the treasury and the judiciary might be made "self-sustaining" by letting these buildings to private persons for hire. The analogy will be complete if we suppose the civil, naval, and military officers to be required, in each case, to pay out of their private funds or their salaries the several expenses thus incurred.

Your committee regard the post-office as strictly a department of the government to be used primarily for public purposes, and differing in no essential governmental principle from any other department. But private citizens, it may be said, do not use the other executive offices, including the army and the navy, for private purposes: how comes it, then, that the post-office is an exception? The reason is this: any private use of the former would be inconsistent with the objects for which they were instituted and destructive of their efficiency; but the post-office can well transport the mail matter of private persons at the same time as that of the government, without injury or inconvenience to the public service, and by exacting sufficient postage, without cost to the public treasury.

Certainly the nature of the matter transmitted may afford some reason why its transportation should be under the supervision of government, and by machinery provided by it. Every postal system from the beginning has been established chiefly, if not solely, for the communication of intelligence. Under our own system nothing else is "mailable matter." But this intelligence is in the form of written or printed packets, and to-day both letters and newspapers are transmitted, along with every other conceivable subject of transportation, by private express companies, with "due celerity, certainty, and security," from one end of the Union to the other.

Another reason, perhaps, why the power to establish post-offices and post-roads was committed to the federal government was the necessity and importance of preventing vexatious restrictions and annoyances in the transmission of intelligence from one State to another. This has ever been an evil causing no small mischief in the German confederation. But it must be remembered that the same difficulty would equally exist in the transportation of goods, and of every other article usually intrusted to common carriers; and that in practice, no sort of inconvenience or vexation is experienced in the transmission of intelligence by telegraph, or the transportation of any article upon the railroad, by express or otherwise, from one State through another, to the remotest section of the United States.

Your committee, therefore, are of opinion that, whereas the transmission of government dispatches and intelligence was the primary object of the establishment of the post-office system, so also, it is still, and much more now than at first, the chief reason which justifies its continuance; and that whenever it ceases to be a department of State, to be used in the exercise and execution of some legitimate and necessary function and power of republican government, it ought to be abolished.

Certainly the State might employ special messengers to bear all its dispatches and public intelligence, at home, as it now does on important occasions, or to countries with which it has no postal arrangements abroad; and these messengers would be paid out of the treasury, but the expense would, in that case, be an intolerable burden. Or the government might, except in regard to matters of too great or delicate concern, intrust its communications, if it were wise or economical so to do, to private carriers or express companies, just as it now does to the telegraph, the use of which for public purposes is every day augmenting. But here, again, the expense would be defrayed out of the public funds. No one, in either case, would ask that the several officers transmitting the dispatches or intelligence should be required to pay the expense out of their own means. Why, then, when the government has organized a permanent establishment for its own service, but which, for general convenience and greater security and speed, private citizens are allowed to employ, also, for their own individual purposes, shall it be required to pay for the transmission of its own intelligence by means of its own agencies and machinery? And yet, after all, here is a mere dispute about words, or rather about the mode of payment. Rejecting the proposition that the private citizen shall be taxed a higher rate of postage in order to defray the expense of the transportation of government mail matter, the real question is, whether the State shall pay directly the excess of the expenditures of the Post-Office Department over the receipts at fair rates of postage from private persons using it, or shall pay just the same amount in the shape of postage, at such rates as will make up the deficiency; in other words, shall government keep a postage account and pay it out of the general treasury, or shall it transmit its official dispatches and communications free, and pay, upon another form of account, the increased expenditures of the Post-Office Department—incurred by reason of such free mail matter. In this point of view, your committee deem the controversy of but small moment, and to be determined as a question solely of convenience and economy; and they are clearly of opinion that upon the score of both economy and convenience the latter mode is far preferable. This is the question, unless it be insisted that the officers or agents of the State shall pay out of their own salaries or private fortunes, if any they may have, the postage accounts of their respective offices. But if out of their salaries, then the payment is at last, though meanly and circuitously, out of the public treasury, and a general increase of salaries would be the final and inevitable result, since the amount so put into the treasury, assuming the estimate of the Post-Office Department of $1,800,000 to be correct, if assessed upon officials, executive and legislative, who now enjoy the "franking privilege," would essentially diminish the compensation which they now severally receive. If the payment is to be made out of their own private means, then it is an infraction of the principles of republican government, the imposition of an unjust tax upon public servants, and an exaction without example in any other instance of governmental administration. No less reasonably might the officers of the navy, or the judiciary, or the treasury, be required also to provide from their own fortunes, ships and equipments, or court-houses and custom-houses, for the use of the government. And why, upon the same principle, should not the officers of the army be compelled to pay, in the same manner, for the cost of the transportation of troops and munitions of war from one post to another? The true rule your committee understand to be this: every expense of a public nature, necessary to the faithful and efficient discharge of public duty, the government ought to pay out of the common treasury, because the expenditure is for the common good. Unquestionably, the communication of orders and other public intelligence from one officer to another, whether a superior or subordinate, is not only a part, but a most important part, of official duty, and which, indeed, especially in a country so vast in geographical extent as ours, is indispensable to the existence of the government itself. This would seem to be too clear for argument.

Although the bill referred to your committee prohibits all free matter, as well executive as congressional, and as it stands now would require all postage on government communications to be paid by officials out of their own means, your committee are slow to believe that such an act of injustice and folly was seriously intended. They assume that the purpose of the friends of the measure is to abolish congressional franks altogether, and to pay official or executive postage, as in England, out of the public treasury. To pay for congressional free matter in the same way would be simply a proposed reform, and not an abolition of the privilege. And if both be placed upon the same footing, nothing would be gained to the common treasury, and only the mode of paying the general expenses of the postal system would be changed. One department of government would buy postage stamps from another department of government which had already appropriated for the former the very money with which these stamps had been purchased, and thus the old fable be realized of the two lads who, shut up in a dark room, amassed a fortune each by exchanging garments. It is only by requiring all private persons and officials who use the post-office to pay alike out of their own means the usual and necessary postage rates that any thing is to be really saved to the treasury. And this rule, your committee understand, is to be applied only to members of the legislative department, while the postage of the executive, though the more costly of the two, is to be defrayed out of the general fund. Congress, with marvellous excess of patriotism, is to enact a self-denying ordinance, not applicable in its burdens to any but its own members.

Assuming, then, that the abolition of franks is to be limited really to congressional communications or intelligence, while all other government mail matter is to be carried free or have the postage upon it paid out of the public treasury, your committee proceed to consider whether, in the nature of our system of government, or in any peculiar or accidental circumstances, there exists any reason why a discrimination should in this respect be made against the legislative department and its members, and in favor of the executive and its officials.

In a majority of countries where postal systems exist there is no legislature at all; in others it is but a shadow; in some, merely an office wherein to register the decrees of royalty. If in any such the right to transmit through the King's mails any matter free is conceded to the semblance the legislature, it is strictly a privilege, or possibly a sort of badge of office or distinction. It is a matter of grace, like the license to kill deer in the royal forests—"blowing a horn if the forester be absent, so that the King's venison may not seem to be taken by stealth." In all such states there is little need for sympathy or communication between the representative and the constituent, since elections in some are but mere forms, and in others the executive is the real and sometimes, in whole or in part, the formal constituent of the legislature. In but one country besides our own has the legislative department any real and substantial portion of the power of the government, and even there the post-office system grew up under the auspices of royalty, and at a period when Parliaments were but the registers of the King's good will and pleasure. Postal couriers were employed by King John to convey government dispatches as early as the thirteenth century, and between that period and the reign of James I., when the first postmaster-general, having charge of as well private as public correspondence, was appointed, nothing probably but official letters and packets was transmitted by the King's post. From the beginning down to the time of the Long Parliament the entire system was under the control of the executive as a part of the royal prerogative, and posts were established by proclamation. When in the time of Cromwell, both King and Lords were abolished, and all power consolidated at first in the House of Commons, the post-office passed also under their control, and they succeeded, of course, to the rights and privileges of the executive, and used the mails for the conveyance of their own dispatches and intelligence. Blackstone dates the first *legislative* establishment and regulation of the post-office from this period. At the restoration, in 1660, the system, though then and ever afterwards subject to control by act of Parliament instead of royal proclamation, passed again in its administration into the hands of the King. Pending a bill in the same year for the organization of the post-office, the Commons, "because that the letters of as well the King's council of state as his own and other executive officers passed free through the mails," added a proviso that their letters also should be entitled to the same privilege. The Lords threw out the proviso, and the Commons consented to drop it upon a private assurance from the crown that the exemption should be allowed to the members; and accordingly a warrant was ever afterwards regularly issued from the King to the postmaster-general, directing the allowance to members of Parliament of free letters to the extent of two ounces. This was the origin of the "franking *privilege*;" for privilege it then really was, granted of royal grace, and so it continued for a century, when, in 1764, it was for the first time confirmed and regulated by act of Parliament.

Why, your committee ask, shall the executive dispatches and correspondence pass free through the mails or be paid for out of the common treasury? The reason is twofold: First, because they are official communications passing between superiors and subordinates, between principals and agents upon public business. It is fit, therefore, that the public should pay the expense. Second, the people have a right to know what the executive department is doing, and whether their public servants are fully and faithfully discharging their public duties, to the end that they may be held to a due responsibility. And it is fit again that the people and not their servants should pay the expense. Do not both these considerations apply equally to congressional or legislative communications? The States and the people are the constituents; members of Congress are their representatives; the States and the people are principals; we their agents. They are superiors, we subordinates. How shall responsibility be enforced without knowledge on the part of the States and of the people of what their agents are doing and of how they discharge their trusts? Is it unimportant to the public interests or not necessary for the maintenance, pure and incorrupt, of our institutions as they now exist, that the accountability of the legislative department to the States and the people should be preserved? Is it not the more important and the more essential, inasmuch as it is the business and duty of the legislative to enforce responsibility upon the executive, and thus to stand as the sentinel or custodian of State and popular rights? But *quis custodiat custodes ipsos*, if there shall be no communication between Congress and the people and States? And if there be communication through the instrumentality of the Post-Office Department—a part and parcel of government machinery—why shall the legislative any more than the executive public servant be required to pay the expense out of his own private fortune? The very basis of our government is the responsibility of representatives to their constituents; and free and frequent communication between the two is essential to the enforcement of this responsibility. It is not enough that they may communicate mutually through the newspaper press. The States and the people have a right to send and receive directly to and from their representatives, and to learn in an authentic and official form what has been said and done by these public servants. Your committee will not press the importance of this consideration further; it is too obvious.

If it be urged that the right to frank extends also to merely private communications between individuals, your committee answer that this is at most an abuse and a small one which, if need be, it is easy to cut off. But according to the individual experience and observation of the members of your committee, the number of strictly private business or social letters passing free through the mails is very small. Letters or communications relating in any way to political affairs between representative and constituent your committee do not deem mere private letters. In their judgment it is not necessary that the communication should relate solely to business formally before Congress in order to entitle it to the designation of a public or official letter. If a representative has the right to print and address a communication directed to the whole body of his constituents relating to general politics and public affairs, or solely to the local politics of his own district, why may he not address the same in manuscript to any one of his constituents?

But if franking be really a mere privilege and not a right of the people and a duty of the representative, then your committee demand to know why it shall be conceded in a republican government to the executive department alone and denied to the legislature? Is there any thing in the nature of the government, of the offices, or of the communications that special privileges should be conferred upon the former and not also, or rather, indeed, upon the latter?

Loud complaint is made that the treasury is impoverished by reason of the vast numbers of very costly books and public documents which, it is alleged, would not be printed but for the "franking privilege." Your committee answer that no book or document is printed except by general or special order of Congress or of the Senate or House; and that it is only necessary to refuse to direct the printing of documents and none will be transmitted by mail, and thus the expense both of printing and transportation be saved. But what are these books and documents thus summarily condemned? They are the records of the government in its various departments; the reports of its general or special agents appointed by law. They are the official archives of State, the originals of which are accessible to those only, few in number, who may chance to visit the Federal capital, and which ought to be printed; which the people have a right to see, and to have distributed at public expense either through the mails or by express. Certainly the printing of books, not coming strictly within the class above described, has been of late years carried to an excess which demands rebuke and retrenchment. But let Congress apply the corrective directly, by refusing to print, and not circuitously by abolishing the right to transmit free through the mail.

It is complained, also, as if it were a monstrous abuse, that immense quantities of speeches and pamphlets are franked from the Capitol, especially during a presidential canvass; and tables have been prepared to show that they number millions. Your committee would have millions more, in the same manner, sent out. Every one of them relates to the politics of the country. Every one of them finds its way into the hands of some one or more of the people—of the constituent body to whom this House and every other department of the Government is responsible. They afford public instruction and mould public sentiment. They are printed at the private cost of the members of the Senate or House—a heavy tax and a heavy burden in itself—and it is fit that, meant for the people, they should at least be circulated through the people's mails, and at the people's expense. There is no "privilege" in all this to the member; it is his duty and burden, and the privilege of the constituent.

The free exchange of newspapers is, perhaps, an anomaly in the post-office system, and includes, no doubt, a greater amount of matter than any other passing free through the mails. Yet your committee justify it upon the ground of long and uniform usage—more than a hundred years in duration—and for strong reasons of public policy. It would be not difficult to demonstrate that to cut off free exchanges would go far to break down the whole newspaper press of the country, except a few of the leading journals in the larger cities, and thus to concentrate in these journals all that tremendous power which belongs to this "fourth estate" of Government. Cities would become still more the seats of political power; thither alone would ambitious eyes be directed, and public servants would be compelled to look for responsibility no longer to their own immediate constituents, but to the conductors of a powerful metropolitan press, which already exerts a controlling, though not always wholesome influence over public sentiment throughout the Union. It is the great problem in a Republican Government how to decentralize power, whose natural tendency is to gravitate towards a common centre. Wide extent of country, separate State Governments, conflicting interests, local jealousy, pride and ambition, but, above all, the electric telegraph, have prevented or arrested hitherto in the United States that evil which, for the most part, is suppressed in Europe by a denial of liberty to the press. Still the great journals of our larger cities need no aid from Government. Rejoicing in abundant capital, full of enterprise, commanding a high order of talent of every sort, laying every art, every science, and the whole circle of literature under contribution, and constituting thus a controlling, and certainly a most wonderful element of modern civilization, they are able to stand alone, and Government, indeed, itself is glad sometimes to look to them for support. Your committee would withdraw no privilege, therefore, from the country press—an institution so essential to that equality which is the corner-stone of every truly Democratic State.

For the same reasons, also, your committee propose to continue to the publishers of weekly newspapers the privilege of transmitting to subscribers one copy free of postage within the county of publication.

So far your committee have discussed this question upon principle. We propose, now, briefly to meet and reply to some considerations urged in behalf of the measure on the score of policy.

The clamor just now in favor of this alleged reform, so far as it is disinterested, is founded mainly upon the very great increase of late years in the expenditures of the Post-Office Department. To this your committee answer, that a large part of this increase accrues because of the extension of mail facilities by overland and water to the Pacific coast, and that the free mail matter transported over these routes bears as to the cost but an insignificant proportion to the whole. The evil lies not there. No; the last annual report of the Postmaster-General discloses the secret of this inordinate increase. The *six different routes* to and from the Pacific, cost the Government $2,693,394 13, being an expenditure of $4 14 to each inhabitant of that section of the Union, 600,000 in number, while the cost east of the Rocky Mountains for thirty millions of people, is less than forty-one cents to each person. The annual receipts from these six routes are $339,747 66, showing an excess of expenditures of $1,844,949 66 per annum. One route alone costs $600,000, and yields as revenue the exact sum of $27,229 94. Here, then, is ample room for reform. Will not the "non-franking patriots" of the Senate and House see to it?

Your committee would not, indeed, diminish by one jot the necessary and reasonable mail facilities of that vast and opulent portion of our confederacy, which, lying at so great a distance from the centre, and separated by vast deserts and high mountains, bears yet its full proportion of the burdens of Government without a just measure of its benefits. But a provident and economical adjustment and equalization of these facilities is neither denial nor injustice to the people of the Pacific coast.

Another and yet more important cause of this vast increase in the expenditures of the Post-Office Department is the great reduction, of late years, in the rates of postage. However unwise this too close imitation of the British postal reform may at first have been, your committee are opposed to any return to the higher rates, at least till the experiment of cheap postage shall have been more fully and fairly tried, the Government itself meantime paying its just proportion out of the common treasury for the transportation of its own mail matter free.

It is said that the abolition of franks will cut off millions by retrenching the amount of public printing. Your committee have already replied that not a dollar is expended for printing except by act or resolution of one or both houses of Congress. Let us lay the axe, then, at the root of the evil. But are these books and public documents printed in excess solely because they may be transmitted free? or, rather, is it not that the public printer may be enriched, or reimbursed, at least, what it has cost him to secure his election? If so, the abolition of franks will in nowise tend to arrest the evil.

But it is urged that the mails are loaded down by the weight—*multorum camelorum onus*—of books and public documents, and that thus the cost of mail transportation is greatly enhanced. Now, by far the greater part of free matter is carried upon railroads or in steamboats; and what contractor, we ask, will carry for one dollar a mile less because of the abolition of franks? The department furnishes, and must furnish, the route agents; while the contractors provide, and must provide, the mail cars or apartments, whether there be free mail matter or not; and of what moment is it, in this regard, to either contractor or department, whether there be one bag to transport or twenty?

Again, it is said, and Postmasters-General have repeated it till it has become a sort of *carmen necessarium* to officials, that this great reform is to gain millions to the department. "There is no reason," so it is written down in a late annual report, "why the Post-Office Department, through its contractors, should perform this service *gratuitously* for the *Government* than there is that the steamboats and railroad companies of the country should transport its troops, munitions of war, and stores without compensation." When, your committee beg to know, did the Post-Office Department become a separate Government? When did it "secede?" Hitherto it has been a popular delusion that the General Post-Office was but a branch or department of the government—a part of the machinery by which its constitutional powers and functions were to be executed. It has been supposed the creature of Congress and under their control; and, further, that if Congress should command it to transport certain matter free of postage, it was its duty, as a branch of the executive, to "faithfully execute" such command, even "gratuitously;" leaving it to Congress to supply the means, in such manner as they might see fit. Steamboat and railroad companies being made up of private individuals may, constitutionally, refuse to do that sort of service for the Government without "just compensation;" but your committee cannot concede any such privilege to a mere creature of Congress—a subordinate Department of Government.

But $1,800,000 is to be saved in postages to the Government. How saved? If that vast amount of mail matter, now free, which so greatly enhances, as is said, the cost of transportation, is to be cut off by the abolition of franks, whence is to come the alleged increase of postage by reason of this same matter no longer transported? If books and public documents are no more to be printed, they cannot be transmitted through the mails; and if not transmitted, they cannot be charged with postage. There must be a loss somewhere. But assume that this class of mail matter is still to be transported, or that upon another class, now free, $1,800,000 is to be gained in postages, who is to pay this increased amount? If out of the treasury, Government saves nothing; if those only who receive, the people, pay, then it is but another form of taxation or burden, and far cheaper and better every way would it be that they should pay to private express companies or other common carriers. If those who send, the public servants, are to pay these $1,800,000 into the treasury, no office in the gift of Government—none requiring correspondence—is worth a single year's purchase. If the abolition be confined to congressional franks alone, and that sum is, in this way, to be paid into the treasury, the average amount to each Senator, Representative, and delegate will equal $5,844 15—nearly twice the compensation now allowed to them by law. Divide the burden between those who send and those who receive, and there still remains to each member of Congress nearly $2,500 as his proportion of the tax.

Finally, it is urged that the system of franking is full of abuses. Your committee deny, as to much that is denounced as an abuse, that it deserves the condemnation. As to the residue, it springs from either a defect in the law or a wanton violation of it. If a member of Congress frank a letter not written by himself, or strictly by his order; above all, if he frank envelopes, or packages of envelopes, in blank, to be used by those not entitled to the privilege, he breaks the law, and dishonors his office. If he undertake to frank that which is not mailable matter, or evasively to exceed the limit of two ounces, or mark that as a "public document" which is not, he is, in like manner, guilty of an offence against both law and good morals. It is an act of unveracity which no gentleman, upon reflection, will commit. Yet, strange to say, there are no adequate penalties for any of these offences. Here, then, let the "amending hand" be applied.

Franking by deputy, though, in the judgment of your committee, clearly legal, is a prolific source of abuse. Several times the Post-Office Department, assuming it to be contrary to law, has attempted to arrest it; yet so heavy is the burden of personal franking, especially of speeches and public documents, that the department has never long persisted in its efforts. And your committee are satisfied that a desire on the part of members to evade this burden, or otherwise the heavy tax for the hire of clerks, is the cause of some part, at least, of the opposition to the franking privilege.

To correct abuses, and at the same time to relieve members of Congress in this regard, your committee report a plan which they believe to be efficient, and at the same time secured from abuse, and which they trust may be approved by the House. This plan, along with a few other slight amendments or modifications of existing laws, not enlarging but rather restricting the franking privilege, they propose as a substitute for the Senate bill referred to them, and accordingly report the accompanying bill as a digest or code of regulations for the transmission of free matter through the mails of the United States.

JUSTICE TO THE NORTH-WEST.

REMARKS ON THE MOTION TO EXCUSE MR. HAWKINS, OF FLORIDA, FROM SERVING ON "THE COMMITTEE OF THIRTY-THREE."

In the House of Representatives, December 10, 1860.

COMPELLED, by the rules of the House, to vote upon the question of excusing the gentleman from Florida from serving upon this committee, I desire, in a few words, to submit my own reasons for the vote which I propose to give. With many of the reasons assigned by the gentleman from Florida, I, as a Representative from one of the free States of this Union, have nothing to do; but there are considerations which impel me, as such Representative, to vote for the motion to excuse.

It is idle, sir, to attempt to "coerce" any gentleman to serve upon this committee who assigns such reasons as the gentleman from Florida has given; and in justice to him, and to his State, but above all, to the very purpose of the committee itself, I cannot so vote. You may decline to excuse him; you cannot compel him to discharge, with good will or alacrity, the duties you impose upon him; and what kind of conciliation and compromise is that which begins by forcing a man to serve upon a committee raised for the very purpose of peace? What prospect, in God's name—I speak it reverently—is there of adjustment, when you are obliged to resort to compulsion to make up your committee on compromise and adjustment?

I pass by without comment the consideration so earnestly pressed by the gentleman from Florida, that this proposition might, with far more propriety and effect, have come from the Republican party in this House; that party which has just triumphed in the election which is the culminating point of all our controversies, and of all the dangers which surround us; and that, with great honor to himself and great and soothing good, it may have been, to the whole country, full of excitement and alarm, the gentleman now chairman of this committee (Mr. Corwin), distinguished for his age, his experience, his eloquence, and his moderation—not to speak of his position as the "leader" (so he asserts) of that party—might have assumed upon himself the responsibility of the initiative in that great work of reconciliation and reconstruction which alone can save us now, instead of allowing it to be devolved upon the Representative of that particular spot in Virginia selected by Abolition madness and wickedness as the weakest point of attack along the entire slaveholding borders of this Confederacy.

I pass by also the cumbrous construction of this committee, with the single remark that a council of war never fights, and a committee of thirty-three will never agree upon any thing—upon any thing, certainly, not so weak, so diffused, so diluted, as to be utterly inadequate to the solution of the greatest and gravest and most difficult question ever presented in modern history. I will not so much as suggest, sir, the possibility that the labors of this committee will all end in nothing, and in worse than nothing; nor—approving earnestly of the motive for raising the committee—will I remark even, as the gentleman from Florida has done, upon the peculiar composition of this committee in having men appointed upon it who represent nobody—not even themselves—or who are peculiarly odious or distasteful to the sections from which they come; and fitted, therefore, far more to embarrass and defeat, than to advance the avowed purpose for which the committee was ordered. Of course, sir, I mean no disrespect personally to the Speaker; but in assigning my reasons for refusing to coerce a gentleman to serve upon this committee, I have the right, and mean to exercise it, of just criticism upon its composition, and of suggestion as to the probable result of its labors.

But there is one consideration which will absolutely preclude me from voting to compel any man to act upon your committee. The gentleman from Florida has alluded to it; but he has not stated it quite strong enough. *There is not one single Representative of the Democratic party upon this committee—not from the Northwest alone—but from the sixteen free States of this Union east of the Rocky Mountains.* The Pacific is, indeed, represented. No thanks, sir; it was "Hobson's choice." There is no Republican member from California here; although Mr. Lincoln, through the infinite subdivision of his opponents, has been enabled to secure the electoral vote of that State. The excellent and intelligent gentleman from Oregon (Mr. Stout) is, indeed, upon it, because he is fortunate in having no colleague in this House; though, to speak the truth, remembering the representation of Oregon in certain recent political conventions, I should not have been surprised had that gentleman been supplanted by Horace Greeley; or possibly by the member from Massachusetts (Mr. Thayer), although that member is, I suspect, a little too strongly tinctured, perhaps, with the doctrine of "squatter sovereignty" to suit the times. (Laughter.)

But, I repeat, sir, there is not upon your committee one solitary Representative east of the Rocky Mountains, of that mighty host, numbering one million six hundred thousand men, which for so many years has stood as a vast breakwater against the winds and waves of sectionalism; and upon whose constituent elements, at least, this country must still so much depend in the great events which are thronging thick upon us, for all hope of preservation now or of restoration hereafter. Sir, is any man here insane enough to imagine for a moment that this great Northern and Western Democracy, constituting an essential part, and by far the most numerous part, of that great Democratic party which for half a century moulded the policy and controlled the destinies of this Republic; that party which gave to the country some of her brightest jewels; that party which placed upon your statute-books every important measure of enduring legislation from the beginning of the Government to this day—that such a section of such a party is to be thus utterly ignored, insulted, and thrust aside as of no value? I tell you, you mistake the character of the men you have to deal with. We are in a minority indeed, to-day, at the ballot-box; and *we* bow quietly now to the popular will thus expressed. We are defeated, but not conquered; and he is as a fool in the wisdom of this world, who thinks that in the midst of the stirring and revolutionary times which are upon us, these sixteen hundred thousand men, born free and now the equals of their brethren—men whose every pulse throbs with the spirit of liberty—will tamely submit to be degraded to inferiority and reduced to political servitude. Never, never, while there is but one man left to strike a blow at the oppressor.

Sir, we love this Union; and more than that, we obey the Constitution. We are here a gallant little band of less than thirty men, but representing more than a million and a half of freemen. We are here to maintain the Constitution, which makes the Union, and to exact and to yield that equality of rights which makes the Constitution worth maintaining. We are ready here to do all and to suffer all in the cause of our—thank God!—yet common country; and by no vote or speech or act of ours, here or elsewhere, shall any thing be done to defile, or impair, or to overthrow this the grandest temple of human liberty ever erected in any age. But we demand to worship at the very foot of the altar; and not, as servants or inferiors, in the outer courts of the edifice. And, sir, if the great work of the preservation or of the restoration of this Government is to go on successfully, let me warn gentlemen that it is to this very army of conservative men that you are to look at last for its consummation. If the gentleman from Ohio (Mr. CORWIN), the chairman of this committee, would do any thing effectively to correct public sentiment in our common State, it is to the two hundred and ten thousand men, not of his own party, together with such others of that party as he may be able to carry over with him, that he is to trust for the vindication of such measures, if any, of conciliation and adjustment which his committee may propose, and this House and the Senate may adopt. So, too, it will be in every free State of this Union. And yet that powerful minority, reckoned by millions, and including a country extending from the Atlantic to the Rocky Mountains, made up of men by whose right hands this Government is to be defended and maintained, or restored, are as voiceless upon this committee as the sands upon the sea-shore. Can any good result from a committee so constituted? Ought any man to be compelled to serve upon such a committee?

I speak now as a western man; and I thank the gentleman from Florida heartily for the kindly sentiments towards that great West, to which he has given utterance. Most cordially I reciprocate them, one and all. Sir, we of the Northwest have a deeper interest in the preservation of this Government in its present form, than any other section of the Union. Hemmed in, isolated, cut off from the seaboard upon every side; a thousand miles and more from the mouth of the Mississippi, the free navigation of which, *under the law of nations*, we demand, and will have at every cost; with nothing else but our other great inland seas, the lakes—and their outlet, too, through a foreign country—what is to be our destiny? Sir, we have fifteen hundred miles of southern frontier, and but a little narrow strip of eighty miles or less, from Virginia to Lake Erie, bounding us upon the east. Ohio is the isthmus that connects the South with the British Possessions, and the East with the West. The Rocky Mountains separate us from the Pacific. Where is to be our outlet? What are *we* to do when you shall have broken up and destroyed this Government? We are seven States now, with fourteen Senators and fifty-one Representatives, and a population of nine millions. We have an empire equal in area to the third of all Europe, and we do not mean to be a dependency or province either of the East or of the South; nor yet an inferior or second rate power upon this continent; and if we cannot secure a maritime boundary upon other terms, we will cleave our way to the sea-coast with the sword. A nation of warriors we may be; a tribe of shepherds never. I speak it out, sir, now and here; yet without apprehension of any just cause of complaint or quarrel at any time with either section upon this question.

And yet nearly one-half of the people of that vast empire, which very soon is to perform so important a part in the affairs of this continent, are utterly ignored and excluded from this committee. More than six hundred thousand voters, represented here by sixteen members upon this floor, are silenced and disfranchised in its arrangement. What do you propose to do without their votes at home and our votes here? Or are we both to accept blindly whatsoever your committee may choose graciously to report, and be thankful for it? Sir, we have one State with a Democratic majority upon this floor, and she, at least, had a right to be represented upon your committee. I find no fault, personally, with the gentleman from that State now on the Committee (Mr. KELLOGG), but the Democracy of the Northwest had a right to be heard through the State of Illinois.

Such is your committee; and I cannot and I will not vote to compel any man to serve upon it. The time is short; the danger imminent; the malady deep-seated and of long standing. Whatever is to be done must be done at once, and it must be done thoroughly. Every remedy must go right straight home to the seat of the disease. Let there be no delays, no weak inventions, no temporizing expedients. Otherwise, not secession of a few States only, but total and absolute disruption of this whole Government is inevitable.

Sir, we stand this day in the forum of history. We are acting in the eye of posterity. We have solemn duties to the whole country to perform; and if we do not discharge them instantly and aright—

> "Not poppy, nor mandragora,
> Nor all the drowsy sirups of the world,
> Shall ever medicine us to that sweet sleep,
> Which yesterday we ow'd."

In the name, then, of the Democracy of sixteen of the free States of this Union, I protest against the arrangement of this committee. My motives may be misinterpreted now. Be it so. Time in a little while will vindicate them.

RESPONSE,

Upon being called out at a Serenade to the Hon. George E. Pugh, Washington, December 22, 1860.*

Fellow-Citizens: As a Western man, as a citizen of Ohio, as a long-time friend, and now the colleague and house-mate of the Senator from my State, in whose honor you have assembled, I thank you cordially for this demonstration—a personal compliment to him for the ability and courage which the other day he displayed in the Senate Chamber. No man has deserved it better, and he too, I am sure, thanks you heartily for it. But it is as a testimonial in behalf of the doctrine enforced and the policy pronounced by him on that occasion, that this demonstration has peculiar significance. To-night you are here to indorse the great policy of conciliation, not force; peace, not civil war. The desire nearest the heart of every patriot in this crisis, is the preservation of the Union of these States, as our fathers made it. [Applause.] But the Union can be preserved only by maintaining the Constitution, and the constitutional rights, and above all, the perfect equality of every State and every section of this Confederacy. [Cheers.] That Constitution was made in peace; it has, for now more than seventy years, been preserved by the policy of peace at home, and it can alone be maintained for our children, and their children after them, by that same peace policy.

This Union is not to be held together, this Constitution is not to be cemented by the blood of our citizens poured out in civil war; and coercion is civil war, and it is folly to attempt to disguise its true character under the name and pretence of "enforcing the laws." The people will in the end demand a bloody reckoning upon the heads of those who may thus deceive them. [Loud cheers.] No; let us negotiate, compromise, concede; let us, if need be, give and receive new guarantees for our respective rights; for this is wisdom and true statesmanship; and in this way only can the Government be preserved or restored. At all events let us have no civil war. [Applause.] And, as one living near the borders of what may be, unhappily, and in an evil hour, a divided Confederacy, I am resolved that by no vote, by no speech, by no act of mine shall any thing be done to plunge this my country, into the horrors of a war among brethren.

I lament profoundly indeed the causes which have led to this most alarming crisis in the midst of which we now are. I have labored faith-

* Speeches were also made on this occasion, by Hons. George E. Pugh, John J. Crittenden, George A. Pendleton, Robert Mallory, and others.

fully and right manfully for years to correct and to remove them. I regret also the results which naturally and inevitably have followed them. But if we must separate, let it, in God's name, be in peace. Then we shall be able to reconstruct this Government. If we cannot preserve, we can, and we will, restore it, and become thus the second founders of the Republic. That is our mission, inferior only in glory and honor, and in good, to the mission of those who laid its foundation at first. [Applause].

Preserve peace and we shall yet save this Government; we shall have time to correct public sentiment everywhere, and to agree upon such terms of adjustment as will consolidate the union of these States and make it firmer and stronger than before. But the first drop of blood shed among us in the wicked and murderous insanity of coercion will be the beginning of a civil war, and of massacres and atrocities, the end of which neither you nor your children's children will see, till wearied, impoverished, exhausted, the people of a generation or two hence shall seek for peace and security under the despotism of the two, three, or more military leaders who shall partition this magnificent country of ours between them, by the sword. Hence, citizens of Washington, you are right to be here to-night to testify your approval of that great policy of peace and conciliation which alone can avert these horrors. [Great cheering.]

The Republican party has come into power with the threat of hostility to the rights and institutions of nearly one-half of this Confederacy; and it is just and fit, according to the course of the common law, but, above all, of the great law of self-preservation, that they should be put under bonds not to carry that threat into execution. [Applause.] This is the philosophy of new guarantees for old rights. It is the philosophy of that policy to which the gentleman in whose honor you have assembled, together with myself and others from the North and Northwest, are wholly and resolutely committed. We mean to stand by it. Public sentiment may, indeed, at first be against us; the tide may run heavily the other way for a little while; but thank God we all have nerve enough, and will enough, and faith enough in the people, to know that at last it will turn for peace; and though we may be prostrated for a time by the storm, yet upon the gravestone of every patriot who shall die now in the cause of peace and humanity and the country, shall be written, "*Resurgam*"—I shall rise again. And it will be a glorious resurrection. [Loud and continued applause.] From the Senate Chamber, then, from the Hall of Representatives, and from this assemblage to-night, let the word go forth to the hearts of the people throughout the length and breadth of the land, that come what may of secession, disruption, and political discord and strife, the sword at least shall not be drawn by the rival sections, nor our quarrels ever be submitted to its stern arbitrament. [Applause].

A voice—Let South Carolina go to——

South Carolina is bound, I trust, upon no such mission [loud and deafening applause], travelling in no such direction. [Cheers.] But I hope and believe that if security but be given to her for the full and undisturbed enjoyment of the same rights and no more, she must ask no more—[A Voice.—She don't ask more]—which she is entitled to now in the Union and under the Constitution; if the new guarantees for old rights, proposed by Mr. Crittenden, or similar guarantees, ample enough to settle finally and forever this pestilent anti-slavery agitation, which, for a quarter of a century, having shaken the temple of this Union, is now about to topple it down in ruin upon our heads—if these shall be given in the same spirit with which the Constitution itself was made and agreed to, South Carolina will gladly return to that Confederacy, in the founding of which, as in the war of the Revolution which preceded it, her heroes and patriots and statesmen bore so gallant and honorable and distinguished a part.. [Cheers.]

Fellow-citizens, I am all over, and altogether, a Union man. I would preserve it in all its integrity and worth. But, I repeat, that this cannot be done by coercion—by the sword. He who would resort to force—military force, is a disunionist, call himself what he may, and disguise it though he may under the pretext of executing the laws and preserving the Union. He is a "disunionist," whether he knows it and means it or not. Hence I am for peace and for compromise, fixed, irrepealable compromise, so that we may secure peace; but I am for peace in any event—peace upon both sides and upon all sides, now and forever.

THE GREAT AMERICAN REVOLUTION OF 1861.

Speech delivered in the House of Representatives, Feb. 20, 1861.*

The special order—namely, the Report of the Committee of Thirty-Three—being under consideration—Mr. VALLANDIGHAM addressed the House as follows:

MR. SPEAKER: It was my purpose, some three months ago, to speak

* This is that famous speech in which Mr. VALLANDIGHAM is said to have proposed to divide the Union into "*four distinct nationalities.*" The whole speech is here

solely upon the question of peace and war between the two great sections of the Union, and to defend, at length, the position which, in the very beginning of this crisis, and almost alone, I assumed against the employment of military force by the Federal Government to execute its laws and restore its authority within the States which might secede. Subsequent events have rendered this unnecessary. Within the three months, or more, since the Presidential election, so rapid has been the progress of events, and such the magnitude which the movement in the South has attained, that the country has been forced—as this House and the incoming Administration will at last be forced, in spite of their warlike purposes now—to regard it as no longer a mere casual and temporary rebellion of discontented individuals, but a great and terrible REVOLUTION, which threatens now to result in permanent dissolution of the Union, and division into two or more rival, if not hostile, confederacies. Before this dread reality, the atrocious and fruitless policy of a war of coercion to preserve or to restore the Union has, outside, at least, of these walls and of this capital, rapidly dissolved. The people have taken the subject up, and have reflected upon it, till, to-day in the South, almost as one man, and by a very large majority, as I believe, in the North, and especially in the West, they are resolved, that, whatever else of calamity may befall us, that horrible scourge of CIVIL WAR shall be averted. Sir, I rejoice that the hard Anglo-Saxon sense and pious and humane impulses of the American people have rejected the specious disguise of words without wisdom, which appealed to them to enforce the laws, collect the revenue, maintain the Union, and restore the Federal authority by the perilous edge of battle, and that thus early in the revolution they are resolved to compel us, their Representatives, belligerent as you of the Republican party here may now be, to the choice of peaceable disunion upon the one hand, or Union through adjustment and conciliation upon the other. Born, sir, upon the soil of the United States—attached to my country from earliest boyhood, loving and revering her with some part, at least, of the spirit of Greek and Roman patriotism—between these two alternatives, with all my mind, with all my heart, with all my strength of body and of soul, living

given: also, the proposed amendments to the Constitution. It is not easy to imagine a greater perversion of the plain and obvious meaning of language than has been exhibited in this case. The reader will not be surprised to find that this speech, made in the hour of most imminent peril, when the greatest calamity any nation has ever endured was impending, so far from being, as has been so often and so falsely asserted, a proposition to divide the Union into "four distinct nationalities," was, in fact, a most wise and prudent suggestion, evincing the deepest political sagacity and foresight. If adopted, the country would have been saved that great waste and slaughter which have already wearied and sickened the heart of humanity, and of which the end is not yet. Even now, it may not be too late to make good use of some features of the plan here proposed.

or dying, at home or in exile, I am for the Union which made it what it is; and therefore, I am also for such terms of peace and adjustment as will maintain that Union now and forever. This, then, is the question which to-day I propose to discuss:

How shall the Union of these States be Restored and Preserved?

Sir, it is with becoming modesty, and with something of awe, that I approach the discussion of a question which the ablest statesmen of the country have failed to solve. But the country expects even the humblest of her children to serve her in this, the hour of her sore trial. This is my apology.

Devoted as I am to the Union, I have yet no eulogies to pronounce upon it to-day. It needs none. Its highest eulogy is the history of this country for the last seventy years. The triumphs of war, and the arts of peace—science, civilization, wealth, population, commerce, trade, manufactures, literature, education, justice, tranquillity, security to life, to person, to property—material happiness, common defence, national renown, all that is implied in the "blessings of liberty"—these, and more, have been its fruits from the beginning to this hour. These have enshrined it in the hearts of the people; and, before God, I believe they will restore and preserve it. And, to-day, they demand of us, their ambassadors and Representatives, to tell them how this great work is to be accomplished.

Sir, it has well been said that it is not to be done by eulogies. Eulogy is for times of peace. Neither is it to be done by lamentations over its decline and fall. These are for the poet and the historian, or for the exiled statesman who may chance to sit amid the ruins of desolated cities. Ours is a practical work, and it is the business of the wise and practical statesman to inquire first what the causes are of the evils for which he is required to devise a remedy.

Sir, the subjects of mere partisan controversy which have been chiefly discussed here and in the country, so far, are not the causes, but only the symptoms or developments of the malady which is to be healed. These causes are to be found in the nature of man, and in the peculiar nature of our system of governments. Thirst for power and place, or pre-eminence—in a word, ambition—is one of the strongest and earliest developed passions of man. It is as discernible in the school-boy as in the statesman. It belongs alike to the individual and to the masses of men, and is exhibited in every gradation of society, from the family up to the highest development of the State. In all voluntary associations of any kind, and in every ecclesiastical organization, also, it is equally manifested. It is the sin by which the angels fell. No form of government is exempt from it; for even the absolute monarch is obliged to execute his power through the instrumentality of agents; and ambition here courts one master instead of many masters. As between foreign States, it manifests itself in schemes of conquest and territorial aggrandizement. In despotisms it is shown in intrigues, assassinations, and revolts. In constitutional monarchies, and in aristocracies, it exhibits itself in contests among the different orders of society, and the several interests of agriculture, trade, commerce, and the professions. In democracies it is seen everywhere, and in its highest development; for here all the avenues to political place and preferment, and emolument, too, are open to every citizen; and all movements, and all interests of society, and every great question—moral, social, religious, scientific, no matter what—assumes, at some time or other, a political complexion, and forms a part of the election issues and legislation of the day. Here, when combined with interest, and where the action of the Government may be made a source of wealth, then honor, virtue, patriotism, religion, all perish before it. No restraints and no compacts can bind it.

In a federal republic all these evils are found in their amplest proportions, and take the form also of rivalries between the States; or more commonly, or finally, at least, especially where geographical and climatic divisions exist, or where several contiguous States are in the same interest, and sometimes where they are similar in institutions or modes of thought, or in habits and customs, of sectional jealousies and controversies, which end always, sooner or later, in either a dissolution of the union between them, or the destruction of the Federal character of the Government. But, however exhibited—whether in federative or in consolidated governments, or whatever the development may be—the great primary cause is always the same: the feeling that might makes right; that the strong ought to govern the weak; that the will of the mere and absolute majority of numbers ought always to control; that fifty men may do what they please with forty-nine; and that minorities have no rights, or at least that they shall have no means of enforcing their rights, and no remedy for the violation of them. And thus it is that the strong man oppresses the weak, and strong communities, States, and sections aggress upon the rights of weaker States, communities, and sections. This is the principle; but I propose to speak of it, to-day, only in its development in the political, and not in the personal or domestic relations.

Sir, it is to repress this principle that governments, with their complex machinery, are instituted among men; though in their abuse, indeed, governments may themselves become the worst engines of oppression. For this purpose treaties are entered into, and the law of nations acknowledged between foreign States. Constitutions and municipal laws and compacts are ordained, or enacted, or concluded, to secure the same great end. No men understood this, the philosophy and aim of all just government, better than the framers of our Federal Constitution. No men tried more faithfully to secure the Government which they were instituting from this mischief; and, had the country over which it was established been circumscribed by nature to the limits which it then had, their work would have, perhaps, been perfect, enduring for ages. But the wisest among them did not foresee—who, indeed, that was less than omniscient, could have foreseen?—the amazing rapidity with which new settlements and new States have sprung up, as if by enchantment, in the wilderness; or that political necessity, or lust for territorial aggrandizement, would, in sixty years, have given us new Territories and States equal in extent to the entire area of the country for which they were then framing a Government? They were not priests or prophets to that God of MANIFEST DESTINY whom we now worship, and will continue to worship, whether united into one Confederacy still, or divided into many. And yet it is this very acquisition of territory which has given strength, though not birth, to that sectionalism which already has broken in pieces this, the noblest Government ever devised by the wit of man. Not foreseeing the evil, or the necessity, they did not guard against its results. Believing that the great danger to the system which they were about to inaugurate lay rather in the jealousy of the State Governments toward the power and authority delegated to the Federal Government, they defended it diligently against that danger. Apprehending that the larger States might aggress upon the rights of the smaller States, they provided that no State should, without its consent, be deprived of its equal suffrage in the Senate. Lest the legislative department might encroach upon the executive, they gave to the President the self-protecting power of a qualified veto; and, in turn, made the President impeachable by the two Houses of Congress. Satisfied that the several State Governments were strong enough to protect themselves from Federal aggressions, if, indeed, not too strong for the efficiency of the General Government, they thus devised a system of internal checks and balances looking chiefly to the security of the several departments from aggression upon each other, and to prevent the system from being used to the oppression of individuals. I think, sir, that the debates in the Federal Convention, and in the conventions of the several States called to ratify the Constitution, as well as the contemporaneous letters and publications of the time, will support me in the statement, that the friends of the Constitution wholly under-estimated the power and influence of the Government which they were establishing. Certainly, sir, many of the ablest statesmen of that day earnestly desired a stronger Government; and it was the policy of Mr. Hamilton, and of the Federal party, which he created, to strengthen the General Government; and hence the funding and protective systems, the national bank, and other similar schemes of finance, along with the "general-welfare doctrine," and a liberal construction of the Constitution.

Sir, the framers of the Constitution—and I speak it reverently, but with the freedom of history—failed to foresee the strength and centralizing tendencies of the Federal Government. They mistook wholly the real danger to the system. They looked for it in the aggressions of the large States upon the small States, without regard to geographical position, and accordingly guarded jealously in that direction, giving, for this purpose, as I have said, the power of a self-protecting veto in the Senate to the small States, by means of their equal suffrage in that Chamber, and forbidding even amendment of the Constitution, in this particular, without the consent of every State. But, they seem wholly to have overlooked the danger of SECTIONAL COMBINATIONS as against other sections, and to the injury and oppression of other sections, to secure possession of the several departments of the Federal Government, and of the vast powers and influence which belong to them. In like manner, too, they seem to have utterly under-estimated SLAVERY as a disturbing element in the system, possibly because it existed still in almost every State, but chiefly because the growth and manufacture of cotton had scarce yet been commenced in the United States—because cotton was not yet crowned King. The vast extent of the patronage of the Executive, and the immense power and influence which it exerts, seem also to have been altogether under-estimated. And independent of all these, or rather, perhaps, in connection with them, there were inherent defects, incident to the nature of all governments; some of them peculiar to our system, and to the circumstances of the country, and the character of the people over which it was instituted, which no human sagacity could have foreseen, but which have led to evils, mischiefs, and abuses, which time and experience alone have disclosed. The men who made our Government were human; they were *men*, and they made it for men of like passions and infirmities with themselves.

I propose now, sir, to inquire into the practical workings of the system; the experiment—as the fathers themselves called it—after seventy years of trial.

No man will deny—no American, at least, and I speak to-day to and for Americans—that in its results it has been the most successful of any similar Government ever established; and yet, in the very midst of its highest development and its perfect success, in the very hour of its might, while "towering in its pride of place," it has suddenly been stricken down by a revolution which it is powerless to control. Sir, if I could believe, as the gentleman from Tennessee (Mr. Etheridge) would seem to have me believe, that for more than half a century the South has had all that she ever asked, and more than she ever deserved, and that now, at last, a few discontented spirits have been able to precipitate already seven States into insurrection and rebellion, because they are displeased with the results of a presidential election; or, if I could persuade myself, with the gentleman from Massachusetts (Mr. Adams), that thirteen States, or fifteen States, and eleven or twelve millions of people have been already drawn, or may soon be drawn, into a revolt against the grandest and most beneficent Government, in form and in practice, that ever existed, from no other than the trivial and most frivolous causes which he has assigned, then I should, indeed, regard this revolution, in the midst of which we are, as the most extraordinary phenomenon ever recorded in history. But the muse of history will, I venture to say, not so write it down upon the scroll which she still holds in her hand, in that grand old Hall of Representatives, where, linked to time, solemnly and sadly she numbers out yet the fleeting hours of this perishing Republic. No; believe me, Representatives, the causes for these movements lie deeper, and are of longer duration, than all this. If not, then the malady needs no extreme medicine, no healing remedies nothing, nothing. Time, patience, forbearance, quiet—these, these alone will restore the Union in a few months. But, sir, I have not so read the history of this country, especially for the last fourteen years. The causes, I repeat, are to be found in the practical workings of the system, and are to be removed only by remedies which go down to the very root of the evil; not, indeed, by eradicating the passions which give it birth and strength—for even religion fails to accomplish that impossible mission—but by checking or taking away the power with which these passions are armed for their work of evil and mischief.

I find, then, sir, the first or remote cause which has led to the incipient dismemberment of the Union, in the infinite honors and emoluments, the immense, and continually increasing, power and patronage of the Federal Government. Every admission of new States, every acquisition of new territory, every increase of wealth, population, or resources of any kind; all moral, social, intellectual, or inventive development; the press, the telegraph, the railroad, and the application of steam in every form —whatsoever there is of greatness at home, or of national honor and glory abroad—all, all has inured to the aggrandizement of this central government. Part of this, certainly, is the result of causes which no constitutional restriction, no party policy, and no statesmanship can control; but much of it, nevertheless, from infringements of the Constitution, and from usurpations, abuses, corruptions, and mal-administration of the Government. In the very beginning, as I have said, a fixed policy of strengthening the General Government, in every department, was inaugurated by the Federal party; and this led to the bitter and vehement struggle, in the very first decade of the system, between the Democratic-Republicans and the Federalists; between the advocates of power, and the friends of liberty; those who leaned strongly toward the General Government, and those who were for State rights and State sovereignty—the followers of Hamilton and the disciples of Jefferson—which ended, in 1801, in the overthrow of the Federal party, and the inauguration of the Democratic policy, which demanded a simple Government, a strict construction of the Constitution, no public debt, no protective tariff, no system of internal improvements, no national bank, hard money for the public dues, and economical expenditures; and this policy, after a long and violent contest for more than forty years—a contest marked with various fortune, and occasional defeat, and sometimes temporary departure by its own friends—at last became the established policy of the Government, and so continued until this pestilent sectional question of slavery obliterated old party divisions, and obscured and hid over and covered up for a time—if indeed, it has not removed utterly—some, at least, of the ancient landmarks of the Democratic party. And yet, in spite of the overthrow of the Federal party, in spite of the final defeat of its policy, looking especially and purposely to the strengthening of the General Government, partly from natural causes, as I have said, and partly because the Democratic party has sometimes been false to its professed principles—above all, to its great doctrine of State Rights, and its true and wise policy of economy in expenditures, and decrease in executive patronage and influence—the Federal Government has gone on, steadily increasing in power and strength and honor and consideration and *corruption*, too, from the hour of its inauguration to this day; and when I speak of "corruption," I use the word in the sense in which British statesmen use it—men who understand the word, and who have, for a century and a half, reduced the thing itself to a science and a system, and have made it an element of very great strength in the British Government.

Nor, sir, is this mischief, if mischief indeed it be, confined wholly to any one department of the General Government? The Federal judiciary—to begin with it—here and in the States, dazzles the imagination and invites the ambition of the lawyers, that not most numerous but yet most powerful class of citizens, by its superior honors, its great emoluments, its life-tenure, its faith in precedents, and its settled forms and ancient practice, untouched by codes and unshaken by crude and reckless and hasty legislation. Here, in this venerable forum, where States at home and States and empires from abroad, and the Federal Government itself, are accustomed to contend for the judgment of the court, whatever there yet remains of ancient and black-letter law; whatever of veneration and regard for the names and memories, and the volumes of Littleton, and Coke, and Croke, and Plowden, and the year books; or for silk gowns, and for all else, too, that is valuable in legal archæology, has taken refuge, and stands intrenched. All that there was of form and ceremony and dignity and decorum, in the beginning of the Government, is still to be found here, and only here; all but the bench and bar of forty years ago—the Marshalls, and the Storys, the Harpers, the Pinckneys, the Wirts, and the Websters of an age gone by.

Still, the circle of honor through the judiciary is a narrow one, and it lies open to but few; and yet, in times past, the judiciary has done much to enlarge the powers and increase the consideration and importance of the central Government.

But it is the Senate and the House of Representatives which are the great objects of ambition, and the seats of power. All the legislative powers of this great and mighty Republic, whose name and authority and majesty are known and felt and feared, too, throughout the earth, are vested in the Congress of the United States. War, revenues, credit, disbursement, commerce, coinage, the postal system, the punishment of crimes upon the high seas, and against the law of nations, the admission of new States, the disposition of the public lands, armies, navies, the militia—all belong to it to control, together with an unnumbered, innumerable, and most indefinable host of implied or derivative powers: whence funding systems, banks, protective tariffs, internal improvements, distributions, surveys, explorations, railroads, land grants, submarine telegraphs, postal steam navigation and post-roads upon the high seas, plunder schemes, speculations, and peculations, pensions, claims, the acquisition and government of Territories, and a long train of usurpations and abuses; all tending—legitimate powers and illegitimate assumptions of power alike—to aggrandize the central Government, and to make its possession and control the highest object of a corrupt, wicked, perverted, and peculating ambition, in any party or any section.

But great and imposing as the powers, honors, and consideration of Congress are, the Executive department is scarce inferior in any thing, and, in some things, is far superior to it. Your President stands in the place of a king. There is a divinity that doth hedge him in; it is the divinity of PATRONAGE. He is the god whose priests are a hundred and fifty thousand, and whose worshippers a host whom no man can number; and the sacrifices of these priests and worshippers are literally "a broken spirit." Sir, your President is commander-in-chief of your armies, your navies, and of the militia—four millions of men. He carries on war, concludes peace, and makes treaties of every sort. Through his qualified veto, he is a participant in the entire legislation of the Government, and it behooves the whole army of speculators, jobbers, contractors, and claimants, to propitiate him as well as Senators and Representatives. He calls the Congress together on extraordinary occasions, and adjourns them in case of disagreement. He appoints and receives ambassadors and all other diplomatic agents; appoints judges of the Supreme Court, and of other judicial tribunals; cabinet ministers; collectors of customs, and postmasters, and controls the appointment of a hundred and fifty thousand other officers, of every grade, from Secretary of State down to the humblest tide-waiter. All that is implied in the word "patronage," and all that is meant by that other word, the "spoils"—*res detestabilis et caduca*—a word and a thing unknown to the fathers of the Republic, all belong to him to control. His power of appointment and removal at discretion makes him the master of every man who would look to the Executive for honor or emolument; and its tremendous influence is reflected back upon the Senate and this House, on every Senator or Representative who would reward his friends for their support at home, or secure new friends for a re-election. The Constitution forbids titles of nobility; yet your President is the fountain of honor. Sir, to pass by the utter and extraordinary perversion of the original purpose of the Constitution in the choice of electors for the President—a perversion the result of caucuses, national conventions, and other party machinery, and which has led to those violent and debauching presidential struggles, every four years, for possession of the immense spoils of the executive office—no department has, in other respects also, so utterly outstripped the estimate of the founders of the Government, except, indeed, of the few who, like Patrick Henry, were derided as ghost-seers and hypochondriacs.

When the elder Adams was President, the great east-room of the White House—where now, or lately, on gala days, are gathered the ambassadors and ministers of a hundred courts, from Mexico to Japan, and the assembled wit and fashion and beauty and distinction of the thirty-three States of the Union—was then used by the excellent and patriotic wife of the President as a drying-room for—not the maids of honor—but the washerwoman of the palace.

Sir, there is an incident connected with the early settlement of this city—still the capitol of the Republic, selected as the seat of Government, by Washington, the Father of the Republic, and bearing his honored name—an incident which shows how much he and the other great men who made the Constitution under-estimated the power and importance of the Executive. This capitol, within which we now deliberate, *fronts to the east.* There all your Presidents are inaugurated; and it was the design and the expectation of the founders of the city that it should extend to the eastward. There, sir—there, in that direction—was to be the future Rome of the American continent. The Executive mansion was meant to be in the rear, and to be kept in the rear of the Chambers of the Legislature. A long vista through the original forest trees—a sort of American mall—was to connect them together; and the President was expected to enter below stairs, and at the back door, into this capitol. But he was to be kept for the most part *trans Tiberem*—on the other side of the Tiber. The low, marshy ground to the westward, it was supposed, would forever forbid the building up of a city between the seats of legislative and executive magistracy; and the whole—if, indeed, ever laid out at all—might have become a great national park. But behold the strange perversity of man! The city has all gone to the westward. The rear of the capitol has now become its front. Pennsylvania Avenue, instead of a suburban drive, is now a grand thoroughfare, the chief artery which conveys the blood from that which is now the centre or heart of the system—the President. The Executive mansion—that old castle, with bad fires, and without bells, to the sore discomfort of Mistress Abigail Adams—is now, and has been for years, the great object of attraction; and whereas, in the beginning of the "taverns"—for that was the name given them sixty years ago—all clustered around this capitol, I observe that now the greatest, most flourishing, and best patronized "hotel" has established itself within bow-shot of the White House. Sir, the power of executive gravitation has proved too strong for the framers of the Government and the founders of the city. Westward the course of architecture has taken its way; and certainly, sir—certainly—it is not because of any especial attraction about that most venerable of ancient marts—old Georgetown.

But to resume, sir. Nothing adds so much to the power and influence of the Executive as a large revenue and heavy expenditures; and if a public debt be added, so much the worse. Every dollar more borrowed or collected, and every dollar more spent, is just so much added to the power and value of the executive office. Nothing in the political history of the country has been so marked as the steady, but enormous, increase in the taxation and disbursement of the Federal Government. Fifteen years ago—to go back no further—just previous to the Mexican War, the receipts of the Treasury were $29,000,000, and the expenditures $27,000,000; while four years ago—only ten years later—the receipts had run up to $69,000,000, and the expenditures to $71,000,000—the latter being always, or nearly always, a little in advance of the former. Nature, it is said, sir, abhors a vacuum: but government—our government, at least—would seem to abhor a plethoric treasury. There are always surgeons, volunteers too, at that, if need be, of a very famous school of surgery, who are ready to resort, upon all occasions, to financial phlebotomy. Verily, sir—verily these surgeons of the executive household have great faith in a low fiscal regimen.

The collection and disbursement of $80,000,000 a year, for four years, is a prize worth every sacrifice. The power of the sword, the command of armies and navies and the militia, is itself a tremendous power; and, from the signs around us, from all that everywhere meets the eye or falls upon the ear, at every step throughout this capital, I am afraid that now at length, and before the close of the last quarter of the first century of the Republic, it is about to assume a terrible significancy, and that the reign of military despotism is henceforth to be dated from this year. But, great as this power is, it is nothing—nothing as yet in this country—compared with the power of the purse. He who commands that unnumbered host of eager and hungry expectants whose eyes are fixed upon the Treasury, to say nothing of that other host of seekers of office, is mightier far than the commander of military legions. The gentleman from Tennessee (Mr. Etheridge) entertained us the other day with a glowing picture of the exodus of the present incumbents about the executive offices and elsewhere. Sir, I should be pleased, when he next addresses the House, to have his fine powers of wit and eloquence tested by a description of the flight of the incoming locusts about the fourth of March. Certainly, sir—certainly—the departure of the army of fat, sleek, contented, well-fed and well-clad office-holders, whose natural *habitat* is the Treasury building, or some other of the same sort, is a picture melancholy enough to excite commiseration in even the hardest and the stoniest heart. But the ingress of that other mighty host of office-seekers, fifty to one—lean, lank, cadaverous, hungry, hollow-eyed, with bones bursting through their garments, and long, skinny fingers, eager to clutch the spoils; and stung, too, with the *œstus* of that practical sort of patriotism which loves the country for its material benefits, would require some part, at least, of the powers of those diabolical old painters of the Spanish or Italian school. The gentleman will pardon me, but I am sure that even he is not equal to it.

Such, Mr. Speaker, is the central Government of the United States, and such its powers and honors and emoluments; and every year adds strength to them. Against the centralizing tendencies and influences of such a Government, the States, separately, cannot contend. Neither ambition nor avarice, the love of honor, or the love of gain, find any thing to satisfy their large desires in the State governments. Sir, the State executives have no cabinets, no veto for the most part, no army, no navy, no militia, except upon the peace establishment, and that commonly despised; no foreign appointments, and no diplomatic intercourse; no treaties, no post-office, no land-office, no great revenues to disburse; small salaries, and no patronage—in short, sir, nothing to arouse ambition, or to excite avarice. The Legislatures of the States have a most valuable, but not the most dignified, field of labor. They declare no war, levy no imposts, regulate no external commerce, coin no money, establish no post-routes, oceanic or overland; make no land grants, emit no bills of credit of their own, publish no *Globe*, have no franking privilege, and their Senators and Representatives serve the State for a few hundred dollars a year. The State judiciaries, however important the litigation before them may be to the parties, attract commonly but small interest from the public; and, of late years, no great or splendid legal reputation is to be acquired, outside of a few of the larger cities at least, either upon the bench or at the bar of the State courts. Whatever, sir, the dignity or power or consideration of the United States may be, that of each State is but the one thirty-fourth part of it; and, indeed, for some years past, the control of the State governments has, to a great extent, been sought after chiefly as an instrumentality for securing control of legislative, executive, or judicial position in the Federal Government. And all this mischief—for mischief certainly I must regard it—has been steadily aggravated by the policy pursued in nearly all the States, of diminishing, in every way, in their constitutions, and by their laws, the dignity, power, and consideration of the several departments of their State governments. Short tenures, low salaries, biennial sessions, crude, hasty, and continually changing legislation, new constitutions every ten years, and whatever else may be classed under the head of reform, falsely so called, have been the bane of State sovereignty and importance. Indeed, for years past, State constitutions, laws, and institutions of every sort, seem to have been regarded as but so many subjects for rude and wanton experiments at the hands of reckless ideologists or demagogues. But, besides all this, the infinite subdivision of political power in the States, from the chief departments of State down through counties, townships, school-districts, cities, towns, and villages, all of which certainly is very necessary and proper in a democratic Government, tends very much of itself to decrease the dignity and importance of the States. In short, sir, in nearly all the States, and especially in the new States, the great purpose of the politicians would seem to have been, to ascertain just how feeble and simple and insignificant their governments could be made—just how near to a pure and perfect democracy our representative form of republicanism can be carried. All this, sir, would have been well, and consistent enough, no doubt, if the States were totally disconnected, or if the Federal Government could have been kept down equally low, simple, and democratic. Certainly, this is the true idea of a strictly democratic form and administration of government; and the nearer it is approached, the purer and better the system—in theory, at least. But the experiment having been fairly tried, and the fact settled, that in a country so large, wealthy, populous, and enterprising as ours is, it is impossible to reduce down, or to keep down, the central Government to one of economy and simplicity, it is the true wisdom and policy of the States to see to it that their own separate governments are not rendered any more insignificant, at least, than they are already.

Such, sir, I repeat, then, is the central Government of the United States, and such its great and tremendous powers and honors and emoluments. With such powers, such honors, such patronage, and such revenues, is it any wonder, I ask, that every thing, yes, even virtue, truth, justice, patriotism, and the Constitution itself, should be sacrificed to obtain possession of it? There is no such glittering prize to be contended for every four or two years anywhere throughout the whole earth; and accordingly, from the beginning, and every year more and more, it has been the object of the highest and lowest, the purest, and the most corrupt ambition known among men. Parties and combinations have existed from the first, and have been changed, and reorganized, and built up, and cast down, from the earliest period of our history to this day, all for the purpose of controlling the powers and honors and the moneys of the central Government. For a good many years parties were organized upon questions of finance or of political economy. Upon the subjects of a permanent public debt, a national bank, the public deposits, a protective tariff, internal improvements, the disposition of the public lands, and other questions of a similar character, all of them looking to the special interests of the moneyed classes, parties were, for a long while, divided. The different kinds of capitalists sometimes also disagreed among themselves—the manufacturer with the commercial men of the country; and, in this manner, party issues were occasionally made up. But the great dividing line, at last, was always between capital and labor—between the few who had money, and who wanted to use the Government to increase and "protect" it, as the phrase goes, and the many who had little, but wanted to keep it, and who only asked Government to let them alone. Money, money, sir, was at the bottom of the political contests of the times; and nothing so curiously demonstrates the immense power of money, as the fact, that in a country where there is no entailment of estates, no law of primogeniture, no means of keeping up vast accumulations of wealth in particular families, no exclusive privileges, and where universal suffrage prevails, these contests should have continued, with various fortune, for full half a century. But, at the last, the opponents of Democracy, known at different periods of the struggle by many different names, but around whom the moneyed interests always rallied, were overborne, and utterly dispersed. The Whig party, their last refuge, the last and ablest of the economic parties died out; and the politicians who were not of the Democratic party, with a good many more, also, who had been of it, but who had deserted it, or whom it had deserted, were obliged to resort to some other and new element for an organization which might be made strong enough to conquer and to destroy the Democracy, and thus obtain control of the Federal Government. And most unfortunately for the peace of the country, and for the perpetuity, I fear, of the Union itself, they found the nucleus of such an organization ready formed to their hands—an organization odious, indeed, in name, but founded upon two of the most powerful passions of the human heart: SECTIONALISM, which is only a narrow and localized patriotism, and ANTI-SLAVERY, or love of freedom, which commonly is powerful just in proportion as it is very near coming home to one's own self, or very far off, so that either interest, or the imagination can have full power to act.

And here let me remark, that it had so happened that almost, if not quite, from the beginning of the Government, the South, or slaveholding section of the Union—partly because the people of the South are chiefly an agricultural and producing, a non-commercial and non-manufacturing people, and partly because there is no conflict, or little conflict among them between labor and capital, inasmuch as to a considerable extent, capital owns a large class of their laborers not of the white race; and it may be also, because, as Mr. Burke said, many years ago, the holders of slaves are "by far the most proud and jealous of their freedom," and because the aristocracy of birth and family, and of talent, is more highly esteemed among them than the aristocracy of wealth—but no matter from what cause, the fact was that the South, for fifty years, was nearly always on the side of the Democratic party. It was the natural ally of the Democracy of the North, and especially of the West. Geographical position and identity of interests bound us together; and till this sectional question of slavery arose, the South and the new States of the West were always together; and the latter in the beginning, at least, always Democratic. Sir, there was not a triumph of the Democratic party in half a century, which was not won by the aid of the statesmen and the people of the South. I would not be understood, however, as intimating that the South was ever slow to appropriate her full share of the spoils—the *opima spolia* of victory, or especially that the politicians of that great and noble old Commonwealth of Virginia—God bless her—were ever remarkable for the grace of self-denial in this regard—not at all. But it was natural, sir, that they who had been so many times, and for so many years, baffled and defeated by the aid of the South, should entertain no very kindly feelings towards her. And here I must not omit to say, that all this time there was a powerful minority in the whole South, sometimes a majority in the whole South, and always in some of the States of the South, who belonged to the several parties which, at different times, contended with the Democracy for the possession and control of the Federal Government. Parties, in those days, were not sectional, but extended into every State, and every part of the Union. And, indeed, in the Convention of 1787, the possibility, or, at least, the probability, of sectional combinations, seems, as I have already said, to have been almost wholly overlooked. Washington, it is true, in his Farewell Address, warned us against them, but it was rather as a distant vision than as a near reality; and a few years later, Mr. Jefferson speaks of a possibility of the people of the Mississippi Valley seceding from the East; for even then a division of the Union, North and South, or by slave lines in the Union, or out of it, seems scarcely to have been contemplated. The letter of Mr. Jefferson upon this subject, dated in 1803, is a curious one; and I commend it to the attention of gentlemen upon both sides of the House.

So long, sir, as the South maintained its equality in the Senate, and something like equality in population, strength, and material resources in the country, there was little to invite aggression, while there were the means, also, to repel it. But, in the course of time, the South lost its equality in the other wing of the capitol, and every year the disparity between the two sections became greater and greater. Meantime, too, the anti-slavery sentiment, which had lain dormant at the North for many years after the inauguration of the Federal Government, began, just about the time of the emancipation in the British West Indies, to develop itself in great strength, and with wonderful rapidity. It had appeared, indeed, with much violence at the period of the admission of Missouri, and even then shook the Union to its foundation. And yet, how little a sectional controversy, based upon such a question, had been foreseen by the founders of the Government, may be learned from Mr. Jefferson's letter to Mr. Holmes, in 1820, where he speaks of it falling upon his ear like "a fire-bell in the night." Said he:

" considered it, at once, as the death-knell of the Union. It is hushed, indeed, for the moment; but this is a reprieve only, not a final sentence. A geographical line, *coinciding with a marked principle, moral and political*,"—

Sir, it is this very coincidence of geographical line with the marked principle, moral and political, of slavery, which I propose to reach and to obliterate in the only way possible; by running other lines coinciding with other and less dangerous principles, none of them moral, and, above all, with other and conflicting interests—

"A geographical line, coinciding with a marked principle, moral and political, once conceived and held up to the angry passions of men, will never be obliterated, and every new irritation will mark it deeper and deeper." . . . .
. . . "I regret that I am now to die in the belief that the useless sacrifice of themselves, by the generations of 1776, to acquire self-government and happiness to their country, is to be thrown away by the unwise and unworthy passions of their sons; and that my only consolation is to be that I shall not live to weep over it."

Fortunate man! He did not live to weep over it. To-day he sleeps quietly beneath the soil of his own Monticello, unconscious that the mighty fabric of government which he helped to rear—a government whose foundations were laid by the hands of so many patriots and sages, and cemented by the blood of so many martyrs and heroes—hastens now, day by day, to its fall. What recks he, or that other great man, his compeer, fortunate in life and opportune alike in death, whose dust they keep at Quincy, of those dreadful notes of preparation in every State for civil strife and fraternal carnage; or of that martial array which already has changed this once peaceful capital into a beleaguered city? Fortunate men! They died while the Constitution yet survived, while the Union survived, while the spirit of fraternal affection still lived, and the love of true American liberty lingered yet in the hearts of their descendants.

Sir, the antagonism of parties founded on money or questions of political economy having died out, and the balance of power between the North and the South being now lost, and the strength and dignity, and the revenues and disbursements—the patronage and spoils—of the Federal Government having grown to an enormous size, was any thing more natural than the organization, *upon any basis peculiar to the stronger section* of a sectional party, to secure so splendid and tempting a prize? Or was any thing more inevitable than that the "marked principle, moral and political," of slavery, *coinciding with the very geographical line which divided the two sections*, and appealing so strongly to Northern sentiments and prejudices, and against which it was impossible for any man or any party long to contend, should be revived? Unhappily, too, just about this time, the acquisition of a very large territory from Mexico, not foreseen or provided for by the Missouri Compromise, opened wide the door for this very question of slavery, in a form every way the most favorable to the agitators. The Wilmot Proviso, or Congressional prohibition—now, indeed, exploded, but which, nevertheless, received in some form or other, the indorsement of every free State then in the Union—it was proposed to establish over the whole territory thus acquired, as well south of 36° 30′ as north of that latitude. The proposition, upon the other hand, to extend the Missouri Compromise line to the Pacific, was rejected by the votes of almost the entire Whig party, and of a large majority, I believe, of the Democratic party of the free States. That, sir, was the fatal mistake of the North; and in tribulation and anguish will she and the other sections of the Union, and our posterity, too, for ages, it may be, weep tears of bloody repentance and regret over it.

This controversy, however, sir, after having again shaken the Union to its centre, was at last, though with great difficulty, adjusted through the compromise measures of 1850, by the last of the great statesmen of the second period of the Republic. But four years afterwards, upon the bill to organize the territories of Kansas and Nebraska, upon the principles of the legislation of 1850, the imprisoned winds—*Eurus, Notusque, creberque procellis Africus*—were all again let loose with more than the rage of a tropical hurricane. The Missouri restriction, which for years had been denounced as a wicked and atrocious concession to slavery, and which, some thirty years before, had consigned almost every free State Senator or Representative who supported it, to political oblivion, became now a most sacred compact, which it was sacrilege to touch. A distinguished Senator, late the Governor of Ohio, who had entitled his great speech against the adjustment measures of 1850, "*Union and Freedom without Compromise*," now put forth his elaborate defence, four years later, of the Missouri restriction, with the rubric or text, in ambitious characters, "*Maintain Plighted Faith.*" But, right or wrong, wise or unwise, at the time, as the repeal of that restriction may have seemed, subsequent acts and events have made it both a delusion and a snare. Yes, sir, I confess it. I, who, as a private citizen, was one of its earliest defenders, make open confession of it here to-day. It was this which gave a new and terrible vitality to the languishing element of abolitionism, and which precipitated, at least, a crisis which, I fear, was, nevertheless, sooner or later, inevitable. It is the crisis of which the President elect spoke three years ago. It is, indeed, reached. Would to God it were passed, also, in peace.

But, sir, whether the leaders of the movement against the repeal of the Missouri restriction were consistent or inconsistent, honest or dishonest, the great mass of the people of the free States were roused, for a time, to the highest indignation by it; and, inasmuch as the Whig party was just then falling to pieces, wicked, or reckless, or short-sighted men eagerly seized upon this unsettled condition of the public mind, to reorganize the Free Soil party of 1848, under a new and captivating name, but very nearly upon the principles of the Buffalo platform of that year, thus abandoning the extreme abolition sentiments of the Liberty party, and bringing up the great majority of the Whig party, and not a few of the Democratic party, also, to the Free Soil and non-slavery extension principle; and by this compromise, forming and consolidating that powerful party, which, for the first time in our history, by a mere sectional plurality—in a minority, in fact, by a million of votes—has obtained possession of the power and patronage of the central government. Sir, if all this had happened solely by accident, and were likely never to be repeated, portentous as it might be of present evil, it would have caused, and ought to have caused, none of the disasters which have already followed. But the DREAD SECRET once disclosed, that the immense powers and revenues and honors and spoils of this great and mighty republic may be easily won, by a mere sectional majority, upon a popular sectional issue, will never die; and new aggressions and new issues must continually spring from it. This is the philosophy and the justification of the alarm and consternation which have shaken the South from the Potomac to the Gulf. It is the philosophy, and the justification, too, of the amendment of the gentleman from Massachusetts (Mr. Adams), and of all the other propositions for new adjustments and new guarantees. Sir, the gentleman from New York (Mr. Sedgwick) was right when he said that there never was any great event which did not spring from some adequate cause. The South is afraid of your sectional majority, organized and consolidated upon the abstract principle of hostility to slavery generally, and the practical application of that principle to the exclusion of slavery from all the Territories, and its restriction, by the power of that sectional majority, to where it now exists. And if this be not the fundamental doctrine of the Republican party, I shall be greatly obliged to some gentleman of that party to tell me what its fundamental doctrine is.

But unjust and oppressive as the South feel their exclusion from the common territories of the State to be, they know well, also, that the propelling power of a great moral and religious principle, as it is regarded in the North, added to the still more enduring, persistent, and prudent passion of ambition, of thirst for power and place, for the honors and emoluments of such a government as ours, with its half a million of dependents and expectants, and its eighty millions of revenues and disbursements, all, all to be secured by the Aladdin's lamp of a sectional majority, cannot be arrested or extinguished by any thing short of the suppression of the power which makes it potent for mischief. And nothing less than this, be assured, will satisfy any considerable number of even the more moderate of the people of the border slave States, and certainly without it there is not the slightest hope of the return of the States upon the Gulf, and thus of a restoration of the Union as it existed but three months ago. The statesmen and the people of all these States well know, also, that, by the civil law of every country, among individuals, and by the law of nations, as between sovereign and foreign States, the power to aggress, along with the threat and the preparation to aggress, is a good cause why an individual or a State should be required to give some adequate assurance that the power shall not be used to execute the threat; or, otherwise, that the power shall itself be taken away. Apply now, sir, these principles to the case in hand. The North has the power; that power is in the hands of the Republican party, and already they have resolved to use it for the exclusion of the South from all the Territories. There shall be no more extension of slavery. More than this: the leaders of the party—many of them leaders and founders of the old Liberty Guard, the original Abolition party of the North—the very men who brought the masses of the Whig party, and many of the Democratic party, from utter indifference and non-intervention years ago upon the question of slavery, up to the point of no more slavery extension, and persuaded them, in spite of the warning voice of Washington, in the very face of the appalling danger of disunion, to unite, for this purpose, in a powerful sectional party, for the first time in the history of the government—these self-same leaders proclaim now, not, indeed, as present doctrines or purposes of the Republican party, but as solemn abstract truths, as fixed, existing facts, that there is a "higher law" than the Constitution, and an "irrepressible conflict" of principle and interest, between the dominant and the minority sections of the Union, and that one or the other must conquer in the conflict. Sir, in this contest with ballots, who is it that must conquer—the section of the minority, or the section of the majority?

And now, sir, when sentiments like these are held, and proclaimed—deliberately, solemnly, repeatedly proclaimed—by men, one of whom is now the President elect, and the other the Secretary of State of the incoming Administration, is it at all surprising that the States of the South should be filled with excitement and alarm, or that they should demand, as almost with one voice they have demanded, adequate and complete guarantees for their rights, and security against aggression? Right or wrong, justifiably or without cause, they have done it; and I lament to say, that some of these States have even gone so far as to throw off wholly the authority of the Federal Government, and withdraw themselves from the Union. Sir, I will not discuss the right of secession. It is of no possible avail now, either to maintain or to condemn it; yet it is vain to tell me that States *cannot* secede. Seven States *have* seceded; they now refuse any longer to recognize the authority of this government, and already have entered into a new confederacy, and set up a provisional government of their own. In three months their agents and commissioners will return from Europe with the recognition of Great Britain and France, and of the other great powers of the continent. Other States at home are preparing to unite with this new confederacy, if you do not grant to them their just and equitable demands. The question is no longer one of the mere preservation of the Union. That was the question when we met in this Chamber some two months ago. Unhappily, that day has passed by; and while your "perilous Committee of Thirty-three" debated and deliberated to gain time—yes, to gain time—for that was the insane and most unstatesmanlike cry in the beginning of the session, star after star shot madly from our political firmament. The question to-day is: How shall we now keep the States we have, and restore those which are lost? Ay, sir, *restore*, till every wanderer shall have returned, and not one be missing from the "starry flock."

If, then, Mr. Speaker, I have justly and truly stated the causes which have led to those most disastrous results, if, indeed, the control of the immense powers, honors, and revenues—the spoils—of the Federal Government, in a word, if the possession of power, and the temptation to abuse it, be the primary cause of the present dismemberment of the United States, ought not every remedy proposed to reach at once the very seat of the disease? And why, sir, may not the malady be healed? Why cannot this controversy be adjusted? Has, indeed, the union of these States received the immedicable wound? I do not believe it. Never was there a political crisis for which wise, courageous, and disinterested statesmen could more speedily devise a remedy. British statesmen would have adjusted it in a few weeks. Twice certainly, if not three times, in this century, they have healed troubles threatening a dissolution of the monarchy and civil war, and each time healed them by yielding promptly to the necessities which pressed upon them, giving up principles and measures to which they had every way for years been committed. They have learned wisdom from the obstinacy of the king, who lost to Great Britain her thirteen colonies; and have been taught, by that memorable lesson, to concede and to compromise in time, and to do it radically; and history has pronounced it statesmanship, not weakness. In each case, too, they yielded up, not doctrines and a policy which they were seeking for the first time to establish, but the ancient and settled principles, usages, and institutions of the realm; and they yielded up these to save others yet more essential, and to maintain the integrity of the empire. They did save it, and did maintain it; and, to-day, Great Britain is stronger and more prosperous, and more secure than any government on the globe.

Sir, no man had, for a longer time, or with a more inexorable firmness, opposed Catholic emancipation than the Duke of Wellington; yet, when the issue came, at last, between emancipation or civil war, the hero of a hundred battle-fields, the conqueror at Waterloo, one of the greatest military commanders of modern times, yes, the IRON DUKE, lost not a moment, but yielded to the storm, and himself led the party which carried the great measure of peace and compromise, through the very citadel of conservatism—the House of Lords. Sir, he sought no middle ground, no half-way measure, confessing weakness, promising something, doing nothing. And in that memorable debate he spoke words of wisdom, moderation, and true courage, which I commend to gentlemen in this House—to our Wellington outside of it, and to all others, anywhere, whose parched jaws seem ravenous for blood. He said:

"It has been my fortune to have seen much of war—more than most men. I have been constantly engaged in the active duties of the military profession, from boyhood until I have grown gray. My life has been passed in familiarity with scenes of death and human suffering. Circumstances have placed me in countries where the war was internal—between opposite parties in the same nation; and, rather than a country I loved should be visited with the calamities which I have seen, *with the unutterable horrors of civil war, I would run any risk—I would make any sacrifice—I would freely lay down my life.* There is nothing which destroys property and prosperity, and demoralizes character, to the extent which civil war does. By it the hand of man is raised against his neighbor, against his brother, and against his father; the servant betrays his master, and the master ruins his servant. *Yet this is the resource to which we must have looked—these are the means which we must have applied, in order to have put an end to this state of things, if we had not embraced the option of bringing forward the measure for which I hold myself responsible.*"

Two years later, sir, in a yet more dangerous crisis upon the Reform Bill, which the Commons had rejected, and when civil commotion and discord, if not revolution, were again threatened, and it became necessary to dissolve the Parliament, and, for that purpose, to secure the consent of a king adverse to the dissolution, the Lord Chancellor of England, one of the most extraordinary men of the age—by, perhaps, the boldest and most hazardous experiment ever tried upon royalty—surprised the king into consent, assuring him, that the further existence of the Parliament was incompatible with the peace and safety of the kingdom; and having, without the royal command, summoned the great officers of State, prepared the crown, the robes, the king's speech, and whatever else was needed, and, at the risk of the penalties of high treason, ordered, also, the attendance of the troops required by the usages of the ceremony, he hurried the king to the Chamber of the House of Lords, where, in the presence of the Commons, the Parliament was dissolved, while each House was still in high debate, and without other notice in advance than the sound of the cannon which announced his majesty's approach. Yet all this was done in the midst of threatened insurrection and rebellion; when the Duke of Wellington, the Duke of Cumberland, and other noblemen were assaulted in the streets, and their houses broken into and mobbed; when London itself was threatened with capture, and the dying Sir Walter Scott was hooted and reviled by ruffians at the polls. It was done while the kingdom was one vast mob; while the cry rang through all England, Ireland, and Scotland, that the Bill must be carried *through* Parliament or *over* Parliament—if possible, by peaceable means—if not possible, then by force; and when the Prime Minister declared, in the House of Commons, that, by reason of its defeat, "much blood would be shed in the struggle between the contending parties, and that he was perfectly convinced that the British Constitution would perish in the conflict." And, sir, when all else failed, the king himself at last gave permission, in writing, to Earl Grey and the Lord Chancellor, to create as many new peers as might be necessary to secure a majority for the Reform Bill in the House of Lords.

Such, sir, is British statesmanship. They remember, but we have forgotten, the lessons which our fathers taught them. Sir, it will be the opprobrium of American statesmanship forever, that this controversy of ours shall be permitted to end in final and perpetual dismemberment of the Union.

I propose, now, sir, to consider briefly, the several propositions before the House looking to the adjustment of our difficulties by Constitutional amendment, in connection, also, with those which I have myself had the honor to submit.

Philosophically or logically considered, there are two ways in which the work before us may be effected: the first, by removing the temptation to aggress; the second, by taking the power away. Now, sir, I am free to confess that I do not see how any amendment of the Constitution can diminish the powers, dignity, or patronage of the Federal Government, consistently with the just distribution of power between the several departments; or between the States and the general Government, consistently with its necessary strength and efficiency. The evil here, lies rather in the administration than in the organization of the system; and a large part of it is inherent in the administration of every government. The virtue and intelligence of the people, and the capacity and honesty of their representatives, in every department, must be intrusted with the mitigation and correction of the mischief. The less the legislation of every kind, the smaller the revenues and fewer the disbursements; the less the Government shall have to do, every way, with debt, credit, moneyed influences, and jobs, and schemes of every sort, the longer peace can be maintained; and the more the number of the employés and dependents on Government can be reduced, the less will be the patronage and the corruption of the system, and the less, therefore, the motive to sacrifice truth and justice, and to overleap the Constitution to secure the control of it. In other words, the more you diminish temptation, the more you will deliver us from the evil.

But I pass this point by without further remark, inasmuch as none of the plans of adjustment proposed—either here or in the Senate—look to any change of the Constitution in this respect. They all aim—every one of them—at checking the POWER to aggress; and, except the amendment of the gentleman from Massachusetts (Mr. Adams), which goes much further than mine in giving a negative upon one subject to every slave State in the Union, they propose to effect their purpose by mere constitutional prohibitions. It is not my purpose, sir, to demand a vote upon the propositions which I have myself submitted. I have not the party position, nor the power behind me, nor with me, nor the age, nor the experience which would justify me in assuming the lead in any great measure of peace and conciliation; but I believe, and very respectfully I suggest it, that something similar, at least, to these propositions will form a part of any adequate and final adjustment which may restore all the States to the Federal Union. No, sir; I am able now only to follow where others may lead.

I shall vote for the amendment of the gentleman from Massachusetts (Mr. Adams)—though it does not go far enough—because it ignores and denies the moral or religious element of the anti-slavery agitation, and thus removes, so far at least, its most dangerous sting—*fanaticism*—and, dealing with the question as one of mere policy and economy, of pure politics alone, proposes a new and most comprehensive guarantee for the peculiar institution of the States of the South. I shall vote, also, for the Crittenden propositions—as an experiment, and only as an experiment—because they proceed upon the same general idea which marks the Adams amendment; and whereas, for the sake of peace and the Union, the latter would give a new security to slavery in the States, the former for the self-same great and paramount object of Union and peace, proposes to give a new security also to slavery in the Territories south of the latitude 36° 30′. If the Union is worth the price which the gentleman from Massachusetts volunteers to pay to maintain it, is it not richly worth the very small additional price which the Senator from Kentucky demands as the possible condition of preserving it? Sir, it is the old parable of the Roman Sibyl; and to-morrow she will return with fewer volumes, and, it may be, at a higher price.

I shall vote to try the Crittenden propositions, because, also, I believe that they are perhaps the least which even the more moderate of the slave States would, under any circumstances, be willing to accept; and because, North, South, and West, the people seem to have taken hold of them, and to demand them of us, as an experiment, at least. I am ready to try, also, if need be, the propositions of the Border State Committee, or of the Peace Congress; or any other fair, honorable, and reasonable terms of adjustment, which may so much as promise, even, to heal our present troubles, and to restore the Union of these States. Sir, I am ready and willing and anxious to try all things and to do all things "which may become a man," to secure that great object which is nearest to my heart.

But, judging all of these propositions, nevertheless, by the lights of philosophy and statesmanship, and as I believe they will be regarded by the historian who shall come after us, I find in them all two capital defects, which will, in the end, prove them to be both unsatisfactory to large numbers alike of the people of the free and the slave States, and wholly inadequate to the great purpose of the reconstruction and future preservation of the Union. None of them—except that of the gentleman from Massachusetts (Mr. Adams), and his in one particular only—proposes to give to the minority section any veto or self-protecting power against those aggressions, the temptation to which, and the danger from which, are the very cause or reason for the demand for any new guarantees at all. They who complain of violated faith in the past, are met only with new promises of good faith for the future; they who tell you that you have broken the Constitution heretofore, are answered with proposed additions to the Constitution, so that there may be more room for breaches hereafter. The only protection here offered against the aggressive spirit of the majority, is the simple pledge of power that it will not abuse itself, nor aggress, nor usurp, nor amplify itself to attain its ends. You place, in the distance, the highest honors, the largest emoluments, the most glittering of all prizes, and then you propose, as it were, to exact a promise from the race-horse that he will accommodate his speed to the slow-moving pace of the tortoise. Sir, if I meant terms of equality, I would give the tortoise a good ways the start in the race.

My point of objection, therefore, is that you do not allow to that very minority which, because it is a minority, and because it is afraid of your aggressions, is now about to secede and withdraw itself from your Government, and set up a separate confederacy of its own, you do not allow to it the power of self-protection within the Union. If, Representatives, you are sincere in your protestations that you do not mean to aggress upon the rights of this minority, you deny yourselves nothing by these new guarantees. If you do mean to aggress, then this minority has a right to demand self-protection and security.

But, sir, there remains yet another, and a still stronger objection to these several propositions. Every one of them proposes to recognize, and to embody in the Constitution, that very sort of sectionalism which is the immediate instrumentality of the present dismemberment of these States, and the existence of which is, in my judgment, utterly inconsistent with the peace and stability of the Union. Every one of them recognizes and perpetuates the division line between slave labor and free labor, that self-same "*geographical line, coinciding with the marked principle, moral and political*," of slavery, which so startled the prophetic ear of Jefferson, and which he foretold, forty years ago, every irritation would mark deeper and deeper, till, at last, it would destroy the Union itself. They, one and all, recognize slavery as an existing and paramount element in the politics of the country, and yet only promise that the non-slaveholding majority section, immensely in the majority, will not aggress upon the rights or trespass upon the interests of the slaveholding minority section, immensely in the minority. *Adeo senuerunt Jupiter et Mars?*

Sir, just so long as slavery is recognized as an element in politics at all—just so long as the dividing line between the slave labor and the free labor States is kept up as the only line, with the disparity between them growing every day greater and greater—just so long it will be impossible to keep the peace, and maintain a Federal Union between them. However sufficient any of these plans of adjustment might have been one year ago, or even in December last, when proposed, and prior to the secession of any of the States, I fear that they will be found utterly inadequate to restore the Union now. I do not believe that, alone, they will avail to bring back the States which have seceded, and, therefore, to withhold the other slave States from ultimate secession; for, surely, no man fit to be a statesman can fail to foresee that unless the cotton States can be returned to the Union, the border States must and will, sooner or later, follow them out of it. As between two confederacies—the one non-slaveholding, and the other slaveholding—all the States of the South must belong to the latter, except, possibly, Maryland and Delaware, and they, of course, could remain with the former only upon the understanding that, just as soon as practicable, slavery should be abolished within their limits. If fifteen slave States cannot protect themselves, and feel secure in a Union with eighteen anti-slavery States, how can eight slave States maintain their position and their rights in a Union with nineteen, or with thirty anti-slavery States? The question, therefore, is not merely, What will keep Virginia in the Union, but also, what will bring Georgia back? And here let me say, that I do not doubt that there is a large and powerful Union sentiment still surviving in all the States which have seceded, South Carolina alone, perhaps, excepted; and that if the people of those States can be assured that they shall have the power to protect themselves, by their own action, *within the Union*, they will gladly return to it, very greatly preferring protection within to security outside of it. Just now, indeed, the fear of danger, and your persistent and obstinate refusal to enable them to guard against it, have delivered the people of those States over into the hands, and under the control, of the real secessionists and disunionists among them; but give them security, and the means of enforcing it; above all, dry up this pestilent fountain of slavery agitation, as a political element, in both sections, and, my word for it, the ties of a common ancestry, a common kindred, and common language; the bonds of a common interest, common danger, and common safety; the recollections of the past, and of associations not yet dissolved, and the bright hopes of a future to all of us, more glorious and resplendent than any other country ever saw; ay, sir, and visions, too, of that old flag of the Union, and of the music of the Union, and precious memories of the statesmen and heroes of the dark days of the Revolution, will fill their souls yet again with desires and yearnings intense for the glories, the honors, and the material benefits, too, of that Union which their fathers and our fathers made; and they will return to it, not as the prodigal, but with songs and rejoicing, as the Hebrews returned from the captivity to the ancient city of their kings.

Proceeding, sir, upon the principles which I have already considered, and applying them to the causes which, step by step, have led to our present troubles, I have ventured, with great deference, to submit the propositions, which are upon the table of the House. While not inconsistent with any of the other pending plans of adjustment, they are, in my judgment, and again I speak it with becoming deference, fully adequate to secure that protection from aggression, without which there can be no confidence, and, therefore, no peace and no restoration for the Union.

There are two maxims, sir, applicable to all constitutional reform, both of which it has been my purpose to follow. In the first place, not to amend more, or further, than is necessary for the mischief to be remedied, and next, to follow strictly the principles of the Constitution which is to be amended; and corollary to these, I might add, that in framing amendments, the words and phrases of the Constitution ought, so far as practicable, to be adopted.

I propose then, sir, to do as all others in the Senate and the House have done, so far—to recognize the existence of sections as a fixed fact, which, lamentable as it is, can no longer be denied or suppressed; but, for the reasons I have already stated, I propose to establish four instead of two grand sections of the Union, all of them well known, or easily designated by marked, natural, or geographical lines and boundaries. I propose four sections instead of two; because, if two only are recognized, the natural and inevitable division will be into slaveholding and non-slaveholding sections; and it is this very division, either by constitutional enactment, or by common consent, as hitherto, which, in my deliberate judgment and deepest conviction, it concerns the peace and stability of the Union, should be forever hereafter ignored. Till then, there cannot be, and will not be, perfect union and peace between these United States; because, in the first place, the nature of the question is such that it stirs up, necessarily, as forty years of strife conclusively proves, the strongest and the bitterest passions and antagonism possible among men; and, in the next place, because the non-slaveholding section has now, and will have to the end, a steadily increasing majority, and enormously disproportioned weight and influence in the government; thus combining that which never can be very long resisted in any government—the temptation and the power to aggress.

Sir, it was not the mere geographical line which so startled Mr. Jefferson, in 1820; but the coincidence of that line with the marked principle, moral and political, of slavery. And now, sir, to remove this very mischief, which he predicted, and which has already happened, it is essential that this coincidence should be obliterated; and the repeated failure, for years past, of all other compromises, based upon a recognition of this coincidence, has proved, beyond doubt, that it cannot be obliterated, unless it be by other and conflicting lines of principle and interests. I propose, therefore, to multiply the sections, and thus efface the slave-labor and free-labor division, and, at the same time, and in this manner, to diminish the relative power of each section. And to prevent combinations among these different sections, I propose, also, to allow a vote in the Senate by sections, upon demand of one third of the Senators of any section, and to require the concurrence of a majority of the Senators of each section in the passage of any measure, in which, by the Constitution, it is necessary that the House, and therefore, also, the President, should concur. All this, sir, is perfectly consistent with the principles of the Constitution, as shown in the division of the legislative department into the two Houses of Congress; the veto power; the two-thirds vote of both Houses necessary to pass a bill over the veto; the provisions in regard to the ratification of treaties, and amendments to the Constitution; but especially in the equal representation and suffrage of each State in the Senate, whereby the vote of Delaware, with a hundred thousand inhabitants, *vetoes* the vote of New York, with her population of nearly four millions. If the protection of the smaller States against the possible aggressions of the larger States, required, in the judgment of the framers of the Constitution, this peculiar, and, apparently, inequitable provision, why shall not the protection, by a similar power of veto, of the smaller and weaker sections against the aggressions of the larger and stronger sections, not be now allowed, when time and experience have proved the necessity of just such a check upon the majority? Does any one doubt that, if the men who made the Constitution had foreseen that the real danger to the system lay, not in aggression by the large upon the small States, but in geographical combinations of the strong sections against the weak, they would have guarded jealously against that mischief, just as they did against the danger, to which they mistakenly believed the government to be exposed? And if this protection, sir, be now demanded by the minority as the price of the Union, so just and reasonable a provision ought not, for a moment, to be denied. Far better this than secession and disruption. This would, indeed, enable the minority to fight for their rights in the Union, instead of breaking it to pieces to secure them outside of it.

Certainly, sir, it is in the nature of a veto power to each section in the Senate; but necessity requires it, secession demands it, just as twice, in the history of the Roman Commonwealth, secession demanded, and received the power of the tribunitian veto, as the price of a restoration of the Republic. The secession to the Sacred Mount secured, just as a second secession, half a century later, restored the veto of tribunes of the people, and reinvigorated and preserved the Roman constitution for three hundred years. Vetoes, checks, balances, concurrent majorities—these, sir, are the true conservators of free government.

But it is not in legislation alone that the danger, or the temptation to aggress, is to be found. Of the tremendous power and influence of the Executive I have already spoken. And, indeed, the present revolutionary movements are the result of the apprehension of executive usurpation and encroachments, to the injury of the rights of the South. But for secession, because of this apprehended danger, the legislative department would have remained, for the present at least, in other and safer hands. Hence the necessity for equal protection and guarantee against sectional combinations and majorities, to secure the election of the President, and to control him when elected. I propose, therefore, that a concurrent majority of the electors, or States, or Senators, as the case may require, of each section, shall be necessary to the choice of President and Vice-President; and lest, by reason of this increased complexity, there may be a failure of choice oftener than heretofore, I propose also a special election in such case, and an extension of the term, in all cases, to six years. This is the outline of the plan; the details may be learned in full from the joint resolution itself; and I will not detain the House by any further explanation now.

Sir, the natural and inevitable result of these amendments will be to preclude the possibility of sectional parties and combinations to obtain possession of either the legislative or the executive power and patronage of the Federal Government; and, if not to suppress totally, at least very greatly to diminish the evil results of national caucuses, conventions, and other similar party appliances. It will no longer be possible to elect a President by the votes of a mere dominant and majority section. Sectional issues must cease, as the basis, at least, of large party organizations. Ambition, or lust for power and place, must look no longer to its own section, but to the whole country; and he who would be President, or in any way the foremost among his countrymen, must consult, henceforth, the combined good, and the good-will, too, of all the sections, and in this way, consistently with the Constitution, can the "general welfare" be best attained. Thus, indeed, will the result be, instead of a narrow, illiberal, and sectional policy, an enlarged patriotism and extended public spirit.

If it be urged that the plan is too complex, and, therefore, impracticable, I answer that was the objection, in the beginning, to the whole Federal system, and to almost every part of it. It is the argument of the French Republicans against the division of the legislative department into two Chambers; and it was the argument especially urged at first against the entire plan or idea of the electoral colleges for the choice of a President. But, if complex, I answer again, it will prevent more evil than good. If it suspend some legislation for a time, I answer the world is governed too much. If it cause delay, sometimes, in both legislation and the choice of President, I answer yet again, better, far better this, than disunion and the ten thousand complexities, peaceful and belligerent, which must attend it. Better, infinitely better this, in the Union, than separate confederacies outside of it, with either perpetual war or entangling and complicated alliances, offensive and defensive, from henceforth forever. To the South I say: If you are afraid of free State aggressions by Congress or the Executive, here is abundant protection for even the most timid. To the Republican party of the North and West I say: If you really tremble, as, for years past you would have had us believe, over that terrible, but somewhat mythical monster—the SLAVE POWER—here, too, is the utmost security for you against the possibility of its aggressions. And, from first to last, allow me to say that, being wholly negative in its provisions, this plan can only prevent evil, and not work any positive evil itself. It is a shield for defence, not a sword for aggression. In one word, let me add, that the whole purpose and idea of this plan of adjustment, which I propose, is to give to the several sections *inside* of the Union that power of self-protection which they are resolved, or will some day or other be resolved, to secure for themselves *outside* of the Union.

I propose further, sir, that neither Congress nor a Territorial Legislature, shall have power to interfere with the equal right of migration, from all sections, into the Territories of the United States; and that neither shall have power to destroy or impair any rights, of either person or property, in these Territories; and, finally, that new States, either when annexed, or when formed out of any of the Territories, with the consent of Congress, shall be admitted into the Union with any constitution, republican in form, which the people of such States may ordain.

And now, gentlemen of the South, why cannot you accept it? The Federal Government has never yet, in any way, aggressed upon your rights. Hitherto, indeed, it has been in your own, or at least in friendly hands. You only fear, being in the minority, that it will aggress, because it has now fallen under the control of those who, you believe, have the temptation, the will, and the power to aggress. But this plan of adjustment proposes to take away the power; and of what avail will the temptation, or the will then be, without the power to execute? Both must soon perish.

And why cannot you of the Republican party accept it? There is not a word about slavery in it, from beginning to end—I mean in the amendments. It is silent upon the question. South of 36° 30′, and east of the Rio Grande, there is scarce any territory which is not now within the limits of some existing State; and west of that river and of the Rocky Mountains, as well as north of 36° 30′, and east of those mountains, though any new State should establish slavery, still her vote would be counted in the Senate and in the electoral colleges, with the non-slaveholding section, to which she would belong; just as if, within the limits of the South, any State should abolish slavery, or any new State, not tolerating slavery, should be admitted, the vote of such State would also be cast with the section of the South. However slavery might be extended, as a mere form of civilization or of labor, there could be no extension of it as a mere aggressive political element in the government. If the South only demand that the Federal Government shall not be used aggressively to prohibit the extension of slavery; if she does not desire to use it herself, upon the other hand, positively to extend the institution, then she may well be satisfied; and if you of the Republican party do not really mean to aggress upon slavery where it now exists; if you are not, in fact, opposed to the admission of any more slave States; if, indeed, you do not any longer propose to use the powers of the Federal Government, positively and aggressively, to prohibit slavery in the Territories, but are satisfied to allow it to take its natural course, according to the laws of interest or of climate, then you, too, may well be content with this plan of adjustment, since it does not demand of you, openly and publicly, to deny, abjure, and renounce, in so many words, the more moderate principles and doctrines which you have this session professed. And yet candor obliges me to declare, that this plan of settlement, and every other plan, whatsoever, which is of the slightest value—even the amendment of the gentleman from Massachusetts (Mr. Adams), is a virtual dissolution of the Republican party, as a mere sectional and anti-slavery organization; and this, too, will, in my judgment, be equally the result, whether we compromise at all, and the Union be thus restored, or whether it be finally and forever dissolved. The people of the North and the West will never trust the destroyers—for destroyers, indeed, you will be, if you reject all fair terms of adjustment—the destroyers of our government, and such a government as this, with the administration and control of any other. You have now the executive department, as the result of the late election. Better, far better, reorganize and nationalize your party, and keep the government for four years in peace, and with a Union of thirty-four States, than with the shadow and mockery of a broken and disjointed Union of sixteen or nineteen States, ending, at last, in total and hopeless dissolution.

Having thus, sir, guarded diligently the rights of the several States and sections, and given to each section also the power to protect itself, inside of the Union, from aggression, I propose next to limit and to regulate the alleged right of SECESSION, since this, from a dormant abstraction, has now become a practical question of tremendous import. As long, sir, as secession remained an untried and only menaced experiment, that confidence, without which no government can be stable or efficient, was not shaken because it was believed that actual secession would never be tried; or, if tried, that it must speedily and ingloriously fail. The popular faith, cherished for years, has been that the Union could not be dissolved. To that faith the Republican party was indebted for its success in the late election; and we, who predicted its dissolution, were smitten upon the cheek, and condemned to feed upon bread of affliction, and water of affliction, like the prophet whom Ahab hated. But partial dissolution has already occurred. Secession has been tried, and has proved a speedy and a terrible success. The practicability of doing it, and the way to do it, have both been established. Sir, the experiment may readily be repeated—it will be repeated. And is it not madness and folly, then, to call back, by adjustment, the States which have seceded, or to hold back the States which are threatening to secede, without providing some safeguard against the renewal of this most simple and disastrous experiment? Can foreign nations have any confidence, hereafter, in the stability of a government which may so readily, speedily, and quietly be dissolved? Can we have any confidence among ourselves?

If it be said that it would have availed nothing to check secession in the Gulf States, even had there been a constitutional prohibition of it. I answer, perhaps not, if it had been total and absolute—for there would have been no alternative but submission or revolution; and hence, I propose only to define and restrain, and to regulate this alleged right. But I deny that, if a particular mode of secession had been prescribed by the Constitution, and thus every other mode prohibited, it would have been possible to have secured, in any of the seceding States—no, not even in South Carolina—a majority in favor of separate State secession, or secession in any other way than that provided in the Constitution. No, sir; it was the almost universal belief in the cotton States in the unlimited right of secession—a doctrine recognized by few in the free States, but held to by a great many, if not very generally, all over the slave States—which made secession so easy. It is hard to bring any considerable number of the people of the United States—suddenly, at least—up to the point of a palpable violation of the Constitution; but it is easy, very easy, to draw them into any act which seems to be only the exercise of one right for the purpose of securing and preserving the higher rights of life, liberty, person, and property for a whole State, or a whole section. Sir, it is because of this very idea or notion among the people of the Gulf States, that they were exercising a right reserved under the Constitution, that secession there, and the establishment of a new confederacy and provisional government, have been marked by so much rapidity, order, and method—all through the ballot-box, and not with the halter, or at the point of the bayonet, over oppressed minorities—and, for the most part, with so few of the excesses and irregularities which have characterized the progress of other revolutions. I would not prohibit totally the right of secession, lest violent revolutions should follow; for where laws and constitutions are to be overleaped, and they who make the revolution avow it to be a revolution, and claim no right except the universal rights of man, such revolutions are commonly violent and bloody within themselves; and, even if not, they cannot be resisted by the established authorities, except at the cost of civil war; while, if submitted to in silence, they tend to demoralize all government. It is of vital importance, therefore, every way, in my judgment, that the exercise of this certainly *quasi*-revolutionary right should be defined, limited, and restrained; and, accordingly, I propose that no State shall secede without the consent of the legislatures of all the States of the section to which the State proposing to secede may belong. This is, obviously, a most reasonable restraint; and yet, of its sufficiency no man can doubt, when he remembers that, in the present crisis of the country, had this provision existed, no State could have obtained the absolute consent, at least, of even one-half of the States of the South.

Such, Mr. Speaker, is the plan which, with great deference, and yet with great confidence, too, in its efficiency, I would propose for the adjustment of our controversies, and for the restoration and preservation of the Union which our fathers made. Like all human contrivances, certainly, it is imperfect, and subject to objection. But something searching, radical, extreme, going to the very foundations of government, and reaching the seat of the malady, must be done, and that right speedily, while the fracture is yet fresh and reunion is possible. Two months ago, when I last addressed the House, imploring you for immediate action, less, much less, would have sufficed; but we learned no wisdom from the lessons of the past—and now, indeed, not poppy, nor mandragora, nor other drowsy sirup is of any value to arrest that revolution, in the midst of which we are to-day—a revolution the grandest and the saddest of modern times.

The following are the amendments to the Constitution, proposed by Mr. Vallandigham, on the 7th of February, 1861, to the support of which the foregoing speech is devoted:

JOINT RESOLUTION.

Whereas the Constitution of the United States is a grant of specific powers, delegated to the Federal Government by the people of the several States, all powers not delegated to it, nor prohibited to the States, being reserved to the States, respectively, or to the people; and whereas it is the tendency of stronger governments to enlarge their powers and jurisdiction at the expense of weaker governments, and of majorities to usurp and abuse power, and oppress minorities, to arrest and hold in check which tendency, compacts and constitutions are made; and whereas the only effectual constitutional security for the rights of minorities—whether as people or as States—is the power expressly reserved in constitutions, of protecting those rights by their own action; and whereas this mode of protection, by checks and guarantees, is recognized in the Federal Constitution, as well in the case of the equality of the States in representation and in suffrage in the Senate, as in the provision for overruling the veto of the President, and for amending the Constitution, not to enumerate other examples; and whereas, unhappily, because of the vast extent and diversified interests and institutions of the several

States of the Union, sectional divisions can no longer be suppressed; and whereas it concerns the peace and stability of the Federal Union and Government, that a division of the States into mere slaveholding and non-slaveholding sections, causing, hitherto—and from the nature and necessity of the case—inflammatory and disastrous controversies, upon the subject of slavery, ending, already, in present disruption of the Union—should be forever hereafter ignored; and whereas this important end is best to be obtained by the recognition of other sections without regard to slavery, neither of which sections shall alone be strong enough to oppress or control the others, and each be vested with the power to protect itself from aggressions: Therefore,

Resolved, by the Senate and House of Representatives of the United States of America, in Congress assembled (two-thirds of both Houses concurring), That the following Articles be, and are hereby, proposed as amendments to the Constitution of the United States, which shall be valid, to all intents and purposes, as part of said Constitution, when ratified by Conventions in three-fourths of the several States:

ARTICLE XIII.

SEC. 1. The United States are divided into four sections, as follows:

The States of Maine, New Hampshire, Vermont, Massachusetts, Rhode Island, Connecticut, New York, New Jersey, and Pennsylvania, and all new States annexed and admitted into the Union, or formed or erected within the jurisdiction of any of said States, or by the junction of two or more of the same, or of parts thereof, or out of territory acquired north of said States, shall constitute one section, to be known as the NORTH.

The States of Ohio, Indiana, Illinois, Michigan, Wisconsin, Minnesota, Iowa, and Kansas, and all new States annexed or admitted into the Union, or erected within the jurisdiction of any of said States, or by the junction of two or more of the same, or of parts thereof, or out of territory now held or hereafter acquired north of latitude 36° 30′, and east of the crest of the Rocky Mountains, shall constitute another section, to be known as the WEST.

The States of Oregon, and California, and all new States annexed and admitted into the Union, or formed or erected within the jurisdiction of any of said States, or by the junction of two or more of the same, or of parts thereof, or out of territory now held, or hereafter acquired, west of the crest of the Rocky Mountains and of the Rio Grande, shall constitute another section, to be known as the PACIFIC.

The States of Delaware, Maryland, Virginia, North Carolina, South Carolina, Georgia, Florida, Alabama, Mississippi, Louisiana, Texas, Arkansas, Tennessee, Kentucky, and Missouri, and all new States annexed and admitted into the Union, or formed or erected within the jurisdiction of any of said States, or by the junction of two or more of the same, or of parts thereof, or out of territory acquired east of the Rio Grande, and south of latitude 36° 30′, shall constitute another section, to be known as the SOUTH.

SEC. 2. On demand of one-third of the Senators of any one of the sections, on any bill, order, resolution, or vote, to which the concurrence of the House of Representatives may be necessary, except on a question of adjournment, a vote shall be had by sections, and a majority of the Senators from each section voting, shall be necessary to the passage of such bill, order, or resolution, and to the validity of every such vote.

SEC. 3. Two of the electors for President and Vice-President shall be appointed by each State, in such manner as the Legislature thereof may direct, for the State at large. The other electors, to which each State may be entitled, shall be chosen in the respective Congressional districts into which the State may, at the regular decennial period, have been divided, by the electors of each district, having the qualifications requisite for electors of the most numerous branch of the State Legislature. A majority of all the electors in each of the four sections in this article established, shall be necessary to the choice of President and Vice-President; and the concurrence of a majority of the States of each section shall be necessary to the choice of President by the House of Representatives, and of the Senators from each section to the choice of Vice-President by the Senate, whenever the right of choice shall devolve upon them respectively.

SEC. 4. The President and Vice-President shall hold their office each during the term of six years; and neither shall be eligible to more than one term, except by the votes of two-thirds of all the electors of each section, or of the States of each section, whenever the right of choice of President shall devolve upon the House of Representatives, or of Senators from each section, whenever the right of choice of Vice-President shall devolve upon the Senate.

SEC. 5. The Congress shall, by law, provide for the case of failure by the House of Representatives to choose a President, and of the Senate to choose a Vice-President, whenever the right of choice shall devolve upon them respectively, declaring what officer shall then act as President; and such officer shall act accordingly until a President shall be elected. The Congress shall also provide by law for a special election for President and Vice-President in such case, to be held and completed within six months from the expiration of the term of office of the last preceding President, and to be conducted in all respects as provided for in the Constitution for regular elections of the same officer, except that if the House of Representatives shall not choose a President, should the right of choice devolve upon them, within twenty days from the opening of the certificates and counting of the electoral votes, then the Vice-President shall act as President, as in the case of the death, or other constitutional disability of the President. The term of office of the President chosen under such special election, shall continue six years from the fourth day of March preceding such election.

ARTICLE XIV.

No State shall secede without the consent of the Legislatures of the States of the section to which the State, proposing to secede, belongs. The President shall have power to adjust with seceding States all questions arising by reason of their secession; but the terms of adjustment shall be submitted to the Congress for their approval before the same shall be valid.

ARTICLE XV.

Neither the Congress nor a Territorial Legislature shall have power to interfere with the right of the citizens of any of the States, within either of the sections, to migrate upon equal terms with the citizens of the States within either of the other sections to the Territories of the United States: nor shall either the Congress or a Territorial Legislature have power to destroy or impair any rights of either person or property in the Territories.

New States annexed for admission into the Union, or formed or erected within the jurisdiction of other States, or by the junction of two or more States, or parts of States; and States formed, with the consent of the Congress, out of any territory of the United States, shall be entitled to admission upon an equal footing with the original States, under any constitution establishing a government, republican in form, which the people thereof may ordain, whenever such States, if formed out of any territory of the United States, shall contain, within an area of not less than sixty thousand square miles, a population equal to the then existing ratio of representation, for one member of the House of Representatives.

A card, from which the following is extracted, was published by Mr. Vallandigham in the *Cincinnati Enquirer*, on the 10th of November, 1860, a few days after the Presidential election :

"And, now, let me add that I did say—not in Washington, not at a dinner-table, not in the presence of 'fire-eaters,' but in the city of New York, in a public assembly of Northern men, and in a public speech at the Cooper Institute, on the 2d of November, 1860—that, 'if any one or more of the States of this Union should, at any time, secede—for reasons, of the sufficiency and justice of which, before God, and the great tribunal of history, they alone may judge—much as I should deplore it, *I never would, as a Representative in the Congress of the United States, vote one dollar of money, whereby one drop of American blood should be shed in a civil war.*' That sentiment, thus uttered in the presence of thousands of the merchants and solid men of the free and patriotic city of New York, was received with vehement and long-continued applause, the entire vast assemblage rising as one man, and cheering for some minutes. And I now deliberately repeat and reaffirm it, resolved, though I stand alone, though all others yield, and fall away, to make it good to the last moment of my public life. No menace, no public clamor, no taunts, no sneers, nor foul detraction, from any quarter, shall drive me from my firm purpose. Ours is a government of opinion, not of force—a Union of free will, not of arms; and coercion is civil war—a war of sections, a war of States, waged by a race, compounded and made up of all other races, full of intellect, of courage, of will unconquerable, and, when set on fire by passion, the most belligerent and most ferocious on the globe—a civil war, full of horrors, which no imagination can conceive and no pen portray. If Abraham Lincoln is wise, looking truth and danger full in the face, he will take counsel of the 'old men,' the moderates of his party, and advise peace, negotiation, concession; but if, like the foolish son of a wise king, he reject these wholesome counsels, and hearken only to the madmen who threaten chastisement with scorpions, let him see to it, lest it be recorded at last that none remained to serve him, 'save the house of Judah only.' At least, if he will forget the secession of the Ten Tribes, will he not remember and learn a lesson of wisdom from the secession of the Thirteen Colonies?"

In answer to a gross telegraphic misrepresentation of this proposition, Mr. Vallandigham explained and defended it, in a card to the *Cincinnati Enquirer*, dated February 14, 1861, as follows:

"My proposition looks *solely to the restoration and maintenance of the Union forever*, by suggesting a mode of voting in the United States Senate, and the electoral colleges, by which the causes which have led to our present troubles may, in the future, be guarded against *without secession and disunion;* and, also, the agitation of the slavery question, as an element in our national politics, *be forever hereafter arrested.* My object—the sole motive by which I have been guided, from the beginning of this most fatal revolution—is to MAINTAIN THE UNION, and not destroy it. When all possible hope is gone, and the Union irretrievably broken, then, but not till then, I will be for a Western confederacy."

Referring to a statement in a leading Abolition paper, Mr. VALLANDIGHAM, in a communication to the *Cincinnati Enquirer*, under date of Washington, D. C., December 18, 1862, said:

"Now, Mr. Vallandigham never proposed to divide 'the Republic into four distinct nationalities.' So far as any such proposition has been suggested at all, it was by General Scott, who even went so far as to name the probable capitals of three of those 'nationalities.' My proposition, on the contrary, was to maintain the existing Union, or 'nationality' forever, by dividing or arranging the States into sections *within the Union, under the Constitution*, for the purpose of voting in the Senate and electoral colleges."

LETTER TO R. H. HENDRICKSON, AND OTHERS, OF MIDDLETOWN, OHIO.

DAYTON, *May* 13, 1861.

GENTLEMEN: Yours of the 9th instant, requesting my opinion upon certain points, connected with what you justly style the present "inglorious, and it may be, bloody war," has been received. That opinion was long since formed, and was repeatedly set forth through the press, or by speech and vote in the House of Representatives, last winter, and reaffirmed in a card, dated on the 17th of last month, a few days after the commencement of the war.* But inasmuch as I never had occasion to discuss this particular question at length, I beg leave to adopt the following admirable summary of the case, in an extract from a carefully-prepared and exceedingly able speech of the Hon. Stephen A. Douglas, in the Senate of the United States, March 15th, 1861 :

"I prefer such an amicable settlement to peaceable disunion, and I prefer it a thousand times to civil war. If we can adopt such amendments as will be satisfactory to Virginia, North Carolina, Tennessee, and the other border States, the plan of pacification which will satisfy them, will create a Union party in the Cotton States, which will soon embrace a large majority of the people in those States, and bring them back of their own free will and accord; and thus restore, strengthen, and perpetuate the glorious old Union forever. I repeat, whatever guarantees will satisfy Maryland and the border States (the States now in the Union), will create a Union party in the seceded States, that will bring them back by the voluntary action of their own people. You can restore and preserve the government in that mode. You can do it in no other.

"War is disunion. War is final, eternal separation. Hence, disguise it as you may, every Union man in America must advocate such amendments to the Constitution as will preserve peace and restore the Union; while every disunionist, whether openly or secretly plotting its destruction, is the advocate of peaceful secession, or of war, as the surest means of rendering reunion and reconstruction impossible. I have too much respect for his intellect to believe, for one moment, that there is a man for war who is not a disunionist *per se*. Hence I do not mean, if I can prevent it, that the enemies of the Union—men plotting to destroy it—shall drag this country into war, under the pretext of protecting the public property, and enforcing the laws, and collecting revenue, when their object is disunion, and war the means of accomplishing a cherished purpose.

"The disunionists, therefore, are divided into two classes: the one open, the other secret disunionists. The one is in favor of peaceful secession, and a recognition of independence; the other is in favor of war, as the surest means of accomplishing the object, and making the separation final and eternal. I am a Union man, and hence against war; but if the Union must be temporarily broken by a revolution, and the establishment of a *de facto* government by some of the States, let no act be done that will prevent restoration and future preservation. Peace is the only policy that can lead to that result.

"But we are told, and we hear it repeated everywhere, that we must

* See Supplement, *post*, page 554.

find out whether we have got a government. 'Have we a government?' is the question, and we are told we must test that question by using the military power to put down all discontented spirits. Sir, this question, 'Have we a government?' has been propounded by every tyrant who has tried to keep his feet on the necks of the people, since the world began. When the barons demanded Magna Charta from King John, at Runnymede, he exclaimed, 'Have we a government?' and called for his army to put down the discontented barons. When Charles I. attempted to collect the ship-money, in disregard of the rights of the people, and was resisted by them, he exclaimed, 'Have we a government? We cannot treat with rebels; put down the traitors; we must show that we have a government.' When James II. was driven from the throne of England, for trampling on the liberties of the people, he called for his army, and exclaimed, 'Let us show that we have a government!' When George III. called upon his army to put down the rebellion in America, Lord North cried lustily, 'No compromise with traitors; let us demonstrate that we have a government.' When, in 1848, the people rose upon their tyrants all over Europe, and demanded guarantees for their rights, every crowned head exclaimed, 'Have we a government?' and appealed to the army to vindicate their authority, and enforce the law.

"Sir, the history of the world does not fail to condemn the folly, weakness, and wickedness of that government which draws its sword upon its own people, when they demanded guarantees for their rights. This cry, that we must have a government, is merely following the example of the besotted Bourbons, who never learned any thing by misfortune, never forgave an injury, never forgot an affront. Must we demonstrate that we have got a government, and coerce obedience without reference to the justice or injustice of the complaints? Sir, whenever ten millions of people proclaim to you, with one unanimous voice, that they apprehend their rights, their firesides, and their family altars, are in danger, it becomes a wise government to listen to the appeal, and to remove the apprehension. History does not record an example where any human government has been strong enough to crush ten millions of people into subjection, when they believed their rights and liberties were imperiled, without first converting the government itself into a despotism, and destroying the last vestige of freedom."

These were the sentiments of the Democratic party, of the Constitutional Union party, and of a large majority of the Republican presses and party, only six weeks ago. They are mine. I voted them repeatedly, along with every Democrat and Union man in the House. I have seen nothing to change, and much to confirm them since; especially in the secession, within the last thirty days, of Virginia, Arkansas, North Carolina, and Tennessee, taking with them four millions and a half of people, immense wealth, inexhaustible resources, five hundred thousand fighting men, and the grave of Washington and Jackson. I shall vote them again.

Waiving the question of the doubtful legality of the first proclamation of April 15th, calling on the militia for "three months," under the act of 1795, I will yet vote to pay them, because they had no motive but supposed duty, and patriotism, to move them; and, moreover, they will have rendered almost the entire service required of them, before Congress shall meet. But the audacious usurpation of President Lincoln, for which he deserves impeachment, in daring, against the very letter of the Constitution, and without a shadow of law, to "raise and support armies," and to "provide and maintain a navy," for three or five years, by mere executive proclamation, I will not vote to sustain or ratify—never. Millions for defense: not a dollar or a man for aggressive and offensive civil war.

The war has had many motives for its commencement; it can have but one result, whether it last one year or fifty years—final, eternal separation—disunion. As for the conquest and subjugation of the South, I will not impeach the intelligence of any man among you, by assuming that you dream of it as at any time or in any way possible. Remember the warning of Lord Chatham to the British Parliament: "My Lords, you cannot conquer America." A public debt of hundreds of millions, weighing us and our posterity down for generations, we cannot escape. Fortunate shall we be if we escape with our liberties. Indeed, it is no longer so much a question of war with the South, as whether we ourselves are to have constitutions and a republican form of government hereafter in the North and West.

In brief: I am for the Constitution first, and at all hazards for whatever can now be saved of the Union next; and for Peace always, as essential to the preservation of either. But whatever any one may think of the war, one thing, at least, every lover of liberty ought to demand inexorably: that it shall be carried on strictly subject to the Constitution.

The peace policy was tried: it arrested secession, and promised a restoration of the Union. The policy of war is now upon trial: in twenty days it has driven four States and four millions and a half of people out of the Union, and into the Confederacy of the South. In a little while longer it will drive out, also, two or four more States, and two millions or three millions of people. War may, indeed, be the policy of the East; but peace is a necessity to the West.

I would have volunteered nothing, gentlemen, at this time, in regard to this civil war; but, as constituents, you had a right to know my opinions and position; and briefly, but most frankly, you have them.

My only answer to those who indulge in slander and vituperation, was given in the card of the 17th of April, herewith inclosed.*

EXECUTIVE USURPATION.

Speech delivered in the House of Representatives, July 10, 1861.†

"After some time be past."

THE House was in Committee of the Whole, the subject under consideration, The State of the Union, when Mr. Vallandigham, obtaining the floor, said:

MR. CHAIRMAN: In the Constitution of the United States, which the other day we swore to support, and by the authority of which we are here assembled now, it is written:

> "All legislative powers herein granted, shall be vested in a Congress of the United States."

It is further written, also, that the Congress, to which all legislative powers granted, are thus committed—

> "Shall make no law abridging the freedom of speech or of the press."

And, it is yet further written, in protection of Senators and Repre-

* See Supplement, page 554.

† This speech was delivered soon after the opening of the extra session of Congress, convened on the 4th of July, 1861. No speech was ever delivered in the midst of greater personal danger—not even Cicero's defence of Milo. The galleries were filled with an excited soldiery and infuriated partisans threatening assassination. A leading Abolition paper in New York had, two days before, declared that, if an attempt was made to speak for peace, "the aisles of the Hall would run with blood." Arbitrary arrests for opinion and speech, had already been commenced. Almost without sympathy upon his own side of the House, and with a fierce, insolent, and overwhelming majority upon the other side, Mr. Vallandigham, calm, and unawed, met every peril, and spoke as firmly, solemnly, and earnestly, as under ordinary circumstances. The "motto" prefixed to the speech is from Lord Bacon's Will, and is significant, interpreted, as it has now been, by the light of two years' experience. Some three hundred thousand copies of the speech, in various forms, were published and circulated in the United States. It was published, also, in England and on the Continent.

sentatives, in that freedom of debate here, without which there can be no liberty, that—

"For any speech or debate in either House, they shall not be questioned in any other place."

Holding up the shield of the Constitution, and standing here in the place, and with the manhood of a Representative of the people, I propose to myself to-day, the ancient freedom of speech used within these walls, though with somewhat more, I trust, of decency and discretion, than have sometimes been exhibited here. Sir, I do not propose to discuss the direct question of this civil war, in which we are engaged. Its present prosecution is a foregone conclusion; and a wise man never wastes his strength on a fruitless enterprise. My position shall, at present, for the most part, be indicated by my votes, and by the resolutions and motions which I may submit. But there are many questions incident to the war, and to its prosecution, about which I have somewhat to say now.

Mr. Chairman, the President, in the message before us, demands the extraordinary loan of $400,000,000—an amount nearly ten times greater than the entire public debt, State and Federal, at the close of the Revolution, in 1783, and four times as much as the total expenditures during the three years' war with Great Britain, in 1812.

Sir, that same Constitution, which I again hold up, and to which I give my whole heart, and my utmost loyalty, commits to Congress alone the power to borrow money, and to fix the purposes to which it shall be applied, and expressly limits army appropriations to the term of two years. Each Senator and Representative, therefore, must judge for himself, upon his conscience and his oath, and before God and the country, of the justice and wisdom and policy of the President's demand; and whenever this House shall have become but a mere office, wherein to register the decrees of the Executive, it will be high time to abolish it. But I have a right, I believe, sir, to say that, however, gentlemen upon this side of the Chamber may differ finally as to the war, we are yet firmly and inexorably united in one thing, at least, and that is in the determination that our own rights and dignities and privileges, as the Representatives of the people, shall be maintained in their spirit, and to the very letter. And, be this as it may, I do know that there are some here present who are resolved to assert and to exercise these rights with becoming decency and moderation, certainly, but, at the same time, fully, freely, and at every hazard.

Sir, it is an ancient and wise practice of the English Commons, to precede all votes of supplies by an inquiry into abuses and grievances, and especially into any infractions of the Constitution and the laws by the Executive. Let us follow this safe practice. We are now in Committee of the Whole on the State of the Union; and in the exercise of my right and my duty as a Representative, and availing myself of the latitude of debate allowed here, I propose to consider the present State of the Union, and supply, also, some few of the many omissions of the President in the message before us. Sir, he has undertaken to give us information of the state of the Union, as the Constitution requires him to do; and it was his duty, as an honest Executive, to make that information full, impartial, and complete, instead of spreading before us a labored and lawyerly vindication of his own course of policy—a policy which has precipitated us into a terrible and bloody revolution. He admits the fact; he admits that, to-day, we are in the midst of a general civil war, not now a mere petty insurrection, to be suppressed in twenty days, by a proclamation and a *posse comitatus* of three months' militia.

Sir, it has been the misfortune of the President, from the beginning, that he has totally and wholly under-estimated the magnitude and character of the Revolution with which he had to deal, or surely he never would have ventured upon the wicked and hazardous experiment of calling thirty millions of people to arms among themselves, without the counsel and authority of Congress. But when, at last, he found himself hemmed in by the revolution, and this city in danger, as he declares, and waked up thus, as the proclamation of the 15th of April proves him to have waked up, to the reality and significance of the movement, why did he not forthwith assemble Congress, and throw himself upon the wisdom and patriotism of the Representatives of the States, and of the people, instead of usurping powers which the Constitution has expressly conferred upon us? Ay, sir, and powers which Congress had, but a little while before, repeatedly and emphatically refused to exercise, or to permit him to exercise? But I shall recur to this point again.

Sir, the President, in this message, has undertaken also to give us a summary of the causes which have led to the present revolution. He has made out a case—he might, in my judgment, have made out a much stronger case—against the secessionists and disunionists of the South. All this, sir, is very well, as far as it goes. But the President does not go back far enough, nor in the right direction. He forgets the still stronger case against the abolitionists and disunionists of the North and West. He omits to tell us that secession and disunion had a New England origin, and began in Massachusetts, in 1804, at the time of the Louisiana purchase; were revived by the Hartford Convention, in 1814; and culminated during the war with Great Britain, in sending Commissioners to Washington, to settle the terms for a peaceable separation of New England from the other States of the Union. He forgets to remind us and the country, that this present revolution began forty years ago, in the vehement, persistent, offensive, most irritating, and unprovoked agitation of the slavery question in the North and West, from the time of the Missouri controversy, with some short intervals, down to the present hour. Sir, if his statement of the case be the whole truth, and wholly correct, then the Democratic party, and every member of it, and the Whig party, too, and its predecessors, have been guilty, for sixty years, of an unjust, unconstitutional, and most wicked policy in administering the affairs of the government.

But, sir, the President ignores totally the violent and long-continued denunciation of slavery and slaveholders, and especially since 1835—I appeal to Jackson's message for the date and proof—until at last a political anti-slavery organization was formed in the North and West, which continued to gain strength, year after year, till, at length, it had destroyed and usurped the place of the Whig party, and finally obtained control of every free State in the Union, and elected himself, through free State votes alone, to the Presidency of the United States. He chooses to pass over the fact, that the party to which he thus owes his place and his present power of mischief, is wholly and totally a sectional organization; and, as such, condemned by Washington, by Jefferson, by Jackson, Webster, and Clay, and by all the founders and preservers of the Republic, and utterly inconsistent with the principles, or with the peace, the stability, or the existence even, of our Federal system. Sir, there never was an hour, from the organization of this sectional party, when it was not predicted by the wisest men and truest patriots, and when it ought not to have been known by every intelligent man in the country, that it must, sooner or later, precipitate a revolution, and the dissolution of the Union. The President forgets already that, on the 4th of March, he declared that the platform of that party was "a law unto him," by which he meant to be governed in his administration; and yet that platform announced that whereas there were two separate and distinct kinds of labor and forms of civilization in the two different sections of the Union, yet that the entire national domain, belonging in common to all the States, should be taken, possessed, and held by one section alone, and consecrated to that kind of labor and form of civilization alone, which prevailed in that section which, by mere numerical superiority, had chosen the President, and now has, and for some years past has had, a majority in the Senate, as from the beginning of the Government it had also in the House. He omits, too, to tell the country and the world—for he speaks, and we all speak now, to the world, and to posterity—that he himself, and his prime minister, the Secretary of State, declared, three years ago, and have maintained ever since, that there was an "irrepressible conflict" between the two sections of this Union; that the Union could not endure part slave and part free; and that the whole power and influence of the Federal Government must henceforth be exerted to circumscribe and hem in slavery within its existing limits.

And now, sir, how comes it that the President has forgotten to remind us, also, that wh■ the party thus committed to the principle of deadly hate and hostility to the slave institutions of the South, and the men who had proclaimed the doctrine of the irrepressible conflict, and who in the dilemma or alternative of this conflict, were resolved that "the cotton and rice fields of South Carolina, and the sugar plantations of Louisiana, should ultimately be tilled by free labor," had obtained power and place in the common Government of the States, the South, except one State, chose first to demand solemn constitutional guarantees for protection against the abuse of the tremendous power and patronage and influence of the Federal Government, for the purpose of securing the great end of the sectional conflict, before resorting to secession or revolution at all? Did he not know—how could he be ignorant?—that, at the last session of Congress, every substantive proposition for adjustment and compromise, except that offered by the gentleman from Illinois (Mr. Kellogg), and we all know how it was received—came from the South? Stop a moment, and let us see.

The Committee of Thirty-three was moved for in this House by a gentleman from Virginia, the second day of the session, and received the vote of every Southern Representative present, except only the members from South Carolina, who declined to vote. In the Senate, the Committee of Thirteen was proposed by a Senator from Kentucky (Mr. Powell), and received the silent acquiescence of every Southern Senator present. The Crittenden propositions, too, were submitted also by another Senator from Kentucky (Mr. Crittenden), now a member of this House; a man, venerable for his years, loved for his virtues, distinguished for his services, honored for his patriotism; for four-and-forty years a Senator, or in other public office; devoted from the first hour of his manhood to the Union of these States; and who, though he himself proved his courage fifty years ago, upon the battle-field against the foreign enemies of his country, is now, thank God, still for compromise at home, to-day. Fortunate in a long and well-spent life of public service and private worth, he is unfortunate only that he has survived a Union, and, I fear, a Constitution, younger than himself.

The Border State propositions, also, were projected by a gentleman from Maryland, not now a member of this House, and presented by a gentleman from Tennessee (Mr. Etheridge), now the Clerk of this House. And yet all these propositions, coming thus from the South, were severally and repeatedly rejected by the almost united vote of the

Republican party in the Senate and the House. The Crittenden propositions, with which Mr. Davis, now President of the Confederate States, and Mr. Toombs, his Secretary of State, both declared, in the Senate, that they would be satisfied, and for which every Southern Senator and Representative voted—never, on any occasion, received one solitary vote from the Republican party in either House.

The Adams or Corwin amendment, so called—reported from the Committee of Thirty-three, and the only substantive amendment proposed from the Republican side—was but a bare promise that Congress should never be authorized to do what no sane man ever believed *Congress* would attempt to do—abolish Slavery in the States where it exists; and yet, even this proposition, moderate as it was, and for which every Southern member present voted—except one—was carried through this House by but one majority, after long and tedious delay, and with the utmost difficulty—sixty-five Republican members, with the resolute and determined gentleman from Pennsylvania (Mr. Hickman) at their head, having voted against it and fought against it to the very last.

And not this only, but, as a part of the history of the last session, let me remind you that bills were introduced into this House, proposing to abolish and close up certain Southern ports of entry; to authorize the President to blockade the Southern coast, and to call out the militia, and accept the services of volunteers—not for three years merely—but without any limit as to either numbers or time, for the very purpose of enforcing the laws, collecting the revenue, and protecting the public property—and were pressed, vehemently and earnestly, in this House, *prior to the arrival of the President in this city*, and were then—though seven States had seceded, and set up a government of their own—voted down, postponed, thrust aside, or in some other way disposed of, sometimes by large majorities in this House, till, at last, Congress adjourned without any action at all. Peace, then seemed to be the policy of all parties.

Thus, sir, the case stood, at twelve o'clock on the 4th of March last, when, from the eastern portico of this capitol, and in the presence of twenty thousand of his countrymen, but enveloped in a cloud of soldiery, which no other American President ever saw, Abraham Lincoln took the oath of office to support the Constitution, and delivered his inaugural—a message, I regret to say, not written in the direct and straightforward language which becomes an American President and an American statesman, and which was expected from the plain, blunt, honest man of the Northwest—but with the forked tongue and crooked counsel of the New York politician, leaving thirty millions of people in doubt whether it meant peace or war. But, whatever may have been the secret purpose and meaning of the inaugural, practically, for six weeks, the policy of peace prevailed; and they were weeks of happiness to the patriot, and prosperity to the country. Business revived; trade returned; commerce flourished. Never was there a fairer prospect before any people. Secession in the past languished, and was spiritless and harmless; secession in the future was arrested, and perished. By overwhelming majorities, Virginia, Kentucky, North Carolina, Tennessee, and Missouri—all declared for the old Union, and every heart beat high with hope, that, in due course of time, and through faith and patience and peace, and by ultimate and adequate compromise, every State would be restored to it. It is true, indeed, sir, that the Republican party, with great unanimity, and great earnestness and determination, had resolved against all conciliation and compromise. But, on the other hand, the whole Democratic party, and the whole Constitutional Union party, were equally resolved that there should be no civil war, upon any pretext: and both sides prepared for an appeal to that great and final arbiter of all disputes in a free country—the people.

Sir, I do not propose to inquire, now, whether the President and his Cabinet were sincere and in earnest, and meant, really, to persevere to the end in the policy of peace; or whether, from the first, they meant civil war, and only waited to gain time till they were fairly seated in power, and had disposed, too, of that prodigious horde of spoilsmen and office-seekers which came down, at the first, like an avalanche upon them. But I do know that the people believed them sincere, and cordially ratified and approved of the policy of peace—not as they subsequently responded to the policy of war, in a whirlwind of passion and madness—but calmly and soberly, and as the result of their deliberate and most solemn judgment; and believing that civil war was absolute and eternal disunion, while secession was but partial and temporary, they cordially indorsed, also, the proposed evacuation of Sumter, and the other forts and public property within the seceded States. Nor, sir, will I stop, now, to explore the several causes which either led to a change in the apparent policy, or an early development of the original and real purposes of the Administration. But there are two which I cannot pass by. And the first of these was PARTY NECESSITY, or the clamor of politicians, and especially of certain wicked, reckless, and unprincipled conductors of a partisan press. The peace policy was crushing out the Republican party. Under that policy, sir, it was melting away like snow before the sun. The general elections in Rhode Island and Connecticut, and municipal elections in New York and in the Western States, gave abundant evidence that the people were resolved upon the most ample and satisfactory constitutional guarantees to the South, as the price of a restoration of the Union. And then it was, sir, that the long and agonizing howl of defeated and disappointed politicians came up before the Administration. The newspaper press teemed with appeals and threats to the President. The mails groaned under the weight of letters demanding a change of policy; while a secret conclave of the Governors of Massachusetts, New York, Ohio, and other States, assembled here, promised men and money to support the President in the irrepressible conflict which they now invoked. And thus it was, sir, that the necessities of a party in the pangs of dissolution, in the very hour and article of death, demanding vigorous measures, which could result in nothing but civil war, renewed secession, and absolute and eternal disunion, were preferred and hearkened to before the peace and harmony and prosperity of the whole country.

But there was another and yet stronger impelling cause, without which this horrid calamity of civil war might have been postponed, and, perhaps, finally averted. One of the last and worst acts of a Congress which, born in bitterness and nurtured in convulsion, literally did those things which it ought not to have done, and left undone those things which it ought to have done, was the passage of an obscure, ill-considered, ill-digested, and unstatesmanlike high protective tariff act, commonly known as "THE MORRILL TARIFF." Just about the same time, too, the Confederate Congress, at Montgomery, adopted our old tariff of 1857, which we had rejected to make way for the Morrill act, fixing their rate of duties at five, fifteen, and twenty per cent. lower than ours. The result was as inevitable as the laws of trade are inexorable. Trade and commerce—and especially the trade and commerce of the West—began to look to the South. Turned out of their natural course, years ago, by the canals and railroads of Pennsylvania and New York, and diverted eastward at a heavy cost to the West, they threatened now to resume their ancient and accustomed channels—the water-courses—the Ohio and the Mississippi. And political association and union, it was well known, must soon follow the direction of trade and interest. The city of New York, the great commercial emporium of the Union, and the North-west, the chief granary of the Union—began to clamor now, loudly, for a repeal of the pernicious and ruinous tariff. Threatened thus with the loss of both political power and wealth, or the repeal of the tariff, and, at last, of both, New England—and Pennsylvania, too, the land of Penn, cradled in peace—demanded, now, coercion and civil war, with all its horrors, as the price of preserving either from destruction. The subjugation of the South—ay, sir, the *subjugation* of the South!—I am not talking to children or fools; for there is not a man in this House fit to be a Representative here, who does not know that the South cannot be forced to yield obedience to your laws and authority again, until you have conquered and subjugated her—the subjugation of the South, and the closing up of her ports—first, by force, in war, and afterwards, by tariff-laws, in peace—was deliberately resolved upon by the East. And, sir, when once this policy was begun, these self-same motives of waning commerce, and threatened loss of trade, impelled the great city of New York, and her merchants and her politicians and her press—with here and there an honorable exception—to place herself in the very front rank among the worshippers of Moloch. Much, indeed, of that outburst and uprising in the North, which followed the proclamation of the 15th of April, as well, perhaps, as the proclamation itself, was called forth, not so much by the fall of Sumter—an event long anticipated—as by the notion that the "insurrection," as it was called, might be crushed out in a few weeks, if not by the display, certainly, at least, by the presence of an overwhelming force.

These, sir, were the chief causes which, along with others, led to a change in the policy of the Administration, and, instead of peace, forced us, headlong, into civil war, with all its accumulated horrors.

But, whatever may have been the causes or the motives for the act, it is certain that there was a change in the policy which the Administration meant to adopt, or which, at least, they led the country to believe they intended to pursue. I will not venture, now, to assert, what may yet, some day, be made to appear, that the subsequent acts of the Administration, and its enormous and persistent infractions of the Constitution, its high-handed usurpations of power, formed any part of a deliberate conspiracy to overthrow the present form of Federal-republican government, and to establish a strong centralized government in its stead. No, sir; whatever their purposes now, I rather think that, in the beginning, they rushed, heedlessly and headlong, into the gulf, believing that, as the seat of war was then far distant and difficult of access, the display of vigor in re-enforcing Sumter and Pickens, and in calling out seventy-five thousand militia, upon the firing of the first gun, and, above all, in that exceedingly happy and original conceit of commanding the insurgent States to "disperse in twenty days," would not, on the one hand, precipitate a crisis; while, upon the other, it would satisfy its own violent partisans, and thus revive and restore the falling fortunes of the Republican party.

I can hardly conceive, sir, that the President and his advisers could be guilty of the exceeding folly of expecting to carry on a general civil war by a mere *posse comitatus* of three-months' militia. It may be, indeed, that, with wicked and most desperate cunning, the President meant all this as a mere entering-wedge to that which was to rive the oak asunder; or, possibly, as a test, to learn the public sentiment of the North and West. But however that may be, the rapid secession and movements of Virginia, North Carolina, Arkansas, and Tennessee, taking with them, as I have said elsewhere, four millions and a half of people, immense wealth, inexhaustible resources, five hundred thousand fighting men, and the graves of Washington and Jackson, and bringing up, too, in one single day, the frontier from the Gulf to the Ohio and the Potomac, together with the abandonment, by the one side, and the occupation, by the other, of Harper's Ferry and the Norfolk navy-yard; and the fierce gust and whirlwind of passion in the North, compelled either a sudden waking-up of the President and his advisers to the frightful significancy of the act which they had committed, in heedlessly breaking the vase which imprisoned the slumbering demon of civil war, or else a premature but most rapid development of the daring plot to foster and promote secession, and then to set up a new and strong form of government in the States which might remain in the Union.

But, whatever may have been the purpose, I assert here, to-day, as a Representative, that every principal act of the Administration since has been a glaring usurpation of power, and a palpable and dangerous violation of that very Constitution which this civil war is professedly waged to support. Sir, I pass by the proclamation of the 15th of April, summoning the militia, not to defend this capital—there is not a word about the capital in the proclamation, and there was then no possible danger to it from any quarter, but to retake and occupy forts and property a thousand miles off—summoning, I say, the militia to suppress the so-called insurrection. I do not believe, indeed, and no man believed in February last, when Mr. Stanton, of Ohio, introduced his bill to enlarge the act of 1795, that that act ever contemplated the case of a general revolution, and of resistance by an organized government. But no matter. The militia thus called out, with a shadow, at least, of authority, and for a period extending one month beyond the assembling of Congress, were amply sufficient to protect the capital against any force which was then likely to be sent against it—and the event has proved it—and ample enough, also, to suppress the outbreak in Maryland. Every other principal act of the Administration might well have been postponed, and ought to have been postponed, until the meeting of Congress; or, if the exigencies of the occasion demanded it, Congress should forthwith have been assembled. What if two or three States should not have been represented, although even this need not have happened; but better this, a thousand times, than that the Constitution should be repeatedly and flagrantly violated, and public liberty and private right trampled under foot. As for Harper's Ferry and the Norfolk navy-yard, they rather needed protection against the Administration, by whose orders millions of property were wantonly destroyed, which was not in the slightest danger from any quarter, at the date of the proclamation.

But, sir, Congress was not assembled at once, as Congress should have been, and the great question of civil war submitted to their deliberations. The representatives of the States and of the people were not allowed the slightest voice in this, the most momentous question ever presented to any government. The entire responsibility of the whole work was at once assumed by the Executive, and all the powers required for the purposes in hand were boldly usurped from either the States or the people, or from the legislative department; while the voice of the judiciary, that last refuge and hope of liberty, was turned away from with contempt.

Sir, the right of blockade—and I begin with it—is a belligerent right, incident to a state of war, and it cannot be exercised until war has been declared or recognized; and Congress alone can declare or recognize war. But Congress had not declared or recognized war. On the contrary, they had, but a little while before, expressly refused to declare it, or to arm the President with the power to make it. And thus the President, in declaring a blockade of certain ports in the States of the South, and in applying to it the rules governing blockades as between independent powers, violated the Constitution.

But if, on the other hand, he meant to deal with these States as still in the Union, and subject to Federal authority, then he usurped a power which belongs to Congress alone—the power to abolish and close up ports of entry; a power, too, which Congress had, also, but a few weeks before, refused to exercise. And yet, without the repeal or abolition of ports of entry, any attempt, by either Congress or the President, to blockade these ports, is a violation of the spirit, if not of the letter, of that clause of the Constitution which declares that "no preference shall be given, by any regulation of commerce or revenue, to the ports of one State over those of another."

Sir, upon this point I do not speak without the highest authority. In the very midst of the South Carolina nullification controversy, it was suggested, that in the recess of Congress, and without a law to govern him, the President, Andrew Jackson, meant to send down a fleet to Charleston and blockade the port. But the bare suggestion called forth the indignant protest of Daniel Webster, himself the archenemy of nullification, and whose highest honors were won in the three years' conflict in the Senate Chamber, with its ablest champions. In an address, in October, 1832, at Worcester, Massachusetts, to a National Republican convention—it was before the birth, or christening at least, of the Whig party—the great expounder of the Constitution said:

"We are told, sir, that the President will immediately employ the military force, and at once blockade Charleston. A military remedy—a remedy by direct belligerent operation, has thus been suggested, and nothing else has been suggested, as the intended means of preserving the Union. Sir, there is no little reason to think that this suggestion is true. We cannot be altogether unmindful of the past, and, therefore, we cannot be altogether unapprehensive for the future. For one, sir, I raise my voice, beforehand, against the unauthorized employment of military power, and against superseding the authority of the laws, by an armed force, under pretence of putting down nullification. *The President has no authority to blockade Charleston.*"

Jackson! Jackson, sir! the great Jackson! did not dare to do it without authority of Congress; but our Jackson of to-day, the little Jackson at the other end of the avenue, and the mimic Jacksons around him, do blockade, not only Charleston harbor, but the whole Southern coast, three thousand miles in extent, by a single stroke of the pen.

"The President has no authority to employ military force till he shall be duly required,"—

Mark the word:

"*required* so to do by law and the civil authorities. His duty is to cause the laws to be executed. His duty is to support *the civil authority*,"—

As in the Merryman case, forsooth; but I shall recur to that hereafter:

"His duty is, if the laws be resisted, to employ the military force of the country, if necessary, for their support and execution; *but to do all this in compliance only with law and with decisions of the tribunals.* If, by any ingenious devices, those who resist the laws escape from the reach of judicial authority, as it is now provided to be exercised, it is entirely competent to *Congress* to make such new provisions as the exigency of the case may demand."

Treason, sir, rank treason, all this to-day. And yet, thirty years ago, it was true Union patriotism and sound constitutional law! Sir, I prefer the wisdom and stern fidelity to principle of the fathers.

Such was the voice of Webster, and such, too, let me add, the voice, in his last great speech in the Senate, of the Douglas whose death the land now mourns.

Next after the blockade, sir, in the catalogue of daring Executive usurpations, comes the proclamation of the 3d of May, and the orders of the War and Navy Departments in pursuance of it—a proclamation and usurpation which would have cost any English sovereign his head at any time within the last two hundred years. Sir, the Constitution not only confines to Congress the right to declare war, but expressly provides that "Congress (not the President) shall have power to raise and support armies;" and to "provide and maintain a navy." In pursuance of this authority, Congress, years ago, had fixed the number of officers and of the regiments, of the different kinds of service; and also, the number of ships, officers, marines, and seamen which should compose the navy. Not only that, but Congress has repeatedly, within the last five years, refused to increase the regular army. More than that still: in February and March last, the House, upon several test votes, repeatedly and expressly refused to authorize the President to accept the service of volunteers for the very purpose of protecting the public property, enforcing the laws, and collecting the revenue. And yet, the President, of his own mere will and authority, and without the shadow of right, has proceeded to increase, and has increased, the standing army by twenty-five thousand men; the navy by eighteen thousand; and has called for, and accepted the services of, forty regiments of volunteers for three years, numbering forty-two thousand men, and making thus a grand army, or military force, raised by executive proclamation alone, without the sanction of Congress, without warrant of law, and in direct violation of the Constitution, and of his oath of office, of eighty-five thousand soldiers enlisted for three and five years, and already in the field. And yet, the President now asks us to support the army which he has thus raised, to ratify his usurpations by a law *ex post facto*, and thus to make ourselves parties to our own degradation, and to his infractions of the Constitution. Meanwhile, however, he has taken good care not only to enlist the men, organize the regiments, and muster them into service, but to provide, in advance, for a horde of forlorn, worn-out, and broken-down politicians of his own party, by appointing, either by himself, or through the Governors of the States, major-generals, brigadier-generals, colonels, lieutenant-colonels, majors, captains, lieutenants, adjutants, quarter-masters, and surgeons, without any limit as to numbers, and without so much as once saying to Congress, "By your leave, gentlemen."

Beginning with this wide breach of the Constitution, this enormous usurpation of the most dangerous of all powers—the power of the sword—other infractions and assumptions were easy; and after public liberty, private right soon fell. The privacy of the telegraph was invaded, in the search after treason and traitors; although it turns out, significantly enough, that the only victim, so far, is one of the appointees and especial pets of the Administration. The telegraphic dispatches, preserved under every pledge of secrecy, for the protection and safety of the telegraph companies, were seized and carried away without search-warrant, without probable cause, without oath, and without description of the places to be searched, or of the things to be seized, and in plain violation of the right of the people to be secure in their houses, persons, *papers*, and effects, against unreasonable searches and seizures. One step more, sir, will bring upon us search and seizure of the public mails; and, finally, as in the worst days of English oppression—as in the times of the Russells and the Sydneys, of English martyrdom—of the drawers and secretaries of the private citizen; though even then tyrants had the grace to look to the forms of the law, and the execution was judicial murder, not military slaughter. But who shall say that the future Nero of America, shall have the modesty of his Roman predecessor, in extenuation of whose character it is written by the great historian, *Subtraxit occulos, jussitque scelera non spectavit.*

Sir, the rights of property having been thus wantonly violated, it needed but a little stretch of usurpation to invade the sanctity of the person; and a victim was not long wanting. A private citizen of Maryland, not subject to the rules and articles of war—not in a case arising in the land or naval forces, nor in the militia, when in actual service—is seized in his own house, in the dead hour of night, not by any civil officer, nor upon any civil process, but by a band of armed soldiers, under the verbal orders of a military chief, and is ruthlessly torn from his wife and his children, and hurried off to a fortress of the United States—and that fortress, as if in mockery, the very one over whose ramparts had floated that star-spangled banner, which "in the dawn's early light," gladdened the eyes and inspired the soul of the patriot prisoner, who in the midst of battle, and upon the deck of one of the enemy's ships, made it memorable by the noblest of American national lyrics.

And, sir, when the highest judicial officer of the land, the Chief Justice of the Supreme Court, upon whose shoulders "when the judicial ermine fell, it touched nothing less spotless than itself," the aged, the venerable, the gentle, and pure-minded Taney, who, but a little while before, had administered to the President the oath to support the Constitution, and to execute the laws, issued, as by law it was his sworn duty to issue, the high prerogative writ of *habeas corpus*—that great writ of right, that main bulwark of personal liberty, commanding the body of the accused to be brought before him, that justice and right might be done by due course of law, and without denial or delay, the gates of the fortress, its cannon turned towards, and in plain sight of the city, where the court sat, and frowning from the ramparts, were closed against the officer of the law, and the answer returned that the officer in command had, by the authority of the President, *suspended* the writ of *habeas corpus.* And thus it is, sir, that the accused has ever since been held a prisoner without due process of law; without bail; without presentment by a grand jury; without speedy, or public trial by a petit jury, of his own State or district, or any trial at all;

without information of the nature and cause of the accusation; without being confronted with the witnesses against him; without compulsory process to obtain witnesses in his favor; and without the assistance of counsel for his defence. And this is our boasted American liberty? And thus it is, too, sir, that here, here, in America, in the seventy-third year of the Republic, that great writ and security of personal freedom, which it cost the patriots and freemen of England six hundred years of labor and toil, and blood to extort and to hold fast from venal judges and tyrant kings; written in the great charter at Runnymede, by the iron barons, who made the simple Latin and uncouth words of the times, *nullus liber homo*, in the language of Chatham, worth all the classics; recovered and confirmed a hundred times afterwards, as often as violated and stolen away, and finally, and firmly secured at last by the great act of Charles II., and transferred thence to our own Constitution and laws, has been wantonly and ruthlessly trampled in the dust. Ay, sir, that great writ, bearing, by special command of Parliament, those other uncouth, but magic words, *per statutum tricessimo primo Caroli secundi regis*, which no English judge, no English minister, no king or queen of England, dare disobey; that writ, brought over by our fathers, and cherished by them, as a priceless inheritance of liberty, an American President has contemptuously set at defiance. Nay, more, he has ordered his subordinate military chiefs to suspend it at their discretion! And, yet, after all this, he coolly comes before this House and the Senate, and the country, and pleads that he is only preserving and protecting the Constitution; and demands and expects of this House and of the Senate, and the country, their thanks for his usurpations; while, outside of this capitol, his myrmidons are clamoring for impeachment of the Chief Justice, as engaged in a conspiracy to break down the Federal Government.

Sir, however much necessity—the tyrant's plea—may be urged in extenuation of the usurpations and infractions of the President in regard to public liberty, there can be no such apology or defence for his invasions of private right. What overruling necessity required the violation of the sanctity of private property and private confidence? What great public danger demanded the arrest and imprisonment, without trial by common law, of one single private citizen, for an act done weeks before, openly, and by authority of his State? If guilty of treason, was not the judicial power ample enough and strong enough for his conviction and punishment? What, then, was needed in his case, but the precedent under which other men, in other places, might become the victims of executive suspicion and displeasure?

As to the pretence, sir, that the President has the Constitutional right to suspend the writ of *habeas corpus*, I will not waste time in arguing it. The case is as plain as words can make it. It is a legislative power; it is found only in the legislative article; it belongs to Congress only to do it. Subordinate officers have disobeyed it: General Wilkinson disobeyed it, but he sent his prisoners on for judicial trial; General Jackson disobeyed it, and was reprimanded by James Madison; but no President, nobody but Congress, ever before assumed the right to suspend it. And, sir, that other pretence of necessity, I repeat, cannot be allowed. It had no existence in fact. The Constitution cannot be preserved by violating it. It is an offence to the intelligence of this House, and of the country, to pretend that all this, and the other gross and multiplied infractions of the Constitution and usurpations of power were done by the President and his advisers out of pure love and devotion to the Constitution. But if so, sir, then they have but one step further to take, and declare, in the language of Sir Boyle Roche, in the Irish House of Commons, that such is the depth of their attachment to it, that they are prepared to give up, not merely a part, but the whole of the Constitution, *to preserve the remainder.* And yet, if indeed this pretext of necessity be well founded, then let me say, that a cause which demands the sacrifice of the Constitution and of the dearest securities of property, liberty, and life, cannot be just; certainly it is not worth the sacrifice.

Sir, I am obliged to pass by, for want of time, other grave and dangerous infractions and usurpations of the President since the 4th of March. I only allude casually to the quartering of soldiers in private houses without the consent of the owners, and without any manner having been prescribed by law; to the subversion in a part, at least, of Maryland of her own State Government and of the authorities under it; to the censorship over the telegraph, and the infringement, repeatedly, in one or more of the States, of the right of the people to keep and to bear arms for their defence. But if all these things, I ask, have been done in the first two months after the commencement of this war, and by men not military chieftains, and unused to arbitrary power, what may we not expect to see in three years, and by the successful heroes of the fight? Sir, the power and rights of the States and the people, and of their Representatives, have been usurped; the sanctity of the private house and of private property has been invaded; and the liberty of the person wantonly and wickedly stricken down; free speech, too, has been repeatedly denied; and all this under the plea of necessity. Sir, the right of petition will follow next—nay, it has already been shaken; the freedom of the press will soon fall after it; and let me whisper in your ear, that there will be few to mourn over its loss, unless, indeed, its ancient high and honorable character shall be rescued and redeemed from its present reckless mendacity and degradation. Freedom of religion will yield too, at last, amid the exultant shouts of millions, who have seen its holy temples defiled, and its white robes of a former innocency trampled now under the polluting hoofs of an ambitious and faithless or fanatical clergy. Meantime national banks, bankrupt laws, a vast and permanent public debt, high tariffs, heavy direct taxation, enormous expenditure, gigantic and stupendous peculation, anarchy first, and a strong government afterwards—no more State lines, no more State governments, but a consolidated monarchy or vast centralized military despotism must all follow in the history of the future, as in the history of the past they have, centuries ago, been written. Sir, I have said nothing, and have time to say nothing now, of the immense indebtedness and the vast expenditures which have already accrued, nor of the folly and mismanagement of the war so far, nor of the atrocious and shameless peculations and frauds which have disgraced it in the State governments and the Federal Government from the beginning. The avenging hour for all these will come hereafter, and I pass them by now.

I have finished now, Mr. Chairman, what I proposed to say at this time upon the message of the President. As to my own position in regard to this most unhappy civil war, I have only to say that I stand to-day just where I stood upon the 4th of March last; where the whole Democratic party, and the whole Constitutional Union party, and a vast majority, as I believe, of the people of the United States, stood too. I am for *peace*, speedy, immediate, honorable PEACE, with all its blessings. Others may have changed—I have not. I question not their motives nor quarrel with their course. It is vain and futile for them to question or to quarrel with mine. My duty shall be discharged—calmly, firmly, quietly, and regardless of consequences. The approving voice of a conscience void of offence, and the approving judgment which shall follow "after some time be past," these, God help me, are my trust and my support.

Sir, I have spoken freely and fearlessly to-day, as became an American Representative and an American citizen; one firmly resolved, come what may, not to lose his own Constitutional liberties, nor to surrender his own Constitutional rights in the vain effort to impose these rights and liberties upon ten millions of unwilling people. I have spoken earnestly, too, but yet not as one unmindful of the solemnity of the scenes which surround us upon every side to-day. Sir, when the Congress of the United States assembled here on the 3d of December, 1860, just seven months ago, the Senate was composed of sixty-six Senators, representing the thirty-three States of the Union, and this House of two hundred and thirty-seven members—every State being present. It was a grand and solemn spectacle—the ambassadors of three-and-thirty sovereignties and thirty-one millions of people, the mightiest republic on earth, in general Congress assembled. In the Senate, too, and this House, were some of the ablest and most distinguished statesmen of the country; men whose names were familiar to the whole country—some of them destined to pass into history. The new wings of the capitol had then but just recently been finished, in all their gorgeous magnificence, and, except a hundred marines at the navy-yard, not a soldier was within forty miles of Washington.

Sir, the Congress of the United States meets here again to-day; but how changed the scene! Instead of thirty-four States, twenty-three only, one less than the number forty years ago, are here, or in the other wing of the capitol. Forty-six Senators and a hundred and seventy-three Representatives constitute the Congress of the now United States. And of these, eight Senators and twenty-four Representatives, from four States only, linger here yet as deputies from that great South which, from the beginning of the Government, contributed so much to mould its policy, to build up its greatness, and to control its destinies. All the other States of that South are gone. Twenty-two Senators and sixty-five Representatives no longer answer to their names. The vacant seats are, indeed, still here; and the escutcheons of their respective States look down now solemnly and sadly from these vaulted ceilings. But the Virginia of Washington and Henry and Madison, of Marshall and Jefferson, of Randolph and Monroe, the birth-place of Clay, the mother of States and of Presidents; the Carolinas of Pinckney and Sumter and Marion, of Calhoun and Macon; and Tennessee, the home and burial-place of Jackson; and other States, too, once most loyal and true, are no longer here. The voices and footsteps of the great dead of the past two ages of the Republic linger still, it may be in echo, along the stately corridors of this capitol; but their descendants, from nearly one half of the States of the Republic, will meet with us no more within these marble halls. But in the parks and lawns, and upon the broad avenues of this spacious city, seventy thousand soldiers have supplied their places; and the morning drum-beat from a score of encampments, within sight of this beleaguered capitol, gives melancholy warning to the Representatives of the States and of the people, that AMID ARMS LAWS ARE SILENT.

Sir, some years hence—I would fain hope some months hence, if I dare—the present generation will demand to know the cause of all this; and, some ages hereafter, the grand and impartial tribunal of history will make solemn and diligent inquest of the authors of this terrible revolution.

ADDENDUM.

In reply to a question by Mr. HOLMAN, of Indiana, in regard to supporting the Government, Mr. VALLANDIGHAM said he would answer in the words of the following resolution, which he had prepared, and proposed to offer at a future time:

Resolved, That the Federal Government is the agent of the people of the several States comprising the Union; that it consists of three distinct departments—the legislative, the executive, and the judicial—each equally a part of the Government, and equally entitled to the confidence and support of the States and the people; and that it is the duty of every patriot to sustain the several departments of the Government in the exercise of all the Constitutional powers of each which may be necessary and proper for the preservation of the Government in its principles and in its vigor and integrity, and to stand by and defend to the utmost the flag which represents the Government, the Union, and the country.

REMARKS,

ON HIS PROPOSITION TO APPOINT COMMISSIONERS TO ACCOMPANY THE ARMY.

In the House of Representatives, July 12, 1861.

THE Army Bill being under consideration, Mr. VALLANDIGHAM offered the following proviso:

"*Provided, further*, That before the President shall have the right to call out any more volunteers than are already in the service, he shall appoint seven commissioners, whose mission shall be to accompany the Army on its march, to receive and consider such propositions, if any, as may at any time be submitted from the Executive of the so-called Confederate States, or of any one of them, looking to a suspension of hostilities and the return of said States, or any one of them, to the Union, and to obedience to the Federal Constitution and authority."

Mr. V. spoke in support of the amendment as follows:

Mr. CHAIRMAN. I do not rise to debate this question at length—the hour for that discussion has not yet come—but simply to remind gentlemen on both sides of the House that when, four years ago, the obscure and far-distant Territory of Utah, with little less than one hundred thousand inhabitants, and insignificant in power and resources, was in armed rebellion against the Government of the United States, the President appointed two commissioners to accompany the Army upon a like mission of generous forbearance and humanity.

Mr. LOVEJOY. I make the point of order that the amendment is irrelevant.

The CHAIRMAN. The Chairman overrules the point of order.

Mr. VALLANDIGHAM. I rise simply to remind the House of that significant fact, and to inquire whether, if, in a case like that, where the lives and fortunes of a people so few, so insignificant, and so odious in their manners and their institutions, were concerned, this great and powerful Government thought it becoming, in a spirit of justice and moderation, to send commissioners to accompany, and indeed to precede, the Army on its march, for the purpose of receiving propositions of submission and of return to obedience to the authority of the Federal Government, we ought not now, in this great revolution—this great rebellion, if you prefer the word—to exhibit somewhat also of the same spirit of moderation and forbearance; and while the legislative department is engaged in voting hundreds of thousands of men and hundreds of millions of dollars, we ought not, bearing the sword in one hand, to go forth with the olive-branch in the other?

I offer the amendment in good faith, and for the purpose of ascertaining whether there be such a disposition in the House. For my own part, sir, while I would not in the beginning have given a dollar or a man to commence this war, I am willing—now that we are in the midst of it without any act of ours—to vote just as many men and just as much money as may be necessary to protect and defend the Federal Government. It would be both treason and madness now to disarm the Government in the presence of an enemy of two hundred thousand men in the field against it. But I will not vote millions of men and money blindly, for bills interpreted by the message, and in speeches on this floor, to mean bitter and relentless hostility to and subjugation of the South. It is against an aggressive and invasive warfare that I raise my vote and voice. I desire not to be misunderstood. I would suspend hostilities for present negotiation, to try the temper of the South—the Union men, at least, of the South. But as the war is upon us, there must be an army in the field; there must be money appropriated to maintain it; but I will give no more of men and no more of money than is necessary to keep that army in the position, and ready to strike, until it can be ascertained whether there is a Union sentiment in the South, and whether there be indeed any real and sober and well-founded disposition among the people of those States to return to the Union and to their obedience to the authority of this Government. I trust that this amendment will receive that consideration which I believe it justly deserves.

[This proposition to appoint commissioners *solely* for the purpose of a *restoration of the Union* by the return of the seceded States, received only twenty-one votes.]

THE TARIFF—TEA, COFFEE, AND SUGAR.

Remarks in the House of Representatives, December 23, 1861.

MR. SPEAKER:—I desire to say that, at the last session, I opposed, in common with all the gentlemen upon this side of the House, the tariff and tax bill; and in some brief remarks then submitted, I predicted that the result of increasing the duties would be a great and disastrous diminution of the importations, and by consequence of the revenue from customs.

We have before us now the annual report of the Secretary of the Treasury, four months later, admitting that his estimate of receipts from duties on articles imported, or to be imported, during the current fiscal year, must already be reduced by $25,000,000. Such has been the effect of the "Morrill tariff" of 1861, and the act of August, amending it. Yet, instead of pursuing a course of policy which every principle of political economy demands, and promoting an increase of the revenues by reducing duties and encouraging importations, we are about still further to diminish the revenues by increasing the duty to such an extent as will, in a little while, amount to prohibition. Why, sir, in portions of the Northwest it already requires four bushels of corn to buy one pound of coffee. Corn, in Illinois is selling at seven cents a bushel, and in some places has been used as fuel, instead of wood, because it is now cheaper. Yet gentlemen of the Eastern States are continually applying the same Sangradian panacea, holding fast to the absurd notion that an increase of duty will always and inevitably be followed by a corresponding increase of revenue. They still insist, whenever the receipts run low, on adding to the tariff of duties, without remembering that the natural effect of the increase, even in ordinary times, is to diminish importations, and that now, especially, the loss of the cotton export, amounting last year to $191,000,000, or, deducting the precious metals, to nearly two-thirds of our entire exportation, and the depressing influence every way of the present crisis, have already cut down the importations to nearly one-half, as compared with the last five or six years. In the port of New York alone the falling off amounts to about one hundred millions of dollars. How, I beg to know, are you to have revenue from imports when nothing is imported? *Ex nihilo nihil fit.*

But not so think the wise men of the East. The more you fetter commerce the more they believe it will flourish. The higher you make the duties the more will revenue flow into your Treasury. Do gentlemen forget that customs duty is a voluntary tax, and that beyond a certain point no one will tax himself of his own free will? When times are prosperous and money plenty, and trade and commerce are brisk, men will buy much, though the price be raised. But in times of depression, when wages are low, money scarce, and employment difficult to be had —in just such times, in short, as are now upon us—merchants will not import because consumers will not purchase if the price be high. The true policy, therefore, clearly is to lower the impost and encourage importation, and not to add to all the other causes which now combine to destroy this main source of revenue, the killing effect of increased duties. This is quackery, not statesmanship; and I predict to-day that your high tariffs will not realize for the current year even the revised and amended estimate of the Secretary of the Treasury.

Now, sir, I submit the question without going into the argument further, that at the least, this bill should be postponed until the entire tariff system can be digested and accommodated to the changed condition of the country; until it can be made literally and strictly a revenue tariff—a war tariff, if you please. As it now stands, it is an incongruous amalgam of three separate acts and two or three different systems of duties—the *ad valorem*, the specific, and a compound of the two. I think, sir, that the bill should certainly go over for two or three weeks, until the whole subject can be arranged, collated and harmonized. This can be done without the slightest loss to the revenue. How much, sir, does the gentleman from Vermont expect to realize within the next three weeks from the passage of this act? Will there be an extraordinary importation of tea from China and Japan within that time? Will there be any such of coffee and sugar? What is in the wind? As to the latter article of sugar, let me say further, that the West has heretofore received its sugars mostly from the lower States on the Mississippi; but an embargo has been laid on the trade of that river ever since April or May last. You have shut up, blockaded, the Mississippi for us; and more effectually, too, than any port on the southern coast. Since that time our sugars have been received from the East, and the price has of course been very greatly enhanced. In addition to thus cutting us off from our market, you increased the duties upon sugars at the late session; and now you propose, in hot haste, to raise that duty still higher, and thus to place the article wholly beyond the reach of most of those in the West who are accustomed to regard it as a necessary of life; and I believe, sir, that it is consumed perhaps to a larger extent there than in the States of the East.

It seems to me, Mr. Speaker, that some other surer and wiser mode ought to be devised for increasing the waning revenues of the Government. Your expenditures are $500,000,000; your income but $50,000,000, enough to last just one month. If the Constitution did not forbid a tax upon exports, something might, in that way, be added, because there has been a very large increase of exportations within the last six months. But even in that case, I have not the slightest doubt you would, upon each recurring pressure, raise the duties, too, and thus break down your exports, as you have already your imports by the same folly. True, the country is benefited to a large extent, doubtless by this heavy exportation, and the West receives a share of that benefit. But let it be remembered that this increased exportation from the West through the seaports of the East, arises from the fact that the navigation of the Mississippi has been closed to us, and thus the products which heretofore we were accustomed to carry down that river have been forced to find a market in foreign countries. Cut off as we are from all other means of outlet except by way of the lakes, and thus, in part, through a foreign country, and with our railroads leading to the East, for the most part in the hands of Eastern directors or bondholders, the tariff of freights has at the same time been fully doubled, thus increasing the burdens upon our trade both ways, so largely as to amount in a little while longer to absolute prohibition; while, to make the matter still worse, that great and natural channel of railroad communication, also, from the southern portions of the Northwest eastward, the Baltimore and Ohio railroad, has been closed for all purposes of travel and transportation for the last six months, and it seems almost impossible for some cause—surely not "military necessity," but shall I say base selfishness on the part of more northern and eastern or rival roads?—to procure the opening of it upon any terms.

Sir, I have spoken so far solely for the purpose of directing the attention of the House and the country to this subject, and not with any vain notion of being hearkened to now or here. The bill will pass forthwith, and just as you received it from the Treasury Department. It has been impossible to obtain even from this side of the House, the poor privilege of the yeas and nays upon the question of suspending the rules to allow it to be reported; and it is vain to offer opposition to the measure. Let it pass. But I am resolved that the record shall be made up for the GREAT HEREAFTER, and that the responsibility for this and other kindred measures shall be fixed just where it belongs.

CHARGES OF DISLOYALTY: 1862.*

MR. SPEAKER: I was just waiting for an opportunity to call the attention of the House to that statement myself, having received it from some unknown source a moment ago. I do not know, of course, what the motive just now of the gentleman from Pennsylvania may be, nor do I care. My purpose then was just what it is now, to give a plain, direct, emphatic contradiction—a flat denial to the infamous statement and insinuation contained in the newspaper paragraph just read. I never wrote a letter or a line upon political subjects, least of all, on the question of secession, to the *Baltimore South*, or to any other paper, or to any man south of Mason and Dixon's line, since this revolt began—never; and I defy the production of it. The charge is false, infamous, scandalous; and, it is beyond endurance, too, that a man's reputation shall be at the mercy of every scavenger employed to visit the haunts of vice in a great city, a mere local editor of an irresponsible newspaper, who may choose to parade before the country false and malicious libels like this. I avail myself of this opportunity, to say that I enter into no defence, and shall enter into none, until some letter shall be produced here which I have written, or authorized to be written, referring to "bleeding Dixie," or making any suggestion "how the Yankees might be defeated." If any such are in existence, I pro-

* During the Thirty-Seventh Congress there was a strong outside pressure against Mr. Vallandigham, and, on the part of many members of that body, a great willingness to yield to the pressure. And yet no successful attempt to impeach, or even to cast reproach upon his loyalty, has ever been made. The efforts in that direction, made seven times in Congress, were only a reproach to the parties by whom they were made.

On the 7th of January, 1862, Mr. Vallandigham, in reply to Mr. Hutchins, of Ohio, said:

"To-day the magnitude and true character of the war stand confessed, and its real purposes begin to be revealed; and I am justified, or soon will be justified by thousands, who, a little while ago, condemned me. But I appealed, in the beginning, as I appeal now, alike to the near and the distant future; and by the judgment of that impartial tribunal, even in the present generation, I will abide, or, if my name and memory shall fade away out of the record of these times, then will these calumnies perish with them."

But, of these attacks. the most important and serious was that made in the House of Representatives on the 19th of February, 1862, by Mr. Hickman, of Pennsylvania, who offered a resolution, "instructing the Committee on the Judiciary to inquire into the truth of certain charges of disloyalty, made in the local columns of a Baltimore newspaper, against C. L. Vallandigham, of Ohio."

Mr. Vallandigham spoke in reply, as above.

nounce them, here and now, utter and impudent forgeries. I have said that I enter upon no defence. I deny that it is the duty or the right of any member to rise here, and call for investigation founded upon statements like this; and I only regret that I did not have the opportunity to denounce this report before the chairman of the Committee on the Judiciary rose, and, in this formal manner, called the attention of the House to it—himself the accuser and the judge. Sir, I have for five years been a member of this House, and I never rose to a personal explanation but once, and that to correct a report of the proceedings of the House. I have always considered such mere personal explanations and controversies with the press, as unbecoming the dignity of the House.

Nevertheless, I did intend to make this the first exception in my congressional career, and to say—and I wish my words reported, not only at the desk here officially, but in the gallery—that I denounce, in advance, this foul and infamous statement, that I have been in treasonable, or even suspicious correspondence with any one in that State—loyal though it is to the Union—or in any other State, or have ever uttered one sentiment inconsistent with my duty, not only as a member of this House, but as a citizen of the United States—one who has taken a solemn oath to support the Constitution, and who, thank God, has never tainted that oath in thought, or word, or deed. I have had the right, and have exercised it, and as God liveth, and my soul liveth, and as He is my judge, I will exercise it still in this House, and out of it, of vindicating the rights of the American citizen; and beyond that I have never gone. My sentiments will be found in the records of the House, except as I have made them public otherwise, and they will be found nowhere else. There, sir, is their sole repository. And foreseeing, more than a year ago, but especially in the early part of December, 1860, the magnitude and true character of the revolution or rebellion into which this country was about to be plunged, I then resolved not to write, although your own mails still carried the letters, nor have I written, one solitary syllable or line—as to the Gulf States, months even before secession began—to any one residing in a seceded State. And yet, the gentleman avails himself now of this paragraph, to give dignity and importance to charges of the falsest and most infamous character. Had the letter been produced; had the charge come in any tangible or authentic shape; had any editor of any respectable newspaper, even, indorsed the accusation, and made it specific, there might have been some apology; but the gentleman knows well that this base insinuation was placed in the local columns of a vile newspaper, put there by some person who had never seen any such letter.

Sir, I meet this first specific charge of disloyalty, made responsibly here—I meet it at the very threshold, as becomes a man and a Representative—by an emphatic but contemptuous denial. This is due to the House; it is due to myself.

Mr. Richardson. I hope the gentleman from Pennsylvania will allow me to make a single remark.

Mr. Hickman. Certainly.

Mr. Richardson. Mr. Speaker: I want to hear nothing about disloyalty on this side of the House while there is a class of members here upon the other side of the House who have declared that they will vote for no proposition to carry on the War, unless it is prosecuted in a particular line, and for the abolition of slavery. *They* would subvert the Constitution and the Government, and I denounce them as traitors, and they ought to be brought to trial, condemnation, and execution.

Mr. Hickman. Mr. Speaker: The motives which actuated me in introducing the resolution in question ought not to be doubted. The severe charge contained in the article in question is made against the gentleman from Ohio, a member of this House. Even a suspicion, a mere suspicion, would justify such an investigation as this resolution contemplates. But the gentleman from Ohio, as well as other members upon this floor, knows that the suspicions which have existed against him—I do not say whether justly or unjustly—have been numerous, and in circulation for a long time past. It is the duty of this House to purge itself of unworthy members. I do not assert whether the gentleman from Ohio occupies, properly or improperly, his seat upon this floor. By offering this resolution I do not prejudge him. If he were the most intimate friend I had on earth, accused as the gentleman from Ohio is in the paragraph in question, I should deem it my solemn duty to urge the investigation which is here suggested. But, sir, this charge does not come in a very questionable shape. It appears as an original article in the *Baltimore Clipper*, and is, therefore, presumed to be editorial, or at least under the supervision of the editor. It, to all appearances, emanates from a responsible source.

But, sir, I suggest further, that the suppression of the newspaper in question, the *Baltimore South*, and the seizure of its office of publication, was made under the direct authority of the Government, and it is to be presumed that the effects of the office are, at this time, in the custody of the Government, or of the agents of the Government, and, therefore, the information communicated in this paper must have come through the Government, or the agents of the Government. It is responsible in its origin, as far as we can judge. Now, sir, I refer the gentleman from Ohio, as my answer to the suggestion that I was not justified in offering this resolution under the circumstances, to page 69 of the last edition of the Manual. The first paragraph of section thirteen, headed "Examination of Witnesses," reads as follows:

"Common fame is a good ground for the House to proceed to inquiry, and even to accusation."

This, sir, is more than common fame. I repeat, that it is, so far as it appears, a direct charge by the editor of a responsible newspaper. The information comes, we must believe, through the Government, or the agents of the Government, and it is, therefore, more than common fame. It is good ground, at least, for instituting an inquiry.

Mr. VALLANDIGHAM. I desire to ask the gentleman from Pennsylvania whether he does not know that this is a mere local item, and that the author of it does not even pretend to have seen the letters.

Mr. HICKMAN. I do not understand what the gentleman means by saying that the author of the paragraph has not seen them.

Mr. VALLANDIGHAM. I say he does not profess to have seen them, and I *know* that he never did, for they never were written, do not now exist, and never did exist.

Mr. HICKMAN. Who never saw them?

Mr. VALLANDIGHAM. The author of that paragraph in the local columns of this newspaper.

Mr. HICKMAN. He never saw the letters!

Mr. VALLANDIGHAM. He does not profess even to have seen them.

Mr. HICKMAN. Whether it is a local item or not, it is an original article in a responsible newspaper, and is, therefore, presumed to have been inserted under the direct supervision of the editor, if not written by him.

Mr. VALLANDIGHAM. The gentleman from Pennsylvania has alluded to suspicions existing heretofore. Now, I desire to know of him, whether he ever heard of any specific item on which any such suspicions ever rested—any thing other than words spoken in this House or made public over my own name?

Mr. HICKMAN. Yes, sir.

Mr. VALLANDIGHAM. Well, let us have it.

Mr. HICKMAN. I have heard a thousand.

Mr. VALLANDIGHAM. Name a single one.

Mr. HICKMAN. I do not desire to do any injustice to the gentleman from Ohio.

Mr. VALLANDIGHAM. I have asked the gentleman, and I demand a direct answer to my question, whether he can specify one single item?

Mr. HICKMAN. I will reply to it directly.

Mr. VALLANDIGHAM. Or does the gentleman mean merely the newspaper slanders that have been published against me, and which I have denounced as false, over and over again, in cards, and on the floor of this House?

Mr. HICKMAN. I know nothing about that, sir. I know that suspicions may well exist, and I know they do exist, where denials accompany them.

Mr. VALLANDIGHAM. Yes; I know that fact in the gentleman's own case.

Mr. HICKMAN. I have no controversy with the gentleman from Ohio, nor am I here to defend myself in the course which I have taken. Let him defend himself, and allow me to take care of myself, as I expect to be able to do.

Mr. RICHARDSON. Will the gentleman from Pennsylvania allow me——

Mr. HICKMAN. I will not suffer any interruption except by the gentleman from Ohio. He has a right to interrupt me, and I am glad he does so, because I do not want to put the gentleman from Ohio in any false position any more than I would desire to be myself placed in one; and I will not do it. I do say, most distinctly, that suspicions have existed against the loyalty of the gentleman from Ohio; and I would not have referred to them at all if I had not been satisfied that he himself knew of the existence of those suspicions as well as I did. Indeed, the remarks which preceded my rising on this floor indicated the fact, more clearly than I myself could indicate it by any thing that I could say, that he was in possession of a knowledge of the existence of those suspicions, for he got up to repel them, not merely such as are contained in this article in question, but in general terms—general suspicions and imputations against his character. That was deemed right by him, sir. I have nothing to say against it.

Now, the gentleman asks for specifications. I am called upon by him to refresh my memory, and to give an instance. I will give him one or two. I may not be able to give more at this time. Perhaps, if he were to give me time, I would be able to refer him to many more instances.

Mr. VALLANDIGHAM. Mr. Speaker——

Mr. HICKMAN. The gentleman must allow me to answer his question, and then he may interrupt me. I must reply to one inquiry at a time. I am now on the witness-stand—brought to it by the gentleman from Ohio. I am on cross-examination, and he must allow me to answer one question before he propounds to me another. Now, sir, I refer to the fact of the Breckinridge meeting in the city of Baltimore, where the gentleman from Ohio attended, and which gave rise to very many suspicions, allow me to say; at least I have heard a great many expressed. Allow me again to refer to the fact of his attending a certain dinner in Kentucky, which was given, I believe, in his honor, or which was, at least, published as such in the papers.

Mr. VALLANDIGHAM. Allow me, right there——

Mr. HICKMAN. Allow me first——

Mr. VALLANDIGHAM. That is a specific charge, which I wish to answer.

Mr. HICKMAN. Not this moment.

Mr. VALLANDIGHAM. I appeal to the gentleman's honor.

Mr. HICKMAN. I will treat the gentleman from Ohio fairly. He must receive all my answer before he asks me another question.

Mr. VALLANDIGHAM. Let him oblige me by replying to me specifically.

Mr. HICKMAN. I am not done with my answer, and I refuse to yield the floor until I finish my answer. I am entitled to be treated here properly, as well as the gentleman from Ohio. I will extend to him all the courtesy that can possibly be demanded by any gentleman. That is my habit, I trust. There are many other items. There was the speech which the gentleman made at the July session in this House—a speech which was understood to be one of general accusation and crimination against the Government and against the party having the conduct of this war. It gave rise to a great many suspicions; and the gentleman from Ohio, with his intelligence, ought not to be ignorant of all these facts. Well, sir, will not conversation naturally arise in consequence of these facts? And I appeal to every member of this House whether they have not heard suspicion upon suspicion against the loyalty of the gentleman from Ohio. Is it not a common rumor, sir, that he is suspected? I allege that it is a common rumor in the Northern States, and among the loyal people of the Loyal States, that the gentleman from Ohio is, at least, open to grave suspicion, if not to direct imputation. That is my answer. Now I will hear the gentleman.

Mr. VALLANDIGHAM. In reply to the specification, and the only one, which the gentleman has been able to point out, relating to a public dinner in Kentucky, allow me to tell him that my foot has not pressed the soil of Kentucky since the 10th day of July, 1852, when, as a member of a committee appointed by the Common Council of the city where I reside, I followed the remains of that great and noble man, and true patriot, Henry Clay, to their last resting-place. I have partaken of no dinners there, or elsewhere, of a political character, nor did I ever attend any Breckinridge meeting at Baltimore, or elsewhere, at any time. This is my answer to that, the only specification. And yet, the gentleman dares attempt to support that falsehood, which I here denounce as such, by alluding to suspicions which have been created and set afloat throughout the whole country, not merely against me, but against hundreds and thousands of others, in whose veins runs blood as patriotic and loyal as ever flowed since the world began. I tell the gentleman that, in years past, I have heard his loyalty to the Union questioned. I have known of things which would have justified me—had I relied on authority similar to that to which he has attempted to give dignity—in introducing similar resolutions to make inquiry into his purpose to disrupt this Union by the doctrines which he has held, and the opinions which he has expressed. And yet, opinions and sentiments, uttered here, are "the head and the front of my offending." It has "this extent, no more."

And, sir, I replied, some time ago, to two others, which, I doubt not, the gentleman would have dragged now out of the mire and slough into which they have fallen, but that they were answered, when thrust into debate by the gentleman before me (Mr. Hutchins). I refer to the charge that I had once uttered the absurd declaration that the soldiery of the North and West should pass over my dead body before they should invade the Southern States. I denied it then, and will not repeat the denial now.

Nor need I refer again to that other charge, that I had uttered, in debate, here or elsewhere, the sentiment that I preferred peace to the Union; I have heretofore met that charge with a prompt and emphatic contradiction, and no evidence has been found to sustain it. Referring to that and other charges and insinuations, on the 7th of January last, I said to my colleague:

"As to my record here at the extra session, or during the present session, it remains, and will remain."

And just here, sir, in reference to the speech to which the gentleman alluded, delivered on this floor, in the exercise of my constitutional right as a member of this house, on the 10th of July last, I defy him—I hurl the defiance into his teeth—to point to one single disloyal sentiment or sentence in it. I proceeded to say, further, on the 7th of last month:

"I do neither retract one sentiment that I have uttered, nor would I obliterate a single vote which I have given. I speak of the record, as it will appear hereafter, and, indeed, stands now upon the Journals of this House and in the Congressional Globe. And there is no other record, thank God, and no act or word or thought of mine, and never has been from the beginning, in public or in private, of which any patriot ought to be ashamed. Sir, it is the record, as I made it, and as it exists here to-day; and not as a mendacious and shameless press have attempted to make it up for me. Let us see who will grow tired of his record first. Consistency, firmness, and sanity, in the midst of general madness—these made up my offence. But 'Time, the avenger,' sets all things even; and I abide his leisure."

And am I now to be told, that because of a speech made upon this floor, under the protection of the Constitution, in the exercise and discharge of my solemn right and duty, under the oath which I have taken, that I am to-day to be arraigned here, and the accusation supported by the addition of mere vague rumors and suspicions, which have been bruited over and over again, as I have said, against not myself only, but against hundreds and thousands, also, of other most patriotic and loyal men?

The gentleman from Pennsylvania makes the charge that I attended a certain dinner in the State of Kentucky. Sir, I was invited to that State, and have been frequently, by as true and loyal men as there are in that State to-day. I accepted no invitation, and never went at all I have already named the last and only time when I stood upon the soil of Kentucky. But I know of nothing now—whatever there may have been in the past—certainly nothing to-day about Kentucky that should prevent a loyal and patriotic man from visiting a State which has given birth or residence to so many patriots, to so many statesmen, and to orators of such renown.

Yet that is all, the grand aggregate of the charges, except this miserable falsehood which some wretched scavenger, prowling about the streets and alleys and gutters of the city of Baltimore, has seen fit to put forth in the local columns of a contemptible newspaper; so that the member from Pennsylvania may rise in his place and prefer charges against the loyalty and patriotism of a man who has never faltered in his devotion to the flag of his country—to that flag which hangs now upon the wall over against him; one who has bowed down and worshipped this holy emblem of the Constitution and of the old Union of these States, in his heart's core, ay, in his very heart of hearts, from the time he first knew aught to this hour; and who now would give life, and all that he is or hopes to be in the present or the future, to see that glorious banner of the Union—known and honored once over the whole earth and the whole sea—with no stripe erased, and not one star blotted out, floating forever over the free, united, harmonious old Union of every State once a part of it, and a hundred more yet unborn. I AM THAT MAN; and yet he dares to demand that I shall be brought up before the secret tribunal of the Judiciary Committee—that committee of which he is chairman, and thus both judge and accuser—to answer to the charge of disloyalty to the Union!

Sir, I hurl back the insinuation. Bring forward the specific charge; wait till you have found something—and you will wait long—something which I have written, or something I have said, that would indicate any thing in my bosom which he who loves his country ought not to read or hear. In every sentiment that I have expressed, in every vote that I have given, in my whole public life, outside this House, before I was a member of it, and since it has been my fortune to sit here, I have had but one motive, and that was the real, substantial, permanent good of my country. I have differed with the majority of the House, differed with the party in power, differed with the Administration, as, thank God, I do and have the right to differ, as to the best means of preserving the Union, and of maintaining the Constitution and securing the true interests of my country; and that is my offence, that the crime, and the only crime, of which I have been guilty.

Mr. Speaker, if, in the Thirty-fifth Congress, I or some other member had seen fit to seize upon the denunciations, long-continued, bitter, and persistent against that member (Mr. Hickman)—for he, too, has suffered, and he ought to have had the manhood to remember, in this the hour of sore persecution, that he himself has been the victim of slanders and detraction, peradventure—for, sir, I would do him the justice which he denies to me—what, I say, if I had risen and made a vile paragraph in some paper published in his own town, or elsewhere, the subject of inquiry and investigation, and had attempted to cast yet further suspicion upon him, by reference to language uttered here in debate, which he had the right to utter, or by charges vague and false, and without the shadow of a foundation except the malignant breath of partisan suspicion and slander, what would have been his record, in the volumes of your reports, and the Congressional Globe, going down to his children after him? But, sir, it is not in the power of the gentleman to tarnish the honor of my name, or to blast the fair fame and character for loyalty which I have earned—dearly earned, with labor, and patience, and faith, from the beginning of my public career. From my boyhood, at all times and in every place, I have never looked to any thing but the permanent, solid, and real interests of my country.

Beyond this, Mr. Speaker, I deem it unnecessary to extend what I have to say. I would have said not a word, but that I know this Committee will find nothing, and that they will be obliged, therefore, to

22

report—a majority of them cheerfully, I doubt not—that nothing exists to justify any charge or suspicion such as the member from Pennsylvania has suggested here to-day. I avail myself of the occasion thus forced on me, to repel this foul and slanderous assault upon my loyalty, promptly, earnestly, indignantly, yes, scornfully, and upon the very threshold. Sir, I do not choose to delay week after week, until your partisan press shall have sounded the alarm; and till an organization shall have been effected for the purpose of dragooning two-thirds of this House into an outrage upon the rights of one of the Representatives of the people, which is without example except in the worst of times. I meet it and hurl it back defiantly here and now.

Why, sir, suppose that the course which the member from Pennsylvania now proposes, had been pursued in many cases which I could name in years past; suppose that his had been the standard of accusation, and irresponsible newspaper paragraphs had been regarded as evidence of disloyalty or want of attachment to the Constitution and the Union; nay, more, if a yet severer test had been applied, what would have been the fate of some members of this House, or of certain Senators at the other end of the capitol, some years ago? What punishment might not have been meted out to the predecessor (Mr. Giddings, of my colleague on the other side of the House? How long would he have occupied a seat here? Where would the Senator from Massachusetts (Mr. Sumner) have been? Where the other Senator from Massachusetts (Mr. Wilson)? Where the Senator from New Hampshire (Mr. Hale)? Where the three Senators—Mr. Seward, Mr. Chase, and Mr. Hale, two of them now in the Cabinet, and the other in the Senate still—who, in 1850, twelve years ago, on the 11th of February, voted to receive, refer, print, and consider a petition praying for the dissolution of the Union of these States? Yet I am to be singled out now by these very men, or their minions, for attack; and they who have waited and watched, by day and by night, with the vigilance of the hawk and the ferocity of the hyena, from the beginning of this great revolt, that they might catch some unguarded remark, some idle word spoken, something written carelessly or rashly, some secret thought graven yet upon the lineaments of my face, which they might torture into evidence of disloyalty, seize now upon the foul and infectious gleanings of an anonymous wretch who earns a precarious subsistence by feeding the local columns of a pestilent newspaper, and, while it is yet wet from the press, hurry it, reeking with falsehood, into this House, and seek to dignify it with an importance demanding the consideration of the House and of the country.

Sir, let the member from Pennsylvania go on. I challenge the inquiry, unworthy of notice as the charge is, but I scorn the spirit which has provoked it. Let it go on.

Mr. HICKMAN then replied briefly; and, in the course of his remarks, said: "As the gentleman has called upon me, I will answer further. Does he not know of a camp in Kentucky having been called by his name—that disloyal men there called their camp Camp Vallandigham? That would not indicate that in Kentucky they regarded him as a man loyal to the Federal Union.

Mr. VALLANDIGHAM. Is there not a town—and it may be a camp, too—in Kentucky by the name of Hickman? (Laughter.)

Mr. HICKMAN. Thank God! disloyal men have never called one of their camps by my name. There are a great many Hickmans in Kentucky, but I have not the pleasure of their acquaintance. I have heard of but one Vallandigham.

Mr. VALLANDIGHAM. And there are a great many Vallandighams there, too.

Mr. HICKMAN, after a few words further, withdrew his resolutions; and there the matter ended.

NOTE.—On the 21st of April, 1862, Benjamin F. Wade, of Ohio, attacked Mr. Vallandigham in the Senate, in the following language:

"I accuse them (the Democratic party) of deliberate purpose to assail, through the judicial tribunals, and through the Senate and House of Representatives of the United States, and everywhere else, and to overawe, intimidate, and trample under foot, if they can, the men who boldly stand forth in defence of their country, now imperilled by this gigantic rebellion. I have watched it long. I have seen it in secret. I have seen its movements ever since that party got together, with a colleague of mine in the other House, as chairman of the Committee on Resolutions—a man who never had any sympathy with the Republic, but whose every breath is devoted to its destruction, just as far as his heart dare permit him to go."—*Congressional Globe*, page 1735.

Quoting the foregoing extract, in the House, on the 24th of April, Mr. Vallandigham said:

"Now, sir, here in my place in the House, and as a Representative, I denounce—and I speak it advisedly—the author of that speech as a liar, a scoundrel, and a coward. His name is Benjamin F Wade."

In June, 1862, Shellabarger and Gurley, of Ohio, presented printed petitions from citizens of their own districts—none from Mr. Vallandigham's—asking for his expulsion from the House as "a traitor and a disgrace to the State of Ohio." The petitions were referred to the Committee on the Judiciary, consisting of the following members: John Hickman, chairman; John A. Bingham, William Kellogg, Albert G. Porter, Benjamin F. Thomas, Alexander S. Diven, James F. Wilson, George H. Pendleton, and Henry May—all of them Republicans, except May and Pendleton. This Committee, on the very same day on which the petitions were presented, by a unanimous vote, ordered them to be reported back, and laid upon the table; and accordingly, on the first day that the Committee was called—July 3, 1862—Mr. Bingham reported them back, and, on his motion, they were laid on the table, no evidence whatever of either "treason" or "disgrace," having been produced to the Committee.

SPEECH ON THE "UNITED STATES NOTE" BILL,

In the House of Representatives, February 3, 1862.

It has been my habit, Mr. Chairman, to premeditate, whenever premeditation was possible, whatever I have had to say in this House; for no man has a right, in my judgment, to obtrude his immature and undigested thoughts and opinions upon a deliberative assembly. From the laboratory of his mind and the store-house of his memory, it is his duty to bring forth, at all times, as the occasion may permit, whatever is most valuable; and there is no such thing as inspiration in matters of either law or legislation, and least of all, certainly, upon questions of finance. And just at this moment, especially, the country and the Government demand sound philosophy and stern facts; not vain theories, or what is worse still, delusive and hazardous experiments and contrivances. *Experimentum in vili corpore;* and never was the maxim more applicable.

If, therefore, sir, I have prepared myself now a little more elaborately than heretofore, the complexity, delicacy, and magnitude, not to say novelty, of the subject in late years, are my justification. And I do, from my heart, and with the deepest sincerity, lament that I am not now master of the whole science of political economy and finance; and am unable, therefore, and because that I have not that divine order of intellect, which is able to seize hold of it, and to comprehend and fathom it as if by intuition, to discuss it as its immeasurable importance demands. It happened to me, sir, to come into public life, and even to attain majority, after the great questions of currency and revenue, in the administrations of Jackson, Van Buren, and Tyler had, for the most part, been settled, and to be familiar, therefore, chiefly with a subject, the discussion of which I would to God had never been obtruded upon Congress, or the country, and which, even now, I would forever banish from both. But at intervals, in years past, and with labor and diligence for some months past, I have sought to master the facts and principles, and to penetrate somewhat into the philosophical mysteries of these great questions, and to apply them firmly and faithfully to the present and approaching condition of the country. Committed fully to any measure, and all measures of finance, necessary to sustain, as well the honor as the credit of the country in which I was born, and the integrity of the Government of which I am a part, and especially to adequate and just taxation for that purpose, I propose to-day to discuss the subjects involved in this bill to the best of my ability, and with becoming candor and freedom, and I may add earnestness, too; for I have the profoundest conviction of their incalculable importance to the interests, present and future, of the United States, and of the people of this whole continent.

Nor am I to be deterred from a faithful discharge of my duty, by the consciousness that my voice may not be hearkened to here, or in the country, because of the continued, persistent, but most groundless and malignant assaults and misrepresentations to which, for months past, I have been subjected. Sir, I am not here to reply to them to-day. Neither am I to be driven from the line of duty by them. "Strike—but hear." Whatever a silenced or a mendacious press, outside of this House, may choose to withhold or to say, no man who is fit to be a member of this House, will allow his speech or his votes or his public conduct here to be controlled by his personal hates or prejudices. Sir, I recant nothing, and would expunge nothing from the record of the past, so far as I am concerned. But my path of duty now, as a Representative, is as clear as the sun at broad noon. The Ship of State is upon the rocks. I was not the helmsman who drove her there; nor had I part or lot in directing her course. But now, when the sole question is, how shall she be rescued? I will not any longer, or, at least, not just now, inquire who has done the mischief. So long as they who held control insisted that she was upon her true course, and in no danger, but prosperously upon her voyage, though in the midst of the storm, I had a right to resist, and did resist and denounce the madness which was driving her headlong to destruction. But now, that the shipwreck stands confessed, I recognize, and here declare, it to be as much my duty to labor for her preservation, as it is theirs who stranded her upon the beach. Within her sides she bears still all that I have or hope for, now or hereafter, in this life; and he is a madman or a traitor, who would see her perish without an effort to save. Whoever shrinks now is responsible, also, for some part, at least, of the ruin which shall follow.

In this spirit it is, sir, that I approach this great question; and I thank the House kindly for the attention which they seem inclined to accord to me, and assure them that it shall not be abused.

I do not agree, Mr. Chairman, with the gentleman who opened this debate [Mr. Spaulding], that this bill is a war measure. Certainly, sir, it has been forced upon us by the war; but if peace were restored to-morrow these $100,000,000 of Treasury notes would be just as essential to the public credit as they are to-day. The argument of "military necessity" has been carried quite far enough already, without being now urged in behalf of the proposition—so unconstitutional, disastrous, and unjust—to make paper-money a legal tender in discharge of all debts. I support this measure—not, indeed, as reported—impossible—but as I would have it amended—because it is absolutely essential to even the ordinary credit of the Government, and because, without it, I see nothing but bankruptcy to the Government in the midst of immense aggregate wealth among the people. The credit of the country is the honor and strength and support of the country, and it must be maintained at all hazards, and no matter who is President, or what party is in power. And I am not willing to hazard the entire credit, and honor, and good faith of the country, because the Administration may, perchance, use this recuperated credit, to continue a war which I have not approved. "War is disunion," said Mr. Douglas, and bankruptcy is disunion, and as a true Union man, I have opposed the first, as I shall labor now to avert the last.

But to return. No scheme of loan, or taxation, or national bank, or currency, or other similar contrivance, can be devised and put into operation in time to avert the ruin. Therefore the Government must fall back upon Treasury notes, for its present support. But a single question is presented: what shall be their form, and how shall they be floated? But inasmuch as the Government has no money, no gold and silver coin—which is the only *money* in the world—these notes, incapable, therefore, of being the representatives of money, must take its place as a substitute. They must become currency, and pass or "run" from hand to hand. But Treasury notes, bearing interest, and payable at a future day, are not fitted to run or pass as money. They are as mere ordinary promissory notes; and though often issued in this form —and, indeed, never before in any other, except once, within the last fifty years—they never, at any time, passed into general circulation, or even circulation at all. They are a particular form of loan or indebtedness, or security, and fit subjects for speculation on the stock exchange, but are neither money, nor the representatives of, nor a substitute for money. If made payable on demand, they need bear no interest, since the great element of value in a paper currency is not profit but credit. Therefore, intending that Treasury notes should circulate and become a sort of currency, this bill proposes, as did also the act of July, 1861, that they shall bear no interest, and be payable in gold and silver. This, unquestionably, is the legal and inevitable inference from the language of the act and the bill, so far as appears upon their face.

But neither the act nor the bill, the present nor the original bill, prescribes expressly in what they shall be paid. But both are "payable." Payable in what? Gold and silver, which is the only money that by law can be received for the public dues, or disbursed in payment of debts owing by the United States, except that the Treasury notes already authorized, are declared receivable also in payment of debts due to the Government.

Sir, this bill is in two particulars modelled, though imperfectly, after the act of 1815; and, to that extent, I approve of the idea or theory upon which it proceeds. The issue of notes without interest, and to circulate as currency between the Government and its creditors and debtors, is for temporary purposes, and to meet the immediate and pressing necessities of the government—and this is the only justification for their issue—and they are to be funded or converted, at the will of the holder, into six per cent. stock, redeemable twenty years after date; and so far they are, therefore, not mere government paper-money, like the Continental bills of the Revolution, or the French assignats, or the Austrian notes of 1809. Nevertheless, sir, there are capital objections to this bill, which ought, in my judgment, to condemn it to unanimous reprobation and defeat.

In the first place, sir, it precedes where it ought to follow. It assumes that the promise to tax will give credit before a dollar of tax has been laid; much less collected. On the faith of this credit, it expects the free circulation of $50,000,000 already issued, and the $100,000,000 proposed to be issued under its own provisions. But, as if fearful—and most justly, too—that the promise may not be received for performance, and that, at last, no adequate tax may be assessed, or, if assessed, collected, it proceeds to declare these notes to be money—actual, substantial, tangible, and veritable MONEY—and to be a legal tender in satisfaction of all debts, public and private, corporate and individual, State and United States. The judgments of the State courts are to be discharged in these notes, and State taxes to be paid in them. All debts owing by the United States are to be liquidated in them. They are even to be received in payment of each other, and one promissory note of the Government is, by compulsion of law, and, of course, if need be, at last, by armed force, to be taken in full discharge of another promissory note issued by the same Government. These notes, sir, are declared "payable to bearer." Payable in what? Gold and silver and Treasury notes. But the Government is truly apostolic in its poverty. Silver and gold it has none. Therefore one Treasury note is a full, authorized, compulsory discharge of another Treasury note. Peter is to be robbed to pay Paul; and Paul in turn is to pay Peter for a debt of his own out of the fruits of the robbery. In plain English, and without metaphor, one promise to pay is to be made a legal tender in satisfaction of another promise to pay; and the promise of the Government to pay in paper, is to discharge the obligation of the contract of the individual debtor to pay his creditor in gold and silver. And this is the grand financial contrivance of the Secretary of the Treasury, with the concurrence of one half of the Ways and Means!

Sir, if it were fifty-fold as constitutional as, in my deliberate judgment, it is unconstitutional in letter, and abhorrent to the spirit and principles of that instrument, it could not command my support. I will not renew the discussion of the question of constitutional power to make Government paper, or any other paper, a legal tender in payment of any debts, public or private, present or prospective. My colleague from the first district [Mr. Pendleton] the other day, with a clearness and force never exceeded in this Hall, disposed of that question forever. His argument has not been answered; and, pardon me, sir, it never will be. I concur in it all, thoroughly and totally, upon this point. Sir, disguise it as you may, this bill is but a FORCED LOAN from the people. It is an abuse and a stretch of power which no Government, except one either in the first throes of revolutionary madness and desperation, or in the last agonies of dissolution, or in the midst of the most imminent danger of either bankruptcy or conquest and overthrow, and no king or potentate, except a usurper, ever ventured to exert. If voluntarily submitted to, or by fear or power enforced, it will corrupt, derange, and debase the currency, and afflict the country with financial and commercial disaster and ruin, and shake the foundations of public and private credit for half a century to come. But we shall be fortunate if it does not precipitate a revolution, sooner or later, in our own midst. In ordinary times, certainly not; but let us not forget that we are in the very crisis of a convulsion, equalled by but few in the history of the world, and where no man can reckon the course, or momentum, or extent of any movement according to any of the ordinary laws which govern human affairs. But independent of all this, tried by the plainest principles of finance, the commonest maxims of political economy, as exhibited and enforced in the experience of other nations, this bold, but ill-advised and most hazardous experiment of forcing a paper currency upon the people, ought to be met by the Representatives of the people with unanimous and emphatic condemnation. Otherwise, the experiment, if successful, will be followed by other enormous issues, till not a dollar of gold or silver will be seen again in your day or mine, and but little of ordinary bank paper. Exportation, hoarding, melting, and manufacture into articles of luxury of every kind, will follow as the legitimate and inevitable consequence of your irredeemable Government paper currency. The golden age of America henceforth will belong only to the *Saturnia regna* of poets and mythologists.

Nor is this all, nor the worst. An immense inflation or bloat in this wonderful paper-money which our financial Midas by his touch is to convert into gold, must come next. Cheap in material, easy of issue, worked by steam, signed by machinery, there will be no end to the legions of paper devils which shall pour forth from the loins of the Secretary. Sir, let the army rejoice; there will be no more "shoddy," for there will be no more rags out of which to manufacture it.

And now, sir, what must follow from all this? First, that which never has failed in times of bloated currency—high prices, extravagant speculation, enormous sudden fortunes, immense fictitious wealth, general insanity. These belong to all inordinate and excessive paper issues, and even to plethoras in the circulation of gold and silver, if such plethoras could occur. But the evil will not stop here. Every banker, every lender, every merchant, every business man, and every seller of real or personal estate, or of any thing else, compelled to receive in payment for whatever he lends or sells, an irredeemable paper-money, dependent for its value solely upon force, and without the smallest credit, and himself having no confidence in the Government, and no special good-will to the borrower or buyer who forces him to take its paper, will demand a still higher price, by way of insurance, than if the currency were sound and safe, no matter how much inflated.

And now, sir, what is to be the result of all this? What else but the result from like causes in years past in foreign countries and in our own? It is written in the commercial convulsions and sufferings of France in 1720, and of England a century later, and of the United States in 1837. The collapse follows the inflation, and is terrible and disastrous just in proportion as the bubble has been magnificent. Your legal tender laws will avail nothing. They have been tried before; tried in this country and tried abroad; and have always failed in the end. The regent of France proclaimed them in Law's time, in 1717; and what followed? Let M. Thiers answer:

> "Violent and vexatious as the measures were to sustain the credit of the notes, they were insufficient to give them a value which they did not possess. *Dishonest debtors alone used them to pay their debts.* Coin was secretly used for daily purchases, and was concealed with care. Many accumulated it clandestinely. The greater part buried it in the earth, and the rich realizers used every artifice to transfer it to foreign countries. Another portion of our coin left France; and although the exportation of specie is not necessarily injurious, it was so at this time, since it left behind only a false paper currency and an imaginary capital."

But again, sir, this bill declares these notes to be "payable *at the pleasure of the United States.*" Was ever such a proposition before this submitted by any legitimate, established Government? Did any of the multitudinous Mexican usurpers, in the midst of the direst convulsions of that most distracted of all countries, even in his severest straits, ever "pronounce" any thing more unjust and monstrous? Sir, these notes are not to be the basis of a future loan; they are not kites to raise the wind with. They are to be paid out in discharge of past liabilities for debts which already exist; for honest and fair indebtedness for past services rendered or value already received, as between the Government and the citizen. All these debts were payable in gold and silver only—in the current coin and lawful money—the hard money—of the country. In the absence of any express stipulation or law to the contrary—and not in one case out of a hundred probably has any such existed—they are all payable by cash in hand or on demand. And yet payment at all of this very class of debts is, by the terms of this bill, to be postponed indefinitely, unless indeed the creditor will accept bonds at six per cent., depreciated, it may be, and if this bill pass in its present form, will be, to eighty or ninety cents on the dollar, and redeemable in twenty years. The Government proposes to settle with its creditors, and to execute its promissory notes payable whenever it is ready or finds it convenient to pay. In other words, the debtor dictates terms to the creditor, and declares that a debt payable in cash down or on demand shall be paid at the pleasure of the debtor, or otherwise, in either case, shall be utterly extinguished. O most wonderful, righteous, and equitable Secretary!

Sir, there is no subject so delicate as credit. What is it? Confidence, trust, faith. In its very nature it is voluntary, and you can no more coerce credit than you can compel belief in a particular creed or religion, or love between man and woman. It withers before suspicion, and languishes and dies at the sight of force. Sir, in the reign of Henry VIII., Parliament passed "an act for the *abolishing of diversity of opinion* in certain articles concerning the Christian religion." How much worse or more absurd, I ask, was that act than the bill before us? Good faith is the foundation of all credit; but this bill proposes, not bold and outright, but timid—I will not say cowardly—and indirect repudiation. More than this: it is an open confession of bankruptcy. If the Government has solid means, it needs no notes. If it has credit, why declare its notes lawful money and a legal tender, equal with gold? If it has neither means nor credit, it is exactly what is meant by a bankrupt.

But yet, again, this bill styles the paper which it authorizes to be issued, "United States notes." Well, sir, words are things, and this change of name is for some purpose. What is it? I have carefully examined every Treasury note act and act referring to Treasury notes, public and private, from the first, in 1812, to the present time, eighty-two in number; and in not one, not one, are notes of this description called any thing but Treasury notes. Sometimes they have been issued as a convenient form of temporary loan; at other times as evidence of indebtedness by the Treasury. But they were always, upon their face, limited to the Treasury department, and were never known in any act by any other name than "Treasury notes." They never were intended to furnish a permanent or even a general circulation as a commercial currency. They were thus maintained to be not "bills of credit," within the then well-understood meaning of that term, and, therefore, not unconstitutional. The act of 1815 styled them Treasury notes, though issued in sums of less than one hundred dollars, payable to bearer, without interest, transferable by delivery, and therefore capable of passing as currency. So did the act of July, 1861; and more than that, so did both the title and the body of this same bill, as first reported on the 7th of January.

Sir, who invented this new-fangled term, "United States notes," and why was it invented? What new light struck in upon the Secretary between the seventh and the twenty-second of the same month? And what are these United States notes but "bills of credit," the very bills so abhorrent to the framers of the Constitution? Most appropriately I may say with Mr. Webster, that "if the genius of the old Confederation were now to rise up in the midst of us, he could not furnish us from the abundant stores of his recollection with a more perfect model of paper-money;" and I am forced to add, also, or a worse model, too.

Here, sir, is one of the Continental bills of November, 1776. It bears small resemblance to the delicate paper issues and exquisite engravings of the present day in the United States. It smacks a little of the poverty of "Dixie" as is said. Instead of the effigies of Lincoln, it bears on its face a veritable but rudely-carved woodcut of the wild boar of the forest. It was bad money, sir, but issued in a noble cause. It is redolent of liberty; it smells of habeas corpus, free speech, a free press, free ballot, the right of petition, the consent of the governed, the right of the people to govern, public indictment, speedy public trial, trial by jury, and all the great rights of political and individual liberty for which martyrs have died and heroes contended for ages—although I am not quite sure, sir, that even now it is altogether without somewhat of the odor of rebellion lingering about it. But even this Continental bill purports to be payable, though not paid, in specie. It recites that "this bill entitles the bearer to receive four Spanish milled dollars, or the value thereof in gold and silver, according to a resolution of Congress, passed at Philadelphia, Nov. 2, 1776," and it is issued in the name of "the United Colonies."

But though in the midst of a revolution, and struggling for liberty and life, and in the darkest hour of that sore trial—it was just previous to the victory at Trenton—it never occurred to the just men and patriots of that day to usurp the power to make this paper-money a legal tender, and to force it, by this usurpation, into credit and circulation by the strong arm of the law; and to that extent—and it is great—the United States notes proposed by this bill are fifty-fold worse and more to be abhorred than Continental money. But this paper of 1776 bears no interest, is payable to bearer, payable in gold and silver, payable at no particular time, intended to circulate permanently and generally as money, and without a dollar of tax or revenue to support it. The men of that day relied on patriotism to keep their bills in credit; and yet we know that even then, in the purest and best times of the Republic, they sank in value till at the close of the war $1,000 in paper were worth but one dollar in specie. In short, sir, they so utterly depreciated that to this day, if a profane man would describe any thing as totally and hopelessly worthless, he would say of it that it was "not worth a Continental—*dollar*."

And here, sir, before I pass from this subject, allow me to say that a very grave error has been fallen into in this debate. The notes of the Bank of England were not made a legal tender during the suspension from 1797 to 1823. The bank was, by act of Parliament, prohibited from paying in specie. The taxes were then very heavy, the expenditures enormous, and the notes of the bank were received as cash in payment of the public dues. For this reason, mainly, and not because they were, either directly or in effect, a legal tender, the notes, until the issues of the bank became excessive, did not depreciate, at least until also gold had begun to disappear in spite of penal legislation. But in three years the depreciation began, and from 1800 to 1814, it varied from eight to twenty-five per cent. In 1816, after the war, it was sixteen and three-fourths. And yet there were public men then, just as some are found now, to maintain that the value of paper-money had not fallen, but that the value of gold had risen. It was precisely the argument over again, of the French National Assembly, nearly twenty years earlier—*it was not the assignat which had lost, but the franc which had gained.* But, sir, the act also of 1834 which, it is said, declared the notes of the bank a legal tender, has been totally misunderstood. They are not now and never were a legal tender as between the bank which issues them and its creditors, or the holders of its notes. Not at all, sir. A proposition so iniquitous and monstrous never was enacted into law by English legislators. It belongs to the present Secretary of the

Treasury of the United States, in the year of grace, 1862. Justly did Mr. Canning boast, in 1811, that

"Never did the wildest and most hostile prophesier of ruin to the finances of England, venture to predict that a time should come when, by the avowal of Parliament, nominal amount in paper, without reference to any real standard value in gold, would be the payment of the public creditor."

But neither are these notes a legal tender at all, except so long as the bank pays specie, and of course, while they are equivalent to, if not convertible at any moment all over England into gold: so that in fact the observation of Mr. Burke, seventy years ago, is equally just and true now:

"Our paper is of value in commerce, because in law it is of none. It is powerful on 'Change, because in Westminster Hall it is impotent."

And now, sir, what are your United States notes? They, too, are payable to bearer; payable—not to be paid—in gold and silver, payable "at the pleasure of the United States," and meant to circulate generally and permanently as currency, at least till the Secretary's grand fiscal machine, his magnificent NATIONAL PAPER-MILL, founded upon the very stocks provided for by this bill, can be put in operation, when this sort of bills of credit is to be supplanted by another sort of bills of credit, which are to become the sole currency of the country, and to drive all gold and silver, and ordinary bank paper, out of circulation. This, sir, is what is meant by the phrase in the third line of the bill, "for temporary purposes," and nothing else is meant. And now sir, how, meantime, are these United States notes to be floated? By voluntary credit, founded on adequate taxation? Not at all, sir. Taxation to nearly or perhaps two-thirds the same amount would, as I shall presently prove, float these notes at par with gold and silver indefinitely. But if taxation is meant, then no other means of credit are needed. How comes it, then, that force, coercion, is to be resorted to to compel these notes into circulation? The faith of the United States, supported by taxation, is to be abandoned, and this paper-money is to be floated in every commercial and business transaction of the country by main force of law, and not voluntary credit because of the solvency of the United States, till a year or two hence the Secretary shall have stocks enough to enable him to execute his financial schemes and contrivances in full. This, then, is the first step in the direction of his grand fiscal and monetary agent which is to maintain the credit of the Government and supply the sole paper currency of the country; and in further proof, I refer to the fact that in his late annual report, the Secretary styles the notes to be "prepared for circulation under national direction," and issued by this monster FISCALITY, "United States notes." These, then, sir, are the reasons why the ancient, approved, constitutional term

"Treasury note," sanctioned by eighty-two acts of Congress, and sustained by judicial decisions, is to be cast off and abandoned for one just freshly coined for the new financial nomenclature of the Secretary of the Treasury.

But I have yet another objection to this bill. Secreted innocently in the first section, I find the following:

"And any holders of said United States notes depositing any sum not less than fifty dollars, or other than a multiple of fifty, with the Treasurer of the United States, or either of the Assistant Treasurers, or either of the designated depositaries at Cincinnati or Baltimore, shall receive in exchange therefor duplicate certificates of deposit, one of which may be transmitted to the Secretary of the Treasury, who shall thereupon issue to the holder an equal amount in bonds of the United States, coupon or registered, as may be desired, bearing interest at the rate of six per cent., and redeemable, at the pleasure of the Government, after twenty years from date; *or in sums not less than* $2,500, *for which, if requested, the Secretary, if he deem it expedient, may issue similar bonds, the principal and interest of which may be expressed in the currency of any foreign country, and payable there.*"

So that whoever, though a citizen of the United States, can gather together $2,500 of these notes, may convert them into stocks expressed in the currency of a foreign country, with principal and interest payable there, and of course in gold and silver or its equivalent; while he who holds fifty dollars or upwards, but less than $2,500, is obliged to receive domestic bonds, payable at home, principal and interest, in "United States notes," or the continental money of 1862. And now, sir, what is the effect of all this? The bonds issued are to be of the same amount as the face value of the United States notes, no matter how much the latter may be depreciated, and they will depreciate in spite or because of your legal tender clause; and not only this, but the face value of the bonds finally, and meantime of the interest, is to be increased by the rate of foreign exchange, whatever it may be at the time of the payment of either principal or interest. Nor is this all. The purpose of this provision, discriminating so palpably and unjustly between the great and the small creditors of the Government, and providing for specie payments to one class, and paper payments to another, is to enable the Secretary to fund his United States notes in stocks of a higher value than those expressed in the home paper currency, so that a surer, speedier, and more profitable accumulation of stocks may be had for the darling object of the Secretary, his grand fiscal contrivance. A twofold purpose will thus be subserved: first, an earlier investment or funding of these notes; second, a more valuable class of stocks for banking operations. To the banker also who shall invest in these bonds, payable in a foreign currency and country, there will accrue, not only the difference between the real value of the United States notes, and the par or face value of the bonds, and the premium upon foreign exchange, but also the profits to be derived from the seven per cent. interest on the notes to be circulated by the new banks, and sometimes, if not regularly, where the bank is distant from the city of New York, or perhaps Philadelphia and Boston—say in the Northwest—the factitious exchange, equal to from six to eighteen per cent. per annum, amounting, with the other profits of banking, in all to from twenty to forty per cent. to the holder of these stocks who shall invest them in the Secretary's new banks. But the operation does not stop here. The interest on these will be paid, of course, in gold or its equivalent; and other United States notes, issued or reissued under this bill, will be bought at their depreciated value as compared with gold, and converted into new stocks, payable in a foreign country and currency; and thus the circle of profits upon an increased capital will again be travelled round, till the untold millions of stocks provided for in the first section of this bill and the $500,000,000 authorized by the second section, shall have all been exhausted.

Sir, there is no need for the amendment suggested the other day by the chairman of the Ways and Means, providing for the payment of the interest on these stocks in gold and silver. He is not in the secret. There will be no bonds issued, and none are intended or expected to be issued, except those payable in a foreign currency and country, and of course in specie. No wonder, sir, that every adventurer and stock-jobber and speculator and kite-flyer and contractor, too, outside of this House is pressing this monstrous scheme, worthy of John Law's most daring genius, gigantic in its proportions, corrupting in its success, and desolating as an earthquake in its final ruin. No wonder the Ways and Means and the country are afflicted daily with "spouting wretches" and scribbling wretches, who raise the magic howl that whoever opposes this great American bubble of 1862, following close upon the great "national loan" bubble of 1861, is in sympathy with the rebellion, and giving aid to traitors. Let us see, now, who and how many will dare to stand up against this clamor, and to hold fast to the Constitution, and cling firmly to the real interests and final safety and preservation of the country.

Sir, it is altogether aside from my present point of argument to urge in reply that this very demand for stocks, payable in the currency of a foreign country, will not only hasten the funding of the notes, and extend the loan, and thus the resources of the Government, but will keep up the credit and par circulation of the notes themselves. Certainly, sir: that is part of the idea of the scheme; and, to a certain extent, the result anticipated will follow in this last particular also. But the bulls and the bears will have something to do with that, too; and the authors of the contrivance themselves have not confidence that this demand would of itself float these $150,000,000 of notes at their par value, or any thing near it; else why do they propose to resort to that very element which above all others tends to destroy credit—*force?*

But I have not done with this section yet, sir. There is no end to the stocks which, payable in the home paper currency provided for by this bill, or a foreign specie currency, are to be issued. The United States notes are to be reissued indefinitely as soon as funded, and funded indefinitely as fast as reissued. The wheel of fortune is to be perpetually in motion, and at every revolution is to throw out new notes and new stocks, till superseded by the grand machine for manufacturing a national currency suggested by the Secretary in his annual report.

And now, sir, besides this emission of notes and bonds as multitudinous as the sands of the sea-shore, the second section provides for the issue of $500,000,000 more. It recites that it is "to enable the Secretary to fund the *Treasury* notes and floating debt of the United States." "Treasury" notes indeed! What Treasury notes? None are proposed to be issued by this bill; and all issued under existing laws, including the acts of July and August, 1861, are to be funded in the same manner as provided for in this section; unless, indeed, the object of the section be, after all, only to enable the Secretary to convert all the outstanding Treasury notes issued under existing laws, except the $50,000,000 demand notes, amounting, according to the gentleman from New York [Mr. Spaulding], to $103,000,000, into bonds, expressed in a foreign currency and country, and payable there, so as to still further increase the amount of the more valuable and profitable class of stocks which are to constitute the basis of the new national bank. The "United States notes"—not "Treasury" notes—authorized by the first section of this bill, and the demand notes issued under the act of July last, are to be funded according to the provisions of the section itself.

Then, sir, we have here some $103,000,000 of old-fashioned Treasury notes payable at a future day and bearing interest. We have also the floating debt estimated by the gentleman from New York [Mr. Spaulding] at $100,000,000, though in my belief, it is more than double that sum. But why authorize $500,000,000 of stock wherewith to fund two or three hundred millions of dollars of Treasury notes and floating debt? The secret lurks quietly in the last sentence of the section:

> "And the Secretary of the Treasury may *also* exchange such bonds at any time for lawful money of the United States."

Sir, what does all this mean? What will be "lawful money" of the United States if this bill pass! The issue of bonds is expressly declared to be for the funding of Treasury notes and the floating debt of the United States; and the Secretary is authorized to issue them to any creditor of the United States who will receive them at their par value in satisfaction of his demands. He may also exchange them for Treasury notes heretofore issued, or which may be issued, under the provisions of this bill, although this bill provides not at all for Treasury notes, either in its title or in the body of it, but only for the newly devised "United States notes." And yet this is the bill which the gentleman from New York [Mr. Spaulding] declared, without a smile, to be "simple and perspicuous in its terms, and easy of execution!" Sir, I am very sure he never could have written it; nor, I apprehend, has he ever scrutinized its language or its provisions with critical accuracy.

But not only are these stocks to be issued in lieu of Treasury notes or discharge of floating debt, but the Secretary may also "exchange" them for the lawful money of the United States. Sir, I pass by the singular inaccuracy of providing for the "exchange" of bonds for gold and silver, or money of any kind, as a mere verbal criticism. But are these bonds, too, to be issued for the United States notes of the first section? These notes are expressly declared to be "lawful money," and was it not enough to provide for the eternal circle, the endless chain of issue and funding and funding and reissue of the first section? No doubt the real object of this provision is to enable the Secretary to sell these bonds for cash, and thus to create a new debt, instead of funding or transmitting a debt which may exist previous to and independent of the bonds. Why not, then, say so openly in the title and in the body of the bill? But I oppose this provision, and prefer that the notes and bonds provided for in this bill shall both be issued, not for the purpose of raising money, but to discharge debts otherwise incurred. In no other way, I fear, can you expect to float these United States notes or Treasury notes, whichever you may call them, at par with gold and silver, or the notes of specie-paying banks.

And now, sir, what, I beg to know, is the object of all this, if it be not to create an enormous and endless public debt, to be interwoven with every political, social, and business relation of life; to subjugate the States and the people perpetually to the Federal Government, and therefore never to be extinguished? The seven years of famine are upon us, and our modern Joseph is to buy in the property of the whole people, and lease it out to them again as tenants at a perpetual rent. Sir, I commend to him the ancient and significant Hebrew proverb: *Quum lateres duplicantur venit Moses*—when the bricks are doubled, Moses comes.

I propose, then, Mr. Chairman, a substitute for the bill, omitting so much of it as purports to make these notes a legal tender. But I go further. The Treasury notes authorized by the act of July last, and those provided for by this bill, are both declared to be payable, the one on demand, and the other " at the pleasure of the United States." Payable in what? You have no gold and silver. You can borrow none. You propose to collect $150,000,000 in taxes and imposts. But you issue at the same time $150,000,000 of Treasury notes, declared to be money, made a legal tender, receivable for the public dues, and to be circulated generally as currency; and you thus drive gold and silver into vaults and hiding places, or under ground, and bank paper out of existence. What, then, can you, will you receive, except these self-same notes again into your Treasury? And if so, what but Treasury notes will you have to pay out? Sir, your bill is a delusion and a snare. These are not demand notes. They are not to be payable to bearer, nor to any one else, at any time, nor at any place. They are not to be "paid" at all. They are to be funded or converted into six per cent. stocks, redeemable in twenty years. Sir, the public credit cannot be maintained by a public lie. Your notes are not money; they will not circulate as currency; they will not be taken as a legal tender, and in discharge of judgments and contracts and State debts, or private debts, though you should send them forth bearing ten times the image and superscription—the fair face and form of Abraham Lincoln, now President and Cæsar of the American Republic.

Sir, I propose to abandon this false pretence, and to change the form of the note itself. A Government note, payable on demand, or at the pleasure of the Government, to bearer, in gold and silver, is necessarily and inevitably a delusion and an absurdity. If the Government has gold and silver wherewith to pay, it need issue no Treasury notes. The necessity and the justification for their issue cannot exist till the Government is without gold and silver or its equivalent, obtained either by taxation or upon formal loan. And whenever it issues notes it confesses that it relies for the time, not upon funds in hand, but on credit because of funds to be had at a future day. And when the note is payable at a future day certain, there is no fraud and no deception. Not so when it purports to be payable on demand, or at no fixed time at all, and certainly not when payable at the pleasure of the debtor, the United States. Recall, then, as I propose, your outstanding demand notes, and conform those which you authorize now by this bill to what they really are, and do not send them forth seeking credit or to be forced upon the people by the strong arm, and yet branded with falsehood upon their face.

Instead of this compound of delusion and force, I propose a form of Treasury note depending solely for its value and circulation upon the consent of the creditor or holder and the solvency and credit of the Government. And as without taxation there can be no credit, it is founded wholly upon the basis of a not far from equal, and at all times certainly an adequate, taxation. It proceeds upon the assumption—first, that the Government is indebted in the amount proposed, and must provide for its creditors, in payment, that which is equivalent to currency or cash; and, secondly, upon the right of property which the Government has in so much of the wealth of the country as is necessary to carry on its legitimate and constitutional operations, and to maintain its credit. Upon these two corner-stones it rests. The Government is to issue in payment of its debts due to others that which it is to receive in satisfaction of the debts due from others to itself. It is to tax the people to the extent of a hundred or a hundred and fifty millions of dollars to maintain its good faith and its integrity every way; and it is to furnish the people with the medium, not the means, of payment. If this scheme fail, if these notes have no credit and do not circulate as substitutes for so much money, always good in satisfaction of so much debt due by the people to their Government, it will be either because there is no sufficient taxation laid, or if laid, not collected, or because of direct and successful repudiation. And if any of these, then the Government cannot be maintained any longer, and is not worth preserving.

But we need apprehend none of these results, I trust. The country is full of wealth and resources; it is able, and, for the purpose of maintaining the honor and credit of the Government, which are the credit and honor of every citizen in it, willing, I doubt not, to pay any amount of taxation which may be demanded. We have full constitutional power to tax. Here is a coercion which I recognize and approve. True, as Mr. Burke said, it is no more possible to tax and to please, than to love and to be wise. But is it not wonderful that gentlemen who are so fearful of their popularity that they will not resort to the constitutional coercion of taxation, are yet willing and eager to force upon the people instead of taxes, the unconstitutional, despotic, and most disastrous coercion of a paper currency to be received in satisfaction of every debt, and to enter into, and derange every contract, and taint and degrade every commercial and every business transaction of every kind, under penalty of forfeiture or confiscation of the debt? Coerce taxes, sir, and you secure a firm credit, and a full and, what is better, a free and voluntary circulation of your Government paper, intermingling naturally with the whole circle of the financial and commercial concerns of the States and of the people, without the violence, derangement, and convulsion of a forced and odious and abhorred paper currency. If you are afraid of the people, be afraid to do wrong, not to do right.

Sir, instead of force, the substitute proposes to rely for the credit and circulation of these Treasury notes—Treasury certificates they really are, but I prefer the long-established and accepted name—first, upon their convertibility at the will of the holder into six per cent stock; and as they bear no interest at all, the holders will naturally seek to fund them whenever United States stocks shall have been restored to their par value. And this will happen whenever, and not before, its solid revenue shall have been made sufficient for its ordinary expenses, and the punctual and certain payment of the interest on the public debt, present and prospective, and the collection of that revenue made absolutely sure. Whenever *doubt* upon that question is removed, your stocks will go up to par, and will remain there or above it. Why does not this bill, instead of force, rely upon credit obtained by the right to fund these notes bearing no interest, in bonds with interest at six per cent.? Because your stocks are already at ninety cents on the dollar, and of course no capitalist will invest par notes in bonds ten per cent. below par. And why are your stocks thus depreciated? Because there is a *doubt* whether the interest will be paid punctually and surely at maturity. And, pardon me, sir, you never can remove that doubt by legislation or force, but only by revenue.

Sir, I have not referred to-day to a sinking fund as an object of immediate importance; because if revenue enough can be secured just now to pay the very large interest on the public debt, we shall have done well enough at present, without attempting to find ways and means to discharge it, till the enormous drain of millions a day shall in some way or other have been arrested. Sufficient unto the day will that evil be. I concur, indeed, thoroughly in the principle which affirms that no debt ought to be created without at the same time providing means wherewith to pay it finally. But that principle should have been remembered before, or at least at the time when, the prodigious expenditures of the Government were commenced; and it is impossible to act upon it just now, when there is scarce a dollar to be had for the most pressing wants of the Treasury. Let us seize the earliest moment for it when it shall have become practicable, and meantime be content to find means for the current and most essential expenses of the Government.

But, Mr. Chairman, the fundamental idea of this substitute is to support and float these $150,000,000, by a nearly equal amount of taxation and revenue, payable of course in these notes. The Government owes the people and the people owe the Government, each $150,000,000, and these notes are primarily to be used as a common medium of payment between them. Unquestionably so long as this relation of mutual debts and credits subsists in nearly the same proportion, these notes will float in general circulation and in payments, or exchanges, or other commercial and business transactions between citizen and citizen, even without the funding clause; but this clause is essential inasmuch as the expenditures of the Government very greatly exceed the $150,000,000, and because the debt present and future is unhappily to last for many years to come. But these notes will have this advantage over bank paper, that they are receivable at par with gold and silver in payment of Government dues, while it is not. The refusal, therefore, of the banks to receive and circulate them will avail nothing to depreciate their value, since their credit and circulation will depend, not on bank favor, but on taxes of a nearly equal amount which must be paid, at all events, and may be paid in these same notes. They will thus be beyond the reach of bull, bear, or banker.

Will they circulate as money, and answer its purposes as well to the creditors as the debtors of the Government, sustained as they are by all these elements of credit? Sir, I do not depend solely on theory and deduction upon this point. We are not without examples at home and abroad. North Carolina, after the Revolution, and previous to the adoption of the present Constitution, issued between four and five hundred thousand dollars, of paper, receivable in payment of her public dues. She declared it also a legal tender, but her ratification of the Constitution in November, 1789, of course abrogated that provision; and yet, supported by taxation sufficient to pay her debts and carry on her State government, this immense amount of paper-money remained in circulation for more than twenty years at par with gold and silver during the whole time, although her revenue was less than one-fourth of the whole amount of this currency. In like manner Russia, as late as 1827, had a fixed paper circulation of upward of $120,000,000, in the form of bank-bills, but having nothing to sustain it, except that it was receivable in payment of her public dues; and yet it continued for years at par, although her revenue did not exceed $90,000,000 annually. And in 1838 Mr. Clay declared that if the Government used only gold and silver, and its own credit, it could even with the then small revenue of some $30,000,000 keep $40,000,000 of Treasury drafts in circulation at par all over the Union, though they should bear not a cent of interest, and not be fundable at last in interest-bearing stocks; and I do not now doubt that one-third, possibly one-half more of these Treasury notes, than of any given amount of fixed, undoubted, and punctually paid revenue, could be floated at par to-day.

I do not propose, Mr. Chairman, or pretend that these Treasury notes are to be convertible into gold and silver. They are not payable on demand; they are not payable to bearer, nor payable at all. They are not *to be* paid, but to circulate as a currency receivable in Government dues, and finally to be funded in twenty years' stocks. They are not promises to pay, and therefore are not paper-money. They do not represent gold and silver, of which the Government has none; and if it had wherewith to pay notes on demand, it would be under no necessity and have no justification for issuing or circulating these notes at all. They represent only Government dues, and their value rests on the credit of the Government—on its right and power to collect such an amount of taxes as may be needed to sustain that credit. The United States are to cease in part for a time to be a specie-paying, hard-money Government. I deplore it profoundly. But imperious necessity demands it. There is no alternative, no matter what evils may follow. It is the best possible that can be done under the circumstances; and that is the only apology for suspending, even to that extent, the Independent Treasury, as wise and beneficent a measure as ever was devised. And yet it is one thing for the Government to receive and pay out its own paper or notes in its own business, and quite another to receive and pay out the paper bills or promises of a bank as cash; and as to this last, the Independent Treasury system remains unchanged.

But I utterly deny, sir, the right of the Federal Government to provide a paper currency intended primarily to circulate as money, and meet the demands of business and commercial transactions, and to the exclusion of all other paper. It is not the intent or object of the substitute to furnish such a currency for the country. Its purpose is to provide a new but temporary medium, receivable for the public dues and sufficient only to meet the increased fiscal action of the Government. It is not to supersede either gold and silver or bank paper in ordinary business and commercial affairs. The tendency of all paper, indeed, is to expel specie from circulation; and it always will, to a greater or less extent, where it is a mere substitute for it, and the more so just in proportion as there is a want of confidence in it. But this bill proposes a paper in addition to the present currency of the country, an addition made necessary by the immensely increased disbursements, and by and by, of the revenues of the Government. Sir, the whole amount of specie and bank paper actually in circulation in the United States, on the 1st of May, when this increase began, was about $400,000,000, of which amount some $300,000,000 were in the States still called loyal. Of the whole amount, the Government employed in various ways $87,000,000; leaving $313,000,000 for the ordinary commercial and business transactions of the country; of which amount about $213,000,000 were circulated in the loyal States. Meantime in nine months, though one-third of the States have seceded, the expenditures and operations of the Government have gone up in the remaining two-thirds, from $87,000,000 to $600,000,000. To meet this immensely increased fiscal action, we have but $213,000,000 of currency, gold and silver and bank paper, not including the $50,000,000 of demand notes now in circulation.

It is true, sir, that in the generally deranged and embarrassed condition of the country, a large part of the $213,000,000 has been withdrawn from ordinary and private business and commerce, and used in aid of the transactions of Government. But with all this there remains some hundreds of millions needed still. It cannot, indeed, be all supplied in this way, because the limit to the credit of the Government, by virtue of which it can float Treasury notes, is not the amount of its expenditures and indebtedness, but of its solid revenues. There is, however, abundant room, as I have just shown, for the circulation of these notes, primarily, and therefore constitutionally, as a medium between the Government and its tax-payers and tax-consumers; but, secondarily, as a part of, and not a substitute for, the common currency of the country. And it is a consideration of no small value to the Government, and bringing no loss to the people, that as long as they circulate there will be a large saving of interest, equivalent in one year, at six per cent., to the sum of $900,000; a considerable item, in ordinary times at least.

And they have this further advantage also over Treasury notes bearing interest and payable at a future day, that the latter bear interest from the day they are put out, but the former only from the time they cease to circulate and are funded—another large item in the way of economy. Nor is there any danger, sir, that they will continue in circulation after the necessity which compels and justifies their issue shall have ceased. As soon as the credit of the Government is restored, and its bonds are at par or command a premium, and when its enormous receipts and disbursements shall have been diminished, not only will it be the interest of all capitalists to fund them, but especially of the banks to drive them into stocks and thus out of circulation. That day, indeed, may be far distant.

Such, Mr. Chairman, is the substitute which I have submitted. It differs essentially from the bill. The one relies on force, the other upon credit; the one looks to the direct and despotic coercion of law and arms, the other to the indirect and ordinary coercion of taxation; the bill would override both the letter and the spirit of the Constitution; the substitute follows and complies with both; the former shocks every principle not only of justice between the Government and the citizen, but of sound political economy; the latter recognizes the eternal and immutable rules of justice, and conforms itself strictly to the fixed and inexorable laws of commerce and trade; and finally, the one would provide an unlimited, irredeemable, depreciated paper-money forced by fear of violence or confiscation, upon the whole people; while the other proposes only a voluntary, limited, and temporary currency to circulate primarily between the creditors and the debtors of the Government.

The difference is radical. It is the difference between the broad road and the narrow way. The Secretary has chosen the former and death is at the end of it.

> "Oh for that warning voice, which he, who saw
> The Apocalypse, heard cry in Heaven aloud!"

To my political friends let me now appeal for support, not only of this substitute, but of the taxation which must follow it as essential to the maintenance of the good faith and credit of the Government. Forego the little paltry advantage which might be secured from opposition to the taxes necessary for that purpose. Impair not the estate in order to injure or annoy the tenant. But I put it upon higher and nobler grounds. There is not a member of this House, I take it for granted, who does not desire and hope and look for an ultimate, if not a speedy restoration of the Union of these States just as our fathers made it. If there be one who does not, no matter on which side of the House he sits, he has no business here. I have differed with the Administration as to the means, and differ widely still, but never as to the end; if, indeed, reunion, the old Union, be the end and purpose for which they are contending. But, I repeat it, bankruptcy is disunion and dissolution in the worst form, and would instantly end the war, the Government, and the Union forever.

Finally, sir, if the committee and the House shall proceed upon the principles of justice and sound political economy which have been hitherto observed by every wise Government, and above all by this Government from the beginning, in the maintenance of its credit and good faith, I will lend a ready and an earnest support to every measure framed in conformity with these principles, and intended and calculated to build up and to sustain the public credit and good faith. Otherwise, I cannot and I will not vote to bring down upon the wretched people of this once happy and prosperous country, the triple ruin of a forced currency, enormous taxation, and a public debt never to be extinguished.

APPENDIX.

The following are the material sections of Mr. VALLANDIGHAM's substitute:

That to meet the necessities of the Treasury of the United States, and to provide a currency receivable for the public dues, the Secretary of the Treasury, with the approbation of the President of the United States, is hereby authorized to issue, on the faith of the United States, Treasury notes in any amount not exceeding $150,000,000, not bearing interest, transferable by delivery, and of such denominations as he may deem expedient, not greater than $1,000, nor less than five dollars each: *Provided, however*, That $50,000,000 of said notes shall be in lieu of the demand Treasury notes authorized to be issued by the act of July 17, 1861; which said demand notes, so far as issued, shall be taken up as rapidly as practicable, and the notes herein provided for substituted for them, and no more of said demand notes shall be issued or reissued after the passage of this act: *And provided further*, That the amount of the two kinds of notes together shall at no time exceed the sum of $150,000,000; and the Treasury notes herein authorized shall be receivable in payment of all taxes, duties, imposts, excises, debts, and demands of every kind due to the United States, and may be paid out, under the direction of the Secretary of the Treasury, by any disbursing officer of the United States to any creditor of the United States who will consent to receive the same, at the par value thereof, in discharge of the debt or claim of such creditor; and any holder thereof depositing any sum not less than $100, or some multiple of one hundred, with the Treasurer of the United States, or either of the Assistant Treasurers, or either of the designated depositaries at Cincinnati or Baltimore, shall receive in exchange therefor duplicate certificates of deposit, one of which may be transmitted to the Secretary of the Treasury, who shall thereupon issue to the holder an equal amount of bonds of the United States, coupon or registered, as may by said holder be desired, bearing interest at the rate of six per centum per annum, payable semi-annually, and redeemable at the pleasure of the United States after twenty years from the date thereof; and any holder of said notes, being a citizen or subject and resident of any foreign country, depositing, as aforesaid, any sum therein not less than $2,500, shall, if he demand it, receive similar bonds at the above-named rate of interest, payable semi-annually, the principal and interest of which shall be expressed in the currency of any foreign country, and payable there. And said United States Treasury notes shall be received the same as coin, at their par value, in the sale or negotiation of any bonds that may be hereafter sold or negotiated by the Secretary of the Treasury, with the approbation of the President of the United States, to any person being a citizen and resident of the United States, and may be reissued from time to time, as the exigencies of the public interests shall require: *Provided, however*, That this right to reissue shall not continue longer than two years from the passage of this act, unless Congress shall hereafter otherwise provide.

SEC. 2. *And be it further enacted*, That the form of said Treasury notes shall be as follows: "The United States will receive this Treasury note in payment of all taxes, duties, imposts, excises, debts, and demands of every kind due to the United States, to the value of five dollars," or whatever sum or denomination may be expressed thereon, as hereinbefore provided for.

SEC. 3. *And be it further enacted*, That to enable the Secretary of the Treasury to fund the floating debt of the United States, he is hereby authorized, with the approbation of the President of the United States, to issue on the credit of the United States, coupon bonds, or registered bonds, to an amount not exceeding $200,000,000, redeemable at the pleasure of the United States after twenty years from date, and bearing interest at the rate of six per cent. per annum, payable semi-annually. And said bonds shall be of such denominations, not less than fifty dollars, as the Secretary of the Treasury, with the approbation of the President of the United States, may determine upon; or where any creditor of the floating debt of the United States, in any sum of not less than $2,500, being a citizen or subject and resident of any foreign country shall demand it, said bonds shall be issued to such creditor, the principal and interest therein being expressed in the currency of any foreign country, and payable there: *Provided, however*, That none of said bonds shall issue except at their par value; and to such creditors of the floating debt of the United States as shall elect to receive them in satisfaction of their demands: *Provided further, also*, That the claims and demands of such creditors shall, in all cases, have been first audited and settled by the proper accounting officers of the Treasury.

ADDRESS

OF DEMOCRATIC MEMBERS OF THE HOUSE OF REPRESENTATIVES OF THE UNITED STATES, TO THE DEMOCRACY OF THE UNITED STATES.

WASHINGTON, D. C., *May* 8, 1862.*

FELLOW-CITIZENS:—The perilous condition of the country demands that we should counsel together. Party organization, restricted within proper limits, is a positive good, and indeed essential to the preservation of public liberty. Without it the best government would soon degenerate into the worst of tyrannies. In despotisms the chief use of power is in crushing out party opposition. In our own country the experience of the last twelve months proves, more than any lesson in history, the necessity of party organization. The present Administration was chosen by a party, and in all civil acts and appointments has recognized, and still does, its fealty and obligations to that party. There must and will be an opposition. The public safety and good demand it. Shall it be a new organization or an old one? The Democratic party was founded more than sixty years ago. It has never been disbanded. To-day it numbers one million five hundred thousand electors in the States still loyal to the Union. Its recent numerous victories in municipal elections in the Western and Middle States prove its vitality. Within the last ten months it has held State conventions and nominated full Democratic tickets in every free State in the Union. Of no other party opposed to the Republicans can the same be said.

SHALL THE DEMOCRATIC PARTY BE NOW DISBANDED?

Why should it? Are its ancient PRINCIPLES wrong? What are they? Let its platforms for thirty years speak:

"*Resolved*, That the American Democracy place their trust in the intelligence, the patriotism, and the discriminating justice of the American people.

* This Address was signed by William A. Richardson, Anthony L. Knapp, and James C. Robinson, *of Illinois*; John Law, and Daniel W. Voorhees, *of Indiana*; William Allen, Chilton A. White, Warren P. Noble, George H. Pendleton, and Clement L. Vallandigham, *of Ohio*; Nehemiah Perry, *of New Jersey*; Philip Johnson, and Sydenham E. Ancona, *of Pennsylvania*; and George K. Shiel, *of Oregon*.

"That we regard this as a distinctive feature in our political creed, which we are proud to maintain before the world, as the great moral element in a form of Government springing from and upheld by the POPULAR WILL; and we contrast it with the creed and practice of Federalism, under whatever name or form, which seeks to palsy the will of the constituent, and which conceives no imposture too monstrous for the popular credulity.

"That the Federal Government is one of limited power, derived *solely* from the CONSTITUTION; and the grants of power made therein ought to be strictly construed by all the departments and agents of the Government; and that it is inexpedient and dangerous to exercise doubtful constitutional powers."

And as explanatory of these the following from Mr. Jefferson's first inaugural:

"The support of the STATE GOVERNMENTS in all their rights as the most competent administrations of our domestic concerns, and the surest bulwarks against anti-republican tendencies.

"The preservation of the GENERAL GOVERNMENT in its whole constitutional vigor as the sheet-anchor of our peace at home and safety abroad.

"A jealous care of the right of election by the people.

"THE SUPREMACY OF THE CIVIL OVER THE MILITARY AUTHORITY.

"Economy in the public expense, that labor may be lightly burdened.

"The honest payment of our debts and sacred preservation of the public faith.

"FREEDOM OF RELIGION, FREEDOM OF THE PRESS, AND FREEDOM OF PERSON UNDER PROTECTION OF THE HABEAS CORPUS, AND TRIAL BY JURIES IMPARTIALLY SELECTED."

Such, Democrats, are the principles of your party, essential to public liberty and to the stability and wise administration of the Government, alike in peace and war. They are the principles upon which the Constitution and the Union were founded; and under the control of a party which adheres to them, the Constitution would be maintained and the Union could not be dissolved.

Is the POLICY of the Democratic party wrong that it should be disbanded?

Its policy is consistent with its principles, and may be summed up, from the beginning, as follows: The support of liberty as against power; of the people as against their agents and servants; and of State rights as against consolidation and centralized despotism; a simple Government; no public debt; low taxes; no high protective tariff; no general system of internal improvements by Federal authority; no National Bank; hard money for the Federal public dues; no assumption of State debts; expansion of territory; self-government for the Territories, subject only to the Constitution; the absolute compatibility of a Union of the States, "part slave and part free;" the admission of new States, with or without slavery, as they may elect; non-interference by the Federal Government with slavery in State and Territory, or in the District of Columbia; and, finally, as set forth in the Cincinnati Platform, in 1856, and reaffirmed in 1860, absolute and eternal "repudiation of ALL SECTIONAL PARTIES AND PLATFORMS concerning domestic slavery which seek to embroil the States and incite to treason and armed resistance to law in the Territories, *and whose avowed purposes, if consummated, must end in* CIVIL WAR AND DISUNION."

Such was the ancient and the recent policy of the Democratic party, running through a period of sixty years—a policy consistent with the principles of the Constitution, and absolutely essential to the preservation of the Union.

Does the HISTORY of the Democratic party prove that it ought to be abandoned? "By their fruits shall ye know them." Sectional parties do not achieve Union triumphs. For sixty years from the inauguration of Jefferson on the 4th of March, 1801, the Democratic party, with short intervals, controlled the power and the policy of the Federal Government. For forty-eight years out of these sixty, Democratic men ruled the country; for forty-four years and eight months the Democratic policy prevailed. During this period Louisiana, Florida, Texas, New Mexico, and California were successively annexed to our territory, with an area more than twice as large as all the original Thirteen States together. Seventeen new States were admitted under strictly Democratic administrations—one under the Administration of Fillmore. From five millions, the population increased to thirty-one millions. The Revolutionary debt was extinguished. Two foreign wars were successfully prosecuted, with a moderate outlay and a small army and navy, and without the suspension of the habeas corpus; without one infraction of the Constitution; without one usurpation of power; without suppressing a single newspaper; without imprisoning a single editor; without limit to the freedom of press, or of speech in or out of Congress, but in the midst of the grossest abuse of both; and without the arrest of a single "traitor," though the HARTFORD CONVENTION sat during one of the wars, and in the other Senators invited the enemy to "GREET OUR VOLUNTEERS WITH BLOODY HANDS AND WELCOME THEM TO HOSPITABLE GRAVES."

During all this time wealth increased, business of all kinds multiplied, prosperity smiled on every side; taxes were low; wages were high; the North and the South furnished a market for each other's products at good prices; public liberty was secure; private rights undisturbed; every man's house was his castle; the courts were open to all; no passports for travel; no secret police; no spies; no informers; no bastiles; the right to assemble peaceably; the right to petition; freedom of religion, freedom of speech, a free ballot, and a free press; and all this time the Constitution maintained and the Union of the States preserved.

Such were the choice fruits of Democratic principles and policy, carried out through the whole period during which the Democratic party held the power and administered the Federal Government. Such has been the history of that party. It is a Union party, for it preserved the Union, by wisdom, peace, and compromise, for more than half a century.

Then neither the ancient principles, the policy, nor the past history of the Democratic party require nor would justify its disbandment.

Is there any thing in the present crisis which demands it? The more immediate issue is,

TO MAINTAIN THE CONSTITUTION AS IT IS, AND TO RESTORE THE UNION AS IT WAS.

To maintain the Constitution is to respect the rights of the States and the liberties of the citizen. It is to adhere faithfully to the very principles and policy which the Democratic party has professed for more than half a century. Let its history, and the results, from the beginning, prove whether it has practised them. We appeal proudly to the record.

The first step towards a restoration of the Union as it was is to maintain the Constitution as it is. So long as it was maintained in fact, and not threatened with infraction in spirit and in letter, actual or imminent, the Union was unbroken.

To restore the Union, it is essential, first, to give assurance to every State and to the people of every section that their rights and liberties and property will be secure within the Union under the Constitution. What assurance so doubly sure as the restoration to power of that ancient, organized, consolidated Democratic party which for sixty years *did* secure the property, rights, and liberties of the States and of the people; and thus did maintain the Constitution and preserve the Union, and with them the multiplied blessings which distinguished us above all other nations?

To restore the Union is to crush out sectionalism North and South. To begin the great work of restoration through the ballot is to KILL ABOLITION. The bitter waters of secession flowed first and are fed still from the unclean fountain of abolition. That fountain must be dried up. Armies may break down the power of the Confederate Government in the South; but the work of restoration can be carried on only through political organization and the ballot in the North and West. In this great work we cordially invite the co-operation of all men of every party, who are opposed to the fell spirit of abolition, and who, in sincerity, desire the Constitution as it is, and the Union as it was.

Let the dead past bury its dead. Rally, lovers of the Union, the Constitution, and of Liberty, to the standard of the Democratic party, already in the field and confident of victory. That party is the natural and persistent enemy of abolition. Upon this question its record as a national organization, however it may have been at times with particular men or in particular States, is clear and unquestionable. From the beginning of the anti-slavery agitation to the period of the last Democratic National Convention it has held but one language in regard to it. Let the record speak:

"*Resolved*, That Congress has no power under the Constitution to interfere with or control the domestic institutions of the several States, and that such States are the sole and proper judges of every thing appertaining to their own affairs not prohibited by the Constitution; that all efforts of the Abolitionists or others made to induce Congress to interfere with questions of slavery, or to take incipient steps in relation thereto, are calculated to lead to the most alarming and dangerous consequences, and that all such efforts have an inevitable tendency to diminish the happiness of the people and endanger the stability and permanency of the Union, and ought not to be countenanced by any friend of our political institutions."

Upon these principles alone, so far as relates to slavery, can the Union as it was be restored; and no other Union, except the UNITY OF DESPOTISM, can be maintained in this country; and this last we will resist, as our fathers did, with our lives, our fortunes, and our sacred honor.

But it is said that you must disband the Democratic party, "to support the government." We answer that the Democratic party has always supported THE GOVERNMENT; and while it was in power preserved the government in all its vigor and integrity, not by force and arms, but by wisdom, sound policy, and peace. But it never did admit, and never will, that this Administration, or any Administration, is "the Government." It holds, and ever has held, that the Federal Government is the agent of the people of the several States composing the Union; that it consists of three distinct departments—the legislative, the executive, and the judicial—each equally a part of the government, and equally entitled to the confidence and support of the States and the people; and that it is the duty of every patriot to sustain the several departments of the government in the exercise of all the constitutional powers of each, which may be necessary and proper for the preservation of the government, in its principles and in its vigor and integrity, and to stand by and defend to the utmost, the flag which represents the government, the Union, and the country.

In this sense the Democratic party has always sustained, and will now sustain, the government against all foes, at home or abroad, in the North or the South, open or concealed, in office or out of office, in peace or in war.

If this is what the Republican party mean by supporting the government, it is an idle thing to abandon the old and tried Democratic party, which for so many years, and through so many trials, supported, preserved, and maintained the government of the Union. But if their real purpose be to aid the ancient enemies of the Democracy, in subverting our present Constitution and form of government, and, under pretence of saving the Union, to erect a strong centralized despotism on its ruins, the Democratic party will resist them as the worst enemy to the Constitution and the Union, and to free government everywhere.

We do not propose to consider now the causes which led to the present unhappy civil war. A fitter time will come hereafter for such discussion. But we remind you now that Compromise made your Union, and Compromise fifteen months ago would have saved it. Repeated efforts were made at the last session of the Thirty-Sixth Congress to this end. At every stage, the great mass of the South, with the whole Democratic party, and the whole Constitutional Union party, of the North and West, united in favor of certain amendments to the Constitution—and chief among them, the well known "Crittenden Propositions," which would have averted civil war, and maintained the Union. At every stage, all proposed amendments inconsistent with the sectional doctrines of the Chicago Platform, were strenuously and unanimously resisted, and defeated, by the Republican party. The "Crittenden Propositions" never received a single Republican vote, in either House. For the proof we appeal to the Journals of Congress and to the Congressional Globe.

We scorn to reply to the charge that the Democratic party is opposed to granting aid and support to the Federal Government, in maintaining its safety, integrity, and constitutional supremacy, and in favor of disbanding our armies, and succumbing to the South. The charge is libellous and false. No man has advocated any such proposition. Democrats recognize it as their duty as patriots, to support the government in all constitutional, necessary, and proper efforts to maintain its safety, integrity, and constitutional authority; but at the same time they are inflexibly opposed to waging war against any of the States or people of this Union, in any spirit of oppression, or for any purpose of conquest or subjugation, or of overthrowing or interfering with the rights or established institutions of any State. Above all, the Democratic party will not support the Administration in any thing which looks or tends to the loss of our political or personal rights and liberties, or a change of our present Democratic form of government.

But no, Democrats, it is not the support of the government, in restoring the Union, which the party in power require of you. You are asked to give up your principles, your policy, and your party, and to stand by the Administration in all its acts. Above all, it is demanded of you that you yield at least a silent support to their whole policy, and to withhold all scrutiny into their public conduct, of every kind, lest you should "embarrass the Administration." You are thus asked to renounce one of the first principles and the chief security of a Democratic government—the right to hold public servants responsible to their master, the people; to render the representative accountable to the constituent; the ancient and undoubted prerogative of Americans to canvass public measures and public men. It is this "high constitutional privilege" which Daniel Webster declared he would "defend and exercise, within the House and out of the House, and in all places; in time of war, in time of peace, and at all times!" It is a right secured by the Constitution; a right inestimable to the people, and formidable to tyrants only.

If ever there was a time when the existence and consolidation of the Democratic party, upon its principles and policy, was a vital necessity to public and private liberty, it is now.

Unquestionably the Constitution gives ample power to the several departments of the government to carry on war, strictly subject to its provisions, and, in case of civil war, with perfect security to citizens of the loyal States. Every act necessary for the safety and efficiency of the government, and for a complete and most vigorous trial of its strength, is yet wholly consistent with the observance of every provision of that instrument, and of the laws in pursuance of it, if the sole motives of those in power were the suppression of the "rebellion," and no more. And yet the history of the Administration for the twelve months past has been, and continues to be, a history of repeated usurpations of power, and of violations of the Constitution, and of the public and private rights of the citizen. For the proof we appeal to facts, too recent to need recital here, and too flagrant and heinous for the calm narrative which we propose. Similar acts were done, and a like policy pursued in the threatened war with France in the time of John Adams, and with the same ultimate purpose. But in two or three years the people forced them into an honorable peace with France, rebuked the excesses and abuses of power, vindicated the Constitution, and turned over the Federal Government to the principles and policy of the Democratic party. To the "sober second thought" of the people, therefore, and to the ballot-box, we now appeal when again in like peril with our fathers.

But if every Democrat concurred in the policy of prosecuting the war to the utter subjugation of the South, and for the subversion of her State Governments and her institutions, without a Convention of the States, and without an overture for peace, we should just as resolutely resist the disbanding of the Democratic party. It is the only party capable of carrying on a war; it is the only party which has ever conducted a war to a successful issue, and the only party which has done it without abuse of power, without molestation to the rights of any class of citizens, and with due regard to economy. All this it has done: all this, if need be, it is able to do again. If success, then, in a military point of view be required, the Democratic party alone can command it.

To conclude: Inviting all men, without distinction of State, section, or party, who are for the Constitution as it is, and the Union as it was, to unite with us in this great work upon terms of perfect equality, we insist that—

The restoration of the Union, whether through peace or by war, demands the continued organization and success of the Democratic party;

The preservation of the Constitution demands it;

The maintenance of liberty and free democratical government demands it;

The restoration of a sound system of internal policy demands it;

Economy and honesty in the public expenditures, now at the rate of nearly four millions of dollars a day, demand it;

The rapid accumulation of an enormous and permanent public debt, demand it—a public debt, or liability, already one thousand millions of dollars, and equal, at the present rate, in three years, to England's debt of a century and a half in growth;

The heavy taxation, direct and indirect, State and Federal, already more than two hundred millions of dollars a year, eating out the substance of the people, and augmenting every year, demands it;

Reduced wages, low prices, depression of trade, decay of business, scarcity of work, and impending ruin on every side, demand it;

And, finally, the restoration of the concord, good feeling, and prosperity of former years, demands that the Democratic party shall be maintained, and made victorious.

SPEECH ON PUBLIC DEBT, LIABILITY, AND EXPENDITURES,

In the House of Representatives, June 30, 1862.

MR. SPEAKER:—Desiring on Friday last to leave for home at an early hour this morning, it would greatly have suited my convenience to have addressed the House on that day; but inasmuch as the chairman of the Committee of the Whole [Mr. Dawes], after due deliberation and upon solemn advice, decreed that it was not in order, pending a revenue measure, to discuss the general subject of revenue and expenditures, but only the particular items of the bill, I was obliged to remain, in order that I might speak to-day.

Of this I will not now complain. It is but a part of the sum of human disappointments to which we are all subject.

The bill before us appropriates $200,000, and pledges the faith of the United States to the extent of $10,000,000 more. While, as a Western man, I should gladly support any measure really and honestly for the interest of the West, I am constrained to oppose this bill. I am against it, first, because, in my deliberate judgment, it is wholly without constitutional warrant. I oppose it further, because the debt and expenditures of the Government to-day are too great to justify any such further assumption of liability as this measure contemplates. And it is upon this point alone that I now propose to address the House.

My purpose is not to produce an electioneering document. At the instance of others, if at all, and not by any act of mine, shall my remarks of to-day be published and distributed in pamphlet. My object is to vindicate the truth of financial history; to ascertain, as nearly as may be possible, the actual and full amount of the debt, liability, and expenditures of the Government—a debt, every dollar of which fairly and honestly incurred, must be paid; for REPUDIATION is but treason in another form.

I desire also to vindicate gentlemen on this side of the Chamber who have so gratuitously, wantonly, and unjustly been censured and assailed even to the extent of insinuations against their loyalty, for but repeating the statements of others as to the enormous expenditures and indebtedness of the Government. I propose further to justify by the proof, those Republican members of the Senate and this House upon whose authority we of the Democratic party here and through the country have made the statements which have so alarmed the Secretary of the Treasury and his retainers. Official accuracy and veracity of any kind are rare virtues in this day, and wherever found, are worthy of special commemoration and praise.

Sir, I see nothing to be gained, but much, very much to be lost by the vain effort to conceal the real extent of the public debt and expenditures. In private life, nothing so much indicates, and generally nothing so certainly precedes disastrous bankruptcy, as an attempt dishonestly to cover up or withhold the true condition of a business man in embarrassed circumstances. And the same principle applies equally to a government.

The gentleman from Indiana [Mr. Voorhees], and the other Democratic members of this House, who put forth recently a certain "address" to the people, have been unsparingly denounced here and elsewhere for asserting that the public debt to-day, the end of the present fiscal year, amounts to from seven hundred to one thousand million dollars, and that the expenditures average now from two to near four million dollars a day.

Now, sir, upon what authority did we assert, and had we a right to assert it? No Democratic member of this House has access, or at least familiar access, to the Treasury Department: none certainly to its secrets. We have not the means of knowing, by the inspection of its records, what amount of indebtedness has already been incurred, nor what the expenditures are. Such access and means of knowledge belong alone to the Republican members of the Senate and House of Representatives, and above all to the members of that party which compose the Committee of Ways and Means in the House, and the Committee on Finance in the Senate, and whose business it is to deal with the Treasury.

A large, a generous charity, therefore, I say, ought to be extended to us who, after three and four months' repeated and specific statements officially from Senators and Representatives as to the amount of debt and expenditures, have but put upon record before the people that which we derived from their authority. I propose then, sir, in the first place, to review and collate what has been said upon this subject within the past eleven months in this House and the Senate.

On the 25th of July, 1861, the chairman of the Committee of Ways and Means said:

"It must be recollected that the demand on the Treasury is well nigh *a million dollars a day*."—*Congressional Globe, extra session*, 1861, p. 267.

Again, on the 5th of August, 1861, ten days later, he said:

"I am alarmed at the expense we are incurring. This day, and *every day* for some time, the nation has incurred an expense of some *one million two hundred and fifty thousand dollars*. I cannot see where the money is to come from."—*Ibid.*, p. 448.

That, sir, was before the notion that the Constitution authorized the making of the promissory notes of the United States, or any thing else except gold and silver, a "legal tender," had ever entered the brain of any one, and before the Secretary of the Treasury had compassed and devised his extraordinary scheme of a grand national paper-mill for the manufacture of money by steam.

Again, the gentleman from Massachusetts [Mr. Dawes], who was thrust forward here the other day as the advocate to defend, upon special retainer, and abet the Secretary of the Treasury in his deliberate effort to underestimate the true amount of the public debt and daily expenditures of the Government, and who, by some sort of financial legerdemain, contrived to prove them to be somewhat less than one million dollars a day, himself, on the 13th of January last, said:

"Mr. Speaker, it takes $2,000,000 *every day* to support the Army in the field."

Mark you, not as he here subsequently suggested, that on that particular 13th of January, or the day before or the day after, or any other one day, that was the expenditure, but "every day." And this, too, for the Army alone.

But he proceeds:

"One hundred millions have been expended since we met here in the *beginning of December, upon an Army in repose.*"

Ah! indeed. Why, sir, that is at the rate of $2,380,000 a day for the preceding six weeks, with the Army "in repose." He adds:

"What they will be when that great day shall arrive—if it shall ever arrive—when our eyes shall be gladdened with the sight of the Army in motion, *I do not know*."—*Congressional Globe*, 1861–2, vol. 2, p. 299.

Well, sir, our eyes were at length "gladdened with the sight of the Army in motion." The grand Army of the Potomac did actually move; and yet then of all others precisely is the time which the gentleman selects for severe censure upon members on this side of the House for intimating the mere suspicion that the expenses which he could not even estimate, might be seven or eight hundred thousand dollars more a day with the Army "in motion" than his own statement of the expenditure for the same Army "in repose."

But he proceeds again:

Another $100,000,000 will go with this, as the $100,000,000 more I have here enumerated, outside of the daily support of the Army, have gone"—

Outside of the daily support of the Army, indeed! Why, sir, that is $200,000,000 in six weeks, or at the rate of $4,760,000 a day. Oh, what a "traitor" to assert it!

"Another one hundred million dollars, I say, must be added to this before the 4th of March!"

How long before the 4th of March? But $300,000,000 for full three months, are $1,200,000,000 a year; or, if he means only $200,000,000, that itself is at the rate of $800,000,000 a year for the Army alone, to say nothing of the other legitimate expenses of the Government, nor of the gigantic plunder and peculation which have disgraced it.

But the gentleman from Massachusetts proceeds next in elegiac strain:

"Sir, what it may cost to put down this rebellion, I care very little, provided it may be put down; but, sir, faith without works is dead, and I am free to confess that my faith sometimes fails—my faith in men, not in the cause."

Thus heavily and despairingly, on the 13th of January, the Pilgrim of Massachusetts bore upon his vicarious back the huge burden or pack of the sin of this Administration's indebtedness, as he struggled on sorrowfully in the financial Slough of Despond. What cross—what sort of a "cross" it was, at the sight of which, some months later, this vast burden rolled from his shoulders, no doubt some future Democratic Bunyan, languishing in the cells or casemates of your military prisons, will hereafter disclose.

On the 28th of January, 1862, the gentleman from New York [Mr. Spaulding], a member of the Committee of Ways and Means, said:

"But with the Navy and an Army of six hundred thousand in the field, requiring, with the other expenses of the Government, an *average* daily expenditure of *more* than one million six hundred thousand dollars"—

How much more? But at that sum alone, it equals $584,000,000—

this new system of banking will not afford relief to the Treasury in time to enable the Secretary to meet the pressing demands that are made upon him."—*Congressional Globe*, 1861–2, p. 524.

Again, on the 4th of February, 1862, the gentleman from New York [Mr. Roscoe Conklin], assuming to estimate the expenditure, ordinary and extraordinary, from that date to July 1, 1862, at $300,000,000, said:

"This last item is at the rate of $2,000,000 per day for one hundred and fifty days. If $45,000,000 a month is taken as the estimate, the item will be $225,000,000. But it will then reach $300,000,000, because there is an item of a hundred million nearly which will be payable at the close of the war, growing out of bounty acts, and it has been nowhere included."

And estimating the entire debt to July 1, 1862, at $806,000,000, he exclaimed:

"Eight hundred and six millions! Who can credit these figures when he remembers that the world's greatest tragedian closed his bloody drama at St. Helena, leaving the public debt of France less than seventy million of pounds?"

Rank disloyalty, all this! Sir, had I presumed to speak thus, my fidelity to my country would have been utterly denied, and the gentleman from Massachusetts would have added at least one page more to the suspicions and innuendoes of his speech of the 27th of May. The gentleman from New York adds:

"This enormous debt amounts, for each congressional district represented upon this floor, to $4,210,000, and when the war is ended, it will be more than five million dollars. Let every gentleman ponder upon the fact that there is more than three hundred thousand dollars of interest to be paid every year by his congressional district."—*Congressional Globe*, 1861–62, p. 635.

Again, the gentleman from New Hampshire [Mr. Edwards], setting down the public debt at a more moderate figure than any one else, nevertheless declared it "appalling," estimating it at $650,000,000 upon the 1st of July, 1862.

The Chairman of the Committee of Ways and Means again, on the 6th of February, said:

"The *daily* expenses of the Government are now about $2,000,000. To carry us on till the next meeting of Congress would take $600,000,000 more, making, before legislation could be had at next session, about $700,000,000 to be provided for. We have already appropriated $350,000,000, making our entire debt $1,050,000,000."—*Congressional Globe*, 1861–62, p. 687.

On the 12th of the same month, the Chairman of the Committee on Finance in the Senate, the Senator from Maine [Mr. Fessenden] said:

"Sir we are contracting a large debt. At the end of this fiscal year (July 1, 1862), I suppose it will be, in round numbers, $750,000,000; and at the end of the succeeding year, if the war should continue, $1,500,000,000."—*Congressional Globe*, 1861–62, p. 765.

Still further, on the 19th of February, the gentleman from New York [Mr. Spaulding] said:

"One million six hundred thousand does not cover the *daily* expenditures."—*Congressional Globe*, 1861–62, p. 883.

And, on the same day, the gentleman from Maine [Mr. Pike] estimated our "enormous expenditures at from one to two million dollars a day."—*Congressional Globe*, 1861–62, p. 887.

Still further, the Chairman of the Committee of the Ways and Means [Mr. Stevens], on the 20th of February, 1862, said:

"Now, in less than a year, taking the public debt at what my colleague makes it—*I make it more*—$1,200,000,000, what will the interest be upon it at seven and three-tenths per cent., for it will all centre at that rate of interest?"—*Congressional Globe*, 1861–62, p. 900.

And again, on the 8th of April:

"I suppose our debt on the 1st of July next will not be less than $800,000,000 When, some time since, I had occasion to address the House on the Treasury note bill, I stated our expenses at $2,000,000. They are now, and *have been for some time past* over three million dollars *a day*. It is plain, therefore, that the sum I have stated will be rather *below* than above our indebtedness at the end of this fiscal year."—*Congressional Globe*, 1861–62, p. 1577.

And the Senator from Maine [Mr. Fessenden], again, on the 30th of May, declared that, taking the old debt and the appropriations for the years 1861–62, the whole amount would reach $670,000,000, and added:

"The Senator can judge for himself whether, taking into consideration the odds and ends, unsettled claims, deficiencies, etc., which will be likely to come in upon us, we shall fall short of $700,000,000."—*Congressional Globe*, 1861–62, p. 2446.

On the 6th of June, the Chairman of the Finance Committee of the Senate [Mr. Fessenden] said:

"I gave the other day, and I can give perhaps a little more accurately to-day, the amount of those appropriations for the present year. The appropriations for the year ending June 30th, 1862, were, at the second session of the Thirty-Sixth Congress, $71,000,000, and at the special session, and at this session of Congress, thus far, $535,000,000, making $606,000,000. Then if you add to that the old debt of $70,000,000, you have $676,000,000 as the total amount. Gentlemen must be perfectly aware from their experience, when you take into consideration the state of the country at the present time, the contracts that have been made, the outstanding claims, the expenditures of which no record, necessarily, can be made in a time like this, with so vast an expenditure, and the deficiencies that we are called upon almost every day of the session to meet, that you may safely add twenty or thirty million dollars to that estimate which I have thus stated, and in that way you have got a little over seven hundred millions. I see no escape from the conclusion, that at the end of the year, taking the appropriations and liabilities together, we certainly make no unreasonable estimate, if we call the amount of what is owing from us, provided nothing has been paid, seven hundred million dollars."—*Congressional Globe*, 1861–62, p. 2606.

Such, sir, were the repeated and reiterated statements of Senators and Representatives, all of them of the Republican party—the chairman of the Ways and Means in the House, the chairman of the Finance Committee of the Senate, the organs, in this Capitol, of the Treasury Department, the official mouthpieces of the Secretary, men having daily access to, and in daily communication with him—statements not uttered once and at random, but repeated over and over again, and with all possible accuracy and minuteness of detail. Charity, a little charity, I pray you, sir, toward those of us, who having no entrance within the inner courts of the temple of the Treasury, and no right to penetrate its hidden mysteries, are forced to content ourselves with standing in awe at its vestibule that we may catch the whispered echoes of the oracle within.

And now, sir, I propose to prove beyond an honest controversy, that the statements of the Republican Senators and Representatives, upon whose authority we of the Democratic party repeated them, were justified to the fullest extent, by the estimates, by the appropriations, by the authorized indebtedness, and by the actual indebtedness, as appears from official records the authenticity and verity of which cannot be impeached.

First, as to the "ESTIMATES." These, indeed, are by no means reliable, because every two or three months, and possibly every two or three weeks, we have additional estimates from the Treasury Department to supply the continually recurring deficiencies. There is a discrepancy between the estimates for the present fiscal year, made in July last, and those submitted on the 1st of December, of $213,904,000. The estimates of the 1st of July, were $318,519,000; and yet, during a short session of five weeks, Congress appropriated over and above these estimates the sum of $47,985,000. Last December the Secretary of the Treasury sent in supplementary estimates, asking additional appropriations to the extent of $213,904,000. On the 15th page of his annual report, of that date, he sums up the total of estimated expenditures for the fiscal year 1862 at $543,406,000, or at the rate of $1,500,000 every day in the year. Deducting the estimate of receipts, $36,809,000, you have as the amount of debt to-day, estimated by the Secretary of the Treasury himself seven months ago, the sum of $506,596,000. To this add the debt up to July 1, 1861, of $90,867,000, and you have a sum total of $597,464,519. And yet, with even this enormous amount, he has been forced since to confess errors to the extent of two or three hundred millions of dollars in his estimate for the year. And on the 28th of January, the gentleman from New York [Mr. Spaulding], declaring that the Secretary "substantially agreed with him as to what the expenses would be," summed up the debt at $650,000,000, or nearly $53,000,000 more than the Secretary, in his report, had set it down only seven weeks earlier.

I pass next to the "APPROPRIATIONS." What further deficiencies are to come in, or are now pending, I know not; but the amount of appropriations already made by Congress for the fiscal year ending today (June 30th), is $608,126,496; and for the coming fiscal year, 1862–63, the appropriations provided for in bills now between the two Houses, having passed one or the other, are for the Army alone $521,980,445, or at the rate of $820 a man, and for the naval service $42,427,771—an aggregate of $564,408,000 for the Army and Navy alone. Adding to that $1,818,000 for the Indian Department, you have $566,227,000. And to this must be added $28,318,000 in bills already become laws in all, the sum of $594,543,000 for the next fiscal year, making as the grand aggregate of the appropriations already provided for by this Congress since the 4th of July last, the enormous sum of $1,104,976,881 66.

I proceed next to ascertain the amount of AUTHORIZED INDEBTEDNESS, for which this House, the Senate, and the President have pledged the faith of the Government. In the first place, the appropriations, as I have said, amount to $581,526,000. Deducting from that the estimated receipts, adding to them $9,000,000 for error, from customs, lands, and all other ordinary sources, $46,000,000, we have $535,526,000. But this does not include the $10,200,000 proposed to be pledged by this bill for the ship canal from Lake Michigan to the Mississippi River, nor the $64,860,000 for the Pacific railroad, for which the faith of the Government is now pledged, nor the $3,500,000 for the enlargement of the locks of the Oswego and Erie canal, nor the $5,000,000 for the ship canal around the falls of Niagara, nor the other one hundred projects of disinterested patriots and philanthropic projectors in this House and outside of it, for augmenting the number, and extending still more widely the circulation of the "legal tender" notes of the United States.

There is yet another form of authorized indebtedness—loans and Treasury notes. By the act of July 17, 1861, we empowered the Secretary of Treasury to contract a debt of $250,000,000 in bonds, at his discretion. By the act of the 25th of February, 1862, $500,000,000 more in bonds were authorized, and $100,000,000 in Treasury notes; and by an act passed a day or two subsequently, $10,000,000, in addition, of demand notes; and by the act which has already passed this House, is now pending in the Senate, and will probably become a law in a few days, $150,000,000 more of "legal tender," making of authorized indebtedness in these two forms a grand aggregate of $1,010,000,000.

And now, sir, for the purpose of arriving at a fair estimate of the daily expenditures of the Government, I propose to take the ARMY as the test or standard. According to the statement of the Adjutant-General, May 21, 1862, furnished to the chairman of the Military Committee of the Senate, and the report of the Secretary of War in December last, the number of men in the regular and volunteer forces on the 21st of May was 637,988, divided thus: regulars, 20,334; volunteers, 617,654. On the 21st of May there were in these two arms of the military service, 26 major-generals, 207 brigadier-generals, 1,200 staff-officers, including brigade surgeons and additional paymasters, one retired Lieutenant-General drawing whole pay, and a full quota of officers attached to the department of the adjutant-general, quartermaster, subsistence, pay, ordnance, inspector-general, and medical departments, and the corps of engineers and topographical engineers.

Now, from statements made up at the pay office, I present here a sum total for pay and subsistence alone, including forage and servants, of the regular and volunteer army, amounting to $17,290,916 72 a month, being at the rate of $207,491,000 a year, and $576,363 a day; and this, let it be remembered, for pay and subsistence alone. What the actual amount of other expenditures for the Army are in full, it is utterly impossible to learn, in advance of actual returns, which cannot be had for some months to come; but I have ascertained the proportion which pay and subsistence bear to the other expenses in time of peace, by the actual expenditure returned, and in time of war, by estimate for the present year, and I find it to be exactly two-fifths. Assuming that as a basis of calculation, we have $518,745,500 a year as the total expenses of the Army, $3,000,000 less, by the way, than the appropriations already made for the coming year, being at the rate of $43,228,000 a month, and $1,440,000 a day.

These other expenses, sir, include cost of clothing, camp and garrison equipage, ordnance and medical stores, supplies, purchase of cavalry and artillery horses (to be replaced at least once in four months), medical and hospital department (in time of war enormously beyond any thing in time of peace), the transportation and subsistence of prisoners of war, and the purchase of arms, ordnance stores, gunpowder, and lead, amounting in the appropriations already made for the current fiscal year to $35,000,000, or not far from the sum for which contracts were made by authority of the late Secretary of War, Mr. Cameron. But above and beyond all as to cost, is "transportation" (by railroad, steamboats, sailing vessels, and wagon trains), including, in time of war as a very heavy item, the transportation of the sick and wounded. Now, sir, I submit to the candid judgment of the House, that it is but a fair and reasonable estimate to say, that at least twenty per cent. also should be added to the aggregate of these and other expenses, not including pay and subsistence of the Army, for additional cost and waste, and wear and tear, or destruction or capture in time of war. Adding this, you have a total expenditure of $580,996,400 a year; or $49,249,000 a month, and $1,642,485 a day, for the Army alone.

To this I add now the expenditures for the Navy. Having no means of actual knowledge of the amount, I apply the only or at least the next best test, the appropriations for the current fiscal year, amounting at the last three sessions of Congress to the sum of $101,778,762 30. Adding this to the Army expenditure, you have, as the aggregate, the sum of $682,775,162 30, being at the rate of $56,897,930 per month, and $1,896,598 per day for the entire year round. Sir, the gentleman from Massachusetts [Mr. Dawes] was right, except that, tried by his own standard, his "disloyalty" was a little more exaggerated than mine.

So much, sir, for the cost of the Army and the Navy.

But there is yet another army: the horde of *thieves and plunderers*, less numerous, it may be, but more formidable, more consuming far to the Treasury than the legions of the brave men who go forth baring their bosoms to the storm of battle. These are the cankers of troubled times and a fierce strife—

"A pitchy cloud
Of locusts warping on the *eastern* winds."

They are the "somebodies" who, with the aid of their official allies in high places, have, in the language of the gentleman from Massachusetts [Mr. Dawes], on the 25th of April last, in the days of his innocency and before his fall, "plundered the Treasury well nigh in that single year, the first year of a Republican Administration, of as much as the entire current yearly expenses of the Government during that Administration (Mr. Buchanan's) which the people hurled from power because of its corruption."

And there is yet another army, sir, to be paid and subsisted—an army more reputable certainly than your plunderers, but more in numbers also and not less devastating in their march. I mean the host of assessors and tax gatherers whom you are to-day enlisting to go forth into every dwelling-house, every business house, upon every farm, into every city, every town, every village, and every hamlet, into palace and hovel alike, throughout the land, carrying anxiety and dismay at every step.

And these constitute the very priesthood of that accursed Trinity of WAR, TAXATION, and EMANCIPATION, before whose cruel shrine the gentleman from Maine [Mr. Pike] bows down in idolatrous worship; a Trinity compared with which Juggernaut is merciful and the Ganges humane; a Trinity upon whose bloody and consuming altar the fairest country and the noblest structure of government the world ever saw is offered up day by day as a sacrifice.*

I proceed now, sir, to the question of the actual indebtedness and liabilities to-day. On the 4th of March, 1861, the public debt was $72,289,278 68. On the 28th of January, 1862, that debt, according to the statement of the Treasury Department, as produced here by the gentleman from New York [Mr. Spaulding], amounted to the sum of $306,764,613 34. On the 29th of May, 1862, according to the letter of the Secretary of Treasury, the debt was $491,445,984 11. Deducting the $90,867,828 68 of debt to July 1, 1861, there remains the sum of $400,578,155 43 as the amount of debt incurred during the present fiscal year up to May 29th. Thus, the increase from January 28, 1862, to that date—a period of three months—is shown, not by conjecture, but by the record, to have been $184,681,370 77, being at the rate of $61,560,456 a month, and $2,052,000 a day, or very nearly the exact sum estimated in January and February, in debate here and in the Senate, as the average daily expenditure.

And now, sir, as to the statement or letter of the Secretary of the Treasury, submitted on the 4th of June, as a sort of codicil to the speech of the gentleman from Massachusetts, I have a word to say. On the 8th of January I offered a resolution calling on the Secretary of the Treasury for a statement of the floating debt. It was adopted; and after three weeks incubation, he hatched out the following answer:

> "I transmitted without delay copies of this resolution to the heads of other Executive Departments, and required them to furnish me such statements as would enable me to furnish the information desired. As soon as the necessary information shall be received, the result will be transmitted to the House."

* "Our duty to-day is to tax and fight. Twin brothers of great power; to them in good time shall be added a third; and whether he shall be of Executive parentage, or generated in Congress, or spring, like Minerva, full grown from the head of our Army, I care not. Come he will, and his name shall be Emancipation. And these three—TAX, FIGHT, EMANCIPATE—shall be the TRINITY of our salvation. In this sign we shall conquer."—*Speech of Mr. Pike, of Maine, in the House of Representatives, Feb. 5, 1862: Congressional Globe, p.* 658.

Well, sir, inasmuch as the result has never been transmitted to this House, I have a right to assume that the necessary information has never been obtained. In that assumption I am fully sustained by the declaration of the Secretary of the Treasury, on the 31st of May—two days after this statement was made out—to the chairman of the Finance Committee in the Senate. I read from the official report of the debates in that body:

"Mr. FESSENDEN. The Secretary of the Treasury speaks simply of what appears on the books of his office. I know it from his own mouth, for I asked this question, 'How much is our indebtedness?' He gave me the amount. Said I, 'How much is the unliquidated floating debt?' He replied, '*How should I know? I have no means of telling.*'"

Such, sir, was the declaration of the Secretary of the Treasury, in reference to the floating debt as late as the last of May; and it is to be construed as a part of his letter to this House.

But this statement is not the public debt to July 1, 1862. Thirty-two days' expenditure must be added to it, which, at the rate of Army and Navy expenditures above, would make $60,791,000, or assuming the entire daily expenditure at $2,000,000 in round numbers, then $64,000,000, or an aggregate of $555,445,984 11.

Again, this statement purports to be what it is not—"the public debt" to May 29, 1862. It is only the funded and liquidated debt, that for which the Government has executed its paper in due form of law. It is that which, in the language of the Senator from Maine, appears on the books of the Treasury, and no more.

Again, it does not include what was in process of liquidation, which the Secretary of the Treasury estimated, as stated in the Senate by the Senator from New York [Mr. Harris], on the 31st of May, at $20,000,000.

Again, it does not include the floating and unliquidated debt, the amount of which the Secretary of the Treasury declared he did not know, and had no means of telling. Have we no means of conjecture? Let us see.

On the 28th day of January last, the gentleman from New York [Mr. Spaulding] said:

"There are now over one hundred million dollars of accrued indebtedness, in different forms, that should be paid at an early day."—*Congressional Globe*, p. 523.

On the 6th of February the chairman of the Committee of Ways and Means said:

"There is now a floating debt, audited and unaudited, of at least one hundred and eighty million dollars."

And the gentleman from New York [Mr. Roscoe Conkling], on the same day, estimated it at $200,000,000. I need here but barely to allude to the declaration of the Senator from Iowa, [Mr. Grimes,] on the 31st of May:

"That there was none of us who knew any thing about it, and that no man could compute it."

Sir, this floating or unliquidated debt is made up of all the liabilities or obligations of every kind against the Government, for which it has not executed its public Government paper in some form or other. It is in the nature of book account, but very much broader. And just here let me say that with quite as much fairness and honesty might some merchant doing an immense and widely extended business undertake, when charged with impending bankruptcy, to prove his solvency and show the amount of his indebtedness by producing a memorandum of promissory notes issued or bonds executed by him, as the Secretary of the Treasury to palm off upon the country a table or statement of the funded debt as a full or fair exhibit of the indebtedness and liabilities of the Government.

The floating debt includes the unsettled accounts for the pay and subsistence of the Army and Navy, for arms, ordnance, ammunition, military stores, medical stores, transportation, and whatever else enters into the province of the Paymaster-General or the Quartermaster-General. So, too, it includes all the unsettled accounts of the Navy Department—a Department having the care of a Navy of some fifteen hundred vessels, or more, from the largest and noblest steam frigate down to the humblest transport; one half, or more, of them hired at from fifty dollars to seven hundred and fifty dollars a day; and covering a sea and river coast of nearly four thousand miles in extent.

Sir, the Secretary does not pretend to include any part of these liabilities in his statement; and yet, in two months, for the Army and Navy alone, they would amount to $113,795,000. But if only the pay and subsistence accounts were in arrear, the amount would be $34,581,832. But the two months not included, were the months of March and April, in which a large part of the Army of the Mississippi valley was transported southward into Kentucky and Tennessee, and the entire Army of the Potomac was carried by an immense fleet of transports—and these are still in the service—from opposite Washington to the peninsula between the York and James Rivers. Now, it does seem to me that I fix a most moderate estimate—I should be glad, as a tax-payer and a citizen of the United States, to find that I have over-estimated it—when I assume the floating debt to be $140,000,000, or half way between the estimate in January of the gentleman from New York [Mr. Spaulding] and that of the chairman of the Committee of Ways and Means.

Again, the statement of the Secretary of the Treasury does not include the balance due to the States for advances. We have already appropriated $25,000,000 for that purpose, and accounts to the extent of $15,000,000 have been presented at the Treasury Department; and it is there estimated that the sum total will reach from twenty to twenty-five million dollars. Estimating it at $22,000,000, and deducting the $7,500,000 already paid, there remain $14,500,000 yet to be paid.

Again, it does not include bounties already due, and for the payment of which a bill appropriating $5,028,000 has passed this House, and is now in the Senate; nor does it include pensions already due, not less than $4,000,000 in amount.

Again, it does not include the unpaid interest on the public debt up to July 1, 1862, the amount of which I am only able to conjecture from the estimates of the Secretary of the Treasury, and the appropriations. Assuming these as tests, I place it at $14,000,000.

Again, it does not include the liability incurred by the passage of the Pacific railroad bill, estimated by the gentleman from Pennsylvania [Mr. Campbell] at $64,800,000. Nor does it include the liability assumed by the enlistment act of July 1861, for bounties, $56,700,000. These, indeed, are not yet payable; but the liability is absolute, and must continually increase with new enlistments.

Sir, I may say nothing here of the cost assumed by the pledge given by Congress and the Executive, to pay for the slaves of loyal citizens in the border slave States, equal, at the rate fixed for the District of Columbia, an average of $300 for each slave, to $1,000,000,000. I pass it wholly by in the reckoning, because, in my deliberate judgment the States and the people, North and South—for the West I speak confidently—will indignantly repudiate and rebuke both the pledge and its authors.

Again, this statement does not include claims for damages—actual, not speculative—for property of loyal citizens taken and destroyed by Federal authority. Of course it would be but the merest conjecture to estimate the amount, but assuming the lowest conceivable limit, I put it down at $50,000,000.

Again, it does not include the expenses of collecting the internal tax. By the act of August, 1861, the States that should assume the collection of the direct tax were allowed fifteen per cent. It would be fair, in my judgment, to set down the cost of collection, under the bill we have just passed, at twenty per cent.; but that I may allow no possible room for cavil, I estimate it at only ten per cent.; which, assuming the amount of tax collected under both tax bills to be

$113,925,000, the estimate of the gentleman from Vermont [Mr. Morrill] would give the sum of $11,392,000.

And now, sir, so far further as this statement is to be regarded, and for that purpose it was put forth as a test of expenditures, these items also must be added:

1. Receipts from customs, lands, and other ordinary sources, estimated by the Secretary of the Treasury, in December, at $36,809,731 24, but which he has shown in his letter of the 11th of June to this House, to have reached in the month of May the sum of $6,900,000, at the rate of $82,000,000 a year, or nearly $50,000,000 more than his estimate. I assume them to be $46,000,000.

2. The actual receipts of the Post-Office Department, which, if a statement made the other day by the Chairman of the Committee on the Post-Office and Post-Roads [Mr. Colfax] be correct, I may fairly set down at $8,000,000. To this also must be added, what I am unable to estimate, the amount of the direct tax which the States have already paid into the Treasury. Pennsylvania, I understand, has paid; so has Maryland; and Ohio also, in part at least.

I present now, sir, in conclusion, the following summary of debt, expenditure, and liabilities to July 1, 1862:

To May 29, 1862	$491,445,984 11
Add thirty-two days to July 1, at $2,000,000 a day	64,000,000 00
"In process of liquidation," May 29	20,000,000 00
Floating debt, deducting preceding item	120,000,000 00
Balance due the States for advances	14,500,000 00
Bounties already payable	5,028,000 00
Pensions already payable	4,000,000 00
Interest on public debt to July 1, 1862	14,000,000 00
Aggregate of certain and fixed items	732,473,984 11
Add for liability incurred by Pacific railroad bill	64,800,000 00
For bounties pledged by the enlistment act of July, 1861, but not yet payable	56,700,000 00
For expenses of collecting internal taxes	11,392,500 00
Total actual debt and absolute liabilities already accrued or assumed	865,366,484 11
Add liability for pensions to or on behalf of all who may be injured or die in battle or by sickness in the service—estimated	10,000,000 00
For contingencies and for claims for damages to loyal citizens for property taken or destroyed by authority of the United States	50,000,000 00
Total of actual and absolute and contingent liabilities	925,366,484 11
Deducting from this the debt to March 4, 1861	72,289,278 68
There remain	853,077,205 43

Add receipts from customs, lands, and other ordinary sources, from March 1, 1861, to July 1, 1862	$49,396,424 00
From Post Office Department within same period	10,087,324 00
Grand aggregate of actual debt and expenditures and absolute and contingent liabilities, chargeable to this Administration during the first fifteen months of its existence	$912,560,953 43

Being at the rate of for every month, $60,837,330.
For every day, $2,027,911.

And yet, according to the Senator from Iowa [Mr. Grimes], this is not the full amount by perhaps $100,000,000; and, indeed, is some six hundred million dollars less than his own actual but loose estimate

Such is the appalling exhibit of the debt, liability, and expenditures of this Government within the past fifteen months; and now, sir, I submit, in view of all these things, that it would have been decent and becoming in the gentlemen who have so lavishly bestowed their censure upon others, had they been content to expose error, if error there had been, without imputation, or unfairness and dishonesty, and, above all, without insinuations of disloyalty to the Government under which we were born, and to the preservation of which, unimpaired, just as we received it from our fathers, we are committed unalterably by every tie of birth, and kindred, and language, by every obligation of allegiance and of honor, and by every sentiment and sympathy of our hearts.

Sir, I put these facts and figures upon record for no present partisan purpose, but that they may remain and abide the test of the future, when conjecture shall have become certainty, and the Treasury Department have been obliged to yield up the secrets of its prison-house.

COLUMBUS DEMOCRATIC CONVENTION.

Speech before the Democratic State Convention, July 4, 1862.*

Mr. President and Fellow-Democrats of the State of Ohio: I am obliged again to regret that the lateness of the hour precludes me

* The Convention that met in Columbus, on the 4th of July, 1862, was one of the largest, most enthusiastic, and harmonious ever convened in Ohio. It assembled on the east side of the State House. Governor Medary was elected President. Its immediate object was to nominate candidates for State officers. These were soon agreed upon, in every case unanimously. A series of resolutions were then read and adopted, when loud and continued calls were made for Mr. Vallandigham, who, having ascended the platform, was greeted with rapturous applause. He spoke as above.

from addressing you either in the manner or upon the particular subjects which otherwise I should prefer. This is my misfortune again to-day, as last night; but speaking thus, without premeditation, and upon such matters chiefly as may occur to me at the moment, if I should happen to get fairly under headway, it may turn out to be your misfortune. (Laughter.) I congratulate the Democracy of Ohio, that, in the midst of great public trial and calamity, of persecution for devotion to the doctrines of the fathers who laid deep and strong the foundations of the Constitution and the Union under which this country has grown great and been prosperous,—the fathers, by whose principles, one and all, the party to which we are proud to belong has always been guided —to-day we have assembled in numbers greater than at any former convention in Ohio. I congratulate you that, despite the threats which have been uttered, and the denunciations which have been poured out upon that time-honored and most patriotic organization, peaceably and in quiet, with enthusiasm and earnestness of purpose, we are here met; and, in harmony, which is the secret of strength and the harbinger of success, have discharged the duties for which we were called together. There was a time when it was questionable if, in free America—in the United States, boasting of their liberties for more than eighty years—a party to which this country is indebted for most that is great, grand, and glorious—would have been permitted peaceably to assemble to exercise its political rights, and perform its appropriate functions. Threats have even been made, in times more recent, that this most essential of all political rights, secured to us by the precious blood of our fathers, in a seven years' revolutionary war, should no longer be enjoyed. The Democrats of our noble sister State of Indiana, second-born daughter of the Northwest, have been menaced, within the last ten days, with a military organization and the bayonet, to put down their party. I hold in my hand a telegraphic dispatch from the capital of that State, boasting of this infamous purpose. I will read it, gentlemen, because I know that the same dastardly menaces have been proclaimed against the Democrats of Ohio, and because I am here to-day to rebuke them, as becomes a freeborn man who is resolved to perish——(Great applause, in the midst of which the rest of the sentence was lost.)

Some months ago, a Democratic State Convention was held in Indiana. It was a Convention of the party founded by Thomas Jefferson, built up by Madison and Monroe, and consolidated by Andrew Jackson (applause)—a party under whose principles and policy, from thirteen States, we have grown to thirty-four, for thirty-four there were, true and loyal to this Union, before the Presidential election of 1860 —a party under whose wise and liberal policy the course of empire westward did take its way, until the symbol of American power—the stars and stripes—waved proudly from the Atlantic to the Pacific, over the breadth of a whole continent—a party which, by peace and compromise, and through harmony, wisdom, and sound policy, brought us up from feeble and impoverished colonies, struggling in the midst of defeat and disaster in the war of the Revolution, to a mighty empire, foremost among the powers of the earth, the foundations of whose greatness were laid, broad and firm, in that noble Constitution, and that grand old Union which the Democratic party has ever maintained and defended. The Democratic party, with such principles, and such a history and record to point to, held a State Convention, in pursuance of its usages for more than thirty years, and under the rights secured by a State and Federal Constitution, older still, in the capital of the State of Indiana. And yet, referring to this party and its Convention, the correspondent of a disloyal and pestilent, but influential newspaper, in the chief city of Ohio, dared to send over the telegraphic wires, wires wholly under the military control of the Administration, which permits nothing to be transmitted not acceptable to its censors, a dispatch in these words:

"The fellows are frightened, evidently not without cause."

Well, gentlemen, I know not how far Democrats of Indiana may be frightened—and a nobler and more fearless body of men never lived—but I see thousands of Democrats before me, to whom fear and reproach are alike unknown. Frightened at what? Frightened by whom? We are made of sterner stuff.

"The militia of the State," he adds, "will, probably, be put upon a war footing very shortly."

And who, I pray, are the militia of the State? They are not made up of the leaders of the Republican party in Indiana or Ohio, I know. I never knew that sort of politicians to go into any such organization, in peace or in war. No men have ever been more bitter and unrelenting in their opposition to, and ridicule of, the militia, and none know it better than I—as my friend before me, by his smile, reminds me, that one of my own offences is that I am a militia brigadier in favor of the next foreign war.

But who are the militia? They are the freeborn, strong-armed, stout-hearted Democrats of Indiana, as they are of Ohio. Let them be put on a war footing. Good! We have hosts of them in the army already, and on a war footing, but who are as sound Democrats and as much devoted to the principles of the party, as they were the hour they enlisted. They have been in the South, and I have the authority of hundreds of officers and privates in that gallant army for saying, that not only are the original Democrats in it more devoted to the party to-day than ever before, but that hundreds, also, who went hence Republicans, have returned, or will return, cured of the disease. (Laughter and applause.) Sir, the army is, fortunately, most fortunately for the country, turning out to be a sort of political hospital or sanitary institution, and I only regret that there are not many more Republican patients in it. (Laughter.)

Well, put the militia upon a war footing. Put arms in their hands. They never can be made the butchers or jailers of their fellow-citizens, but the guardians rather of free speech and a free press, and of the ballot-box. Standing armies of mercenaries, not the militia of a country, are the customary instruments of tyranny and usurpation.

But this correspondent proceeds:

"If the sympathizers with treason and traitors"—

We sympathize with treason and traitors! We, who have stood by the Constitution and the Union from the organization of the party, in our fathers' day, and in our own day, in every hour of trial, in peace and in war, in victory and in defeat, amid disaster, and when prosperity beamed upon us—we to be branded as enemies to our country, by those whose traitor fathers burned blue lights as signals for a foreign foe, or met in Hartford Convention to plot treason and disunion fifty years ago! We false to the Constitution and to our Government, the bones of whose fathers lie buried on every battle-field of the war of 1812, from the massacre at the River Raisin to the splendid victory at New Orleans; we, who bore aloft the proud banner of the Republic, and planted it in triumph upon the palace of the Montezumas; we, by whose wisdom in council, and courage in the field, for seventy years, the Constitution and the Union, and the country which has grown great under them, have been preserved and defended; we to be denounced as sympathizing with treason and traitors, by the men who, for twenty years, have labored day and night for the success of those principles and of that policy and that party which are now destroying the grandest Union, the noblest Constitution, and the fairest country, on the globe! Talk to me about sympathizing with disunion, with treason, and with traitors! I tell you, men of Ohio, that in six months, in three months, in six weeks it may be, sooner or later, but sometime, these very men, and their masters in Washington, whose bidding they do, will be the advocates of the eternal dissolution of this Union, and denounce all who oppose it as enemies to the peace of the country. Foreign intervention and the repeated and most serious disasters which have lately befallen our arms, will speedily force the issue of separation and Southern independence—*disunion*—or of Union by negotiation and compromise. Between these two I am—and I here publicly proclaim it—for the Union, the whole Union, and nothing less, if, by any possibility, I can have it; if not, then for so much of it as can yet be rescued and preserved; and in any event, and under all circumstances, for the Union which God ordained, of the Mississippi Valley, and all which may cling to it, under the old name, the old Constitution, and the old flag, with all their precious memories, with the battle-fields of the past, and the songs and the proud history of the past—with the birth-place and the burial-place of Washington the founder and Jackson the preserver of the Constitution as it is, and of the Union as it was. (Great applause).

But this correspondent again proceeds:

"If the sympathizers with treason and traitors meditate to carry out their plans in this quarter"—

What plans? Just such as to-day have been the business of this Convention; the plans of that old Union party, laying down a platform, and nominating Democrats to fill the offices, and control the policy of the government, to the end that the Constitution may be again maintained, the Union restored, and peace, prosperity, and happiness, once more drop healing from their wings—

"plans," the fellow proceeds, "in this quarter, they will, doubtless, find the work quite as hot as they bargained for."

And I tell the cowardly miscreant who telegraphed the threat, that he, and those behind him, will find the work fifty-fold hotter when they begin it, than they had reckoned on, both here and in Indiana.

"Ten thousand stand of arms," he adds, "have been ordered for the State troops."

For what? To put down the Democratic party? Sir, that is a work which cannot be done by ten, or twenty, or fifty thousand stand of arms in the hands of any such dastards, in office or out of it. If so full of valor, and so thirsty for blood, let them enlist under the call just issued for troops in Ohio and Indiana. Let them go down and fight the armies of the "rebels" in the South, and let Democrats fight the unarmed, but more insidious and dangerous, Abolition rebels of the North and West, through the ballot-box.

Forty thousand additional troops, I estimate it, are called for, in the proclamation of yesterday, from the State of Ohio. Where are the forty thousand Wide-Awakes of 1860, armed with their portable lamp-posts, and drilled to the music of the Chicago platform? Sir, I propose that thirty-five thousand of them be conscripted forthwith. They will never enlist; they never do. They are "Home Guards"—men who stay vigorously at home, to slander and abuse and threaten

Democrats, whose fathers or brothers or sons are in the Union armies, or have fallen in battle. I speak generally—certainly there are exceptions. But I will engage that if the records of the old Wide-Awake clubs, in the several cities and towns of Ohio, shall be produced, and the Republicans will detail or draft thirty-five thousand from the lists, I will find five thousand strong-armed, stout-hearted, brave and loyal Democrats, to go down and see that they don't run away at the first fire. (Great laughter.)

Sympathizers with treason and traitors! Secessionists! Sir, it is about time that we have heard the last of this. The Democracy of Ohio, and of the United States, are resolved that an end shall be put to this sort of slander and abuse. But I do not propose to discuss this particular subject further now. ("Go on, go on.")

Well, then, from that which concerns the Democratic party, to a word, a single word, about what relates to myself; and I beg pardon for the digression. I am rejoiced that it has been permitted to me to be here present, to-day, in person before you. Had you believed the reports of the Republican press, you would, no doubt, have expected to see, probably, the most extraordinary compound of leprous and unsightly flesh and blood ever exhibited. (Laughter.) Well, my friends, you see that I am not quite "monstrous," at least, bear no especial resemblance to the beast of the Apocalypse, either in heads or horns, but am a man of like fashion with yourselves. To the Republican party alone, and its press and its orators, I am indebted, no doubt, for a large part of the "curiosity" which, I am sorry to say, I seem to have excited, and which has brought out even some of them, as if to "see the elephant." They have never meant to be friendly toward me, I know; but as I see some of them now within my vision, let me whisper in their ears, that I never had better friends, and no man had, since the world began. They have advertised me free of cost, absolutely free of cost, for the last fifteen months; yes, I may say, for some five years past, all over the United States. Thus, gentlemen, I have had my share of what Jefferson called the unction, the holy oil, with which the Democratic priesthood has always been anointed—slander, detraction, and calumny, without stint. Really, I am not sure that with me it has not reached "extreme unction," though I am by no means ready, and do not mean to depart yet. Well, I will not complain. It has cost me not a single night's loss of sleep, from the beginning. My appetite, if you will pardon the reference—if you will allow me, as Lincoln would say, to "blab" upon so delicate a subject—has been in no degree impaired by it. Others before me, and with me, have endured the same. Here is my excellent friend near me (Governor Medary). O, blessed martyr! (Great applause.) For one-and-sixty years the storms of partisan persecution and malignity, in every form, have beaten upon his head; but though time and toil have made it gray, the heart beneath beats still, to-day, as sound and true to its instincts of Democracy and patriotism, and of humanity, too, as when he laid his first offerings upon the altar of his country, just forty years ago. What others have heroically suffered in ages past, we, too, can endure.

We are all, indeed, still in the midst of trials. Here, before me, is the gentleman of whom I have just spoken, whom you have honored with the presidency of this noble Convention, for forty years a Democratic editor—for forty years devoted to the Constitution and the Union of these States—a man who, through evil and through good report, has adhered, with the faith of a devotee and the firmness of a martyr, to the principles and policy of that grand old party of the Union; and now that the frosts of threescore years have descended and whitened his head—he, I say, has lived to see the paper, to which he gives the labor and the wisdom of his declining years, prohibited from circulation through a part of the mails as "disloyal" to the government! (Cries of "No, no, shame!") Samuel Medary disloyal! and Wendell Phillips a patriot! Sir, it is not many months since, that in the city of Washington, in that magnificent building, erected by the charity of an Englishman, who loved America—I would there were more like him—that art and science might the more widely flourish in this country—the Smithsonian Institute—Wendell Phillips addressed an assemblage of men as false to the Union and the Constitution as himself. Upon the platform was the Speaker of the House of Representatives, the third officer in the government; by his side the Vice-President of the United States; and between these two, in proportions long drawn out, the form of "Honest Old Abraham Lincoln." Am I mistaken, and was it at another and earlier abolition lecture by that other disunionist, Horace Greeley, in the same place—there have been many of them—that Lincoln attended? The Speaker and Vice-President, I know, were there; and with these two or three witnesses before him, and in presence of the priesthood of Abolitionism, the Sumners and Wilsons, the Lovejoys and the Wades of the House and Senate, surrounded by these, the very architects of disunion, he proclaimed that "for nineteen years he had labored to take nineteen States out of the Union." And yet, this most spotted traitor, pleading for disunion, in the City of Washington, where women are arrested for the wearing of red, white, and blue upon their bonnets, and babes of eighteen months are dragged from the little willow wagons, drawn by their nurses, because certain colors, called seditious, are found upon their swaddling-clothes! The next day, or soon after, this same Wendell

Phillips did dine with, or was otherwise entertained, by his Excellency, the President of the United States, who related to him one of his choicest anecdotes. Yet Democratic editors, Democratic Senators and Representatives, and those holding other official positions, by the grace of the States or of the people, are "traitors" forsooth, because they would adhere to the principles and organization of their noble and patriotic old party! Such are some of the exhibitions which Washington has witnessed during the past winter.

Congress, too, has been in session. Sir, I saw it announced in one of the disloyal papers of this city yesterday, that Jefferson Davis, and Toombs, and Yancey, and Rhett, and other secessionists of the South, would derive much comfort from this day's meeting. Well, sir, I have just come from a body of men which I would not, for a moment, pretend to compare for statesmanship, respectability, or patriotism, with this Convention. That body has devoted its time and attention to doing more, in six months, for the cause of secessionism, than Beauregard and Lee and Johnston and all the Southern generals combined have been able to accomplish in one year.

Its legislation has been almost wholly for the "Almighty African." From the prayer in the morning—for, gentlemen, we are a pious body, we are—making long faces, and sometimes wry faces, too (laughter),—we open with prayer, but there is not much of the Almighty Maker of heaven and earth in it—from the prayer to the motion to adjourn, it is negro in every shape and form in which he can, by any possibility, be served up. But it is not only the negro inside of the House and Senate, but, outside, also. The city of Washington has, within the past three weeks, been converted into one universal hospital; every church, except one for each denomination, has been seized for hospital purposes. But while the sanctuaries of the Ever-living God—the God of Abraham, Isaac, and Jacob—not the new god of the Burlingames and Sumners and other Abolitionists, not that god whose gospel is written in the new bible of Abolition—but the Ever-living Jehovah God, have been confiscated for hospitals, every theatre, every concert-saloon, every other place of amusement, from the highest to the lowest, from the spacious theatre in which a Forrest exhibits to an enraptured audience his graphic renderings of the immortal creations of Shakspeare, down to the basest den of revelry and drunkenness, is open still—just as in the Inferno of the great Italian poet, it is said—

"The gates of hell stand open night and day."

Sir, if these places of amusement—innocent some of them, but not holy, certainly—had first been seized as hospitals for the comfort and cure of the thousands of brave and honest men who went forth believing in their hearts that they were to battle for the Constitution and the

Union, but who now lie wasting away upon their lonely pallets, with no wife, or sister, or mother there to soothe, groaning in agony, with every description of wound which the devilish ingenuity of man can inflict by weapons whose invention would seem to have been inspired by the very spirit of the author of all human woe and suffering—wounds, too, rankling and festering for the want of surgical aid—if those places, I say, had first been seized, and then it had become necessary, for the comfort or life of the thousands of other sick and wounded who are borne into the city every day, to occupy the churches of Washington, I know of no better or holier purpose to which they could have been devoted. And now, sir, not far from that stately Capitol, within whose marble walls Abolition treason now runs riot, is a building, "Green's Row" by name, *rented by the Government*, in which one thousand one hundred fugitive slaves—"contrabands," in the precious slang of the infamous Butler—daily receive the rations of the soldier, which are paid for out of the taxes levied upon the people. One hundred thousand dollars a day are taken from the public treasury for the support of fugitive slaves there and elsewhere; while the army of Shields, and other Union armies in the field, even so late as six weeks ago, marched barefooted, bareheaded, and in their drawers, for many weary miles, without so much as a cracker or a crust of bread with which to allay their hunger. Ay, sir, while many a gallant young soldier of Ohio, just blooming into manhood, who heard the cry that went up fifteen months ago, "Rally to defend the flag, and for the rescue of the Capital," and went forth to battle, with honesty in his heart, his life in his hand, with courage in every fibre, and patriotism in every vein, lies wan and sad on his pallet in the hospital, your surgeons are forced to divide their time and care between the wounded soldiers and these vagabond fugitive slaves, who have been seduced or forced from the service of their masters. These things, and much more—I have told you not a tithe of all—are done in Washington. We know it there, though it is withheld from the people; and while every falsehood which the ingenuity of man can invent to delude and deceive, is transmitted or allowed by the telegraphic censors of the Administration—themselves usurpers unknown to the Constitution and laws—these facts are not permitted to reach the people of the United States.

Your newspapers, the natural watch-dogs of liberty, are threatened with suppression, if but the half or the hundredth part of the truth be told. And now, too, when but one other means remains for the redress of this and the hundred other political grievances under which the land groans—party organization and public assemblages of the people—even these, too, are threatened with suppression by armed force. Ay, sir, that very party, which, not many years ago, bore upon every banner the motto, "Free Speech and a Free Press," now, day by day, forbids the transmission through your mails of the papers from which you derive your knowledge of public events, and which advocate the principles you cherish. And Democratic editors, too, are seized, "kidnapped," in the midnight hour—torn from their families—gagged—their wives with officers over them menacing violence if they but ask one farewell grasp of the hand, one parting kiss—thrust into a close carriage, in the felon hour of midnight, and with violence dragged to this capital, and here forced upon an express train and hurried off to a military fortress of the United States. Yes, men of Ohio, to a fortress that bears the honored name of that first martyr to American liberty—the Warren of Bunker Hill; or, it may be, to that other Bastile, desecrating that other name sacred in American history, and honored throughout the earth—the name of that man who forsook home and gave up rank and title, and, in the first flush of youth and manhood, came to our shores and linked his fortunes with the American cause—the prisoner of Olmutz, the brave and gallant Lafayette. Ay, freemen of the West, fortresses bearing these honored names, and meant for the defence of the country against foreign foes, and out of whose casemates bristle cannon planted to hurl death and destruction at armed invaders, echo now with the groans and are watered by the tears—not of men only from States seceded and in rebellion, or captured in war, but from the loyal States of the North and the West, and from that party which has contributed nearly three-fourths of the soldiers in the field to-day. Are these things to be borne? ("Never; no, never.") If you have the spirit of freemen in you, bear them not! (Great applause, and cries of "That's it, that's the talk.") What is life worth? What are property and personal liberty and political liberty worth; of what value are all these things, if we, born of an ancestry of freemen, boasting, in the very first hours of our boyhood, of a more extended liberty than was ever vouchsafed to any other people, are to fail now in this the hour of sore trial, to demand and to defend them at every hazard? Freedom of the press! Is the man who sits in the White House at Washington, and who owes all his power to the press and the ballot, is he now to play the tyrant over us? ("No; never, never!") Shall the man who sits at one end of a telegraphic wire in the War Department, or the Department of State —a mere clerk, it may be, a servant of servants—sit down, and by one single click of the instrument, order some minion of his, a thousand miles off, to arrest Samuel Medary, or Judge Ranney, or Judge Thurman, and hurry them to a Bastile? ("No; it can't be done; we will never allow it.") The Constitution says: "No man shall be held to answer for crime except on due process of law." Our fathers, six hundred years ago, assembled upon the plains of Runnymede, in old England, and rescued from tyrant hands, by arms and firm resolve, the God-given right to be free. Our fathers, in the time of James I., and of Charles I., and James II., endured trial and persecution and loss of life and of liberty, rather than submit to oppression and wrong. John Hampden—glorious John Hampden! the first gentleman of England—arrested upon an illegal executive warrant—went calmly and heroically to the cells of a prison rather than pay twenty shillings of an illegally-assessed tax, laid in defiance of the Constitution and laws of England, and of the rights and privileges of Englishmen. And all history is full of like examples. William Tell brooked the tyrant's frown in his day and generation, in defence of these same rights, in the noble Republic of the Swiss; and that gallant little people, hemmed in among the Alps, though surrounded on every side by despots whose legions numbered more than the whole population of Switzerland, have, by that same indomitable spirit of freedom, maintained their rights, their liberties, and their independence, to this hour. And are Americans now to offer themselves up a servile sacrifice upon the altar of arbitrary power? Sir, I have misread the signs of the times, and the temper of the people, if there is not already a spirit in the land which is about to speak in thunder-tones to those who stretch forth still the strong arm of despotic power—"Thus far shalt thou come, and no farther. We made you; you are our servants." That, sir, was the language which I was taught to apply to men in office when I was a youth, or in first manhood and a private citizen, and afterward, when holding office as the gift of the people, to hear applied to me; and I bore the title proudly. And I asked then, as I ask now, no other or better reward than, "Well done, good and faithful servant." (Cries of "You shall have it; you deserve it.") But to-day, they who are our servants, creatures made out of nothing by the power of the people, whose little brief authority was breathed into their nostrils by the people, would now, forsooth, become the masters of the people; while the organs and instruments of the people—the press and public assemblages—are to be suppressed; and the Constitution, with its right of petition, and of due process of law, and trial by jury, and the laws, and all else which makes life worth possessing, are to be sacrificed now upon the tyrant's plea that it is necessary to save the Government, the Union. Sir, we did save the Union for years—yes, we did. We were the "Union-savers," not eighteen months ago. Then there was not an epithet in the whole vocabulary of political Billingsgate so opprobrious in the eyes of a Republican, when applied to the Democratic party, as "Union-shriekers," or "Union-savers." I remember, in my own city, on the day of the Presidential election, in 1860—I remember it well, for I had that day travelled several hundred miles to vote for Stephen A. Douglas for the Presidency—that, in a ward where the judges of election were all Democrats, your patriotic Wide-Awakes, strutting in unctuous uniform, came up, hour after hour, thrusting their Lincoln tickets twixt thumb and finger at the judges, with the taunt and sneer, "*Save the Union! save the Union!*" And yet now, forsooth, we are "traitors" and "secessionists!" And old gray-bearded and gray-headed men, who lived and voted in the times of Jefferson and Madison and Monroe and Jackson—men who have fought and bled upon the battle-field, and who fondly indulged the delusion, for forty years, that they were patriots, wake up suddenly to-day to find themselves "traitors!"—sneered at, reviled and insulted by striplings "whose fathers they would have disdained to have set with the dogs of their flocks." Of all these things an inquisition, searching and terrible, will yet be made, as sure and as sudden, too, it may be, as the day of judgment. We of the loyal States—we of the loyal party of the country, the Democratic party—we, the loyal citizens of the United States, the editors of loyal newspapers—we, who gather together in loyal assemblages, like this, and are addressed by truly loyal and Union men, as I know you are to-day and at this moment ("That's so; that's the truth")—we, forsooth, are to be now denied our privileges and our rights as Americans and as freemen; we are to be threatened with bayonets at the ballot-box, and bayonets to disperse Democratic meetings! Again I ask, why do they not take up their muskets and march to the South, and, like brave men, meet the embattled hosts of the confederates in open arms, instead of threatening, craven-like, to fight unarmed Democrats at home—possibly unarmed, and possibly not? (Laughter and applause, and a remark, "That was well put in.") If so belligerent, so eager to shed that last drop of blood, let them volunteer to re-enforce the broken and shattered columns of McClellan in front of Richmond, sacrificed as he has been by the devilish machinations of Abolition, and there mingle their blood with the blood of the thousands who have already perished on those fatal battle-fields. But no; the whistle of the bullet and the song of the shell are not the sort of music to fall pleasantly upon the ears of this Home-Guard Republican soldiery.

With reason, therefore, fellow-citizens, I congratulate you to-day upon the victory which you have achieved. A great poet has said:

"Peace hath her victories,
No less renowned than war."

To-day the cause of free government has triumphed. A victory of the Constitution, a victory of the Union has been won, but is yet to be made complete by the men who go forth from this, the first political battle-field of the campaign, bearing upon their banners that noble legend, that grand inscription, THE CONSTITUTION AS IT IS, AND THE UNION AS IT WAS. (Great cheering.) In that sign shall you conquer. Let it be inscribed upon every ballot, emblazoned upon every banner, flung abroad to every breeze, whispered in the zephyr, and thundered in the tempest, till its echoes shall rouse the fainting spirit of every patriot and freeman in the land. It is the creed of the truly loyal Democracy of the United States. In behalf of this great cause it is, that we are now, if need be, to do and to suffer, in political warfare, whatever may be demanded of freemen who know their rights, and knowing, dare maintain them. Is there any one man, in all this vast assemblage, afraid to meet all the responsibilities which an earnest and inexorable discharge of duty may require at his hands, in the canvass before us? ("No, no, not one.") If but one, let him go home, and hide his head for very shame:

"Who would be a traitor knave?
Who would fill a coward's grave?
Who so base as be a slave?
Let him turn and flee."

It is no contest of arms to which you are invited. Your fathers, your brothers, your sons, are already, by thousands and hundreds of thousands, on the battle-field. To-day their bones lie bleaching upon the soil of every Southern State, from South Carolina to Missouri. It is to another conflict, men of Ohio, that you are summoned, but a conflict, nevertheless, which will demand of you some portion, at least, of that same determined courage, that same unconquerable will, that same inexorable spirit of endurance, which make the hero upon the military battle-field. I have mistaken the temper of the men who are here today, I have misread the firm purpose that speaks in every eye, and beams from every countenance, which stiffens every sinew, and throbs in every breast; I have misread it all, if you are not resolved to go home, and there maintain, at all hazards, and by every sacrifice, the principles, the policy, and the organization of that party, to which again, and yet again, I declare unto you, this government and country are indebted for all that have made them grand, glorious, and great. (Cheers and great applause.)*

* Mr. Vallandigham's reception at Columbus was one of the proudest and most gratifying that could have been given. He arrived from Washington on the 3d, and about midnight, on that evening, a crowd surrounded his hotel, and called him out for a speech. And, again, on the evening of the 4th, another speech was demanded and given from the balcony of the hotel—three speeches within twenty hours.

STATE OF THE COUNTRY.

Speech delivered at Dayton, August 2, 1862.*

Mr. Vallandigham began by an allusion to the fact that he had arranged to be absent from the city, on a visit to an aged and very near relative, but that, meantime, false charges, and rumors also as to intended arrests, were started. My rule, said he, is always to meet such things a little more than half way. Conscious of rectitude, I mean, face to face with every foe and every danger, to do all, and to bear all, that may become a man; and, therefore, at much inconvenience, I have postponed my visit, and am here to-night, surrounded by thousands of such constituents and friends as no man ever had.

He then referred to the spring election, and its result in this city, upon a direct issue against himself, presented to and accepted by his friends—the triumphant election of the whole Democratic city ticket; and observed that the lesson to our enemies was a severe one, and that they ought to learn from it that there was such a thing as abusing a man so persistently, wantonly, and wickedly, as to make him immensely popular.

Mr. V. next gave a full and minute narrative of the infamous conspiracy just exploded, to procure his arrest as "implicated" with two clergymen from the "Border States," who had been guests at his house. Nothing had been found; both of them were promptly released, and the whole plot had failed. But those concerned in it, some of them "Christians," were known, and would be remembered. A telegraphic dispatch had been prepared by one of the conspirators, and

* The reign of terror was at its height, and the most serious apprehensions were entertained for the personal safety of Mr. Vallandigham, when he announced his determination to address the public in Dayton. As the hour for the meeting approached, the brave and true men of Montgomery and adjacent counties were seen coming in, until fully seven thousand were assembled on the south side of the Court-House. The men who had sworn that he should never again speak in Dayton, very wisely concluded that discretion was better than valor. Of this speech, Governor Medary, republishing it in *The Crisis*, said:

"It should be read by every voter in the United States. Nothing equal to it has been made during the past few years. Seldom has it ever been equalled for power, pathos, purity of diction, and truthfulness in point of facts. Elevated in tone, statesmanlike in conception, it thrills the reader as though fresh from a Roman Senate, in the hour of Rome's most terrible trials for freedom and existence. It should be read in every school-house, to the assembled people, before the elections on the second Tuesday of next October."

The above report is full in some parts, in others condensed.

sent off to the *New York Tribune*, from Dayton, though dated at Columbus, announcing his (Mr. V.'s) "arrest;" and it had never been contradicted to this day.* Democrats, said he, have never received any justice at the hand of the telegraph, and never will, till after the 4th of March, 1865, when, with every thing else, it will be in Democratic hands. The Republican party are teaching us many things, and may find us apt scholars, possibly improving on their lessons, if they shall finally succeed in overthrowing all constitution, law and order. But I trust that it will never come to this.

I am for obedience to all laws and constitutions. No man can be a good democrat who is not in favor of law and order. No matter how distasteful constitutions and laws may be, they must be obeyed. I am opposed to all mobs, and opposed also—inexorably opposed, above every thing—to all violations of constitution and law by men in authority—public servants. The danger from usurpations and violations by them is fifty-fold greater than from any other quarter, because these violations and usurpations come clothed with the false semblance of authority. Those parts of our constitutions and laws which command or restrain the people must be obeyed; but still more must those also which limit and restrain public servants, from the President down. There are rights of the people, to secure which constitutions were ordained, and they must and will be exacted at all hazards; and among the most sacred of these rights, are free speech, a free press, public assemblages, political liberty, and, above all, or at least at the foundation of all, PERSONAL LIBERTY, or freedom from illegal and arbitrary arrests. It was a right, secured in Greece, while she was free, and in Rome in her purer days. But it is peculiarly an Anglo-Saxon right; and it has cost more struggles in England to hold it fast than any other. The right is declared, in the strongest language, in the GREAT CHARTER, in the time of King John, six hundred years ago. Here is the pledge wrung from the tyrant by men, few of whom could read or write, but who were resolved to be free:

> "No freeman shall be arrested, or imprisoned, or disseized (of property), or outlawed, or banished, *or any ways injured*, nor will we pass sentence upon him, nor send trial upon him, UNLESS BY THE LEGAL JUDGMENT OF HIS PEERS, OR BY THE LAW OF THE LAND."

This is the "keystone of English liberty," the pride and boast of every Englishman. The violation of it cost one English monarch his head, another his crown, and a third his most valuable colonies; and to-day, if Queen Victoria were to attempt to suspend it by telegraph,

* A full account of the transaction here referred to, was published in the *Dayton Empire*, Aug. 5, 1862.

or by executive order, or order of privy council in any way, she would be a refugee in a foreign land before a fortnight.

Eighty years later, this sacred and invaluable right to be free from arrest, except by law, was confirmed; and in 1627, by the celebrated Petition of Right, drawn up by that great lawyer, Lord Coke, was again confirmed and extended, as follows:

> "No man, *of what estate or condition that he be*, shall be put out of his land, or tenements, nor *arrested, nor imprisoned*, nor disinherited, nor put to death, without being brought to answer BY DUE PROCESS OF LAW."

And it was further provided that no commissioner should be appointed to try any one by "martial law," who was not in the army, "lest by color of them, any of his Majesty's subjects be destroyed, or put to death, contrary to the laws and franchises of the land."

Next came the Habeas Corpus Act of 1679, to secure the rights asserted by the Great Charter and its confirmations, a statute by virtue of which, says Lord Campbell—and with shame I confess now to the justice of the proud boast—"Personal liberty has been more effectually guarded in England than it has in any country in the world."

Next after this came the Bill of Rights of 1689, enacted by the profoundest statesmen and wisest patriots which England ever had. These great and brave men, after that, by arms, they had driven James II. from the throne, for his repeated violations of the rights of Englishmen, declared that he had been guilty of an attempt to subvert the laws and liberties of the kingdom; among other things—

> "1. By assuming and exercising a power of dispensing with and *suspending of laws* and the execution of laws, *without consent of Parliament.*
>
> "2. By committing and prosecuting divers worthy prelates, for humbly petitioning to be excused from concurring to the said assumed power.
>
> "7. By violating the freedom of election of members to serve in Parliament.
>
> "All which," say they, "are utterly and directly contrary to the known laws and statutes and freedom of this realm."

These, sir, are the "liberties of Englishmen." They are the liberties which were brought over by our ancestors from England, and embodied in all our constitutions and laws. In 1641, twenty years after the first settlement of Massachusetts, that infant colony declared, in her "Body of Liberties," that

> "No man's life shall be taken away, no man's honor or good name shall be stained, *no man's person shall be arrested*, restrained, banished, dismembered, nor any ways punished, no man shall be deprived of his wife or children, no man's goods or estate shall be taken away from him, nor any way endamaged under color of law or countenance of authority, unless it be by virtue or equity of some express law of the country, warranting the same, etc.

"No man's person shall be restrained or imprisoned *by any authority whatsoever*, before the law hath sentenced him thereto, if he can put in sufficient security, bail, or mainprise," etc.

So, also, in the Declaration of Independence, July 4th, 1776, among the many grievances set forth against the king, are the following:

"He has affected to render the military independent of, and superior to, the civil power:

"For depriving us, in many cases, of the benefits of trial by jury:

"For transporting us beyond seas to be tried for pretended offences."

In the Virginia "Bill of Rights" of 1776, written also by Jefferson, it is declared that—

"All power is vested in, and consequently derived from, the people; that magistrates are their trustees and servants, and *at all times* amenable to them.

"All power of suspending laws, or the execution of laws, by any authority, *without consent of the representatives of the people*, is injurious to their rights, and ought not to be exercised.

"*In all cases* the military should be under strict subordination to, and governed by, the civil power.

"Freedom of the press is one of the great bulwarks of liberty, and can never be restrained but by despotic governments."

And yet again; in the "Declaration of Rights" of Massachusetts, in 1780, it is laid down that—

"No person shall be held to answer for any crime or offence, until the same is fully and plainly, substantially and formally, described to him. And *no person shall be arrested, imprisoned*, or despoiled, or deprived of his property, immunities, or privileges, put out of the protection of the law, exiled or deprived of his life, liberty, or estate, *but by the judgment of his peers, or the law of the land.*

"Every person has a right to be secure from all unreasonable searches and seizures of his person, his houses, his papers, and all his possessions.

"The liberty of the press is essential to the security of freedom in a State.

"The people have a right to keep and bear arms for the common defence. The military power shall *always* be held in *exact subordination* to the civil authority, and be governed by it.

"The people have a right, in an orderly and peaceable manner, to assemble, to consult upon the common good.

"The power of suspending the laws ought never to be exercised *but by the Legislature*, or by authority derived from it, to be exercised in *such particular cases only* as the Legislature shall expressly provide for.

"No person can, *in any case*, be subjected to *law martial*, or to any penalties or pains, by virtue of that law (except those employed in the army or navy, and except the militia in actual service), *but by authority of the Legislature.*"

Such were the liberties of Americans in the Revolutionary period of our history, and before it; and they have been embodied in all our constitutions ever since.

Let the present Constitution of Ohio speak. In our "Bill of Rights" we declare that—

"All political power is inherent in the people.

"The people have the right to assemble together in a peaceable manner, to consult for their common good; to instruct their representatives, and to petition the General Assembly for the redress of grievances.

"The people have the right to bear arms for their defence and security. The military shall be in *strict subordination* to the civil power.

"The privilege of the writ of *habeas corpus* shall not be suspended, unless, in cases of rebellion or invasion, the public safety require it. No power of suspending laws shall ever be exercised *except by the General Assembly.*

"In any trial in any court, the party accused shall be allowed *a speedy public trial*, by an impartial jury of the county or district in which the offence is alleged to have been committed.

"Every citizen may freely speak, write, and publish his sentiments *on all subjects*, being responsible for the abuse of the right; and no law shall be passed to abridge the liberty of speech or of the press.

"The right of the people to be secure in their persons, houses, papers, and possessions, against unreasonable searches and seizures, shall not be violated.

"All courts shall be open, and justice administered without denial or delay."

Similar provisions exist in every State constitution in the United States, thus securing every citizen from State tyranny and oppression. Nor is the Federal Constitution less ample and explicit. Hear it:

"All legislative powers herein granted shall be vested in a Congress of the United States."

"The privilege of the writ of *habeas corpus* shall not be suspended, unless when, in cases of rebellion or invasion, the public safety require it."

Now, sir, from the beginning of the Government down to the year 1861, no lawyer, no jurist, no statesman, no writer upon the Constitution, ever pretended that the President, or any other authority, could suspend the privilege of this writ, except Congress alone.

But I read further:

"The judicial power shall extend to *all cases* in law and equity arising under this Constitution, the laws of the United States, and treaties made, or which shall be made, under their authority.

"The trial of all crimes, except in cases of impeachment, shall be by jury, and such trial shall be held in the State where the said crimes shall have been committed.

"Treason against the United States shall consist only in levying war against them, or in adhering to their enemies, giving them aid and comfort. No person shall be convicted of treason unless on the testimony of two witnesses to the same *overt act*, or on confession in open court.

"Congress shall make no law respecting an establishment of religion, or prohibiting the free exercise thereof; or abridging the freedom of speech, or of the press; or the right of the people peaceably to assemble, and to petition the government for a redress of grievances.

"The right of the people to keep and bear arms shall not be infringed.

"The right of the people to be secure in their persons, houses, papers, and effects, against unreasonable searches and seizures, shall not be violated; and no warrant shall issue but upon probable cause, supported by oath or affirmation, and particularly describing the place to be searched, and the persons and things to be seized.

"No person shall be held to answer for a capital or otherwise infamous crime, unless on a presentment or indictment of a grand jury, except in cases arising in the land and naval forces, or in the militia, when in actual service, in time of war and public danger; NOR SHALL BE DEPRIVED OF LIFE, LIBERTY, OR PROPERTY, WITHOUT DUE PROCESS OF LAW; nor shall private property be taken for public use without just compensation.

"In all criminal prosecutions, the accused shall enjoy the right to a speedy and public trial by an impartial jury of the State and district wherein the crime shall have been committed, which district shall have been previously ascertained by law; and to be informed of the nature and cause of the accusation; to be confronted with the witnesses against him; to have compulsory process for obtaining witnesses in his favor, and to have the assistance of counsel for his defence.

"The powers not delegated to the United States by the Constitution, nor prohibited by it to the States, are reserved to the States respectively, or to the people."

These, thus repeated and multiplied over and over again, are the Magna Charta of American freemen. They constitute the *Body of American Liberties*. They cost much blood and treasure, and are worth the most precious treasure and blood of the whole country. Let them be maintained at every hazard and sacrifice. They are dearer in time of war and public danger, than in time of peace. They are secured by the Constitution, and can only be forfeited in accordance with the Constitution. I abhor and denounce the monstrous doctrine, so rife of late, that the Constitution is suspended in time of war; or that the powers under it are enlarged; or, at least, that there is a "war power" above and greater than the Constitution. Sir, that instrument was made for war as well as peace. It expressly gives to Congress the right to declare war, raise armies, provide navies, and call out the militia to execute the laws, suppress insurrection, put down rebellion, and repel invasion. Every power, the very utmost necessary and proper for carrying on any war, foreign or domestic, is explicitly given. The "tyrant's plea" of *necessity* is false. No power that ought to be exercised is withheld, and every usurpation is utterly without excuse. Whoever maintains that the framers of the Constitution failed to make it good enough and strong enough for any crisis—for war and for peace—libels Washington and Madison and Hamilton, and the other patriots of '87. And the man who denounces "sticklers" for the Constitution, and declares that he can tell a "traitor" by his crying out for the Constitution, is himself a traitor or a fool. Keep an eye on him.

We have no hope for ourselves, or our children, except in the Constitution. The President, more than any other man, is bound to obey it. He takes a solemn oath to support it. It is his duty to act according to law. Among the personal rights under the Constitution is that of *habeas corpus.* The uniform testimony of courts and statesmen is that it can be suspended only by Congress. If the President can suspend it, it can only be by proclamation, declaring where, and for how long it is suspended. He has no right to send a dispatch for the arrest of any citizen of the United States, and to say that, by that act, his minions are authorized to suspend the writ. Better to live in Austria, in Turkey, or under any other admitted despotism, than where the President, the servant of the people, shall seize, without "due process of law," and carry off to prison any citizen under the pretence of treason.

These guarantees were not in the original Constitution, but demanded by the States and the people, and added afterwards. They were added for fear some President might be elected who would claim to have the power, if not expressly withheld by the Constitution. What are they? Freedom of speech, of the press, peaceable assemblages, the right to keep and bear arms, freedom from illegal arrest. Yet you have been told that we shall not be allowed to enjoy these rights—that "executive orders" shall be issued against us—that men who represent the voice of the people shall not be heard—that the press shall be muzzled, and men's mouths gagged, and no censure or criticism of the acts of the President, or of the officials under him, shall be permitted, under penalty of arrest and imprisonment; and, thus, that our personal and political liberties shall be disregarded, and the Constitution trampled under foot.

Well, sir, we shall see about it. "No person shall be deprived of life, liberty, or property, without *due process of law.*" Every civil officer knows what "due process of law" is, and, when armed with such due process, it is the duty of every person to obey. But whoever comes with any other papers, or any pretence of authority, by telegraphic dispatch, or otherwise, from the Secretary of War, Commander-in-Chief, or President, deserves to be met as a burglar. It is a desecration of the citizen. There is a statute against it. Let such persons be met by the law. Every house is a castle, the poor man's cottage as well as the rich man's palace, in which he may defy arbitrary power. Such is the law in England. In the language of Lord Chatham, in that noblest outburst of English eloquence, "The poorest man in his cottage may bid defiance to all the forces of the Crown. It may be frail; its roof may shake; the wind may blow through it; the storm may enter; the rain may enter; *but the King of England cannot enter it.* All his power dares not cross the threshold of that ruined tenement." (Tremendous cheering.)

This right is equally sacred and secured to us here in America, and we will never yield it up, least of all to our own public servants. The sooner it is made known to this Administration that the people who created it, and put it in power, will maintain their rights, the less trouble there will be. I but repeat the declaration of the two hundred thousand Democratic voters of Ohio—fifty thousand of them in the army from this State—that freedom cannot be violated by the Administration. Hear the resolution of that Democracy, in State Convention assembled, on the 4th of July last:

"That we view with indignation and alarm the illegal and unconstitutional seizure and imprisonment, for alleged political offences, of our citizens, without judicial process, in States where such process was unobstructed, but by executive order, by telegraph, or otherwise; and call upon all who uphold the Union, the Constitution, and the laws, to unite with us in denouncing and repelling such flagrant violation of the State and Federal Constitutions and tyrannical infraction of the rights and liberties of American citizens; and that the people of this State CANNOT SAFELY, AND WILL NOT SUBMIT to have the freedom of speech and the freedom of the press, the two great essential bulwarks of civil liberty, put down by unwarranted and despotic exertion of power."

Sir, the men who urge on these violations know not what they do. The title to your lands, to your personal property, the legal right to all you have, rests in obedience to constitution and laws. Let this terrible truth be proclaimed everywhere, that whenever, either through infraction and usurpation by the President, or by violence, the Constitution is no longer of binding force and the highest rule of action, then we are at the mercy of mere power, military power at last. This is despotism, absolute, unmixed, cruel despotism—a despotism enforcing its orders to-day by arbitrary imprisonments, and to-morrow by bloody executions. Let all men who love the peace, good order, and happiness of society, who desire that the rights of all classes, and that rights of all kinds shall be maintained, lift up their voices against the arbitrary and unconstitutional acts of the party in power. Men of the Republican party, it is your day now: to-morrow, it may be, it will be ours. Be warned in time. Stand by the Constitution—by law and order. Do nothing by usurpation or violence. It must react—it will react—and there is no raging flood, no mountain torrent, neither the whirlwind, the surging ocean, nor the avalanche, like the madness of an oppressed and outraged people. Do men, who are inciting to mobs and acts of violence, or applauding usurpation and infraction of Constitution and law, not know that they are those who suffer most and worst in the end? Do they imagine that they whose nights, sacred, by God's appointment, to silence and rest, have been invaded without process of law, and their wives and children terror-stricken by arbitrary arrests of husbands and fathers—editors and public men of the loyal States, who have languished, for opinion's sake, within Bastiles for months—will have no day of reckoning for all these enormities? Sir, that great reaction has set in; it hastens on. Oh, that you may allow it to be under the Constitution and according to law—but come it will; and be assured—be assured—that when that great day of account does come, BY THE MEASURE YOU HAVE METED OUT TO US, BY THAT MEASURE SHALL IT BE METED OUT TO YOU AGAIN. Remember, remember, that wrongs like these burn deep into the innermost recesses of our souls, steeling them against atonement and mercy; and that when the inevitable change which already is hurrying on upon the wings of the wind, shall have arrived, that same power, by virtue of which you imprison us, will be in our hands. Be warned in time. All history has been written in vain, if our day does not come, and come right speedily:

"For time at last sets all things even—
And if we do but watch the hour,
There never yet was human power
Which could evade, if unforgiven,
The patient search and vigil long
Of him who treasures up a wrong."

I speak it not as a menace, but by way of entreaty, that your hereafter in this life depends upon your adherence to the laws and Constitution. And yet I am amazed to learn that men of wealth and position in this city—lawyers, clergy, merchants, and others—are proclaiming that those in authority have a right to disobey the Constitution and laws, and ought to disobey them, to secure objects which cannot be had without disregarding all law and the personal and political rights of the citizen. Do these men know what they do? Have they read history?

Mr. VALLANDIGHAM here referred, at length, to Greece, Rome, England, and the French Revolution, for historic parallels, reading from the 10th and 14th chapters of Allison's History of Europe. He quoted the "Law of Suspected Persons," under which all France was divided into twelve classes liable to arrest; among them the following:

"1. All those who, in the assemblies of the people, discourage their enthusiasm by cries, menaces, or *crafty discourses.* 2. All those who more prudently speak only of the misfortunes of the Republic, and are always ready to spread bad news with an affected air of sorrow. 3. All those who have changed their conduct and language according to the course of events, who were mute on the crimes of the Royalists, and loudly exclaimed against the slight faults of the Republicans. 10. Those who speak with contempt of the constituted authorities, the ensigns of the law, the popular societies, or the 'defenders of liberty,'" etc.

Having read these passages, Mr. VALLANDIGHAM proceeded:

Sir, fifty thousand "Revolutionary Committees" sprang up in France to execute this terrible decree. They numbered five hundred and forty thousand members, each one a special marshal or policeman to enforce it; and in a few weeks seven hundred thousand citizens were suspected of "disloyalty." The prisons were speedily loaded with victims in every part of France. "Let them quake in their cells," said Collot d'Herbois, in the Convention; "let the base traitors tremble at the successes of our enemies; let a mine be dug under their prisons, and at the approach of those whom they call their liberators, let a spark blow them into the air."

Mr. VALLANDIGHAM then read a passage concluding as follows:

"Night came, but with it no diminution of the anxiety of the people. Every family early assembled its members; with trembling looks they gazed round the room, fearful that the very walls might harbor traitors. The sound of a foot, the stroke of a hammer, a voice in the streets, froze all hearts with horror. If a knock was heard at the door, every one, in agonized suspense, expected his fate. Unable to endure such protracted misery, numbers committed suicide."

Sir, all of these enormities sprang first from a disregard of law and right in little things, or in violations declared to be "necessary;" and advanced step by step, till they culminated in the bloody and accumulated atrocities of Marât, Danton, and Robespierre, when, by execution or massacre, tens of thousands perished. All history is but a repetition of itself; and what has been, may be. You of the Republican party did not believe me, two years and more ago, when I foretold that Abolition and sectionalism must and would produce civil war. And you do not believe me now. Neither did the antediluvians believe Noah; but the Flood came.

It is the history of the past, that, in times of great public danger, the provisions of the law will not be respected. It was that which made France go into such great excesses. They began with the savans and lawyers of France, who taught the multitude that constitutions and laws and personal rights did not stand in their way; and that men might be imprisoned or put to death without process of law. In such cases, power falls always, at last, into the hands of the worst of men.

Let the day of reckoning come, and these men will perish as they have done in all ages. Robespierre died horribly in atonement for his crimes; and, as the axe fell upon his neck, a woman exclaimed in tones of terrible exultation: "Murderer of my kindred, your agony fills me with joy; descend to hell, covered with the curses of every mother in France!"

Sir, by the memories of the past, by the history of the tyrannies of Greece and Rome, and the terrors of the French Revolution, I call on all men to demand of the Administration that it obey the Constitution. If any man be a traitor, guilty of any act of treason—not for opinion's sake, not for political differences—let him be proceeded against according to law, and, if guilty, let him perish on a gallows as high as Haman's. It is because I would avoid these horrors that I call on the President to keep the exercise of the military law where the Constitution keeps it, in the army and navy—and to see to it that no man, not in the army and navy, shall be arrested without "due process of law."

Hear the Constitution again: "No person shall be deprived of life, liberty, or property, without due process of law." "The accused shall enjoy the right to a speedy and public trial by an impartial jury." Was this, was either of these rights "enjoyed" by Flanders, of Malone, in New York, a Democratic editor, who was dragged from his family, imprisoned for months, and then released without charge against him, and without redress for the wrong? Were they enjoyed by James A. McMaster? Were they not flagrantly violated in the person of James W. Wall, the honored son of a patriot Senator of New Jersey? Have they been allowed to any one arrested by "Executive order?" Sir, this Administration has no constitutional or legal authority to make these arrests. I have as good a right to arrest the President, or any one of his Cabinet, as he or they have to arrest me or any other citizen in this manner. The Constitution is broad enough and strong enough for any emergency. It points out the mode of arrest and trial wherever there is actual or suspected guilt. Let it be obeyed. I, too, have sworn to support that Constitution; and, more than that, *I have done it.* I demand that all men, from the humblest citizen up to the President, shall be made to obey it likewise. In no other way can we have liberty, order, security. I was born a freeman. I shall die a freeman. It is appointed to all men once to die; and death never comes too soon to one in the discharge of his duty. I have chosen my course—have pursued it—have adhered to it to this hour, and will to the end, regardless of consequences. My opinions are immovable; fire cannot melt them out of me. I scorn the mob. I defy arbitrary power. I may be imprisoned for opinion's sake—never for crime; never because false to the country of my birth, or disloyal to the Constitution which I worship. Other patriots, in other ages, have suffered before me. I may die for the cause; be it so; but the "immortal fire shall outlast the humble organ which conveys it, and the breath of liberty, like the word of the holy man, will not die with the prophet, but survive him." (Loud cheers).

And, meantime, men of Dayton, the opinions which I entertain, the deep convictions that control me in that course which, before Almighty God, I believe can alone maintain the Constitution and restore the Union as our fathers made it, I never, never will yield up. Neither height, nor depth, neither death nor life, nor principalities, nor powers, nor things present, nor things to come—no, nor the knife of the assassin, shall move me from my firm purpose. (Great and long-continued cheering).

The President professes to think that the Union can be restored by arms. I do not. A Union founded on consent can never be cemented by force. This is the testimony of the Fathers. It was his own. He said in his Inaugural, but sixteen months ago:

> "Suppose you go to war, you cannot fight always; and when, after *much loss on both sides, and no gain on either*, you cease fighting, the old identical questions as to terms of intercourse are upon you."

I agree with him in that. But now we are in the midst of war, and they who really think that war will maintain the Constitution and restore the Union, ought to fight. I am for the Union in any event. It is an impelling necessity, it is manifest destiny, certainly in the Valley of the Mississippi, that we be one people. We never can fulfil the Great Mission appointed for us without it. But, under Providence, it can only be brought about through the wisdom, courage, and integrity of the people.

At a late "war meeting," so-called, in this city, it was charged by an ex-Governor of the State, of "tin-cup" memory, that I proposed to divide this country into four confederacies or republics. It is false, and he knew it. I proposed only to divide the Senate into four divisions, and to change the mode of electing the President. And this I did in order to preserve, not to destroy the Union. And still my heart's desire and prayer is to see it restored just as our fathers made it.

And now, men of Montgomery, I have somewhat to say upon what Mr. Lincoln, in his late proclamation, has most justly and truly called, "this unnecessary and injurious CIVIL WAR." I am for suppressing rebellion—I am. I always have been. Perhaps my mode is not that of other men; but I have the right—and mean to exercise it still—of judging for myself of the true and proper mode. I think mine would have prevented it at first; and even after it began, would have ended it long since. It must, it will be tried at last, if ever any thing is to be accomplished. But I have had no power to try it. They who have the power have determined upon another way—with what success, judge ye—and, like a good citizen, I resist not, but stand by to see the result of the experiment. If it is successful in maintaining the Constitution and restoring the Union, I will make full, open, explicit confession that I was wrong, utterly, totally wrong, and will retire to private life the residue of my days. But if it fail—let the people judge then between me and my accusers.

I repeat it: I am for suppressing all rebellion—both rebellions. There are two—the Secession Rebellion South, and the Abolition Rebellion North and West. I am against both; for putting down both.

Since you have resolved that there shall be war, I commit the armed Rebellion South, to the soldiers of the Army, three-fourths of them Democrats, young Democrats. I commit it to Halleck and Buel, and Morgan, and others, and to that abused, persecuted, outraged general and patriot, George B. McClellan. (Great cheering). If he cannot do it, it is because, in the nature of things, it is not possible that it be done in that way. The plan proposed by him was the only one which even so much as promised success. And it implied a restoration of the Union as it was, and, meantime, the maintenance of the Constitution as it is. That is the reason why he has been so persecuted by abolition rebels and disunionists. But it is the proud boast of himself and his friends, that in spite of all their abuse and calumny, he has calmly and steadfastly pursued his policy. All our victories were the result of that policy; all our reverses followed his supersession. From that hour to this, these has been no victory. Defeat has not lost him the confidence of the people. He has the devoted and enthusiastic affection of his soldiers; and he has the calmness, the firmness, and the unshaken consistency and persistency of purpose which will enable him to triumph in the end, at least, over his enemies at home. To him, therefore, and to the Army, I commit the Secession Rebellion of the South. I waste no breath in idle denunciation of an enemy a thousand miles off. Cursing will not put down men in arms, else there would have been an end to this armed rebellion long ago. As Governor Richardson suggested in Congress, the Jericho of Secession is not to be thrown down by the blowing of Abolition horns. Whoever among the Abolitionists would curse Secession, let him enlist, and then he will show his faith by his works, and your armies will be full in a week. Let every man who would invite others to go, first go himself. I have never interfered with enlistments. While the war lasts, our armies, for many reasons, must not be disbanded; so I said in Congress more than a year ago. Without enlistments they cannot be kept up; and if any man, subject to military duty, really thinks that the Union can be restored by force and arms, and only in that way, let him enlist; it is his duty to enlist; he is "disloyal" if he does not enlist. (Cries of "Good, good; that's the talk.") Whoever shall be drafted, should a draft be ordered according to Constitution and law, is in duty bound, no matter what he thinks of the war, to either go, or find a substitute, or pay the fine which the law imposes; he has no right to resist, and none to run away.

I have said that, in my deliberate and solemn judgment, war cannot restore the Union, but, if continued long enough, must destroy it; and, it may be, our own liberties also. "War," said Douglas, "is disunion; war is final, eternal separation." The Administration do not seem to think so. The country, just now, does not think so. Mr. Lincoln says, that war is the right way to restore the Union. I think there is another, a better, the only way to do it. He has the power to try his; I have not. War is upon us; and from the beginning, believing as I did, and yet powerless for good, I laid down the rule for myself, and have faithfully adhered to it, and will to the end, neither to vote for or against any purely war measure of the Administration. Wherever I have voted upon any question, my course has been governed by other considerations than those having reference to my opinions on the war. Accordingly, I have not voted for any army bill, or navy bill, or army or navy appropriation bill, since the meeting of Congress on the 4th of July, 1861. Neither have I voted against any such bill from the beginning. I appeal to the *Globe*, and to the Journals of the House, for the proof. These facts I refer to, because you are my constituents, and have a right to know them. One thing, however, we all must demand of the Administration: that the war be conducted according to the Constitution, and for a constitutional purpose.

But, men of Dayton, there is another and different, yet most desperate rebellion to be dealt with—the ABOLITION REBELLION of the North and West. It, too, must be put down; speedily and firmly put down, if we would save the country. In my judgment, you will never suppress the armed Secession Rebellion till you have crushed under foot the pestilent Abolition Rebellion first. Ask the officers and soldiers of the army, and they will tell you the same thing. A Representative, and exempt, therefore, from military service, I believe it my duty to stay at home and fight the Abolition rebels of the North and West. In the exercise of my constitutional rights, which cannot, and shall not be taken away, I propose to do my part toward putting down this, the earliest and most desperate and malignant rebellion. It must be met by reason and appeals to the people, through the press and in public assemblages, and be put down at the ballot-box. But if the overt rebellion in Wisconsin and in Ohio, at Urbana, in 1857, and Cleveland, in 1859 (the one at Urbana an armed rebellion), had been promptly and severely punished as they ought to have been, we never would have had any other.

Here Mr. V. traced briefly the history of the slavery question from the beginning to the present day. In 1787, it had been settled by the compromises of the Constitution, and all had been peace, quiet, and prosperity, till the terrible "Missouri Question," which struck upon the ear of Jefferson "like a fire-bell in the night." That had been settled by COMPROMISE, and we had quiet and peace again for fifteen years, till the systematic and organized anti-slavery agitation began, in 1835, at which time it was so bitterly denounced by President Jackson. But it continued gaining strength every year, till it ended, as every wise man foresaw it must end, in an "unnecessary and injurious CIVIL WAR." Fifteen years ago there were Secession disunionists South, just as there were Abolition disunionists in the North and West. The former were in public places, State and Federal; but as soon as they proclaimed their disunion proclivities, or were even suspected of them, they were speedily ejected from office, even in South Carolina. In 1851, every Southern State, without exception, carried the Union ticket upon a direct issue; and for years no disunionist, in the South, could be elected to any office. How was it, meantime, in the North and West? From absolute odium and weakness, Abolitionism steadily increased in position and power, till the Senate began to be filled with Abolitionists, open or in disguise, and the House of Representatives also; and till every free State, in every branch of its government, fell into the hands of active and aggressive anti-slavery men; and, finally, a President was elected by a sectional anti-slavery party, on a sectional anti-slavery platform, who himself declared that this Union could not endure "part slave and part free." And yet, at the South, even after secession began, it was with difficulty that any State was induced to secede, except South Carolina. In every other cotton State, there was a large minority against secession; and up to April 15th, 1861, North Carolina, Virginia, Tennessee, and Arkansas refused, by large majorities, to secede, while Delaware, Maryland, Kentucky, and Missouri adhere to the Union to this day. In the very midst of secession, if any fair and adequate compromise had been proposed by Congress, especially if the "Crittenden propositions" of December, 1860, had been adopted, secession would have perished. Mr. Davis and Mr. Toombs both declared that they would be content. That is the statement of Mr. Pugh. It is the testimony of Mr. Douglas also. But those propositions never received a solitary Republican vote in either the Senate or the House. "Hence, the sole responsibility for our disagreement," said Douglas, on the 3d of January, 1861, "and the only difficulty in the way of our amicable adjustment, is with the Republican party."

Sir, these are facts which it is useless to deny, and senseless to quarrel with; and they are part of the many circumstances upon which I found my immovable hope of a final restoration of the Union, in spite of the folly and madness and wickedness every day exhibited, uniting the South, and dividing the North and West.

The South is now well nigh united as one man; and for nearly three months we have met with little else than defeat. What united the South? What changed the fortunes of the war? In the beginning it was declared to be for the Union and the Constitution. These were noble objects, and success attended our arms. Before the Battle of Bull

Run, Mr. Crittenden sought to offer his now often quoted resolution, defining the objects of the war, and the Republicans did not allow it to be even so much as received. It was met with sneers and contempt. The day after the battle, when Washington was full of escaped soldiers, and fugacious Congressmen from the battle-field, it was offered again, and without objection. But two men, both Republicans, voted against that part of it. I voted for that part of it, but not for the first, because it did not speak the whole truth ; because it did not denounce the Abolition disunionists of the North and West also, and hold them responsible too. Six hundred thousand men were soon afterward enlisted. The victories of Hatteras, Port Royal, Mill Springs, Donelson, Roanoke, Winchester, Newbern, Island Ten, New Orleans, Norfolk, and others, all followed. Then was the hour for wisdom and sound policy. But, no ; it was the exact time selected by Abolitionism for the very saturnalia of its folly and madness. Every scheme and project of emancipation, execution, and confiscation, Congressional and Executive, of the whole session, was pressed forward, and many of them consummated during this same period of victory. The war was everywhere to be perverted from the spirit of the "Crittenden resolution." And with what result? The South, before that time divided, was now united as one man. Even the border slave States were shaken to the centre, and thousands of their citizens driven into the Confederate service. The armies of the South were rapidly filled up. A spirit was breathed into each man's breast which made him a host. It was these things, and such infamous orders as Butler's at New Orleans, which inspired their armies, making them invincible—and not overwhelming numbers. Victory everywhere was theirs. McDowell, The Seven Pines, Front Royal, Winchester, Cross Keys, Port Republic, James Island, Vicksburg, and the Great Seven Days Battle of Richmond, all followed. The men, and the women, too, of the South, said, If indiscriminate execution, confiscation, and emancipation are to be the rule of the Federal Government, let us perish rather on the battle-field.

This is what Abolitionism has cost us already—an unnecessary and injurious civil war; a united South; a divided North and West; a diminished Federal army ; an increased Confederate army ; the one dispirited, the other confident ; fifteen months of most vigorous war, with the largest army and most numerous navy of modern times; and yet not a single State restored ; but a public debt of a thousand millions of dollars incurred, and two hundred and fifty thousand brave men lost to the army, no man knows how. For all this, Abolitionism is responsible. Let it answer at the bar of public opinion. Let the people judge. Let the inexorable sentence go forth, and just and speedy judgment be executed upon it.

These, men of Dayton, are my opinions. They are my convictions. And yet, for these I am denounced as "disloyal!" What is loyalty in the United States? Obedience, faithfulness to law, or, in Norman-French, to LOI; and there is no higher law than the Constitution. Whoever obeys the laws is loyal; whoever breaks them, whether one in authority, or a private citizen, is disloyal. There is no such thing here yet, thank God, as loyalty to a President, or to any Administration. And yet, I have heard of loyalty to Abraham Lincoln, to a man, a public servant, whom the people made, and can unmake! Whoever talks thus is fit only to be a slave. If these men mean that I am opposed to the Administration and party in power, and to the doctrines and policy of Abolition, and think them false to the Constitution, and disastrous to the country; if they mean that I am a Democrat, devoted to the principles and policy, and faithful to the organization of that grand old party which made this country what it is, and am for the old Constitution and the old Union, then I am disloyal, and bless God for it. But if they mean that I am false to the Constitution, untrue to the Union, or disloyal to the country of my birth, in thought, or word, or deed, then, in the language of an eloquent citizen of Indiana (Mr. Voorhees), "they lie in their teeth, in their throats, and in their hearts." (Loud cheers.)

Who is an Abolitionist? Whoever is for indiscriminate confiscation, in order to strike at slavery, is an Abolitionist. Whoever is for emancipation and purchase of the slaves of the border States, and the pretended colonization of them abroad, but really their importation North and West, to compete with our own white labor, is an Abolitionist. Whoever would reduce the Southern States to Territories, in order to strike down slavery in them by Federal power, is an Abolitionist. Whoever is in favor of arming the slaves, or of declaring slavery abolished by executive or military proclamation, is an Abolitionist. And, finally, whoever is for converting the war, directly or indirectly, into a crusade for the abolition of slavery, is an Abolitionist of the worst sort; and he who votes for those who favor these things, is also an Abolitionist in practice, no matter what his professions or his party name may be. Whoever is opposed to these projects and votes accordingly, and is for the Constitution as it is, and the Union as it was, is a truly loyal citizen, whether he fights Secession rebels in the field, or Abolition rebels at the ballot-box.

And now, men of Montgomery, if you desire that the rebellion at the South shall be suppressed, that the Confederate armies shall be dissolved, and that the Constitution shall be maintained, the Union restored, and all laws obeyed, unite with me at the ballot-box in speedily and forever crushing out the execrable Abolition rebellion in the North and West. Whoever feels it his duty to fight armed rebels at the South, let him enlist at once; let him not buy up a substitute, but go himself. Whoever remains at home, it is his duty to join with me against Abolition rebels in our midst. This is loyalty; this is fidelity to the Union. The hour of trial and of vindication will soon come. The GREAT HEREAFTER is at hand. In six months—I repeat it—in three months, in six weeks, it may be—sooner or later, come meantime what may, the question will be, eternal separation, or the Union through compromise. Which will you then choose—not now, not yet; for amid arms reason, too, is silent—but when it does come? Come it will, and then you must choose between the Union which our fathers made, or a hopeless, cheerless, eternal, and belligerent disunion. I believe that the Administration will declare for separation. Then, as now and ever, I shall be for the Union, and against separation. Sir, the choice must be made, and made soon. We have already an enormous debt. A thousand millions would not pay it. We spend three millions a day. How long can you stand that? Our army of six hundred and thirty-seven thousand last January, has melted away to four hundred thousand; and now three hundred thousand more volunteers are demanded, and will soon be in the field. Yet, only fifteen months ago, just seventy-five thousand militia were called out, and the "insurgents" officially commanded to disperse in twenty days! A government paper currency of hundreds of millions is upon us; and a taxation the most onerous and unjust ever levied upon any but a conquered people. A tariff, too, of from forty-one to one hundred and thirteen per cent., as if to heap up the utmost measure of the load, is now added. Stand in the doorway of your farm-house, and behold and feel nothing, nothing not taxed, except the air you breathe, and the bright sunlight or starlight of heaven! And yet you must pay it, to the uttermost farthing. None but a madman or a traitor will talk of resistance or repudiation. It was not so in Democratic times. For sixty years that party governed this country in peace and prosperity, and with wisdom and sound policy. Try it again. I am a party man, more from conviction than inclination. There must be parties under every free government, and if there are not good parties, there will be bad ones; and "when bad men combine," said Burke, "good men must associate." Why did the Democratic party always govern this country wisely and well, and all other parties fail? Because our institutions are Democratic, and the principles and policy of the Democratic party are consistent with them; just as a piece of mechanism can only be made to work upon the principle or theory on which it is constructed. That is the philosophy of the historic fact. But the Democratic party could not conduct the British government three months without signal and disastrous failure. Let the people lay these things to heart. Let them restore the Democratic party to power, if they would be rescued at last. And, meantime, if the President would be sustained, let him resist fearlessly the spirit of Abolitionism; let him adhere to the Constitution; and himself obey all laws, and execute all laws; let him unmuzzle the press, and unfetter the tongue, and give freedom again to assemblages of the people, and to elections; let him liberate his so-called prisoners of State, and henceforth arrest no man without due process of law; in a word, let him look to love, not fear; to law, not terror, as the support of his administration; and every true patriot in the land will rally round him; and then, in God's good time, our eyes shall yet be gladdened, dark as the hour now is, with the blessed vision of the Constitution maintained, the Union restored, and the old flag of our country known and honored once again in every land, and upon every sea. (Great and long-continued cheering.)

ADDRESS,

Accepting the Nomination of the Democratic Congressional District Convention, at Hamilton, Ohio, September 4, 1862.

DEMOCRATS OF THE THIRD DISTRICT:

Just after the congressional election in 1860, acknowledging my very many and great obligations to you for past favors, I declared my fixed purpose to decline another candidacy. In this mind I continued through all the extraordinary changes of the past two years. I learned, indeed, some time ago, from many sources, and upon unmistakable evidence, that it was the general desire of the Democracy of the District that I should be their candidate again, and I thanked them for the confidence implied. But recently circumstances have changed. The "reign of terror" has been renewed with more severity than ever before. Freedom of the press and of speech has been repeatedly and causelessly stricken down. Political and personal liberty has, over and over again, been assailed by illegal and arbitrary arrests; and thus a determined purpose evinced to break down the ancient, customary, and constitutional means of opposition to the political party in power, under the false and tyrannical pretence that it is "opposition to the Government." To shrink from a canvass pressed upon me by the unanimous voice of the Democracy of the District, would be cowardice now. You have never deserted me; I will not, in this hour of peculiar trial and peril, desert you. With many and most heartfelt thanks, therefore, I accept the unanimous nomination just tendered to me, content with your indorsement here to-day, and the ratification of it by the Democrats, and other loyal Union men of the District, at the polls, as of more value than an election purchased by the sacrifice of the party and the principles which my judgment and conscience approve, and which I have adhered to and maintained from my very boyhood to this day; a party, too, the success of which is so essential, at this moment, to the reunion of the States, and the peace and prosperity of the country; for, if there be any one fact proved now beyond a reasonable doubt, it is the utter incompetency of the party in power to successfully administer the government. I know, indeed, that the district in which I have been three times honored with an election, has been changed by a "no party" partisan Legislature, and made heavily Republican, for the purpose of preventing the return of a Democrat; and that at the election last fall, the counties which now compose this district, gave the Republican or fusion candidate for governor a very large majority. But districts made for party purposes have more than once been changed by the people at the polls, and greater majorities than this many times overcome, as was, indeed, done last spring, even in the district as now constituted. In any event, the vindication of Democratic principles and the Democratic cause is, at this time especially, of far more importance than mere success in any election.

At your demand, therefore, men of the Third District, I accept the nomination, and present myself to the people for their suffrages, upon no other platform than THE CONSTITUTION AS IT IS, AND THE UNION AS IT WAS.

It is a platform broad enough for every patriot. Whoever is for it, I ask his support. Whoever is against it, I would not have his vote. Every faculty of body and mind which I possess shall be exerted unremittingly for the great purpose implied in this platform.

As a Representative, it is my duty to visit the constituency of the old district, still a part of the new, and to render to them an account of my stewardship as a public servant. As a candidate, I have a right to address the people upon all political questions, and they have a right to hear me.

Says the Constitution:

"Members of the House of Representatives shall be chosen every second year by the people."

And again:

"Congress shall make no law abridging the freedom of speech, or of the press; or the right of the people peaceably to assemble, and to petition the government for a redress of grievances."

Our State Constitution is still more explicit:

"The people have the right to assemble together in a peaceable manner, to consult for their common good; to instruct their representatives, and to petition the General Assembly for the redress of grievances."

These high and essential constitutional rights the Democrats, and other loyal Union men of this district everywhere, and I, as their candidate, mean to exercise to the fullest extent. And it will tend much toward the quiet and good feeling of communities, if all idle talk, such as that the Democratic candidate shall not speak in this place or that place, be dispensed with; for, let it be understood, once for all, that wherever, in any part of any county in the district, it is deemed convenient and proper to advertise a Democratic meeting, IT WILL BE HELD; AND, GOD WILLING, I WILL ADDRESS IT*

ADDRESS,

Accepting a Cane presented by the Ladies of Dayton, Nov. 21, 1862.†

MR. LOWE: With a grateful heart I receive this cane from the ladies for whom you have just spoken. Valuable in itself, it is to me far more valuable because of the kindly motives which have induced its presentation; but especially as a testimony of their approbation of my conduct as a public man, in the recent and present perilous times of the country. From them I accept it as a large recompense for whatever of calumny and reproach I have endured for the last eighteen months, because of my adherence to principle and a course of public policy which, in my conscience and judgment, I believed essential to the restoration of the Union and the best interests of my country. Such honors are bestowed commonly upon the heroes of military warfare. But if I merit any part of the praise which you have so eloquently expressed, it is moral heroism, which, to-night, is honored by these ceremonies. It is the victories of PEACE which you here celebrate.

* Mr. V. then defined his position as to State defence, expressed in the following resolution, which he offered, and which was adopted unanimously:

"*Resolved,* That it is the highest duty of the citizen, whenever his country or State is invaded, to rush to its rescue, by arms, if he is capable of military service, and by money or otherwise, every way, if he is not; and that the Democracy, as a part of the people of this district, laying aside all party feeling for that purpose, are ready, with life and fortune, to do their part in discharging this patriotic duty."

† The presentation was made at the residence of Judge MORSE, near Dayton, at a pleasant evening entertainment. THOMAS O. LOWE, Esq., presented the cane on behalf of the ladies in a handsome speech.

Her triumphs are, indeed, grander, and her conquests nobler than any achieved by the military hero upon the battle-field. And it is especially fitting that these honors should be paid to the cause—though I, myself, may deserve them not—by THE WOMEN of the country; and, while I lament that so many among them should have forgotten the softness of their sex, and the mild teachings of a religion, essential, indeed, to man, but especially congenial to woman's nature, yet I rejoice that so many, also, have laid not aside the ornament of a meek and quiet spirit, but remembered and clung yet the more steadfastly to the gospel of peace and love, even amid the phrensy of a desolating and demoralizing civil war. True to woman's mission, they are, or will be the wives, mothers, daughters, and sisters, who, by precept, example, or association, shall bring back yet the present, or educate a new generation which shall restore peace, the Union, and constitutional liberty, with all their virtues and their blessings, once more to this bleeding and distracted country. If, indeed, sir, I have exhibited any part of the high qualities of courage, fortitude, and immovable devotion to THE GOOD AND THE RIGHT, which, on behalf of these ladies, you have so kindly attributed to me, it is to one of their own sex, more than to any other human agency, that I am indebted for them—MY MOTHER. In childhood, in boyhood, and in youth, in the midst of many trials, from her teachings, and by her example, I learned those lessons, and formed the character and habits—if it be so—which fitted me, with courage and endurance, and unfaltering faith, to struggle with the terrible times in the midst of which we live.

Congratulating the ladies on the selection of yourself as their representative upon this occasion, and thanking you cordially for the many kind things you have been pleased to say, I accept this beautiful present, with my most grateful acknowledgments to one and all here assembled.

SPEECH ON THE GREAT CIVIL WAR IN AMERICA.

In the House of Representatives, Jan. 14, 1863.*

Bellum atrox, lugubre, incertum victis et victoribus.—TACITUS.

MR. SPEAKER: Indorsed at the recent election, within the same district for which I still hold a seat on this floor, by a majority four times greater than ever before, I speak to-day in the name and by the authority of the people who, for six years, have intrusted me with the office

* See Supplement, p. 573.

of a Representative. Loyal, in the true and highest sense of the word, to the Constitution and the Union, they have proved themselves devotedly attached to, and worthy of, the liberties to secure which the Union and the Constitution were established. With candor and freedom, therefore, as their Representative, and much plainness of speech, but with the dignity and decency due to this presence, I propose to consider the STATE OF THE UNION to-day, and to inquire what the duty is of every public man and every citizen in this the very crisis of the Great Revolution.

It is now two years, sir, since Congress assembled soon after the Presidential election. A sectional anti-slavery party had then just succeeded through the forms of the Constitution. For the first time a President had been chosen upon a platform of avowed hostility to an institution peculiar to nearly one-half of the States of the Union, and who had himself proclaimed that there was an irrepressible conflict, because of that institution, between the States; and that the Union could not endure "part slave and part free." Congress met, therefore, in the midst of the profoundest agitation, not here only, but throughout the entire South. Revolution glared upon us. Repeated efforts for conciliation and compromise were attempted, in Congress and out of it. All were rejected by the party just coming into power, except only the promise in the last hours of the session, and that, too, against the consent of a majority of that party both in the Senate and House: that Congress—not the Executive—should never be authorized to abolish or interfere with slavery in the States where it existed. South Carolina seceded; Georgia, Alabama, Florida, Mississippi, Louisiana, and Texas speedily followed. The Confederate Government was established. The other slave States held back. Virginia demanded a peace congress. The commissioners met, and, after some time, agreed upon terms of final adjustment. But neither in the Senate nor the House were they allowed even a respectful consideration. The President elect left his home in February, and journeyed towards this capital, jesting as he came; proclaiming that the crisis was only artificial, and that "nobody was hurt." He entered this city under cover of night and in disguise. On the 4th of March he was inaugurated, surrounded by soldiery; and, swearing to support the Constitution of the United States, announced in the same breath that the platform of his party should be the law unto him. From that moment all hope of peaceable adjustment fled. But for a little while, either with unsteadfast sincerity or in premeditated deceit, the policy of peace was proclaimed, even to the evacuation of Sumter and the other Federal forts and arsenals in the seceded States. Why that policy was suddenly abandoned, time will fully disclose. But just after the spring elections, and the secret meeting in this city of the Governors of several Northern and Western States, a fleet of eight vessels, carrying fourteen hundred men, was sent down ostensibly to provision Fort Sumter. The authorities of South Carolina eagerly accepted the challenge, and bombarded the fort into surrender, while the fleet fired not a gun, but, just as soon as the flag was struck, bore away and returned to the North. It was Sunday, the 14th of April, 1861; and that day the President, in fatal haste, and without the advice or consent of Congress, issued his proclamation, dated the next day, calling out seventy-five thousand militia for three months, to repossess the forts, places, and property seized from the United States, and commanding the insurgents to disperse in twenty days. Again the gauge was taken up by the South, and thus the flames of a civil war, the grandest, bloodiest, and saddest in history, lighted up the whole heavens. Virginia forthwith seceded. North Carolina, Tennessee, and Arkansas, followed; Delaware, Maryland, Kentucky, and Missouri were in a blaze of agitation, and within a week from the proclamation, the line of the Confederate States was transferred from the cotton States to the Potomac, and almost to the Ohio and the Missouri, and their population and fighting men doubled.

In the North and West, too, the storm raged with the fury of a hurricane. Never in history was any thing equal to it. Men, women, and children, native and foreign-born, Church and State, clergy and laymen, were all swept along with the current. Distinction of age, sex, station, party, perished in an instant. Thousands bent before the tempest; and here and there only was one found bold enough, foolhardy enough it may have been, to bend not, and him it smote as a consuming fire. The spirit of persecution for opinion's sake, almost extinct in the old world, now, by some mysterious transmigration, appeared incarnate in the new. Social relations were dissolved; friendships broken up; the ties of family and kindred snapped asunder. Stripes and hanging were everywhere threatened, sometimes executed. Assassination was invoked; slander sharpened his tooth; falsehood crushed truth to the earth; reason fled; madness reigned. Not justice only escaped to the skies, but peace returned to the bosom of God, whence she came. The gospel of love perished; hate sat enthroned, and the sacrifices of blood smoked upon every altar.

But the reign of the mob was inaugurated only to be supplanted by the iron domination of arbitrary power. Constitutional limitation was broken down; habeas corpus fell; liberty of the press, of speech, of the person, of the mails, of travel, of one's own house, and of religion; the right to bear arms, due process of law, judicial trial, trial by jury, trial at all; every badge and muniment of freedom in republican government or kingly government—all went down at a blow; and the chief law-officer of the crown—I beg pardon, sir, but it is easy now to fall into this courtly language—the Attorney-General, first of all men, proclaimed in the United States the maxim of Roman servility: Whatever pleases the President, that is law! Prisoners of state were then first heard of here. Midnight and arbitrary arrests commenced; travel was interdicted; trade embargoed; passports demanded; bastiles were introduced; strange oaths invented; a secret police organized; "piping" began; informers multiplied; spies now first appeared in America. The right to declare war, to raise and support armies, and to provide and maintain a navy, was usurped by the Executive; and in a little more than two months a land and naval force of over three hundred thousand men was in the field or upon the sea. An army of public plunderers followed, and corruption struggled with power in friendly strife for the mastery at home.

On the 4th of July Congress met, not to seek peace; not to rebuke usurpation nor to restrain power; not certainly to deliberate; not even to legislate, but to register and ratify the edicts and acts of the Executive; and in your language, sir, upon the first day of the session, to invoke a universal baptism of fire and blood amid the roar of cannon and the din of battle. Free speech was had only at the risk of a prison; possibly of life. Opposition was silenced by the fierce clamor of "disloyalty." All business not of war was voted out of order. Five hundred thousand men, an immense navy, and two hundred and fifty millions of money were speedily granted. In twenty, at most in sixty days, the rebellion was to be crushed out. To doubt it was treason. Abject submission was demanded. Lay down your arms, sue for peace, surrender your leaders—forfeiture, death—this was the only language heard on this floor. The galleries responded; the corridors echoed; and contractors and placemen and other venal patriots everywhere gnashed upon the friends of peace as they passed by. In five weeks seventy-eight public and private acts and joint resolutions, with declaratory resolutions, in the Senate and House, quite as numerous, all full of slaughter, were hurried through without delay and almost without debate.

Thus was CIVIL WAR inaugurated in America. Can any man to-day see the end of it?

And now pardon me, sir, if I pause here a moment to define my own position at that time upon this great question.

Sir, I am one of that number who have opposed abolitionism, or the political development of the anti-slavery sentiment of the North and West, from the beginning. In school, at college, at the bar, in public assemblies, in the Legislature, in Congress, boy and man, as a private citizen and in public life, in time of peace and in time of war, at all times and at every sacrifice, I have fought against it. It cost me ten years' exclusion from office and honor, at that period of life when honors are sweetest. No matter: I learned early to do right and to wait. Sir, it is but the development of the spirit of intermeddling, whose children are strife and murder. Cain troubled himself about the sacrifices of Abel, and slew him. Most of the wars, contentions, litigation, and bloodshed, from the beginning of time, have been its fruits. The spirit of non-intervention is the very spirit of peace and concord. I do not believe that if slavery had never existed here we would have had no sectional controversies. This very civil war might have happened fifty, perhaps a hundred years later. Other and stronger causes of discontent and of disunion, it may be, have existed between other States and sections, and are now being developed every day into maturity. The spirit of intervention assumed the form of abolitionism because slavery was odious in name and by association to the Northern mind, and because it was that which most obviously marks the different civilizations of the two sections. The South herself, in her early and later efforts to rid herself of it, had exposed the weak and offensive parts of slavery to the world. Abolition intermeddling taught her at last to search for and defend the assumed social, economic, and political merit and values of the institution. But there never was an hour from the beginning when it did not seem to me as clear as the sun at broad noon, that the agitation in any form, in the North and West, of the slavery question, must sooner or later end in disunion and civil war.

This was the opinion and prediction for years of Whig and Democratic statesmen alike; and after the unfortunate dissolution of the Whig party in 1854, and the organization of the present Republican party upon an exclusively anti-slavery and sectional basis, the event was inevitable; because, in the then existing temper of the public mind, and after the education through the press, and by the pulpit, the lecture and the political canvass for twenty years, of a generation, taught to hate slavery and the South, the success of that party, possessed, as it was, of every engine of political, business, social, and religious influence, was certain. It was only a question of time, and short time. Such was its strength, indeed, that I do not believe that the union of the Democratic party, in 1860, on any candidate, even though he had been supported also by the entire so-called conservative or anti-Lincoln vote of the country, would have availed to defeat it; and if it had, the success of the Abolition party would only have been postponed four years longer. The disease had fastened too strongly upon the system to be healed until it had run its course. The doctrine of the "irrepressible conflict" had been taught too long, and accepted too widely and earnestly, to die out until it should culminate in secession and disunion; and, if coercion were resorted to, then in civil war. I believed from the first that it was the purpose of some of the apostles of that doctrine to force a collision between the North and the South, either to bring about a separation, or to find a vain, but bloody pretext for abolishing slavery in the States. In any event, I knew, or I thought I knew, that the end was certain collision, and death to the Union.

Believing thus, I have for years past denounced those who taught that doctrine with all the vehemence, the bitterness, if you choose—I thought it a righteous, a patriotic bitterness—of an earnest and impassioned nature. Thinking thus, I forewarned all who believed the doctrine, or followed the party which taught it, with a sincerity and a depth of conviction as profound as ever penetrated the heart of man. And when, for eight years past, over and over again, I have proclaimed to the people that the success of a sectional anti-slavery party would be the beginning of disunion and civil war in America, I believed it. I did. I had read history, and studied human nature, and meditated for years upon the character of our institutions and form of government, and of the people South as well as North; and I could not doubt the event. But the people did not believe me, nor those older and wiser and greater than I. They rejected the prophecy and stoned the prophets. The candidate of the Republican party was chosen President. Secession began. Civil war was imminent. It was no petty insurrection; no temporary combination to obstruct the execution of the laws in certain States; but a revolution, systematic, deliberate, determined, and with the consent of a majority of the people of each State which seceded. Causeless it may have been; wicked it may have been; but there it was; not to be railed at, still less to be laughed at, but to be dealt with by statesmen as a fact. No display of vigor or force alone, however sudden or great, could have arrested it, even at the outset. It was disunion at last. The wolf had come. But civil war had not yet followed. In my deliberate and most solemn judgment, there was but one wise and masterly mode of dealing with it. Non-coercion would avert civil war, and compromise crush out both Abolitionism and Secession. The parent and the child would thus both perish. But a resort to force would at once precipitate war, hasten secession, extend disunion, and, while it lasted, utterly cut off all hope of compromise. I believed that war, if long enough continued, would be final, eternal disunion. I said it; I meant it; and, accordingly, to the utmost of my ability and influence, I exerted myself in behalf of the policy of non-coercion. It was adopted by Mr. Buchanan's Administration, with the almost unanimous consent of the Democratic and Constitutional Union parties in and out of Congress; and, in February, with the concurrence of a majority of the Republican party in the Senate and this House. But that party, most disastrously for the country, refused all compromise. How, indeed, could they accept any? That which the South demanded, and the Democratic and conservative parties of the North and West were willing to grant, and which alone could avail to keep the peace and save the Union, implied a surrender of the sole vital element of the party and its platform—of the very principle, in fact, upon which it had just won the contest for the Presidency; not, indeed, by a majority of the popular vote—the majority was nearly a million against it—but under the forms of the Constitution. Sir, the crime, the "high crime" of the Republican party was not so much its refusal to compromise, as its original organization upon a basis and doctrine wholly inconsistent with the stability of the Constitution and the peace of the Union.

But to resume: the session of Congress expired. The President elect was inaugurated; and now, if only the policy of non-coercion could be maintained, and war thus averted, time would do its work in the North and the South, and final peaceable adjustment and reunion be secured. Some time in March it was announced that the President had resolved to continue the policy of his predecessor, and even go a step further, and evacuate Sumter and the other Federal forts and arsenals in the seceded States. His own party acquiesced; the whole country rejoiced. The policy of non-coercion had triumphed, and for once, sir, in my life, I found myself in an immense majority. No man then pretended that a Union founded in consent, could be cemented by force. Nay, more, the President and the Secretary of State went further. Said Mr. Seward, in an official diplomatic letter to Mr. Adams:

> "For these reasons, he (the President) would not be disposed to reject a cardinal dogma of theirs (the Secessionists), namely, that the Federal Government could not reduce the seceding States to obedience by conquest, although he were disposed to question that proposition. But in fact the President willingly accepts it as true. Only an imperial or despotic government could subjugate thoroughly disaffected and insurrectionary members of the State."

Pardon me, sir, but I beg to know whether this conviction of the President and his Secretary, is not the philosophy of the persistent and most vigorous efforts made by this Administration, and first of all through this same Secretary, the moment war broke out, and ever since till the late elections, to convert the United States into an imperial or despotic government? But Mr. Seward adds, and I agree with him:

> "This Federal Republican system of ours is, of all forms of government, the very one which is most unfitted for such a labor."

This, sir, was on the 10th of April, and yet that very day the fleet was under sail for Charleston. The policy of peace had been abandoned. Collision followed; the militia were ordered out; civil war began.

Now, sir, on the 14th of April, I believed that coercion would bring on war, and war disunion. More than that, I believed, what you all in your hearts believe to-day, that the South could never be conquered—never. And not that only, but I was satisfied—and you of the Abolition party have now proved it to the world—that the secret but real purpose of the war was to abolish slavery in the States. In any event, I did not doubt that, whatever might be the momentary impulses of those in power, and whatever pledges they might make, in the midst of the fury, for the Constitution, the Union, and the flag, yet the natural and inexorable logic of revolutions would, sooner or later, drive them into that policy, and with it to its final but inevitable result, the change of our present democratical form of government into an imperial despotism.

These were my convictions on the 14th of April. Had I changed them on the 15th, when I read the President's proclamation, and become convinced that I had been wrong all my life, and that all history was a fable, and all human nature false in its development from the beginning of time, I would have changed my public conduct also. But my convictions did not change. I thought that, if war was disunion on the 14th of April, it was equally disunion on the 15th, and at all times. Believing this, I could not, as an honest man, a Union man, and a patriot, lend an active support to the war; and I did not. I had rather my right arm were plucked from its socket and cast into eternal burnings than, with my convictions, to have thus defiled my soul with the guilt of moral perjury. Sir, I was not taught in that school which proclaims that "all is fair in politics." I loathe, abhor, and detest the execrable maxim. I stamp upon it. No State can endure a single generation whose public men practise it. Whoever teaches it is a corrupter of youth. What we most want in these times, and at all times, is honest and independent public men. That man who is dishonest in politics, is not honest at heart in any thing; and sometimes moral cowardice is dishonesty. Do right; and trust to God, and truth, and the people. Perish office, perish honors, perish life itself—but do the thing that is right, and do it like a man. I did it. Certainly, sir, I could not doubt what he must suffer who dare defy the opinions and the passions, not to say the madness, of twenty millions of people. Had I not read history? Did I not know human nature? But I appealed to TIME; and right nobly hath the avenger answered me.

I did not support the war; and to-day I bless God, that not the smell of so much as one drop of its blood is upon my garments. Sir, I censure no brave man who rushed patriotically into this war; neither will I quarrel with any one, here or elsewhere, who gave to it an honest support. Had their convictions been mine, I, too, would doubtless have done as they did. With my convictions I could not.

But I was a Representative. War existed—by whose act no matter—not mine. The President, the Senate, the House, and the country, all said that there should be war—war for the Union; a union of consent and good-will. Our Southern brethren were to be whipped back into love and fellowship at the point of the bayonet. O, monstrous delusion! I can comprehend a war to compel a people to accept a master; to change a form of government; to give up territory; to abolish a domestic institution—in short, a war of conquest and subjugation; but a war for union! Was the Union thus made? Was it ever thus preserved? Sir, history will record that, after nearly six thousand years of folly and wickedness in every form and administration of government—theocratic, democratic, monarchic, oligarchic, despotic, and mixed—it was reserved to American statesmanship, in the nineteenth century of the Christian era, to try the grand experiment, on a scale the most costly and gigantic in its proportions, of creating love by force, and developing fraternal affection by war? And history will record, too, on the same page, the utter, disastrous, and most bloody failure of the experiment.

But to return: the country was at war; and I belonged to that school of politics which teaches that when we are at war, the Government—I do not mean the Executive alone, but the Government—is entitled to demand and have, without resistance, such number of men, and such amount of money and supplies generally, as may be necessary for the war, until an appeal can be had to the people. Before that tribunal alone, in the first instance, must the question of the continuance of the war be tried. This was Mr. Calhoun's opinion, and he laid it down very broadly and strongly in a speech on the loan bill, in 1841. Speaking of supplies, he said:

"I hold that there is a distinction in this respect between a state of peace and war. In the latter, the right of withholding supplies ought ever to be held subordinate to the energetic and successful prosecution of the war. I go further, and regard the witholding supplies, *with a view of forcing the country into a dishonorable peace*, as not only to be what it has been called, moral treason, but very little short of actual treason itself."

Upon this principle, sir, he acted afterwards in the Mexican War. Speaking of that war, in 1847, he said:

"Every Senator knows that I was opposed to the war; but none knows but myself the depth of that opposition. With my conception of its character and consequences, it was impossible for me to vote for it."

And again, in 1848:

"But, after the war was declared, by authority of the Government, *I acquiesced in what I could not prevent, and which it was impossible for me to arrest:* and I then felt it to be my duty to limit my efforts to *give such direction to the war* as would, as far as possible, *prevent the evils and dangers with which it threatened the country and its institutions.*"

Sir, I adopt all this as my own position and my defence; though, perhaps, in a civil war I might fairly go further in opposition. I could not, with my convictions, vote men and money for this war, and I would not, as a Representative, vote against them. I meant that, without opposition, the President might take all the men and all the money he should demand, and then to hold him to a strict accountability before the people for the results. Not believing the soldiers responsible for the war, or its purposes, or its consequences, I have never withheld my vote where their separate interests were concerned. But I have denounced, from the beginning, the usurpations and the infractions, one and all, of law and Constitution, by the President and those under him; their repeated and persistent arbitrary arrests, the suspension of *habeas corpus*, the violation of freedom of the mails, of the private house, of the press and of speech, and all the other multiplied wrongs and outrages upon public liberty and private right, which have made this country one of the worst despotisms on earth for the past twenty months; and I will continue to rebuke and denounce them to the end; and the people, thank God! have at last heard and heeded, and rebuked them, too. To the record and to time I appeal again for my justification.

And now, sir, I recur to the state of the Union to-day. What is it? Sir, twenty months have elapsed, but the rebellion is not crushed out; its military power has not been broken; the insurgents have not dispersed. The Union is not restored; nor the Constitution maintained; nor the laws enforced. Twenty, sixty, ninety, three hundred, six hundred days have passed; a thousand millions been expended; and three hundred thousand lives lost or bodies mangled; and to-day the Confederate flag is still near the Potomac and the Ohio, and the Confederate Government stronger, many times, than at the beginning. Not a State has been restored, not any part of any State has voluntarily returned to the Union. And has any thing been wanting that Congress, or the States, or the people in their most generous enthusiasm, their most impassionate patriotism, could bestow? Was it power? And did not the party of the Executive control the entire Federal Government, every State Government, every county, every city, town, and village in the North and West? Was it patronage? All belonged to it. Was it influence? What more? Did not the school, the college, the church, the press, the secret orders, the municipality, the corporation, railroads, telegraphs, express companies, the voluntary association, all, all yield it to the utmost? Was it unanimity? Never was an Administration so supported in England or America. Five men and half a score of newspapers made up the Opposition. Was it enthusiasm? The enthusiasm was fanatical. There has been nothing like it since the Crusades. Was it confidence? Sir, the faith of the people exceeded that of the patriarch. They gave up Constitution, law, right, liberty, all at your demand for arbitrary power that the rebellion might, as you promised, be crushed out in three months, and the Union restored. Was credit needed? You took control of a country, young, vigorous, and inexhaustible in wealth and resources, and of a Government almost free from public debt, and whose good faith had never been tarnished. Your great national loan bubble failed miserably, as it deserved to fail; but the bankers and merchants of Philadelphia, New York, and Boston lent you more than their entire banking capital. And when that failed too, you forced credit by declaring your paper promises to pay, a legal tender for all debts. Was money wanted? You had all the revenues of the United States, diminished indeed, but still in gold. The whole wealth of the country, to the last dollar, lay at your feet. Private individuals, municipal corporations, the State governments, all, in their frenzy, gave you money or means with reckless prodigality. The great Eastern cities lent you $150,000,000. Congress voted, first, $250,000,000, and next $500,000,000 more in loans; and then, first $50,000,000, next $10,000,000, then $90,000,000, and, in July last, $150,000,000 in Treasury notes; and the Secretary has issued also a paper "postage currency," in sums as low as five cents, limited in amount only by his discretion. Nay, more: already since the 4th of July, 1861, this House has appropriated $2,017,864,000, almost every dollar without debate, and without a recorded vote. A thousand millions have been expended since the 15th of April, 1861; and a public debt or liability of $1,500,000,000 already incurred. And to support all this stupendous outlay and indebtedness, a system of taxation, direct and indirect, has been inaugurated, the most onerous and unjust ever imposed upon any but a conquered people.

Money and credit, then, you have had in prodigal profusion. And were men wanted? More than a million rushed to arms! Seventy-five thousand first (and the country stood aghast at the multitude), then eighty-three thousand more were demanded; and three hundred and ten thousand responded to the call. The President next asked for four hundred thousand, and Congress, in their generous confidence, gave him five hundred thousand; and, not to be outdone, he took six hundred and thirty-seven thousand. Half of these melted away in their first campaign; and the President demanded three hundred thousand more for the war, and then drafted yet another three hundred thousand for nine months. The fabled hosts of Xerxes have been outnumbered. And yet victory, strangely, follows the standard of the foe. From Great Bethel to Vicksburg, the battle has not been to the strong. Yet every disaster, except the last, has been followed by a call for more troops, and every time, so far, they have been promptly furnished. From the beginning the war has been conducted like a political campaign, and it has been the folly of the party in power that they have assumed, that numbers alone would win the field in a contest not with ballots but with musket and sword. But numbers, you have had almost without number—the largest, best appointed, best armed, fed, and clad host of brave men, well organized and well disciplined, ever marshalled. A Navy, too, not the most formidable perhaps, but the most numerous and gallant, and the costliest in the world, and against a foe, almost without a navy at all. Thus, with twenty millions of people, and every element of strength and force at command—power, patronage, influence, unanimity, enthusiasm, confidence, credit, money, men, an Army and a Navy the largest and the noblest ever set in the field, or afloat upon the sea; with the support, almost servile, of every State, county, and municipality in the North and West, with a Congress swift to do the bidding of the Executive; without opposition anywhere at home; and with an arbitrary power which neither the Czar of Russia, nor the Emperor of Austria dare exercise; yet after nearly two years of more vigorous prosecution of war than ever recorded in history; after more skirmishes, combats, and battles than Alexander, Cæsar, or the first Napoleon ever fought in any five years of their military career, you have utterly, signally, disastrously—I will not say ignominiously—failed to subdue ten millions of "rebels," whom you had taught the people of the North and West not only to hate, but to despise. Rebels, did I say? Yes, your fathers were rebels, or your grandfathers. He, who now before me on canvas looks down so sadly upon us, the false, degenerate, and imbecile guardians of the great Republic which he founded, was a rebel. And yet we, cradled ourselves in rebellion, and who have fostered and fraternized with every insurrection in the nineteenth century everywhere throughout the globe, would now, forsooth, make the word "rebel" a reproach. Rebels certainly they are; but all the persistent and stupendous efforts of the most gigantic warfare of modern times have, through your incompetency and folly, availed nothing to crush them out, cut off though they have been, by your blockade, from all the world, and dependent only upon their own courage and resources. And yet, they were to be utterly conquered and subdued in six weeks, or three months! Sir, my judgment was made up, and expressed from the first. I learned it from Chatham: "My lords, you cannot conquer America." And you have not conquered the South. You never will. It is not in the nature of things possible; much less under your auspices. But money you have expended without limit, and blood poured out like water. Defeat, debt, taxation, sepulchres, these are your trophies. In vain, the people gave you treasure, and the soldier yielded up his life. "Fight, tax, emancipate, let these," said the gentleman from Maine (Mr. Pike), at the last session, "be the trinity of our salvation." Sir, they have become the trinity of your deep damnation. The war for the Union is, in your hands, a most bloody and costly failure. The President confessed it on the 22d of September, solemnly, officially, and under the broad seal of the United States. And he has now repeated the confession. The priests and rabbis of abolition taught him that God would not prosper such a cause. War for the Union was abandoned; war for the negro openly begun, and with stronger battalions than before. With what success? Let the dead at Fredericksburg and Vicksburg answer.

And now, sir, can this war continue? Whence the money to carry it on? Where the men? Can you borrow? From whom? Can you tax more? Will the people bear it? Wait till you have collected what is already levied. How many millions more of "legal tender"—to day forty-seven per cent. below the par of gold—can you float? Will men enlist now at any price? Ah, sir, it is easier to die at home. I beg pardon; but I trust I am not "discouraging enlistments." If I am, then first arrest Lincoln, Stanton, Halleck, and some of your other generals, and I will retract; yes I will recant. But can you draft again? Ask New England—New York. Ask Massachusetts. Where are the nine hundred thousand? Ask not Ohio—the Northwest. She thought you in earnest, and gave you all, all—more than you demanded.

"The wife whose babe first smiled that day,
The fair, fond bride of yester eve,
And aged sire and matron gray,
Saw the loved warriors haste away,
And deemed it sin to grieve."

Sir, in blood she has atoned for her credulity; and now there is mourning in every house, and distress and sadness in every heart. Shall she give you any more?

But ought this war to continue? I answer, no—not a day, not an hour. What then? Shall we separate? Again I answer, no, no, no! What then? And now, sir, I come to the grandest and most solemn problem of statesmanship from the beginning of time;

and to the God of heaven, illuminer of hearts and minds, I would humbly appeal for some measure, at least, of light and wisdom and strength to explore and reveal the dark but possible future of this land.

CAN THE UNION OF THESE STATES BE RESTORED? HOW SHALL IT BE DONE?

And why not? Is it historically impossible? Sir, the frequent civil wars and conflicts between the States of Greece did not prevent their cordial union to resist the Persian invasion; nor did even the thirty years Peloponnesian war, springing, in part, from the abduction of slaves, and embittered and disastrous as it was—let Thucydides speak—wholly destroy the fellowship of those States. The wise Romans ended the three years Social War, after many bloody battles and much atrocity, by admitting the States of Italy to all the rights and privileges of Roman citizenship—the very object to secure which these States had taken up arms. The border wars between Scotland and England, running through centuries, did not prevent the final union, in peace and by adjustment, of the two kingdoms under one monarch. Compromise did at last what ages of coercion and attempted conquest had failed to effect. England kept the crown, while Scotland gave the king to wear it; and the memories of Wallace, and the Bruce of Bannockburn, became part of the glories of British history. I pass by the union of Ireland with England—a union of force, which God and just men abhor; and yet precisely "the Union as it should be" of the Abolitionists of America. Sir, the rivalries of the houses of York and Lancaster, filled all England with cruelty and slaughter; yet compromise and intermarriage ended the strife at last, and the white rose and the red were blended in one. Who dreamed a month before the death of Cromwell that in two years the people of England, after twenty years of civil war and usurpation, would, with great unanimity, restore the house of Stuart, in the person of its most worthless prince, whose father, but eleven years before, they had beheaded? And who could have foretold, in the beginning of 1812, that within some three years, Napoleon would be in exile upon a desert island, and the Bourbons restored? Armed foreign intervention did it; but it is a strange history. Or who then expected to see a nephew of Napoleon, thirty-five years later, with the consent of the people, supplant the Bourbon, and reign Emperor of France? Sir, many States and people, once separate, have become united in the course of ages, through natural causes, and without conquest; but I remember a single instance only, in history, of States or peoples once united, and speaking the same language, who have been forced permanently asunder by civil strife or war, unless they were separated by distance or vast natural boundaries. The secession of the Ten Tribes is the exception; these parted without actual war; and their subsequent history is not encouraging to secession. But when Moses, the greatest of all statesmen, would secure a distinct nationality and government to the Hebrews, he left Egypt, and established his people in a distant country. In modern times, the Netherlands, three centuries ago, won their independence by the sword; but France and the English channel separated them from Spain. So did our Thirteen Colonies; but the Atlantic ocean divided us from England. So did Mexico, and other Spanish colonies in America, but the same ocean divided them from Spain. Cuba and the Canadas still adhere to the parent governments. And who now, North or South, in Europe or America, looking into history, shall presumptuously say, that because of civil war the reunion of these States is impossible? War, indeed, while it lasts, is disunion, and, if it lasts long enough, will be final, eternal separation first, and anarchy and despotism afterward. Hence, I would hasten peace now, to-day, by every honorable appliance.

Are there physical causes which render reunion impracticable? None. Where other causes do not control, rivers unite; but mountains, deserts, and great bodies of water—*oceani dissociabiles*—separate a people. Vast forests originally, and the lakes now also, divide us—not very widely or wholly—from the Canadas, though we speak the same language, and are similar in manners, laws, and institutions. Our chief navigable rivers run from North to South. Most of our bays and arms of the sea take the same direction. So do our ranges of mountains. Natural causes all tend to Union, except as between the Pacific coast and the country east of the Rocky Mountains to the Atlantic. It is "manifest destiny." Union is empire. Hence, hitherto we have continually extended our territory, and the Union with it, South and West. The Louisiana purchase, Florida, and Texas all attest it. We passed desert and forest, and scaled even the Rocky Mountains, to extend the Union to the Pacific. Sir, there is no natural boundary between the North and the South, and no line of latitude upon which to separate; and if ever a line of longitude shall be established it will be east of the Mississippi valley. The Alleghanies are no longer a barrier. Highways ascend them everywhere, and the railroad now climbs their summits, and spans their chasms, or penetrates their rockiest sides. The electric telegraph follows, and, stretching its connecting wires along the clouds, there mingles its vocal lightnings with the fires of heaven.

But if disunionists in the East will force a separation of any of these States, and a boundary, purely conventional, is at last to be marked out, it must, and it will be either from Lake Erie upon the shortest line to the Ohio River, or from Manhattan to the Canadas.

And now, sir, is there any difference of race here so radical as to forbid reunion? I do not refer to the negro race, styled now, in unctuous official phrase, by the President, "Americans of African descent." Certainly, sir, there are two white races in the United States, both from the same common stock, and yet so distinct—one of them so peculiar—that they develop different forms of civilization, and might belong, almost, to different types of mankind. But the boundary of these two races is not at all marked by the line which divides the slaveholding from the non-slaveholding States. If race is to be the geographical limit of disunion, then Mason and Dixon's can never be the line.

Next, sir, do not the causes which, in the beginning, impelled to Union, still exist in their utmost force and extent? What were they?

First, the common descent—and, therefore, consanguinity—of the great mass of the people from the Anglo-Saxon stock. Had the Canadas been settled, originally, by the English, they would, doubtless, have followed the fortunes of the Thirteen Colonies. Next, a common language, one of the strongest of the ligaments which bind a people. Had we been contiguous to Great Britain, either the causes which led to a separation would have never existed, or else been speedily removed; or, afterward, we would long since have been reunited as equals, and with all the rights of Englishmen. And along with these were similar, at least not essentially dissimilar, manners, habits, laws, religion, and institutions of all kinds, except one. The common defence was another powerful incentive, and is named in the Constitution as one among the objects of the "more perfect Union" of 1787. Stronger yet than all these, perhaps, but made up of all of them, was a common interest. Variety of climate and soil, and, therefore, of production, implying, also, extent of country, is not an element of separation, but, added to contiguity, becomes a part of the ligament of interest, and is one of its toughest strands. Variety of production is the parent of the earliest commerce and trade; and these, in their full development, are, as between foreign nations, hostages for peace; and between States and people united, they are the firmest bonds of union. But, after all, the strongest of the many original impelling causes to the Union was the securing of domestic tranquillity. The statesmen of 1787 well knew that between thirteen independent but contiguous States, without a natural boundary, and with nothing to separate them, except the machinery of similar governments, there must be a perpetual, in fact, an "irrepressible conflict" of jurisdiction and interest, which, there being no other common arbiter, could only be terminated by the conflict of the sword. And the statesmen of 1863 ought to know that two or more confederate governments, made up of similar States, having no natural boundary either, and separated only by different governments, cannot endure long together in peace, unless one or more of them be either too pusillanimous for rivalry, or too insignificant to provoke it, or too weak to resist aggression.

These, sir, along with the establishment of justice, and the securing of the general welfare, and of the blessings of liberty to themselves and their posterity, made up the causes and motives which impelled our fathers to the Union at first.

And now, sir, what one of them is wanting? What one diminished? On the contrary, many of them are stronger to-day than in the beginning. Migration and intermarriage have strengthened the ties of consanguinity. Commerce, trade, and production, have immensely multiplied. Cotton, almost unknown here in 1787, is now the chief product and export of the country. It has set in motion three-fourths of the spindles of New England, and given employment, directly or remotely, to full half the shipping, trade, and commerce of the United States. More than that: cotton has kept the peace between England and America for thirty years; and, had the people of the North been as wise and practical as the statesmen of Great Britain, it would have maintained union and peace here. But we are being taught in our first century, and at our own cost, the lessons which England learned through the long and bloody experience of eight hundred years. We shall be wiser next time. Let not cotton be king, but peacemaker, and inherit the blessing.

A common interest, then, still remains to us. And union for the common defence, at the end of this war, taxed, indebted, impoverished, exhausted, as both sections must be, and with foreign fleets and armies around us, will be fifty-fold more essential than ever before. And finally, sir, without union, our domestic tranquillity must forever remain unsettled. If it cannot be maintained within the Union, how, then, outside of it, without an exodus or colonization of the people of one section or the other to a distant country? Sir, I repeat, that two governments so interlinked and bound together every way, by physical and social ligaments, cannot exist in peace without a common arbiter. Will treaties bind us? What better treaty than the Constitution? What more solemn, more durable? Shall we settle our disputes then by arbitration and compromise? Sir, let us arbitrate and compromise now, inside of the Union. Certainly it will be quite as easy.

And now, sir, to all these original causes and motives which impelled to Union at first, must be added certain artificial ligaments, which eighty years of association under a common Government have most fully developed. Chief among these are canals, steam navigation, railroads, express companies, the post-office, the newspaper press, and that terrible agent of good and evil mixed—"spirit of health, and yet goblin damned," if free, the gentlest minister of truth and liberty: when enslaved, the supplest instrument of falsehood and tyranny—the magnetic telegraph. All these have multiplied the speed or the quantity of trade, travel, communication, migration, and intercourse of all kinds, between the different States and sections; and thus, so long as a healthy condition of the body-politic continued, they became powerful cementing agencies of union. The numerous voluntary associations, artistic, literary, charitable, social, and scientific, until corrupted and made fanatical; the various ecclesiastical organizations, until they divided; and the political parties, so long as they remained all national, and none sectional, were also among the strong ties which bound us together. And yet all of these, perverted and abused for some years in the hands of bad or fanatical men, became still more powerful instrumentalities in the fatal work of disunion; just as the veins and arteries of the human body, designed to convey the vitalizing fluid through every part of it, will carry also, and with increased rapidity it may be, the subtle poison which takes life away. Nor is this all. It was through their agency that the imprisoned winds of civil war were all let loose at first with such sudden and appalling fury; and, kept in motion by political power, they have ministered to that fury ever since. But, potent alike for good and evil, they may yet, under the control of the people, and in the hands of wise, good, and patriotic men, be made the most effective agencies, under Providence, in the reunion of these States.

Other ties, also, less material in their nature, but hardly less persuasive in their influence, have grown up under the Union. Long association, a common history, national reputation, treaties and diplomatic intercourse abroad, admission of new States, a common jurisprudence, great men whose names and fame are the patrimony of the whole country, patriotic music and songs, common battle-fields, and glory won under the same flag. These make up the poetry of the Union; and yet, as in the marriage relation, and the family, with similar influences, they are stronger than hooks of steel. He was a wise statesman, though he may never have held an office, who said: "Let me write the songs of a people, and I care not who makes their laws." Why is the Marseillaise prohibited in France? Sir, Hail Columbia and the Star-Spangled Banner—Pennsylvania gave us one, and Maryland the other—have done more for the Union than all the legislation and all the debates in this capital for forty years; and they will do more yet again than all your armies, though you call out another million of men into the field. Sir, I would add "Yankee Doodle;" but first let me be assured that Yankee Doodle loves the Union more than he hates the slaveholder.*

And now, sir, I propose to briefly consider the causes which led to disunion and the present civil war; and to inquire whether they are eternal and ineradicable in their nature, and at the same time powerful enough to overcome all the causes and considerations which impel to reunion.

Having, two years ago, discussed fully and elaborately the more abstruse and remote causes whence civil commotions in all governments, and those also which are peculiar to our complex and Federal system, such as the consolidating tendencies of the General Government, because of executive power and patronage, and of the tariff, and taxation and disbursement generally, all unjust and burdensome to the West equally with the South, I pass them by now.

What then, I ask, is the immediate, direct cause of disunion and this civil war? Slavery, it is answered. Sir, that is the philosophy of the rustic in the play—"that a great cause of the night, is lack of the sun." Certainly slavery was in one sense—very obscure, indeed—the cause of the war. Had there been no slavery here, this particular war about slavery would never have been waged. In a like sense, the Holy Sepulchre was the cause of the war of the Crusades, and had Troy or Carthage never existed, there never would have been Trojan or Carthaginian war, and no such personages as Hector and Hannibal; and no Iliad or Æneid would ever have been written. But far better say that the negro is the cause of the war; for had there been no negro here, there would be no war just now. What then? Exterminate him? Who demands it? Colonize him? How? Where? When? At whose cost? Sir, let us have an end of this folly.

But slavery is the cause of the war. Why? Because the South obstinately and wickedly refused to restrict or abolish it at the demand of the philosophers or fanatics and demagogues of the North and West. Then, sir, it was abolition, the purpose to abolish or interfere with and hem in slavery, which caused disunion and war. Slavery is only the subject, but Abolition the cause of this civil war. It was the persistent and determined agitation in the free States of the question of abolishing slavery in the South, because of the alleged "irrepressible conflict" between the forms of labor in the two sections, or, in the false and mis-

* In truth, the song was written in derision by a British officer, and not by an American.

chievous cant of the day, between freedom and slavery, that forced a collision of arms at last. Sir, that conflict was not confined to the Territories. It was expressly proclaimed by its apostles, as between the States also—against the institution of domestic slavery everywhere. But, assuming the platforms of the Republican party as a standard, and stating the case most strongly in favor of that party, it was the refusal of the South to consent that slavery should be excluded from the Territories, that led to the continued agitation, North and South, of that question, and finally to disunion and civil war. Sir, I will not be answered now by the old clamor about "the aggressions of the slave power." That miserable spectre, that unreal mockery, has been exorcised and expelled by debt and taxation and blood. If that power did govern this country for the sixty years preceding this terrible revolution, then the sooner this Administration and Government return to the principles and policy of Southern statesmanship, the better for the country; and that, sir, is already, or soon will be, the judgment of the people. But I deny that it was the "slave power" that governed for so many years, and so wisely and well. It was the Democratic party, and its principles and policy, moulded and controlled, indeed, largely by Southern statesmen. Neither will I be stopped by that other cry of mingled fanaticism and hypocrisy, about the sin and barbarism of African slavery. Sir, I see more of barbarism and sin, a thousand times, in the continuance of this war, the dissolution of the Union, the breaking up of this Government, and the enslavement of the white race, by debt and taxes and arbitrary power. The day of fanatics and sophists and enthusiasts, thank God, is gone at last; and though the age of chivalry may not, the age of practical statesmanship is about to return. Sir, I accept the language and intent of the Indiana resolution, to the full—"that in considering terms of settlement, we will look only to the welfare, peace, and safety of the white race, without reference to the effect that settlement may have upon the condition of the African." And when we have done this, my word for it, the safety, peace, and welfare of the African will have been best secured. Sir, there is fifty-fold less of anti-slavery sentiment to-day in the West than there was two years ago; and if this war be continued, there will be still less a year hence. The people there begin, at last, to comprehend, that domestic slavery in the South is a question, not of morals, or religion, or humanity, but a form of labor, perfectly compatible with the dignity of free white labor in the same community, and with national vigor, power, and prosperity, and especially with military strength. They have learned, or begin to learn, that the evils of the system affect the master alone, or the community and State in which it exists; and that we of the free States partake of all the material benefits of the institution, unmixed with any part of its mischief. They believe, also, in the subordination of the negro race to the white, where they both exist together, and that the condition of subordination, as established in the South, is far better every way, for the negro, than the hard servitude of poverty, degradation, and crime, to which he is subjected in the free States. All this, sir, may be "pro-slaveryism," if there be such a word. Perhaps it is; but the people of the West begin now to think it wisdom and good sense. We will not establish slavery in our own midst; neither will we abolish it, or interfere with it outside of our own limits.

Sir, an anti-slavery paper in New York (*the Tribune*), the most influential, and therefore, most dangerous, of all of that class—it would exhibit more of dignity, and command more of influence, if it were always to discuss public questions and public men with decent respect—laying aside now the epithets of "secessionist" and "traitor," has returned to its ancient political nomenclature, and calls certain members of this House "pro-slavery." Well, sir, in the old sense of the term, as applied to the Democratic party, I will not object. I said, years ago, and it is a fitting time now to repeat it:

> "If to love my country; to cherish the Union; to revere the Constitution; if to abhor the madness, and hate the treason, which would lift up a sacrilegious hand against either; if to read that in the past, to behold it in the present, to foresee it in the future of this land, which is of more value to us, and to the world, for ages to come, than all the multiplied millions who have inhabited Africa, from the creation to this day!—if this it is to be pro-slavery, then in every nerve, fibre, vein, bone, tendon, joint, and ligament, from the topmost hair of the head to the last extremity of the foot, I am all over and altogether a pro-slavery man."

And now, sir, I come to the great and controlling question, within which the whole issue of union or disunion is bound up. Is there "an irrepressible conflict" between the slaveholding and non-slaveholding States? Must "the cotton and rice fields of South Carolina, and the sugar plantations of Louisiana," in the language of Mr. Seward, "be ultimately tilled by free labor, and Charleston and New Orleans become marts for legitimate merchandise alone, or else the rye-fields and wheat-fields of Massachusetts and New York again be surrendered by their farmers to slave culture and the production of slaves, and Boston and New York become, once more, markets for trade in the bodies and souls of men?" If so, then there is an end of all union, and forever. You cannot abolish slavery by the sword; still less by proclamations, though the President were to "proclaim" every month. Of what possible avail was his proclamation of September? Did the South submit? Was she even alarmed? And yet, he has now fulmined another "bull against the comet"—*brutum fulmen*—and threatening servile insurrection, with all its horrors, has yet coolly appealed to the judgment of mankind, and invoked the blessing of the God of peace and love! But declaring it a military necessity, an essential measure of war, to subdue the rebels, yet, with admirable wisdom, he expressly exempts from its operation the only States, and parts of States, in the South, where he has the military power to execute it.

Neither, sir, can you abolish slavery by argument. As well attempt to abolish marriage, or the relation of paternity. The South is resolved to maintain it at every hazard, and by every sacrifice; and if "this Union cannot endure, part slave and part free," then it is already and finally dissolved. Talk not to me of "West Virginia." Tell me not of Missouri trampled under the feet of your soldiery. As well talk to me of Ireland. Sir, the destiny of those States must abide the issue of the war. But Kentucky you may find tougher. And Maryland—

"E'en in her ashes live their wonted fires."

Nor will Delaware be found wanting in the day of trial.

But I deny the doctrine. It is full of disunion and civil war. It is disunion itself. Whoever first taught it ought to be dealt with as not only hostile to the Union, but an enemy of the human race. Sir, the fundamental idea of the Constitution is the perfect and eternal compatibility of a union of States, "part slave and part free;" else the Constitution never would have been framed, nor the Union founded; and seventy years of successful experiment have approved the wisdom of the plan. In my deliberate judgment, a confederacy, made up of slaveholding and non-slaveholding States, is, in the nature of things, the strongest of all popular governments. African slavery has been, and is, eminently conservative. It makes the absolute political equality of the white race everywhere practicable. It dispenses with the English order of nobility, and leaves every white man, North and South, owning slaves or owning none, the equal of every other white man. It has reconciled universal suffrage, throughout the free States, with the stability of government. I speak not now of its material benefits to the North and West, which are many and more obvious. But the South, too, has profited many ways by a union with the non-slaveholding States. Enterprise, industry, self-reliance, perseverance, and the other hardy virtues of a people living in a higher latitude, and without hereditary servants, she has learned or received from the North. Sir, it is easy, I know, to denounce all this, and to revile him who utters it. Be it so. The English is, of all languages, the most copious in words of bitterness and reproach. "Pour on: I will endure."

Then, sir, there is not an "irrepressible conflict" between slave labor and free labor. There is no conflict at all. Both exist together in perfect harmony in the South. The master and the slave, the white laborer and the black, work together in the same field, or the same shop, and without the slightest sense of degradation. They are not equals, either socially or politically. And why, then, cannot Ohio, having only free labor, live in harmony with Kentucky, which has both slave and free? Above all, why cannot Massachusetts allow the same right of choice to South Carolina, separated as they are a thousand miles, by other States, who would keep the peace, and live in good-will? Why this civil war? Whence disunion? Not from slavery—not because the South chooses to have two kinds of labor instead of one—but from *sectionalism*, always and everywhere a disintegrating principle. Sectional jealousy and hate—these, sir, are the only elements of conflict between these States; and, though powerful, they are yet not at all irrepressible. They exist between families, communities, towns, cities, counties, and States; and if not repressed, would dissolve all society and government. They exist, also, between other sections than the North and South. Sectionalism East, many years ago, saw the South and West united by the ties of geographical position, migration, intermarriage, and interest, and thus strong enough to control the power and policy of the Union. It found us divided only by different forms of labor, and, with consummate, but most guilty sagacity, it seized upon the question of slavery as the surest and most powerful instrumentality by which to separate the West from the South, and bind her wholly to the North. Encouraged every way, from abroad, by those who were jealous of our prosperity and greatness, and who knew the secret of our strength, it proclaimed the "irrepressible conflict" between slave labor and free labor. It taught the people of the North to forget both their duty and their interests; and, aided by the artificial ligaments and influences, which money and enterprise had created between the seaboard and the Northwest, it persuaded the people of that section, also, to yield up every tie which binds them to the great valley of the Mississippi, and to join, their political fortunes especially, wholly with the East. It resisted the fugitive slave law, and demanded the exclusion of slavery from all the Territories, and from this District, and clamored against the admission of any more slave States into the Union. It organized a sectional anti-slavery party, and thus drew to its aid, as well political ambition and interest, as fanaticism; and, after twenty-five years of incessant and vehement agitation, it obtained possession, finally, and upon that issue, of the Federal Government, and of every State government, North and West. And, to-day, we are in the midst of the greatest, most cruel, most destructive civil war ever waged. But two years, sir, of blood, and debt, and taxation, and incipient commercial ruin, are teaching the people of the West, and, I trust, of the North, also, the folly and madness of this crusade against African slavery, and the wisdom and necessity of a union of the States, as our fathers made it, "part slave and part free."

What then, sir, with so many causes impelling to reunion, keeps us apart to-day? Hate, passion, antagonism, revenge—all heated seven times hotter by war. Sir, these, while they last, are the most powerful of all motives with a people, and with the individual man; but, fortunately, they are the least durable. They hold a divided sway in the same bosoms with the nobler qualities of love, justice, reason, placability; and, except when at their height, are weaker than the sense of interest, and always, in States, at least, give way to it at last. No statesman who yields himself up to them can govern wisely or well; and no State whose policy is controlled by them can either prosper or endure. But war is both their offspring and their aliment, and, while it lasts, all other motives are subordinate. The virtues of peace cannot flourish, cannot even find development in the midst of fighting; and this civil war keeps in motion all the centrifugal forces of the Union, and gives to them increased strength and activity every day. But such, and so many and powerful, in my judgment, are the cementing or centripetal agencies impelling us together, that nothing but perpetual war and strife can keep us always divided.

Sir, I do not under-estimate the power of the prejudices of section or, what is much stronger, of race. Prejudice is colder, and, therefore, more durable than the passions of hate and revenge, or the spirit of antagonism. But, as I have already said, its boundary in the United States is not Mason and Dixon's line. The long standing mutual jealousies of New England and the South do not primarily grow out of slavery. They are deeper, and will always be the chief obstacle in the way of full and absolute reunion. They are founded in difference of manners, habits, and social life, and different notions about politics, morals, and religion. Sir, after all, this whole war is not so much one of sections—least of all, between the slaveholding and non-slaveholding sections—as of races, representing not difference in blood, but mind and its development, and different types of civilization. It is the old conflict of the Cavalier and the Roundhead, the Liberalist and the Puritan; or, rather, it is a conflict, upon new issues, of the ideas and elements represented by those names. It is a war of the Yankee and the Southron. Said a Boston writer, the other day, eulogizing a New England officer who fell at Fredericksburg: "This is Massachusetts' war; Massachusetts and South Carolina made it." But, in the beginning, the Roundhead outwitted the Cavalier, and by a skilful use of slavery and the negro, united all New England first, and afterwards the entire North and West, and finally sent out to battle against him Celt and Saxon, German and Knickerbocker, Catholic and Episcopalian, and even a part of his own household, and of the descendants of his own stock. Said Mr. Jefferson, when New England threatened secession, some sixty years ago: "No, let us keep the Yankees to quarrel with." Ah, sir, he forgot that quarrelling is always a hazardous experiment; and, after some time, the countrymen of Adams proved themselves too sharp at that work for the countrymen of Jefferson. But every day the contest now tends again to its natural and original elements. In many parts of the Northwest—I might add, of Pennsylvania, New Jersey, and New York city—the prejudice against the "Yankee" has always been almost as bitter as in the South. Suppressed for a little while by the anti-slavery sentiment and the war, it threatens now to break forth in one of those great, but unfortunate, popular uprisings, in the midst of which reason and justice are, for the time, utterly silenced. I speak advisedly, and let New England heed, else she, and the whole East, too, in their struggle for power, may learn yet, from the West, the same lesson which civil war taught to Rome, that *evulgato imperii arcano, posse principem alibi, quam Romæ fieri.* The people of the West demand peace, and they begin to more than suspect that New England is in the way. The storm rages; and they believe that she, not slavery, is the cause. The ship is sore tried; and passengers and crew are now almost ready to propitiate the waves, by throwing the ill-omened prophet overboard. In plain English—not very classic, but most expressive—they threaten to "set New England out in the cold."

And now, sir, I, who have not a drop of New England blood in my veins, but was born in Ohio, and am wholly of Southern ancestry—with a slight cross of Pennsylvania Scotch-Irish—would speak a word to the men of the West and the South, in behalf of New England. Sir, some years ago, in the midst of high sectional controversies, and speaking as a Western man, I said some things harsh of the North, which now, in a more catholic spirit, as a United States man, and for the sake of reunion, I would recall. My prejudices, indeed, upon this subject, are as strong as any man's; but in this, the day of great national humiliation and calamity, let the voice of prejudice be hushed.

Sir, they who would exclude New England in any reconstruction of the Union, assume that all New Englanders are "Yankees" and Puritans, and that the Puritan or pragmatical element, or type of civilization, has always held undisputed sway. Well, sir, Yankees, certainly, they are, in one sense; and so to Old England we are all Yankees, North and South; and to the South just now, or a little while ago, we, of the Middle and Western States, also, are, or were, Yankees, too. But there is really a very large, and most liberal and conservative non-Puritan element in the population of New England, which, for many years, struggled for the mastery, and sometimes held it. It divided Maine,

New Hampshire, and Connecticut, and once controlled Rhode Island wholly. It held the sway during the Revolution, and at the period when the Constitution was founded, and for some years afterwards. Mr. Calhoun said, very justly, in 1847, that to the wisdom and enlarged patriotism of Sherman and Ellsworth, on the slavery question, we were indebted for this admirable Government, and that, along with Paterson, of New Jersey, "their names ought to be engraven on brass, and live forever." And Mr. Webster, in 1830, in one of those grand historic word-paintings, in which he was so great a master, said of Massachusetts and South Carolina: "Hand in hand they stood around the Administration of Washington, and felt his own great arm lean on them for support." Indeed, sir, it was not till some thirty years ago that the narrow, presumptuous, intermeddling, and fanatical spirit of the old Puritan element began to reappear in a form very much more aggressive and destructive than at first, and threatened to obtain absolute mastery in Church, and School, and State. A little earlier it had struggled hard, but the conservatives proved too strong for it; and so long as the great statesmen and jurists of the Whig and Democratic parties survived, it made small progress, though John Quincy Adams gave to it the strength of his great name. But after their death, it broke in as a flood, and swept away the last vestige of the ancient, liberal, and tolerating conservatism. Then every form and development of fanaticism sprang up in rank and most luxuriant growth, till abolitionism, the chief fungus of all, overspread the whole of New England first, and then the middle States, and finally every State in the Northwest.

Certainly, sir, the more liberal or non-Puritan element was mainly, though not altogether, from the old Puritan stock, or largely crossed with it. But even within the first ten years after the landing of the Pilgrims, a more enlarged and tolerating civilization was introduced. Roger Williams, not of the Mayflower, though a Puritan himself, and thoroughly imbued with all its peculiarities of cant and creed and form of worship, seems yet to have had naturally a more liberal spirit; and, first, perhaps, of all men, some three or more years before the Ark and the Dove touched the shores of the St. Mary's, in Maryland, taught the sublime doctrine of freedom of opinion and practice in religion. Threatened first with banishment to England, so as to "remove as far as possible, the infection of his principles," and, afterward, actually banished beyond the jurisdiction of Massachusetts, because, in the language of the sentence of the General Court, "he broached and divulged divers new and strange doctrines against the authority of magistrates" over the religious opinions of men, thereby disturbing the peace of the colony, he became the founder of Rhode Island, and, indeed, of a large part of New England society. And, whether from his teachings and example, and in the persons of his descendants, and those of his associates, or from other causes and another stock, there has always been a large infusion throughout New England of what may be called the *Roger Williams element*, as distinguished from the extreme Puritan or *Mayflower and Plymouth Rock* type of the New Englander; and its influence, till late years, has always been powerful.

Sir, I would not deny nor disparage the austere virtues of the old Puritans of England or America. But I do believe that, in the very nature of things, no community could exist long in peace, and no government endure long alone, or become great, where that element, in its earliest or its more recent form, holds supreme control. And, it is my solemn conviction, that there can be no possible or durable reunion of these States, until it shall have been again subordinated to other and more liberal and conservative elements, and, above all, until its worst and most mischievous development, Abolitionism, has been utterly extinguished. Sir, the peace of the Union and of this continent demands it. But, fortunately, those very elements exist abundantly in New England herself; and to her I look with confidence to secure to them the mastery within her limits. In fact, sir, the true voice of New England has, for some years past, been but rarely heard, here or elsewhere, in public affairs. Men now control her politics, and are in high places, State and Federal, who, twenty years ago, could not have been chosen selectmen in old Massachusetts. But, let her remember, at last, her ancient renown; let her turn from vain-glorious admiration of the stone monuments of her heroes and patriots of a former age, to generous emulation of the noble and manly virtues which they were designed to commemorate. Let us hear less from her of the Pilgrim Fathers and the Mayflower and of Plymouth Rock, and more of Roger Williams and his compatriots, and his toleration. Let her banish, now and forever, her dreamers and her sophists and her fanatics, and call back again into her State administration, and into the national councils, "her men of might, her grand in soul"—some of them still live—and she will yet escape the dangers which now threaten her with isolation.

Then, sir, while I am inexorably hostile to Puritan domination in religion or morals or literature or politics, I am not in favor of the proposed exclusion of New England. I would have the Union as it was, and, first, New England as she was. But if New England will have no union with slaveholders, if she is not content with "the Union as it was," then, upon her own head be the responsibility for secession; and there will be no more coercion now; I at least, will be exactly consistent.

And now, sir, can the central States, New York, New Jersey, and Pennsylvania, consent to separation? Can New York city? Sir, the

trade of the South made her largely what she is. She was the factor and banker of the South. Cotton filled her harbor with shipping, and her banks with gold. But in an evil hour, the foolish, I will not say bad "men of Gotham" persuaded her merchant princes—against their first lesson in business—that she could retain or force back the Southern trade by war. War, indeed, has given her, just now, a new business and trade, greater and more profitable than the old; but with disunion, that, too, must perish. And let not Wall street, or any other great interest, mercantile, manufacturing, or commercial, imagine that it shall have power enough, or wealth enough, to stand in the way of reunion through peace. Let them learn, one and all, that a public man, who has the people as his support, is stronger than they, though he may not be worth a million, nor even one dollar. A little while ago the banks said that they were king, but President Jackson speedily taught them their mistake. Next, railroads assumed to be king; and cotton once vaunted largely his kingship. Sir, these are only of the royal family—princes of the blood. There is but one king on earth. Politics is king.

But to return: New Jersey, too, is bound closely to the South, and the South to her; and more and longer than any other State, she remembered both her duty to the Constitution and her interest in the Union. And Pennsylvania, a sort of middle ground, just between the North and the South, and extending, also, to the West, is united by nearer, if not stronger ties, to every section than any other one State, unless it be Ohio. She was—she is yet—the keystone in the great but now crumbling arch of the Union. She is a border State; and, more than that, she has less within her of the fanatical or disturbing element than any of the States. The people of Pennsylvania are quiet, peaceable, practical, and enterprising, without being aggressive. They have more of the honest old English and German thrift than any other. No people mind more diligently their own business. They have but one idiosyncrasy or specialty—the tariff; and even that is really far more a matter of tradition than of substantial interest. The industry, enterprise, and thrift of Pennsylvania are abundantly able to take care of themselves against any competition. In any event, the Union is of more value, many times, to her, than any local interest.

But other ties also bind these States—Pennsylvania and New Jersey, especially—to the South, and the South to them. Only an imaginary line separates the former from Delaware and Maryland. The Delaware River, common to both Pennsylvania and New Jersey, flows into Delaware Bay. The Susquehanna empties its waters, through Pennsylvania and Maryland, into the Chesapeake. And that great watershed itself, extending to Norfolk, and, therefore, almost to the North Carolina line, does belong, and must ever belong, in common, to the central and southern States, under one government; or else the line of separation will be the Potomac to its head-waters. All of Delaware and Maryland, and the counties of Accomac and Northampton, in Virginia, would, in that event, follow the fortunes of the northern confederacy. In fact, sir, disagreeable as the idea may be to many within their limits, on both sides, no man who looks at the map and then reflects upon history and the force of natural causes, and considers the present actual and the future probable position of the hostile armies and navies at the end of this war, ought for a moment to doubt that either the States and counties which I have named, must go with the North, or Pennsylvania and New Jersey with the South. Military force on either side cannot control the destiny of the States lying between the mouth of the Chesapeake and the Hudson. And if that bay were itself made the line, Delaware, and the eastern shore of Maryland and Virginia, would belong to the North; while Norfolk, the only capacious harbor on the southeastern coast, must be commanded by the guns of some new fortress upon Cape Charles; and Baltimore, the now queenly city, seated then upon the very boundary of two rival, yes, hostile, confederacies, would rapidly fall into decay.

And now, sir, I will not ask whether the Northwest can consent to separation from the South. Never. Nature forbids. We are only a part of the great Valley of the Mississippi. There is no line of latitude upon which to separate. Neither party would desire the old line of 36° 30′ on both sides of the river; and there is no natural boundary east and west. The nearest to it are the Ohio and Missouri Rivers. But that line would leave Cincinnati and St. Louis, as border cities, like Baltimore, to decay, and, extending fifteen hundred miles in length, would become the scene of an eternal border warfare, without example even in the worst of times. Sir, we cannot, ought not, will not, separate from the South. And if you of the East who have found this war against the South, and for the negro, gratifying to your hate or profitable to your purse, will continue it till a separation be forced between the slaveholding and your non-slaveholding States, then, believe me, and accept it, as you did not the other solemn warnings of years past, the day which divides the North from the South, that self-same day decrees eternal divorce between the West and the East.

Sir, our destiny is fixed. There is not one drop of rain which, descending from the heavens and fertilizing our soil, causes it to yield an abundant harvest, but flows into the Mississippi, and there mingling with the waters of that mighty river, finds its way, at last, to the Gulf of Mexico. And we must and will follow it with travel and trade—not by treaty, but by right—freely, peaceably, and without restriction or tribute, under the same government and flag, to its home in the bosom of that gulf. Sir, we will not remain, after separation from the South, a province or appanage of the East, to bear her burdens and pay her taxes; nor, hemmed in and isolated as we are, and without a sea-coast, could we long remain a distinct confederacy. But wherever we go, married to the South or the East, we bring with us three-fourths of the territories of that valley to the Rocky Mountains, and it may be to the Pacific—the grandest and most magnificent dowry that bride ever had to bestow.

Then, sir, New England, freed at last from the domination of her sophisters, dreamers, and bigots, and restored to the control once more of her former liberal, tolerant, and conservative civilization, will not stand in the way of the reunion of these States upon terms of fair and honorable adjustment. And in this great work the central free and border slave States, too, will unite heart and hand. To the West it is a necessity, and she demands it. And let not the States now called Confederate insist upon separation and independence. What did they demand at first? Security against Abolitionism within the Union: protection from the "irrepressible conflict," and the domination of the absolute numerical majority: a change of public opinion, and consequently of political parties in the North and West, so that their local institutions and domestic peace should no longer be endangered. And now, sir, after two years of persistent and most gigantic effort on the part of this Administration to compel them to submit, but with utter and signal failure, the people of the free States are now, or are fast becoming, satisfied that the price of the Union is the utter suppression of Abolitionism or anti-slavery as a political element, and the complete subordination of the spirit of fanaticism and intermeddling which gave it birth. In any event, they are ready now, if I have not greatly misread the signs of the times, to return to the old constitutional and actual basis of fifty years ago: three-fifths rule of representation, speedy rendition of fugitives from labor, equal rights in the Territories, no more slavery agitation anywhere, and transit and temporary sojourn with slaves, without molestation, in the free States. Without all these there could be neither peace nor permanence to a restored union of States "part slave and part free." With it, the South, in addition to all the other great and multiplied benefits of union, would be far more secure in her slave property, her domestic institutions, than under a separate government. Sir, let no man, North, or West, tell me that this would perpetuate African slavery. I know it. But so does the Constitution. I repeat, sir, it is the price of the Union. Whoever hates negro slavery more than he loves the Union must demand separation at last. I think that you can never abolish slavery by fighting. Certainly you never can till you have first destroyed the South, and then, in the language, first of Mr. Douglas and afterward of Mr. Seward, converted this Government into an imperial despotism. And, sir, whenever I am forced to a choice between the loss, to my own country and race, of personal and political liberty, with all its blessings, and the involuntary domestic servitude of the negro, I shall not hesitate one moment to choose the latter alternative. The sole question, to-day, is between the Union, with slavery, or final disunion, and, I think, anarchy and despotism. I am for the Union. It was good enough for my fathers. It is good enough for us, and our children after us.

And, sir, let no man in the South tell me that she has been invaded, and that all the horrors implied in those most terrible of words, civil war, have been visited upon her. I know that, too. But we, also, of the North and West, in every State, and by thousands, who have dared so much as to question the principles and policy, or doubt the honesty, of this Administration and its party, have suffered every thing that the worst despotism could inflict, except only loss of life itself upon the scaffold. Some even have died for the cause, by the hand of the assassin. And can we forget? Never, never. Time will but burn the memory of these wrongs deeper into our hearts. But shall we break up the Union? Shall we destroy the Government, because usurping tyrants have held possession, and perverted it to the most cruel of oppressions? Was it ever so done in any other country? In Athens? Rome? England? Anywhere? No, sir; let us expel the usurper, and restore the Constitution and laws, the rights of the States, and the liberties of the people; and then, in the country of our fathers, under the Union of our fathers, and the old flag—the symbol once again of the free and the brave—let us fulfil the grand mission which Providence has appointed for us among the nations of the earth.

And now, sir, if it be the will of all sections to unite, then upon what terms? Sir, between the South and most of the States of the North, and all of the West, there is but one subject in controversy—slavery. It is the only question, said Mr. Calhoun, twenty-five years ago, of sufficient magnitude and potency to divide this Union; and divide it it will, he added, or drench the country in blood, if not arrested. It has done both. But settle it on the original basis of the Constitution, and give to each section the power to protect itself within the Union, and now, after the terrible lessons of the past two years, the Union will be stronger than before, and, indeed, endure for ages. Woe to the man, North or South, who, to the third or fourth generation, should teach men disunion.

And now the way to reunion: what so easy? Behold to-day two separate governments in one country, and without a natural dividing line; with two presidents and cabinets, and a double Congress; and yet, each under a Constitution so exactly similar, the one to the other, that a stranger could scarce discern the difference. Was ever folly and madness like this? Sir, it is not in the nature of things that it should so continue long.

But why speak of ways or terms of reunion now? The will is yet wanting in both sections. Union is consent, and good-will, and fraternal affection. War is force, hate, revenge. Is the country tired at last of war? Has the experiment been tried long enough? Has sufficient blood been shed, treasure expended, and misery inflicted in both the North and the South? What then? Stop fighting. Make an armistice—no formal treaty. Withdraw your Army from the seceded States. Reduce both armies to a fair and sufficient peace establishment. Declare absolute free trade between the North and South. Buy and sell. Agree upon a *Zollverein.* Recall your fleets. Break up your blockade. Reduce your navy. Restore travel. Open up railroads. Re-establish the telegraph. Reunite your express companies. No more Monitors and iron-clads, but set your friendly steamers and steamships again in motion. Visit the North and West. Visit the South. Exchange newspapers. Migrate. Intermarry. Let slavery alone. Hold elections at the appointed times. Let us choose a new President in sixty-four. And when the gospel of peace shall have descended again from Heaven into their hearts, and the gospel of abolition and of hate been expelled, let your clergy and the churches meet again in Christian intercourse, North and South. Let the secret orders and voluntary associations everywhere reunite as brethren once more. In short, give to all the natural, and all the artificial causes which impel us together, their fullest sway. Let time do his office—drying tears, dispelling sorrows, mellowing passion, and making herb and grass and tree to grow again upon the hundred battle-fields of this terrible war.

"But this is recognition." It is not formal recognition, to which I will not consent. Recognition now, and attempted permanent treaties about boundary, travel, and trade, and partition of Territories would end in a war fiercer and more disastrous than before. Recognition is absolute disunion; and not between the slave and the free States, but with Delaware and Maryland as part of the North, and Kentucky and Missouri part of the West. But wherever the actual line, every evil and mischief of disunion is implied in it. And, for similar reasons, sir, I would not, at this time, press hastily a convention of the States. The men who now would hold seats in such a convention, would, upon both sides, if both agreed to attend, come together full of the hate and bitterness inseparable from a civil war. No, sir; let passion have time to cool, and reason to resume its sway. It cost thirty years of desperate and most wicked patience and industry to destroy or impair the magnificent temple of this Union. Let us be content if, within three years, we shall be able to restore it.

But, certainly, what I propose is informal, practical recognition. And that is precisely what exists to-day, and has existed, more or less defined, from the first. Flags of truce, exchange of prisoners, and all your other observances of the laws, forms, and courtesies of war, are acts of recognition. Sir, does any man doubt, to-day, that there is a Confederate Government at Richmond, and that it is a "belligerent?" Even the Secretary of State has discovered it at last, though he has written ponderous folios of polished rhetoric to prove that it is not. Will continual war then, without extended and substantial success, make the Confederate States any the less a government in fact?

"But it confesses disunion." Yes, just as the surgeon, who sets your fractured limb in splints, in order that it may be healed, admits that it is broken. "But the Government will have failed to crush out the rebellion." Sir, it has failed. You went to war to prove that we had a Government. With what result? To the people of the loyal States it has, in your hands, been the Government of King Stork, but to the Confederate States, of King Log. "But the rebellion will have triumphed." Better triumph to-day than ten years hence. But I deny it. The rebellion will, at last, be crushed out, in the only way in which it ever was possible. "But no one will be hung at the end of war." Neither will there be, though the war should last half a century, except by the mob or the hand of arbitrary power. But, really, sir, if there is to be no hanging, let this Administration, and all who have done its bidding everywhere, rejoice and be exceeding glad.

And now, sir, allow me a word upon a subject of very great interest at this moment, and most important, it may be, in its influence upon the future—FOREIGN MEDIATION. I speak not of armed and hostile intervention, which I would resist as long as but one man was left to strike a blow at the invader. But friendly mediation—the kindly offer of an impartial power to stand as a daysman between the contending parties in this most bloody and exhausting strife—ought to be met in a spirit as cordial and ready as that in which it is proffered. It would be churlish to refuse. Certainly, it is not consistent with the former dignity of this Government to ask for mediation; neither, sir, would it befit its ancient magnanimity to reject it. As proposed by the Emperor of France, I would accept it at once. Now is the auspicious moment. It is the speediest, easiest, most graceful mode of suspending hostilities. Let us hear no more of the mediation of the cannon and the sword. The day for all that has gone by. Let us be statesmen at last. Sir, I give thanks, that some, at least, among the Republican party, seem ready now to lift themselves up to the height of this great argument, and to deal with it in the spirit of the patriots and great men of other countries and ages, and of the better days of the United States.

And now, sir, whatever may have been the motives of England, France, and the other great powers of Europe, in witholding recognition so long from the Confederate States, the South and the North are both indebted to them for an immense public service. The South has proved her ability to maintain herself by her own strength and resources, without foreign aid, moral or material. And the North and West—the whole country, indeed—these great powers have served incalculably, by holding back a solemn proclamation to the world that the Union of these States was finally and formally dissolved. They have left to us every motive and every chance for reunion; and if that has been the purpose of England especially—our rival so long, interested more than any other in disunion, and the consequent weakening of our great naval and commercial power, and suffering, too, as she has suffered, so long and severely because of this war—I do not hesitate to say that she has performed an act of unselfish heroism without example in history. Was such, indeed, her purpose? Let her answer before the impartial tribunal of posterity. In any event, after the great reaction in public sentiment in the North and West, to be followed, after some time, by a like reaction in the South, foreign recognition now of the Confederate States could avail little to delay or prevent final reunion, if, as I firmly believe, reunion be not only possible, but inevitable.

Sir, I have not spoken of foreign arbitration. That is quite another question. I think it impracticable, and fear it as dangerous. The very powers—or any other power—which have hesitated to aid disunion directly or by force, might, as authorized arbiters, most readily pronounce for it at last. Very grand, indeed, would be the tribunal before which the great question of the Union of these States, and the final destiny of this continent, for ages, should be heard, and historic, through all time, the ambassadors who should argue it. And, if both belligerents consent, let the subjects in controversy be referred to Switzerland, or Russia, or any other impartial and incorruptible power or state in Europe. But, at last, sir, the people of these several States here, at home, must be the final arbiters of this great quarrel in America; and the people and States of the Northwest, the mediators who shall stand, like the prophet, betwixt the living and the dead, that the plague of disunion may be stayed.

Sir, this war, horrible as it is, has taught us all some of the most important and salutary lessons which a people ever learned.

First, it has annihilated, in twenty months, all the false and pernicious theories and teachings of Abolitionism for thirty years, and which a mere appeal to facts and arguments could not have untaught in half a century. We have learned that the South is not weak, dependent, unenterprising, or corrupted by slavery, luxury, and idleness; but powerful, earnest, warlike, enduring, self-supporting, full of energy, and inexhaustible in resources. We have been taught, and now confess it openly, that African slavery, instead of being a source of weakness to the South, is one of her main elements of strength; and hence the "military necessity," we are told, of abolishing slavery in order to suppress the rebellion. We have learned, also, that the non-slaveholding white men of the South, millions in number, are immovably attached to the institution, and are its chief support; and Abolitionists have found out, to their infinite surprise and disgust, that the slave is not "panting for freedom," nor pining in silent, but, revengeful grief over cruelty and oppression inflicted upon him, but happy, contented, attached deeply to his master, and unwilling—at least not eager—to accept the precious boon of freedom, which they have proffered him. I appeal to the President for the proof. I appeal to the fact, that fewer slaves have escaped, even from Virginia, in now nearly two years, than Arnold and Cornwallis carried away in six months of invasion, in 1781. Finally, sir, we have learned, and the South, too, what the history of the world ages ago, and our own history might have taught us, that servile insurrection is the least of the dangers to which she is exposed. Hence, in my deliberate judgment, African slavery, as an institution, will come out of this conflict fifty-fold stronger than when the war began.

The South, too, sir, has learned most important lessons; and among them, that personal courage is a quality common to all sections, and that in battle, the men of the North, and especially of the West, are their equals. Hitherto there has been a mutual, and most mischievous mistake upon both sides. The men of the South overvalued their own personal courage, and undervalued ours, and we, too, readily consented; but at the same time they exaggerated our aggregate strength and resources, and underestimated their own; and we fell into the same error; and hence, the original and fatal mistake, or vice, of the military policy of the North, and which has already broken down the war by its own weight—the belief that we could bring overwhelming numbers and power into the field, and upon the sea, and crush out the South at a blow. But twenty months of terrible warfare have corrected many errors, and taught us the wisdom of a century. And now, sir, every one of these lessons will profit us all for ages to come; and if we do but reunite, will bind us in a closer, firmer, more durable union than ever before.

I have finished now, Mr. Speaker, what I desired to say at this time, upon the great question of the reunion of these States. I have spoken freely and boldly—not wisely, it may be, for the present, or for myself personally, but most wisely for the future and for my country. Not courting censure, I yet do not shrink from it. My own immediate personal interests, and my chances just now for the more material rewards of ambition, I again surrender as hostages to that GREAT HEREAFTER, the echo of whose footsteps already I hear along the highway of time. Whoever, here or elsewhere, believes that war can restore the Union of these States; whoever would have a war for the abolition of slavery, or disunion; and he who demands Southern independence and final separation—let him speak, for him I have offended. Devoted to the Union from the beginning, I will not desert it now in this the hour of its sorest trial.

Sir, it was the day-dream of my boyhood, the cherished desire of my heart in youth, that I might live to see the hundredth anniversary of our national independence, and, as orator of the day, exult in the expanding glories and greatness of the still United States. That vision lingers yet before my eyes, obscured, indeed, by the clouds and thick darkness and the blood of civil war. But, sir, if the men of this generation are wise enough to profit by the hard experience of the past two years, and will turn their hearts now from bloody intents to the words and arts of peace, that day will find us again the United States. And if not earlier, as I would desire and believe, at least upon that day let the great work of reunion be consummated; that henceforth, for ages, the States and the people who shall fill up this mighty continent, united under one Constitution, and in one Union, and the same destiny, shall celebrate it as the birthday both of Independence and of the Great Restoration.

Sir, I repeat it, we are in the midst of the very crisis of this revolution. If, to-day, we secure peace, and begin the work of reunion, we shall yet escape; if not, I see nothing before us but universal political and social revolution, anarchy, and bloodshed, compared with which, the Reign of Terror in France was a merciful visitation.

THE CONSCRIPTION BILL.—ARBITRARY ARRESTS.

Speech delivered in the House of Representatives, February 23, 1863.*

Mr. Speaker: I do not propose to discuss this bill at any great length in this House. I am satisfied that there is a settled purpose to enact it into a law, so far as it is possible for the action of the Senate and House, and the President to make it such. I appeal, therefore, from you, from them, directly to the country; to a forum where there is no military committee, no previous question, no hour rule, and where the people themselves are the masters. I commend the spirit in which this discussion was commenced by the chairman of the military committee (Mr. Olin), and I do it the more cheerfully because, unfortunately, he is not always in so good a temper as he was to-day; and I trust that throughout the debate, and on its close, he will exhibit that same disposition which characterized his opening remarks. Only let me caution him that he cannot dictate to the minority here what course they shall pursue. But, sir, I regret that I cannot extend the commendation to the gentleman from Pennsylvania (Mr. Campbell), who addressed the House a little while ago. His speech was extremely offensive, and calculated to stir up a spirit of bitterness and strife, not at all consistent with that in which debates in this House should be conducted. If he, or any other gentleman of the majority, imagines that any one here is to be deterred by threats, from the expression of his opinions, or from giving such votes as he may see fit to give, he has utterly misapprehended the temper and determination of those who sit on this side of the Chamber. His threat I hurl back with defiance into his teeth. I spurn it. I spit upon it. That is not the argument to be addressed to equals here; and I, therefore, most respectfully suggest, that hereafter, all such be dispensed with, and that we shall be spared personal denunciation, and insinuations against the loyalty of men who sit with me here; men whose devotion to the Constitution, and attachment to the Union of these States is as ardent and immovable as yours, and who only differ

* Upon this bill a debate ensued, which, for power, eloquence, strength of argument, and bold defence of constitutional rights, has not often been equalled. Inspired with the courage always given to those who are right, Vallandigham, Voorhees, Pendleton, Cox, Biddle, and others, standing unmoved against the strong current of despotism, boldly assailed the most dangerous and vulnerable features of the Bill. At the most exciting moment of the conflict, Mr. V. addressed the House. Bingham, of Ohio, thought his "assumptions unworthy of any man who had grown to man's estate under the shelter of the Constitution." Voorhees replied he "had held the House spell-bound with one of the ablest arguments he had ever heard."

from you as to the mode of securing the great object nearest their hearts.

[Here Mr. VALLANDIGHAM yielded the floor to Mr. CAMPBELL at his request for an explanation, which being made in highly offensive language, Mr. V. declined to yield longer, saying, amid applause in the gallery, "That is enough. Not another moment after that. I yielded the floor in the spirit of a gentleman, and not to be met in the manner of a blackguard." A scene of confusion on the floor and in the galleries, followed for some moments, after which Mr. V. resumed as follows :]

I think, Mr. Speaker, that this lesson has not been lost; and that it is sufficiently impressed now upon the minds of the audience that this is a legislative, and is supposed to be a deliberative, assembly, and that no breach of decorum or order should occur among them, whatever may be the conduct of any of us on the floor.

The member from Pennsylvania (Mr. Campbell) alluded to-day, generally, to gentlemen on this side of the House. There was no mistaking the application. The language and gesture were both plain enough. He ventured also, approvingly, to call our attention to the opinions and course of conduct of some Democrats in the State of New York, as if we were to learn our lessons in Democracy, or in any thing else, from that quarter. I do not know, certainly, to whom he alluded. Perhaps it was to a gentleman who spoke, not long since, in the city of New York, and advocated on that occasion, what is called in stereotype phrase "the vigorous prosecution of the war," and who, but two months previously, addressed assemblages in the same State and city, in which he proposed only to take Richmond, and then let the "wayward sisters depart in peace." Now I know of no one on this side of the Chamber occupying such a position; and I, certainly, will not go to that quarter to learn lessons in patriotism or Democracy.

I have already said, that it is not my purpose to debate the general merits of this Bill at large, and for the reason, that I am satisfied that argument is of no avail here. I appeal, therefore, to the people. Before them, I propose to try this great question—the question of constitutional power, and of the unwise and injudicious exercise of it in this Bill. We have been compelled, repeatedly, since the 4th of March, 1861, to appeal to the same tribunal. We appealed to it at the recent election. And the people did pronounce judgment upon our appeal. The member from Pennsylvania ought to have heard their sentence, and I venture to say that he did hear it, on the night of the election. In Ohio they spoke as with the voice of many waters. The very question, of summary and arbitrary arrests, now sanctioned in this Bill, was submitted, as a direct issue, to the people of that State, as also of other States, and their verdict was rendered upon it. The Democratic Convention of Ohio, assembled on the 4th of July in the city of Columbus, the largest and best ever held in the State, among other resolutions, of the same temper and spirit, adopted this without a dissenting voice:

> "And we utterly condemn and denounce the repeated and gross violation, by the Executive of the United States, of the rights thus secured by the Constitution; and we also utterly repudiate and condemn the monstrous dogma, that in time of war the Constitution is suspended, or its power in any respect enlarged beyond the letter and true meaning of that instrument.
>
> "And we view, also, with indignation and alarm, the illegal and unconstitutional seizure and imprisonment, for illeged political offences, of our citizens, without judicial process, in States where such process is unobstructed, but by Executive order by telegraph, or otherwise, and call upon all who uphold the Union, the Constitution, and the laws, to unite with us, in denouncing and repelling such flagrant violation of the State and Federal Constitutions, and tyrannical infraction of the rights and liberties of American citizens; and that the people of this State CANNOT SAFELY, AND WILL NOT, SUBMIT to have the freedom of speech and freedom of the press, the two great and essential bulwarks of civil liberty, put down by unwarranted and despotic exertion of power."

On that, the judgment of the people was given at the October elections, and the party candidates nominated by the Convention which adopted that resolution, were triumphantly elected. So, too, with the candidates of the same party in the States of Wisconsin, Illinois, Indiana, Pennsylvania, New Jersey, and New York. And, sir, that "healthy reaction," recently, of which the member from Pennsylvania (Mr. Campbell) affected to boast, has escaped my keenest sense of vision. I see only that handwriting on the wall which the fingers of the people wrote against him and his party, and this whole Administration, at the ballot-box, in October and November last. Talk to me, indeed, of the leniency of the Executive! too few arrests! too much forbearance by those in power! Sir, it s the people who have been too lenient. They have submitted to your oppressions and wrongs as no free people ought ever to submit. But the day of patient endurance has gone by at last. Mistake them not. They will be lenient no longer. Abide by the Constitution, stand by the laws, restore the Union, if *you* can restore it—not by force—you have tried that and failed. Try some other method now—the ancient, the approved, the reasonable way—the way in which the Union was first made. Surrender it not now—not yet—never. But unity is not Union; and attempt not, at your peril—I warn you—to coerce unity by the utter destruction of the Constitution and of the rights of the States and the liberties of the people. Union is liberty and consent: unity is despotism and force. For what was the Union ordained? As a splendid edifice, to attract the gaze and admiration of the world? As a magnificent temple—a stupendous superstructure of marble and iron, like this

Capitol, upon whose lofty dome the bronzed image—hollow and inanimate—of Freedom is soon to stand erect in colossal mockery, while the true spirit, the living Goddess of Liberty, veils her eyes and turns away her face in sorrow, because, upon the altar established here, and dedicated by our fathers to her worship—you, a false and most disloyal priesthood, offer up, night and morning, the mingled sacrifices of servitude and despotism? No, sir. It was for the sake of the altar, the service, the religion, the devotees, that the temple of the Union was first erected; and when these are all gone, let the edifice itself perish. Never—never—never will the people consent to lose their own personal and political rights and liberties, to the end that you may delude and mock them with the splendid unity of despotism.

Sir, what are the bills which have passed, or are still before the House? The bill to give the President entire control of the currency—the purse—of the country. A tax-bill to clothe him with power over the whole property of the country. A bill to put all power in his hands over the personal liberties of the people. A bill to indemnify him, and all under him, for every act of oppression and outrage already consummated. A bill to enable him to suspend the writ of *habeas corpus*, in order to justify or protect him, and every minion of his, in the arrests which he or they may choose to make—arrests, too, for mere opinion's sake. Sir, some two hundred years ago, men were burned at the stake, subjected to the horrors of the Inquisition, to all the tortures that the devilish ingenuity of man could invent—for what? For opinions on questions of religion—of man's duty and relation to his God. And now, to-day, for opinions on questions political, under a free government, in a country whose liberties were purchased by our fathers by seven years' outpouring of blood, and expenditure of treasure—we have lived to see men, the born heirs of this precious inheritance, subjected to arrest and cruel imprisonment at the caprice of a President, or a secretary, or a constable. And, as if that were not enough, a bill is introduced here, to-day, and pressed forward to a vote, with the right of debate, indeed—extorted from you by the minority—but without the right to amend, with no more than the mere privilege of protest—a bill which enables the President to bring under his power, as Commander-in-chief, every man in the United States between the ages of twenty and forty-five—three millions of men. And, as if not satisfied with that, this bill provides, further, that every other citizen, man, woman, and child, under twenty years of age and over forty-five, including those that may be exempt between these ages, shall be also, at the mercy,—so far as his personal liberty is concerned—of some miserable "provost-marshal" with the rank of a captain of cavalry, who is never to see service in the field; and every Congressional district in the United States is to be governed—yes, governed—by this petty satrap—this military eunuch—this Baba—and he even may be black—who is to do the bidding of your Sultan, or his Grand Vizier. Sir, you have but one step further to go—give him the symbols of his office—the Turkish bow-string and the sack.

What is it, sir, but a bill to abrogate the Constitution, to repeal all existing laws, to destroy all rights, to strike down the judiciary, and erect, upon the ruins of civil and political liberty, a stupendous superstructure of despotism. And for what? To enforce law? No, sir. It is admitted now, by the legislation of Congress, and by the two proclamations of the President; it is admitted by common consent, that the war is for the abolition of negro slavery, to secure freedom to the black man. You tell me, some of you, I know, that it is so prosecuted because this is the only way to restore the Union; but others openly and candidly confess that the purpose of the prosecution of the war is to abolish slavery. And thus, sir, it is that the freedom of the negro is to be purchased, under this bill, at the sacrifice of every right of the white men of the United States.

Sir, I am opposed—earnestly, inexorably opposed—to this measure. If there were not another man in this House to vote against it—if there were none to raise his voice against it—I at least, dare stand here alone in my place, as a Representative, undismayed, unseduced, unterrified, and heedless of the miserable cry of "disloyalty," of sympathy with the rebellion, and with rebels, to denounce it as the very consummation of the conspiracy against the Constitution and the liberties of my country.

Sir, I yield to no man in devotion to the Union. I am for maintaining it upon the principles on which it was first formed; and I would have it, at every sacrifice, except of liberty, which is "the life of the nation." I have stood by it in boyhood and in manhood, to this hour; and I will not now consent to yield it up; nor am I to be driven from an earnest and persistent support of the only means by which it can be restored, either by the threats of the party of the Administration here, or because of affected sneers and contemptuous refusals to listen, now, to reunion, by the party of the Administration at Richmond. I never was weak enough to cower before the reign of terror inaugurated by the men in power here, nor vain enough to expect favorable responses now, or terms of settlement, from the men in power, or the presses under their control, in the South. Neither will ever compromise this great quarrel, nor agree to peace on the basis of reunion; but I repeat it—stop fighting, and let time and natural causes operate—uncontrolled by military influences—and the ballot there, as the ballot here, will do its work. I am for the Union of these States; and but for my profound conviction that it can never be restored by force and arms; or, if so restored, could not be maintained, and would not be worth maintaining, I would have united, at first—even now would unite, cordially—in giving, as I have acquiesced, silently, in your taking, all the men and all the money you have demanded. But I did not believe, and do not now believe, that the war could end in any thing but final defeat; and if it should last long enough, then in disunion; or, if successful upon the principles now proclaimed, that it must and would end in the establishment of an imperial military despotism—not only in the South—but in the North and West. And to that I never will submit. No, rather, I am ready first to yield up property, and my own personal liberty—nay, life itself.

Sir, I do not propose to discuss now the question of the constitutionality of this measure. The gentleman from Ohio, who preceded me (Mr. White), has spared me the necessity of an argument on that point. He has shown that, between the Army of the United States, of which, by the Constitution, the President of the United States is the Commander-in-chief, and the militia, belonging to the States, there is a wide, and clearly marked line of distinction. The distinction is fully and strongly defined in the Constitution; and has been recognized in the entire legislation and practice of the Government from the beginning. The States have the right, and have always exercised it, of appointing the officers of their militia, and you have no power to take it away. Sir, this bill was originally introduced in the Senate as a militia bill, and as such, it recognized the right of the States to appoint the officers; but finding it impossible, upon that basis, to give to the Executive of the United States, the entire control of the millions thus organized into a military force, as the conspirators against State rights and popular liberty desire, the original bill was abandoned; and to-day behold here a stupendous Conscription Bill, for a standing army of more than three millions of men, forced from their homes, their families, their fields, and their workshops—an army organized, officered, and commanded by the servant President, now the master Dictator, of the United States. And for what? Foreign war? Home defence? No; but for coercion, invasion, and the abolition of negro slavery by force. Sir, the conscription of Russia is mild and merciful and just, compared with this. And yet, the enforcement of that conscription has just stirred again the slumbering spirit of insurrection in Poland, though the heel of despotic power has trodden upon the necks of her people for a century.

Where now are your taunts and denunciations, heaped upon the Confederate Government for its conscription, when you, yourselves, become the humble imitators of that government, and bring in here a Conscription Bill, more odious even than that passed by the Confederate Congress at Richmond? Sir, the chairman of the military committee rejoiced that for the last two years the army had been filled up by voluntary enlistments. Yes, your army has hitherto been thus filled up by the men of the North and West. One million two hundred and thirty-seven thousand men—for most of the drafted men enlisted, or procured substitutes—have voluntarily surrendered their civil rights, subjected themselves to military law, and thus passed under the command and within the control of the President of the United States. It is not for me to complain of that. It was their own act—done of their own free will and accord—unless bounties, promises, and persuasion may be regarded as coercion. The work you proposed was gigantic, and your means proportionate to it. And what has been the result? What do you propose now? What is this Bill? A confession that the people are no longer ready to enlist; that they are not willing to carry on this war longer, until some effort has been made to settle this great controversy in some other way than by the sword. And yet, in addition to the 1,237,000 men who have voluntarily enlisted, you propose now to force the entire body of the people, between the ages of twenty and forty-five, under military law, and within the control of the President, as Commander-in-chief of the Army, for three years, or during the war—which is to say "for life;" ay, sir, for life, and half your army has already found, or will yet find, that their enlistment was for life too.

I repeat it, sir, this bill is a confession that the people of the country are against this war. It is a solemn admission, upon the record in the legislation of Congress, that they will not voluntarily consent to wage it any longer. And yet, ignoring every principle upon which the Government was founded, this measure is an attempt, by compulsion, to carry it on against the will of the people. Sir, what does all this mean? You were a majority at first, the people were almost unanimously with you, and they were generous and enthusiastic in your support. You abused your power, and your trust, and you failed to do the work which you promised. You have lost the confidence, lost the hearts of the people. You are now a minority at home. And yet, what a spectacle is exhibited here to-night! You, an accidental, temporary majority in this House, condemned and repudiated by the people, are exhausting the few remaining hours of your political life, in attempting to defeat the popular will, and to compel, by the most desperate and despotic of expedients ever resorted to, the submission of the majority of the people, at home, to the minority, their servants, here. Sir, this experiment has been tried before, in other ages and countries, and its issue always, among a people born free, or fit to be free, has been expulsion or death to the conspirators and tyrants.

I make no threats. They are not arguments fit to be addressed to equals in a legislative assembly; but there is truth, solemn alarming truth, in what has been said, to-day, by gentlemen on this side of the Chamber. Have a care, have a care, I entreat you, that you do not press these measures too far. I shall do nothing to stir up an already excited people—not because of any fear of your contemptible petty provost-marshals, but because I desire to see no violence or revolution in the North or West. Yet I warn you now, that whenever, against the will of the people, and to perpetuate power and office in a popular government which they have taken from you, you undertake to enforce this bill, and, like the destroying angel in Egypt, enter every house for the first-born sons of the people—remember Poland. You cannot, and will not be permitted to establish a military despotism. Be not encouraged by the submission of other nations. The people of Austria, of Russia, of Spain, of Italy, have never known the independence and liberty of freemen. France, in seventy years, has witnessed seven principal revolutions—the last brought about in a single day, by the arbitrary attempt of the king to suppress freedom of speech and of the press, and next the free assembling of the people; and when he would have retraced his steps and restored these liberties, a voice from the galleries, not filled with clerks and plunderers and place-men, uttered the sentiments and will of the people of France, in words now historic:—"It is too late." The people of England never submitted, and would not now submit, for a moment, to the despotism which you propose to inaugurate in America. England cannot, to-day, fill up her standing armies by conscription. Even the "press gang," unknown to her laws, but for a time acquiesced in, has long since been declared illegal; and a sweeping conscription like this now, would hurl not only the ministry from power, but the queen from her throne.

Sir, so far as this bill is a mere military measure, I might have been content to have given a silent vote against it; but there are two provisions in it hostile, both to the letter and spirit of the Constitution, and inconsistent with the avowed scope and purpose of the bill itself; and certainly, as I read them in the light of events which have occurred in the past two years, of a character which demands that the majority of this House shall strike them out. There is nothing in the argument, that we have no time to send the bill back to the Senate, lest it should be lost. The presiding officers of both Houses are friends of the bill, and will constitute committees of conference of men favorable to it. They will agree at once, and can at any moment between this and the 4th of March, present their report as a question of the highest privilege; and you have a two-thirds majority in both branches to adopt it.

With these provisions of the bill stricken out, leaving it simply as a military measure, to be tested by the great question of peace or war, I would be willing that the majority of the House should take the responsibility of passing it without further debate; although, even then, you would place every man in the United States, between the ages of twenty and forty-five, under military law, and within the control, everywhere, of the President, except the very few who are exempt; but you would leave the shadow, at least, of liberty to all men not between these ages, or not subject to draft under this bill, and to the women and children of the country too.

Sir, these two provisions propose to go a step further, and include every one, man, woman, and child, and to place him or her under the arbitrary power, not only of the President and his cabinet, but of some two hundred and fifty other petty officers, captains of cavalry, appointed by him. There is no distinction of sex, and none of age. These provisions, sir, are contained in the seventh and twenty-fifth sections of the bill. What are they? I comment not on the appointment of a general provost-marshal of the United States, and provost-marshals in every Congressional District. Let that pass. But what do you propose to make the duty of each provost-marshal in carrying out the draft? Among other things, that he shall "inquire into, and report to the provost-marshal general"—what? Treason? No. Felony? No. Breach of the peace, or violation of the law of any kind? No; but "treasonable practices;" yes, treasonable practices. What mean you by these strange, ominous words? Whence come they? Sir, they are no more new or original than any other of the cast-off rags filched by this Administration from the lumber-house of other and more antiquated despotisms. The history of European tyranny has taught us somewhat of this doctrine of constructive treason. Treasonable practices! Sir, the very language is borrowed from the British monarchs, some hundreds of years ago. It brings up the old, identical quarrel of the fourteenth century. Treasonable practices! It was this that called forth that English Act of Parliament of twenty-fifth Edward III., from which we have borrowed the noble provision against constructive treason, in the Constitution of the United States. Arbitrary arrests, for no crime known, defined or limited by law, but for pretended offences, herded together under the general and most comprehensive name of "treasonable practices," had been so frequent, in the worst periods of English history, that in the language of the Act of Henry the Fourth, "no man knew how to behave himself, or what to do or say, for doubt of the pains of treason."

The statute of Edward the Third had cut all these fungous, toadstool treasons up by the root; and yet, so prompt is arbitrary power to denounce all opposition to it as treasonable, that, as Lord Hale observes,

> "Things were so carried by parties and factions, in the succeeding reign of Richard the Second, that this statute was but little observed, but as this or that party got the better. So the crime of high treason was, in a manner, arbitrarily imposed and adjudged *to the disadvantage of the party which was to be judged;* which by various vicissitudes and revolutions, mischiefed all parties, first and last, and left a great unsettledness and unquietness in the minds of the people, and was one of the occasions of the unhappiness of the king."

And he adds, that

> "It came to pass that almost every offence that was, *or seemed to be*, a breach of the faith and allegiance due to the king, was, by *construction, consequence, and interpretation*, raised into the offence of high treason."

Richard the Second procured an Act of Parliament—even he did not pretend to have power to do it by proclamation—declaring that the bare purpose to depose the king, and to place another in his stead, without any overt act, was treason; and yet, as Blackstone remarks, so little effect have over-violent laws to prevent crime, that within two years afterward this very prince was both deposed and put to death. Still the struggle for arbitrary and despotic power continued; and up to the time of Charles the First, at various periods, almost every conceivable offence relating to the government, and every form of opposition to the king, was declared high treason. Among these were execrations against the king; calling him opprobrious names by public writing; refusing to abjure the Pope; marrying without license, certain of the king's near relatives; derogating from his royal style or title; impugning his supremacy, or assembling riotously to the number of twelve, and refusing to disperse on proclamation. But steadily, in better times, the people and the Parliament of England returned to the spirit and letter of the Act of Edward the Third, passed by a Parliament which now, for five hundred years, has been known and honored as *Parliamentum Benedictum*, the "blessed Parliament"—just as this Congress will be known, for ages to come, as "The Accursed Congress"—and among many other acts, it was declared by a statute, in the first year of the Fourth Henry's reign, that "*in no time to come* any treason be judged, otherwise than as ordained by the statute of king Edward the Third." And for nearly two hundred years, it has been the aim of the lawyers and judges of England to adhere to the plain letter, spirit, and intent of that act, "to be extended," in the language of Erskine, in his noble defence of Hardy, "by no new or occasional constructions—to be strained by no fancied analogies—to be measured by no rules of political expediency—to be judged of by no theory—to be determined by the wisdom of no individual, however wise—but to be expounded by the simple, genuine letter of the law."

Such, sir, is the law of treason in England to-day; and so much of the just and admirable statute of Edward as is applicable to our form of government, was embodied in the Constitution of the United States. The men of 1787 were well read in history and in English constitutional law. They knew that monarchs and governments, in all ages, had struggled to extend the limits of treason, so as to include all opposition to those in power. They had learned the maxim that, miserable is the servitude where the law is either uncertain or unknown, and had studied and valued the profound declaration of Montesquieu, that "if the crime of treason be indeterminate, that alone is sufficient to make any government degenerate into arbitrary power." Hear Madison, in the *Federalist:*

"As *new-fangled and artificial treasons* have been the great engines by which violent factions, the natural offspring of free governments, have usually *wreaked their alternate malignity on each other*, the convention have, with great judgment, opposed a barrier to this peculiar danger, by inserting a constitutional definition of the crime, fixing the proof necessary for the conviction of it, and restraining the Congress, even in punishing it, from extending the consequences of guilt beyond the person of its author."

And Story, not foreseeing the possibility of such a party or Administration as is now in power, declared it "*an impassable barrier* against arbitrary constructions, either by the courts or by Congress, upon the crime of treason." "Congress"—that, sir, is the word, for he never dreamed that the President, or, still less, his clerks, the cabinet ministers, would attempt to declare and punish treasons. And yet, what have we lived to hear in America daily, not in political harangues, or the press only, but in official proclamations and in bills in Congress! Yes, your high officials talk now of "treasonable practices," as glibly "as girls of thirteen do of puppy dogs." Treasonable practices! Disloyalty! Who imported these precious phrases, and gave them a legal settlement here? Your Secretary of War. He it was who, by command of our most noble President, authorized every marshal, every sheriff, every township constable, or city policeman, in every State in the Union, to fix, in his own imagination, what he might choose to call a treasonable or disloyal practice, and then to arrest any citizen at his discretion, without an accusing oath, and without due process, or any process of law. And now, sir, all this monstrous tyranny, against the whole spirit and the very letter of the Constitution, is to be deliberately embodied in an Act of Congress! Your petty provost-marshals are to determine what treasonable practices are, and "inquire into," detect, spy out, eavesdrop, ensnare, and then inform, report to the chief spy at Washington. These, sir, are now to be our American liberties under your Administration. There is not a crowned head in Europe who dare venture on such an experiment. How long think you this people will submit? But words, too—conversation or public speech—are to be adjudged "treasonable practices." Men, women, and children are to be haled to prison for free speech. Whoever shall denounce or oppose this Administration—whoever may affirm that war will not restore the Union, and teach men the gospel of peace, may be reported and arrested, upon some old grudge, and by some ancient enemy, it may be, and imprisoned as guilty of a treasonable practice.

Sir, there can be but one treasonable practice, under the Constitution, in the United States. Admonished by the lessons of English history, the framers of that instrument defined what treason is. It is the only offence defined in the Constitution. We know what it is. Every man can tell whether he has committed treason. He has but to look into the Constitution to find out. But neither the Executive, nor Congress, nor both combined, nor the courts, have a right to declare, either by pretended law, or by construction, that any other offence shall be treason, except that defined and limited in this instrument. What is treason? It is the highest offence known to the law—the most execrable crime known to the human heart—the crime of *læsæ majestatis;* of the parricide who lifts his hand against the country of his birth or his adoption. "Treason against the United States," says the Constitution, "shall consist ONLY in levying war against them, or in adhering to their enemies, giving them aid and comfort." (Here a Republican member nodded several times and smiled, and Mr. V. said:) Ah, sir, I understand you. But was Lord Chatham guilty of legal treason, treasonable aid and comfort, when he denounced the war against the Colonies, and rejoiced that America had resisted? Was Burke, or Fox, or Barré guilty, when defending the Americans, in the British Parliament, and demanding conciliation and peace? Were even the Federalists guilty of treason, as defined in the Constitution, for "giving aid and comfort" to the enemy, in the war of 1812? Were the Whigs in 1846? Was the Ohio Senator liable to punishment, under the Constitution, and by law, who said, sixteen years ago, in the Senate Chamber, when we were at war with Mexico, "If I were a Mexican as I am an American, I would greet your volunteers with bloody hands, and welcome them to hospitable graves?" Was Abraham Lincoln guilty, because he denounced that same war, while a Representative on the floor of this house? Was all this "adhering to the enemy, giving them aid and comfort," within the meaning of this provision?

A MEMBER. The Democratic papers said so.

Mr. VALLANDIGHAM. Sir, I am speaking now as a lawyer, and as a legislator, to legislators and lawyers acting under oath and the other special and solemn sanctions of this Chamber, and not in the loose language of the political canvass. And I repeat, sir, that if such had been the intent of the Constitution, the whole Federal party, and the whole Whig party, and their Representatives in this and the other Chamber, might have been indicted and punished as traitors. Yet, not one of them was ever arrested. And shall they, or their descendants, undertake now to denounce and to punish, as guilty of treason, every man who opposes the policy of this Administration, or is against this civil war, and for peace upon honorable terms? I hope, in spite of the hundreds of your provost-marshals, and all your threats, that there will be so much of opposition to the war, as will compel the Administration to show a decent respect for, and yield some sort of obedience to, the Constitution and laws, and to the rights and liberties of the States and of the people.

But to return; the Constitution not only defines the crime of treason, but, in its jealous care to guard against the abuses of tyrannic power, it expressly ascertains the character of the proof, and the number of witnesses necessary for conviction, and limits the punishment to the person of the offender, thus going beyond both the statute of Edward, and the common law. And yet every one of these provisions is ignored or violated by this bill.

"No person," says the Constitution, "shall be convicted of treason"—as just defined—"unless on the testimony of *two witnesses.*"

Where, when, and by whom, sir, are the two witnesses to be examined, and under what oath? By your provost-marshals, your captains of cavalry? By the jailers of your military bastiles, and inside of forts Warren and Lafayette? Before arrest, upon arrest, while in prison, when discharged, or at any time at all? Has any witness ever been examined in any case heretofore? What means the Constitution by declaring that no person shall be *convicted* of treason "unless on the *testimony of two witnesses?*" Clearly, conviction in a judicial court, upon testimony openly given under oath, with all the sanctions and safeguards of a judicial trial to the party accused. And if any doubt there could be upon this point, it is removed by the sixth article of the amendments.

But the Constitution proceeds:

"Unless on the testimony of two witnesses *to the same overt act.*"

But words, and still less, thoughts or opinions, sir, are not acts; and yet, nearly every case of arbitrary arrest and imprisonment, in the wholly loyal States at least, has been for words spoken or written, or for thoughts, or opinions supposed to be entertained by the party arrested. And that, too, sir, is precisely what is intended by this bill.

But further:

"The testimony of two witnesses to the same overt act, *or confession in open court*"

What court? The court of some deputy provost-marshal at home, or of your provost-marshal general, or Judge-Advocate General, here in Washington? The court of a military bastile, whose gates are shut day and night against every officer of the law, and whose very casemates are closed to the light and air of heaven? Call you that "open court?" Not so the Constitution. It means judicial court, law court, with judge and jury and witnesses and counsel; and to speak of it as anything else, is a confusion of language, and an insult to intelligence and common sense. Yet, to-night, you deliberately propose to enact the illegal and unconstitutional executive orders, or proclamations, of last summer, into the semblance and form of law.

"To inquire into treasonable practices," says the bill. So, then, your provost-marshals are to be deputy spies to the grand spy, holding his secret inquisitions here in Washington, upon secret reports, sent by telegraph perhaps, or through the mails, both under the control of the Executive. What right has he to arrest and hold me without a hearing, because some deputy spy of his chooses to report me guilty of "disloyalty," or of "treasonable practices?" Is this the liberty secured by the Constitution? Sir, let me tell you, that if the purpose of this bill be to crush out all opposition to the Administration and the party in power, you have no constitutional right to enact it, and not force enough to compel the people, your masters, to submit.

But the enormity of the measure does not stop here. Says the Constitution:

"Congress shall make no law abridging the freedom of speech, or of the press."

And yet speech—mere words, derogatory to the President, or in opposition to his Administration, and his party and policy, have over and over again, been reported by the spies and informers and shadows, or other minions, of the men in power, as "disloyal practices," for which hundreds of free American citizens, of Caucasian, not African, descent, have been arrested and imprisoned for months, without public accusation, and without trial by jury, or trial at all. Even upon pretence of guilt of that most vague and indefinite, but most comprehensive of all offences, "discouraging enlistments," men have been seized at midnight, and dragged from their beds, their homes, and their families, to be shut up in the stone casemates of your military fortresses, as felons. And now, by this bill, you propose to declare, in the form and semblance of law, that whoever "counsels or dissuades" any one from the performance of the military duty required under this conscription, shall be summarily arrested by your provost-marshals, and held, without trial, till the draft shall have been completed. Sir, even the "Sedition Law" of '98 was constitutional, merciful, and just, compared with this execrable enactment. Wisely did Hamilton ask, in the *Federalist*, "What signifies a declaration that the liberty of the press (or of speech) shall be inviolably preserved, when its security must altogether depend on public opinion, *and on the general spirit of the people*, and of the Government."

But this extraordinary bill does not stop here.

"No person," says the Constitution,—"*no* person shall be held to answer for a capital or otherwise infamous crime, unless on a presentment or indictment of a grand jury, except in cases arising in the land and naval force, or in the militia when in actual service in time of war or public danger; nor be deprived of life, liberty, or property, without due process of law."

Note the exception. Every man not in the military service, is exempt from arrest, except by due process of law, or, being arrested without it, is entitled to demand immediate inquiry and discharge, or bail; and if held, then presentment or indictment by a grand jury in a civil court, and according to the law of the land. And yet you now propose, by this Bill, in addition to the 1,237,000 men who have voluntarily surrendered that great right of freemen, second only to the ballot—and, indeed, essential to it—to take it away forcibly, and against their consent, from three millions more, whose only crime is that they happen to have been so born as to be now between the ages of twenty and forty-five. Do it, if you can, under the Constitution; and when you have thus forced them into the military service, they will be subject to military law, and not entitled to arrest only upon due process of law, nor to indictment by a grand jury in a civil court. But you cannot, you shall not—because the Constitution forbids it—deprive the whole people, also, of the United States of these rights, "inestimable to them, and formidable to tyrants only," under "the war power," or upon pretence of "military necessity," and by virtue of an act of Congress creating and defining new treasons, new offences, not only unknown to the Constitution, but expressly excluded by it.

But again:

"In all criminal prosecutions,"—

and wherever a penalty is to be imposed, imprisonment or fine inflicted, it is a criminal prosecution—

"In all criminal prosecutions," says the Constitution, "the accused shall enjoy the right to a speedy and public trial, by an impartial jury of the State and district wherein the crime shall have been committed, which district shall have been previously ascertained by law; and to be informed of the nature and cause of the accusation; to be confronted with the witnesses against him; to have compulsory process for obtaining witnesses in his favor, and to have the assistance of counsel for his defence."

Do you propose to allow any of these rights? No, sir—none—not one; but, in the twenty-fifth section, you empower these provost-marshals of yours to arrest any man—men not under military law—whom he may charge, or any one else may charge before him, with "counselling or dissuading" from military service, and to hold him in confinement indefinitely, until the draft has been completed. Sir, has it been completed in Connecticut yet? Is it complete in New York? Has it been given up? If so now, nevertheless it was in process of pretended execution for months. In any event, you propose, here, to leave to the discretion of the Executive the time during which all persons arrested, under the provisions of this Bill, shall be held in confinement upon that summary and arbitrary arrest; and when he sees fit, and then only, shall the accused be delivered over to the civil authorities for trial. And is this the speedy and public trial by jury, which the Constitution secures to every citizen not in the military service?

"The State and district wherein the crime"—

Yes, crime, for crime it must be, known to and defined by law, to justify the arrest—

"Shall have been committed, which district shall have been previously ascertained by law."

Do you mean to obey that, and to observe State lines, or district lines in arrests and imprisonments? Has it ever been done? Were not Keyes, and Olds, and Mahoney, and Sheward, and my friend here to the left (Mr. Allen, of Illinois), and my other friend from Maryland (Mr. May), dragged from their several States and districts, to New York, or Massachusetts, or to this city? The pirate, the murderer, the counterfeiter, the thief—you would have seized by due and sworn process of law, and tried forthwith, by jury, at home; but honorable and guiltless citizens, members of this House, your peers upon this floor, were thrust, and may, again, under this bill, be thrust into distant dungeons and bastiles, upon the pretence of some crawling, verminous spy and informer, that they have "dissuaded" some one from obedience to the draft, or are otherwise guilty of some "treasonable practice."

"And to be informed of the nature and cause of the accusation."

How? By presentment or indictment of a grand jury. When? "Speedily," says the Constitution. "When the draft is completed," says this bill; and the President shall determine that. But who is to limit and define "counselling or dissuading" from military service? Who shall ascertain and inform the accused of the "nature and cause" of a "treasonable practice?" Who, of all the thousand victims of arbitrary arrests within the last twenty-two months, even to this day, has been informed of the charge against him, although long since released? Yet even the Roman pro-consul, in a conquered province, refused to send up a prisoner, without signifying the crimes with which he was charged.

"To be confronted with the witnesses against him."

Witnesses, indeed! Fortunate will be the accused if there be any witnesses against him. But is your deputy provost-marshal to call them? O, no; he is only to "inquire into, and report." Is your provost-marshal general? What! call witnesses from the remotest parts of the Union, to a secret inquisition here in Washington. Has any "prisoner of State," hitherto, been confronted with witnesses, at any time? Has he even been allowed to know so much as the names of his accusers? Yet, Festus could boast, that it was not the manner of the Romans, to punish any man, "before that he, which is accused, have the accusers face to face."

"To have compulsory process for obtaining witnesses in his favor."

Sir, the compulsory process will be, under this bill, as it has been from the first, to compel the absence rather, of not only the witnesses, but the friends and nearest relatives of the accused; even the wife of his bosom, and his children—the inmates of his own household. Newspapers, the Bible, letters from home, except under surveillance, a breath of air, a sight of the waves of the sea, or of the mild, blue sky, the song of birds, whatever was denied to the prisoner of Chillon, and more too; yes, even a solitary lamp in the casemate, where a dying prisoner struggled with death, all have been refused to the American citizen accused of disloyal speech or opinions, by this most just and merciful Administration.

And, finally, says the Constitution:

"To have the assistance of counsel for his defence."

And yet your Secretary of State, the "conservative" Seward—the confederate of Weed, that treacherous, dissembling foe to constitutional liberty, and the true interests of his country—forbade his prisoners to employ counsel, under penalty of prolonged imprisonment. Yes, charged with treasonable practices, yet the demand for counsel was to be dealt with as equal to treason itself. Here is an order, signed by a minion of Mr. Seward, and read to the prisoners at Fort Lafayette, on the 3d of December, 1861:

"I am instructed, by the Secretary of State, to inform you, that the Department of State, of the United States, *will not recognize any one as an attorney for political prisoners*, and will look with distrust upon all applications for release through such channels; and that such applications *will be regarded as additional reasons for declining to release the prisoners.*"

And here is another order to the same effect, dated "Department of State, Washington, November 27, 1861," signed by William H. Seward himself, and read to the prisoners at Fort Warren, on the 29th of November, 1861:

"Discountenancing and repudiating all such practices."

The disloyal practice, forsooth, of employing counsel:

"The Secretary of State desires that all the State prisoners may understand *that they are expected to revoke all such engagements now existing, and avoid any hereafter*, as they can only lead to new complications and embarrassments to the cases of prisoners, on whose behalf *the Government might be disposed to act with liberality.*"

Most magnanimous Secretary! Liberality toward men guilty of no crime, but who, though they had been murderers or pirates, were entitled, by the plain letter of the Constitution, to have "the assistance of counsel for their defence." Sir, there was but one step further possible, and that short step was taken some months later, when the prisoners of State were required to make oath, as the condition of their discharge, that they would not seek their constitutional and legal remedy in Court, for the wrongs and outrages inflicted upon them.

Sir, incredible as all this will seem some years hence, it has happened, all of it, and more yet untold, within the last twenty months, in the United States. Under executive usurpation, and by virtue of presidential proclamations and cabinet orders, it has been done without law and against Constitution; and now it is proposed, I repeat, to sanction and authorize it all, by an equally unconstitutional and void act of Congress. Sir, legislative tyranny is no more tolerable than executive tyranny. It is a vain thing to seek to cloak all this under the false semblance of law. Liberty is no more guarded or secured, and arbitrary power no more hedged in and limited here, than under the executive orders of last summer. We know what has already been done, and we will submit to it no longer. Away, then, with your vain clamor about disloyalty, your miserable mockery of treasonable practices. We have read, with virtuous indignation, in history, ages ago, of an Englishman executed for treason, in saying that he would make his son heir to the crown, meaning of his own tavern-house, which bore the sign of the crown; and of that other Englishman, whose favorite buck the king had killed, and who suffered death as a traitor, for wishing, in a fit of vexation, that the buck, horns and all, were embowelled in the body of the king. But what have we not lived to see in our own time? Sir, not many months ago, this Administration, in its great and tender mercy toward the six hundred and forty prisoners of State, confined, for treasonable practices, at Camp Chase, near the capital of Ohio, appointed a commissioner, an extra-judicial functionary, unknown to the Constitution and laws, to hear and determine the cases of the several parties accused, and with power to discharge at his discretion, or to banish to Johnson's Island, in Lake Erie. Among the political prisoners called before him, was a lad of fifteen, a newsboy upon the Ohio River, whose only offence proved, upon inquiry, to be, that he owed fifteen cents, the unpaid balance of a debt due to his washer-woman—possibly a woman of color—who had him arrested by the provost-marshal, as guilty of "disloyal practices." And yet, for four weary months the lad had lain in that foul and most loathsome prison, under military charge, lest, peradventure, he should overturn the Government of the United States; or, at least, the Administration of Abraham Lincoln!

SEVERAL MEMBERS ON THE DEMOCRATIC SIDE OF THE HOUSE. Oh no; the case cannot be possible.

Mr. VALLANDIGHAM. It is absolutely true, and it is one only among many such cases. Why, sir, was not the hump-back carrier of the New York *Daily News*, a paper edited by a member of this House, arrested in Connecticut, for selling that paper, and hurried off out of the State, and imprisoned in Fort Lafayette? And yet, Senators and Representatives, catching up the brutal cry of a bloodthirsty but infatuated partisan press, exclaim, "the Government has been too lenient; there ought to have been more arrests!"

Well did Hamilton remark, that "arbitrary imprisonments have been, in all ages, the favorite and most formidable instruments of tyranny;" and not less truly, Blackstone declares, that they are "a less public, a less striking, and therefore a more dangerous engine of arbitrary government," than executions upon the scaffold. And yet, to-night, you seek here, under cloak of an act of Congress, to authorize these arrests and imprisonments, and thus to renew again that reign of terror which smote the hearts of the stoutest among us, last summer, as "the pestilence which walketh in darkness."

But the Constitution provides further, that

"The right of the people to be secure in their persons, houses, papers, and effects, against unreasonable searches and seizures, shall not be violated, and no warrants shall issue, but upon probable cause, supported by oath or affirmation, and particularly describing the place to be searched, and the persons or things to be seized."

Sir, every line, letter, and syllable of this provision has been repeatedly violated, under pretence of securing evidence of disloyal or treasonable practices; and now you propose, by this bill, to sanction the past violations, and authorize new and continued infractions in future. Your provost-marshals, your captains of cavalry, are to "inquire into treasonable practices." How? In any way, sir, that they may see fit; and of course, by search and seizure of person, house, papers or effects; for, sworn and appointed spies and informers as they are, they will be and can be of no higher character, and no more scrupulous of law, or right, or decency, than their predecessors of last summer, appointed under executive proclamations of no more or less validity than this bill, which you seek now to pass into a law. Sir, there is but one step further to take. Put down the peaceable assembling of the people; the right of petition for redress of grievances; the "right of the people to keep and bear arms;" and finally, the right of suffrage and elections, and then these United States, this Republic of ours, will have ceased to exist. And that short step you will soon take, if the States and the people do not firmly and speedily check you in your headlong plunge into despotism. What yet remains? The Constitution declares that:

"The enumeration in the Constitution, of certain rights, shall not be construed to deny or disparage others retained by the people."

And again:

"The powers not delegated to the United States by the Constitution, nor prohibited by it to the States, are reserved to the States respectively, or to the people."

And yet, under the monstrous doctrine, that in war the Constitution is suspended, and that the President as Commander-in-chief, not of the military forces only, but of the whole people of the United States, may, under "the war power," do whatever he shall think necessary and proper to be done, in any State or part of any State, however remote from the scene of warfare, every right of the people is violated or threatened, and every power of the States, usurped. Their last bulwark, the militia, belonging solely to the States, when not called, as such, into the actual service of the United States, you now deliberately propose, by this bill, to sweep away, and to constitute the President supreme military dictator, with a standing army of three millions and more at his command. And for what purpose are the militia to be thus taken from the power and custody of the States? Sir, the opponents of the Constitution anticipated all this, and were denounced as raving incendiaries or distempered enthusiasts. "The Federal Government," said Patrick Henry, in the Virginia Convention,

"Squints towards monarchy. Your President may easily become a king. If ever he violates the laws, *will not the recollection of his crimes teach him to make one bold push for the American throne?* Will not the immense difference between being master of every thing, and being ignominiously tried and punished, powerfully excite him to make this bold push? But, sir, where is the existing force to punish him? Can he not, at the head of his army, beat down all opposition? What then will become of you and your rights? Will not absolute despotism ensue?"*

And yet, for these apprehensions, Henry has been the subject of laughter and pity for seventy years. Sir, the instinctive love of liberty is wiser and more far-seeing than any philosophy.

Hear, now, Alexander Hamilton, in the *Federalist.* Summing up what he calls the exaggerated and improbable suggestions respecting the power of calling for the services of the militia, urged by the opponents of the Constitution, whose writings he compares to some ill-written tale, or romance full of frightful and distorted shapes, he says:

"The militia of New Hampshire (they allege) is to be marched to Georgia; of Georgia to New Hampshire; of New York to Kentucky; and of Kentucky to Lake Champlain. Nay, the debts due to the French and Dutch, are to be paid in militia-men, instead of Louis d'ors and ducats. At one moment, there is to be a large army to lay prostrate the liberties of the people; at another moment, the militia of Virginia are to be dragged from their homes, five or six hundred miles, to tame the republican contumacy of Massachusetts; *and that of Massachusetts is to be transported an equal distance, to subdue the refractory haughtiness of the aristocratic Virginians.* Do persons who rave at this rate, imagine that their eloquence can impose any conceits or absurdities upon the people of America, for infallible truths?"

And yet, sir, just three-quarters of a century later, we have lived to see these raving conceits and absurdities practised, or attempted, as calmly and deliberately as though the power and the right had been expressly conferred.

And now, sir, listen to the answer of Hamilton to all this—himself the friend of a strong government, a Senate for life, and an Executive for life, with the sole and exclusive power over the militia, to be held by the National Government; and the Executive of each State to be appointed by that Government:

"If there should be an army to be made use of as the engine of despotism, what need of the militia? If there should be no army, *whither would the militia, irritated at being required to undertake a distant and distressing expedition, for the purpose of riveting the chains of slavery upon a part of their countrymen, direct their course,* BUT TO THE SEATS OF THE TYRANTS WHO HAD MEDITATED SO FOOLISH, AS WELL AS SO WICKED, A PROJECT; TO CRUSH THEM IN THEIR IMAGINED INTRENCHMENTS OF POWER, AND MAKE THEM AN EXAMPLE OF THE VENGEANCE OF AN ABUSED AND INCENSED PEOPLE? Is this the way in which usurpers stride to dominion over a numerous and enlightened nation?"

Sir, Mr. Hamilton was an earnest, sincere man, and, doubtless, wrote what he believed: he was an able man also, and a philosopher; and

* And the reporter, unable to follow the vehement orator of the Revolution, adds, "Here, Mr. Henry strongly and pathetically expatiated on the probability of the President's enslaving America, and the horrid consequences that must result."

yet how little did he foresee, that just seventy-five years later, that same Government, which he was striving to establish, would, in desperate hands, attempt to seize the whole militia of the Union, and convert them into a standing army, indefinite as to the time of its service, and for the very purpose of not only beating down State sovereignties, but of abolishing even the domestic and social institutions of the States.

Sir, if your objects are constitutional, you have power abundantly under the Constitution, without infraction or usurpation. The men who framed that instrument, made it both for war and peace. Nay more, they expressly provide for the cases of insurrection and rebellion. You have ample power to do all that of right you ought to do—all that the people, your masters, permit under their supreme will, the Constitution. Confine, then, yourselves within these limits, and the rising storm of popular discontent will be hushed.

But I return, now, again, to the arbitrary arrests sanctioned by this Bill, and by that other consummation of despotism, the Indemnity and Suspension Bill, now in the Senate. Sir, this is the very question which, as I said a little while ago, we made a chief issue before the people in the late elections. You did, then, distinctly claim—and you found an Attorney-General and a few other venal or very venerable lawyers to defend the monstrous claim—that the President had the right to suspend the writ of *habeas corpus;* and that every one of these arrests was legal and justifiable. We went before the people with the Constitution and the laws in our hands, and the love of liberty in our hearts; and the verdict of the people was rendered against you. We insisted that Congress alone could suspend the writ of *habeas corpus* when, in cases of rebellion or invasion, the public safety might require it. And to-day, sir, that is beginning to be again the acknowledged doctrine. The Chief-Justice of the Supreme Court of the United States so ruled in the Merriman case; and the Supreme Court of Wisconsin, I rejoice to say, has rendered a like decision; and if the question be ever brought before the Supreme Court of the United States, undoubtedly it will be so decided, finally and forever. You yourselves now admit it; and at this moment, your "Indemnity Bill," a measure more execrable than even this Conscription, and liable to every objection which I have urged against it, undertakes to authorize the President to suspend the writ all over, or in any part of, the United States. Sir, I deny that you can thus delegate your right to the Executive. Even your own power is conditional. You cannot suspend the writ except where the public safety requires it, and then only in cases of rebellion or invasion. A foreign war, not brought home by invasion, to our own soil, does not authorize the suspension, in any case. And who is to judge whether and where there is rebellion or invasion, and whether and when the public safety requires that the writ be suspended? Congress alone, and they cannot substitute the judgment of the President for their own. Such, too, is the opinion of Story: "The right to judge," says he, "whether exigency has arisen, must *exclusively* belong to that body." But not so under the bill which passed this House the other day.

Nor is this all. Congress alone can suspend the writ. When and where? In cases of rebellion or invasion. Where rebellion? Where invasion? Am I to be told, that because there is rebellion in South Carolina, the writ of *habeas corpus* can be suspended in Pennsylvania and Massachusetts where there is none? Is that the meaning of the Constitution? No, sir; the writ can be suspended only where the rebellion or invasion exists—in States, or parts of States alone, where the enemy, foreign or domestic, is found in arms; and moreover, the public safety can require its suspension only where there is rebellion or invasion. Outside of these conditions, Congress has no more authority to suspend the writ, than the President—and least of all, to suspend it without limitation as to time, and generally all over the Union, and in States not invaded or in rebellion. Such an act of Congress is of no more validity, and no more entitled to obedience, than an Executive proclamation; and in any just and impartial court, I venture to affirm that it will be so decided.

But, again, sir, even though the writ be constitutionally suspended, there is no more power in the President to make arbitrary arrests than without it. The gentleman from Rhode Island (Mr. Sheffield) said, very justly—and I am sorry to see him lend any support to this bill—that the suspension of the writ of *habeas corpus* does not authorize arrests, except upon sworn warrant, charging some offence known to the law, and dangerous to the public safety. He is right. It does not; and this was so admitted in the bill which passed the Senate, in 1807. The suspension only denies release upon bail, or a discharge without trial, to parties thus arrested. It suspends no other right or privilege under the Constitution—certainly not the right to a speedy public trial, by jury, in a civil Court. It dispenses with no "due process of law," except only that particular writ. It does not take away the claim for damages to which a party illegally arrested, or legally arrested, but without probable cause, is entitled.

And yet, everywhere, it has been assumed, that a suspension of the writ of *habeas corpus*, is a suspension of the entire Constitution, and of all laws, so far as the personal rights of the citizen are concerned, and that, therefore, the moment it is suspended, either by the President, as heretofore asserted, or by Congress, as now about to be authorized, arbitrary arrests, without sworn warrant, or other due process of law, may be made at the sole pleasure or discretion of the Executive. I tell you no; and that, although we may not be able to take the body of the party arrested from the provost-marshal by writ of *habeas corpus*, every other right and privilege of the Constitution and of the common law remains intact, including the right to resist the wrong-doer or trespasser, who, without due authority, would violate your person, or enter your house, which is your castle; and, after all this, the right also to prosecute on indictment, or for damages, as the nature or aggravation of the case may demand. And yet, as claimed by you of the party in power, the suspension of this writ is a total abrogation of the Constitution and of the liberties of the citizen, and the rights of the States. Why, then, sir, stop with arbitrary arrests and imprisonments? Does any man believe that it will end here? Not so have I learned history. The guillotine! the guillotine! the guillotine follows next.

Sir, when one of those earliest confined in Fort Lafayette—I had it from his own lips—made complaint to the Secretary of State of the injustice of his arrest, and the severity of the treatment to which he had been subjected in the exercise of arbitrary power, no offence being alleged against him, "Why, sir," said the Secretary, with a smile of most significant complacency, "my dear sir, you ought not to complain; *we might have gone further.*" Light flashed upon the mind of the gentleman, and he replied: "Ah! that is true, sir; you had just the same right to behead, as to arrest and imprison me." And shall it come to this? Then, sir, let us see who is beheaded first. It is horrible enough to be imprisoned without crime, but when it becomes a question of life or death, remember the words of the book of Job—"All that a man hath will he give for his life."

Sir, it is this which makes revolutions. A gentleman upon the other side asked, this afternoon, which party was to rise now in revolution. The answer of the able and gallant gentleman from Pennsylvania (Mr. Biddle) was pertinent and just—"No party, but an outraged people." It is not, let me tell you, the leaders of parties who begin revolutions. Never. Did any one of the distinguished characters of the Revolution of 1776, participate in the throwing of the tea into Boston harbor? Who was it? Who, to-day, can name the actors in that now historic scene? It was not Hancock, nor Samuel Adams, nor John Adams, nor Patrick Henry, nor Washington; but men unknown to fame. Good men agitate; obscure men begin real revolutions; great men finally direct and control them. And if, indeed, we are about to pass through the usual stages of revolution, it will not be the leaders of the Democratic party, not I, not the men with me here, to-night—but some man among the people, now unknown and unnoted, who will hurl your tea into the harbor; and it may even be in Boston once again; for the love of liberty, I would fain believe, lingers still under the shadow of the monument on Bunker Hill. But sir, we seek no revolution except through the ballot-box. The conflict to which we challenge you, is not of arms, but of argument. Do you believe in the virtue and intelligence of the people? Do you admit their capacity for self-government? Have they not intelligence enough to understand the right, and virtue enough to pursue it? Come then: meet us through the press, and with free speech, and before the assemblages of the people, and we will argue these questions, as we and our fathers have done from the beginning of the Government—"Are we right, or you right, we wrong, or you wrong?" And by the judgment of the people, we will, one and all, abide.

Sir, I have done now with my objections to this Bill. I have spoken as though the Constitution survived, and was still the supreme law of the land. But if, indeed, there be no Constitution any longer, limiting and restraining the men in power, then there is none binding upon the States or the people. God forbid. We have a Constitution yet, and laws yet. To them I appeal. Give us our rights; give us known and fixed laws; give us the judiciary; arrest us only upon due process of law; give us presentment or indictment by grand juries; speedy and public trial; trial by jury and at home; tell us the nature and cause of the accusation; confront us with witnesses; allow us witnesses in our behalf, and the assistance of counsel for our defence; secure us in our persons, our houses, our papers, and our effects; leave us arms, not for resistance to law or against rightful authority, but to defend ourselves from outrage and violence; give us free speech and a free press; the right peaceably to assemble; and above all, free and undisturbed elections and the ballot—take our sons, take our money, our property, take all else, and we will wait a little, till at the time and in the manner appointed by Constitution and law, we shall eject you from the trusts you have abused, and the seats of power you have dishonored, and other and better men shall reign in your stead.

PEACE—LIBERTY—THE CONSTITUTION.*

LUKE F. COZANS, President of the Association, in a few remarks introduced the orator of the evening, Hon. C. L. VALLANDINGHAM, who on rising was received with loud and protracted cheers. When silence was restored he spoke as follows :

GENTLEMEN :—I was not aware till after my arrival here, a few hours ago, of the stereotyped threats that this man or that man, representing certain sentiments, should not be permitted to speak in the city of New York. Had I known it, I probably would have taken an earlier train and been here a few hours in advance. (Applause.) The spirit of those before me sufficiently proves that the time for all that has gone by. I am here to speak to-night regardless of all threats; and if there were any disagreeable consequences to follow, regardless of those consequences. (Loud cheers.) But there are none, and I am here to speak just such things as, in my judgment, a true patriot and a freeman ought to speak. (Enthusiastic cheers.) I accepted the invitation very cordially, to address this Association, and came at no inconsiderable personal sacrifice, because the exigencies of the times which are again upon us, with threatening aspect, not only justify, but, in my judgment, demand of every public man, that all personal considerations should be laid aside for the public good. I know as well as any one, the pressure that is now made upon the Democratic party, with the vain hope of crushing it out. The men who are in power at Washington, extending their agencies out through the cities and States of the Union and threatening to reinaugurate a reign of terror, may as well know that we comprehend precisely their purpose. I beg leave to assure you that it cannot and will not be permitted to succeed. (Applause.) The people of this country indorsed it once because they were told that it was essential to "the speedy suppression or crushing out of the rebellion" and the restoration of the Union ; and they so loved the Union of these States, that they would consent even for a little while under the false and now broken promises of the men in power, to surrender those liberties, in order that the great object might, as was promised, be accomplished speedily. They have been deceived ; instead of crushing out the rebellion, the effort has been to crush out the spirit of liberty. (Cheers.)

The conspiracy of those in power is not so much for a vigorous

*Speech before the "Democratic Union Association of New York City," March 7, 1863. This speech was made wholly without preparation, and was not revised by Mr. V, till in type. It is included here, not because of any rhetorical excellence in it, but for its historic value.

prosecution of the war against rebels in the South as against the Democracy in peace at home. (Cheers.) And now no effort, however organized, premeditated, or well concerted to restore those times through which we have passed, and which will stand upon the pages of history as the darkest of all the annals of America, will be permitted to succeed, and the sooner they comprehend this, the better and the less trouble there will be in the land. (Applause.) We were born to an inheritance of freedom; the Constitution came to us from our fathers; it guaranteed to us rights and liberties older than the instrument itself—God-given, belonging to the people, belonging to men, because God made them free—and we do not mean to surrender one jot or tittle of those rights and liberties. (Loud cheers.) Yet nothing but the consciousness that just at this moment men desperately wicked have deliberately determined to make one last expiring effort to break down the reaction setting in from the people against the policy of this Administration, against the party in power, and the conviction that it was necessary to meet that effort instantly and everywhere, could have induced me to be here to-night, wearied and exhausted as I am with the labors of the Congress, which, thank God, has just expired. (Laughter and cheers.) Absent from home for many months, my own business neglected, the politics of my own State allowed to pass by for the present—nothing, I say, but these considerations could have induced me to be present to-night; but I rejoice that I am here, and look in the face, and am looked in the face by freemen—men whose eyes speak the determination of their hearts to meet this crisis with whatsoever agencies this Administration may choose to make necessary. (Applause.) Gentlemen, I am no revolutionist; I am in all things as far as practicable, a peace man, and want peace and order in this country. I am ready to submit to many things that I think had better not be attempted, just so long as assemblages of the people and the ballot, which are the great correctives of evil, and which were intended by our fathers to be the machinery by which peaceable revolution should be accomplished in our government, remain untouched; but I say to the Administration:—"Lay not your hands at the foundation of the fabric of our liberties: you may lop off a branch here and there, and it will survive; we may tolerate that for the sake of a greater good hereafter; but whenever you reach forth your hand to strike at the very vitals of public liberty, then the people must and will determine in their sovereign capacity, what remedy the occasion demands. (Cheers.) But we have not as yet come to that. I have seen enough already to satisfy me upon that subject, not in the West only, about which there can be no doubt, but in Philadelphia, the most terror-ridden city in the Union, eighteen months ago. The spirit of the men born within the sound of Independence bell, yet survives in all its grandeur and its majesty (applause); and I think I can answer, not merely from what I see here to-night, but from what elsewhere in other ways I have learned, that the spirit of the people of New York is not behind. This is not, indeed, Cooper Institute. (Laughter.) It may not hold as many people; but this is a spontaneous meeting. It was not prearranged according to a fixed programme; it is not a chronic or periodic assemblage of a certain class of persons for a certain purpose. Sir, I know something about the style in which those meetings are gotten up, and everybody here comprehends them. Their sole effect, so far as they have any, is in distant portions of the country, where they are telegraphed—and at a distance, like every thing else, they look exceedingly charming. They are very much after the fashion of the Cincinnati, so-called and grossly miscalled, Union meeting, not long ago, which was in spirit and in effect a contemptible failure. And very much, too, after the fashion of the meeting at Columbus, of which you have read in the telegraph; or the meeting at Indianapolis. Some operator, true to his vocation, lied. He says that the latter was attended by thirty thousand people. I venture the assertion that not two thousand outside of the city of Indianapolis, were present on the occasion. But, the meeting last night was a preconcerted effort; it was a part of the programme. It was artificial; this is natural. They who spoke there were pleading for power—I speak for liberty. (Loud applause.) They spoke to men in power and holding office; I speak to and for the people. There is not one single office-holder, I venture to say, in this meeting, who does not derive his title from the people. Was there a single one present last night who did? This, then, is the difference. Coming immediately from Washington, having witnessed with the common satisfaction of the people of this country, the expiration of the Thirty-seventh Congress, I am here to speak, in the first place, briefly of some things which have been done in that body during the recent session, and the session which preceded it. I will not go back so far as the extra session when general insanity prevailed throughout the country, and when the representatives of the people were, perhaps, to a large degree excusable; because while they had doubtless contributed to that insanity, it was reflected back upon them again; but after a period given for meditation, after the logic of events had begun to work out, after the experiment of war had been tried for one year, it seems to me that wise men, men in whose hands you can with safety deposit the power that belongs to you, should have meditated a little while, and with some degree of wisdom have proceeded to legislate for the true interests of the country. Did they do it? What has been the legislation financially, to begin with that? Where were we then? What was your currency? Gold. How much have you seen lately of it? You read of it in the stock market, impalpable, invisible—a thing that belongs to the past; it will go into the collections of those who have a curiosity for coins. What is your currency now? ("Greenbacks.") Greenbacks; nor is that all ("Postage stamps"). Postage currency, and to what extent? Nearly a thousand millions already. That is what is offered to you. It is the entertainment to which you were invited, or rather which you were compelled to accept, though not invited to in 1860. Your public debt—what was it then? The enormous sum of seventy-one millions. Would you not be willing to compromise on that to-day? No doubt even they to whom that word "compromise" is most odious, who feel towards it as Romeo towards the word "banishment," would be very willing to settle the debt of this country at seventy-one millions. It is now, actually or prospectively, because the appropriations reach that extent —$2,277,000,000. That is the sum which this Congress has appropriated. They have given to this tremendous debt, the power that belongs to it by the issuing of what is called a government currency, binding everybody by some sort of paper tie, to the government—by the establishment of a grand national paper-mill, a national bank, and through the other schemes of finance which were formed in the brain, or found a lodgment there somehow or other, of the Secretary of the Treasury. They have, by this instrumentality, obtained absolute control of the entire country. Through a tax law, the like of which never was imposed upon any but a conquered people, they have possession actually or prospectively, of the entire property of the people of the country. Thus the purse, through the swift and anxious servility of a Congress which was intended by our fathers to be the watchful guardian of the people's money and the people's property, is now absolutely and unqualifiedly for two years at the disposal of the Executive of the United States. In ordinary times, the control of that purse was regarded by the jealous lovers of liberty, by the men who preceded those in power, by the men who sat in your places twenty, thirty, or forty years ago, as one of the instruments of despotism— then even when our revenue was down as low as twenty millions of dollars. It was then that with jealousy, with the most scrutinizing care, every appropriation of money was allowed to pass through the House of Representatives or the Senate of the United States. And yet this Congress, since the 4th of July, 1861, some twenty months or less, has appropriated, as I have said, the enormous sum, and put it at the disposal of the President of the United States, of $2,277,000-000. And for what? To control that which in part is the life-blood of the nation, its business, its currency, all that enter, into the business transactions of life. Part of it was intended in the beginning as a fund wherewith to set up the negro trade. (Laughter.) It entered the mind of Mr. Lincoln, that the idea of compensated emancipation, as he calls it, must be carried out practically, and it found a place in his message and was repeated in the annual message, and that most delicate term to conceal a most odious thing—compensated emancipation—was given to it with the vain idea of deceiving the people—compensated emancipation meaning, being interpreted into good old-fashioned English, *Greenback Abolition.* (Laughter and cheers.) The minority in the Senate and in the House, through their pertinacity of purpose, surrounded though they were by bayonets and by despotic power on every side, succeeded at last in defeating this scheme for the purchase of negroes; but nearly all the other plans were consummated. Thus, as I have said, the purse was placed under the control of the Executive for two years. You have surrendered it—you cannot take it back again. It has gone into the hands of men, of the party of Abolition—men who, base and coward-like, for the sake of appointment when their terms should expire, after the 4th of March, sold out the precious deposit, which you put in their keeping. (A voice—"What can we do?") We will see. We have the ballot-box yet. (Applause.) We can do what we are doing to-night, and we will do it. (Cheers.) We can vote yet, and we mean to vote, and more than that, we mean that the mandate of that ballot-box shall be carried out at all hazards. (Loud applause.) We meet those men fairly under the Constitution and laws of the land, and propose to try this question before the great tribunal of the people. As I have said before, for this is a time for line upon line and precept upon precept, if they beat us we will submit, because we must submit to what is Constitution and law; but if, on the other hand, we conquer them, then, by the Eternal, they must and shall submit. (Loud cheers.) So much for the money—the purse.

And now, as to that other great weapon of government—the sword. What have your "misrepresentatives" done? They gave, and with your consent, ("Never") yes, they did; and I am sorry it is so, my friends. (A voice—"The Republicans.") No, my dear sir, Democrats did it too. I did not. (Cheers.) If I had had my way there never would have been a necessity for any thing of the kind—the sword never would have been drawn, and we never would have had civil war. The Crittenden propositions would have compromised and settled this difficulty. (Great applause). But Congress, in the beginning, with the concurrence of the people, in a fit of insanity, as I think—no disparagement to them, it was their excessive patriotism that led to it—but they did give first, or recognized, at least, the giving of 75,000 men, then of 87,000, then of 637,000, next of 300,000 more, and

300,000 more yet in the form of a draft, making in all of volunteers some 937,000 men. They went out to the field voluntarily. Your representatives gave to the President the control of that number of men—the power at least to call for them—and they went, and your committees helped them to go. There was no place where more was accomplished in that way than in the city of New York. It was then popular to advocate civil war, to enlist or procure enlistments, and to address war meetings. I am sorry some gentlemen have not heard that it is unpopular now. Their habit seems to get control of their judgment. As long as the people said so, though my judgment humbly disapproved of it, I was content to remain silent, and see the experiment tried. But that was not all. Not only have those 937,000 enlisted men, and the 300,000 drafted men—indeed, I might say the 1,237,000 enlisted men, for the draft was used only to compel and procure enlistments—not only have all these been sent into the field, or at least made to appear on the pay rolls, but in the very expiring hours of the Congress, which died and went to its own place at 12 o'clock on the 4th of March, your misrepresentatives—for such they had become—not speaking the voice of the people, did attempt to clothe the President with the power of conscripting every man in the United States between the ages of twenty and forty-five—to compel him to enter the army and enable the President to keep up a war which, by that bill itself, he and they confess to be against the will of the people. (Applause.) The bill is an admission upon the record, that they cannot, by voluntary enlistment, obtain more soldiers to fight in this war. Now, whereas, the Constitution of the United States makes the distinction between the regular army and the militia of the country; whereas, it forbids States to keep a standing army, and authorizes the United States to do it, but, on the other hand, leaves to the States the control of the militia, and enables the President or Congress only to call out the militia, as such, for certain specified purposes, and for a limited time, reserving to these States the appointment of officers and the discipline of the militia until they are mustered into the service of the United States; this bill yet undertakes to make a standing army of more than three millions of the people for three years or during the war. How long will that be? (A voice—"Nine years.") Thus, so far as it is possible, by an enactment having the form of law, the Congress of the United States have surrendered, absolutely, the entire military power of the country to the President. Now, if in possession of the purse and the sword absolutely and unqualifiedly, for two years, there be any thing else wanting which describes a dictatorship, I beg to know what it is? Why did they not imitate the manhood of the old Roman Senators when the exigency of the Republic, in their judgment, demanded it, and declare Mr. Lincoln a dictator in terms?—that was alone absolutely what they meant—instead of coward-like, undertaking, in the form of law and by the abuse of constitutional power, to give the same authority and the same agencies to establish a despotism, as would have been implied by the direct creation of a dictatorship. (Applause.) That bill passed the Senate without opposition, and much has been said upon the subject, and great gratification has been expressed by some. Gentlemen, it was a mistake, an accident, not intentional. There was not a Democratic, conservative Senator who was not opposed to it, but happening to be absent at the hour when the vote was taken, the dead hour of midnight,

> "When graveyards yawn,
> And hell itself breathes out contagion,"

their votes were not recorded; but when the bill came to the House, the minority there were resolved that it should not pass without a severe scrutiny, without a thorough consideration, without all the resistance, by parliamentary tactics and by speech, to which we had a right to resort. It was announced by the Chairman of the Military Committee that no debate should be allowed upon the bill, and what is called the previous question was demanded, for the purpose of bringing us to an immediate vote. Then it was that that little minority, once only five in number, but grown now to thirty, thank God—(cheers)—having enough to call the yeas and nays, resorted to what is the last refuge of a minority in a legislature, and what very aptly is called "fillibustering." Yes, we "fillibustered" on that bill. (Laughter.) We did not follow the example of the Abolition Senators in Illinois, who, coming fresh from an election, where they had been rebuked and their party repudiated, yet to prevent the enactment of the will of the people into a law, saw fit to run away and break up the Senate. We stood to our posts, and the only complaint they had to prefer against us was that we stood but too well. Nor did we imitate the revolutionary example of the minority in the Indiana Legislature, who went home for the same purpose, and have remained home now for one week. We did not do that; we "filibustered," and in the course of a few hours that little minority compelled that great majority, first, to yield the point of debate, and then to adjourn with the understanding that the bill should be open to a thorough discussion. And it was so opened; and such a discussion as the reporters, who have been there for years, and the oldest members and spectators, have all united in the testimony that the like of it had not been witnessed in that Capitol for more than twenty years. We were few, but

> "Thrice is he armed that hath his quarrel just;"

and ours was the justest cause that ever was struggled for. We spoke with the courage of freemen, fully conscious that we were standing in the very breach against the rushing torrent of despotism, and as we spoke the Felixes of Abolition trembled, and they gave us another day, and at the end of the discussion, so completely had they been mastered that they consented to strike out every provision in that bill that did not relate to it purely as a military measure. That is what we gained by courage and firmness and manhood. (Applause). They had provided for the appointment of a Provost-Marshal in every congressional district, with power to inquire into and report disloyal practices —such as we are engaged in here to-night (laughter)—to report what some Democrat had said in opposition to, not the Government, for Democrats support the Government, but the executive, Abraham Lincoln. That was stricken out. They had authorized the Provost-Marshals—fellows spread all over the country in every congressional district, with the rank of a captain of cavalry, and drawing pay, of course—they had authorized them to summarily arrest everybody who should resist the draft, or counsel resistance, or oppose it in any way, shape, or form, and we compelled them to insert a provision that though a person might be thus arrested, summarily, he should be forthwith handed over to the civil authorities to be dealt with. (Applause.) But, as originally proposed, the bill not only would have but the three or four millions of males between twenty and forty-five, under the military control of the President, as Commander-in-chief, but would also have placed every man, woman, and child, by virtue of the two provisions that were stricken out, also in his power. Our civil rights would have been gone, and our judiciary undermined, and he would have been an absolute and uncontrolled dictator, with the power of Cincinnatus, but without one particle of his virtues. (Cheers.) Yet unfortunately, while this much was accomplished on that bill, the same tyrannical power was conferred by another bill which passed both houses, and is now, so far as forms are concerned, a law of the land—at least an act of the Thirty-seventh Congress. (Laughter.) It authorizes the President whom the people made, whom the people had chosen by the ballot-box under the Constitution and laws, to suspend the writ of *habeas corpus* all over the United States; to say that because there is a rebellion in South Carolina, a man shall not have freedom of speech, freedom of the press, or any of his rights untrammelled in the State of New York, or a thousand miles distant. That was the very question upon which the people passed judgment in the recent elections, more, perhaps, than any other question. The President had assumed to exercise this power by virtue of a proclamation, and had arrogated to himself the prerogative, long since exploded, of the Kings of England. He had exercised this kingly prerogative, and the people had repudiated it; they had said:—"You have no right to suspend this writ, you have no power of arbitrary arrest, and we will not submit to its exercise." Sir, the same argument which was addressed to the people in discussing this question previous to the October and November elections now applies to this so-called act of Congress. The Constitution gives the power to Congress, and to Congress alone, to suspend the writ of *habeas corpus*, but it can only be done in case of invasion or rebellion, and then only when the public safety requires it; and in the opinion of the best jurists of the land, and indeed of every one previous to these times, Congress could only suspend this writ in places actually in rebellion or actually invaded. That is the Constitution. (Cheers.) And whenever this question shall be tried before a court in the State of New York, or Ohio, or Wisconsin, or anywhere else, before honest and fearless judges worthy of the place they occupy, the decision will be that it is unconstitutional. (Loud applause.) Assuming what is not implied and never was in the suspension of the writ of *habeas corpus*, that it gives power of arbitrary arrest, they have affected to make provision for the exercise of such power. But the President has no more authority when the writ of *habeas corpus* is suspended, to lay his hand upon the citizen, than he has before, or than I have; and the suspension of that writ takes away no other civil rights, and no other legal remedy: but the same right of resistance that the common law gives against every trespasser acting without authority of law, and attempting to enter a man's house, which is his castle, applies equally whether the writ be suspended or not. (Great applause.) And the same right of redress in courts of justice, in an action for damages, remains also. That writ may not be issued by the court, but every other right still continues in force for the benefit of him who may be made the victim of the arrest. Now, sir, there being no more right of arrest, notwithstanding this pretended power of suspension, no more necessity for arrest in the States still adhering to the Union, than there was before; I repeat the assertion that whenever an effort is made to exercise arbitrary, unconstitutional, and unwarrantable power, any honest court of justice will decide it to be unconstitutional. (Applause.) But provision is made upon the assumption that the President and Secretary of State and the Secretary of War who are the officers enumerated in the act, will send forth their minions and lay hands upon the freemen of this country. And it is provided in that act, that if any man has been arrested by a warrant issued from the President or either of these secretaries, and the writ returned that he is held by virtue of that authority, he shall remain imprisoned until the next United States District or Circuit Court shall sit; and that then, if the Grand Jury do not find a bill of indictment against him, he shall be—what? Discharged?—yes, discharged. How? Remember that a Grand Jury of fifteen men sworn to do their duty are to make inquisition into the offence and examine the case with the witnesses called only on the part of the United States—and there are wretches enough to be found everywhere ready to commit perjury under such circumstances—yet if that Grand Jury shall find nothing against the man, he is not allowed, as the apostle Paul was, to appeal unto Cæsar. Oh, no. Our Cæsars are the people, and to them the appeal will be made finally. But it is further provided that this citizen, whose innocence has been absolutely established by virtue of his discharge by the Grand Jury, shall not be permitted to go out of that dungeon until he has taken an unconstitutional and most execrable oath—the identical oath that was tendered to other men who have been imprisoned by arbitrary power within your limits and elsewhere. An oath to support the Constitution? No. That would be tolerable in itself, though even that, intolerable under the circumstances, for no man ought to be obliged to take any oath unless there is some occasion for it in a judicial investigation, or when he takes upon himself the duties of an office. The man who is born a citizen of the United States is assumed, and has been from the beginning of this government, to be under a perpetual oath, and the Democrats of the country have always kept that oath. (Cheers.) The foreigner who seeks citizenship takes an express oath to support the Constitution of the United States. The man born under the tyranny of Austria or Russia—these used to be tyrannies before we had one of our own—(Laughter)—that man born thus, with all his ideas formed upon the model of such governments, comes here; and yet it never entered into the heads of our fathers from the beginning down to the present day, to require of him, through the naturalization laws, the taking of any other oath than to withdraw his allegiance to any foreign potentate and support the Constitution, But our own native born citizens, and foreigners who have become citizens, who have taken that oath, are required, notwithstanding their innocence, to take this other oath—and though the informers, despicable as the vermin are, have failed to invent or devise any accusation whereby he can be held, he is required to take it, and if he refuse, he is then to remain imprisoned during the pleasure of the President of the United States. These are our liberties, forsooth! Was it this which you were promised, in 1860, in that grand "Wide Awake" campaign, when banners were borne through your streets inscribed "Free speech, free press, and free men?" And all this has been accomplished, so far as the forms of the law go, by the Congress which has just expired. Now, I repeat again, that if there is any thing wanting to make up a complete and absolute despotism, as iron and inexorable in its character as the worst despotisms of the old world, or the most detestable of modern times, even to Bomba's of Naples, I am unable to comprehend what it is.

All this, gentlemen, infamous and execrable as it is, is enough to make the blood of the coldest man who has one single appreciation in his heart of freedom, to boil with indignation. (Loud applause.) Still, so long as they leave to us free assemblages, free discussion, and a free ballot, I do not want to see, and will not encourage or countenance, any other mode of ridding ourselves of it. ("That's it," and cheers.) We are ready to try these questions in that way; but I have only to repeat what I said a little while ago, that when the attempt is made to take away those other rights, and the only instrumentalities peaceably of reforming and correcting abuses—free assemblages, free speech, free ballot, and free elections—THEN THE HOUR WILL HAVE ARRIVED WHEN IT WILL BE THE DUTY OF FREEMEN TO FIND SOME OTHER AND EFFICIENT MODE OF DEFENDING THEIR LIBERTIES. (Loud and protracted cheering, the whole audience rising to their feet.) Our fathers did not inaugurate the Revolution of 1776, they did not endure the sufferings and privations of a seven years' war to escape from the mild and moderate control of a constitutional monarchy like that of England, to be at last, in the third generation, subjected to a tyranny equal to that of any upon the face of the globe. (Loud applause.)

But, sir, I repeat that it will not, in my judgment, come to this. I do not believe that this Administration will undertake to deprive us of that right. I do not think it will venture, for one moment, to attempt to prevent, under any pretext whatever, the assembling together of the people for the fair discussion of their measures and policy. I do not believe it, because it seems to me with all the folly and madness which have been manifested in those high places, they must foresee what will inevitably follow. Believing this, and believing that the best way of averting the crisis is to demand inexorably and resolutely, with the firmness and dignity of freemen, these rights, and let them know distinctly that we do not mean to surrender them, I am here to-night to speak it just as I have spoken. (Applause.) There is nothing that will encourage or induce this Administration, for one moment, to attempt any such exercise of despotic power, reaching to assemblages of the people and to elections, except the evidences which they are now seeking for—feeling the public pulse—that the people are terrified and ready to surrender their rights. There never was a tyrant that dared to go one step, if he were a wise tyrant, till he saw his people were ready to submit. It is my duty, therefore, as a freeman in the exercise of these rights, to speak thus to this Administration and to all men of the party in power. I do not speak it in the spirit of a revolutionist; I have already disclaimed that. I desire to see nothing resembling it inaugurated in this country. God knows I have read too much in history, of the horrors of revolutions in ages past and in other countries, to wish one single moment to see these scenes repeated in the land which gave me birth. There is no horror that can enter into the imagination of man, none that has ever been enacted upon this globe since it first came from the hand of God, equal to that of a grand convulsive social revolution among such a people as we are, so descended, of such tempers and such wills, and inheriting all the ferocity of the Anglo-Saxon race. I do not desire to see it, but I will never consent to be made a slave. (Loud cheers.) I speak it advisedly. Man has but one life to give up here; and that life is but of little value as compared with the liberties which we would be called upon to surrender, (Cheers.) Other men have given up their lives on the battle-field or the scaffold, for the sake of a great and good cause, and if in God's providence it becomes necessary that lives should be offered up cheerfully in this country, in the midst of the terrific scenes which I have been portraying, then I trust that there is even yet enough of manhood—ay, enough left in the men of this generation to vindicate the truth recorded in holy writ, that God created man and breathed into his nostrils, and made him a living soul. (Cheers.)

I have spoken now of what this Administration and what the Congress of the United States have done. And for what is all this? What is the purpose to be subserved? For the permitted exercise of such tremendous power—for the surrender of every liberty by a people born free—there ought to be some compensation at least. The maintenance of the Constitution, if the Constitution could be maintained by destroying it, would justify that surrender. The restoration of the Union of these States, if it could be restored in this way, would not only justify but demand it, because the value would bear some proportion to the price given. In the beginning you were told that the purpose of all the power, previous to the recent legislation of Congress, given to or usurped by the Executive, was for the maintenance of the Constitution and the restoration of the Union; and with that love for both, which is the highest honor to this people and its only apology (and it will be so recorded) for submitting to what we have done, the people made sacrifices, gave money, sent forth their first-born at the call of the Executive as no other people ever did since the world began. There never was such a struggle in any age or any country. Why? Because the President and all under him did repeatedly and distinctly declare that the sole purpose was to uphold the Constitution which our fathers had made, and the Union which that Constitution established, and to which we owed all our greatness and prosperity. The people of America were willing to sacrifice all these for that great good. It was so said in the President's annual message of the 4th of July, as it had been in his proclamation of the 15th of April, calling forth the militia, in the beginning. It was in the orders and proclamations of every Federal General for the first eight or ten months after he entered the Southern States. The day after the battle of Bull Run, by a vote unanimous save two, Congress declared that the sole purpose of the war should be the maintenance of the Constitution, the restoration of the Union, and the enforcement of the laws; and when these objects were accomplished, the war should cease, without touching the domestic institutions, slavery included, in the Southern States. That pledge was given, and under it an army of six hundred thousand men was at once raised; and it was repeated in every form till towards the close of the second session of Congress. Then the Abolition Senators and Representatives began first to demand a change in the policy of the Administration, they began to proclaim that the war must be no longer for the Union and the Constitution, but for the abolition of slavery in the Southern States. Now, sir, I repeat it and defy contradiction, that not a soldier enlisted, out of the first nine hundred thousand, for any other purpose than the restoration of the Union and the maintenance of the Constitution. There was not one single officer, so far as his public declarations were concerned, whatever may have been the secret purposes of his heart, that did not openly declare that the moment this object was changed to the abolition of slavery, he would throw up his commission and resign. Yes, the very men who, for the last four or five weeks in the army—the officers—I do not mean your private soldiers, they who do picket duty, who stand in the front ranks, who brave the iron hail and leaden rain of the stormy battle-field, the men who sacrifice their lives for the paltry sum of thirteen dollars a month, the noble, brave men, who, if they were at home, would give us their votes, as their sympathies are still with us; I speak of your officers only—your majors, your lieutenant-colonels, colonels, brigadiers, and major-generals, each one of them seeking promotion, and drawing his salary of two, three, four, five, six, and seven thousand dollars a year, and whose interest it is that the war be made eternal. They are the men who have been holding these meetings of regiments so called, concocting resolutions, or rather adopting resolutions concocted in Indianapolis, Columbus, Springfield, or Washington, and sent down to be clothed in form as an expression of the opinion of the regiments, but, in fact, the expression of the officers alone. They are the men who have solemnly declared, at home and in the army, that the moment this became an Abolition war, they would resign and come back to us, and yet they are now sending out these missiles to us their peers—threatening messages that they mean to come back and "whip" the Democratic traitors and secessionists of the North.

Now, I tell these shoulder-strapped gentlemen who are looking to the White House instead of at the enemy, that when they have succeeded in the mission for which they were sent out; when upon the battle-field they have put down those who are now in arms against them, it will be time enough to talk about coming back. But if they imagine for one moment that any man here is to be frightened by their insolent messages, they know not the spirit of the freemen who remain at home. (Applause.) We have three or five to their one, even if they had, what they have not, the soldiers of the army with them. And shall officers and men sent down South to the battle-field to fight against an enemy in arms, turn their backs upon that enemy and their faces upon the men who feed them, who clothe them, and who have given to them all the liberties they ever had, and who, in spite of them, mean to maintain those liberties? (Applause.) Now, sir, I care not whether they are major-generals, brigadiers, colonels, or what not—they can frighten no man who is fit to be a freeman. Do we not understand all this? Do we not know where these resolutions were written? Is not their paternity sufficiently stamped upon their very visage? The precious Governor of Ohio, forsooth, and of Indiana, and Illinois, and others in power in Washington, prepared all these and sent them down, as I have already said, for the purpose of being brought back with the notion that somebody was going to be, not "hurt," but terrified. Sir, I avail myself of this first occasion, to give notice, so far as any thing I may say shall ever reach them, that there is no one frightened by any of these menaces, and that when they return home after this war shall have been ended, to take their places as citizens among us, there is not a single household in the Democratic party, there is not a man in the humblest cottage or cabin of any free American, who will not have those letters and resolutions of theirs, pasted upon the wall, to rise up in judgment against them forever. (Cheers.) They may get promotion just now, from the man in the White House—but they will learn that final promotion cometh not from that quarter, but at the hands of the people. They have their mission to perform—a very serious and a very tedious one; it was to have been accomplished in twenty days, sixty days, ninety days, but it is not done yet. Let them go forward and try that first. We have our mission here; our business is to fight Abolition rebels in our midst. (Loud applause.) We have not interfered with them in the discharge of their duty, and they shall not interfere with us. They are under military law, the command of the President of the United States; of their superiors; we are not.

(Cheers.) We are the masters of these officials. They are liable to be tried at drum-head courts-martial, according to military law, and punished under that law. We are, and we mean to be, tried only by the judicial tribunals in our midst. (Applause.) Let them look, then, to the discipline of their regiments, brigades, and divisions; let them see to it that they make themselves efficient military officers; but while they are at a distance, without the means of communicating with the people or knowing any thing about political questions, let them confine themselves to their legitimate duties, and allow us, unmolested, to attend to ours. But there is not one of those who have participated in these meetings, who did not declare repeatedly at home and in the army, that the moment this was proclaimed to be a war for the abolition of slavery, he would resign his commission; yet now, because we would oppose this war for abolition, because we would maintain the position that we have held from the beginning, they, forsooth, dare to taunt us with treason, and to impeach our fidelity to our country.

Such, then, gentlemen, was the purpose originally declared of this war. Now, what is it to-day? Let any man honestly and conscientiously judge. I speak not as a mere partisan; I speak what will be regarded as historic truth. Look at the legislation of Congress, your confiscation bill, your emancipation schemes, the proclamation of the 22d of September, reiterated on the 1st of January last. Look at the fact that to-day the entire purpose and object of the war, as proclaimed by the Executive and by Congress is the overthrow of slavery in the Southern States. Now, is it not so? What did the men who were accustomed to address war meetings in New York and elsewhere say? What did the gentlemen who spoke last night declare? Months ago, if it should become a war for the abolition of slavery, what did they declare it was their purpose to do? Did they not denounce it? Did they not denounce it even during the last canvass in the State of New York and elsewhere? We did, too. We abide by these declarations to-day, and we mean to make them good. It being then conceded that this is the purpose, we have the testimony of these very men themselves, some of them of the Democratic party, and many of the Republican or Abolition party, that a war against the South, a war for subjugation and to abolish slavery, would end in the destruction of the Union and in the establishment of a despotism in our midst. There is not a man among them that is not on the record in that declaration. Did they believe it? If they did not, I did; and I believe it to-night, and am with every man who does believe that a war carried on upon this basis can never succeed in its purpose—that it must either end in disunion, or in establishing a tyranny at home. What shall we do? If there be any man, and I repeat what I said upon another occasion—if there be any man in the Democratic or Republican party who still thinks that war can restore the Union as it was and maintain the Constitution as it is, I have no quarrel with him to-night. I assume his position for the sake of the argument—it is not mine, and never was; but let it be so for a moment. You say that a war prosecuted for this purpose must thus result. Have you the power to change the purpose? Can you compel Abraham Lincoln to withdraw his proclamation? Can you repeal the legislation of the Congress that is now defunct? If you cannot, the war must go on upon the basis on which it is now prosecuted—and you believe that it will end in death to the Union, the Constitution, and to Liberty.

What position, then, do you occupy before your countrymen in still advocating the so-called vigorous prosecution of the war? Vigorous prosecution! For what? By your own declaration—disunion, separation, destruction, despotism. Dare any man stand before an assembly of freemen and advocate the objects, or the results, at least, of such a war? And yet, what inconsistency for any one claiming intelligence, to declare that although it must so result, and although he has not the power to change the policy of the Administration, it is the duty of every man to support that Administration in its policy. I deny it (cheers); and for one, at least, I will not do it. If I had believed originally, as I did not believe, that it was possible to restore this Union by force, if I had occupied the position of hundreds and thousands of Democrats, as well as the great mass of the Republican party, I would proclaim to-night that, inasmuch as this is the policy, and we have not the power to change it, that then our duty would be, and is, to advocate henceforth to the end, A VIGOROUS PROSECUTION OF PEACE FOR THE UNION. (Loud cheers.) I will not consent to put the entire purse of the country and the sword of the country into the hands of the Executive, giving him despotic and dictatorial power to carry out an object which I avow before my countrymen is the destruction of their liberties, and the overthrow of the Union of these States. I do not comprehend the honesty of such declarations, or of the men who make them. I know that the charge is brought against myself, personally, and against many of us—(A voice—"Never mind.") I have not spent a moment in replying to it—the people will take care of all that. (Applause.) The charge has been made against us—all who are opposed to the policy of this Administration and opposed to this war—that we are for "peace on any terms." It is false. I am not, but I am for an immediate stopping of the war and for honorable peace. I am for peace for the sake of the Union of these States. More than that—I am for peace, and would be, even if the Union could not be restored, as I believe it can be; because, without peace, permitting this Administration for two years to exercise its tremendous powers, the war still existing, you will not have one remnant of civil liberty left among yourselves. (Great applause.) The exercise of these tremendous powers, the apology for which is the existence of this war, is utterly incompatible with the stability of the Constitution and of constitutional liberty. (Cheers.) I am not for "peace on any terms;" I would not be with any country on the globe. Honor is also the life of the nation, and it is never to be sacrificed. I have as high and proud a sense of honor, and have a right to have it, as any man in the South, and I love my country too well, and cherish its honor too profoundly, for one single moment to consent to a dishonorable peace. (A voice—"The whole country.") Yes, the whole country; every State; and I, unlike some of my own party, and unlike thousands of the Abolition party, believe still, before God, that the Union can be reconstructed and will be. (Great applause.) That is my faith, and I mean to cling to it as the wrecked mariner clings to the last plank amid the shipwreck. But when I see that the experiment of blood has failed from the beginning, as I believed it would fail, I am not one of those who proclaim now that we shall have separation and disunion. I am for going back to the instrumentality through which this union was first made, and by which alone it can be restored. (Cheers.) I am for peace, because it is the first step toward conciliation and compromise. You cannot move until you have first taken that indispensable preliminary—a cessation of hostilities. But it is said that the South has refused to accept or listen to any terms whatever. How do you know that? Has it been tried? Now, gentlemen, I know very well what the papers in support of the administration at Richmond say. I know what men in the Senate and House of Representatives at Richmond declare upon this subject; I have read it all. We are indebted to the Abolition papers for the republication of all that. But I do hope that no man who has ever known me in person or by speech, supposed for one moment, that I expected that the children of that revolution, the men who sprang from it, the men who are dependent upon it, or even the men holding power now under it would, while this war lasted, listen to any terms of settlement. I would as soon expect Abraham Lincoln and his cabinet to propose such terms on the basis of the Union of fifty years ago, as Jefferson Davis or any man in Richmond. Now, I am not, perhaps, the most sensitive man in the world, and yet I have a reasonable degree of sensitiveness, and I hope, some common sense with it—but I do not feel, as I am afraid some of our friends do feel, personally slighted, because, while I have advocated a peaceable settlement of our difficulties—conciliation and compromise for the restoration of the Union of these States—I have met with opposition and with hostility from the papers in Richmond. I did not look for it, gentlemen, although I have a better right to it than some of your friends here (A voice—"Van Buren") from my former relation to the Democratic party of the South, when they were acknowledging obedience to the Constitution, and were still in the Union; but I did not expect that Jefferson Davis, and Benjamin, and Hunter, or any of them would, when I opened my arms and said—"Return, prodigal sons," rush with tears to my embrace,—and I do not feel hurt. I am not the least "miffed" by it; and I certainly shall not therefore advocate a vigorous prosecution of the war to punish them. I am afraid some gentlemen imagined, when they gave out this invitation, that it would be, of course, accepted at once; although one of those who first proclaimed it, had even less power than I have, certainly not more—and was very much in the condition of that distinguished personage who, from the top of a certain high mountain, promised all the kingdoms of the world. I do not think that he or I, or any other man while this administration is in place, has the power to conciliate and compromise now. Take the theory for what it is worth, and let men of intelligence judge; let history attest it hereafter. My theory upon that subject, then, is this—stop this war. (Cheers).

Let parties in the South be organized, as parties never will be while the war lasts, upon some other question than repelling invasion. Let opposition parties spring up there, restore all the ordinary instrumentalities, and, as I have said elsewhere, allow all the great and powerful natural causes which impel us to reunion, to operate and have their full effect, and then, through the ballot-box in the South, men will be put in power, elected presidents, constituted cabinets, and chosen senators and representatives (because the people will it so), who will agree to terms of settlement and compromise with the men whom the people of the North and the West will by that time have also made presidents, cabinet ministers, senators, and representatives. (Cheers.) I no more expect the *Richmond Enquirer* to accept these propositions, least of all, now to advocate reunion, than I do the *Chronicle* or *Republican*, or the *Philadelphia Press*, or the *Times* in this city, or the *Evening Post.* But there is a people in the South just like us, as intelligent, as brave, as well-informed, as acute in discerning their own interests and obedient to their own duties as any people; and when they see that duty and interest both combine to demand the reconstruction of the Union of these States, they will do then as their fathers and our fathers did in 1787. The old Confederation had perished. When the Union they established was gone, and the States were resolved again into their original and sole sovereignty, they came together, every State, in a convention of States in Philadelphia, and with Washington as presiding officer, and with him Hamilton, Jay, Sherman, Ellsworth, Pinckney, and Madison—not at the mouth of the cannon, not with the edge of the sword, not at the point of the bayonet, but in council, and in the spirit of conciliation and compromise, they made a new union. (Cheers.) That Union endured for seventy-two years, in peace, prosperity, and happiness, until its foundations were first sapped by the abolitionists. Now, sir, what was done then can be done again, and will be done. The time will come, by and by, when the States of the South, one by one (because the people composing those States resolve upon it), shall come together, when this war shall have terminated and reason resumed its sway, and we have the power to put down fanaticism and abolitionism; and the North and West will come together with them in convention to restore a more perfect union. The Union of 1776, the Union that carried us through the revolutionary war, was dissolved, and yet was reconstructed. Why? Because interest, duty, patriotism, desire for a great and prosperous country, all these contributed to the result. That council chamber made the Union under which we live. The States through their Sovereignties did it, and will do it again. We hear much in condemnation of the doctrine of State Rights, and attempts have been made by execrable oaths to overthrow that great and fundamental doctrine without which the liberties of this people cannot endure an hour. Mr. Lincoln undertook to announce, in his message of the 4th of July, the monstrous absurdity that the Union was older than the Constitution—that is, that the child was older than the parent. But I affirm that it was the State Sovereignties which met in convention and made the Federal Government, and I have here an extraordinary proof of that fact. I doubt whether there are half a score like it in the United States to-day. It is especially pertinent because of the pending election in that State, and also because of the noble, bold, and patriotic stand which the Democracy of Connecticut have assumed. Here, sir, is a piece of coin from the mint of the Sovereign State of Connecticut, coined by her, in the exercise of her high power of sovereignty, and bearing date in 1787. Yes, the Confederation was dissolved, and that State went back again to its sole sovereignty and coined money. I believe it never issued any "greenbacks;" they are a later invention. But here is the evidence of that great fact, which designing men, consolidating empire here at the price of liberty, are desirous continually to ignore. It is a copper coin, with a copper head upon it. (Great laughter, and cheers for the "Copperheads.") It is the head of Liberty. (Renewed applause.) It bears the superscription and image of Freedom. It reads, "By the authority of the State of Connecticut." That was its warrant for circulation.

Now, sir, I have already explained what I believe solemnly to be the only peaceable mode by which the Union of these States can be restored. The idea of accomplishing it by force does seem to me, with all due respect to the twenty odd millions of people who once thought otherwise, the most extraordinary absurdity that ever entered the imagination of man. (Applause.) Despotic governments do not proclaim, as our fathers did in the Declaration of Independence, that all governments derive their just powers from the consent of the governed. That was the foundation upon which this great superstructure of civil liberty, this mighty fabric, was erected, and upon that it prospered; and now that by force, by coercion, the fraternity, the good will, without which there can be no Union, should be sought to be perpetuated, will seem in future ages, to men undisturbed by the passions and prejudices of the day, almost incredible. It will be set down among the fabulous portions of history, and some future Herodotus will relate it, as he does all his other fables, with the preface, "They say." Russia is at this moment engaged in suppressing an insurrection in Poland, and it is a singular coincidence that that insurrection among a people trodden under the heel of despotism for seventy years, without a form of government, without ballot, without free speech, without a free press, without the liberty to assemble, governed by satraps and deputies appointed by the autocrat of Russia, is resistance to a conscription act. But they are a people in whose ashes seem yet to slumber the fires of liberty that once burned bright in the heart of every Polander. (Three cheers for the Poles.) Now, upon the theory of the Russian Empire, the autocrat of Russia has a right and is perfectly consistent in sending his armies to suppress that rebellion; but to expect to accomplish such a result in this country seems, as I have said, an absurdity beyond conception. But I do understand the theory of our government. I do believe that all governments derive their just powers from the consent of the governed, and I know that that consent can be brought about only by the application of reason, or by appeals to the better passions of men. I would resort now to these appeals. I desire to reason this case with the men of the South, when we have got through reasoning it with the men of the North and West. When we have accomplished that work, and re-established all our own liberties, freedom of speech, of the press, and of elections here, then I desire that an appeal shall be made to the South, and that by their consent now, as in 1787, the Union shall be restored. I have that faith in their intelligence, their patriotism, their wisdom and their statesmanship, to believe that this result will be accomplished; and I feel confident that either the men now in power there will be obliged to yield to the popular demand, or failing to yield, will be compelled to do what we propose to compel Lincoln and his party to do on the 4th of March, 1865—to give place to other men. (Cheers.) Without entering into detail, these are my reasons for the faith that is in me, of the reconstruction of the Union of these States; and my conviction is as earnest as ever penetrated the heart of man. I believe it. I speak it thus, because I believe it.

But to return: upon the other theory that the war is prosecuted, inexorably and unchangeably, as a war of aggression—a war to abolish slavery—a war to set free four millions of negroes—I ask whether or not it is our duty, nay, have we a right to lend to it our support in the way of "vigorous prosecution." The President has no right to call upon us; we are under no obligation to respond beyond the limits of a law constitutionally enacted. (Applause.) We have a right to determine this question, to argue it in court and before the people, as well as every other question. Sir, the Democratic party carried on the war of 1812, and never dreamed of forbidding discussion as to its policy. The Democratic party afterward waged the war against Mexico, and never thought of arresting any man—never attempted to suppress freedom of speech or of the press—never locked men in bastiles—never prohibited the circulation of a single newspaper through the mails. (Loud cheers.) This was reserved to the party of Abolition, to the party in power, that undertakes to suppress all these agencies of popular rights and freedom.

Now, what a spectacle has this Congress presented! We went before the people at the October and November elections, and so far as was possible through the press, trammelled as it was, and of speech, trodden down as it was, made our appeal. The people heard it, and answered. They rendered judgment of condemnation against the Administration, and yet after having chosen four Senators—as many as the elections that had taken place permitted us; having changed the political complexion of the House of Representatives; having converted that body into a vast charnel house, a political sepulchre; the men who had been beaten at home spent the last expiring hours of that infamous Congress in attempting to perpetuate their power by force. By legislation seeking to reverse the judgment of the people, they placed themselves in a condition to maintain their power after its constitutional limitation should have expired, or to control the elections. That can be but the purpose of all this. Why should the *habeas corpus* be suspended in the adhering States of this Union? Why shall the President undertake for one single moment to arrest a citizen for the expression of his opinions, or for the assembling together, as we have done to-night, to discuss his policy? What is the purpose of all this?

To suppress the rebellion in the South? They do not arrest anybody there. It is precisely the same weak and execrable policy that was exhibited in the proclamation of freedom to all the slaves inside the Confederate lines, with an exemption of slaves within our military lines, where alone the President has the power to set them free. (Applause.)

Instead of arresting traitors who are within the limits of the Confederate States, he proposes to arrest men in the North and West, whose only crime is, that they choose, in the exercise of their rights as freemen, to condemn his policy; who demand, through the ballot-box, that another party and other men, representing other principles and another policy, shall be put in power. (Cheers). It cannot be done in the United States yet. We have borne enough, but we cannot endure every thing. There is a limit where patience ceases to be a virtue. It has not come yet—I think it will not come. I know it will not, if a spirit of freedom is exhibited by those who have descended from the ancestors who gave us our liberties in this, and in our mother country. I know well, indeed, that we are in the midst of a period of profound darkness, that clouds lower heavily in the horizon above us—another of those fluctuating crises which mark every revolution, is at this moment upon us. He is blind, indeed, who does not see; deaf, indeed, who does not hear the mutterings of the storm. At this moment the whole power of the Administration, all its agencies, secret and public, are being employed to ascertain whether this people is servile enough to submit to the loss of their liberties; and then, with a cowardice which marks all tyrants, if it be found, by the shrinking away of the people and their cowering before threats, the threats will be executed. Yes, of that let there be no doubt. But if the report from the spies and informers who infest all your places, public and private, by order of this Administration, be received at the centre of power in Washington, that this people still love their liberties, and are resolved, at every hazard, to maintain them, then the Administration will yield before that popular resolve. (Cheers). You will then escape, because, unwise as the men in power have proved themselves, by the sad experience of the past, destitute, as they are, of the first principles of true statesmanship, without one spark of that love of liberty which ought to animate the breast of every American citizen; still, I repeat, they are not stolid enough to mistake these signs, which indicate the gathering wrath of an outraged and oppressed people. Let the men in power beware—and I would warn them, though I well know who will conquer if such a struggle shall come—although I know it is not your head or mine that would be stricken off upon the block—still, I know too well the calamities which must be inflicted upon this, the country of my birth, to desire to witness scenes like these in our midst. Let me, then, as a patriot, pretending no love to this Administration, feeling all the natural promptings of the human heart to avenge wrongs which I, as well as others, have endured, and which burn deep within this bosom—ay, wrongs inflicted, or threatened to be inflicted, and causing many a sleepless night and many an anxious hour to myself and the family of my household—with all that, still let me, in the spirit of a patriot, appeal to this Administration, and with a voice of warning, prophetic it may be—I trust not, because I trust the warning will be heeded—let me say to them: Learn a parable from the fig-tree—"When ye see the fig-tree putting forth his leaves, ye know that the summer is nigh." It is not summer; it is winter—"the winter of our discontent." Let them be warned in time, and make no issue with the people, while exercising their constitutional power, which they have a right to do, and carrying out the laws enacted according to the Constitution, by President and Cabinet ministers to the 4th of March, 1865; by representatives the same; by senators till their terms respectively shall have expired. Let all who are under this Administration in peace and quiet hold their offices; let their persons be undisturbed, violated by no mob, punished by no exercise of arbitrary power. Let them fret still their brief hour on this great stage upon which the most wondrous drama of the world's history is now being enacted. In patience let them wait the expiration of their term of power; but meantime, as they value peace in this land, as they would avert a revolution in our midst; as they would see the Constitution maintained, the laws executed, social convulsions turned aside, let them see to it that the people enjoy every jot and tittle of their rights through that Constitution and under the laws, and permit the several States, unobstructed, to exercise their judgment at the ballot-box, and determine whether their party shall remain in power, or whether another party holding other principles, pursuing, or proposing to pursue, another policy, shall reign in their stead. I make no threats—no wise man ever did. (Cheers.) I never yield to threats—therefore, I expect no one else to yield; but, in the spirit of warning, as one who would avert the struggle which this people will make to maintain their liberties, I have spoken; and I would that my voice could penetrate that most impenetrable of all recesses, the precincts of the White House, and that the men who are surrounded there by the parasites of power—the flatterers who are the vermin of courts, with that legion of contractors and placemen who speak not the truth, and represent not the people—that a voice from the people could reach their ears, and that the voice being heard might be heeded. Then shall we escape the convulsions which have visited other countries. The scenes of revolutions in former times will not be re-enacted in our midst; but peaceably and quietly, under the Constitution, and in accordance with law, the changes of administration successively, year after year, will go on in this country, which, before God, I believe, and it is the faith and hope of my heart, is destined yet once again, in peace, happiness, and prosperity, to realize that most splendid of visions that ever fell upon human eyes—one Union, one Constitution, one Destiny.

NOTE.—The following card from Mr. VALLANDIGHAM was called out by a misreport of the foregoing speech, in the New-York *Times:*

NEW YORK, *March* 8, 1863.

To the Editor of the New York Times:

Allow me to say, that the statement of your reporter that I denied that we owed any obedience to the Conscription Act, and your own that I counselled resistance to it by the people of the North, are both incorrect. On the contrary, I expressly counselled the trial of all questions of law before our judicial courts, and all questions of politics before the tribunal of the ballot-box. I am for obedience to all laws—obedience by the people and by men in power also. I am for a free discussion of all questions of law before our judicial courts, and all questions of politics before the tribunal of the ballot-box. I am for a free discussion of all measures and laws whatsoever as in former times; but forcible resistance to none. The ballot-box, and not the cartridge-box, is the instrument for reform and revolution which I would have resorted to. Let this be understood.

REMARKS ON THE RIGHT OF THE PEOPLE TO KEEP AND BEAR ARMS;

Made at a Mass Meeting in Hamilton, Ohio, March 21, 1863.

I WILL not speak disrespectfully of Colonel Carrington. He and I served pleasantly together in the militia of Ohio, on the peace establishment (laughter), and I found him always gentlemanly in his deportment. I am glad to learn that he is still so regarded at Indianapolis. How could he have issued such an order? I know that he is "great" on general orders; but such a one passes my comprehension. I am sure he cannot want to do wrong, for he must know, that two years hence, under the legislation of the late Congress, a Democratic President or Secretary of War—and who knows but I may be Secretary myself? (laughter and cheers)—can strike his name from the roll without even a why or wherefore. It would be well for all ambitious military gentlemen just now to recollect this small fact, and confine themselves strictly to their legal and Constitutional military duties, and to allow others to enjoy their opinions and civil rights unmolested. But to the order. Here it is:

HEAD-QUARTERS, UNITED STATES FORCES,
INDIANAPOLIS, IND., *March* 17, 1863.

" *General Order No.* 15.

"1. THE habit of carrying arms upon the person has greatly increased"—

Well, so it has, and in times of threats and danger like these, it ought to, and in spite of all "orders," it will increase—

"And is prejudicial to peace and good order"—

Sir, restore to us peace and good order, and we will lay aside all arms, and be glad of the chance—(Great applause.)

"As well as a violation of civil law"—

I deny it; but, if so, who gave authority to this gentleman to lecture on civil law in a military order?—

"Especially at this time, it is unnecessary, impolitic, and dangerous."

Was ever the like heard or read of before? "At this time—" at a time when Democrats are threatened with violence everywhere; when mobs are happening every day, and Democratic presses destroyed; when secret societies are being formed all over the country to stimulate to violence; when, at hotels and in depots, and in railroad cars and on the street corners, Democrats are scowled at and menaced, a military order coolly announces that it is unnecessary, impolitic, and dangerous to carry arms! And who signs this order? "Henry B. Carrington, Colonel 18th U. S. Infantry, *Commanding*"—

Commanding what? The 18th U. S. *Infantry*, or at most the United States *forces* of Indiana—but not the people, the free white American citizens of American descent, not in the military service. That is the extent of his authority, and no more. And now, sir, I hold in my hand a general order also—an order binding on all military men and all civilians alike—on colonels and generals and commanders-in-chief—State and Federal. (Applause.) Hear it:

" *The right of the people to* KEEP AND BEAR *arms shall not be infringed.*" By order of the States and people of the United States. George Washington, commanding. (Great cheering.)

That, sir, is General Order No. 1—the Constitution of the United States. (Loud cheers.) Who now is to be obeyed—Carrington or Washington?

But I have another "order" yet.

"The people have a right to *bear arms* for their *defence and security*, and the military shall be in strict subordination to the civil power." (Renewed cheering.)

That, sir, is General Order No. 2—the Constitution of Ohio, by order of the people of Ohio. Here, sir, are our warrants for keeping and bearing arms, and by the blessing of God, we mean to do it; and if the men in power undertake in an evil hour to demand them of us, we will return the Spartan answer, "Come and take them."

But Colonel Carrington's order proceeds:

"The Major-General commanding the Department of the Ohio"—

Commanding whom, again I ask? Only the military forces of the Department of Ohio, but not a single citizen in it—

"Having ordered that all sales of arms, powder, lead, and percussion caps, be prohibited until further orders"—

Where, sir, is the law for all that? Are we a conquered province governed by a military proconsul? And so then it has come to this, that the Constitution is now suspended by a military General Order, No. 15! Sir, the Constitutional right to keep and bear arms, carries with it the right to buy and sell arms; and fire-arms are useless without powder, lead, and percussion caps. It is our right to have them, and we mean to obey General Orders Nos. 1 and 2, instead of No. 15. (Loud applause.)

But I read further—"and that any violation of said order will be followed by the *confiscation* of the goods sold, and the seizure of the stock of the vender."

Is the man deranged? *Confiscation*, indeed! Why, sir, the men who are clothed now with a little brief authority, seem to think of nothing except taxation, emancipation, confiscation, conscription, and every other word ending in t-i-o-n. (Laughter.) But General Order No. 1 says, "No man shall be deprived of property without due process of law;" and General Order No. 2 says, "Private property shall ever be held inviolate, and every person, for an injury done him in his land, *goods*, person, or reputation, shall have remedy by due course of law." And though the writ of *habeas corpus* may be suspended, the writs of replevin and injunction cannot be. (Cries of "Good, good.")

But Order No. 15 proceeds: "And said order having been extended by the Major-General, to cover the entire department, is hereby promulged"—

Yes, promulged—"for immediate observance throughout the State."

Can military insolence go further? Is this the way the military is to be in strict subordination to the civil power? And does the colonel commanding the 18th U. S. Infantry thus undertake to "promulge" a general order suspending or abrogating the Constitution of the United States and of Indiana? Are we living in America or Austria?

And now the fitting commentary on all this attempt to disarm the white man, while public arms are being put into the hands of the negro, is the allusion in the second section of this General Order No. 15, to the recent destruction of a Democratic printing-press, by what the colonel commanding the 18th U. S. Infantry, drawing it mild after the fashion of Sarey Gamp, calls a "popular demonstration;" and yet not one of the perpetrators of this outrage, although soldiers, and under military law, has been punished, nor ever will be. Yet at just such a time of lawless violence, it is proposed that the people shall be disarmed. Never. (Loud cheers.)

Sir, I repeat now what I believe to be the true programme for these times: Try every question of law in your Courts, and every question of politics before the people, and through the ballot-box; maintain your Constitutional civil rights, at all hazards, against military usurpation. Let there be no resistance to law, but meet and repel all mobs and mob violence by force and arms on the spot. (Great and continued cheering.)

PROTEST BEFORE THE MILITARY COMMISSION

*At Cincinnati, May 7, 1863.**

ARRESTED without due "process of law," without warrant from any judicial officer, and now in a military prison, I have been served with a "charge and specifications," as in a Court-Martial or Military Commission.

I am not in either "the land or naval forces of the United States, nor in the militia in the actual service of the United States," and therefore am not triable for any cause, by any such Court, but am subject, by the express terms of the Constitution, to arrest only by due process of law, judicial warrant, regularly issued upon affidavit and by some officer or Court of competent jurisdiction for the trial of citizens, and am now entitled to be tried on an indictment or presentment of a Grand Jury of such Court, to speedy and public trial by an impartial jury of the State of Ohio, to be confronted with witnesses against me,

* The morning of Mr. VALLANDIGHAM'S arrest, May 5, 1863, he wrote a brief address in pencil, and found means to send it out from the Military Prison at Cincinnati, declaring that it was only because of his political opinions and the defending of them before the people, that he was in bonds, and added: "As for myself, I adhere to every principle, and will make good, through imprisonment and by the sacrifice of life itself, every pledge and declaration which I have ever made, uttered, or maintained from the beginning. To you, to the whole people, to TIME, I again appeal. Stand firm! Falter not an instant!"

to have compulsory process for witnesses in my behalf, the assistance of counsel for my defence, and evidence and argument according to the common law and the ways of Judicial Courts.

And all these I here demand as my right as a citizen of the United States, and under the Constitution of the United States.

But the alleged "offence" is not known to the Constitution of the United States, nor to any law thereof. It is words spoken to the people of Ohio in an open and public political meeting, lawfully and peaceably assembled, under the Constitution and upon full notice. It is words of criticism of the public policy of the public servants of the people, by which policy it was alleged that the welfare of the country was not promoted. It was an appeal to the people to change that policy, not by force, but by free elections and the ballot-box. It is not pretended that I counselled disobedience to the Constitution, or resistance to laws and lawful authority. I never have.

Beyond this protest, I have nothing further to submit.

ADDRESS TO THE PEOPLE OF OHIO UPON HIS GOING INTO EXILE.*

MILITARY PRISON, CINCINNATI, OHIO, *May* 22, 1863.

BANISHED from my native State for no crime save Democratic opinions and free speech to you in their defence, and about to go into exile, not of my own will, but by the compulsion of an arbitrary and tyrannic power which I cannot resist, allow me a parting word. Because despotism and superior force so will it, I go within the Confederate lines. I well understand the purpose of this order. But in vain the malice of enemies shall thus contrive to give color to the calumnies and misrepresentations of the past two years. They little comprehend the true character of the man with whom they have to deal. No order of banishment, executed by superior force, can release me from my obligations or deprive me of my rights as a citizen of Ohio and of the United States. My allegiance to my own State and Government I shall recognize, wheresoever I may be, as binding in all things, just the same as though I remained upon their soil. Every sentiment

* Upon arriving at the lines, on the 25th of May, Mr. VALLANDIGHAM said to the Confederate soldiers sent to meet him, the Federal officers also being present: "*I am a citizen of Ohio, and of the United States, still claiming and owing allegiance to both. I am within your lines against my will and by military compulsion, and therefore surrender myself a prisoner of war.*"

and expression of attachment to the Union and devotion to the Constitution—to my country—which I have ever cherished or uttered, shall abide unchanged and unretracted till my return. Meantime, I will not doubt that the people of Ohio, cowering not a moment before either the threats or the exercise of arbitrary power, will, in every trial, prove themselves worthy to be called freemen.

ADDRESS TO THE PEOPLE OF OHIO, UPON ARRIVING IN CANADA.

CLIFTON HOUSE, NIAGARA FALLS, CANADA WEST,
July 15, 1863.

ARRESTED and confined for three weeks in the United States, a prisoner of State; banished thence to the Confederate States, and there held as an alien enemy and prisoner of war, though on parole, fairly and honorably dealt with and given leave to depart, an act possible only by running the blockade at the hazard of being fired on by ships flying the flag of my own country, I found myself a freeman when upon British soil. And to-day under the protection of the British flag, I am here to enjoy and in part to exercise the privileges and rights which usurpers insolently deny me at home. The shallow contrivance of the weak despots at Washington, and their advisers, has been defeated. Nay, it has been turned against them; and I, who for two years was maligned as in secret league with the Confederates, having refused, when in their midst, under circumstances the most favorable, either to identify myself with their cause, or even so much as to remain, preferring rather exile in a foreign land, return now with allegiance to my own State and government, unbroken in word, thought, or deed, and with every declaration and pledge to you while at home, and before I was stolen away, made good in spirit and to the very letter.

Six weeks ago, when just going into banishment because an audacious but most cowardly despotism caused it, I addressed you as a fellow-citizen. To-day and from the very place then selected by me, but after wearisome and most perilous journeyings for more than four thousand miles by land and upon the sea, still in exile, though almost in sight of my native State, I greet you as your Representative. Grateful certainly I am, for the confidence in my integrity and patriotism, implied by the unanimous nomination as candidate for Governor of Ohio, which you gave me while I was yet in the Confederate States.

It was not misplaced; it shall never be abused. But this is the least of all considerations in times like these. I ask no personal sympathy for the personal wrong. No, it is the cause of constitutional liberty and private right cruelly outraged beyond example in a free country, by the President and his servants, which gives public significancy to the action of your Convention. Yours was, indeed, an act of justice to a citizen, who, for his devotion to the rights of the States and the liberties of the people, had been marked for destruction by the hand of arbitrary power. But it was much more. It was an example of courage worthy of the heroic ages of the world; and it was a spectacle and a rebuke to the usurping tyrants, who, having broken up the Union, would now strike down the Constitution, subvert your present Government and establish a formal and proclaimed despotism in its stead. You are the RESTORERS AND DEFENDERS OF CONSTITUTIONAL LIBERTY, and by that proud title history will salute you.

I congratulate you upon your nominations. They whom you have placed upon the ticket with me, are gentlemen of character, ability, integrity, and tried fidelity to the Constitution, the Union, and to Liberty. Their moral and political courage—a quality always rare, and now the most valuable of public virtues—is beyond question. Every way, all these were nominations eminently fit to be made. And even jealousy, I am sure, will now be hushed, if I especially rejoice with you in the nomination of Mr. Pugh as your candidate for Lieutenant-Governor and President of the Senate. A scholar and a gentleman, a soldier in a foreign war, and always a patriot; eminent as a lawyer, and distinguished as an orator and statesman, I hail his acceptance as an omen of the return of the better and more virtuous days of the Republic.

I indorse your noble platform; elegant in style—admirable in sentiment. You present the true issue and commit yourselves to the great mission just now of the Democratic party—to restore and make sure FIRST the rights and liberties declared yours by your constitutions. It is in vain to invite the States and people of the South to return to a Union without a Constitution, and dishonored and polluted by repeated and most aggravated exertions of tyrannic power. It is base in yourselves, and treasonable to your posterity, to surrender these liberties and rights to the creatures whom your own breath created and can destroy. Shall there be free speech, a free press, peaceable assemblages of the people, and a free ballot in Ohio? Shall the people hereafter, as hitherto, have the right to discuss and condemn the principles and policy of the party—the ministry—the men who, for the time, conduct the Government—to demand of their public servants a reckoning of their stewardship, and to place other men and another party in power at their supreme will and pleasure? Shall Order Thirty-Eight or the Constitution be the supreme law of the land? And shall the citizen any more, be arrested by an armed soldiery at midnight, dragged from wife and child and home, to a military prison; thence to a mock military trial; there condemned and then banished as a felon, for the exercise of his rights? That is the issue, and nobly you have met it. It is the very question of free, popular government itself. It is the whole question: upon the one side, liberty; on the other, despotism. The President as the recognized head of his party, accepts the issue. Whatever he wills, that is law. Constitutions, State and Federal, are nothing; acts of legislation nothing; the judiciary less than nothing. In time of war, there is but one will supreme—his will; but one law—military necessity, and he the sole judge. Military orders supersede the Constitution, and military commissions usurp the place of the ordinary courts of justice in the land. Nor are these mere idle claims. For two years and more, by arms, they have been enforced. It was the mission of the weak but presumptuous Burnside—a name infamous forever in the ears of all lovers of constitutional liberty—to try the experiment in Ohio—aided by a judge whom I name not, because he has brought foul dishonor upon the judiciary of my country. In your hands now, men of Ohio, is the final issue of the experiment. The party of the Administration have accepted it. By pledging support to the President, they have justified his outrages upon liberty and the Constitution; and whoever gives his vote to the candidates of that party, commits himself to every act of violence and wrong on the part of the Administration which he upholds; and thus, by the law of retaliation, which is the law of might, would forfeit his own right to liberty, personal and political, whensoever other men and another party shall hold the power. Much more do the candidates themselves. Suffer them not, I entreat you, to evade the issue; and by the judgment of the people we will abide.

And now, finally, let me ask, what is the pretext for all the monstrous acts and claims of arbitrary power which you have so boldly and nobly denounced? "Military necessity." But if, indeed, all these be demanded by military necessity, then, believe me, your liberties are gone, and tyranny is perpetual. For if this civil war is to terminate only by the subjugation or submission of the South to force and arms, the infant to-day will not live to see the end of it. No, in another way only can it be brought to a close. Travelling a thousand miles and more, through nearly one-half of the Confederate States, and sojourning for a time at widely different points, I met not one, man, woman, or child, who was not resolved to perish rather than yield to the pressure of arms even in the most desperate extremity. And whatever may and must be the varying fortune of the war, in all which I recognize the hand of Providence pointing visibly to the ultimate issue of this great trial of the States and people of America, they are better prepared now every way, to make good their inexorable purpose, than at any period since the beginning of the struggle. These may indeed be unwelcome truths; but they are addressed only to candid and honest men. Neither, however, let me add, did I meet any one, whatever his opinions or his station, political or private, who did not declare his readiness, when the war shall have ceased and invading armies been withdrawn, to consider and discuss the question of reunion. And who shall doubt the issue of the argument? I return, therefore, with my opinions and convictions as to war or peace, and my faith as to final results from sound policy and wise statesmanship, not only unchanged, but confirmed and strengthened. And may the God of Heaven and Earth so rule the hearts and minds of Americans everywhere, that with a Constitution maintained, a Union restored, and Liberty henceforth made secure, a grander and nobler destiny shall yet be ours, than that even which blessed our fathers in the first two ages of the Republic.

LETTER TO THE DEMOCRATIC MEETING AT TOLEDO.

TABLE ROCK HOUSE,
NIAGARA FALLS, C. W., *July* 31, 1863.

Messrs. THOMAS DUNLAP, H. P. PLATT, JOHN T. MAHER, JOHN G. ISHAM, J. C. WALES, and others, *Committee, etc.*

GENTLEMEN: Unable to attend your meeting, of the 5th of August, in person, permit me to address you by letter briefly.

I waste no part of your time in personal defence. To the candidates, speakers, and writers of the Administration party, I leave, undisturbed, the brave and chivalrous work of assailing an opponent, absent because the tyrannic power of their master, executed by military force, compels it. The great issue of the day ought not to be subordinated to things merely personal; and I recommend to my friends generally that they imitate the wise Romans, and "carry the war into Africa."

The Democracy of Lucas, postponing all other issues, and ignoring all differences of opinion in regard to them, assemble, of course, to consider what General Fremont, the candidate of the "free speech and free press" Republican party, of 1856, very aptly styles "the uppermost question of the day"—the question of their own constitutional rights and liberties. This is the practical issue in the Ohio campaign, forced by the President and his party upon the people; and boldly met by the Democracy in their nominations, as also in their admirable platform, which, as a candidate, I accept as their solemn and deliberate confession of political faith, and their pledge to the country that they mean to defend the rights asserted in it, with their lives, their fortunes, and their sacred honors. Until these shall have been made secure, it can be neither useful nor possible to discuss any other question not directly connected with it. There is, indeed, just such a question—one second only in importance to that of public liberty—the Union of the States, worth the whole world to the American people. But LIBERTY is the soul of a people; and what shall it profit us to gain the whole world and lose our own soul? The Constitution made the Union, and, when the war began, it was proclaimed to be for the supremacy of the Constitution and laws; and whatever difference of opinion there may have been, even then, as to the mode of securing it, every patriotic citizen of the United States knew what the laws and Constitution were. But what do we see to-day? The opinion and will, from hour to hour, of the President—and such a President!—is solemnly and officially proclaimed superior to the Constitution and the laws, even in the States wholly loyal. So that upon the present policy of the Administration and its party, declared unchangeable, the South is to be forced to submit to the will and opinion of Abraham Lincoln, instead of written fundamental statute and common law. And if we ourselves scorn to yield up our constitutional rights and liberties to this monstrous demand, does any honorable man, any sane man, ask or expect the States and people of the South to surrender, so long as a man survives to strike a blow, or a woman to strengthen his heart or nerve his arm? Upon such a policy this war must and will be interminable. So many square miles may be overrun, so much soil may be conquered, but the hearts of the people never.

How, then, stand the chances of the Union, measured by the two different policies of the Abolition and Democratic parties?

The party of the Administration declares that the States and people of the South shall be forced to lay down their arms and submit. What then? Confiscation of all property, emancipation of all slaves, and execution of all who, directly or indirectly, have taken part in the rebellion: namely, nine-tenths of the whole population; for no general amnesty has ever as yet been so much as suggested by either Congress or the Executive, and unconditional submission is now the least which is demanded. More than this: as to any State which may first submit or be conquered, conscription of every male person, white or black, between twenty and forty-five, for the conquest of the States still in arms.

Nor is this the worst; for inasmuch as all slaves and free negroes South are considered "loyal," and nearly all white men and women "disloyal," and, therefore, as having forfeited all rights, the negroes, then all free, are to be treated as almost the only persons entitled to the several rights and privileges of citizenship, and especially the very soldiers to garrison the South. And now add to all this: suppression of the freedom of speech and of the press, suspension of *habeas corpus*, martial law, arbitrary arrests, imprisonments, banishments, interference with elections, test oaths, appropriation of private houses, seizure of private property, and every other act of oppression, outrage, and despotism, which for two years have been mercilessly practised even in States never in insurrection, but always true to the Union.

This is the entertainment to which, under the present policy of the Administration, dictated by the radicals who control it, the States and people of the South are invited. And repeatedly the question was put to me while among them, "If the citizens of the States still adhering to the Union are continually arrested, imprisoned, banished, or otherwise outraged, merely because of their political opinions, or for censure and criticism of the men and party in power, what would not be done with *us* if we should be conquered or were to submit?" In fact, it is this very policy which, instead of "crushing out the rebellion," crushed out all Union sentiment among them, and made, as it still keeps them, a unit in numbers and spirit, against the force and arms of the Federal Government. It was the repeated confession to me, personally, of several of the most distinguished public men of the Southwest, that if General Buell had been retained in command, and permitted to continue his policy of peace and conciliation—acting the officer and gentleman, observing private rights, respecting private property, returning fugitive slaves, and tolerating all political opinions, whether in sympathy with Secession or not, so long as not carried out into overt acts—the people of Tennessee would have voluntarily returned to the Union six months ago. And they rejoiced in the change of policy and his removal. But the mischief has been consummated, and no success of arms, no number of victories can repair it. Not only another policy, but other instrumentalities, alone can now restore the Union.

What, upon the other hand, does the Democratic party propose to the States and people of the South? Not Confiscation, nor Emancipation, nor Conscription, nor Execution, and certainly not the equality, or, rather, the superiority, of the negro race, but the Constitution with all its guarantees, the rights of the States, and the liberties of the people. We would restore the Union, and with it give them quiet and security in the enjoyment of their rights, properties, and institutions of every kind, as in the beginning of the Government, and before anatics and demagogues made slavery a subject of moral or political agitation. We promise, also, to ourselves, and of course to them, a free press, free speech, free elections, liberty of conscience and opinion, *habeas corpus*, due process of law, judicial trial, trial by jury, no midnight arrests, no martial law, no military orders or commissions, no provost-marshals, no military governors. In short, we ask and offer nothing but the CONSTITUTION, THE UNION, AND THE LAWS.

Which policy, then, let me ask, is best calculated to restore the Union? Which party best able to effect the restoration? All wise and candid men now admit, that even if the military power of the Confederate States could be broken down by force, and her armies dissipated, the final settlement of this great controversy must be the result of statesmanship, not arms—conciliation, not force. And to whom but Democratic statesmen, untainted with Abolitionism, and in whose wisdom and integrity the people of all sections—South as well as North and West—have confidence, can the work be securely committed? Can they accomplish it who come with acts and proclamations of abolition, confiscation, conscription, and death—men who are for no peace or union till slavery is abolished? Believe me, the success of the Democratic ticket this fall, in Ohio, will do more, not only for constitutional liberty, but for the Union, than such men could accomplish in a hundred years.

I need not repeat my often-declared conviction, which time has always vindicated, that the South cannot be conquered by force and arms. But granting, for argument's sake, "the effectual check and waning proportions of the rebellion," as proclaimed now again for the hundredth time, by the organs of the Administration, and that, by the second Monday in January next, all the armies of the Confederates will have been captured or dispersed, and their remaining five hundred thousand square miles of territory overrun and occupied, then the hour for the pacification of the South and conciliation of her people will have arrived. And which party will most readily be hearkened to by them? Who, as Governor of Ohio, will be the most efficient agent in that great and arduous work? Your candidate, committed wholly to the restoration of the Union as it was; or the candidate of the Administration, pledged to a policy full, upon the one hand, of continual exasperation and hate, and on the other, of insurrection and revenge? Very momentous are these questions; for until that shall have been accomplished, there can be neither Constitution nor Union, and no security and no quiet in the land; nor can a single soldier, till then, returns to mother, or wife, or child, or home. Reason together, then, men of Ohio, and judge wisely, ye who love your country, and would restore to its former peace, prosperity, and glory. Continual war and strife are the forbidden fruit of our political Eden, and bear still the primal curse, uttered in tones louder than the voice of the mighty Cataract in whose presence I now write—"*In the day that thou eatest thereof thou shalt surely die.*"

LETTER TO THE DEMOCRATIC MEETING AT DAYTON.

WINDSOR, C. W., *September* 15, 1863.

President of the Democratic Mass Meeting, Dayton, Ohio:

SIR: Complying with the desire of many of my Democratic friends in the city and county where I have for so many years resided, I address them briefly through you.

No further warning or entreaty from me is needed to arouse the people to the importance of the great issue before them, and to the danger which on every side threatens their liberties. The great popular demonstrations, occurring every day throughout the State, prove their zeal and devotion to the cause of Liberty and Union, and that they mean that these two shall in very deed be inseparable. Both these depend largely upon the issue of the Ohio campaign. If that party should succeed, which, upon the one hand, applauds the atrocious acts of Abraham Lincoln and his servants, and indorses the monstrous claim of absolute power over person and property, not to say life itself, set up by him in his recent letters to the Albany and Columbus Committees; and, on the other, accepts as its own, the whole radical policy, "root and branch," of Congress and the Executive in the conduct of the war, there is an end to both. In the North and West, every lover of constitutional liberty looks anxiously to the approaching elections. In the South, the eyes of hundreds of thousands, who yet, in their hearts, love the Union as it was, the old Union which their fathers and our fathers made, and would gladly see it restored in peace and with security to all, are turned now in earnest desire for the triumph of the Democratic party, as their last hope for its restoration. And the very successes of the Federal army do but render this triumph the more important; for while, according to Mr. Lincoln, they have not at all broken the strength or subdued the spirit of the Confederates in arms, they have done much to open the eyes of the people of the States still adhering to the Union, to the fact that the policy of conciliation must at least follow—far better that before any war it had preceded—the policy of coercion. Moreover, the recent extraordinary events in Mexico have greatly augmented the necessity and importance of speedily putting into power the party in whose hands the rights and interest of all States and sections will be secure. Recognition by Mexico and France, and subsequent alliance between them and the Confederate States, are impending dangers, every hour becoming more imminent. Napoleon well knows, and Joseph of Austria also, whom he has enlisted now with him, that if a united government of any kind be restored here, either "the Union as it was" of the Democrats, or "the Union as it should be" of the Abolitionists—a unity of despotism—no Empire, at least no European Empire, would be permitted to continue in Mexico. Hence he, and all whom he can persuade or force with him, will very speedily recognize the Confederate States, on condition of a guarantee of the Mexican Empire, and that by a treaty of alliance offensive and defensive, as did Louis XVI. in 1777. And thus the leaders of the Southern revolt will be enabled to keep the whole people with them, encouraged, as they will be, by the powerful support of the army, the navy, and the credit of France. The alleged mission of Mr. Stephens to Paris clearly points to this result. Unwisely and wickedly rejected by the Court at Washington, where, according to Southern authority, he came with "full powers to treat for peace and settlement," he goes now, as is said, on special embassy to the Court of Versailles. The disastrous results of the success of such embassy, either through him or Mr. Slidell already there, upon the interests and future peace of the Northwest, no man can calculate. Then, indeed, along with permanent disruption of the Union, and other numberless calamities, would the Mississippi be effectually sealed against us, except upon such terms as foreign nations may choose to impose; and thus every city and town upon that great river and its tributaries, would begin to fall into decay. Victories in the field will not at all tend to retard or prevent this alliance and its ruinous results. Now, therefore, is the accepted time, the very hour before the blow be struck, for the people of the North and West to rebuke the radicals and malignants who control public affairs, and prove to the people of the South that they can return to their allegiance to the Constitution, and thus to the Union, "with all the dignity, equality, and rights of their several States unimpaired." I repeat that the success of the Democratic party in Ohio and the other States will go further toward this result than any event which can happen within the next twelve months. Shall the golden moment to aid powerfully in the restoration of the Union as it was, be suffered to pass by?

Upon another subject allow me now a word, not volunteered, but called out and made appropriate by those who assail me.

The candidate of the Administration party is reported to have spoken recently at Columbus, in a public meeting, in substance as follows:

"What will be the effect of electing Mr. Vallandigham Governor of Ohio? I will tell you what the effect of it will be. It will inaugurate civil war in your State. It will bring civil war to your homes, upon the soil of your own State; for I tell you there is a mighty mass of men in this State whose nerves are strung up like steel, who will never permit this dishonor to be consummated in their native State. Another effect will be that it will be an invitation to the rebels in arms to come up and take possession of our soil."

Now I have so often myself been made the subject of false statement and misreport, that I will not hold Mr. Brough responsible for either the sentiment above expressed, or the presumptuous silliness of referring to the election by the people of his opponent, as bringing "dishonor" upon the State. But I know that the proposition itself is beginning to be urged by many of his friends as a menace to the freemen of Ohio; and I choose to meet it flatly.

First. The "invitation to rebels in arms" which my election will signify, will be to lay down their arms and return to the old Union and to obedience to and protection under the Constitution, laws, and flag, secure from Abolition intermeddling and agitation, as before the war, and from conscription, confiscation, execution, emancipation, negro equality, and all exertions of arbitrary, despotic power since.

Second. There will be no "civil war" in Ohio if I am elected Governor, unless Mr. Brough and his party inaugurate it; in which event we will "crush out the rebellion" in a very much shorter space of time than they have employed in putting down the "slaveholders' rebellion." If, however, he means that they will "secede" from the State by voluntary exile to Canada, or elsewhere, there will be no "coercion" in that event. But the threat, if intended to intimidate, is as the idle wind: if meant seriously, it is time that the people should know it, that they may affix the mark of Cain upon the foreheads of these new conspirators against the ballot-box. In any event, he whom a majority of the "qualified electors" of Ohio may choose for their Governor, will be inaugurated, and the vast mass of the people, without distinction of party, will aid, if need be, in the work of keeping the peace of the State, and carrying out the fundamental maxim of popular governments, that the "majority must govern." For let Mr. Brough, and all others who would defeat the will of the people, take notice that "there is a mighty mass of men in Ohio whose nerves are strung up like steel," who mean that the man who is the choice of the people shall be the people's Governor. Should that choice fall upon me, all the duties of the office shall be faithfully and fearlessly discharged. I would myself obey the Constitution and laws, and see to it that all others obeyed them within her limits and jurisdiction. The courts should be open, and restored once more to their rightful authority; justice administered without denial or delay, and the military in strict subordination to the civil power. Habeas corpus should be respected, no citizen arrested except upon due process of law, or held except for trial by the civil tribunals, and none kidnapped from the State.

But while the rights of the State and the liberties of her citizens should be thus strictly enforced, the constitutional and lawful authority and rights of the Federal Government should be obeyed and respected with scrupulous fidelity, no matter who administered it. Whatever the Administration have a right under the Constitution and laws to demand or expect from the State Executive, should be promptly and exactly rendered. In short, I would adopt and thoroughly carry out the two maxims upon this subject laid down by Mr. Jefferson in his inaugural in 1801:

First. "The support of the State Governments in all their rights, as the most competent administrations of our domestic concerns, and the surest bulwarks against anti-republican tendencies."

Second. "The preservation of the General Government in its whole constitutional vigor, as the sheet-anchor of our peace at home and safety abroad."

And in this way would I strive, by the quick and decisive exercise of will and authority whenever necessary and proper, and by cheerful and ready compliance wherever due, to restore the peace, the quiet, the economy, the good order and harmony which, in former years, marked the States, both in their relation to their own citizens and to the Federal Government, and thus, in better times, made the Union secure, and the people prosperous, happy, and contented. This, and not "civil war"—for my "crime" is that I am opposed to civil wars—is what my election would "inaugurate" in Ohio. And now, men of my native State, are not these just the blessings which you and your wives and your children, with longing hearts most earnestly desire? Defend, then, and hold fast in every extremity to, the ballot-box, and labor night and day, I invoke you, to secure these blessings, through that, the appointed potential weapon of freemen.

LETTER TO DEMOCRATIC MEETING AT CARTHAGE, O.

WINDSOR, C. W., *September* 17, 1863.

To the President of the Democratic Mass Meeting at Carthage, Ohio:

SINCE writing to the Mass Convention at Dayton to-day, the monstrous proclamation of the President has appeared, suspending the writ of *Habeas Corpus*, and thus declaring martial law throughout the United States, in every one, and every part of every one of them, and in all their territories. It comes without previous warning. It is announced at a time when the successes of the Federal armies and the reverses of the Confederates are greater than at any period since the beginning of the war; at a time when the lines of the former are more extended, and of the latter more contracted and further removed from the original frontier, than ever before; and at a time when, according to the Secretary of State, the rebellion is at last almost crushed out. It appears in the midst of no riot, tumult, or other popular convulsion anywhere in the States always true to the Union, and no preparation for any; and when even the odious "conscription" is being executed quietly and without resistance wherever announced. It is to continue "during the rebellion"—the President being the sole judge and arbiter of how long the rebellion shall be deemed to last.

At such a time, and under such circumstances, it can have but one object—the pending elections this fall, but especially the Presidential canvass of 1864. It is, indeed, the full development of that of which I have so often warned the people of Ohio and of the United States—the great conspiracy against constitutional liberty and free popular government—the establishment of a "formal and proclaimed despotism" in your midst. Oh, that the warning voice had been heard, feeble though it was, which two years ago, in the beginning of this great struggle, in accents earnest as ever issued from human lips, cried aloud to the people that, one by one, their liberties were about to perish, and that anarchy first and a strong government afterwards, no more State lines, no more State governments, but a consolidated monarchy, or vast centralized military despotism, must all follow in the history of the future, as in the history of the past they had centuries before been written. But that voice found no echo then, save in the columns and corridors of the Capitol. To-day it is lifted up again. And hereafter let no man tell you—least of all the sentinels upon your watch-towers—that there is no danger, no ground for alarm or apprehension. To-day your President is in form, as for two years and more he has been in fact, a Military Dictator. The most incredulous may see at last that the issue is, indeed, whether there shall any longer be Constitution and law in the United States, other than the will, unknown or expressed, of the President; whether freedom of person, of the press, of speech, free political assemblages and a free ballot, shall any more exist among us; and whether the people shall hereafter, as heretofore, choose the Legislatures and Chief Executives of the State and Federal Governments. Shall there be free State elections any longer, or another Presidential election of any sort? Shall popular government or a despotism, unlimited by law and uncontrolled by Judicial Courts, henceforth prevail in the United States? This now, men of Ohio, more than ever, is the issue before you. The revolutionary purpose of the Administration to perpetuate, by intimidation or force, its power in the States and in the General Government, stands now fully revealed. Next, after this declaration of martial law, will follow the armed seizure and occupation of your State by Federal troops, to intimidate or overpower you at the polls. But this monstrous purpose will not and cannot be executed, except the people cringe or cower before the threat or the attempted execution. The time, therefore, has now arrived for the renewed, solemn, inexorable declaration and pledge, by the people to each other, through the press and in public assemblages, that they mean to maintain their liberties at every hazard, and to have and to hold free elections, peaceably if they can, forcibly if they must. By the Constitution of Ohio, no soldier or marine of the United States can gain a residence or become a citizen and elector of the State by being stationed within her limits. By the law of England, and by a provident statute of Pennsylvania, all troops are required to be removed a prescribed distance—not less than two miles—from the place of holding an election; and this, too, is the spirit at least of our own laws. Every qualified elector of Ohio has the right freely, and without molestation of any kind, to vote the ticket of his choice; and if Federal or State troops be present to molest or intimidate—no matter under what pretext—it is the right of the citizens and the duty of the civil officers and of the militia to disperse or arrest the offenders, and to use whatever force may be necessary for that purpose.

I counsel you, one and all, to stand by the Union, maintain the Constitution, support the Government, and obey the laws. But in the name and by the memory of your fathers, and as you would secure the blessings of liberty to yourselves and your children, I invoke you to defend the right of election and the ballot-box by all the means which the exigencies of the case may demand. The hour of your trial has at last come. Be firm and be ready. And God grant that the spirit of the patriots and freemen of other ages and countries, of the heroes of Greece and Rome, the spirit of Bruce and Tell, of Hampden and Sydney, of Henry, and Washington, and Jackson, may be found to survive yet in the men of the present generation in America; and thus that both the form and the substance of constitutional liberty and free popular government be still preserved and made secure among us.*

ADDRESS AFTER THE ELECTION, 1863.

WINDSOR, C. W., *October* 14, 1863.

DEMOCRATS OF OHIO:—You have been beaten—by what means it is idle now to inquire. It is enough that while tens of thousands of soldiers were sent or kept within the State, or held inactive in camp elsewhere, to vote against you, the Confederate enemy were marching upon the Capital of your country.

You were beaten; but a nobler battle for constitutional liberty and free popular government never was fought by any people. And your unconquerable firmness and courage, even in the midst of armed military force, secured you those first of freemen's rights—free speech and a free ballot. The conspiracy of the 5th of May fell before you. Be not discouraged: despair not of the Republic. Maintain your rights, stand firm to your position; never yield up your principles or your organization. Listen not to him who would have you lower your standard in the hour of defeat. No mellowing of your opinions upon any question, even of policy, will avail any thing to conciliate your political foes. They demand nothing less than an absolute surrender of your principles and your organization. Moreover, if there be any hope for the Constitution or liberty, it is in the Democratic party alone; and your fellow-citizens, in a little while longer, will see it. Time and events will force it upon all, except those only who profit by the calamities of their country.

I thank you, one and all, for your sympathies and your suffrages. Be assured, that though still in exile for no offence but my political opinions and the free expression of them to you in peaceable public assembly, you will find me ever steadfast in those opinions, and true to the Constitution and to the State and country of my birth.

* Under the Constitution, the privilege of the writ of habeas corpus can be suspended only "when, in case of rebellion or invasion, *the public safety* may require it." The proclamation of the 15th of September, 1863, recites that, "in the judgment of the President, the public safety does require that the privilege of the said writ shall now be suspended *throughout the United States.*" And yet, on the 3d of October, 1863, less than three weeks later, Mr. LINCOLN set his hand officially to another, a "Thanksgiving" proclamation, reciting that throughout the whole year, "*order had been maintained, the laws respected and obeyed, and harmony had prevailed* EVERYWHERE, *except in the theatre of military conflict.*"

ADDRESS TO THE STUDENTS OF MICHIGAN UNIVERSITY.*

At Windsor, C. W., Nov. 14, 1863.

I THANK you, Young Gentlemen, for this visit. I thank you, sir, especially, Mr. BUSKIRK, for the compliments so handsomely expressed on behalf of your fellows. The applause of the young is the highest praise. They speak the language of the coming generation, and anticipate the judgment of posterity. To that judgment, if it so be that my name shall chance to live in the record of these times, I long since appealed; and, meantime, am content to abide the scrutiny which must precede it. Without further personal allusion, therefore, in reply, allow me to pass to another subject; and, if it be in my power, thus to change a visit of ceremony into one, perhaps, not altogether without profit.

You are students. Some of you still pursue your classical and scientific studies; others prepare yourselves for professional pursuits; all of you are eager to rush into the great world, and be men. Yet in a little while, when you have borne its buffetings with lusty sinews, not one of you but will exclaim with a sigh—

"Ah! happy years! once more who would not be a boy?"

But in the battle of life there is no retreat; and the brave spirits among you will press forward, and the weak falter and perish. You now but prepare yourselves for a life of action; and just in proportion as you are disciplined every way, you will be ready to meet whatever fortune may betide you. "Redeem the time." No injunction is more suggestive. So many days and years you have in pawn to the Almighty Maker of heaven and earth; and those only are reckoned redeemed, which are spent profitably to either the body or the mind. Youth is not the season for ease or pleasure; but for labor and self-denial. Whoever has practised these hardy virtues when a boy, and in early manhood, will, at forty, sound in mind and body, find the lawful and virtuous pleasures of life full of sweetness. Horace was right:

"Multa tulit fecitque puer."

The more ingenuous among you incur another and widely differing hazard. You have endured heat and cold; have refrained from lust and wine; have abjured pleasure. Your vigils have "outwatched the Bear." But youthful ambition is eager and impatient. It sees nothing

* On the 14th of November 1863, a large delegation of the students of the University of Michigan, at Ann Arbor in that State, paid a formal visit to Mr. VALLANDIGHAM at Windsor. They were received in the dining-room of the Hirons House, which was well filled by a select audience, embracing many of the leading citizens of Windsor and Detroit. Mr. C. A. Buskirk, on behalf of the students, delivered an eloquent address, after which Mr. Vallandigham replied as above.

but Fame's Proud Temple, and forgets that it shines afar. It sees not the long and wearisome leagues of hill and valley, of forest and rock, of thicket and jungle, which lie between the goddess and her younger worshippers. It counts every moment of delay and difficulty on the way, as a moment lost. There is, indeed, a false goddess whose fane is near and easy of access. Hard by is the altar of Mammon. Fraud, Falsehood, and Violence are their joint sibyls and priests. A tumultuous crowd of idolatrous and abject worshippers throng around. But Notoriety is not Fame, and her devotees soon perish. Not such let your ambition be; but rather that which Pope, and after him, Lord Mansfield, proclaimed "the pursuit of noble ends by noble means," and yours, too, that popularity which follows, not that which is run after. But to obtain this you must learn early that most difficult of all lessons—TO LABOR AND TO WAIT. At twenty you think forty an old age. At forty, if you have disciplined your minds and not abused your bodies, you will find yourselves younger but far wiser than you are to-day; and the hour of your death will seem more distant and give you less concern. You will feel that there is a lifetime yet before you; and if you are of a strong will and brave spirit, and worthy of a name to live, your past failures and defeats you will regard then as but probation and discipline, and indeed, as so many assurances of final triumph. Press on! but not in haste. The Master of Ravenswood chose a wise motto and not inapt coat of arms—a bull's head, and "I bide my time."

In one other thing be not mistaken: you are not about to finish your studies. When you take leave of the University you but begin them. No man ever attained great and enduring eminence without study—not always of books. Men of action have not leisure at all times for books; but they are students, nevertheless, of the men and things around them; and books are but the written records of things and men remote or of the past. Yet they have this advantage, that whatever they record has passed through the alchemy of the great minds by whom they were written; and, moreover, in them we study men and things divested of the prejudices, the bigotries, and the self-interested influences of that which is present in time or near in space. Especially is this true of history—the most amplifying, liberalizing in its effect upon the mind and soul, of all studies. He who remains a bigot in any thing, has read history to little purpose; and he who would comprehend the present, and discern the future, must give his days and nights to this study. Prophecy uninspired is but history anticipated. Read history, and learn that the patriot, the hero, the statesman, the orator, whom you reverence or admire in the pages of Plutarch and Livy, or of Hume, Gibbon, and Macaulay, was reviled and persecuted in his own day, and suffered death, it may have been, at the hands of the men of his own generation. Ponder, too, the wisdom of Moses, who, before the pleasures and honors of the king's court, preferred rather the Red Sea and forty years in the wilderness, and death and an unknown grave, that he might become a great lawgiver, and the founder of a new religion and of a powerful people.

Most of you, Young Gentlemen, have read the usual course of "ancient classics." It is the fashion of our times to decry this study. But aside from the perennial pleasure, through life, which he receives who seeks these precious fountains, their practical value, also, will not be questioned by him who reflects that our whole language, and especially our scientific nomenclature, is largely derived from the Greek and Latin, and that our entire literature is pervaded by the spirit of these classics, and full of quotations and allusions drawn from them. Cicero's magnificent eulogy upon the studies which Archias taught, is not at all exaggerated when applied to the Grecian and Roman writings which have come down to us. If the modern sculptor study the Apollo Belvidere and the Dying Gladiator, why shall not the modern student study the language of the men who chiselled these wonderful creations out from the solid marble? But most valuable as the mere discipline may be, it is not enough that you content yourselves with the usual course now prescribed in school or college. These writings must be a study, more or less, through life. Let not any say that he has "no time." There is always time and a way for whatever a strong-willed, diligent man may choose to undertake. What is most wanted, is a judicious economy of time, and a wise division of it in the multiplicity of employments, so that but one thing shall be done at a time.

A majority of you, Young Gentlemen, are preparing yourselves for professional pursuits. Whoever would become a Christian clergyman, let him preach the evangely of Bethlehem. Let him confine himself to his legitimate duties, and aspire to be the most faithful and exemplary of the men of his calling.

Whoever would practise surgery and medicine, let his ambition be to reach, as nearly as possible, or to excel, the acquirements and skill of the great men who, in ancient and modern times, have been the ornaments of that profession. The *novum organum* of medicine remains to be written, and he who is to write it has not yet appeared. Why should he not be an American? Why not adorn the University of Michigan?

And you, Young Gentlemen, who prepare for the profession of the law, will have a nobler theatre to act in than any who have gone before you in the United States. Out of the terrible revolution which now convulses every part of our unhappy land will arise questions of constitutional and statute law, of personal liberty, or private right, of property, of life, grander, more numerous, more infinite in variety, and more perplexing than heretofore in any age or country. If just now, "amid arms, laws are silent," in your day, at least, should free government happily in any form survive among us, arms will again yield to the toga, and laws reign supreme. With diligence, therefore, fixed faith, and unalterable purpose, prepare yourselves for the destiny which lies before you; to the end that, in the next generation, you may be among the number of those who, upon the Bench and at the Bar, shall restore and bear aloft to higher renown the already illustrious standard of British and American forensic learning and eloquence. Cowardice and servility before executive power were the disgrace of the English Bar and Bench in the days of the Stuarts; and these, threatening now the honor and the independence of the American judiciary, are among the most alarming portents of the times.

But remember, that while along with the great Hampden the name of the honest and fearless Croke, and of his noble wife, still survive in honor, the time-serving and unjust judges who sat with him, and yielded to political expediency and "military necessity," have perished from history, or are remembered only to be execrated. The blessed memory of Lord Hale is still fragrant; while the name of the bloody Jeffries, who escaped death upon the felon's scaffold only by dying miserably in a felon's cell, is the opprobrium of the English Bench. Algernon Sidney died as a convicted traitor; but in a little while his execution was adjudged judicial murder; and posterity, for six generations, has held him in reverence as a patriot. Finch, King James the Second's attorney-general, procured the conviction and death of the pure and virtuous Lord Russell, as a conspirator against the government; but eight years afterwards, when he would have relieved himself in Parliament from the odium of the act, the indignant clamor of the whole House forced him, in shame and confusion, to resume his seat; and Russell still lives in England and America as a martyr to liberty.

Your courage, your fortitude, your manhood, will also, some day, be severely tried. But, then, remember Curran, whose fame brightens just as the memory of the venal placemen and barristers around him rots with each revolving year, and who, when menaced in court by a file of soldiers, clattering their muskets as he addressed the jury in defence of one charged with treason, exclaimed in manly defiance: "*You may assassinate, but you cannot intimidate me.*" Read, too, the speeches, and admire and imitate the heroic Erskine, the greatest of English barristers, who, against the whole power of the Executive, in time of both foreign war and rebellion, maintained for years the rights and liberties of Englishmen, with undaunted intrepidity. Prepare yourselves, by continual study of the characters and noble emulation of the examples of these and other great and good men of the past, for like scenes in your own day. Nerve your hearts now for the struggle; but remember that ability, however eminent, and intellectual discipline, however exact, are not enough. Without pure morals, correct habits, and fixed integrity, you cannot endure the trial. Be virtuous. Be pious. I use the word in no narrow, sectarian, or theological sense, but in that which Virgil means when he calls Æneas "*pius*"—a piety which belongs to no one sect, nor clime, nor time, nor country, but which everywhere, and at all times, renders to God, and self, and man, whatever is due, and does it in the very spirit of the Sermon on the Mount.

But, Young Gentlemen, while I have thus addressed you as students preparing yourselves for the ordinary business and professions of life, I well know that at any time many of you would be, and in times of such tremendous import as just now are upon us in our own country, all of you are, profoundly interested in POLITICS. Probably you give to them more of your thoughts than to any of your collegiate or professional studies. I know, too, that many of you, even now, look eagerly forward to the time when you will pass from your professions into political life. This is the goal of your ambitious longings. Your hearts are fixed upon it. It is an honorable, a holy ambition; an ambition not to be extinguished, but to be regulated. He is a false teacher who would tell the ingenuous, virtuous, and public-spirited youth of the country that the political service of the country is fit only for the vulgar, the impure, the corrupt. As there are hypocrites in the pulpit, empirics in medicine, pettifoggers at the bar, and pretenders everywhere, so there are demagogues in political life. But there is as well a morality as a philosophy, a science in politics, far above the circle of these reptiles. Unhappily, the low standard of capacity and morals set up and denounced by those who decline public life, and practically but too often acknowledged by politicians, is another of the evil portents which impend our country. Of the corrupting influences of avarice, at all times, I need not speak. But more debasing and dangerous still, in seasons of great public commotion, is the execrable vice of fear. All these combined, make up that most loathsome of all the objects of reproach and scorn, "a scurvy politician." He has borne the same odious character in every country and age. Among the Greeks, he once courted popularity, or place, by pointing out the smugglers of figs, and was cursed as both spy and informer, and thence gave a name to the whole class of demagogues. In Rome, he headed every petty popular tumult, and clamored fiercely for a division of lands and goods.

Curran described him, in his day, in felicitous phrase, as "one who, buoyant by putrefaction, rises as he rots." He is the vermin, the insect of politics, and amid the heats of civil war and convulsion, teems into life thick as gnats in the summer evening air. If any one among you—and I speak to those who would aspire to be leaders among their countrymen—have neither the capacity nor the ambition to be a statesman, let him at least not stoop to become a demagogue. Preach, heal, try causes, work; but scorn to be one of that number who know nothing of politics except the passions and personalities which they excite. If not able to argue upon principles, measures, policies, debate not at all. If you cannot soar, do not creep. Whoever discusses only men in politics, is always largely a slanderer. Principles, not men, is, indeed, not altogether a sound maxim, though little liable to be abused, since personalities always make up so large and controlling an element in mere partisan politics. Better say, principles and men. It is easy to be a politician or demagogue—sail with the wind—float with the current—look not to compass, neither lift up your eyes to the heavens where the constellations and the polestar—bright, glorious emblems of God, and Truth, and the Right—still shine, steadfast, immovable, just as they shone in the beginning of time. *Poeta nascitur.* So it is with the demagogue. But the statesman must be made as well as born. His voyage is through mid-ocean and in storm. He sails under orders. His port is ascertained and prescribed before he sets out, and it is his duty to reach it; and so, like the majestic ocean steamer, he moves on, and,

> "Against the wind, against the tide
> Still steadies with an upright keel!"

Demosthenes, more than two thousand years ago, in his great oration for the Crown, well distinguished between these two characters, declaring that while they were alike in nothing, they differed chiefly in this: that the statesman boldly and honestly proclaimed his opinion before the event, and thus made himself responsible to fortune, to the times, to his countrymen, to the world; while the sycophant or demagogue was silent till the event had happened, and then governed his speech and his conduct accordingly.

And now allow me to add, that though you may be patriots and yet not statesmen, the statesman is always a patriot. His love of country is as well a principle as an emotion. Duty enters largely into it; hence it is stable, enduring. It is not sensational—certainly not a mere feeling of gratitude, least of all in the meaning of that word as defined by Dr. Johnson—"a lively sense of favors yet to be received." He loves his country both wisely and well. He never sacrifices her rea[illegible] high more remote interests, to a popular clamor; and still less at the demand of those who hold the power. Neither will he corrupt the virtue, nor tarnish the honor of his country, to serve her mere sordid interests. Rather will he imitate the example of Aristides, who reporting to the Athenians that a certain proposition was indeed for their immediate advantage, but would bring dishonor upon the State, counselled that they reject it.

I have said nothing about "loyalty." It is a word that belongs justly, but only, to kingly governments. I can comprehend loyalty to a King, and especially to a Queen: but as an American, I choose to adhere to the good and honest old republican word "patriotism," and to cherish the virtue which it has always been used to express.

Aspire, then, Young Gentlemen, you who would pursue a public course, to be patriot-statesmen. Have faith—absolute, unquestioning, immovable—that faith which speaking to itself in the silence and calm of the heart's own beating, says: "If not to-day, or this time, then to-morrow, or next or some other day, at some other time, in some other way, all will be well." Without this, no man ever achieved greatness. Be incorruptible in your integrity; be scrupulous and exact in honor; be inexorable in your deliberate, well-considered purposes; be appalled by no difficulties. Amplify your minds, but still more, be great in soul. It is this which shall lift you up high above the earth, and assimilate you to that which is divine. Without it, you will but creep with dusty, and droiling, and wearied wing. Without it, think not to endure that cruel and crushing weight of doing and suffering which he must bear, who faithfully and with heroism, at any time, but most of all in periods of great public convulsion, would act the part of the patriot-statesman.

SPEECH AFTER HIS RETURN TO OHIO.

At Hamilton, June 15, 1864.

Men of Ohio: To-day I am again in your midst, and upon the soil of my native State. To-day I am once more within the district which for ten years extended to me the highest confidence, and three times honored me as its Representative in the Congress of the United States. I was accused of no crime against the Constitution or laws, and guilty of none. But whenever and wherever thus charged upon due process of law, I am now here ready to answer, before any civil court of competent jurisdiction, to a jury of my countrymen; and meantime to give bail in any sum which any judge or court, State or Federal, may affix; and you, the hundred and eighty-six thousand Democrats of Ohio, I offer as my sureties. Never for one hour have I remained in exile because I recognized any obligation of obedience to the unconstitutional and arbitrary edict. Neither did personal fear ever restrain me. And to-day I return of my own act and pleasure, because it is my constitutional and legal right to return. Only by an exertion of arbitrary power, itself against Constitution and law, and consummated by military force, I was abducted from my home and forced into banishment. The assertion or insinuation of the President, that I was arrested because laboring with some effect to prevent the raising of troops and to encourage desertions from the army, and was responsible for numerous acts of resistance to the draft and to the arrest of deserters, causing "assassination, maiming, and murder;" or that at any time, in any way, I had disobeyed or failed to counsel obedience to lawful authority, or even to the semblance of law, is absolutely false. I appeal for the proof to every speech I ever made upon these questions, and to the very record of the Mock Military Commission, by the trial and sentence of which I was outraged. No; the sole offence then laid to my charge was words of criticism of the public policy of the Administration, addressed to an open and public political meeting of my fellow-citizens of Ohio, lawfully and peaceably assembled. And to-day my only "crime" is that, in the way which they call treason, worship I the Constitution of my fathers. But, for now more than one year, no public man has been arrested, and no newspaper suppressed within the States adhering still to the Union, for the expression of political opinion; while hundreds, in public assembly and through the press, have, with a license and violence in which I never indulged, criticised and condemned the acts and policies of the Administration, and denounced the war, maintaining even the propriety and necessity of the recognition of Southern independence. Indorsed by nearly two hundred thousand freemen of the Democratic party of my native State at the late election, and still with the sympathy and support of millions more, I do not mean any longer to be the only man of that party who is to be the victim of arbitrary power. If Abraham Lincoln seeks my life, let him so declare; but he shall not again restrain me of my personal liberty except upon "due process of law." The unconstitutional and monstrous "Order 38," under which, alone, I was arrested thirteen months ago, was defied and spit upon at your State Convention of 1863, by the gallant gentleman who bore the standard as your candidate for Lieutenant-Governor, and by every Democratic press and public speaker ever since. It is dead. From the first it was against the Constitution and laws, and without validity, and all proceedings under it were and are utterly null, void, and of no effect. The indignant voice of condemnation long since went forth from the vast majority of the people and presses of America, and from all free countries in Europe, with entire unanimity. And more recently, too, the "platform" of an earnest, numerous, and most formidable convention of the sincere Republicans, and still further, the emphatic letter of acceptance by the candidate of that convention, General John C. Fremont—the first candidate, also, of the Republican party for the Presidency eight years ago, upon the rallying cry of free speech and a free press—give renewed hope that, at last, the reign of arbitrary power is about to be brought to an end in the United States. It is neither just nor fit, therefore, that the wrongs inflicted under "Order 38," and the other edicts and acts of such power, should any longer be endured—certainly not by me alone. But every ordinary means of redress has first been exhausted; yet either by the direct agency of the Administration and its subordinates, or through its influence or intimidation, or because of want of jurisdiction in the civil courts to meet a case which no American ever in former times conceived to be possible here, all have failed. Counsel applied in my behalf to an unjust judge for the writ of *habeas corpus*. It was denied; and now the privilege of that writ is suspended by act of Congress and Executive order, in every State. The Democratic Convention of Ohio, one year ago, by a resolution formally presented through a committee of your best and ablest men, in person at Washington, demanded of the President, in behalf of a very large minority of the people, a revocation of the edict of banishment. Pretending that the public safety then required it, he refused; saying at the same time, that "it would afford him pleasure to comply as soon as he could by any means be made to believe that the public safety would not suffer by it." One year has elapsed; yet this hollow pretence is tacitly asserted, and to-day I am here to prove it unfounded in fact. I appealed to the Supreme Court of the United States, and because Congress had never conferred jurisdiction in behalf of a citizen tried by a tribunal unknown for such purposes, to the laws and expressly forbidden by the Constitution, it was powerless to redress the wrong. The time has, therefore, arrived when it becomes me as a citizen of Ohio and of the United States, to demand, and by my own act to vindicate the rights, liberties, and privileges which I never forfeited, but of which for so many months I have been deprived. Wherefore, men of Ohio, I am again in your midst to-day. I owe duties to the State, and am here to discharge them; I have rights as a citizen, and am here to assert them; a wife, and child, and home, and would enjoy all the pleasures which are implied in those cherished words. But I am here for peace, not turbulence; for quiet, not convulsion; for order and law, not anarchy. Let no man of the Democratic party begin any act of violence or disorder; but let none shrink from any responsibility, however urgent, if forced upon him. Careful of the rights of others, let him see to it that he fully and fearlessly exacts his own. Subject to rightful authority in all things, let him submit to excess or usurpation in nothing. Obedient to Constitution and law, let him demand and have the full measure of protection which law and Constitution secure to him.

Men of Ohio! You have already vindicated your right to *hear:* it is now my duty to assert my right to *speak.* Wherefore, as to the sole offence for which I was arrested, imprisoned, and banished—free speech in criticism and condemnation of the Administration; an Administration fitly described in a recent public paper by one of its early supporters as "marked at home by disregard of constitutional rights, by its violations of personal liberty and the liberty of the press, and, as its crowning shame, by its abandonment of the right of asylum, a right especially dear to all free nations abroad." I repeat it here to-day, and will again and yet again, so long as I live, or the Constitution and our present form of government shall survive. The words then spoken and the appeal at that time made, and now enforced by one year more of taxation and debt, and of blood and disaster, entreating the people to change the public servants and their policy, not by force, but peaceably, through the ballot, I now and here reiterate in their utmost extent, and with all their significancy, I repeat them, one and all, in no spirit of challenge or bravado, but as earnest, sober, solemn truth and warning to the people.

Upon another subject allow me here a word:

A powerful, widely-spread, and very dangerous secret, oath-bound combination among the friends of the Administration, known as the "Loyal Union League," exists in every State. Yet the very men who control it charge persistently upon the members of the Democratic party, that they have organized—especially in the Northwest—the "Order of Knights of the Golden Circle," or some other secret society, treasonable or "disloyal" in its character, affiliated with the South, and for the purpose of armed resistance to the authorities of the Federal and State Government. Whether any such ever existed, I do not know; but the charge that organizations of that sort, or having any such purpose, do now exist among members of that party in Ohio or other non-slaveholding States, is totally and positively false. That lawful political or party associations have been established, having as their object the organizing and strengthening of the Democratic party and its success in the coming Presidential election, and designed as a counter-movement to the so-called "Union Leagues," and, therefore, secret in their proceedings, is very probable; and however objectionable hitherto, and in ordinary times, I recognize, to the fullest extent, not the lawfulness only, but the propriety and necessity of such organizations now, for "when bad men combine, good men must associate." But they are no conspiracy against the Government, and their members are not conspirators, but patriots; men not leagued together for the overthrow of the Constitution or the laws, and still less, of liberty, but firmly united for the preservation and support of these great objects. There is, indeed, a "conspiracy" very powerful, very ancient, and I trust that before long I may add, strongly consolidated also, upon sound principles, and destined yet to be triumphant—a conspiracy known as the Democratic party, the present object of which is the overthrow of the Administration in November next, not by force but through THE BALLOT-BOX, and the election of a President who shall be true to his oath, to Liberty, and to the Constitution. This is the sole conspiracy of which I know any thing; and I am proud to be one of the conspirators. If any other exist, looking to unlawful armed resistance to the Federal or State authorities anywhere, in the exercise of their legal and constitutional rights, I admonish all persons concerned, that the act is treason and the penalty death. But I warn also the men in power, that there is a vast multitude, a host whom they cannot number, bound together by the strongest and holiest ties, to defend, by whatever means the exigencies of the times shall demand, their natural and constitutional rights as freemen, at all hazards and to the last extremity.

Three years have now passed, Men of Ohio, and the great issue of Constitutional Liberty and Free Popular Government is still before you. To you I again commit it, confident that in this the time of their greatest peril, you will be found worthy of the ancestors who for so many ages in England and America, on the field, in prison, and upon the scaffold, defended them against tyrants and usurpers whether in council or in arms.

SUPPLEMENT.

"An enthusiasm can be evoked from the hearts of the people before which all opposition will be swept away as by a consuming fire."—*Letter to Sanderson, of Pennsylvania.*

SUPPLEMENT.

IN this SUPPLEMENT will be found extracts from Speeches, Letters, &c., not deemed of sufficient importance to be included at length in the body of the book. These extracts are inserted here, not because of any especial excellency in style or originality of thought, but as giving a fuller and clearer insight into Mr. VALLANDIGHAM'S political and personal sentiments and character, than any mere narrative could express.

THE BENEVOLENT INSTITUTIONS OF THE STATE.

Extract from a Speech (Mr. V.'s first) in the Ohio House of Representatives, December 8, 1845. The speech was noticed thus in the editorial correspondence of the Lancaster, O., *Eagle:* "The youngest Democratic member in the House, Mr. VALLLANDIGHAM, made his debut to-day, on a resolution to print documents. It was a brilliant effort, and produced an electric effect upon the House. He is a splendid young man."

IF there be any one thing more than another, to which the citizens of Ohio may point with proud and generous exultation, it is to her public asylums, to her common schools, to her state prison, by which she has acquired so lofty and honorable a pre-eminence among her sisters of the confederacy. Not the soil of Ohio, not her climate, not the extent of her territory, nor the multiplied variety of her productions; not even the majestic river, which washes her base; not the multitude of her teeming population, nor her wealth, nor her resources, nor her rapid growth, unparalleled in the history of States, challenging the wonder of the world, and realizing the magic creations of the lamp in Oriental fable; not any thing in her whole history and character, has contributed one-half so much to elicit the eulogy and admiration of the intelligent and enlightened of Europe and America, as the asylums, and other public institutions, which the generous benevolence of the people of Ohio, has consecrated to the relief and solace of those, whom, otherwise, the misfortune of birth, or the accidents of life, must have consigned to hopeless despair. For my own part, sir, I never turn my eyes or direct my thoughts toward these buildings—these living monuments of a lofty and substantial charity—and to our common schools, without the warm feelings of a heart—patriotic, I trust—swelling unconsciously in my bosom, and breaking from my lips, though in solitude, in audible accents, "I am a citizen of Ohio."

Mr. Speaker, I do not mean, upon this or upon any occasion, to indulge on this floor, in mere school-boy declamation. I desire, now and always, to speak in language becoming the representative, in part, of this great people. But be assured, be assured that these are the institutions which constitute the true glory and greatness of a

State. Be assured, that when banks and tariffs, and all the other fleeting topics of the day we live in, shall have descended to the oblivion which awaits them alike—when your Senate chambers, your halls of justice, and your monuments shall have bowed themselves to the dust; when you and I, Mr. Speaker, shall "sleep in dull, cold marble;" nay, when, after the lapse of some centuries, this Union shall have been dissolved, our political institutions decayed, their vital spirit yielded up, our greatness all gone, and even our language ceased to fall from living lips—be assured, sir, that the future historian of Ohio, writing her history in a tongue as yet unformed, will record, as foremost and proudest among her glories, these very institutions, which, with great humbleness, yet in all singleness of heart, I have thus eulogized.

PATIENCE, FIRMNESS, AND FAITH.

Extract from remarks on the Bank Bill, in the Ohio House of Representatives, December 30, 1845.

I KNOW, Mr. Speaker, it is easy—very easy—to answer all this with ridicule, and, it may be, with sarcasm and sneer. My venerable friend from Belmont (Mr. Cowen), may find a ready occasion, and may readily embrace it, to open the masked battery of his wit, upon the doctrines I have uttered, and, perhaps, upon me personally. I shall not complain. His wit is Attic, and it is always courteous. But wit is not argument, though it be the weapon with which all great reforms, and all great but new truths, have in all ages been attacked. True, bigots have, in other times, gone farther. The rack and the prison-house have been called into requisition. If I recollect history aright, when Galileo first taught, in an age of superstition and ignorance, that the earth revolved round the sun—not the sun round the earth, men's minds were shocked at his presumption and his blasphemy; and both church and State—both magistrate and ecclesiastic, conspired to cast him into prison. But looking calmly through the bars of his dungeon, and smiling at his persecutors, this great hero of science could exclaim: "You have thrust me into prison, but still the earth goes round." Sir, the same spirit of opposition—of ridicule and persecution—has fought, though not prevailed, against every other great truth, when first put forth to the world. And the present age and generation are not less slow of belief in such truths, than the generations and ages which have gone before us. If any, however, of my friends of the majority, or any, perchance, of the minority, are not yet prepared to agree with me upon this great question, it is their right, under our institutions and laws, to entertain and express whatever opinion they may choose to express or to entertain. But they will remember, that the same great right belongs to me also. Sir, I shall seek no occasion of quarrel with any of them, or with any man, for an honest difference of belief, however erroneous or absurd, or fanatical, his opinions may be. Standing upon the vantage ground of TRUTH, we who hold to these doctrines, shall wait calmly, and wait firmly—we may wait long—till the steady progression of the age, and of public opinion, shall have come up.

Mr. THOMAS felt inclined to congratulate himself upon having heard the principles of the Democratic party frankly and candidly avowed, from the lips of the gentleman who had been styled the leader of that party by its accredited organ.

Mr. VALLANDIGHAM.—The gentleman from Shelby (Mr. Thomas), and his friends with him, are fully welcome to the entire benefit of any thing which may have fallen from me. I have never sought concealment, either upon this question or upon any other. I am not afraid of the truth—I dare speak it openly. It may be unpopular: it may be in advance of the age—it is none the less truth, and I am not therefore, the more afraid to proclaim it. But I spoke for myself only, and undertook not to bind any man by my declarations. I spoke, also, the sentiments, as I believe, of the people of Columbiana. We study no concealment there. My own sentiments were openly proclaimed through the public press, and in the popular assemblages; and that also, as well before the late election, as at other times. I pledged myself, voluntarily, to vote for "the total, immediate, and unconditional repeal" of the banking law of the last session. Yet was I elected almost without opposition. The gentleman from Shelby is also equally welcome to my individual sentiments upon any subject connected with politics, or, if he desire it, upon any other subject—upon the tariff—upon a constitutional treasury—upon Texas, or upon Oregon. Confiding fully in the honesty and intelligence of the people, and in the power of truth, I have nothing to conceal.

Mr. Higgins would inform the gentleman from Shelby (Mr. Thomas), that the Democratic side of the House acknowledged no leaders.

Mr. Vallandigham disclaimed all aspirations for any thing like leadership. Nothing could be further from his expectations, humbly indulged in, than to find himself elevated into a position to lead the great Democratic party of Ohio. It was no part of his ambition, and he had neither the capacity nor the inclination to undertake it.

RETRENCHMENT. SALARIES.

Remarks on the proposed repeal of the "Retrenchment Act," in the Ohio House of Representatives, January 3, 1846.

I further object to the act which it is proposed to repeal, because it fixes the salary or compensation of many officers entirely too low. It is impossible in the long run, to secure good and competent men to fill offices of responsibility, at the present rate of compensation. The laborer is worthy of his hire, and men will not undergo great labor without a reasonable recompense. It is true, so far as concerns members of the Legislature, that the rich who may desire to spend a winter amid the dissipation and gayety of the State capital, or to secure the passage of some favorite measure for their own special benefit, can well afford to come here at two dollars a day. So the mere idler or "loafer" whose ambition rises no higher than the payment of his board, can come profitably at the same price. But few men with families and occupations, can be found able or willing to leave them, and undergo the inconveniences of absence and the fatigues of public business, for a compensation which, with the strictest economy, enables them to meet their expenses. Sir, the "Retrenchment Act," as it stands, is a virtual disfranchisement to poverty, as to nearly all offices. It is but an insidious and indirect property qualification, against the spirit of the Constitution—a qualification which the spirit of the age is fast exploding all over the Union, and which ought not, in a Democratic government, to be tolerated in any shape. It is opposed to the fundamental idea of our institutions, and equally odious whether it exists in the old-fashioned way of a direct requirement of so much property, or in the more modern way of a beggarly salary.

It has indeed been said that there is no lack of office-seekers or office-holders since the act passed. That may be true, sir. Patriots of a certain kind, are always and everywhere abundant. Our case would be hard, indeed, if it were not so. Some men will take office at any price; and such men are always sure to enrich themselves by larceny or peculation. But the question is, how much better men could you not have, if you provided a compensation which would justify the best men in accepting official stations without too great a personal sacrifice. No office ought to be sought after for the purpose of making money by it; but, on the other hand, every office ought to yield enough to pay its incumbent for the labor and responsibility connected with it. If what a man can earn a day, at his trade or business, is to be the criterion of official compensation, then the standard should be brought down to the lowest degree—to the pay of a day-laborer—*fifty cents.* This would be a scale of salary very convenient, very easy of application, and certainly as just as the other: and the legislature, carrying out the principle, ought then to forbid every mechanic, farmer, and workman of every kind, to receive more. But the principle, sir, is all wrong. No two men in the same trade can make the same amount, so that this can afford no fixed or just rule upon the subject.

I hold, sir, that every public servant is entitled to a compensation in proportion to the amount of labor and service which he renders: and to a fair and generous compensation. Republics, especially, where there is little hereditary wealth, and every man depends upon his own exertions, ought not to be niggardly. Officers are public servants, not rulers, as in former times, or in other countries, and ought to have, like other servants, a reasonable and sufficient recompense for their services; though no man ought to be allowed to grow rich from the money of the people.

There is one point, sir, and a very material one, which I omitted when I addressed the House last. The ostensible object of the act of 1844—the object which was then held out as a blind to the eyes of the people, and the only, at least the chief argument, now urged against its repeal, was and is that taxation may be lessened and money put into the public treasury. Well, sir, the law has been in operation two years; it has been fairly tested, and what is the result? By its second section it is provided, by the most pitiful refinement of economy which ever disgraced the public records of any state, that at the close of each session of the General Assembly, the sergeant-at-arms shall gather up the fragments of every kind, and expose them to sale. This elevated duty was afterwards devolved upon the Secretary of State. Well, sir, that duty has been performed to the very letter. And what, think you, was the result of this wonderful sale—this most extraordinary auction? Your Secretary of State—the Secretary of the great commonwealth of Ohio—the third in this grand American Republic—after raking and scraping and nosing in the dust and sweepings and spittle of this honorable body, gathers together the candle ends, and waste paper, and broken snuffers and candlesticks which he has smelled out and rescued from the rubbish, and exposes them at public auction in order that the coffers of the impoverished State of Ohio may be enriched. And what does he realize? *Six dollars and seventy-two cents!* Yes, the magnitudinous sum of six dollars and seventy-two cents! There is no denying it: the report of the Secretary is upon our tables, and not contradicted. Truly, sir, we are growing rich: there is a plethora in the public treasury; the buildings must be enlarged. I shall, I think I shall introduce a bill for the distribution of the surplus revenue; certainly, at least a bill providing that the proceeds of this great annual auction be set apart as a sinking fund to discharge the public debt. But seriously, Mr. Speaker, if this be not, as I have styled it, the *economy of meanness.* I beg to know in what meanness consists. * * *

I have now, Mr. Speaker, given briefly the reasons which govern my judgment as to the vote I am about to give. I am fully awake, sir, to the use which may be made of it. The cry of "retrenchment and reform," has in all ages been perverted to the basest purposes. But I have a deep and abiding confidence in the honesty and intelligence of the people, and I mean now, and upon all occasions, here and elsewhere, to demonstrate the sincerity of my professions. Sir, I come not here with confidence on my lips and distrust in my heart. My convictions of the utter inequity, and the worthlessness, as to its ostensible object, of the act now proposed to be repealed, are deep and unalterable. The almost universal admission upon this floor, that the character of the act is just what I have described it, has greatly strengthened these convictions. The case seems to me plain; and I do believe that the people have as much capacity to perceive it as I have, and honesty enough to concur in the repeal of such an act. Entertaining these opinions, and believing that I am about to do right, I enter fearlessly upon the discharge of my duty, satisfied to abide the judgment of a constituency I am proud to represent. If that judgment be against me, I shall be content; having still within my own bosom, the consoling consciousness that I dared to do what appeared to me to be just.

LEGISLATION—ITS MYSTERIES.

Extract from Remarks on a motion to adjourn *sine die*, in the Ohio House of Representatives, January 28, 1846.

I AM aware, Mr. Speaker, that motions for adjournment at an early day are, not unfrequently, a very small way of manufacturing a very small capital. Such, however, I am satisfied is not the object of the mover of this resolution—such shall not be my object in voting for its passage. I mean to vote for it, because I am sincerely desirous that this House should adjourn at the time proposed. I came here, in part, Mr. Speaker, to see, in the words of a celebrated chancellor of Sweden, "with how little wisdom the world is governed." Well, sir, I have seen it—have looked the business of legislation over—have pryed somewhat into its mysteries, as exhibited in this Legislature—have had enough to satisfy me for the present, and am ready now to return home. It is true that as to some things, I have not been able to see exactly *how they were done.* That perhaps was my own fault, in not keeping a sufficiently sharp look-out, and because I have not been fortunate enough to have obtained admission into the "caucus." No matter. I may see further into it the next time.

SEPULTURE.—CEMETERIES.

Extract from Remarks on the Bill "to Secure the Inviolability of Places of Human Sepulture," in the Ohio House of Representatives, February 11, 1846.

THIS bill, sir, merits a different treatment at the hands of honorable gentlemen. The feelings in which it originates are implanted in us by nature herself, and it is vain for us to undertake to disregard them. They have been recognized, honored, and obeyed in all ages, because they spring up from the human heart in its purest state. There is no man, however humble his condition or whatever his religious belief, who does not attach some sanctity to the dead, and desire that after his life shall have terminated, some tribute of respect be paid to his remains. This is an aspiration, an impulse so natural, that no degradation, be it ever so low, can obliterate it from our hearts. Even the most friendless and forsaken, dying alone, a stranger in a strange land, without a friend to perform, in his dying moments, the last sad offices of affection, desires that his body at least be suffered quietly and decently to rest in its grave. And this is a feeling which has dominion much more over the friends and relatives of the dead, where the dead have been so fortunate as to have left relatives and friends behind them. It is this self-same feeling which in all times has reared the splendid mausoleum of the king, and planted the simple rose-bush over the humble grave of the peasant. There is no nation, however barbarous, but has some funereal monuments; and the rites and the sanctity of sepulture are among all, no matter what their religion, held in the highest regard. The Mussulmen have their cemeteries, spacious and costly, and called beautifully and expressively in their language, "Cities of Silence." Even the simple Indian savages of our continent have their memorials, rude indeed, but still memorials of the burying-places of their fathers. All this springs from our innate feeling of veneration and care for the dead; for those who have passed into that "undiscovered country from whose bourne no traveller returns"—a feeling founded in the consciousness we all possess of the immortality of the soul. But whether the soul be immortal, or suffer annihilation at death, there exists, and has existed in all times, and among all men, an instinctive desire that the body be cared for and guarded, even though it be no longer any more than cold, unanimated clay, resolved again to its original elements. And even the place of one's burial has in every age been a matter of anxious solicitude with the dying. Who that is familiar with that earliest and best of books, coming down to us hallowed by every sanction of antiquity, full of the simple narrative of the patriarchal ages and fresh with the spirit of a newly-created world, but remembers that the first purchase of land upon record, was of the cave of Machpelah for a burying-place, where Abraham was buried and Sarah his wife? Who has not read the last dying aspiration of another of the Hebrew patriarchs, who, calling his chosen son to his side, prayed him with the simple pathos of expiring old age, "Deal kindly and truly with me; bury me not in Egypt, I pray thee; *but I will lie with my fathers;* and thou shalt carry me out of Egypt." And who does not know how religiously the injunction was obeyed; and that four hundred years afterwards the bones of the son, also, were carried up from the land where first buried, and deposited in the sepulchre of the patriarchs. Sir, it is vain to war against these feelings. Nature will assert her mastery. They are too deeply implanted and too universal to be despised in American legislation. Even in those countries where the dead were burned, the ashes were preserved and handed down in costly urns, as a sacred legacy to their children. And superstition lent its aid to enforce the rites of burial, and to secure the sanctity of the grave. The souls of those whose bodies remained unburied were fabled in the mythology of the ancients, to wander a hundred weary years to and fro upon the banks of the river, beyond which lay the Elysian fields, before it was permitted to them to pass over; and the prayer of the wandering spirit of the shipwrecked philosopher, was that a few handfuls of dust might be cast—"*ter pulvere injecto,*"—even by the hand of a stranger, upon his uncovered remains. The last degree of inhumanity, punished according to their notions of future punishment, with the hottest torments of the damned, was for a victorious general to refuse to his vanquished enemy the privilege of burying their dead. The very religion of the ancients forbade the dissection of human corpses; and such dissection was first practised not many centuries ago. Sir, these are feelings which must be respected, no matter, I repeat, whether the soul be mortal or immortal. But if immortal—and who so besotted as to doubt it?—how much more ought the frail tenement in which it has been enclosed, and upon which, it may be, that it now looks down in wistful solicitude, be guarded with the most scrupulous veneration. No matter, either, whether death be an eternal sleep, as some vainly and blasphemously hold, or no more than a temporary slumber till

> Wrapped in fire the realms of ether glow,
> And Heaven's last thunder shakes the earth below.

But much more, even for the sake of the dead, ought protection, and the protection of law, to be extended to their bodies, if, as the Scriptures of truth teach, there is to come a day when that great and tremendous Being who inhabits eternity, shall judge both the quick and the dead—when this corruption shall put on incorruption, and this mortal immortality, and death be swallowed up in victory. He, then, who holds to the faith of the Christian religion, ought the more readily and sacredly to respect the sanctuary of the tomb. It is hard enough, surely, Mr. Speaker, to bear the lengthened and wearisome ills of life, without being denied even the cold repose of an undisturbed grave. There is anguish enough in passing down into the dark valley of the shadow of death, without the superadded torment of the anticipated violation and dissection of our bodies. Shall the weary never be at rest? I appeal to honorable gentlemen; I demand of you each one, what would be your own feelings under such an anticipation? But if you care not for yourself, what emotions would stir your bosom, under the knowledge that the body of the cherished wife of your youth, or of the favorite child of your old age, had been torn from the grave over which you had just bowed in sorrow your stricken soul, watering it with your tears, to be subjected to the merciless process of dissecting by the knife of the faculty, though done with never so much science?

I am aware, Mr. Speaker, that the feelings of which I have just spoken, do not touch the pocket. I know that they do not smack of money, and cannot be coined into gold. They do not find exercise in the digging of a canal, nor in the constructing of a railroad, nor in the establishing of a bank. No; they spring up and hang only as simple flowers over the pure fountains of the human heart. I know, too, the tendency of the age to grossness and sensualism; to laugh at the mere emotions of our nature, and to centre all the care and protection of private association and public government, upon property. But these, sir, I repeat yet again, are not feelings to be despised. You protect against slander; yet the sense of reputation is no more than a mere emotion. Sir, the protection of property is not the sole business of government; nor is the protection of life. The "pursuit of happiness," also, in whatever form, is equally an object of governmental care, so far as such care ought to be extended to any object.

THE PUBLIC DEBT OF OHIO.—REPUDIATION.

Extract from Speech on the "Tax Bill," in the Ohio House of Representatives, Feb. 24, 1846.

THE debt is upon us, and it must be paid, paid to the uttermost farthing. The spectre must be exorcised—this devil must be cast out. There is no alternative between payment and repudiation. And who will hesitate?

Democrats, the Democrats of Ohio, the advocates of repudiation! Sir, I hurl back the slander with indignation. We are a debt-paying, a contract-abiding party. We will not stop to inquire by whom or for what this great debt was accumulated. It is enough to know that it is upon us. Though it were the most improvident that ever hung upon a nation, yet shall it be paid—paid, I repeat, to the uttermost farthing. Ohio repudiate! and for what? Have we not nearly two millions of people, and are they not a people moral, industrious, and enterprising, with sound hearts and strong hands? Have we not millions of fertile acres, full of untold capacity, and tilled by as noble a body of husbandmen as ever held the plough? Are we not rich in commerce, in manufactures, in the mechanical arts, in merchandise, in natural capital, in resources almost boundless, of every kind? No State combines a greater amount of labor and capital, and till recently, none combined them in so just a proportion. Sir, the value of your property cannot fall short of five hundred millions of dollars. The late report of your State Auditor shows a taxable property under the present law, of a hundred and forty-four millions. The wheat crop alone, of your State would in a single year almost liquidate your whole debt. And shall Ohio repudiate? We have not even the ignominious excuse of poverty. Sir, I think I know the people of this State, and I know that they can and will pay the last dollar of their present debt. But beware that you add nothing to it. "The last ounce may break the camel's back," and the people will bear any thing more cheerfully than heavy taxes, wrung out year by year, to feed up a weak and selfish prodigality. * * *

And now let me say to my friends—it is vain for you to war against banks, against monopolies of any sort, so long as you have a public debt. Rank it, too, among your enemies, and a powerful ally to them, and direct your most strenuous efforts to crush it. It is the very centre, the grand redoubt, the rallying-point of the enemy; and until you have carried it, complete victory cannot be yours. Sir, the liquidation of public debts is a Democratic policy.

THE CHARACTER OF THE TRUE STATESMAN.

Extract from a Speech on the Tax Bill, in the Ohio House of Representatives, February 24, 1846.

POLITICS is a science broader in its extent, as fixed, yet more liberal in its principles, more profound and more diversified in its objects, as intricate in its nature, more penetrating and controlling in its effects, wider far in its influence on the happiness of mankind—which is the great end of life—and nobler, every way, than all other human sciences put together. It is a science, the province of which is to carry out, through the agency of man, the designs of the Deity himself. To comprehend such a science in its fullest extent, is the labor of a lifetime, and the business only of a STATESMAN. But by this lofty title I do not mean, in its present degraded acceptation, a miserable partisan, without talents, without character; full of the accumulated vices and deformities which make up the mere vulgar demagogue, a compound of all vileness, the embodiment of every thing despicable; whose very candor is hypocrisy, whose reason is prejudice, whose party is his god; whose atom intellect is exhausted in low intrigue, and his whole research in raking from the mouldering lumber-house of the past, the fleshless skeletons of long-buried falsehoods, to be refined and tortured and galvanized into fresh-born calumnies; or worse, prying, with the instinct of a still lower and baser meanness, into the sanctuary of private life, and bedchamber arrangement. I mean no such detestable character; nor yet one who has merely filled some legislative station with honor to himself and benefit to his immediate constituents No: I mean a STATESMAN, in the broadest, highest, most comprehensive sense—"a mind to comprehend the universe"—bold, sublime, original; from whose all-powerful grasp nothing can escape, to whose piercing gaze nothing is dark, nothing intricate, all clear, and plain, and luminous, as the sun in the firmament; for whose mighty compass immensity itself is scarce too great—a mind inductive, philosophical, inventive, able to originate the mightiest and most extensive plans of national policy, not for a day, but for ages; capable of the loftiest designs, the boldest conceptions, the noblest thoughts—a mind that can take in, at a single glance, the whole compass of State affairs, yet, at the same moment, examine each separately without confusion, analyzing, comparing, arranging, and harmonizing all into one concordant whole—a mind sagacious, unerring, almost divine—a mind that can range at will over all cognate subjects, can glance, with the rapidity of thought, through the dark vista of the past thousands of years, and, in a moment, restraining its flight, pierce, with eagle gaze, into the hidden recesses of the future, "casting the nativity of unborn time," providing against the storm before it has burst, treasuring up the accumulated wisdom of ages, and applying it to the exigencies of the present. A mind thus naturally gifted, must have been developed by years of laborious reading, observation, and study; must have penetrated deep into human nature; must be filled with the whole history of past and present states, adorned with the treasures of science and literature, and enriched with all the multifarious stores of legal and political knowledge. Besides this, an American statesman must be profoundly versed in the history, the interests, separate and relative, of the States; the institutions, political, literary, and religious, of his own country; and must have studied the constitution, laws, nature, and powers of our peculiar system of government, with the deepest and most untiring research. And to these he must add all those qualities which, in public and private life, can ennoble or adorn the human character. His, too, must not have been the mere casual experience of a few months, or years of legislation: his whole life must have been devoted to it.

Such, Mr. Speaker, is the character which I mean, when I speak of a statesman. But I do not affirm that it has ever, as I have drawn it, been exhibited in any age or country; nor yet that it is wholly attainable by any mere "man that is born of a woman." Still less would I maintain, that no one is fit for political life or station, unless he be just such a statesman. Our condition, were such the case, would be lamentable indeed. But the greatest abilities are demanded only for the highest stations and the greatest exigencies, which, comparatively, are few.

THE MEXICAN WAR.

Extracts from Speech of December 22, 1846, on a series of resolutions offered by Mr. VALLANDIGHAM in the Ohio House of Representatives, December 15, 1846, of which the following were two:

"That the war thus brought about and commenced by the aggressions and act of Mexico herself, having been recognized by Congress, according to the forms of the Constitution, is a *Constitutional war*, and a war of the *whole people* of the United States, begun (on our part) and *carried on in pursuance of the Constitution and laws of the Union.*

"That this General Assembly has full confidence in the wisdom and the ability of the Executive of the United States to prosecute the war to a successful and speedy termination by AN HONORABLE PEACE; and that we hereby tender the cordial sympathies and support of this commonwealth, to the said Executive, in the further prosecution of the war."

MR. SPEAKER: the gentleman from Harrison (Mr. Russell), in leading off the opposition to these resolutions, began his speech with a touching allusion to the embarrassment under which he supposed himself to labor. Sir, I can readily believe his embarrassment unaffected. That gentleman always looks embarrassed; he has an embarrassed countenance; and on this occasion, like Mark Antony before the Roman citizens, he would fain have been thought "no orator as Brutus is, but a plain, blunt man," whose deep sense of duty and of the responsibilities imposed upon him as a member of this House, had impelled him, against the promptings of that natural modesty which almost overpowered him, to exhaust a long half hour in diluting the refuse dregs of the late inaugural decoction of Governor Bebb's harangues from the "stump," and pouring them out in bitter profusion upon the Administration, and on the Democratic party generally. But while he is thus embarrassed so greatly between the conflicting calls of duty and the emotions of native modesty, he gravely assumes to read a lecture to the members of this House, for a faithless and selfish forgetfulness of both, in their base scramble for the high places of the State and Federal governments, and hesitates not, in defiance of parliamentary and Christian rule, to impugn the motives of the mover of these resolutions, proclaiming that the applause of the "swell mob," not the obligation of a representative, or the patriotism of a citizen, prompted their introduction. Modestly claiming himself to be moved solely by desire for the public good, that gentleman calmly sets down the speeches and conduct of those who, no less honest and patriotic than himself, happen to differ from him in political sentiment, to the score of self-interested aspirations after office, or the ambition, still more contemptible, to become the first among partisan hacks. He, blushing in virgin embarrassment, is all candor, all fairness, all honesty. His opponents are as arrant and graceless a set of political knaves as ever found a seat among the venal placemen of a First Minister of England. Sir, we are obliged by him: we owe him many compliments. All this is very commendable, and I beg leave to rejoice with him and with his friends, over a début so early and so successful. Above all, I congratulate him upon that sweet felicity of assurance, which enables him to overcome the promptings of that native modesty of his, and cast aside the real embarrassment incident to a member who rises for the first time, to address this House, and arrogating to himself perfect purity of purpose, dash with furious assault upon the conduct and motives of those who have been so unfortunate as to meet his waked wrath. But the gentleman from Harrison is not only modest and pure, honest, faithful and capable, but he is independent also. He aspires to no office; he seeks no place; he crooks not the hinges of his knees to the populace. His judgment and his conscience are alone the rule of his action. He is the very man, *justus et tenax*, so much admired by the old Romans. The people may command corrupt things; the broken heavens may fall down, but the ruins strike him undismayed. He can look calmly and unmoved upon the popular storms which toss us little men to and fro as a reed or a feather; and imitating the sublime fortitude of the Eastern queen, can borrow her language and exclaim, "If I perish, I perish." Well, sir, all this no doubt is very comfortable. I remember to have read somewhere of a French philosopher who held it as a first principle in his creed, that there was no reason on earth why a man should not have a very good opinion of himself. Not meaning to insinuate that the gentleman from Harrison is a disciple of that school of philosophy, I beg to remind him, that however excusable it may be to think highly of his own honesty and independence, charity requires that such self-satisfaction be not indulged in at the expense of others. And let me say to him farther, that the mover of these resolutions is just as honest and independent, and as indifferent to office, and to the unjust censures and opinions of mankind as he is, and not more afraid to avow any sentiments he may conscientiously entertain, or to pursue any course of conduct which he may feel himself called upon to pursue. But I am afraid, I am afraid to meet the honest indignation of my constituents, and especially of that portion of posterity, if any, who may chance to concern themselves about my opinions or conduct as a public man. And more than that, I am afraid to array myself on the side of the enemies of my country. That, sir, is a courage to which I lay no claim, none. I leave it all to the honorable gentleman, if he shall assume it. Let him rejoice in it: I give him joy in its possession. Sir, I offered not these resolutions to entrap the member from Harrison, or any other member. He was not in my eye when I drew them. I offered them because I was a humble friend to the Administration and to the country, and because I found that Administration, and through it the country, ungraciously and fiercely assaulted by men holding high places in this Commonwealth, for what I deemed an honest and faithful discharge of duty.

But the gentleman from Harrison further charges me with ambition.

> "The noble Brutus
> Hath told you Cæsar was ambitious;
> If it were so, it was a grievous fault,
> *And grievously hath Cæsar answered it.*"

Sir, I freely confess that I am not of so stoical a mould of mind as to be indifferent altogether to the honors and glories of the world. But mine, I trust, is that honorable ambition which seeks the attainment of "noble ends by noble means." If I am not without ambition, I yet hope that I shall be found "without the illness which should attend it." Of such ambition I am not ashamed. But the gentleman misapprehends me. I did not speak of the "high places" of the State and the Union as the motives which control my speeches and movements in this House, or as fitting motives to govern any one. Far from it. I have never made office, or even honor, the aim or end of my ambition. They are desirable only so far as they enable the true patriot the more efficiently to do good for his country and for mankind, and not for their own sake. In this spirit and conviction I begin public life, and in it I trust to continue steadfast to the end. * * *

Sir, we have hearkened calmly to the bitter denunciations and mournful wailings over this war, which day after day have been rehearsed in our ears, till vexed with the repetition. We have been reminded of the odium and iniquity of the war, and have had the responsibility laid to our charge. The blood of our brethren, falling in battle, you tell us, cries out, like the blood of the first martyr Abel, against us from the ground. The widow's wail and the orphan's tear are summoned up in judgment against us. The millions, too, of treasure expended, or yet to be spent, in the prosecution of this "unholy crusade against our Mexican brethren," is set down to our account; and the vengeance of heaven and the indignation of the people invoked upon us. Sir, these "incantations of the prophet" disturb not our lightest slumbers. I tell the gentleman that we take the responsibility. We answer for the blood and treasure of this war. But let me admonish him that, held responsible for them, we claim the glory too. Palo Alto is ours; Resaca de la Palma is ours; Monterey is ours; the living glories which encircle the brow of a Taylor are ours; the sepulchral honors which adorn the tomb of a Ringgold are ours. Ours, too, is the bright history of this period. To us belong the admiration of other nations, the gratitude of the present generation, and the applause of posterity in coming time. We consent to share it with none of the revilers of this war. We claim it all, all for ourselves and our children. Sir, if you will howl over its calamities, then in the name of the living, by the blood of the slain, you shall have no part or lot in its glories. * * *

In conclusion, sir, I must be allowed to insist that this discussion has not been so much out of place as some gentlemen seem to think. The State of Ohio is one of the sisters of the great American Confederacy; and within the limits prescribed by the Constitution, an independent and sovereign constituent of the General Government, having intimate connection with all its highest interests. The laws of the Federal Government extend over us: we are bound by them; and must bear our part of the burdens thus imposed, and shed our blood and expend our treasure in the conflicts which that government may bring upon us. As a friend to our peculiar system in its true spirit, and as a State-Rights man, I would be sorry to see the day when the individual States shall cease to feel the deepest solicitude in the acts of the Government of the Union.

SLAVERY.—THE WILMOT PROVISO.—THE UNION.

Remarks, January 21, 1847, on the resolution of Mr. H. G. BLAKE, in the Ohio House of Representatives, requesting our Senators and Representatives to vote for "the exclusion of slavery from the territory of Oregon, and also from any other territory that now is, or may hereafter be, annexed to the United States." The following is the debate, as reported in the *Ohio Statesman.*

MR. ELLISON, of Brown, moved to add these words:

"Excepting in those cases where the welfare and safety of THE UNION may otherwise require."

Mr. FRANKLIN T. BACKUS, of Cuyahoga, moved to amend, by inserting after the word "Union," the words "in the opinion of the chivalry." (A laugh.)

Mr. VALLANDIGHAM rose, and began by rebuking the laughter, and laughing gentlemen, and asked them, if they had forgotten the great Missouri Compromise? That compromise—the principle of concession which was now (1847) laughed at—had saved the Union in 1820. But for the respect which our fathers felt for this principle, and which was then manifested by none more worthily than by Mr. Clay himself, *this Union would have then been dissolved.* Mr. V. declared, for himself, that whenever any question might arise, involving the Union in the alternative, *he would go with his might on that side—on the side of the Union, "now and forever, one and inseparable."* Would any gentleman relinquish the Union rather than tolerate the existence of slavery in the South?

Mr. BACKUS also believed the Compromise (1820) to have been necessary to the perpetuity of the Union. But such an issue was not likely again to occur. *The slaveholding States would be the last to secede and dissolve the Union.* With what face could gentlemen give out their fears on this subject, when they remember the treatment which John Quincy Adams received at their hands, *at the time when he stood up in Congress for a considerate and rational report upon a petition to dissolve the Union.* What a bluster they made, and they were going to expel the old man from the House! Mr. B. affirmed again that we had all been deceived—the slaveholders themselves, by their acts, had manifested the fact, that the very salvation of their system depends upon their remaining in the Union. We had heard enough of these threats to know how to regard them.

Mr. VALLANDIGHAM. The gentleman says that such a portentous issue as that involved in the Missouri question is not likely again to arise. Let him not lay to his soul that flattering unction. But the gentleman from Cuyahoga seems over familiar with this talk of dissolving the Union. That gentleman (Mr. B.) resided in a district *claiming that there now existed cause for dissolving the Union.* He belonged to the district of Joshua R. Giddings, who declared of his constituents, *that they were dissolved from all political connection with the Southern States,* on account of the annexation of Texas. But the mind of the House was not to be drawn off from this question by raising a dispute, whether Mr. Clay ever acted as an honest man. The question was, whether such an exigency as that developed in the Missouri question may not happen again. *What had once happened might happen again*; and let us not become wise above what comes to us as the lessons of the past. The gentleman from Cuyahoga had not answered the question, "If he were to decide between the exclusion of slavery with the dissolution of the Union, and the perpetuation of the Union in connection with that institution, *whether he would prefer to go for dissolution?* He (Mr. V.) trusted the amendment would carry without the mutilation proposed by the gentleman from Cuyahoga. If we were to throw a firebrand toward the South—if we must needs throw down the gauntlet before them, in the shape of these resolutions, they should at least be shaped *so as not to endanger the Union;* they should, by all means, be put in such a guarded form as not to endanger our favored institutions. Mr. V. felt that, perhaps, he had been too much in earnest upon this question. He had spoken from impulse, and, perhaps, with too much freedom and feeling, *because he felt called upon as a patriot and citizen to resist and expose every measure which might work incalculable mischief, not only to ourselves, but to generations yet unborn.*

POLITICAL POSITION AND PRINCIPLES.

Extracts from "Salutatory Address," on assuming editorial charge of the "*Dayton* (Ohio) *Empire*," September 2, 1847.

We will contend calmly and resolutely for all *salutary reforms;* yet not as seeking to change existing institutions solely because they are old, nor clamoring for any innovation simply because it is new. "To innovate is not to reform." Yet no abuse shall escape us because covered by the prescription of ages, or protected by the canonizing authority of great names.

A *radical Democrat* as well from sober conviction as from impulse, we will maintain with calm but determined firmness the doctrines of radical *progressive* Democracy. Ours, however, is not the *sans culotte* democracy of the faubourg calling for two hundred and seventy thousand heads; but our own peculiar, rational, constitutional, American Democracy—that Democracy which is built upon law and order, and governed through reason and by justice—a Democracy the aim of which is to approximate our forms and administration of government as nearly to the standard of unmixed democracies as our circumstances and the well-being of society will admit; to leave as much power with the people in their unorganized capacity as is compatible with the necessities and efficient existence of government, delegating no more to their agents than is requisite for its just and legitimate purposes.

We will contend to the utmost, for the largest wholesome *individual freedom* of action in all things, and oppose with our whole heart, that pernicious and anti-democratic intermeddling of government with those private affairs and relations between man and man, which of right and upon policy ought to be left to the individual citizen himself.

We will maintain *the right of the majority to govern;* not as a natural right, inherent in majorities, but as a political right, subject, therefore, as well to the restrictions imposed upon it by our Constitutions and laws (except in cases justifying a resort to the *ultima ratio populi*, REVOLUTION) as to the natural and imprescriptible rights of the men composing minorities, as individuals. We will war against despotism in all its forms, and to us the despotism of the many is no more tolerable than the despotism of the few.

We will maintain *the will of the people to be the supreme law*, subject to the eternal principles of right and justice, which it belongs not to the people to give or take away; but we will seek for that will primarily in the constitution and laws. The will of the people, as exhibited through the press, through public assemblies, petitions, and above all, the ballot-box, is in itself neither constitution nor law; nor has it the force thereof, though entitled to great respect. But it is the highest evidence of what constitutions and laws the people desire to have ordained and enacted; and to the framers of constitutions, and to legislators as such, we hold it to be, when fully and authentically ascertained, the supreme law, as above limited.

We will support the CONSTITUTION OF THE UNITED STATES, in its whole integrity, as it came to us from "the Fathers," believing it to establish, in principle, the very best form of government which the wisdom of man ever devised.

We will protect and defend, according to our opportunities and abilities, the UNION OF THESE STATES, as in very deed the "Palladium of our political prosperity," "the only rock of our safety," less sacred only than Liberty herself; and we will pander to the sectional prejudices, or the fanaticism, or wounded pride, or disappointed ambition, of no man, or set of men, whereby that Union shall be put in jeopardy.

We will maintain the doctrine of *strict construction*, as applied to all grants of power, in trust, to the agents and servants of the people, and especially to the Constitution of the United States; and we will stand fast to the doctrine, also, of "STATE RIGHTS," as embodied in Mr. Madison's Virginia Report and Mr. Jefferson's Kentucky Resolutions of '98.

Free trade, the Constitutional Treasury, equitable taxation, assessed upon sound financial principles; the collection of no more revenue in the treasury of the General and State government than will suffice, under a wholesome administration of the finances; the faithful and speedy discharge of the State debt, never to be incurred again in time of peace; a revision of our State Constitution without further delay; wholesome and rational economy in all the departments, and all the transactions of government, far removed from the "economy of meanness;" confidence in the people, jealousy of their agents; one term to the Presidency; a fixed tenure to every office under the Federal Government, which will properly admit of it; war before dishonor, but honorable peace always to be preferred to war—these and other kindred principles and measures, will receive our hearty support.

The cause of *popular education* shall receive, in like manner, our cordial sympathy and aid, as of the last necessity to the prosperity and permanence of our institutions.

To the present Administration we will lend that support (whatever it is worth), which an honest, independent man may, and ought to extend, to the Administration of the party to which he belongs.

On these, as on all subjects, our opinions shall be our own, and they shall be candidly, boldly, but courteously expressed. In our editorial intercourse with the public, we shall seek no personal controversy, nor shall any one draw us into any controversy unbecoming a gentleman. Towards all adversaries, between whom and us there shall arise any matter of difference, we will exhibit proper respect, sometimes for their sakes—always for our own.

THE CLERGY AND POLITICS.

Extract from an Editorial Review of a Sermon against the Mexican War, by a Methodist preacher; *Dayton Empire*, December 2, 1847.

THE Saviour, whose Gospel he professes, gave no such example, taught no such doctrine. When the Pharisees, "tempting Him," asked whether it were lawful to pay tribute to Cæsar, a question which then divided the Jewish nation, instead of pandering to their partisan feelings and prejudices, by arraying himself upon the one side or the other, He commanded them to "render unto Cæsar the things which were Cæsar's, and to God the things which were God's." It is no part of the duty of the Christian minister, under the cloak of religion, and in the pharisaical cant of being otherwise recreant to duty, to pronounce his judgment in the pulpit, upon the great political questions, which distract the generation in which he lives. There is an end of all purity and usefulness in the ministry, and with it of the usefulness and purity of religion also, if such a course be tolerated. If the clergy and the church are to be arrayed against the Democratic party, on the question of this war, let us know it, that we may set our battle in array accordingly.

* * * * * * *

In attacking, thus boldly, the abuses of religion by those who essay to preach it, we make no attack on religion itself. We desire to separate, carefully and widely, between the two. We were taught, from earliest infancy, and have sought to practise the lesson ever since, to reverence the religion of the Bible, and to respect those, at least, of its ministers, who walk worthy of their vocation.

THE RIGHT OF REVOLUTION.—"DORRISM."

Extract from an Editorial, in the *Dayton Empire*, March 28, 1848.

THERE is no question in politics, which we have investigated with more diligence, patience, and research, than the above, ever since it was first brought before the public, by the movements in Rhode Island, in 1841 and 1842. If we have erred in our conclusion, it is not because we have spared pains to avoid error. At the same time we recognize, to the fullest extent, what Mr. Calhoun has called "the glorious right of rebellion and revolution." And it is because we hold to and rely upon this, that we reject the other. We know of no "peaceable, constitutional" mode of setting aside existing Constitutions, except in the way which they themselves have prescribed. If the case demands revolution, the mode must be revolutionary. * * * * We say, therefore, boldly, that we are opposed to any movement in Ohio, which shall be based upon the doctrine of "Dorrism," as set up in the Rhode Island affair of 1842. After signal failure then, and recent condemnation by the Supreme Court of the United States, we cannot regard it as a safe doctrine to put in practice in this State. * * *

The difference between this mode of securing a new Constitution and "Dorrism," is manifest as day. The latter begins with the assumption that a numerical majority have a right, natural, inherent, and inalienable, to set aside existing rules and forms as prescribed by constitutions, and proposes by spontaneous movement, without form or color of law, to abrogate an instrument acknowledged to be binding at the time, and to substitute another in its stead. The other, recognizing the right of *Revolution* to the full extent, as laid down in the Declaration of Independence, the Federal Constitution, and the Constitutions of the several States, and among these of Ohio, but denying that these instruments can "formally and peaceably" be set aside, except in the mode which they themselves prescribe, proposes to wait till by a lapse of the powers delegated by the Constitution, and their consequent reversion to the people, that instrument has ceased to exist. In this latter case the forms of the Constitution and law are not looked to, solely because such forms no longer have a being. * * * We are for pursuing a legal and constitutional course, as long as the Constitution and laws have an existence. The extreme medicine of the body politic, must not be made its daily bread.

CONSERVATISM AND PROGRESS—THE TRUE AND THE FALSE.

Extract from Remarks at the "Eighth of January Supper;" Columbus, Ohio, 1850.

WE are apt, sir, in the midst of the all-absorbing topics and occurrences of the day we live in, to forget, sometimes, that there is a Future before us, with its high hopes and its lofty anticipations, and whose unformed destinies are yet to be shaped by the earnest labors of our hands: but much oftener, that there ever has been a great Past, full of vitality, and full of great men and yet greater deeds, and full, too, of lessons and examples fitted to expound the present, and to stir the emulation and develop to the utmost, the genius and faculties of the generation of to-day. I am not, indeed, as yet old enough, Mr. President, to have become, after the manner of Marius, a dweller amid the tombs and monuments and ruins of the past. There is something awfully grand in the contemplation, certainly; and fearful lessons and a terrible discipline to mind and soul, are to be there learned. But they belong not to the business of the hour. There is a dryness and hoariness about them, little calculated to fit us for the struggles and hand-to-hand conflicts of active life. I am no admirer yet—I trust I never shall be—of the "dry-as-dust" conservatism of the past. But there are two Pasts behind us: "the Dead Past and the Living Past. "Let the dead past bury its dead." Our business is with the living past. It is good for us to recur to it for its profound lessons of wisdom, and for the contemplation of its sublime and ennobling exemplars and monuments. There is a purity, a freshness, a reinvigorating stimulus in these fountains of principle and action, which belong not to the turbid and corrupt streams which flow so far removed from their source. It is good for us to drink, now and then, at these fountains. He who will not look to the past, is not fit, said a great and philosophic statesman, to direct the future. And with all our devotion to progress, and all our zeal and absorption in the things of the present, we are yet ever ready to bestow our admiration and regard upon whatever or whomsoever among the events or the men of other times, is great or heroic * * *

The duties which devolve upon us, in the day we live in, if not as arduous, as elevated, and as replete with grand results as in years past, are yet important enough, and equally obligatory upon us. If we cannot achieve liberty, independence, and Union, it is our sacred trust to preserve them. It is our good fortune, also, to live in an age when mental and physical activity and development, are at their highest point. We live in the midst of progress and reform of every kind, ınd when the obsolete and exploded customs and ideas of the dead past are ·apidly passing away. * * * The hour and the man are not yet come; but hey are at hand. False Conservatism may, indeed, sit like the grim giant in the Allegory, and fret, and fume, and champ its chains, and gnash its teeth at the progress and reform which it cannot arrest; or like the owl, its fit emblem, may sit within the shadow and darkness of the dead past, and stare in blindness with ts gray and vacant eyes, and hoot at the light which is breaking in upon its solitudes. But its sceptre is about to depart, and its kingdom to be taken from it. Yet let us not mistake. * * * Several years ago, some workmen digging in one of the principal streets of New York, turned up an ancient mile-stone, on which, in antique and half-obliterated letters, was the inscription, "One mile to New York." A right curious relic of the past, the dead past, sir, was this old mile-stone. Once its inscription was true. Once it *was* one mile to New York. But a century had elapsed; all around had changed. By little and little the city had extended, nearer and nearer, and yet nearer to it, and beyond it, till at last, sinking into the earth, and buried beneath buildings and improvements, it is forgotten; and when, at length, after the lapse of a hundred years, it is turned up again to broad day, in the very heart of the city, it still exclaims, with the spirit and in the very tone of the false conservatism, "One mile to New York." * * * * * * But while we eschew a dead conservatism, we must yet ever bear in mind that all change is not reform, and that we owe "a decent respect" to the opinions, customs, practices, and institutions of those who have gone before us. It is not every kind of progress which is desirable. There is a progress backwards as well as forwards; and a progress, now and then, which leads to defeat and ruin. Nature sometimes interposes impregnable barriers; circumstances often oppose; and progress then rebounds discomfited, and falls hopelessly into the arms of the false conservatism; or, if successful, ends only in destruction. This is not the advancement which we want or advocate. The car of Juggernaut is progressive; but its progress is marked every furlong by the crushed and mangled bodies of human victims. It is the highest of political wisdom accurately to distinguish between the true progress and the false; between that which is fitting and practicable, and that which ends only in mischief and disaster.

THE COMPROMISE MEASURES OF 1850.

These Resolutions were reported by Mr. VALLANDIGHAM, from a committee, and unanimously adopted, at a large public meeting, held, without distinction of party, at Dayton, Ohio, October 26, 1850. He supported them in a speech not reported. He had also spoken at a meeting a few days before, called to denounce the Compromise Measures. Of that speech one paper (Whig) said: "It was ingenious and eloquent. His objection to the course proposed by the resolutions was, that it would lead to further agitation, and tend to endanger the Union."

Another said: "His remarks were earnest, dignified, and appropriate. He strongly deprecated every new attempt to inflame the public mind, while he enforced, in strains of lofty and impassioned eloquence, the duty of every good citizen to observe and maintain the sanction of law, as the only way to secure the peace, order, and happiness of society anywhere."

1. *That we are for the Union as it is, and the Constitution as it is*, and that we will preserve, maintain, and defend both at every hazard, observing, with scrupulous and uncalculating fidelity, every article, requirement, and compromise of the Constitutional compact between these States, to the letter, and in its utmost spirit,

and recognizing no "higher law," between which and the Constitution we know of any conflict.

2. That the Constitution was "the result of a spirit of amity, and of that mutual deference and concession which the peculiarity of our political situation rendered indispensable;" that by amity, conciliation, and compromise alone, can it, and the Union which it established, be preserved; and that it is the duty of all good citizens to frown indignantly upon every attempt, wheresoever or by whomsoever made, to array one section of the Union against the other; to foment jealousies and heart-burnings between them, by systematic and organized misrepresentation, denunciation and calumny, and thereby to render them, in feeling and affection, the inheritors of so noble a common patrimony, purchased by our fathers at so great expense of blood and treasure.

3. That as the friends of peace and concord—as lovers of the Union, and foes, sworn upon the horns of the altar of our common country, to all who seek, and all that tends to its dissolution, we have viewed with anxiety and alarm the perilous crisis brought upon us by years of ceaseless and persevering agitation of the slavery question, in its various forms; and that the Executive and Congress of the United States have deserved well of the Republic, for their patriotic efforts so to compromise and adjust this vexed question, as to leave no good cause for clamor or offence by any portion of the Union.

4. That a strict adherence, in all its parts, to the compromise thus deliberately and solemnly effected, is essential to the restoration and maintenance of peace, harmony, and fraternal affection between the different sections of the Union, and thereby to the preservation of the Union itself; and that good faith imperatively demands that adherence at the hands of all good citizens, whether of the North or of the South.

5. That, believing this compromise the very best which, in view of the circumstances and temper of the times, could have been attained, we are for it as it is, and opposed to all agitation, looking to a repeal or essential modification of any of its parts, and that we will lend no aid or comfort to those who, for any purpose, seek further to agitate and embroil the country upon these questions.

6. That "all obstructions to the execution of the laws, all combinations and associations, under whatever plausible character, with the real design to direct, control, counteract, or awe the regular deliberation and action of the constituted authorities, are destructive of the fundamental principle of our institutions, and of fatal tendency"; that all such efforts, wherever made, or by whomsoever advised, find no answering sympathy in our breast—nothing but loathing and contempt; and that we hereby pledge ourselves to the country, that, so far as in us lies, THE UNION, THE CONSTITUTION, AND THE LAWS, must and shall be maintained.

MONEYED AND MUNICIPAL CORPORATIONS.

Extract from Argument for the plaintiff in error, in the Supreme Court of Ohio, in *The City of Dayton* vs. *Pease*, December Term, 1854.

I DO not propose to enter into any elaborate criticism of these decisions. But allow me, nevertheless, with great respect to the memory of the late Supreme Court, to suggest that they are part of the footsteps of your predecessors wherein, I trust, this Court, as now constituted, has no inclination to tread. I admit, cordially, and now mournfully, the genius and the eloquence of the late lamented Judge Read—[illegible], intellectual meteor, which shot its splendid coruscations of light for a little while, across the heavens, and then went out in utter darkness, upon the distant horizon of the Pacific. Yet I cannot but believe that in the judgment which he gave in Fifteenth Ohio Reports, he was not a little influenced by the peculiar political notions which prevailed then upon the subject of corporations, and which found their way in eloquent, but not very *judicial* language, into that judgment. Concurring, as I then did, and do still, generally, to the uttermost, in his views, upon the great and ever vital question of moneyed corporations, permit me yet to suggest that this holy horror of corporate seals, and the mystic nature of wax, and all that other "transcendentalism," which that late learned and lamented Judge declares "had enveloped both the courts and the profession in a mist, growing out of the airy nothingness of the subject matter, and enabled corporations, like the pestilence which walketh unseen, to do their mischief, and escape responsibility," is by no means to be extended to *all* corporations, and least of all, perhaps, to municipal corporations. There is nothing in the origin, past history, or purposes of such corporations, which ought to subject them to odium or disfavor, or to stricter rules than other public officers, or certainly, at least individuals, exercising like powers. To these corporations, more than to any other proximate cause—more by far than to Magna Charta and the Bill of Rights, the work of the great "iron barons" of King John, and the silken nobles and knights of King James, who drew the rebellious sword or wielded the seditious pen, to enforce and protect their own peculiar rights, we owe it, that the small spark of popular liberty, in that day, was not wholly extinguished, crushed out, in the blood and darkness, and oppressions of the feudal ages. The Senates and Councils of Italy, the Parliaments of France, the Cortez of Spain, would have availed nothing—the House of Commons nothing, with its Pyms and Hampdens, and Sydneys and Russells, of later times, had not the patient and sturdy burghers of the cities and towns, while the kings and barons of Europe, in deadly array, met the infidel hosts, like Sir Kenneth and the Saracen, "under the burning sun of Syria," slowly, but steadily, gone on increasing in wealth, and population, and power. By little and little, availing themselves of the necessities of the nobles, made urgent then by the Crusades, they purchased or extorted privilege upon privilege, till every vestige of their feudal servitude was swept away, and, in the midst of absolutism and oppression elsewhere, a select body of freemen, electing their own officers, and governed by their own ordinances, grew up to a magnitude and strength which, too late, drew the attention and hostility of barons and kings. It was in these corporations that, through the dark ages, the representative idea of government was preserved, which, in our times, and in this country, has been brought to so great perfection. It was the common council and trainbands of a municipal corporation, which gave so great aid to the cause of the people in the first great struggle between power and liberty in the time of the first Charles; and it was the revocation of the charter of a municipality which contributed so greatly to drive the second James from his throne. It was a corporate charter, too, which the sturdy freemen of Connecticut, to save it from destruction, hid within the rough and gnarled, but fostering bosom of the Charter Oak. There may have been no "transcendentalism" in all this, but there *was* a mystic notion, which impelled the honest burghers and citizens of those times, to hold even the wax and the parchment of their charters too sacred, for kings, and the vicegerents of kings, to touch.

Nor is there any thing in the *purposes* for which these corporations are organized, which demands odium, or jealousy even, from the most sensitive lover of liberty. They are but subdivisions of the government, established for the convenience of the more compact communities, or particular consociations of citizens.

They derive all their power from the great body of the people, represented in the legislature; and this power is at any moment liable to be taken away. Their purposes are not the pursuit or aggregation of wealth, nor yet of political power; but the control and management of the internal and municipal affairs of the citizens dwelling within their limits. And in all this they are eminently democratic, acting through a common council or local legislature, the members of which are elected by the citizens, and, from the nature of the case, more directly amenable to their constituents than any other class of representatives.

CAMPAIGN OF 1860.

Extract from Speech at Dayton, May 19, 1860.

HE was not for the North, nor for the South, *but for the whole country;* and yet, in a conflict of sectional interests, he was for THE WEST all the time. In a little while—even after the present year, men east of the mountains would learn that there was a West, which to them has heretofore been an "undiscovered country." *He hoped fervently to see the day when we should hear no more of sections;* but as long as men elsewhere demanded a "united North," and a "united South," he wanted to see a "united West." Still the "United States" was a better term, more patriotic, more constitutional, and more glorious than any of them.

Referring to Mr. Lincoln's "irrepressible conflict" speech of 1858,

Mr. VALLANDIGHAM proceeded for some time to denounce the sentiment of the speech in a vehement and impassionate manner, as revolutionary, disorganizing, subversive of the government, *and ending necessarily in disunion.* Our fathers had founded a government expressly upon the compatibility and harmony of a Union of States, "part slave, and part free," and whoever affirmed the contrary, laid the axe at the very root of the Union.

Extract from Speech at same place, June 30, 1860.

There are now two extreme sectional parties. Six years ago the Abolition sentiments of the free States culminated in the Republican organization. In the course of time *it has brought forth its inevitable fruit,* in the organization, especially in the Gulf or Cotton States, of an extreme Southern or pro-slavery party, *the offspring, but the very antipode of the Republican party.* If either of these is suffered to prevail, *the Union is at an end. Even now it is in peril* from mere conflict between them. But the death of the parent will be the death of the child. Kill the Northern and Western anti-slavery organization, the Republican party, and the extreme Southern pro-slavery, "fire-eating" organization of the Cotton States, will expire in three months. Continue the Republican party—above all, *put it in power, and the antagonism will grow till the whole South will become a unit.* It is our mission here in Ohio, as one of the free States, to conquer and crush out Northern and Western sectionalism, as this is the especial enemy in our midst.

POSITION ON THE WAR; APRIL, 1861.*

DAYTON, OHIO, *April* 17, 1861.

To the Editor of the Cincinnati Enquirer:

I have a word for the Republican press and partisans of Cincinnati and other places abroad, who now daily falsify and misrepresent me and matters which concern me here in Dayton.

* This card, written two days after the President's Proclamation of War, is referred to in the letter to Hendrickson, ante, page 302.

My position in regard to this civil war, which the Lincoln Administration has inaugurated, was long since taken, is well known, and *will be adhered to to the end.* Let that be understood. I have added nothing to it, subtracted nothing from it, said nothing about it publicly, since the war began. I know well that I am right, and that in a little while the "sober second thought of the people" will dissipate the present sudden and fleeting public madness, and will demand to know why thirty millions of people are butchering each other in civil war, and will arrest it speedily. But, meantime, should my own State be invaded, or threatened with invasion, as soon as it may be, then, as a true native-born son of Ohio, acknowledging my first allegiance to be to her, I will aid in defending her to the last extremity, asking no questions. Whoever shall refuse then, or hesitate, will be a traitor and a dastard. And this same rule I apply as well to the people of Virginia, Kentucky, or Missouri, as to any of the free States, North or West.

As to myself: No threats have been made to me personally; none within my hearing; no violence offered; no mob anywhere; none will be; nobody afraid of any, and every statement or rumor in regard to me circulated orally, or published in the Republican press, is basely idle and false. And now let me add, for the benefit of the cowardly slanderers of Cincinnati or elsewhere who libel me daily, that if they have any business with me, I can be found every day and at any time, either at home, or upon the streets of Dayton.

PRIVATE CONFERENCE ON THE WAR AND USURPATION, PROPOSED.

Dayton, Ohio, *May 7th*, 1861.

My Dear Sir:—The almost unanimous uprising of the people in the North and West—called forth by the fatal error, as I think, that the purpose of the Lincoln Administration is to preserve the Union, and that it can be preserved by *civil war*—is being abused to the utter destruction of the Constitution and the inauguration of a military despotism. The first proclamation was, at least, of doubtful legality; the blockade still more so; but the astounding proclamation of May 3d, undertaking by Executive authority alone to "raise and support armies," and to "provide and maintain a navy," discloses at once, the bold conspiracy to usurp all power into the hands of the Executive—since a Congress of partisans surrounded by 30,000 soldiers, can but be the tool of the President. No king of England, since James II., would have dared attempt such a usurpation: England, at no time, since the reign of Henry VIII., would have submitted to it. And all this within twenty days! If there be any spirit of liberty left, is it not time to arouse and strike a blow to rescue the Republic from an impending military despotism? If you agree with me, can we not have a conference of the friends of Constitutional and limited government—of true popular government—say at Chillicothe on the 15th of this month (May), to concert some measures to arouse the people to a sense of the danger which presses upon us? I shall be glad to hear from you.

LETTERS TO SABIN HOUGH; 1861.

Dayton, Ohio, *April* 26.

Rev. Sabin Hough:

Dear Sir:—I thank you *most cordially* for your letter of the 24th. It strengthens me in the truth and right. Its words are fitly and truly spoken. This folly, and madness, and wickedness, must soon have an end. "How long, O, Lord?" We shall see. It is written that "blessed are the peace-makers," and yet the whole church of the Prince of Peace is maddening and thirsting for blood—the blood of our brethren—preaching, praying, *fighting*. Was ever people before delivered over to such folly and wickedness? Truly you have said that it is "from hell and not from Heaven."

I thank you for your pamphlet. I have distributed all but one copy for myself. I send you a copy of my speech of February 20, 1861. But all is over now. It is too late for any thing except peaceable separation.

DAYTON, *April* 30, 1861.

REV. SABIN HOUGH, *Cincinnati, Ohio.*

DEAR SIR:—I have just received yours, and concur with you heartily. The storm is passing, and I hope reason may return, and peace for the present with it. Beyond that I see nothing but separation, first of the free States and slave, and then of the West from the East, and then—I know not what. I have no interest in the *Empire*, but the editor is one of my best friends, and I will adopt your suggestion gladly. On Sunday night in Wesley Chapel (Methodist Episcopal), *divine* services were concluded by singing the "Star Spangled Banner." In the Presbyterian (Dr. Thomas's), an "Ode to Liberty" (negro liberty) was sung by the choir, first being regularly given out by the Doctor from the pulpit. What next?

I shall watch the first favorable chance to move publicly for peace, and restora tion if possible.

DAYTON, OHIO, *September* 4, 1861.

REV. SABIN HOUGH, *Cincinnati, Ohio:*

MY DEAR SIR:—I thank you for your letter. I never received any invitation to speak at the place you mention—so their labor was all lost. But when I undertake to speak, I shall so arrange as to succeed.

Truly, we have fallen upon evil times. But I believe, as God rules, that all will come right in due season.

AFFAIR AT CAMP UPTON, VIRGINIA; 1861.

Telegraphic dispatch of the "Associated Press" to the Washington, Baltimore, and Philadelphia papers.

ALEXANDRIA, *July* 7, 1861.—Mr. VALLANDIGHAM, member of Congress from Ohio, visited the Ohio regiments to-day. While in the camp of the first regiment, a disposition was shown by many to oust him, and, notwithstanding the nerve and courage shown by Mr. VALLANDIGHAM, it is probable they would have succeeded, but for the protection afforded him by the Dayton companies, and a pass from General Scott. He finally retired to the camp of the second regiment, after declaring himself as good a Union man as any of them, and expressing his scorn for the mob spirit shown by his fellow-citizens.

MASON AND SLIDELL.—THE "TRENT" AFFAIR.

ON the 16th of December, 1861, Mr. VALLANDIGHAM offered certain resolutions in the House of Representatives, relating to the seizure of Messrs. Mason and Slidell, on board the British Mail Steamer "Trent." Upon his arrival in Canada, in July, 1863, he was assailed by a Toronto paper, and his Resolutions, and the motives in offering them, both misrepresented—the false copy of the Resolutions which appears in that farrago of stuff and falsehood, "Putnam's Rebellion Record," being substituted for the official copy. The following answer to the assault, explains sufficiently the character and objects of the Resolutions. It is taken from the *Toronto Leader:*

"Mr. VALLANDIGHAM, let it be remembered, was an American Representative, and had the right, and was under the obligation to maintain the honor and dignity of his own country, and was only bound as a statesman, not to indulge in illiberal and abusive language towards a foreign government. On the first day of the session, December 2, 1862, Owen Lovejoy, of Illinois, an ultra Abolition leader of the House of Representatives, offered this resolution: 'That the thanks of Congress are due, and are hereby tendered, to Captain Wilkes, of the United States Navy, for his brave, adroit, and patriotic conduct in the arrest and detention of the traitors James M. Mason and John Slidell.' A little while after, Mr. Colfax, of Indiana, another Administration leader, offered a resolution, proposing to confine Mr. Mason in the 'cell of a convicted felon.' And on the same day a similar resolution was offered by Mr. Odell, a violent 'war man,' as to Mr. Slidell. All these were adopted without objection. About the middle of the month, the steamer brought the news of the extraordinary excitement in England, and of the belligerent determination of the British government. Mr. VALLANDIGHAM perceiving that the very men who had so hastily and valorously indorsed the act of Captain Wilkes, would now back down ingloriously, offered the preamble and resolution quoted by the *Globe*—every substantive word of the former being *quoted* from the language of Secretary Wells, or of Lovejoy and Colfax.

"In offering the resolution, Mr. VALLANDIGHAM said he 'would adhere to it to the last, though he regretted, and would have opposed, if he had had the power, *and prevented the Administration and the House from the folly of taking a position in advance upon, the act of Captain Wilkes.*

"Again, on the 7th of January, 1863, after the surrender, Mr. VALLANDIGHAM addressed the House briefly on the same subject, declaring that the Administration had '*strutted insolently into a quarrel without right,* and basely crept out of it without honor.' And further on, he denounced '*the rash act of Captain Wilkes, and the yet rasher indorsement of the Administration and the country.*' And the same day, in reply to Mr. Hutchins, he said:

"'I did not at the time approve of the resolution of thanks submitted by the gentleman from Illinois (Mr. Lovejoy), and I looked around me in anxious suspense to observe whether there was courage or statesmanship enough on the other side of the House to interpose an objection to it; but there was none. I offered none. Had I objected the cry would have again gone forth—'Behold the enemy of his country; always against her!' I had no responsibility that required me to interfere, and I did not. Then was the time, so far as this House was concerned, to have paused; and, so far as regards this Administration, it was their duty to have acted when Captain Wilkes first anchored the San Jacinto at Fortress Monroe. The law of the case, on the 12th of November last, was precisely what the law was on the 27th of December following. The facts were just as well known and understood four-and-twenty hours after the arrival of these men upon our coast, as they were understood and known when the dispatch of the Secretary was written and the surrender made. Honor would have been saved, and a savor of grace imparted by a voluntary discharge at the first.'

"Mr. VALLANDIGHAM has, at all proper times and places, claimed and exercised the right to criticise and condemn any of the acts or public history of Great Britain, just as he has those of his own country; but he has never had occasion, and least of all in the Trent case, to 'exhaust the whole vocabulary of invective against England."

"AN AMERICAN.

"CLIFTON HOUSE, C. W., *Aug.* 7, 1863."

"LOYALTY."—PATRIOTISM.

Reply to Assaults in the House of Representatives, January 7, 1862.

SIR, if I am charged with the desire of giving aid and comfort to the Southern Confederacy, by maintaining the honor and dignity of my own country against a foreign foe, I hurl back the charge defiantly into the teeth of all concerned, directly or indirectly, openly or tacitly, in the resolutions of the first day of the session. It is too late now, sir, to meet me with this mean and beggarly insinuation. I have had enough of it outside of this House, and will submit to none of it here.

As to my record at the extra session, or during the present session, it remains, and will remain. I do neither retract one sentiment that I have uttered, nor would I obliterate a single vote which I have given. I speak of the record, as it will appear hereafter, and, indeed, stands now upon the Journals of this House, and in the Congressional Globe. And there is no other record, thank God, and no act, or word, or thought of mine, and never has been from the beginning, in public or in private, of which any patriot ought to be ashamed. Sir, it is the record, as I made it, and as it exists here to-day; and not, as a mendacious and shameless press have attempted to make it up for me. Let us see who will grow tired of this record first. Consistency, firmness, and sanity in the midst of general madness—these make up my offence. But "Time, the avenger," sets all things even; and I abide his leisure.

[After quoting a part of his remarks of July 12, 1861 (ante p. 324), Mr. V. proceeds:]

Sir, this was before the battle of Bull Run, and you voted my amendment down almost unanimously. But that was my position then: it was my record in the midst of the crisis of the Revolution. It is true, sir, that in the madness of the hour, amid the bitter and relentless persecution of every man who would not bow the knee to the party in power, and confess unlimited confidence in it, and promise unhesitating support of all that it demanded, usurpations of power, breaches of the Constitution, and all, no man heeded it then: and in common with thousands of as good patriots as ever lived in this or any country—men who would yield up the last drop of their blood in the defence of the Constitution and the Union, and for the maintenance of this Government as our fathers made it, and for the honor of the "Stars and Stripes," emblematic of the principles upon which it was founded—I was hunted and hounded in every State, and by every press, and upon every hustings, by cowards and slanderers, as an enemy to my country.

To-day the magnitude and true character of the war stand confessed, and its real purposes begin to be revealed; and I am justified, or soon will be justified, by thousands, who a little while ago condemned me. But I appealed then, as I appeal now, alike to the near and to the distant future; and by the judgment of that impartial tribunal, even in the present generation, I will abide; or if my name and memory shall fade away out of the record of these times, then will these calumnies perish with them.

FINANCES.—TAXATION.

Remarks on the Direct Tax Resolution, in the House of Representatives, January 15, 1862.

Before I yield the floor to the gentleman from New York, allow me to express the hope that all measures relating to finance may be reported at the earliest practicable moment, and then postponed to a fixed day ahead, so that ample time may be allowed for their consideration. For great, sir, as this civil war is, imminent, too, as the danger of foreign complications, they are, both of them, as nothing in comparison with the daily accumulating and most disastrous financial embarrassments, which are pressing now upon us on every side—not for the present moment only, but for a century, it may be.

The war must come to an end, sooner or later; and in one way or another our foreign complications will be adjusted, with or without war, which could not last long; but the errors or crimes of the financial contrivances and embarrassments of to-day, and their results, will endure to the third and fourth generation of those who shall come after us.

While, then, we ought to begin this work at once, let us not hurry over it. For twenty-six years the pestilent and execrable question of slavery, in every form, has been debated in this House for months in succession. Abolition petitions, the Wilmot Proviso, the Compromise of 1850, the Kansas-Nebraska Bill, the Kansas troubles, and the Lecompton Constitution, each in turn consumed the time of the House for weeks together. And even now, with a public debt already of some seven hundred millions of dollars, increasing, too, at the rate of two millions a day; with an empty treasury, and no means to replenish it; with every fountain of revenue nearly dried up, and even that last resource of the inevitable bankrupt—borrowing—cut off; with all these things staring us full in the face, nevertheless the objects of the war, the conduct of the war, Emancipation, Confiscation, Ball's Bluff, the Trent affair, Government contracts, the Cooly trade, the Coast Survey, the franking privilege, or whatever else may happen to be the especial question of the hour—all of them highly important, certainly, and worthy of due consideration, are debated for days at a time, and even the best-abused man in the House finds no difficulty in obtaining an audience.

Let us prepare, then, at once for the great questions of finance which are before us; but let a time be fixed, and let us debate them day after day, at length, and not wait till the last moment, and then hurry them through, as two bills upon the same subject have already been, without a moment's consideration. The country will be content if they only see that we have gone at the business in earnest, and will not grudge to us an hour spent in legitimate debate. Let the people understand, truly and honestly, the real character and true extent of the burdens we impose upon them, and know and feel that we have faithfully and diligently done the best possible, every way, to protect their interests, and the dread spectre of Repudiation will never be evoked. Let us waste no time in this business; but let us, at the same time, advance slowly, understanding every step of our journey, and then there will be no steps to retrace. Sir, this is immeasurably the most momentous of all the questions which are just now before us; and whoever fails to meet and grapple with it boldly, and to the full extent, is a disunionist; for bankruptcy is disunion and dissolution in the worst form, and will bring the war to an instant end, not as I would have it, by adjustment, fair compromise, and a restoration of the Union, but by immediate, eternal, and ignominious separation.

It is not now any longer a question of "the "vigorous prosecution of the war," as the phrase goes, but absolutely one of simple financial salvation. Taxation, heavy taxation, but upon sound principles, and in the right way, can alone now save us.

I hope I am not giving aid and comfort to the enemy. I know, of course, sir, that I cannot have the ear of those who think that "no good can come out of Nazareth." But I address myself to wiser men, and express again the hope that these measures of finance may be introduced at once, but postponed to a day certain, distant enough to allow the amplest examination of them in advance; and that afterwards they may be considered and discussed at length, and as their immense magnitude and importance demand. If we are not competent to this task, and are expected to take just whatsoever the Secretary of the Treasury on the one hand, or the banks upon the other, or both combined, may choose to submit, let us resign, and go home, to the end that abler and fitter men may be sent here to fill the seats which we dishonor. But the work will be more than half done whenever we shall have boldly, manfully, and honestly taken hold of it.

PROSCRIPTION.—REDRESS.

After the elections in the autumn of 1862, Mr. Vallandigham made many speeches at Democratic "Celebrations." None of them was reported, except in brief abstract. The following is a summary of one, made at Cambridge City, Indiana, November 15, 1862. Mr. V. had spoken at Centreville, Indiana, near Cambridge, on the 20th of October, and had that night, on his way home, been, by order of Governor Morton, "dogged" at Richmond, Indiana, by the United States Marshal for that State, one Rose Garland. Alluding to this, Mr. Vallandigham began thus:

"Is the Marshal of Indiana here to-day? Are his minions about? Is his committee here again? Why liest thou hid now, O sweet-scented *Rose*? Lift up thy delicate head, thou daughter of a mild sky.

"'Quid lates dudum, *Rosa*?'

"Why has not Morton threatened to deck me this time, also, with a *garland* of roses? Ah! I remember me, elections have been held, and the People have spoken. Their voice, as the voice of many waters, has been heard. It has reached the palaces at Washington, and Indianapolis, and Columbus, and penetrated even their darkened and deaf recesses. Lincoln and Morton have heard it, and their knees have smitten together. Tod heard it. The 'Democratic thunder' reached his ears; he knew it, and his 'backbone' softened, and shrivelled, and shrunk before it. *Sic semper tyrannis.* Let us rejoice. The people are once more masters, and henceforth no more shall the rights of the citizen and the courtesies and hospitalities of States be violated. The occupation of marshals and detectives, and spies and informers, and affidavit-makers, is gone, never to return; and their offices, at least the official existence of them, one and all, will soon cease. 'Teach me the measure of my days,' says the Psalmist; and I commend the pious reflection to Lincoln, and Morton, and Tod, and all others under and around, or like them, who have abused power, and outraged the people. The 4th of March, 1865, will end their days. *Habeas corpus* is here. Arbitrary arrests are at an end. The people of New York have restored the great charter of liberty on the 6th of November, and the people of Ohio and Indiana on the 14th day of October. In the midst of a despotism worse than that of Austria, the people of these great States have risen in their might, and pulled down the temple of Abolitionism, never to rise again. Not a vestige of it will be left. Its site will be ploughed over, and salt sowed, after the custom of the Romans, upon the spot where it stood.

In the contest just closed, while the sky was dark, and the storm was gathering—when the old Democratic ship was struggling with the billows—men who had professed to be leaders, who had been foremost when the sky was bright and the wind blew fair, deserted their posts. It was always so. Some were terrified, and fled; others, ambitious men, who would secure power dishonorably, fled; but the people, always true to themselves, retired to their homes, to their farms, and their workshops and their offices, in the hour of trial, to commune with their sober thoughts, and they came forth at the appointed time, and righted the foundering ship. They achieved a victory surprising even to themselves, and perfectly astounding to the Abolitionists.

The railroads, the banks, the telegraph lines, the express companies, and another element that had of late defiled itself in the land—the Churches—were all arrayed against the people. The pure altars of Christianity were polluted, and the disciples had huckstered in the political markets. The Churches had departed from the doctrines of Christ, and Him crucified, and taken up the Negro, and him glorified! There will be no Union, no peace, no hope, no country, until you drive out those who have defiled the temple of the Saviour of mankind, and restore the gospel in its purity. It is time to abandon the Abolition churches. Refuse them support. It is time to speak out.

Mr. VALLANDIGHAM said he was the son of a clergyman, but of one who did not disgrace his calling. He had, of late, quoted freely from the Scriptures in his speeches. Some of his friends remarked it, and he told them he had not attended church lately, and, consequently, he had had time to examine the Bible. In his closet he could find its teachings, but not in the pulpit.

Proscription had been another means used. Men were proscribed in every way. His advice was to meet proscription with proscription. We have as much money as they have—at least, honestly. We have not as many contractors, nor as heavy amounts of stealings hoarded up, but we consume as much as they do, eat as much, wear as much, and, by honest toil, can pay for as much. Proscription is a game that two can play at, and they will be the first to tire of it.

Over all these means, freely and unscrupulously used, we behold the sublime spectacle of twenty millions of freemen making their voices heard, even in the White House. Abraham has heard it, the Cabinet have heard it, and the governors of States have heard it

Mr. VALLANDIGHAM then counselled his Democratic friends to stand by the laws, to seek redress through the courts, and administer that severest of rebukes, to the corrupt—"exclusion from office." We will get satisfaction for our wrongs through the law. He called upon every man who had been unlawfully imprisoned in the walls of a bastile, to seek for redress through the forms of law, as he valued himself and the liberties of his countrymen. England has given us examples of illegal arrest—these usurpers cannot even claim the merit of originality for their tyranny—she has also given us examples of the punishment of the offenders. In England, the person of a subject is inviolate. An Englishman's house or home is his castle. We have a notable instance of what an Englishman's liberty for one hour is considered worth by an English jury. A Secretary of State arrested a British subject, and imprisoned him for one hour. At the end of that time he was released. He brought suit against "my Lord," and recovered a verdict for $5,000. Lord Chief-Justice Pratt, afterward Lord Camden—the advocate of the cause of the Colonies, the friend of America in its youth—made the memorable declaration, in this case: "None but an English jury can estimate the value of an Englishman's liberty for one hour." An Indiana jury may be able to make a like estimate. That is the way we should and will have satisfaction. The people have spoken—they must be heard, and will be heard. "We will have the Union as it was, the Constitution as it is, and the negroes where they are."

Mr. VALLANDIGHAM said that the campaign had only just begun. It must be kept up. We have a wily and unscrupulous antagonism to contend with. The good old times will return. He did believe in the possibility, nay, the probability, of the restoration of the Union as it was. We have commenced the work here, with the ballot-box; with it we have smitten the Philistines hip and thigh. The people of the South, after a little while, will, by the same instrumentality, put down the Secessionists there, as we have the Abolitionists here, and peace and union will once more smile upon the land. That is the sentiment in the ranks of both armies, and if you would to-day put ballots in the hands of the private soldiers of the North and South, the agitators and leaders, who are forcing streams of blood to flow, would be effectually put down. He related several instances of this feeling in the army, and concluded with an elegant peroration, which was received —as the main parts of his speech had been, throughout—by thunders of applause.

PEACE RESOLUTIONS.

On the 16th of December, 1862, Mr. VALLANDIGHAM introduced the following resolutions into the House of Representatives; they were postponed for debate:

"*Resolved*, 1. That the Union as it was must be restored and maintained forever, under the Constitution as it is—the fifth article, providing for amendments, included.

"2. That no final treaty of peace, ending the present civil war, can be permitted to be made *by the Executive, or any other person in the civil or military service of the United States*, on any other basis than the integrity and entirety of the Federal Union, and of the States composing the same as at the beginning of hostilities, and upon that basis peace ought immediately to be made.

"3. That the Government can never permit armed or hostile intervention by any foreign power, in regard to the present civil war.

"4. That the unhappy civil war in which we are engaged was waged, in the beginning, professedly, "not in any spirit of oppression, or for any purpose of conquest or subjugation, or purpose of overthrowing or interfering with the rights or established institutions of the States, but to defend and maintain the supremacy of the Constitution, and to preserve the Union, with all the dignity, equality, and rights of the several States unimpaired," and was so understood and accepted by the people, and especially by the army and navy of the United States; and that, therefore, whoever shall pervert, or attempt to pervert, the same to a war of conquest and subjugation, or for the overthrowing or interfering with the rights or established institutions of any of the States, and to abolish slavery therein, or for the purpose of destroying or impairing the dignity, equality, or rights of any of the States, will be guilty of a flagrant breach of public faith, and of a high crime against the Constitution and the Union.

"5. That whoever shall propose, by Federal authority, to extinguish any of the States of the Union, or to declare any of them extinguished, and to establish territorial governments, or permanent military governments within the same, will be deserving of the censure of this House and of the country.

"6. That whoever shall attempt to establish a dictatorship in the United States, thereby superseding or suspending the constitutional authorities of the Union, or to clothe the President or any other officer, civil or military, with dictatorial or arbitrary power, will be guilty of a high crime against the Constitution and the Union, and public liberty.'"

On the 22d of the same month, Mr. VALLANDIGHAM offered the following, which, also, went over for debate:

"*Resolved*, That, this House earnestly desire that the most speedy and effectual measures be taken for restoring peace in America, and that no time may be lost in proposing an immediate cessation of hostilities, in order to the speedy settlement of the unhappy controversies which brought about this unnecessary and injurious civil war, by just and adequate security against the return of like calamities in time to come; and this House desire to offer the most earnest assurances to the country, that they will in due time cheerfully co-operate with the Executive and the States for the restoration of the Union, by such explicit and most solemn amendments and provisions of the Constitution as may be found necessary for securing the rights of the several States and sections within the Union, under the Constitution."

On the next day, Mr. V. briefly referred to the foregoing resolution, as follows:

"The resolution which I offered yesterday, and which lies over for debate, was originally part of the series submitted by me some time since, and which, as afterward modified, were postponed till the 6th of January. I did not offer it at the same time with the others, because I desired a separate vote upon them; and through the kindness of the member from Illinois (Mr. Lovejoy) and his friends upon the other side of the House, my desire was promptly gratified, just as I anticipated. The resolutions were laid upon the table by a strict party vote, and thus the record for the GREAT HEREAFTER made up, and I am content.

"And now let me add that the resolution of yesterday is but an almost exact transcript of an amendment to the address in answer to the King's speech, proposed in the House of Commons, on the 18th of November, 1777, by the Marquis of Granby, and supported by Lord John Cavendish, Mr. Burke, and the other British patriots of that day. Had I pressed it to a vote, its fate would, I doubt not, have been just the same as that of the amendment itself, which was rejected by the followers of Lord North, by a vote of 243 to 86, in the third year of the American war. That war, sir, as we all know, went on for four years longer, and ended at last in the eternal separation of the Thirteen Colonies from the British Crown. So far as I am concerned, no similar result shall be the issue of our present unhappy war.

"But by speedy, honorable peace, conciliation, and adjustment alone, in my deliberate and most solemn judgment, now as from the very first, can that calamity be averted."

INVASION.—ARREST.—THE TIMES.

The following are extracts from a very imperfect and unrevised report of a speech delivered by Mr. VALLANDIGHAM, at Newark, New Jersey, February 14, 1863:

I SUSPECT that among the other miserable dreams—disappointed nightmare visions that hang in vapory fumes around the imagination of the Secretary of State—it has occurred to him that if he could only invite the Southern Army in force into Pennsylvania, and New Jersey, and Indiana, and Illinois, he would be able to galvanize the dead carcass of this war. (Laughter.) Well, if they invade us, we will write for them precisely the history they have been writing for us for the last few months. The Miami Valley will have some two or three Bull Runs with which to adorn their history, the State of New Jersey will also have several battles, which it is not necessary to allude to, only the picture will be reversed. But I think there is wisdom enough in the men who control the Southern Government not to accommodate the Secretary of State. It has been proclaimed that it never was their purpose to invade the Northern States. It is very true, that if this war is kept up, battles fought, no relenting spirit, no prospect of peace, no sound of concord to reach their ears, they may some day attempt that invasion.

* * * * * * * * * * *

Have any of you known that most terrible of all sensations, haunting you, walking with you, resting with you,—the apprehension of being arrested? Before God, I never have been guilty of any offence against the laws of my country, or the laws written by a higher power—except through the frailties of human nature—but I have learned, in my own person, what of all sensations is the most horrible and oppressive—the fear of arrest. I felt it when, night after night, in my own house—which one of the noblest of Englishmen told me, which my father told me, which the Constitution of my country told me, was my castle—when night after night, from the setting of the sun; from the hour when the gray starlight gathered around that which ought to have been a peaceful and undisturbed home, until day dawned, I watched in suspense for every footfall upon the pavement, and the sound of every carriage that rumbled along the street, lest some execrable minion should dare attempt to cross the threshold of that castle. And it was not in Austria that that happened—not in Russia, not in old Rome, under Nero or Caligula, but in the United States of America, under Abraham Lincoln. (Great applause.) As a man brought up in the Christian religion, under the *ancient regime*, when the gospel was preached, I should forgive transgressors, but I feel in regard to the authors of these acts, that I could join in the exclamation of Queen Elizabeth, when one who had done her a sore wrong asked forgiveness, "May God forgive you, for I cannot!" Forgive! Yes, if you cease now we will be satisfied to resort to the judicial tribunals to avenge those wrongs. Forget! No, not while memory holds a seat in this distracted globe, shall the vigils of those terrible nights be forgotten! And if even the apprehension of arrest fell and scorched thus, like a destroying fire, on the heart of one not subjected to it, what were yours, ye (turning to the late State prisoners on the platform) who felt the horrors of Fort Lafayette and Fort Warren?

* * * * * * * * * * *

We live in extraordinary time. I do not believe that in all history so grand an epoch has ever occurred; so many people and so vast a theatre engaged in civil war, with armies so great, expenditures so enormous, taxation so burdensome.

In the history of the past, just in proportion to the exigencies of the time, have men arisen who have been able to meet them. On every occasion hitherto, the Providence of God has ordained that men should be found fit to deal with the necessities of every nation. Has it been so now? Where are our Statesmen? Not in the person of the President, or the members of his Cabinet. Not in the Senate; not in the House of Representatives; not among your State Executives —certainly not previous to the first of January. Where are the men of might, the lofty in intellect, the grand in soul? (A voice, "in the workshops.") Ay, there are the men; but the instrument is wanted. The workman must have the implement of his trade or he cannot labor. The people must have a statesman equal to the occasion, or the nation is lost. Where are your generals? We had one, but they banished him. (Applause.) It was asked in the Senate the other day what victory he ever won. The reply was, what battle did he ever lose? When we remember the history of this war, it was the most pertinent answer that could have been made. We have been fortunate when we did not lose battles! Where are the men! A great nation is in the very throes and agonies of revolution, and no man has arisen, with power in his hand, stretched forth to save this people. It is what we most need now, and it ought to be the prayer of every true patriot and lover of his country, that God, in his Providence, would raise up a man to lead this people through the red sea of blood, to the promised land of peace.

"Give us the nerve of steel,
The arm of fearless might,
The strength of will that is ready still,
To battle for the right.

"Give us the clear, cold brain,
That is never asleep nor dozing;
But stronger ever by bold endeavor
To wake up the world from its prosing.

"Oh! give us the nerve of steel,
The hand of fearless might,
The heart that can love and feel,
And the head that is always right.

"Our foemen are now abroad,
And the land is filled with crimes,
But our prayer to th' Omnipotent God,
Oh! give us the men for the times!"

A part of the foregoing speech having been grossly misreported in some of the papers, was, in that form read, a few days afterwards, in the House of Representatives, by Mr. THADDEUS STEVENS, as follows: "It is very true that if this war is kept up, battles fought, no relenting spirit, no prospect of peace, no sound of peace to reach their ears, they *ought to be induced* to make that invasion." Mr. VALLANDIGHAM at once interposed, saying:

"I hope the gentleman will give me an opportunity to correct a very gross misreport contained in that part of the speech which he has just read."

Mr. STEVENS. I will certainly, for it is a very grave charge.

Mr. VALLANDIGHAM. It *is* a very grave charge. I concur with the gentleman from Pennsylvania in that. I corrected it the next day by a card in the New York *Tribune*. What I did say was this, that if the Confederates attempt to invade us we will write for them precisely the history they have been writing for us during the last two years: that we will then be able to give them two or three Bull Runs North, to adorn their history, in return for what they have given to us. I said further, in the same connection, that if the war went on indefinitely, with no prospect of peace, no sound of concord, no proposition or prospect of settlement in the future, they might possibly attempt to invade the Northern or Western States; but it never entered my mind, I never conceived for a moment, of such a thing as to give utterance to the sentiment that "they ought to be induced" to invade the North.

THE TRUE POSITION AND DUTY OF THE DEMOCRATIC PARTY.

Letter to ALFRED SANDERSON, Esq., Lancaster, Pennsylvania.

DAYTON, OHIO, *April* 24, 1863.

MY engagements in New York precluded me from accepting your invitation, and addressing you previous to my return West. I expect to go East about the 12th of May or 16th of June, and, if I do, will, if possible, visit Lancaster going or coming, and address your Democracy. Indeed, it will give me great pleasure to comply with your invitation. Should I be able to come, I will advise you in time.

Meanwhile, let me say that every thing depends on keeping the Democratic party up to the full measure of principle and sound policy, true to the Constitution, faithful to the Union, steadfast to the Government which they constitute, and devoted to liberty at the hazard of life itself. Truth and reason, applied to these high and sacred objects, are the only powers or agencies left to the Democracy, and by a bold and manly use alone of them can we succeed in the elections. Every thing else is in the hands of the Abolition party—the Administration. Through the press, but especially by public meetings and open and courageous organization, this use is to be made. Good men individually upon our ticket will not be enough. The people are not now voting for men, but for ideas, principles, policies. No public man is worth a rush now, unless he represents something besides candidacy for an office. Enthusiasm is power—a greater power, especially among the masses, among workingmen and a rural population, than any agency which this Administration can bring to bear, whether it be corruption or force; but there can be no popular enthusiasm for any one, above all just in these times of powerful commotion, unless he is the embodiment, or at least a representative, of some great principle or cause. And to be effective it must be antagonistic to some other and opposite principle or cause; and the stronger and more direct the antagonism, the better. This is essential now.

Last summer and fall the Administration was unsettled, ostensibly at least, in its policy, and its party therefore more or less divided. Not so now. It has a policy, and means steadfastly to adhere to it. Whoever supports the Administration now, supports its policy. All *apology* for temporizing by the Democratic party is utterly gone. The Administration Abolition party is thoroughly consolidated, and unquestionably it is now contending solely for UNITY AND A STRONG CENTRALIZED GOVERNMENT THROUGH WAR, AND, *failing in this, then* DISUNION. And it will rally to its support all men who from any cause, sentiment, or interest, are in favor of either the object or the means. Now the direct antagonism of all this is, UNION AND CONSTITUTIONAL LIBERTY THROUGH AN HONORABLE PEACE. And what nobler principle or idea, what holier cause for the Democratic party to struggle for? Arguments and appeals without number, the strongest ever urged, can be arrayed in its support—from religion, from philosophy, from human nature, politics, history, from the principles of our form of government, and from the utter and inevitable failure of all other means of securing that great end. With all these agencies at our command, an enthusiasm can be evoked from the hearts of the people, before which all opposition will be swept away as by a consuming fire.

THE MILITARY COMMISSION.—THE "CHARGE AND SPECIFICATION;" MAY, 1863.

The following is a full and exact copy of the "Charge and Specification," embodying the *sole* offence or "crime" for which Mr. VALLANDIGHAM was "tried" before Burnside's Military Commission, at Cincinnati, May 6 and 7, 1863.

CHARGE.—Publicly expressing, in violation of General Orders No. 38, from Head-quarters Department of the Ohio, sympathy for those in arms against the Government of the United States, and declaring disloyal sentiments and opinions, with the object and purpose of weakening the power of the Government in its efforts to suppress an unlawful rebellion.

SPECIFICATION.—In this, that the said Clement L. Vallandigham, a citizen of the State of Ohio, on or about the first day of May, 1863, at Mount Vernon, Knox County, Ohio, did publicly address a large meeting of citizens, and did utter sentiments in words, or in effect, as follows, declaring the present war "a wicked, cruel, and unnecessary war;" "a war not being waged for the preservation of the Union;" "a war for the purpose of crushing out liberty and erecting a despotism;" "a war for the freedom of the blacks and the enslavement of the whites;" stating "that if the Administration had so wished, the war could have been honorably terminated months ago;" that "peace might have been honorably obtained by listening to the proposed intermediation of France;" that "propositions by which the Northern States could be won back, and the South guaranteed their rights under the Constitution, had been rejected the day before the late battle of Fredericksburg, by Lincoln and his minions," meaning thereby the President of the United States, and those under him in authority; charging "that the Government of the United States was about to appoint military marshals in every district, to restrain the people of their liberties, to deprive them of their rights and privileges;" characterizing General Orders No. 38, from Head-quarters Department of the Ohio, as "a base usurpation of arbitrary authority," inviting his hearers to resist the same, by saying, "the sooner the people inform the minions of usurped power that they will not submit to such restrictions upon their liberties, the better;" declaring "that he was at all times, and upon all occasions, resolved to do what he could to defeat the attempts now being made to build up a monarchy upon the ruins of our free government;" asserting "that he firmly believed, as he said six months ago, that the men in power are attempting to establish a despotism in this country, more cruel and more oppressive than ever existed before."

All of which opinions and sentiments he well knew did aid, comfort, and encourage those in arms against the Government, and could but induce in his hearers a distrust of their own Government, sympathy for those in arms against it, and a disposition to resist the laws of the land.

RECEPTION AT WINDSOR, C. W.

Soon after arriving at Windsor, on the 24th of August, 1863, Mr. VALLANDIGHAM was welcomed by a deputation of citizens from Detroit, to whom he replied briefly. A summary of his response was published in the Detroit *Free Press* of August 26th, as follows:

MR. VALLANDIGHAM replied, thanking his fellow-citizens for their kindly welcome. He said it was gratifying, personally, but much more as a testimony for the great cause of constitutional liberty. Very strange was the spectacle of an American citizen in exile, receiving a visit from his countrymen upon foreign soil and under the protection of a foreign flag, but in sight of his own country. "It is indeed," said Mr. V., "my country, and as dear to me as when I last trod its soil." It was not fitting that here he should discuss the political questions of that country. The great issue at home was, indeed, common to England and America. It was the question of personal and political liberty, secured in the one by Magna Charta, the Petition of Right, the Statute of Habeas Corpus, and the Bill of Rights; and in the other by the guarantees of our State and Federal constitutions. In better times he would discuss them at home with the ancient freedom of American citizens. Of himself, though so cordially met and kindly referred to, he had nothing to say. He was nothing; the cause every thing. A great struggle was going on in the United States to regain lost liberties—freedom of speech, of the press, and of public assemblages, and to maintain free elections. He had great faith in the ultimate triumph of the people—faith in Providence and faith in the race which, in England and America, had successfully supported their rights and liberties for six hundred years. The race would still vindicate itself in the United States. The right of free election, and all that preceded and was essential to it, must be maintained—peaceably if possible, *but it must be maintained at all hazards.* He counselled obedience to the Constitution and to all laws, and the enforcing of that obedience by all men, those in authority and those not in authority. The ballot was the true and proper remedy in the United States, for all political wrongs; and it was all-sufficient. BUT WHEN THE BALLOT IS DENIED, THEN THE RIGHT OF REVOLUTION BEGINS—NOT THE RIGHT ONLY, BUT THE SACRED DUTY. Give us a free ballot and we want no more. Through this we will regain liberty, maintain the Constitution, uphold the laws, and restore the Union; and thus we will support the government which our fathers made. Claiming the fullest right at home to criticise and condemn the men and acts of the administration, and meaning there, and at the proper time, to again exercise it to the utmost, he, yet on foreign soil, had no word of bitterness to speak. He would only remember now that they represented his country, and forbear.

MISCELLANEOUS.

THE UNION—1849.

Valedictory as Editor of the *Dayton Empire*, June 27, 1849.

WE would stand or fall by them now as then, and throughout life. Of the vital importance to the welfare of the whole country in general, and the Democratic party in particular, of two, in an especial manner, to these principles, every hour has added to our deep conviction. And we would write them as in the rock, upon the hearts of our friends forever:

First, that which is really and most valuable in our American liberties, depends upon the preservation and vigor of THE UNION OF THESE STATES; and therefore, all and every agitation in one section, necessarily generating counter-agitation in the other, ought, *from what quarter soever it may come*, by every patriot and well-wisher of his country, to be "indignantly frowned upon," and arrested ere it be "too late."

NOT "FOR PEACE BEFORE THE UNION."

Card to the *Cincinnati Enquirer*, August 20, 1861.

I NEVER, either in my place in the House of Representatives, or *anywhere else*, said any thing of the kind.

It is a part of that mass of falsehood created and set afloat so persistently for the last few years, in regard to all that concerns me; and is of the same coinage as that other falsehood, that I once said that "Federal troops must pass over my dead body on their way South"—a speech of intense stupidity, which I never, at any time, in any place, in any shape or form, uttered in my life.

But now, allow me, also, to say that I *am* for peace—speedy and honorable peace—*because* I am for the Union, and know, or think I know, that every hour of warfare by so much diminishes the hopes and chances of its restoration. I repeat with Douglas: "War is disunion. War is final, eternal separation;" and with Chatham: "My Lords, you cannot conquer America."

THE UNION—1862.

Remarks against the Bill abolishing Slavery in the District of Columbia, April 11, 1862.

HAD I no other reason, I am opposed to it, because I regard all this class of legislation as tending to prevent a restoration of the Union of these States as it was, and that is the grand object to which I look. I know well, that in a very little while the question will be between the old Union of these States—the Union as our fathers made it—or some new one, or some new unity of government, or eternal separation—disunion. To both these latter I am unalterably and unconditionally opposed. It is to the restoration of the Union as it was, in 1789, and continued for over seventy years, that I am bound to the last hour of my political and personal existence, if it be within the limits of possibility, to restore and maintain that Union.

SOLDIERS.—PAY.—PENSIONS.

Note to Dr. McElwee October 6, 1862.

IN reply to yours of yesterday, I have to say that I supported all the measures in the last Congress looking to the giving of invalid pensions to all soldiers "wounded or incurring disability in the military service." Upon a question like that, no just or humane man could hesitate for a moment. Every soldier who has performed service is entitled to the pay and bounty promised him by law, and all disabled in any way during service are entitled to pensions; and I have never, either directly by vote or indirectly by refusing to vote, withheld either, where the service had been rendered or the disability incurred; nor would I do so.

LAWS.—RIGHTS.—DUTIES.

Remarks at Reception at Dayton, Ohio, March 13, 1863.

It is the determination of the Democratic party to maintain free speech, a free press, and a free ballot, at all hazards. I am for obedience to all laws, and for requiring the men in power to obey them. I would try all questions of Constitution and law before the Courts, and then enforce the decrees of the Courts. I am for trying all political questions by the ballot. I would resist no law by force, but would endure almost every other wrong as long as free discussion, free assemblages of the people, and a free ballot remain, but the moment they are attacked, I would resist. We have a right to change Administrations, policies, and parties, not by forcible revolution, but by the ballot-box; and this right must be maintained at all hazards.

THE SANITARY COMMISSION.

Windsor, C. W., *December* 16, 1863.

Geo. McLaughlin, Esq., *Cincinnati, Ohio:*

Sir:—Yours of the 11th, requesting from me an autograph letter. for the benefit of the Sanitary Commission, has been received, and I cheerfully comply.

The object of the Commission is one of mercy. It is a charity truly Christian, to visit the sick, to heal the wounded, to minister to the maimed, to comfort the afflicted, to relieve the prisoner, to clothe the naked, to feed the hungry, to give drink to them who are athirst, to cheer the widow and the fatherless, to save human life, to alleviate human suffering, and thus to restore some part of that which war always so largely subtracts from the sum of human happiness. That all this is to be wrought out on behalf of those or the families of those who brave wounds and death with heroic courage, upon the many battle-fields of this most sorrowful of wars, gives but still more of value to the merciful purpose. The Commission, if justly, fairly, with integrity and without partiality, it shall perform its pious duties, will prove itself worthy of the noble praise bestowed by Burke upon the benevolent Howard.

SELF-DEFENCE.—PROTECTION.—REPRISALS.*

Windsor, C. W., *March* 7, 1864.

Messrs. Hubbard & Brother, *Dayton, Ohio:*

Gentlemen:—I read, several days ago, the telegraphic announcement of the "riddling" of the *Empire* office by "furloughed soldiers." I offer you no sympathy, for that will avail nothing now or hereafter. I do express to you my profound regret that you were not prepared to inflict on the spot, and in the midst of the assault, the complete puuishment which the assailants deserved; but am gratified to learn that some of them did soon after receive their deserts. But these cowardly acts cannot always be guarded against. And they do not primarily come from the "soldiers." There is, therefore, but one remedy for past and preventa-

*This letter, differing from Mr. Vallandigham's uniform and repeated previous teachings, may be regarded as a recognition by him, of .the melancholy fact that we have at last reached that point in the "Great American Revolution of 1861," where the protection of Constitution and law being no longer enforced by executive or judicial authority, we are obliged to fall back upon our natural rights, not in revenge, but for security.

tive of future injuries; and that is, *instant, summary and ample reprisals upon the persons and property of the men at home, who, by language and conduct, are always inciting these outrages.* No legal nor military punishment is ever inflicted upon the immediate instruments. Retaliation, therefore, is the only and rightful remedy in times like these. I speak advisedly, and recommend it in all cases hereafter. It is of no avail to announce the falsehood that "both parties condemn it," *after* the destruction has been consummated. The time has gone by for obedience without protection. I speak decided language; but the continual recurrence of these outrages—frequently attended with murder, and always without redress—demands it. They *must* be stopped, let the consequences be what they may. Reprisals in such cases are now the only way left for a return to law and order.

LATE, GRUDGING, AND IMPERFECT JUSTICE.

The following appeared in the New York *Tribune* just after the Ohio election in October, 1863. Mr. Greeley is mistaken as to Mr. VALLANDIGHAM'S birth-place. His fathers, for several generations, were born in Virginia: he himself in Ohio. He is in error also as to Mr. V.'s being a "devotee of the Slave Power," etc. Upon this he has spoken for himself:

"Mr. C. L. Vallandigham is very generally regarded by unconditional Unionists as a worse man than our Governor Seymour, and the trimming, balancing, see-sawing politicians of whom he is the most conspicuous. We non-concur in this estimate. 'Val.' is a devotee of the slave power, mistakes slavery for the Constitution, and is as wrong-headed as a man can be; but, for a Copperhead aspirant in these days, *we consider him unusually honest.* He never pretended to desire or favor 'a vigorous prosecution of the war;' for he has from the onset not only detested and execrated the war for the Union, but has frankly and faithfully declared it. * * * * *He does not want the Union divided.* * * * No one can seriously doubt that, had he remained as he was born, a resident of a slave State, he would have been a zealous fighting rebel; his migration to Ohio was a blunder, for which not he but his father is responsible."

PERSONAL NOTICES.

THE following notices of Mr. VALLANDIGHAM, of various dates, are inserted as giving a more correct idea of his person, manners, character, etc., than any more formal description could convey.

AS A MEMBER OF THE OHIO LEGISLATURE; 1845–1847.

Ohio Statesman, December 25, 1845, then edited by C. C. HAZEWELL, now of Boston.

THIS Report (on the Morgan County contested election) is from the pen of Mr. VALLANDIGHAM, the young but most able member from Columbiana. It is one of the most clear, logical, and convincing arguments that it has ever fallen to our lot to read, and should be circulated in all parts of the State. It cannot fail to carry conviction to every impartial mind, and to raise the reputation of its author to a very high point indeed. Columbiana may well be proud of her young member, who has already achieved for himself an enviable name as a debater, for skill and fairness, and as a writer at once powerful and dignified. He is of that class of men whom the Ohio Democracy need, to place them in the position which they occupied a few years ago, and which has been lost, not through any dislike of the people to Democratic principles, but because the party has been unhappily identified with the names and character of two or three detestable individuals, whose utter worthlessness was enough to sink any party. In Mr. VALLANDIGHAM we have such a man as the Democracy of Ohio can rely upon, one who does not think it necessary to disgrace great talents by buffoonery and immorality, in order to achieve a sudden notoriety. A gentleman and a scholar, and thoroughly attached to the principles of Democracy, we can always rely upon him for good services, especially when grave and important matters come up, requiring the action of the highest order of mind, to have them properly discussed and settled.

Written for the *Cincinnati Signal*, by W. M. C., March, 1847.

MR. C. L. VALLANDIGHAM, of Columbiana County, has been, for two successive years, the representative of his county in the popular branch of the Legislature. He entered that body at the early age of twenty-five years, and although the youngest member, came to be regarded, long before the close of the session, as the leader of his party on the floor, which position he maintained during the late short and active session. Mr. VALLANDIGHAM is a native of the State, a fact not unworthy of remark when we reflect that considerably less than *one-fifth* of the members of the present assembly are "to the manner born," and that among the members we recognize no "men of mark," Mr. CUTLER and Mr. VALLANDIGHAM excepted.

Mr. VALLANDIGHAM is slight in figure and altogether youthful in appearance. Ordinarily his manner is in keeping with his appearance, although he is not wanting in dignity when the occasion demands it. Courtesy and urbanity in public as well as private life, have secured for him the esteem of all who know him, without regard to party, while his abilities have commanded their respect. His remark made, somewhat in the tone of reproof, after some characteristic explosion on the part of a turbulent member, that "he hoped he should ever so be a Democrat as not to forget that he was a gentleman," is still remembered. Indeed, in all of Mr. VALLANDIGHAM's intercourse with men, there is evinced a frankness and an obliging, generous feeling which, above all other traits of character, create and retain warm personal friends. In this respect there is no young man in Ohio more fortunate. His friends and well wishers are found among all parties, and their name is Legion. . . . . . Industry and application Mr. VALLANDIGHAM possesses to an eminent degree. As a consequence, he is an invaluable member on whichever legislative committee he is placed—in short, he is an excellent business man, and has all the requisites of a good lawyer. Not that I would be understood as implying that he is a mere man of fact, another name for a dull man and a plodder. Far from it. Mr. VALLANDIGHAM is a man of free—rather too free—fancy; one which sometimes, not often, carries him quite so high that his hearers fear lest, Icarus-like, he may come down wingless to the earth again. He always manages, however, to alight from these flights, with more or less grace, a matter of no little difficulty, even with the most expert cloud-rovers.

Mr. VALLANDIGHAM is decidedly one of the most promising young men in Ohio, and, if he possesses the requisite mental ballast, will attain a high position in the State, to which he is now an honor and an ornament.

Mr. VALLANDIGHAM'S renomination for the Ohio House of Representatives, in June, 1846, was thus noticed by the organ of the Whig party of Carroll county, Ohio:

"Mr. VALLANDIGHAM was a faithful and attentive member of the last Legislature. His gentlemanly deportment and pleasing manners secured him the respect and confidence of all parties; whilst his attention to business and generous sentiments were an honorable exception to the ribaldry which marked many of his partisans in the House; and unless the Whigs of Columbiana County conclude that they shall be represented in the next General Assembly, we shall be pleased to see him elected."

HIS SPEECH OF JANUARY 14, 1863.

THE Washington correspondent of the *Cincinnati Gazette*, a decided political opponent of Mr. VALLANDIGHAM, describing the speech, and the effect of its delivery, relates that the most busy and active members, such as Stevens, Colfax, Wickliffe, Lovejoy, Olin, and others, dropped every thing else, and obtained the best positions for hearing. An effort was making to get a joint session of the military and naval committees to consider a matter to which attention had been called by the Secretary of War. Only three out of *fourteen* members could be got to the committee-room in the course of an hour. Even the reporters in the galleries wake up; the seats are all crowded; the ladies cease their eternal chattering, and lean forward to catch every word.

Describing his manner of commencing, the same writer says:

"He begins boldly, defiantly, even; and is speedily preaching the very doctrine of devils. 'You can never subdue the Seceded States. Two years of fearful experience have taught you that. Why carry on the war? If you persist, it can only end in final separation between the North and South. And in that case, believe it now, as you did not my former warnings, the whole Northwest will go with the South!'

"He waxes more earnest as he approaches this key-note of his harangues, and with an energy and force that makes every hearer—as his moral nature revolts from the bribe—acknowledge, all the more, the splendid force with which the tempter urges his cause, with flashing eye and livid features and extended hand trembling with the passion of his utterance, he hurls the climax of his threatening argument again upon the Republican side of the House: 'Believe me, as you did not the solemn warning of years past, *the day which divides the North from the South, the self-same day decrees eternal divorce between the West and the East.*'

"The group of Republicans standing in the open space before the Clerk's desk, increases; they crowd down the aisles among the Opposition and cluster around the speaker as he resumes: 'Sir, our destiny is fixed. There is not one drop of rain which, descending from the heavens and fertilizing our soil, causes it to yield an abundant harvest, but flows into the Mississippi, and there mingling with the waters of that mighty river, finds its way, at last, into the Gulf of Mexico. And we must and will follow it with travel and trade—not by treaty, but by right—freely, peaceably, and without restriction or tribute, under the same government and flag, to its home in the bosom of that gulf.' It is eloquently spoken, and none are more willing to concede it than his opponents.

"He has spoken for an hour and a half, and accomplished the rare feat of compelling the closest attention of the most disorderly deliberative body in the world, from the beginning to the end. There is then a gradual relaxation, a sudden humming of conversation again on the floor and through the galleries. The Democrats and Border-State men, with faces wreathed in smiles, crowd around their champion with their congratulations. At a single step, the shunned and execrated Vallandigham has risen to the leadership of their party. Deny it, as some of them still may, henceforth it is accomplished."

The Washington correspondent of the *New York Herald* said:

"The speech of Mr. VALLANDIGHAM in the House, to-day, produced a profound sensation. It was bold and able. The Republican side, also, listened intently to it."

The correspondent of the New York *Journal of Commerce* wrote:

"Mr. VALLANDIGHAM'S speech of to-day commanded marked attention, and those who do not agree with him in policy, give him credit for great abilities. He declared himself for the Union as it was, wanted Massachusetts to come back where she was in other days, and in the event of a final separation, prophesied that the Northwest would go with the South, leaving the Northeast 'in the cold;' but still he battled, with great force, for a united country."

The correspondent of the *Boston Herald*, describing the speech and the effect of its delivery, says:

"The long-expected speech of VALLANDIGHAM was delivered in the presence of a large audience in the galleries, and an unusual attendance on the floor. As soon as he arose to address the House, a large number of members of all parties gathered about him. His method of speaking is very attractive. Added to fine appearance of person, he has a good voice and gesture, and always speaks without notes. To-day he was bold and determined; and while his views may be regarded 'as words of brilliant and polished treason,' it was universally admitted to have been a most able speech from that stand-point. He spoke for an hour and a half without interruption of any kind, and had most attentive listeners. I might add, that Vallandigham's great coolness amid the most heated discussions, is one of his peculiarities, and gives him decided advantages over more impassioned antagonists."

Of a similar character is the notice of the Washington correspondent of the *St. Louis Republican*, who writes:

"The peace speech of this Ohio Congressman, in the House, yesterday, was received with remarkable and respectful attention by the Republicans; and it is significant, as the first occasion when that party in Congress calmly listened to the semi-secession doctrines of Vallandigham, or any other peace man. It also attracts attention from every other quarter, and, to-day, is the general subject of comment in the city."

The *Boston Courier* thus spoke:

"This is an extremely able and a very honest speech. No one can read it and help believing that Mr. VALLANDIGHAM is a brave and honest man; and the speech itself affords irresistible evidence that it is his unfaltering devotion to the Union and the Constitution which has led those less loyal to stigmatize him as a secessionist and a traitor. His opinions will answer for themselves: but for its historical value and its strong grasp of the future, the speech ought to have the widest circulation."

The Philadelphia *Constitutional Union* thus refers to it:

"The speech of this distinguished statesman and heroic defender of the Constitution, which we present in full to-day, is the crowning effort of his public life. It rises above the mere cant and humbug of present popularity, into the clear and comprehensive realm of unselfish statesmanship, and discusses the exciting and momentous topics of the day with that measure of candor which their importance demands."

The Republican press limited its denunciations to the *sentiments* of the speech, and no paper whose opinions the public respect, denied its great power and merit as a production of eloquence and logical skill. Even FORNEY, in the Washington *Chronicle*, pronounced it a "*logical and powerful speech.*"

The *Cincinnati Enquirer* said:

"No speech has been made in Congress for years that has produced so great an effect in political circles, has been so universally admired for surpassing ability, for genuine and manly patriotism, for its wise statesmanship, as that of Mr. Vallandigham. It is a valuable and undying contribution to American Congressional eloquence, and will raise its author to a high place among the greatest men of the country. We do not know of a speech made by any of our eminent statesmen that has received higher praise or been more sought for."

The Columbus *Crisis*, edited by Governor MEDARY, said:

"This is no ordinary speech—made by no ordinary man, and under circumstances the most remarkable which ever overtook any nation or people. It will be well if this nation ponders seriously and with judgment over the words of wisdom and burning eloquence which run through every paragraph, sentence, and line.

"The speech of CATO, in the Roman Senate, warning the people against the designs of CÆSAR upon the liberties of the Roman people, contained not more truthful and thrilling interest to that great people about to be sacrificed at the shrine of ambition, than does this speech of the member from the Dayton district, but the true representative of the whole people, of all the States, and the nation as it was, collectively."

AFTER HIS ARREST—1863.

TIME ON VALLANDIGHAM.

From the *Springfield Republican* (Administration paper), May, 1863.

CLEMENT L. VALLANDIGHAM has written from his place of confinement to make an appeal to all Democrats, to his country, and to time, to vindicate his cause against unjust men. The last of these invocations is repeated with an earnestness which indicates a sincere and affecting belief that futurity will restore his rights and honor his memory! Time has indeed not seldom wrought like this to set on high forever those whom all things at first had agreed together to despise and trample on. And there has not been wanting often to such, upon whom were falling the reproaches of the time then present, an ear to catch the distant, reversing, applauding verdict of the patient ages that were following after. It is impressive to witness these changes in the rank of men. The first trial closes, and the court is declared to be adjourned without day, and straight there is arrayed a new and a more august tribunal. The places and the men begin to shift. The prosecuting officer listens to hear his own indictment. The culprit expounds the law. The Cornish Eliot is king in Whitehall, and Charles Stuart lives in "a dark and smoky room" in the tower.

ON HIS NOMINATION FOR GOVERNOR—JUNE, 1863.

From the *Albany Atlas and Argus*.

IT will be noticed that, in the loud outcry of abuse which has stormed about the head of VALLANDIGHAM, not one distinct charge is made against him. No words, even, are quoted from his speeches to convict him of infidelity to the cause of the Union. It is all vague clamor and epithet.

Young, accomplished in person and in manners, he has been called, also, "the most learned man in the West." He is certainly the most eloquent. The old malignants hate him, because of his very elevation of character and talents.

From the *Boston Post*.

Mr. VALLANDIGHAM has high culture and splendid ability. He is urbane in manners, sincere in his convictions, estimable and irreproachable in private life, a gentleman in every sense of the word, because he is an honest man. His political opponents, much as they differ from him, always respect him. The hold he has on his constituents was seen in the vote on his defeat in his district, which, by thousands, was larger than that which made him a member of Congress.

From the *Seneca Falls* (N. Y.) *Reveille*.

VALLANDIGHAM in size is a man of medium stature, and apparently about forty years of age. His address is that of a polished and cultivated gentleman. In conversation he is fluent, easy, and gifted, possessing all the characteristics of an efficient and popular orator. He makes one feel at home in his presence, though constantly impressed with the overshadowing greatness of his mind. We have seldom been more disappointed in the appearance of a public man. Instead of that bold, resolute, defiant personal which we had pictured to ourself, and which is so characteristic of our leading Western politicians, we found him unassuming, courteous, affable, and dignified. That Mr. VALLANDIGHAM is popular at home and among those who know him best, we do not wonder. Few men possess a more fascinating address, or are better calculated to win the affections of the people.

AT NIAGARA FALLS—JULY, 1863.

Correspondence of the *New York News.*

MY card secured me an immediate reception, and I was agreeably surprised to find him in such excellent health and spirits. Never, in the proudest day of his power in Congress, had I seen him more hopeful and tranquil. His agreeable and commanding presence, his well-rounded, symmetrical figure, clear complexion, expressive eye, resolute mouth and chin, a forehead denoting high intellectual powers—presented an *ensemble* that had not suffered by its passage through "Dixie," and one that, though it might easily terrify an Abolition general, almost any other white man would be unwilling to exchange for even the Apollo aspira tions of the handsomest man in the Cabinet of the "Second Washington," who banished him. Surrounded by his family, wife, and one bright-faced little boy, thus I found the banished man.

AT WINDSOR, CANADA WEST—SEPTEMBER, 1863.

From the *Cleveland* (Ohio) *Plaindealer.*

WE never saw Mr. VALLANDIGHAM before, and were very favorably impressed with the man. As we looked upon him, listened to his conversation, witnessed his manners, etc., we could not help thinking, how little he appeared like a "convict candidate for Governor," a "traitor," a "rebel," a "secesher," a "copperhead," or a "butternut."

While our host was engaged in conversation with another guest, we took (reporter-like) a hasty, but accurate (also reporter-like) inventory of the apartment. Mr. VALLANDIGHAM occupies two rooms upon the second story—one a sleeping apartment, which opened out of the little reception-room in which we were sitting, One of the reception-room windows faced the river, giving Mr. VALLANDIGHAM a fine view of Detroit, and also of the United States gunboat Michigan, which has lain moored in the middle of the stream, with its grim and shotted Dahlgren bearing full upon his bedroom, for the last four weeks. The latter gentleman smiled, when we alluded to the Michigan—the fact of an entire gunboat being detailed to guard one man's bedroom seeming to him—as it did to the rest of us—exceedingly ludicrous. The room was plainly furnished, containing a lounge, a few chairs and two tables. Upon the tables was a copious supply of writing materials, a few volumes of the *Congressional Globe*, bundles of newspapers, etc. From the amount of stationery, we concluded that Mr. VALLANDIGHAM'S epistolary correspondence must be extensive.

Mr. VALLANDIGHAM is overrun with visitors from all parts of the country, and is often obliged to lock his doors to secure quiet. In the course of our conversation we remarked that he was probably, at times, troubled with *ennui.* He replied that such was not the case, as the river abounded in excellent fishing, and deer and other wild game could be found in great profusion only about ten miles from Windsor. Thus—Mr. VALLANDIGHAM being an ardent admirer of field-sports—ample means were always at hand wherewith to drive dull care away.

After a half hour's call we took our departure, feeling richly repaid for our visit to the great exile, and also thoroughly impressed with the idea that no amount of senseless, brutal Abolition abuse could dispel the favorable impression that we had formed of CLEMENT L. VALLANDIGHAM.

From the *Rome* (N. Y.) *Sentinel.*

THE picture of VALLANDIGHAM which hangs in our office gives an expression of thought and care which his features assume only at long intervals. Nevertheless the general resemblance was sufficient to enable us in an instant to detect which of the six or eight gentlemen in the room we entered was the one we sought. His features are fuller, his dark hair more sprinkled with gray, his manners more frank, and movements more elastic and evidencing more vigor of health and buoyancy of spirit than we had expected. Without consciously crediting the statements of the Abolition papers that the exile's features were haggard and his look downcast, we had yet supposed, that his life of hard intellectual labor, and his habits of classical study, so evidently revealed in his published addresses, had given an austere and ascetic tinge to his appearance and manners. Nothing could be further from the reality.

From the *Fond du Lac* (Wis.) *Press.*

AN accurate description of the personal appearance of Mr. VALLANDIGHAM, much as it would please our readers, we dare not attempt, except to say that the engravings or photographs that have been published are correct, save that he is a much handsomer man than they represent him to be. He is scarcely turned forty years of age, and is calm and dignified, though frank and cordial in his manners, it being impossible for any one to feel the slightest restraint in his presence, save that which etiquette and good manners require. He lives in plain style, occupying only two small rooms, one of which is occupied as a sleeping apartment; the other serves both as library and reception-room, being furnished with a couple of tables, a rough lounge, and two or three chairs. On the table we noticed files of all the leading daily papers, of both political persuasions, also several standard works, which, upon handling, we found to bear indubitable evidence of having been closely read and studied, as many clauses were marked, and the margins of the pages covered with pencillings, no doubt his own. No man, no matter what his politics may be, can see and talk with Mr. VALLANDIGHAM and not arrive at the conclusion that he is a man of great and mighty intellect, and that he is honest and conscientious in his views upon the great questions which agitate the public mind.

VISIT OF THE STUDENTS OF MICHIGAN UNIVERSITY, NOVEMBER, 1863.

From the *Hillsdale* (Mich.) *Democrat.*

I CONFESS I was somewhat disappointed in the appearance of the man. I had expected a tall, rather slim, and a very proud-looking man—perhaps I may say, fierce looking, eccentric in manners and dress. But, on the contrary, I saw a man neatly and fashionably dressed, with smiling, open countenance, and nothing about him very forcible or striking save his eye. I think I have never in my whole course of life seen an eye which was like it, in every particular,—very large, full, and round. It is constantly betraying the thoughts of his mind, and the feeling of his heart. It gleamed and sparkled, and it trembled and filled with a tear as he pictured his country in the future.

A member of the class addressed him, telling him of our sympathizing with him in his wrongs as a fellow-citizen, and of our appreciation of him as a fearless and conscientious champion of constitutional rights. Mr. VALLANDIGHAM then arose and essayed to speak, but could not; his lip trembled, and a tear stood in his eye. He raised himself to his full height, and looked around for a single moment. That moment I never shall forget. There was not even a breath drawn—all was still as death. Perhaps it was weakness in me; if so, we were all weak, for there was not a dry eye in that large crowd. We saw before us a soul, generous, noble, true; a soul whose every throb was for his country; a soul that communed with every one present, conveying ideas clothed in the eloquence of a silence that drew tears even from reporter's eyes. "Young Gentlemen," said he. The spell was broken—his voice was again under his control; and for a full half hour we sat there, never stirring, hardly breathing, listening with every faculty alive to catch the eloquent words which conveyed thoughts almost inspired. Perhaps it was the occasion, perhaps the emotion of the speaker, that had such an effect upon all present. I say, it *might* have been this, that had such an influence over us that we were far from criticism. But I cannot attribute it wholly to this, but in part to a feeling of humbleness we all have when in the presence of a superior mind.

Long will the participants in that excursion remember it. Long will it be before they forget the mighty truths that a mighty man impressed upon them, in the sincerity, earnestness, and eloquence of one who felt their worth.

"VALLANDIGHAM'S BIRTHPLACE."

From the *Wellsville* (Ohio) *Patriot.*

As the Democratic procession, in New Lisbon, Ohio, on Thursday last, passed the residence of Mrs. Vallandigham, a comfortable two-story brick, surrounded with shade trees and tastefully arranged shrubbery, we observed, suspended across the gateway, a plain white muslin banner, bearing the simple inscription which stands at the head of this paragraph; and upon the grassy lawn near the door of the old homestead, now rendered dear to every freeman, stood the aged mother of CLEMENT L. VALLANDIGHAM, whose name and fame is familiar to the civilized world as the great apostle and champion of human rights during the reign of terror and high-handed usurpations of the Lincoln Administration. To Mrs. V., who is now more than "threescore years and ten," the 17th day of September, 1863, was a proud day. What must have been her feelings when she witnessed that every one, perhaps, of that great procession of freemen, as they passed that plain, unassuming banner, involuntarily sent forth their hearty huzzas in honor of her exiled and persecuted son? And that procession, long and enthusiastic as it was, was but a moiety of the honest sons of Ohio whose inmost hearts beat in unison with theirs.

"Vallandigham's Birthplace!" What associations crowd around it?—the late residence of an aged divine who has long since been gathered to his fathers, and now residence of his widow, who, like the mother of Washington, imparted the nobleness of her own soul to her son. By her instructions in morals, in religion, in purity of purpose and honesty of intentions, from convictions of duty, she raised her son; but little did she think, when bestowing but a mother's care upon him, that before he had scarcely reached the meridian of life, that through official persecution, and banishment from his native State and the home of his adoption, he would become the admired and beloved of millions.

THE NAME OF GLORY.

The following lines are from the pen of THOMAS HUBBARD, of Ohio.

WHAT name of glory do I hear?
    Vallandigham! Vallandigham!
In accents ringing loud and clear—
    Vallandigham! Vallandigham!
From shores which rude Atlantic laves
To calm Pacific's slumbering waves,
Shout men who spurn the gyves of slaves—
    Vallandigham! Vallandigham!

A people by their birthright free—
    Vallandigham! Vallandigham!
Were stricken down, and fell with thee,
    Vallandigham! Vallandigham!
But they will break the tyrant's chain,
The galling fetters rend in twain,
And smite the smiter back again!
    Vallandigham! Vallandigham!

Thy crime was loving Freedom well—
    Vallandigham! Vallandigham!
The crime of the old Switzer Tell!
    Vallandigham! Vallandigham!
Thine were such words as Henry spoke,
Which roused our fathers, till they broke
The tyrant monarch's hated yoke—
    Vallandigham! Vallandigham!

The great warm heart of Burke is thine,
    Vallandigham! Vallandigham!
His love of peace—that love divine—
    Vallandigham! Vallandigham!
Illustrious Chatham spoke in thee,
And generous Barre, bold and free—
Our FIRST EXILE FOR LIBERTY!
    Vallandigham! Vallandigham!

The page of Sidney's, Hampden's fame—
    Vallandigham! Vallandigham!
Will give to future years thy name—
    Vallandigham! Vallandigham!
Hark! Back to thine Ohio home
A million voices bid thee come!
COME! TRIBUNE OF THE PEOPLE, COME!
    Vallandigham! Vallandigham!

www.ingramcontent.com/pod-product-compliance
Lightning Source LLC
LaVergne TN
LVHW021228110826
845150LV00002B/269

* 9 7 8 1 4 2 5 5 6 3 5 5 4 *